40 MOST [...] DISNEY SONGS

ISBN 978-1-70514-240-0

Visit Hal Leonard Online at
www.halleonard.com

World headquarters, contact:
Hal Leonard
7777 West Bluemound Road
Milwaukee, WI 53213
Email: info@halleonard.com

In Europe, contact:
Hal Leonard Europe Limited
1 Red Place
London, W1K 6PL
Email: info@halleonardeurope.com

In Australia, contact:
Hal Leonard Australia Pty. Ltd.
4 Lentara Court
Cheltenham, Victoria, 3192 Australia
Email: info@halleonard.com.au

STRUM AND PICK PATTERNS

This chart contains the suggested strum and pick patterns that are referred to by number at the beginning of each song in this book. The symbols ⊓ and v in the strum patterns refer to down and up strokes, respec
The letters in the pick patterns indicate which right-hand fingers play which strings.

p = thumb
i = index finger
m = middle finger
a = ring finger

For example; Pick Pattern 2
is played: thumb - index - middle - ring

Strum Patterns

Pick Patterns

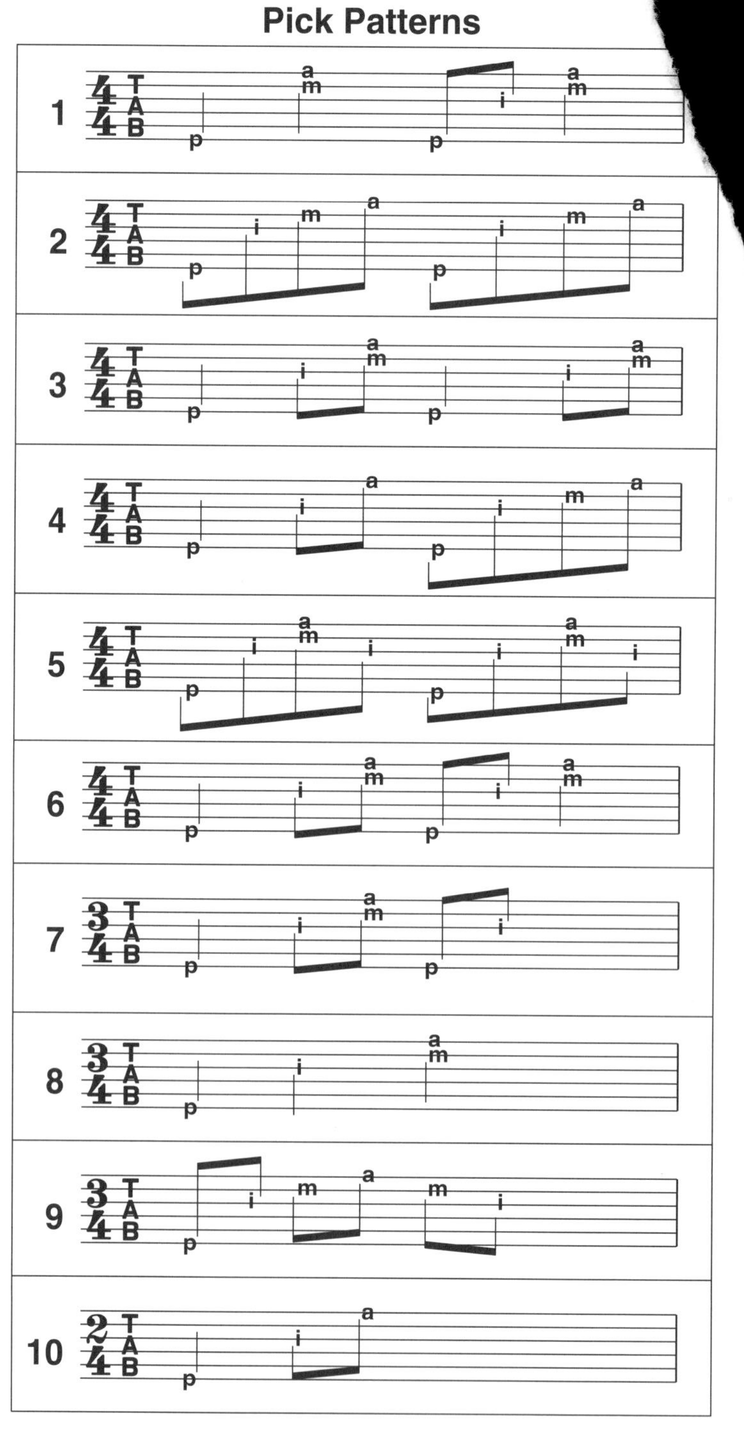

You can use the 3/4 Strum and Pick Patterns in songs written in compound meter (6/8, 9/8, 12/8, etc.). For example, you can accompany a song in 6/8 by playing the 3/4 pattern twice in each measure. The 4/4 Strum and Pick Patterns can be used for songs written in cut time (¢) by doubling the note time values in the patterns. Each pattern would therefore last two measures in cut time.

CONTENTS

Almost There

from THE PRINCESS AND THE FROG

Music and Lyrics by Randy Newman

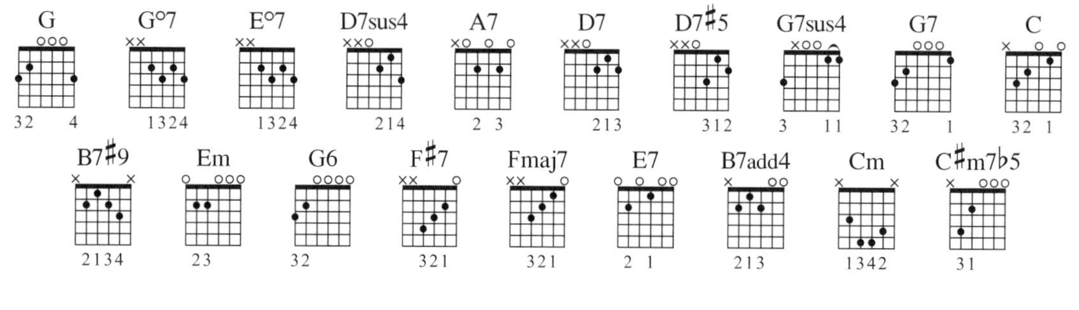

*Capo V

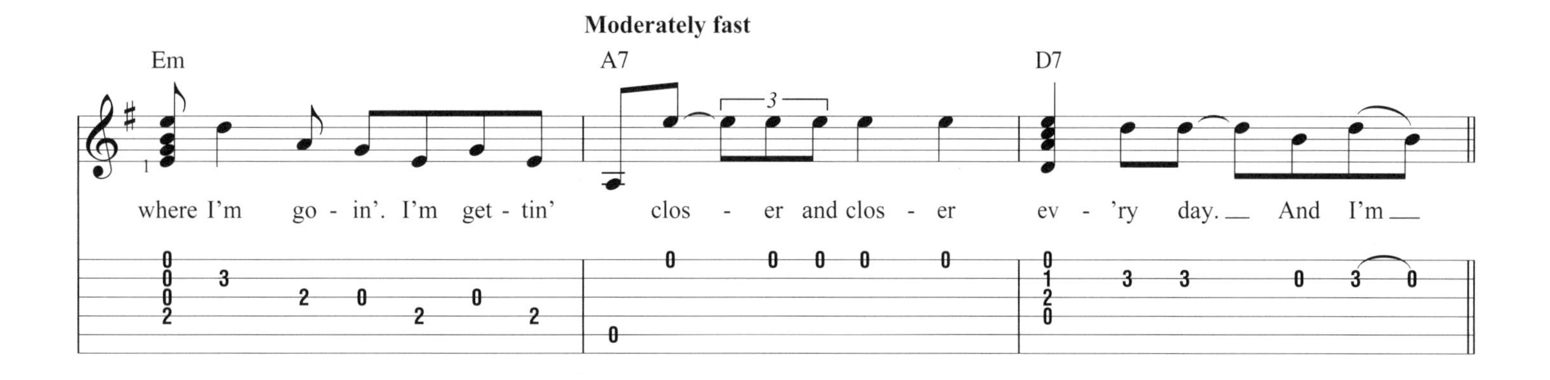
Moderately fast
Em A7 D7
where I'm go - in'. I'm get - tin' clos - er and clos - er ev - 'ry day. And I'm

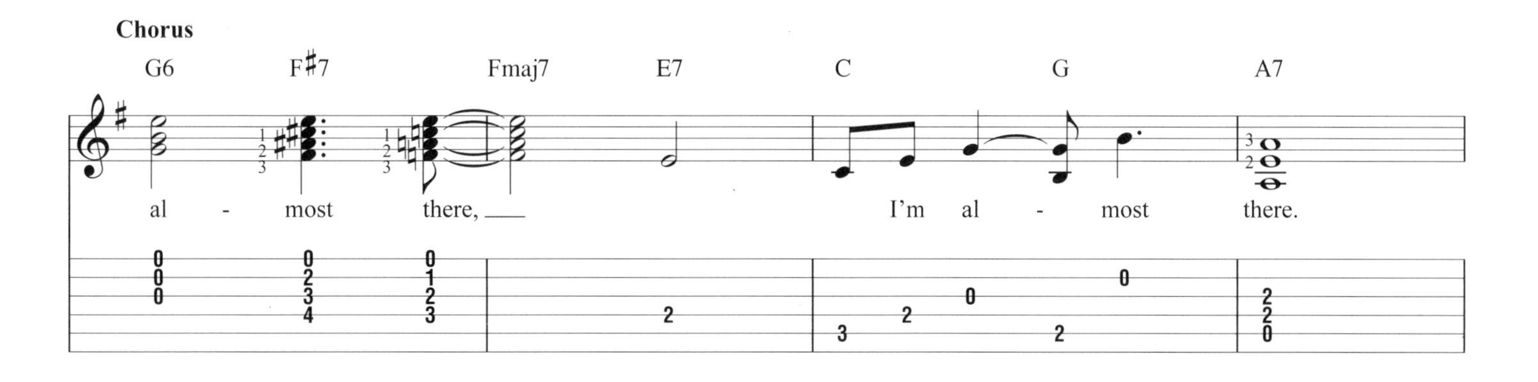
Chorus
G6 F♯7 Fmaj7 E7 C G A7
al - most there, I'm al - most there.

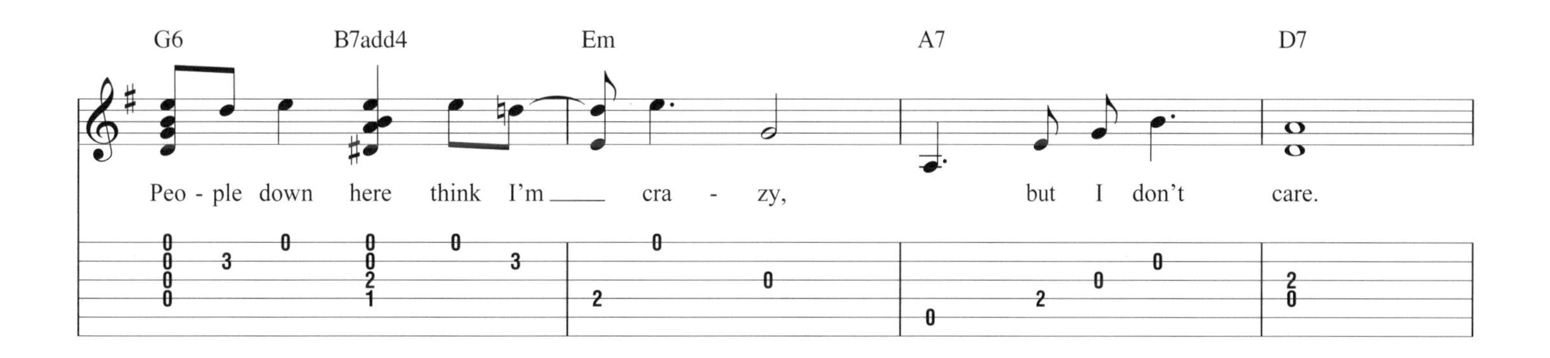
G6 B7add4 Em A7 D7
Peo - ple down here think I'm cra - zy, but I don't care.

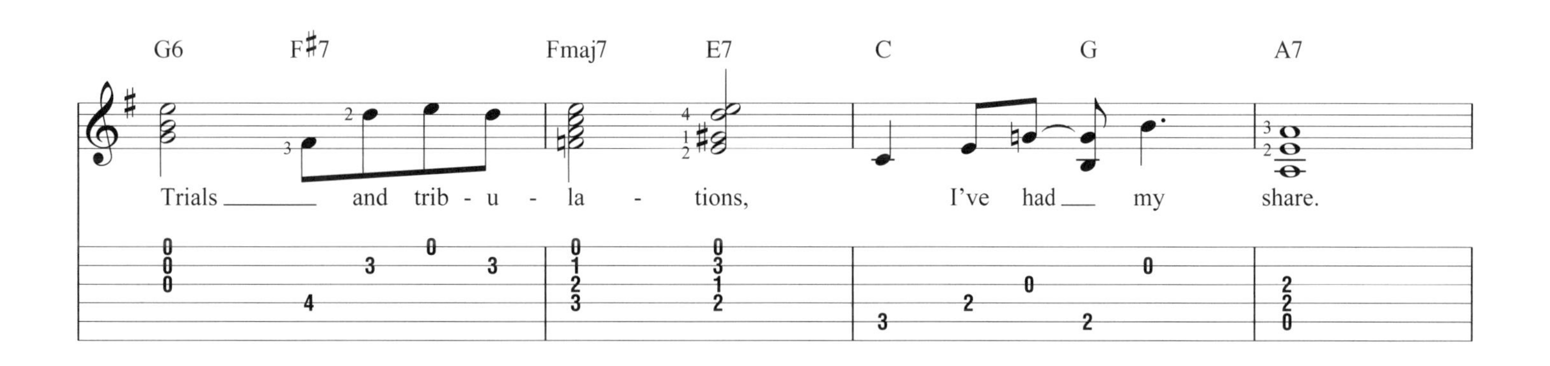
G6 F♯7 Fmaj7 E7 C G A7
Trials and trib - u - la - tions, I've had my share.

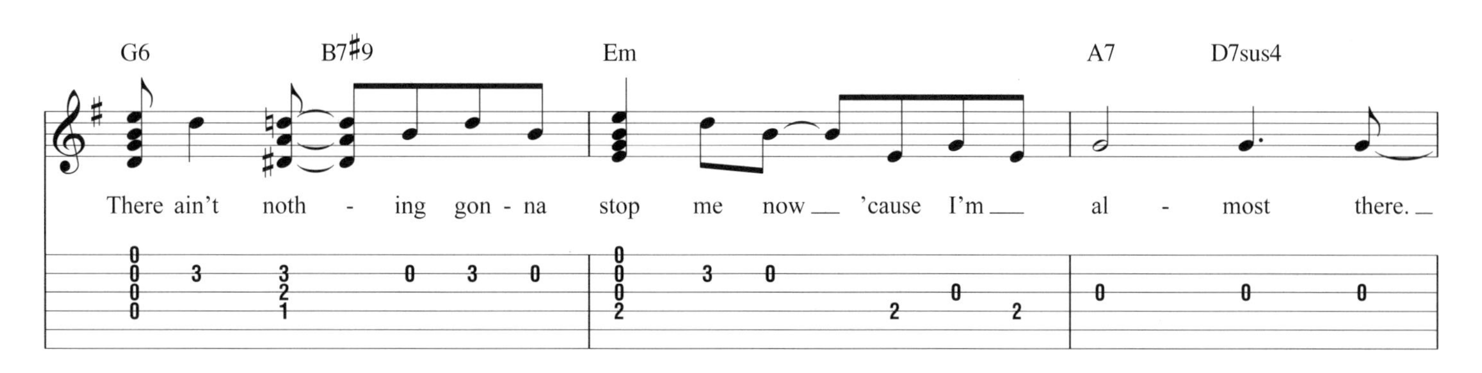
G6 B7♯9 Em A7 D7sus4
There ain't noth - ing gon - na stop me now 'cause I'm al - most there.

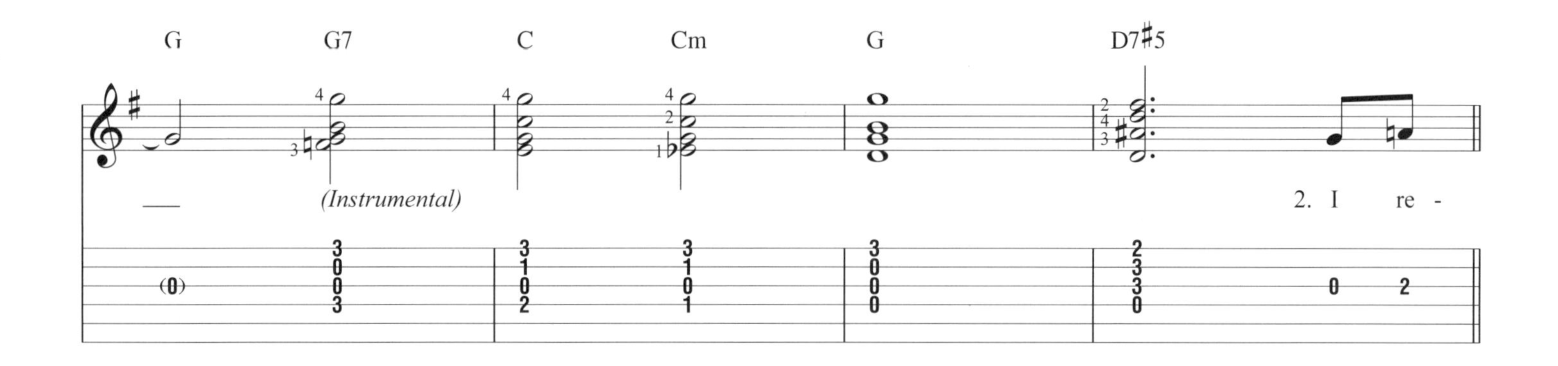
G G7 C Cm G D7♯5
(Instrumental)
2. I re -

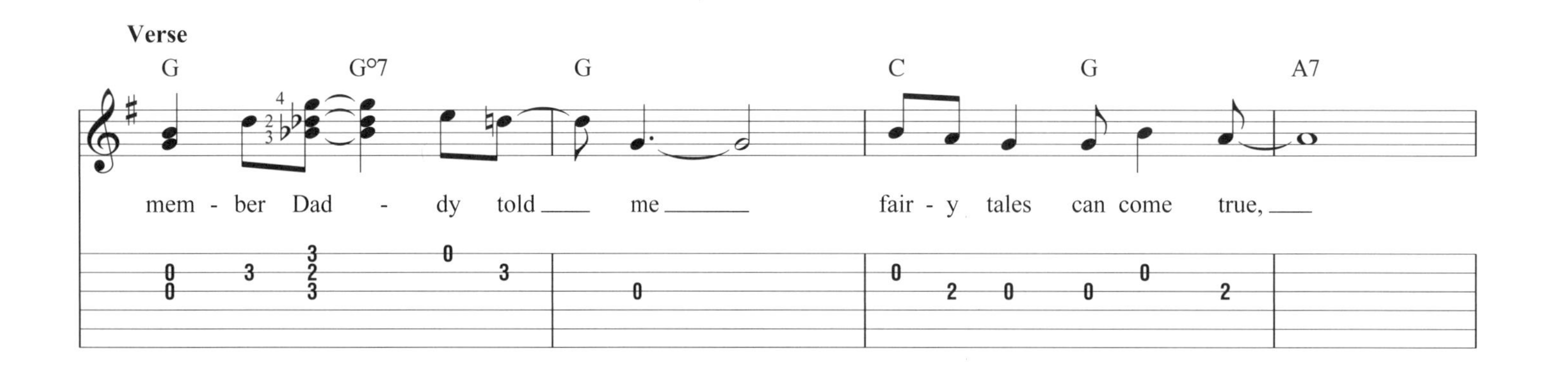
Verse
G G°7 G C G A7
mem - ber Dad - dy told me fair - y tales can come true,

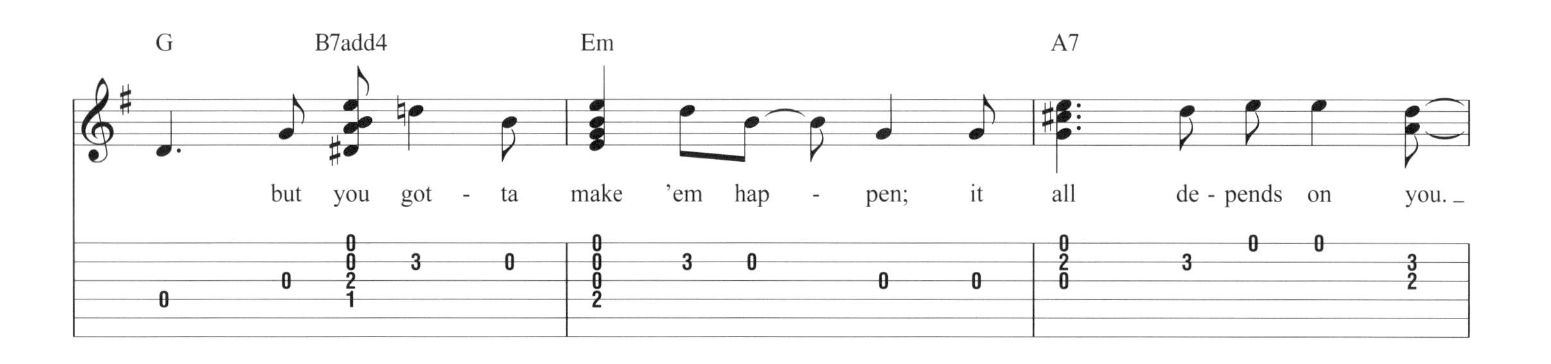
G B7add4 Em A7
but you got - ta make 'em hap - pen; it all de - pends on you.

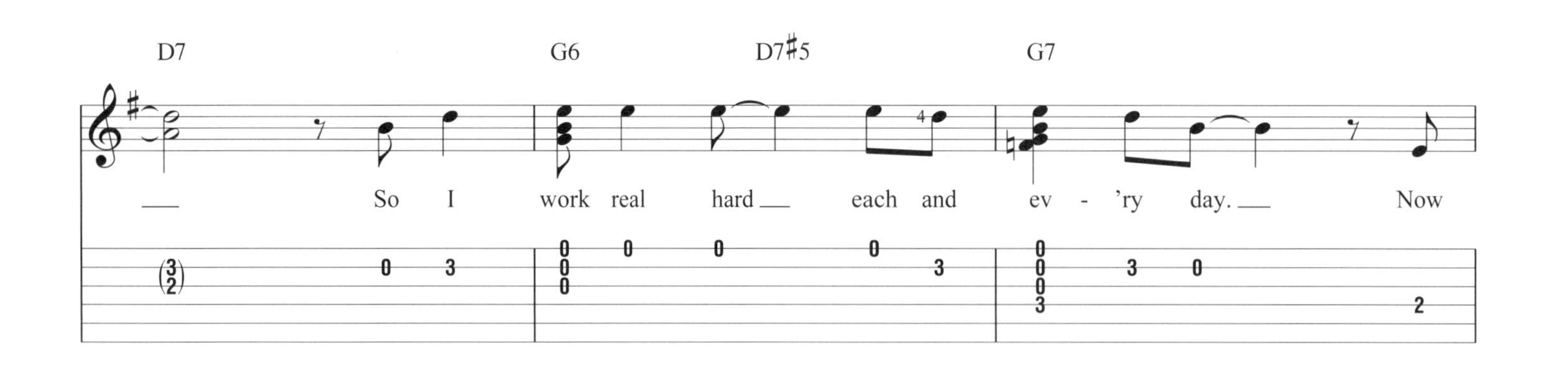
D7 G6 D7♯5 G7
So I work real hard each and ev - 'ry day. Now

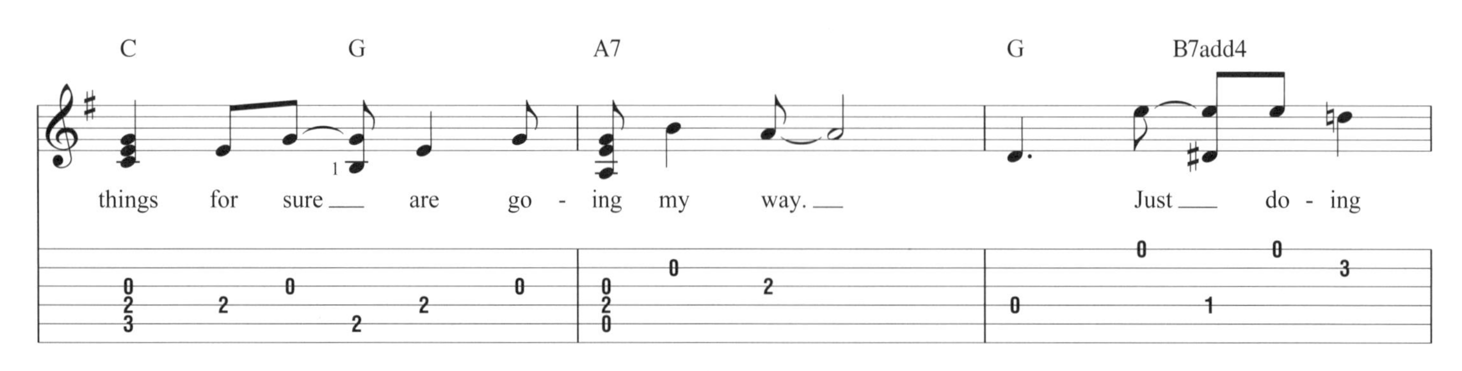
C G A7 G B7add4
things for sure are go - ing my way. Just do - ing

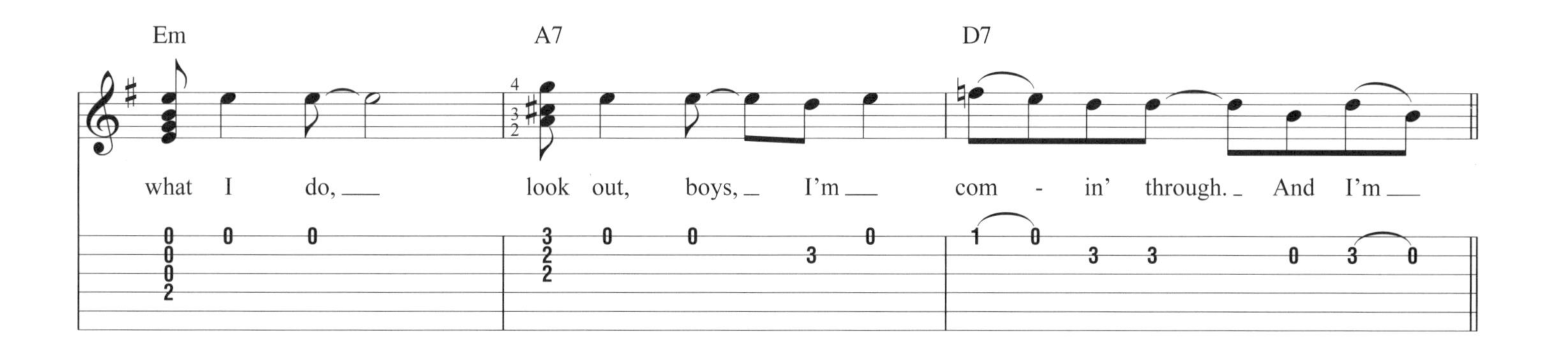
Em A7 D7
what I do, look out, boys, I'm com - in' through. And I'm

Chorus

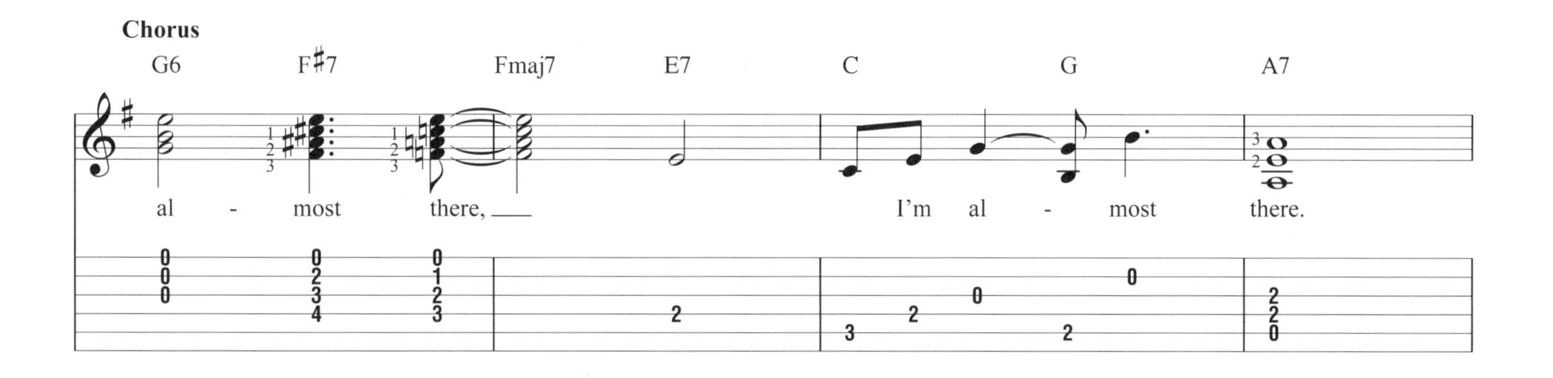
G6 F#7 Fmaj7 E7 C G A7
al - most there, I'm al - most there.

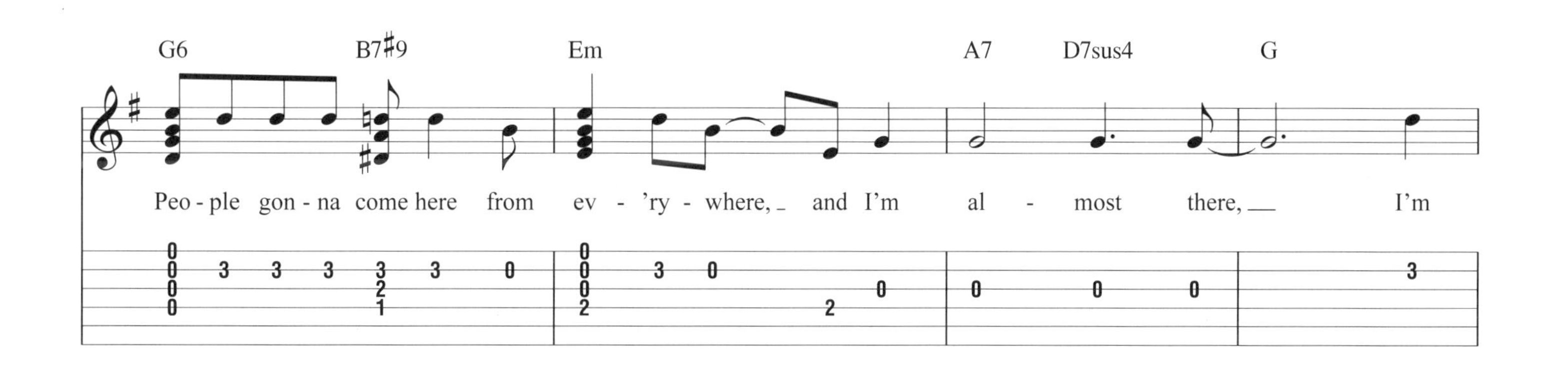
G6 B7#9 Em A7 D7sus4 G
Peo - ple gon - na come here from ev - 'ry - where, and I'm al - most there, I'm

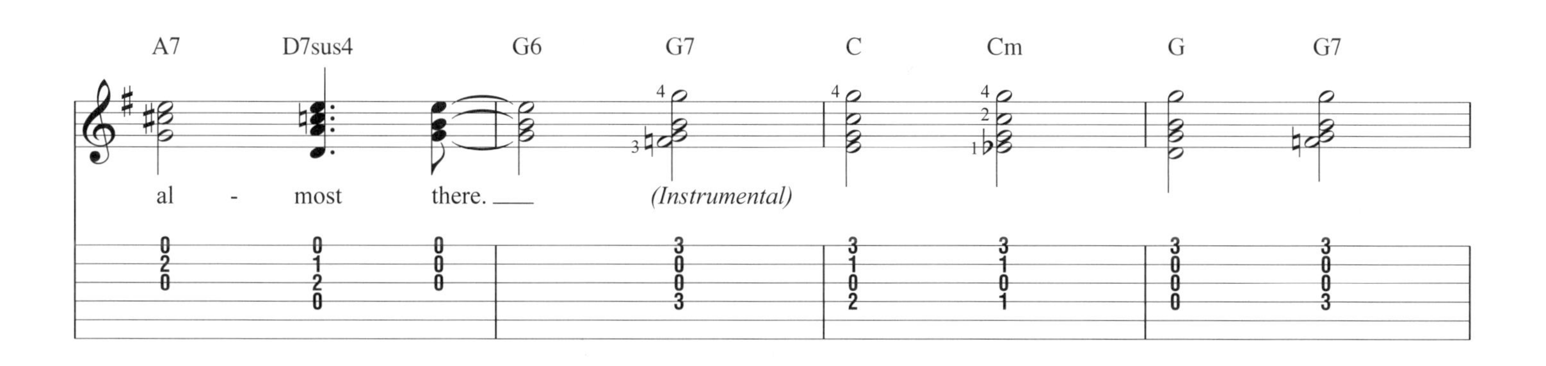
A7 D7sus4 G6 G7 C Cm G G7
al - most there.
(Instrumental)

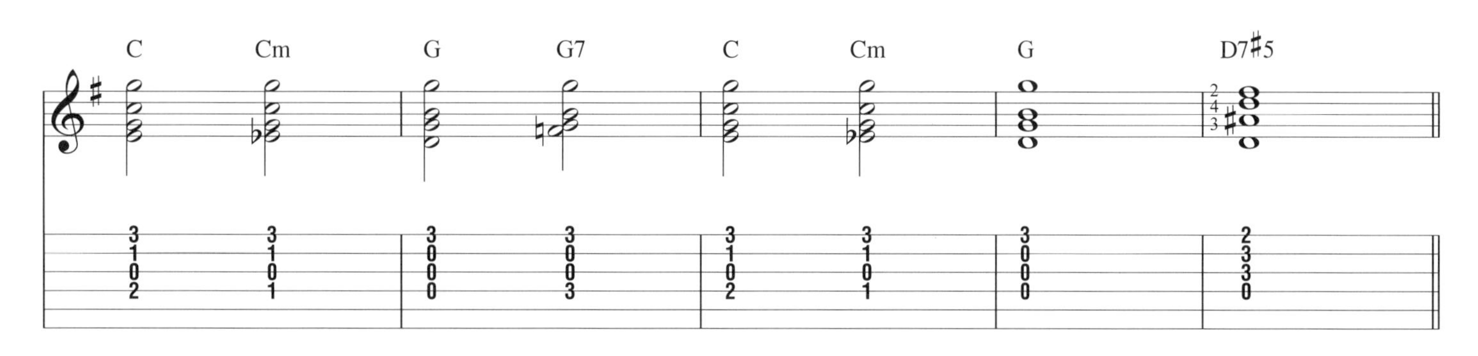
C Cm G G7 C Cm G D7#5

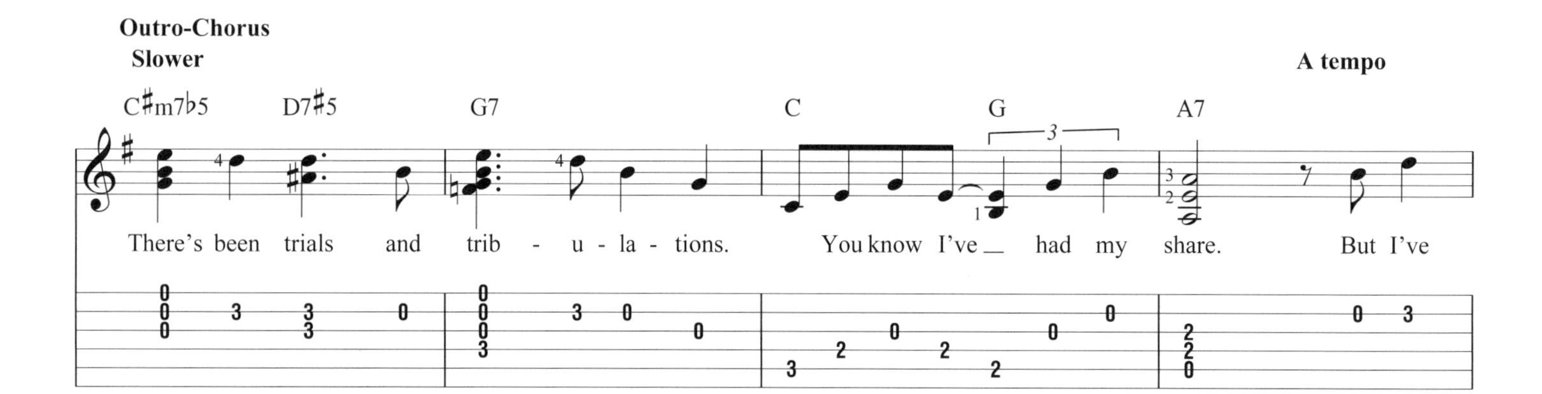
Outro-Chorus
Slower
A tempo
C♯m7♭5 D7♯5 G7 C G A7
There's been trials and trib - u - la - tions. You know I've had my share. But I've

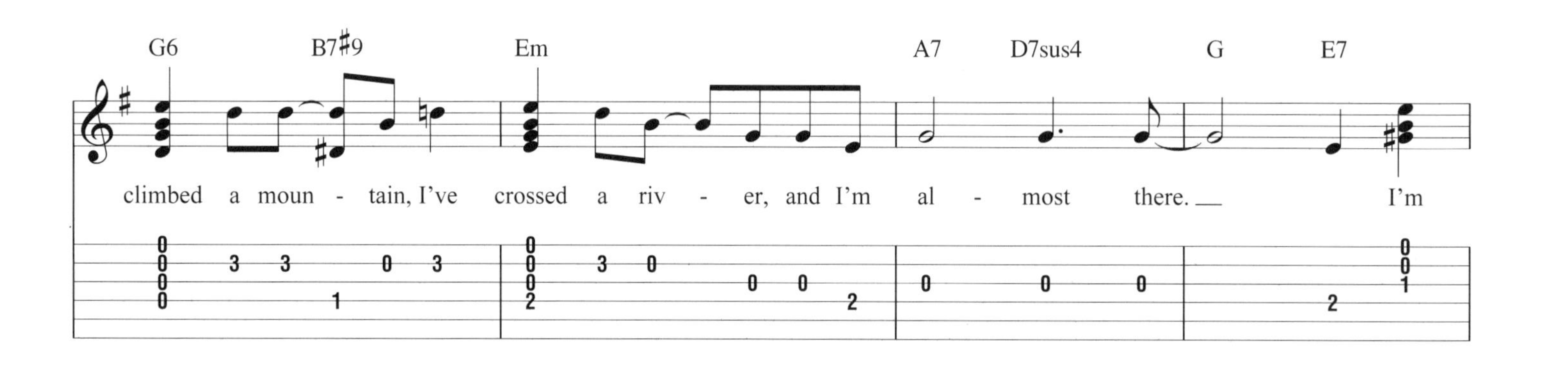
G6 B7♯9 Em A7 D7sus4 G E7
climbed a moun - tain, I've crossed a riv - er, and I'm al - most there. I'm

A7 D7 G E7 A7 D7sus4
al - most there. I'm al - most

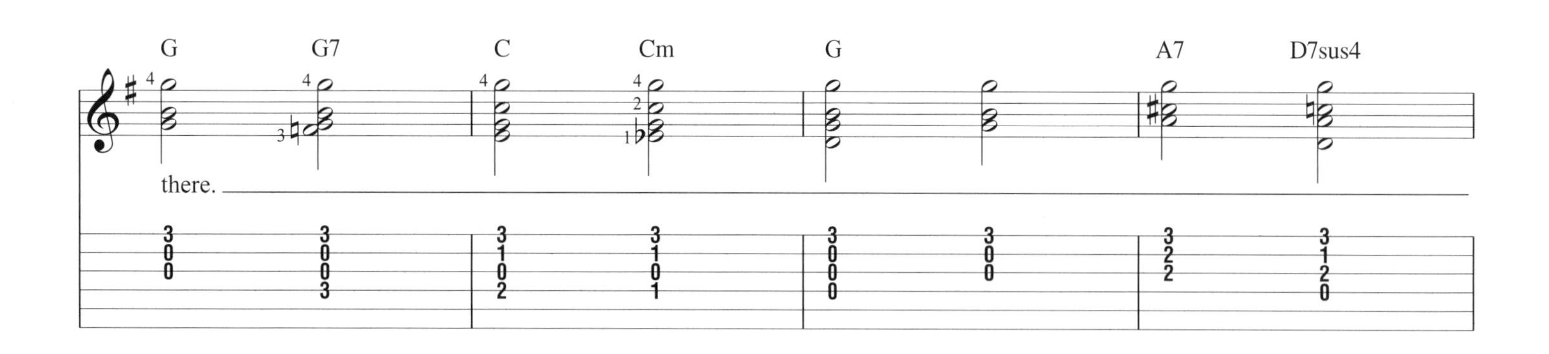
G G7 C Cm G A7 D7sus4
there.

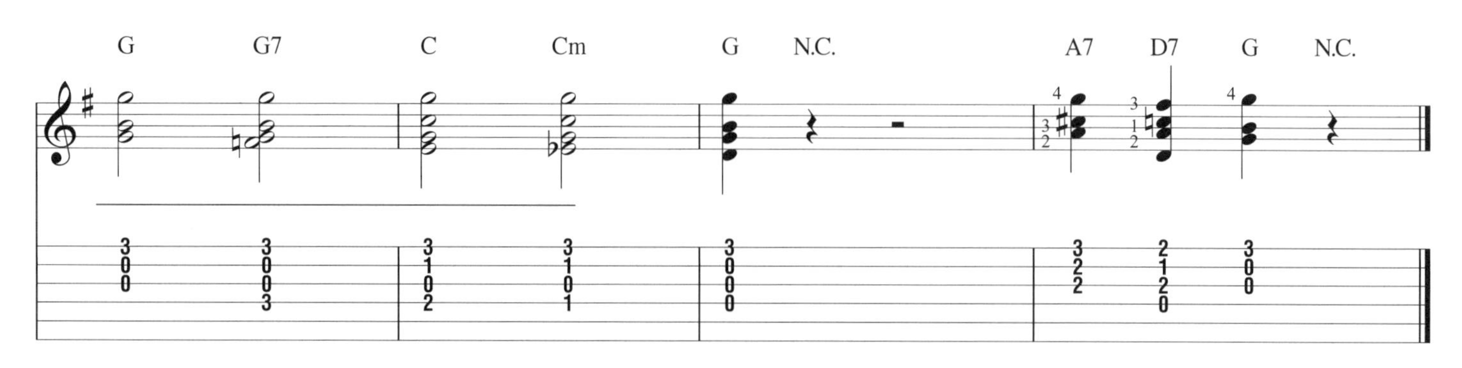
G G7 C Cm G N.C. A7 D7 G N.C.

Beauty and the Beast

from BEAUTY AND THE BEAST
Music by Alan Menken
Lyrics by Howard Ashman

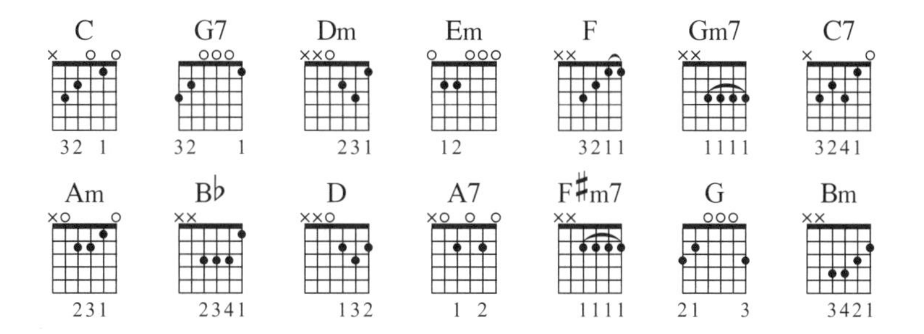

Strum Pattern: 4
Pick Pattern: 2

Verse
Moderately slow

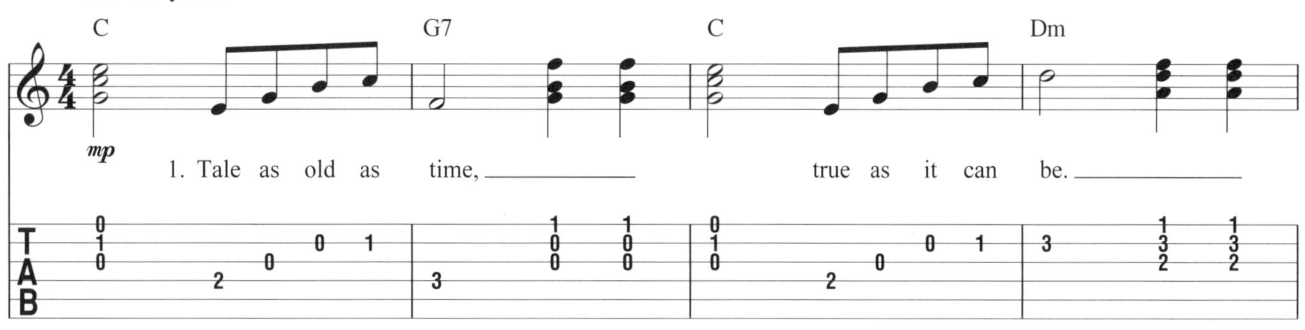

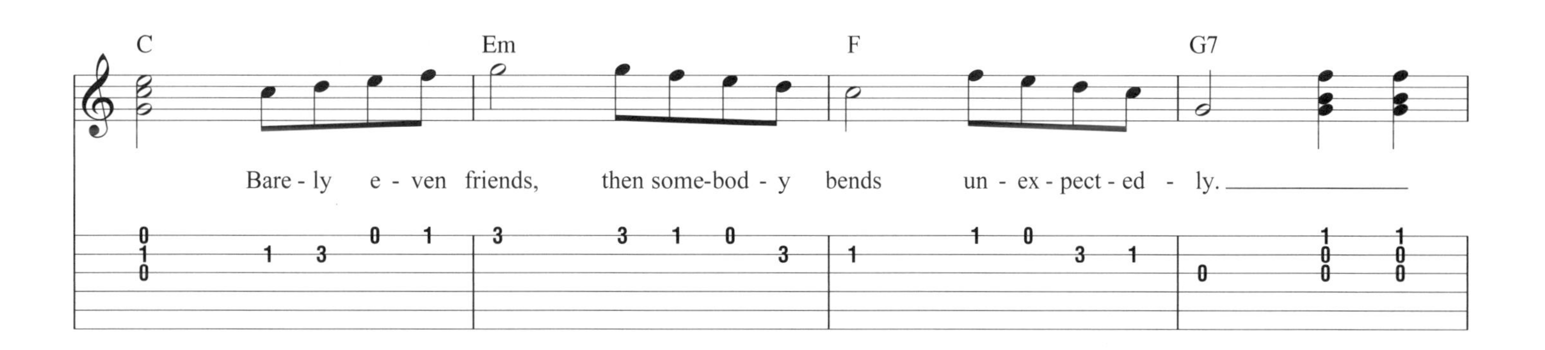

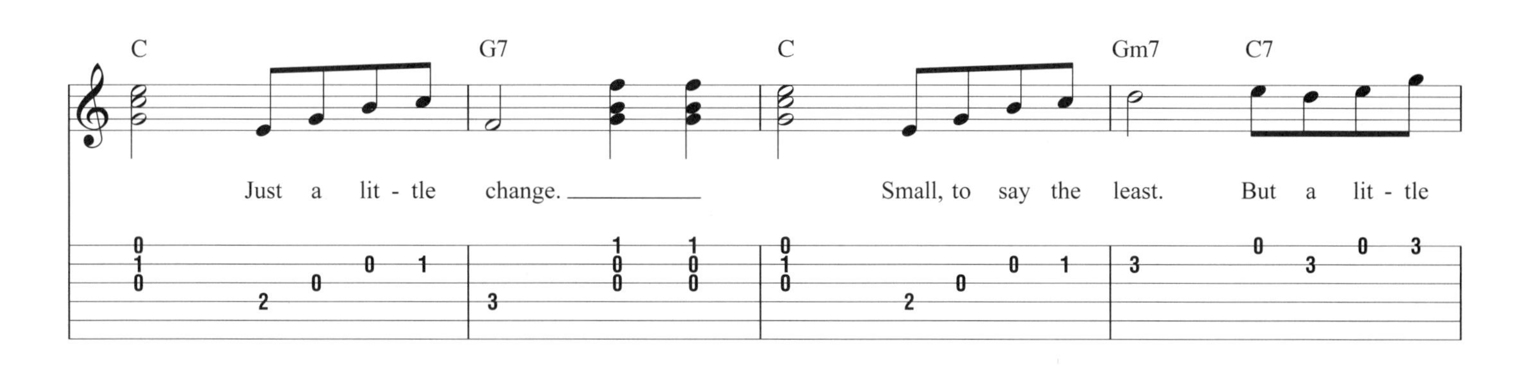

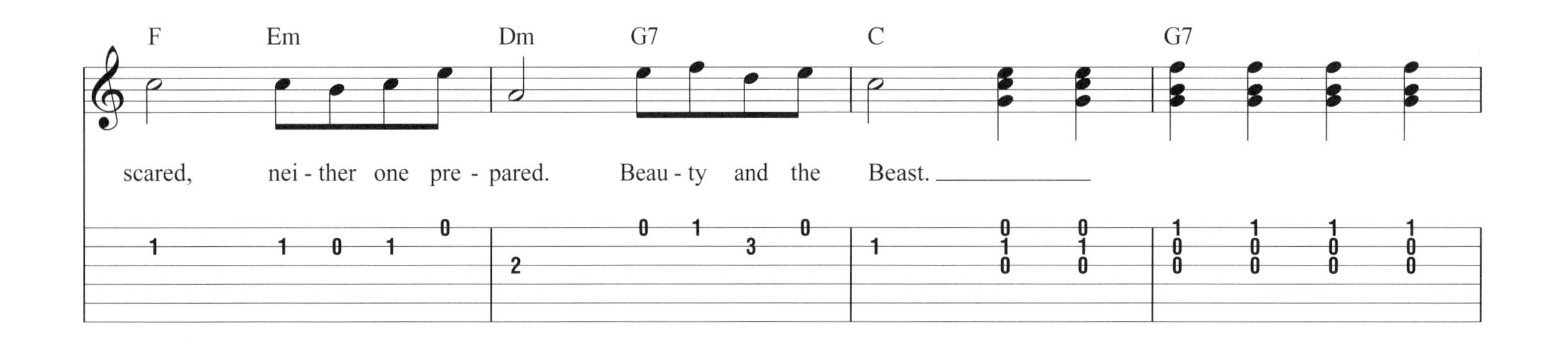
F Em Dm G7 C G7
scared, nei - ther one pre - pared. Beau - ty and the Beast.

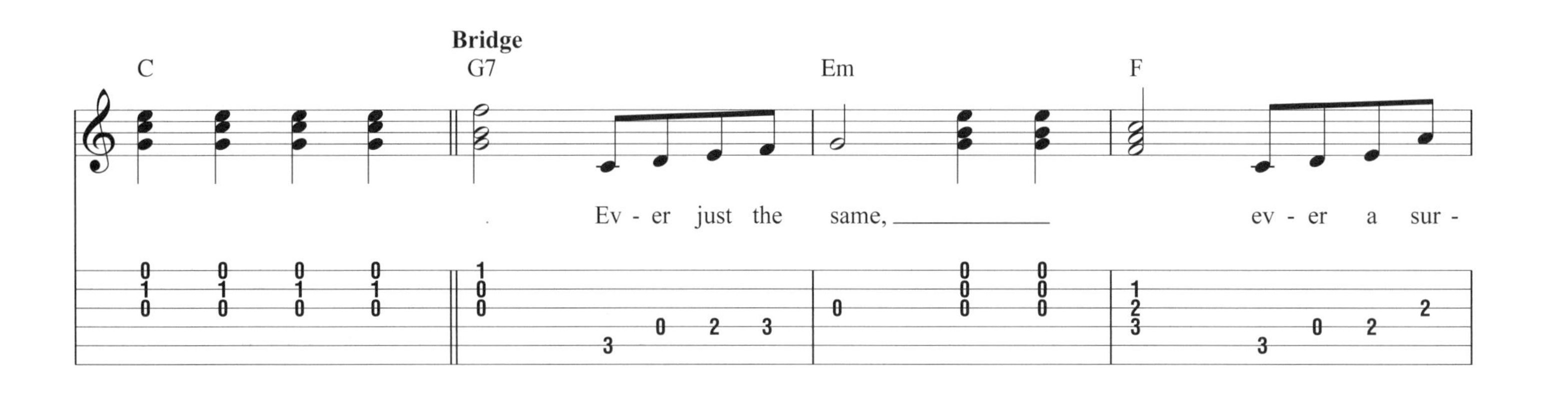
Bridge
C G7 Em F
Ev - er just the same, ev - er a sur -

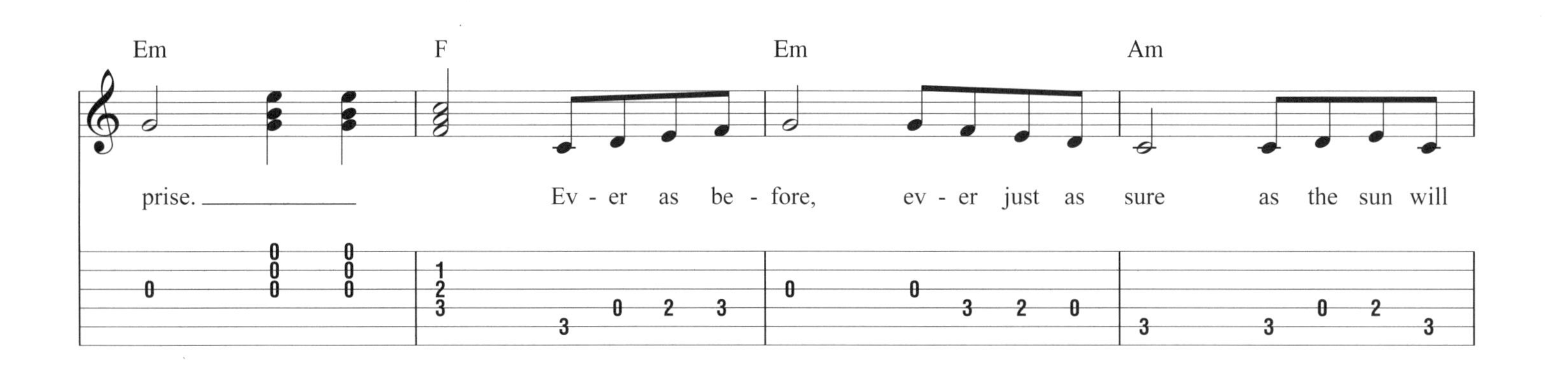
Em F Em Am
prise. Ev - er as be - fore, ev - er just as sure as the sun will

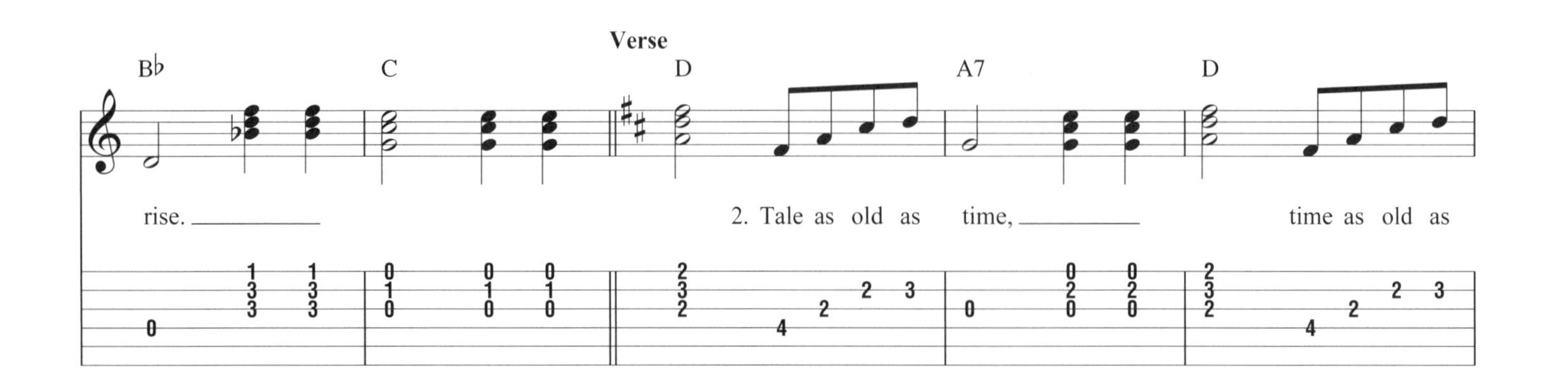
Verse
B♭ C D A7 D
rise. 2. Tale as old as time, time as old as

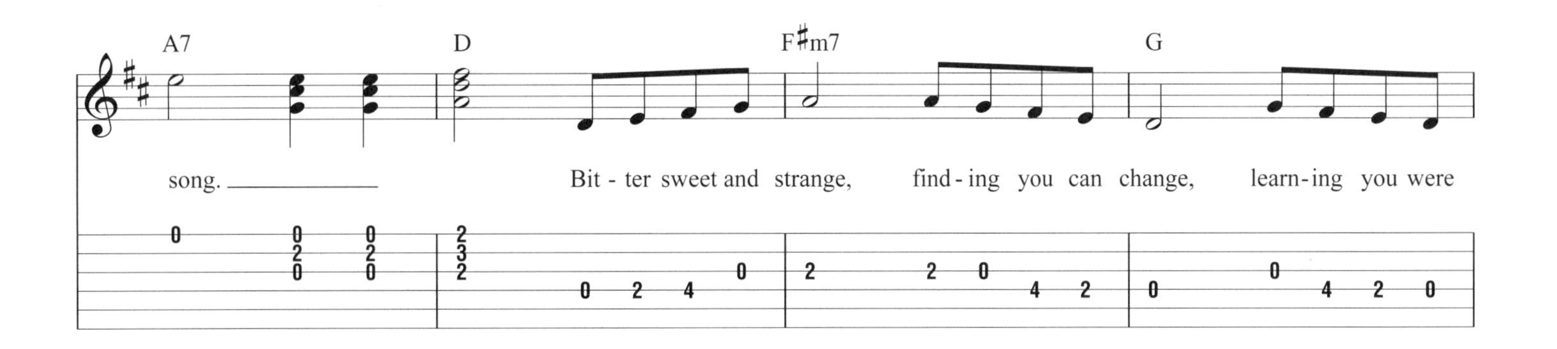
A7 D F♯m7 G
song. Bit - ter sweet and strange, find - ing you can change, learn - ing you were

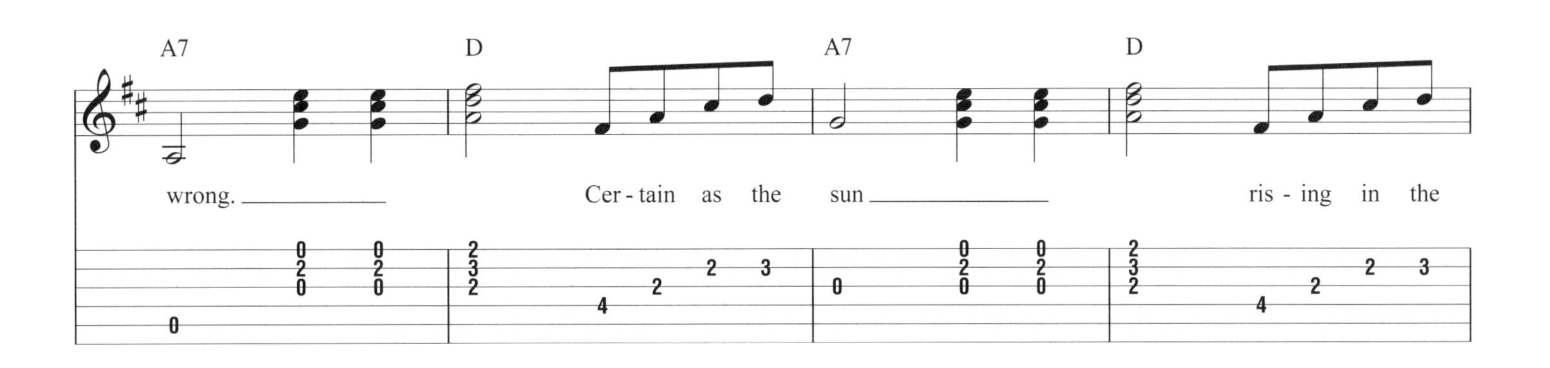
A7 D A7 D
wrong. Cer - tain as the sun ris - ing in the

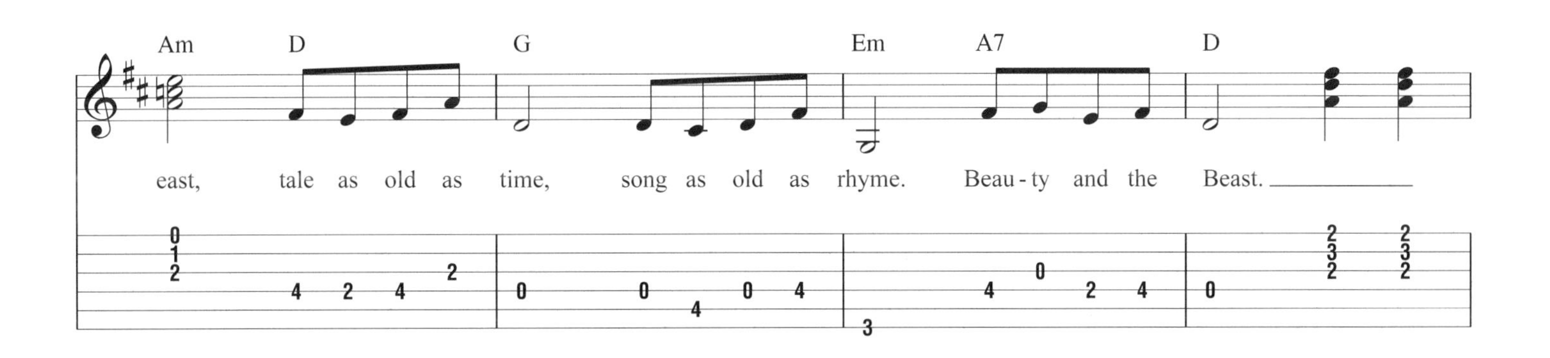
Am D G Em A7 D
east, tale as old as time, song as old as rhyme. Beau - ty and the Beast.

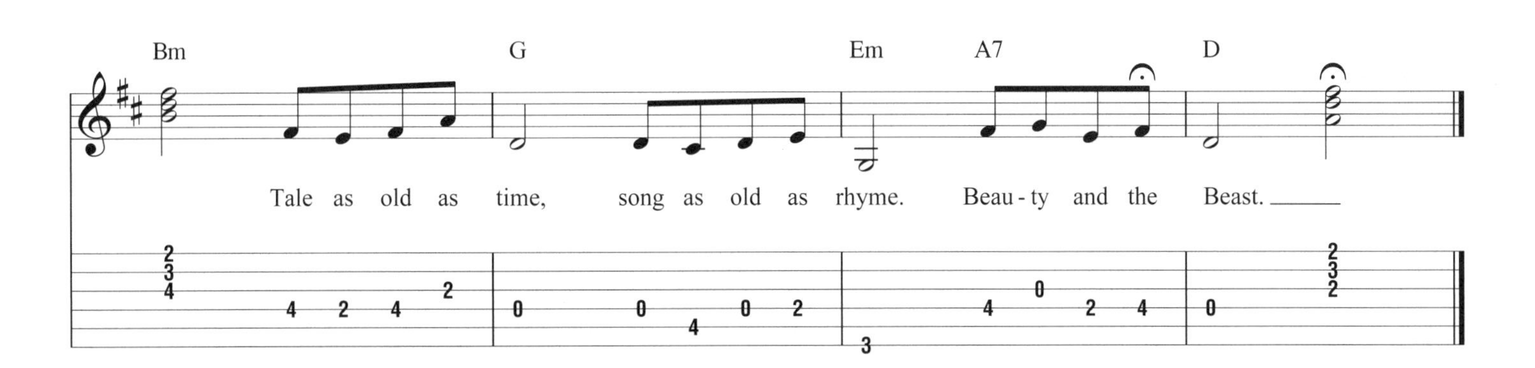
Bm G Em A7 D
Tale as old as time, song as old as rhyme. Beau - ty and the Beast.

Be Our Guest

from BEAUTY AND THE BEAST
Music by Alan Menken
Lyrics by Howard Ashman

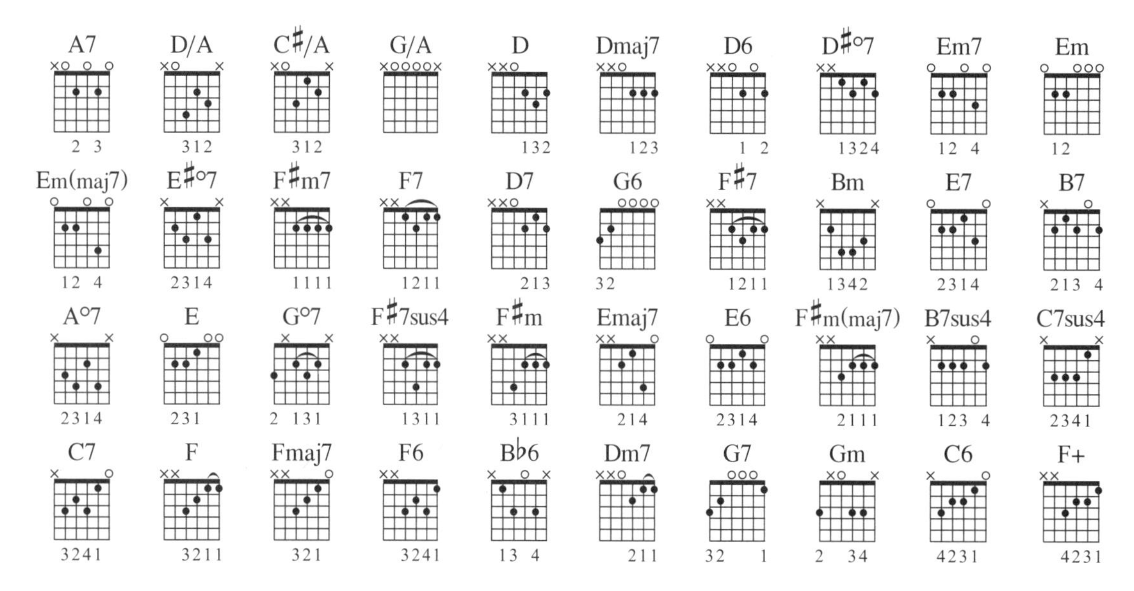

Strum Pattern: 3
Pick Pattern: 3

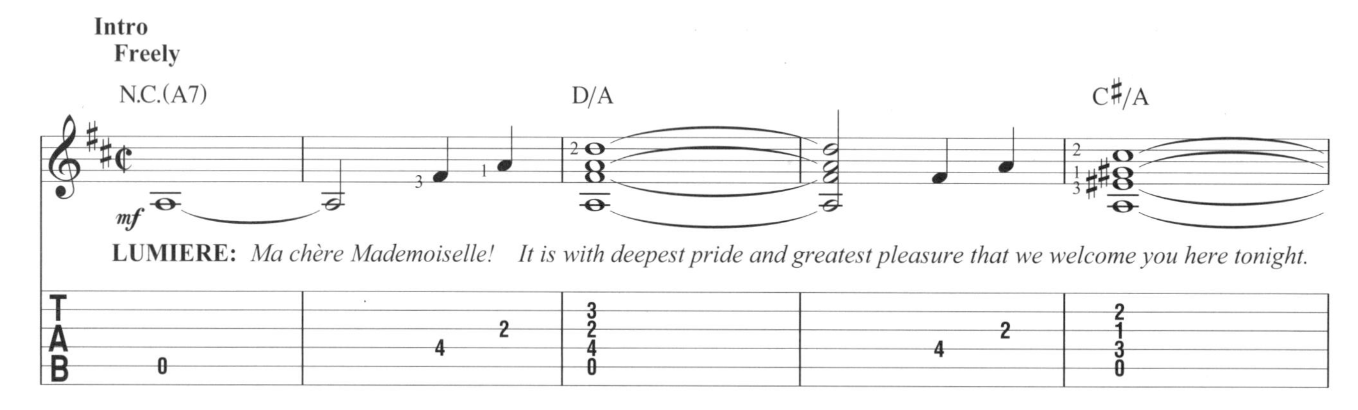

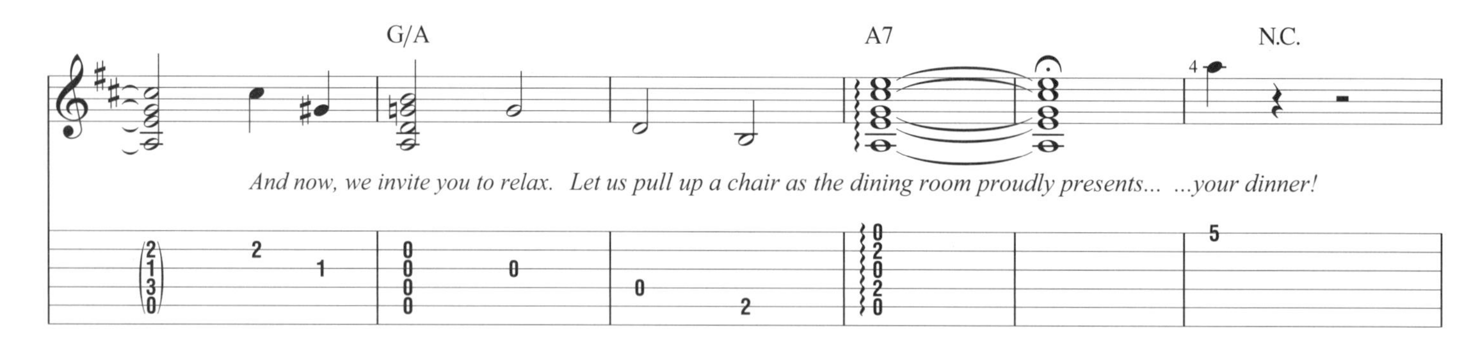

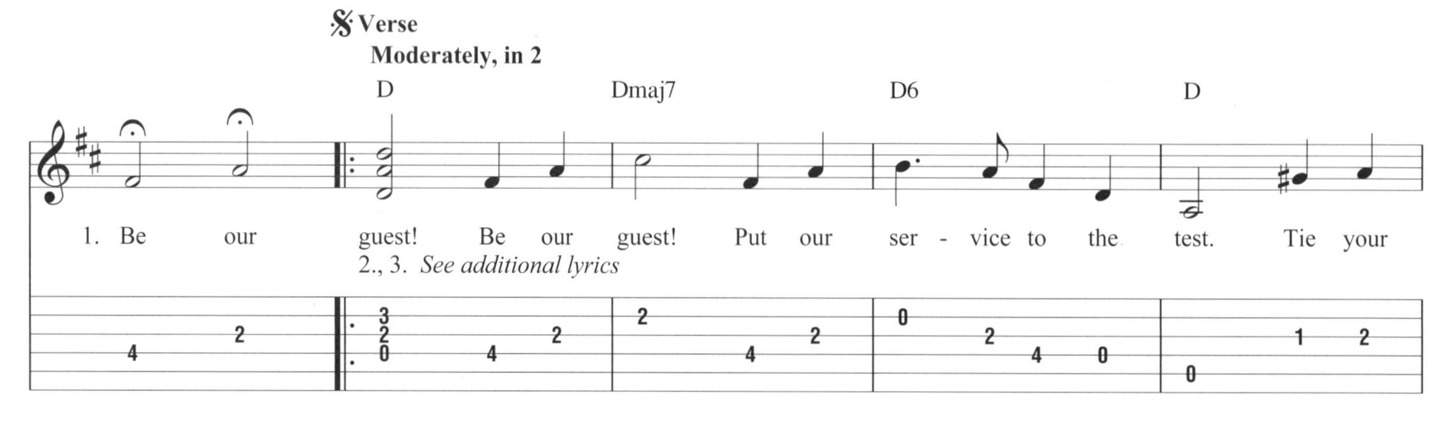

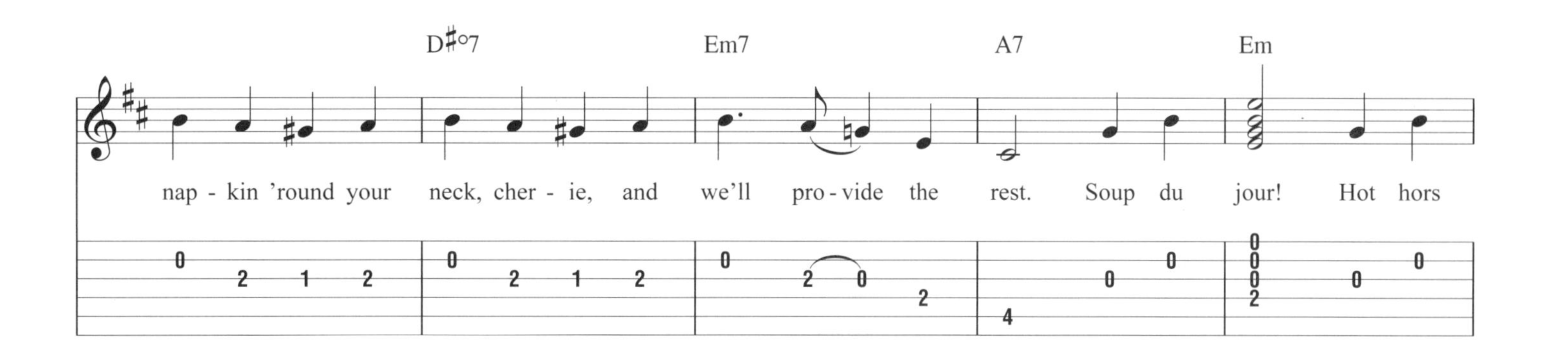
D♯°7 Em7 A7 Em
nap - kin 'round your neck, cher - ie, and we'll pro - vide the rest. Soup du jour! Hot hors

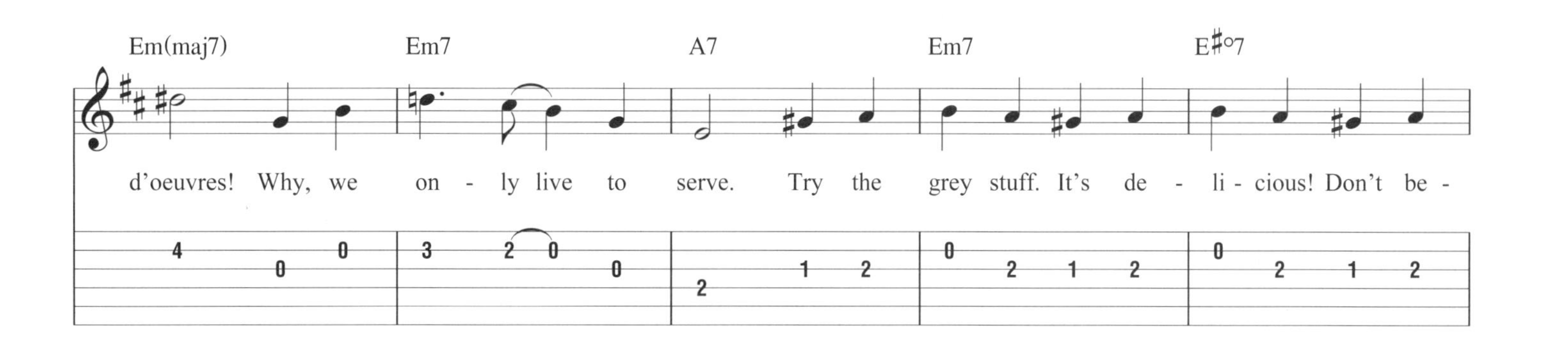
Em(maj7) Em7 A7 Em7 E♯°7
d'oeuvres! Why, we on - ly live to serve. Try the grey stuff. It's de - li - cious! Don't be -

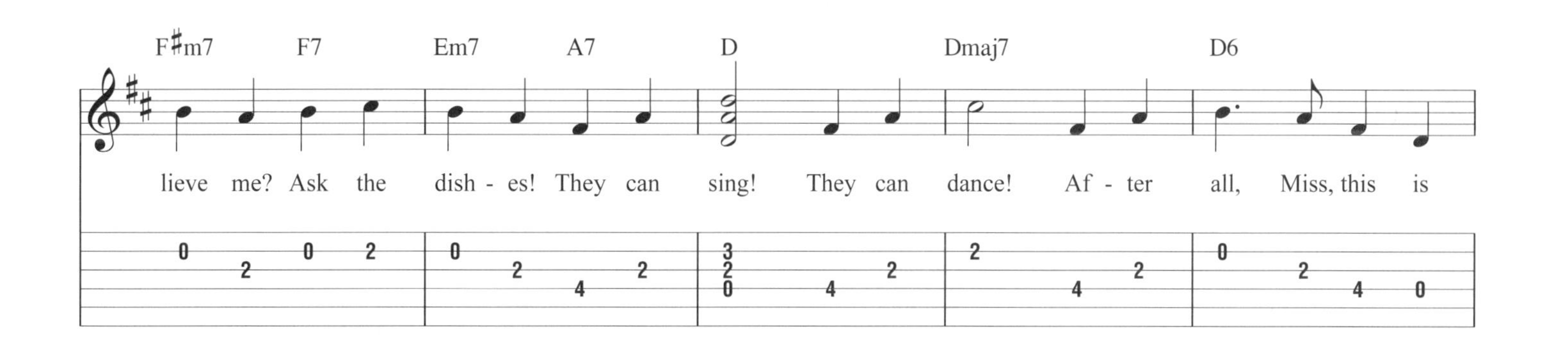
F♯m7 F7 Em7 A7 D Dmaj7 D6
lieve me? Ask the dish - es! They can sing! They can dance! Af - ter all, Miss, this is

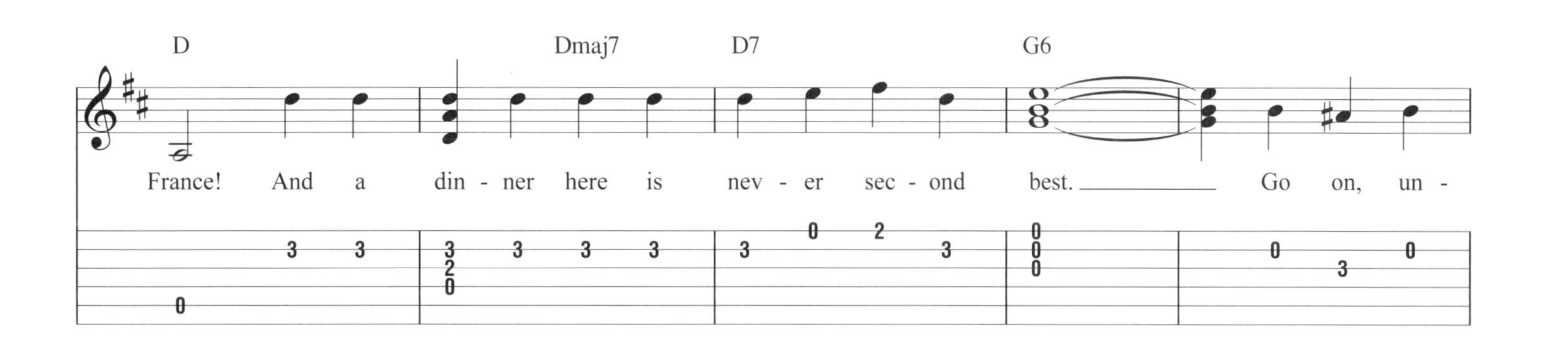
D Dmaj7 D7 G6
France! And a din - ner here is nev - er sec - ond best. Go on, un -

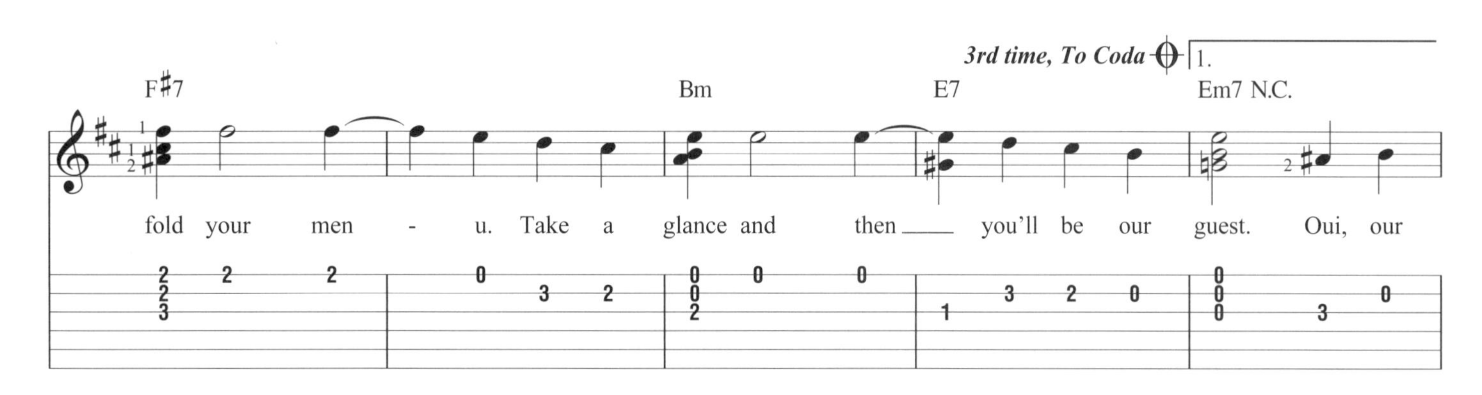
3rd time, To Coda
1.
F♯7 Bm E7 Em7 N.C.
fold your men - u. Take a glance and then you'll be our guest. Oui, our

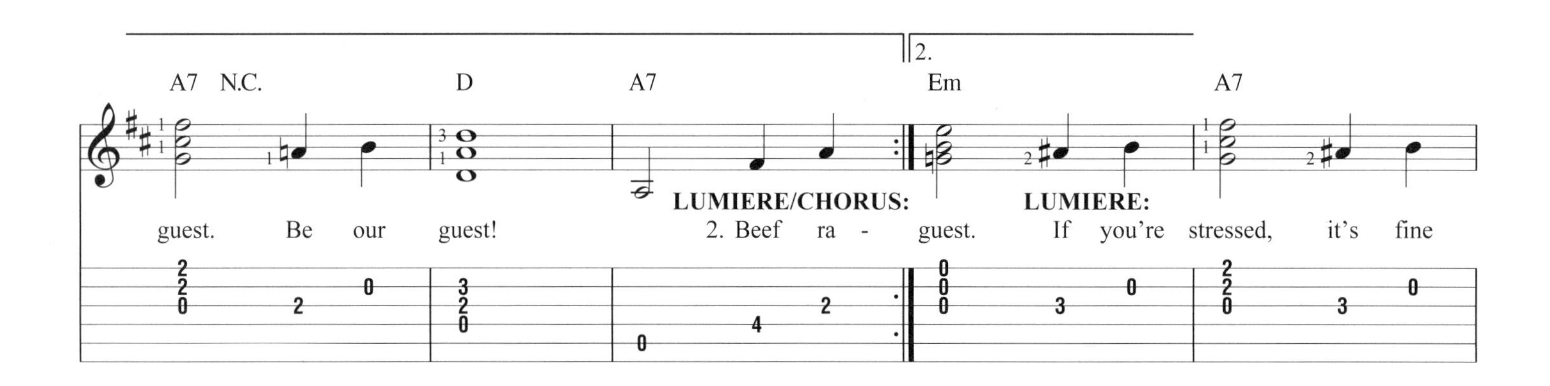
2.
A7 N.C.
D
A7
Em
A7
LUMIERE/CHORUS:
LUMIERE:
guest. Be our guest! 2. Beef ra - guest. If you're stressed, it's fine

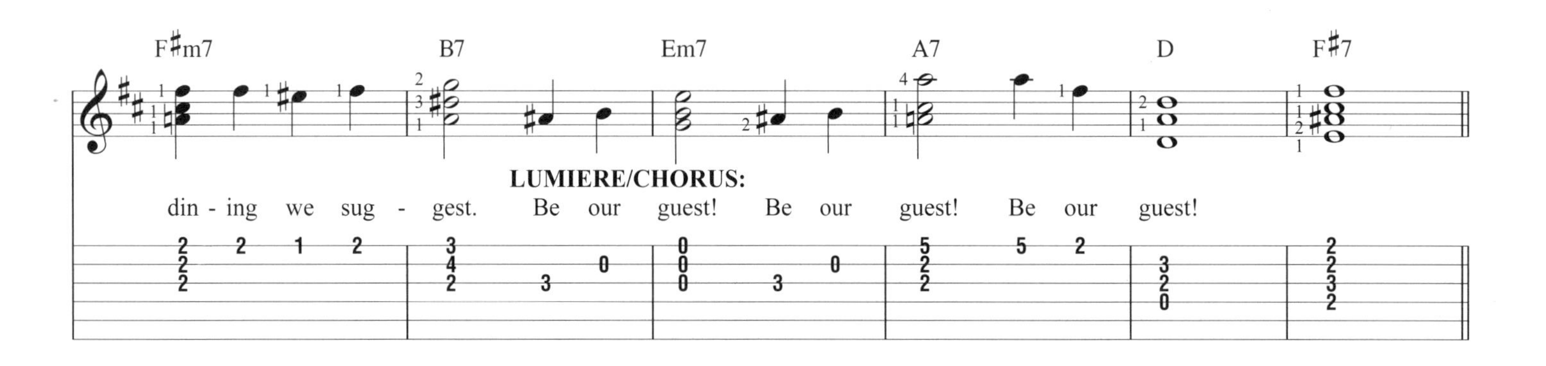
F♯m7
B7
Em7
A7
D
F♯7
LUMIERE/CHORUS:
din - ing we sug - gest. Be our guest! Be our guest! Be our guest!

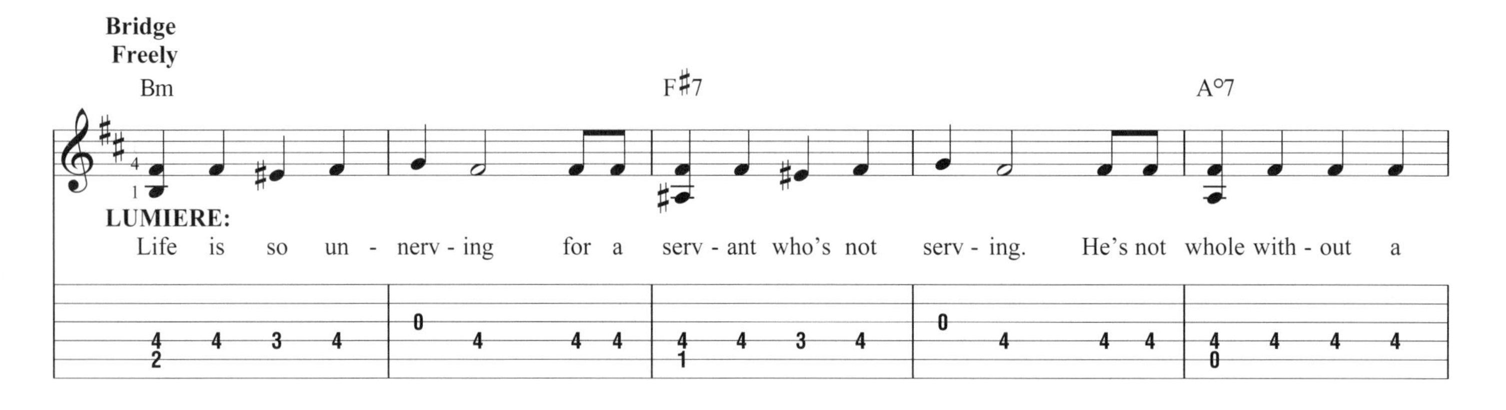
Bridge
Freely
Bm
F♯7
A°7
LUMIERE:
Life is so un - nerv - ing for a serv - ant who's not serv - ing. He's not whole with - out a

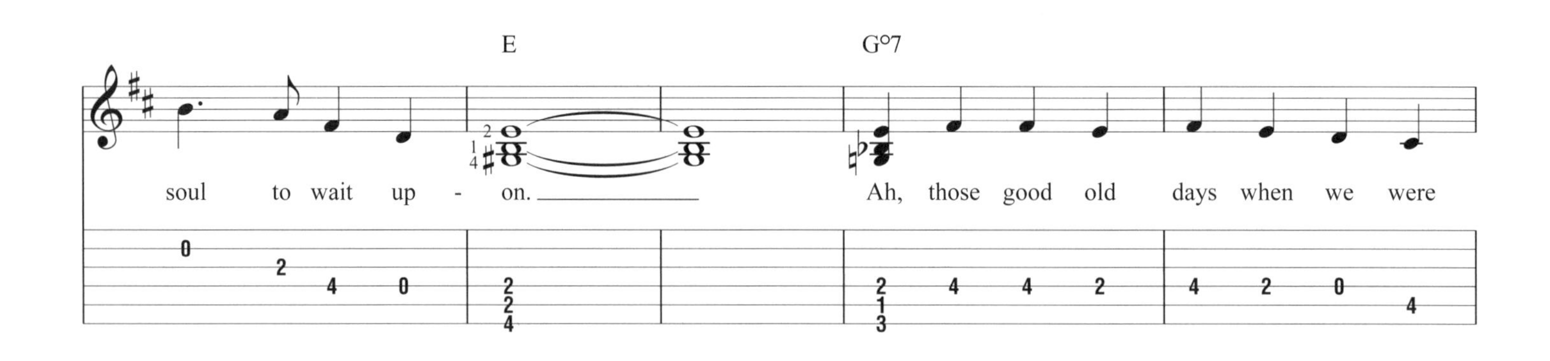
E
G°7
soul to wait up - on.
Ah, those good old days when we were

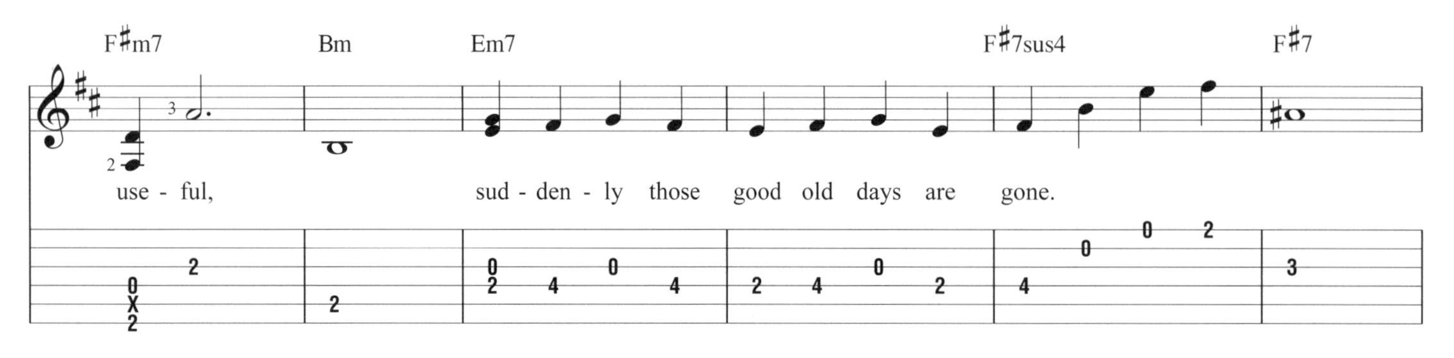
F♯m7
Bm
Em7
F♯7sus4
F♯7
use - ful, sud - den - ly those good old days are gone.

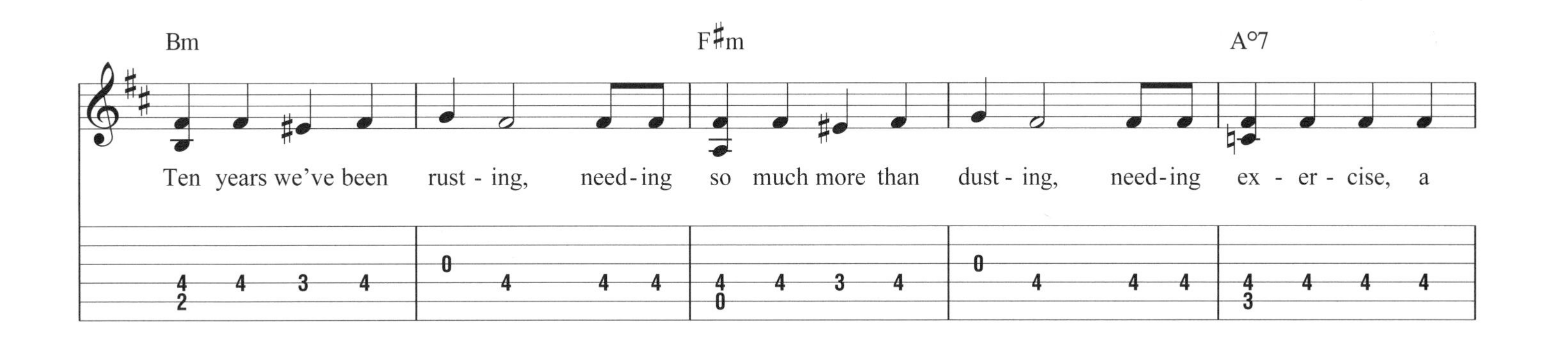
Bm F♯m A°7
Ten years we've been rust - ing, need - ing so much more than dust - ing, need - ing ex - er - cise, a

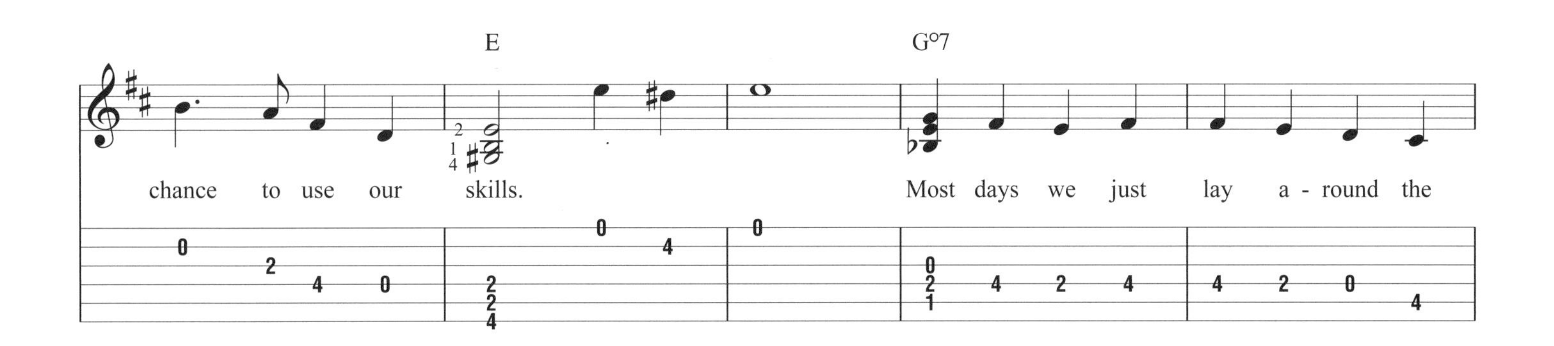
E G°7
chance to use our skills. Most days we just lay a - round the

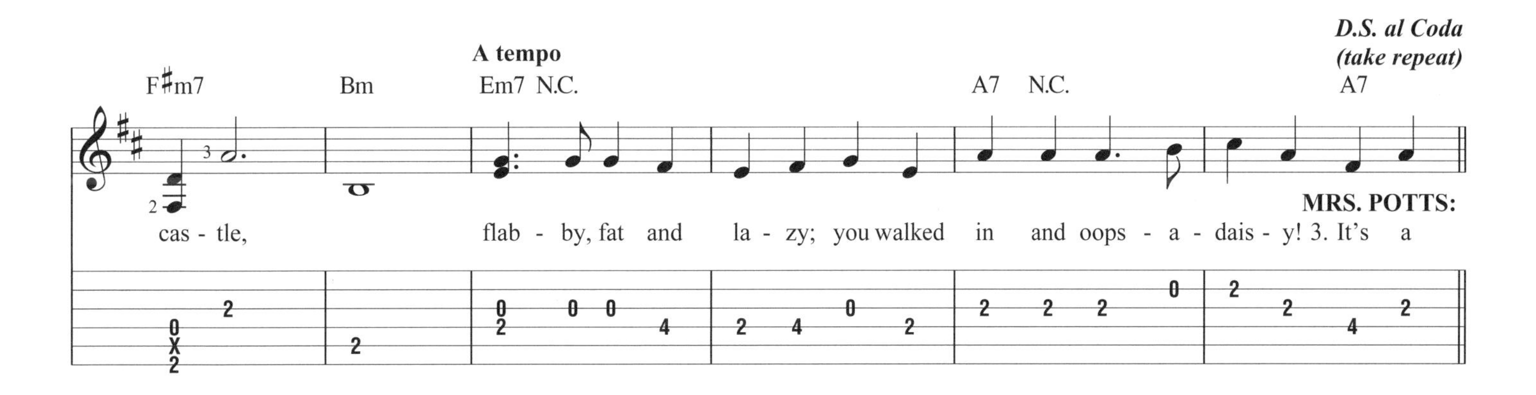
D.S. al Coda
(take repeat)
A tempo
F♯m7 Bm Em7 N.C. A7 N.C. A7
MRS. POTTS:
cas - tle, flab - by, fat and la - zy; you walked in and oops - a - dais - y! 3. It's a

Coda
Em A7 F♯m B7
accel.
CHORUS: MRS. POTTS: CHORUS: ALL:
guest? She's our guest! She's our guest! Be our guest! 4. Be our

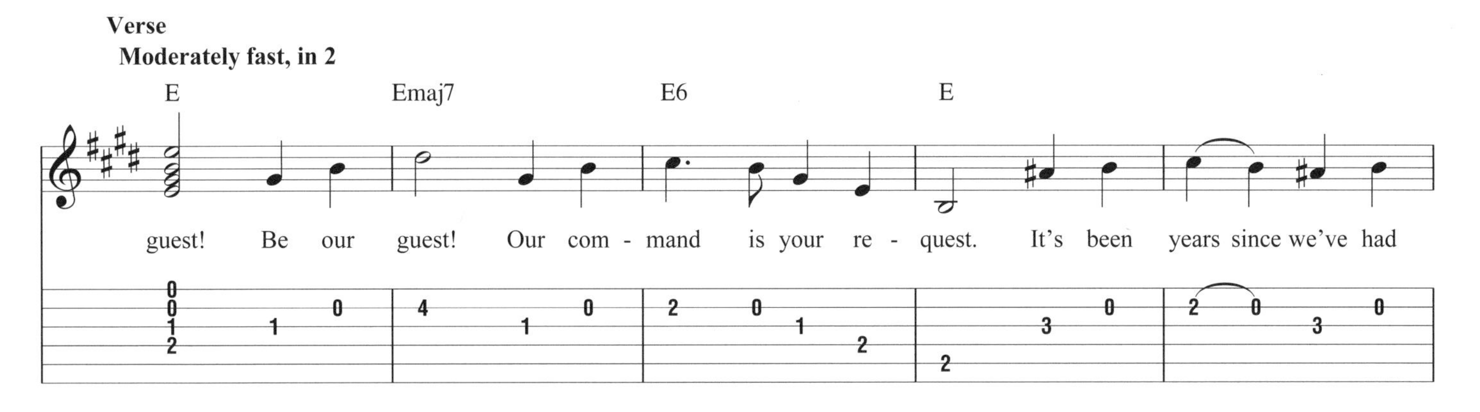
Verse
Moderately fast, in 2
E Emaj7 E6 E
guest! Be our guest! Our com - mand is your re - quest. It's been years since we've had

E♯°7
F♯m7
B7
F♯m
F♯m(maj7)
an - y - bod - y here and we're ob - sessed! With your meal, with your ease, yes in -

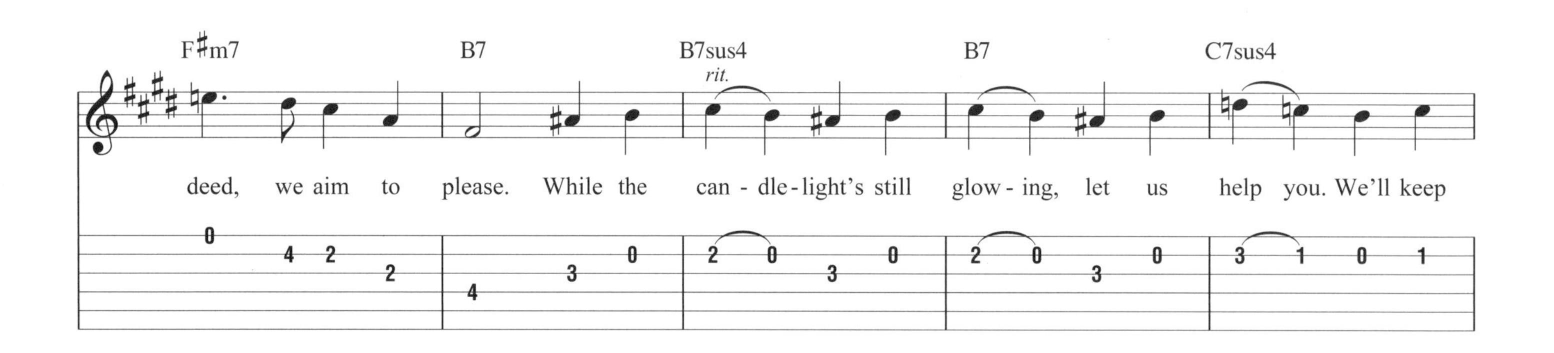
F♯m7
B7
B7sus4
rit.
B7
C7sus4
deed, we aim to please. While the can - dle - light's still glow - ing, let us help you. We'll keep

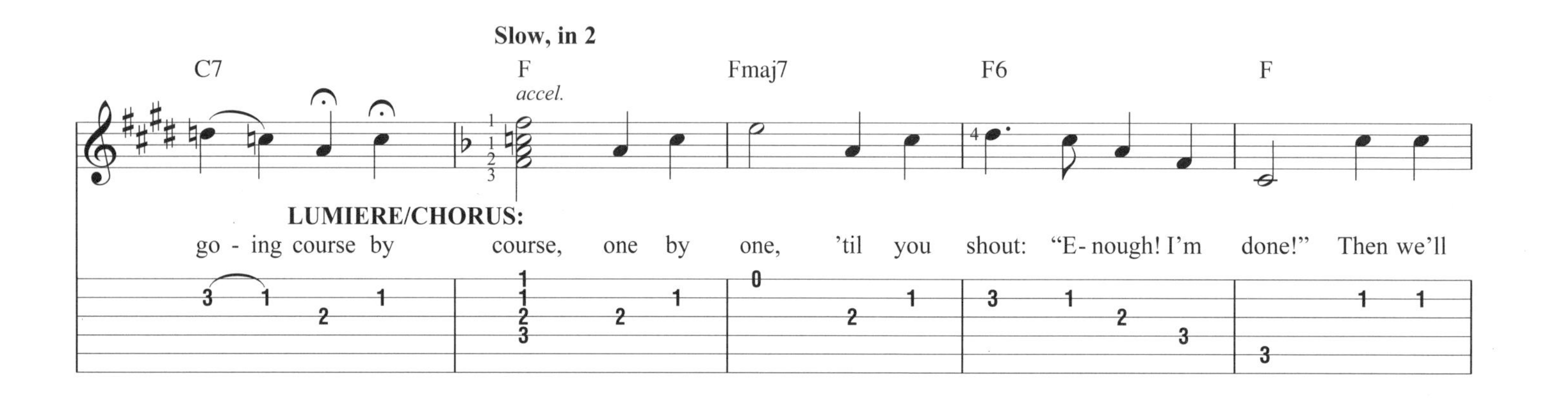
Slow, in 2
C7
F
accel.
Fmaj7
F6
F
LUMIERE/CHORUS:
go - ing course by course, one by one, 'til you shout: "E - nough! I'm done!" Then we'll

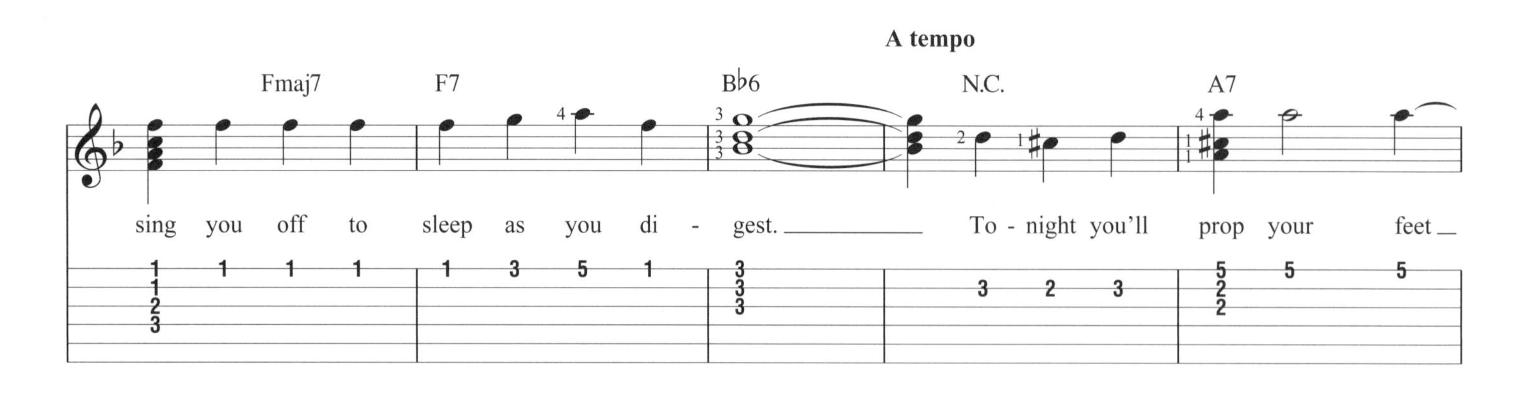
A tempo
Fmaj7
F7
B♭6
N.C.
A7
sing you off to sleep as you di - gest. To - night you'll prop your feet

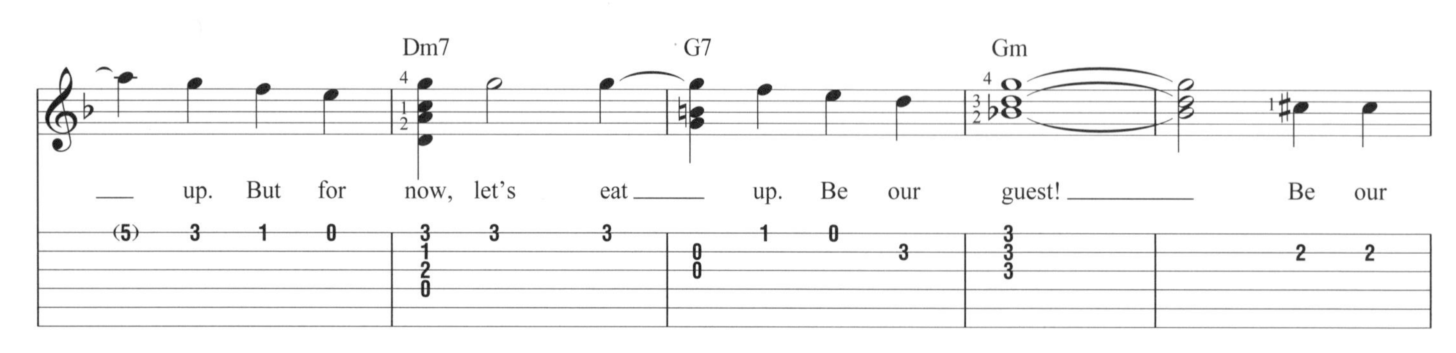
Dm7
G7
Gm
up. But for now, let's eat up. Be our guest! Be our

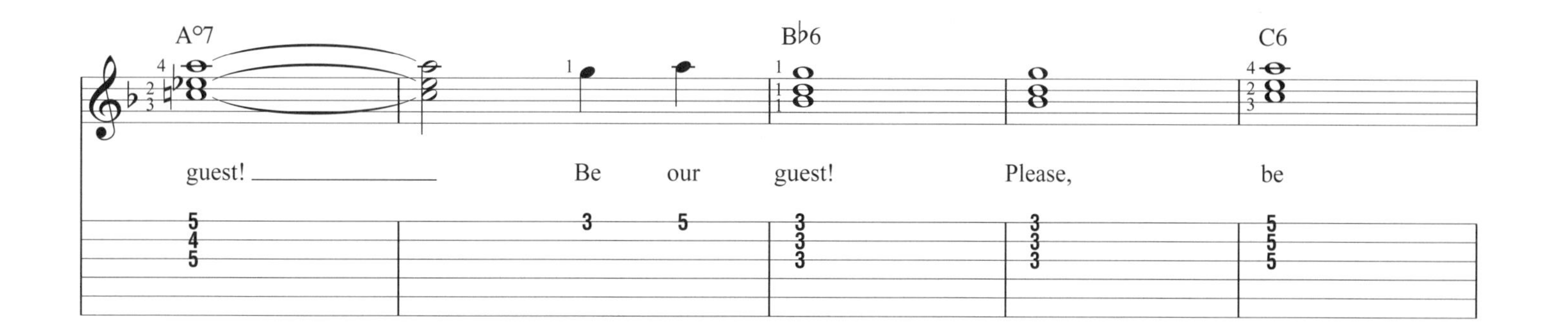

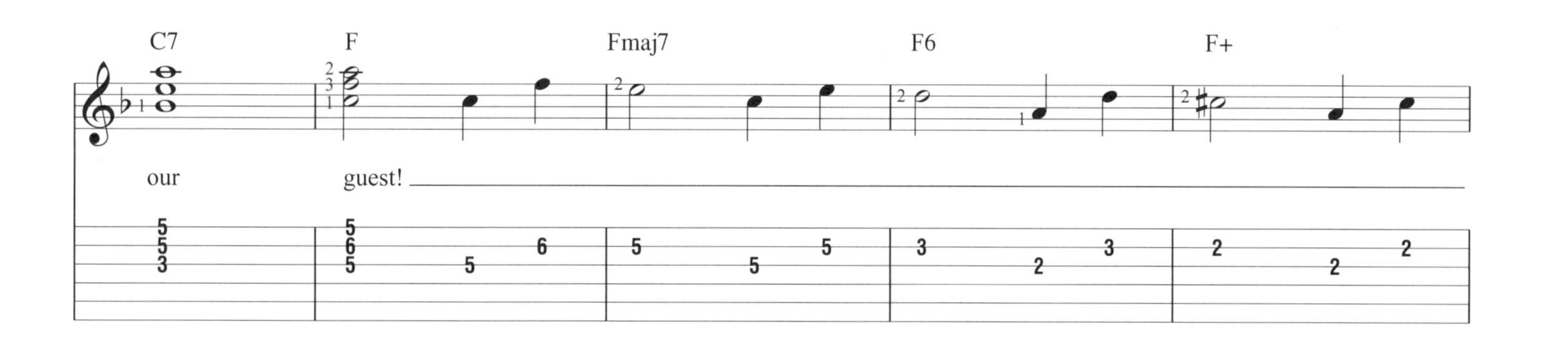

Additional Lyrics

LUMIERE/CHORUS: 2. Beef ragout! Cheese soufflé! Pie and pudding "enflambé!"
LUMIERE: We'll prepare and serve with flare a culinary cabaret.
You're alone and you're scared, but the banquet's all prepared.
No one's gloomy or complaining while the flatware's entertaining.
We tell jokes! I do tricks with my fellow candlesticks.
CHORUS: And it's all in perfect taste. That you can bet.
LUMIERE/CHORUS: Come on and lift your glass. You've won your own free pass
To be our guest. **LUMIERE:** If you're stressed, it's fine dining we suggest.
LUMIERE/CHORUS: Be our guest! Be our guest! Be our guest!

MRS. POTTS: 3. It's a guest! It's a guest! Sakes alive, well, I'll be blessed.
Wine's been poured and, thank the Lord, I've had the napkins freshly pressed.
With dessert she'll want tea. And my dear, that's fine with me.
While the cups do their soft-shoeing, I'll be bubbling, I'll be brewing.
I'll get warm, piping hot. Heaven's sakes, is that a spot?
Clean it up! We want the company impressed.
We've got a lot to do! Is it one lump or two
For you, our guest? **CHORUS:** She's our guest! **MRS. POTTS:** She's our guest! **CHORUS:** Be our guest!

Belle

from BEAUTY AND THE BEAST
Music by Alan Menken
Lyrics by Howard Ashman

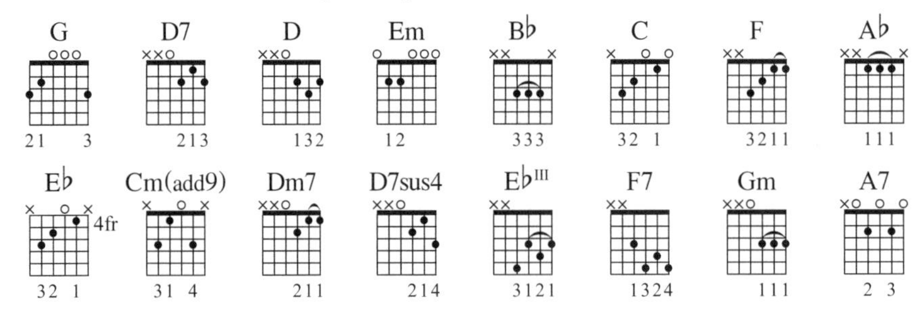

*Capo V

Strum Pattern: 2
Pick Pattern: 3

Verse
Moderately, in 2

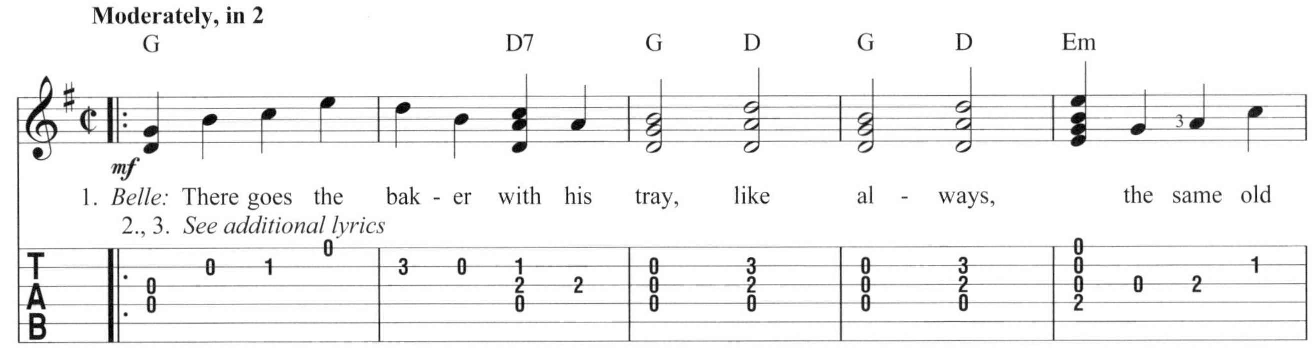

*Optional: To match recording, place capo at 5th fret.

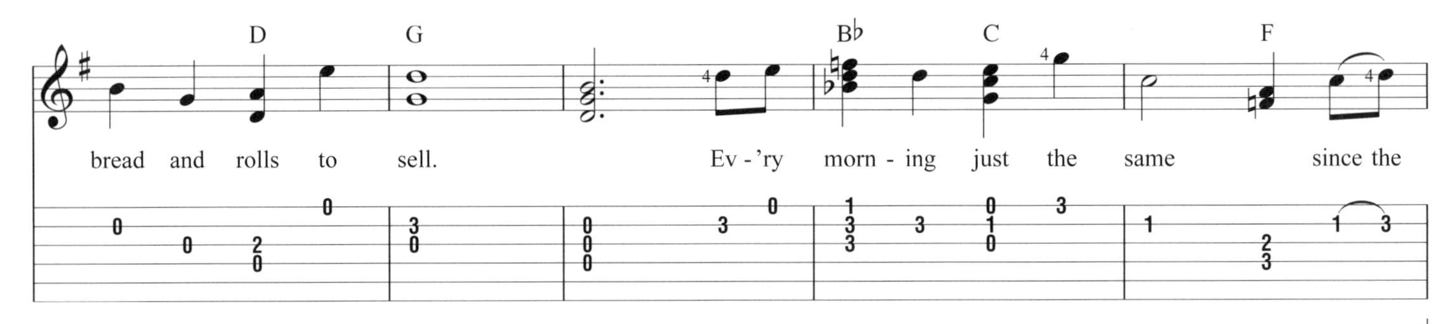

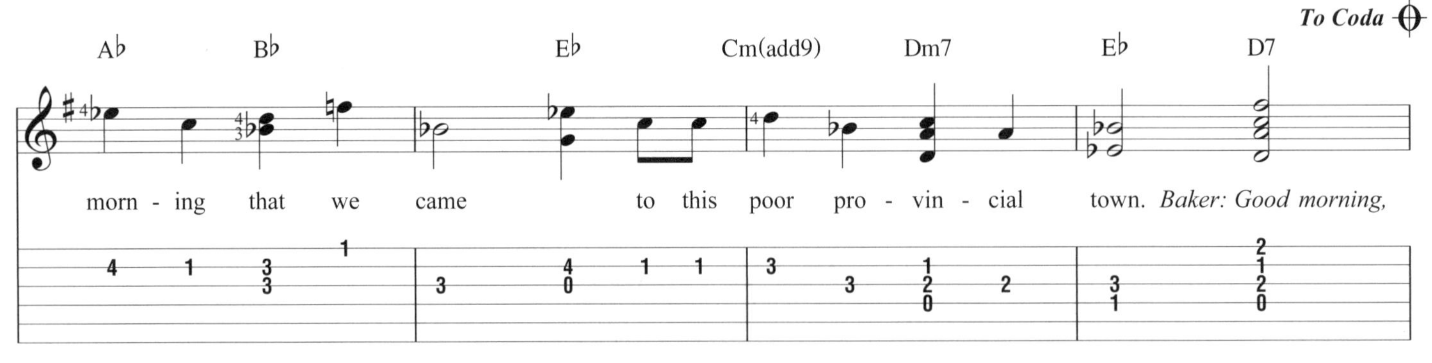

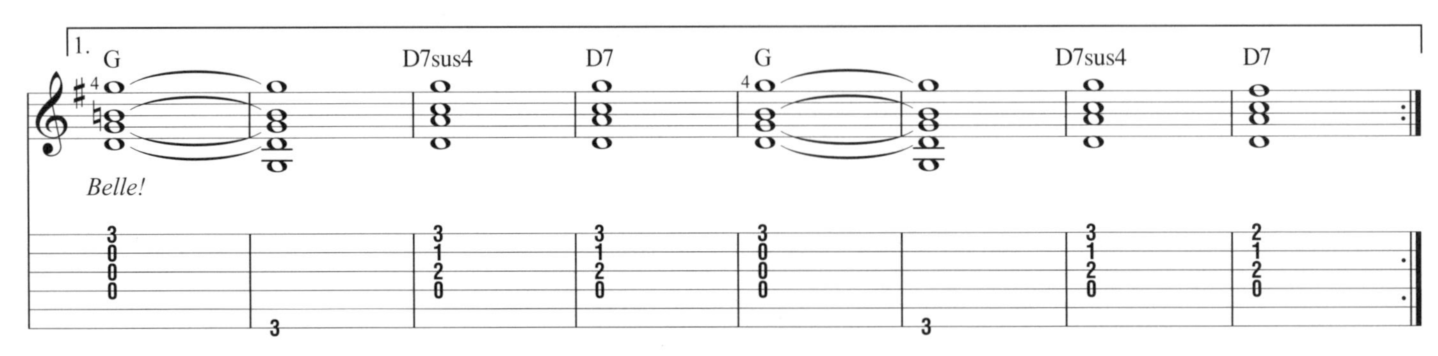

Additional Lyrics

2. *Townsfolk:* Look, there she goes. That girl is strange, no question.
Dazed and distracted, can't you tell?
Never part of any crowd, 'cause her head's up on some cloud.
No denying she's a funny girl, that Belle.

3. *Townsfolk:* Look, there she goes. That girl is so peculiar.
I wonder if she's feeling well.
With a dreamy far-off look, and her nose stuck in a book,
What a puzzle to the rest of us is Belle.

Can You Feel the Love Tonight

from THE LION KING

Music by Elton John
Lyrics by Tim Rice

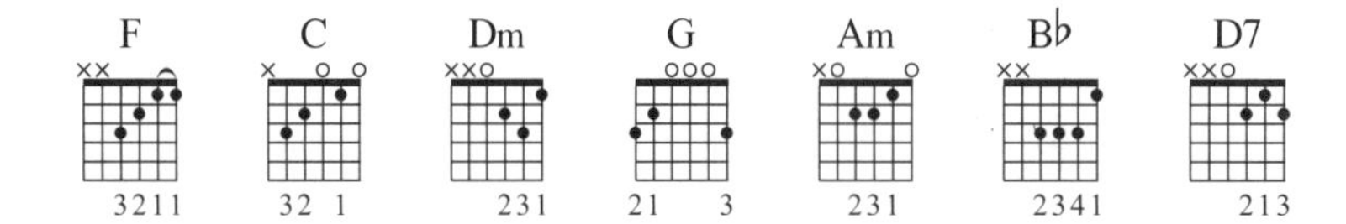

*Tune down 1 step:
(low to high) D-G-C-F-A-D

Strum Pattern: 4
Pick Pattern: 4

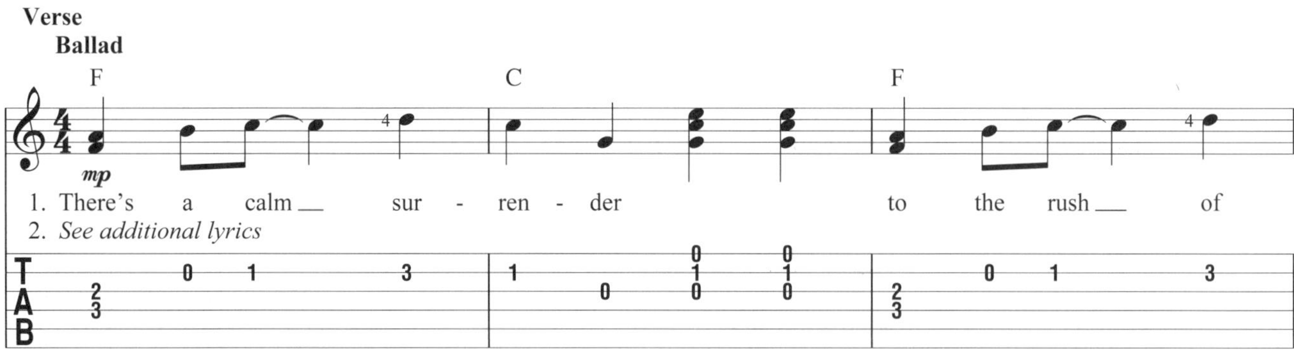

*Optional: To match recording, tune down 1 step.

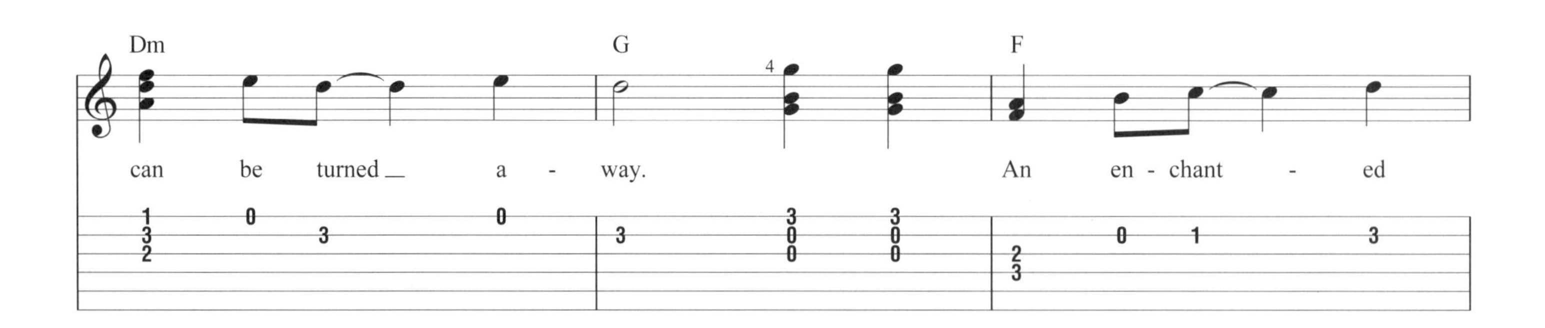

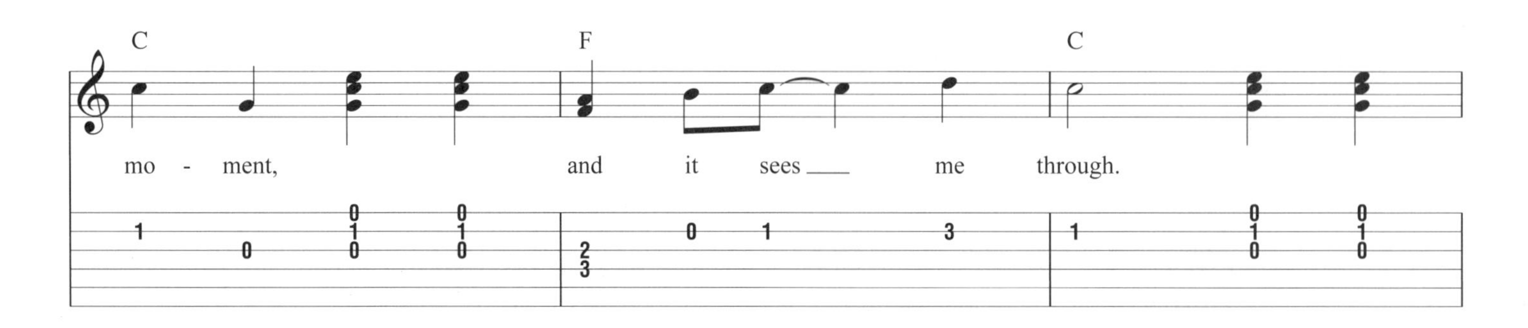

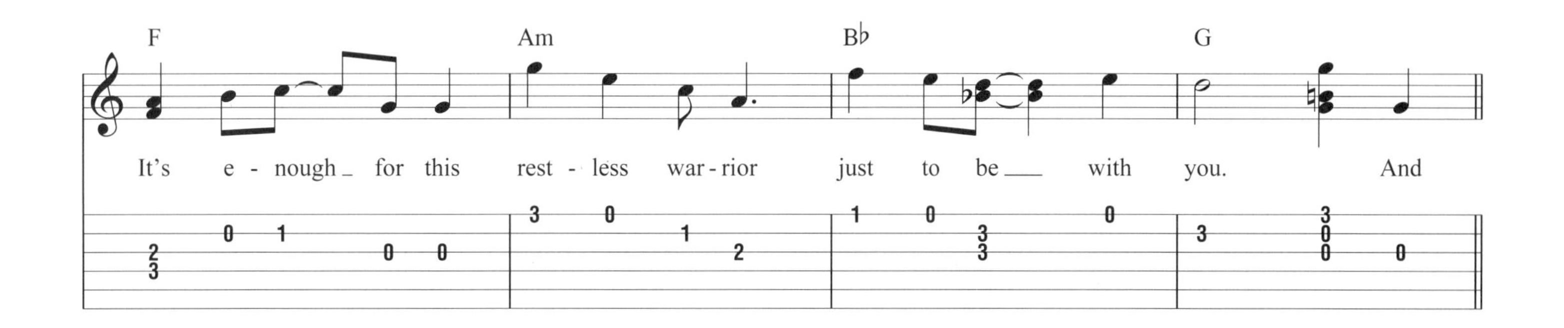
F Am B♭ G
It's e - nough for this rest - less war - rior just to be with you. And

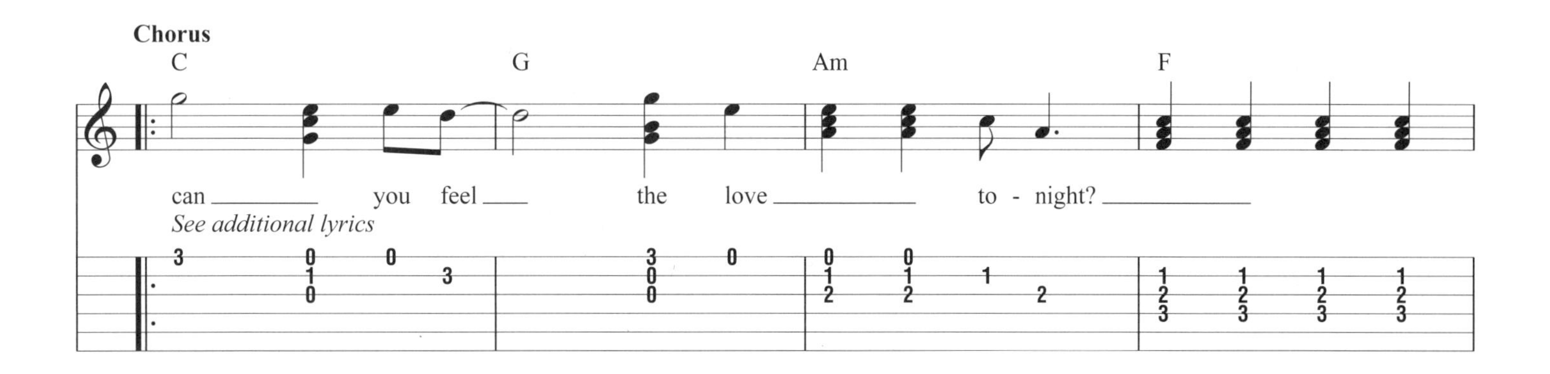
Chorus
C G Am F
can you feel the love to - night?
See additional lyrics

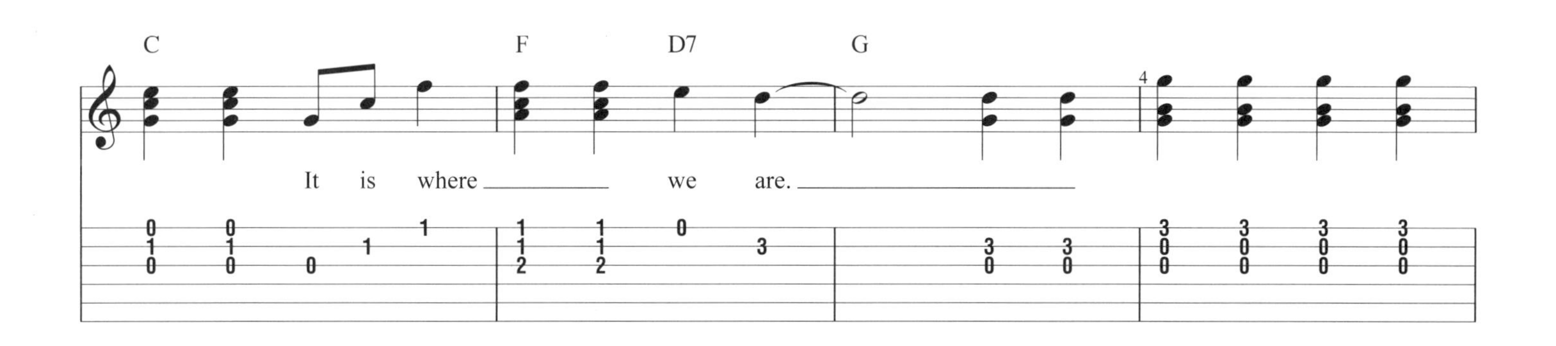
C F D7 G
It is where we are.

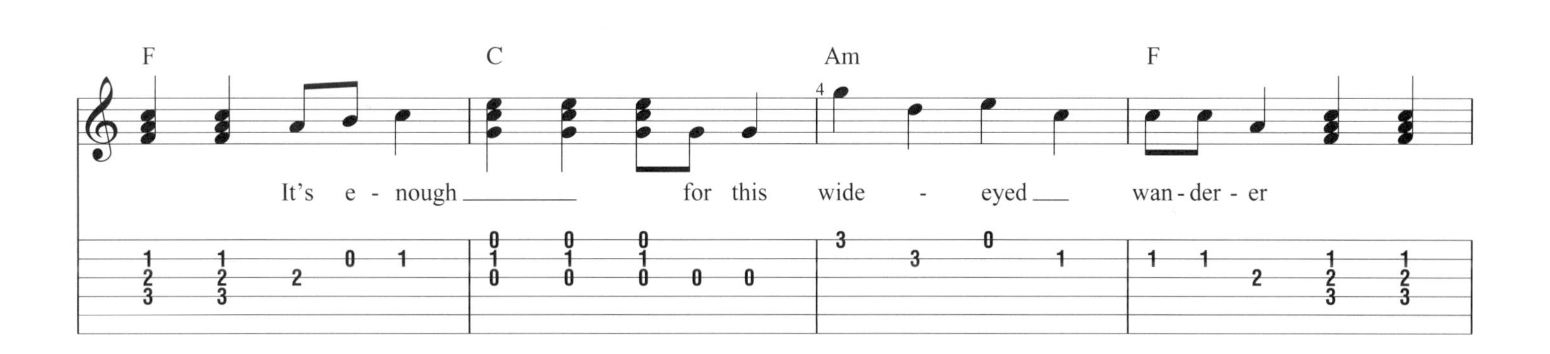
F C Am F
It's e - nough for this wide - eyed wan - der - er

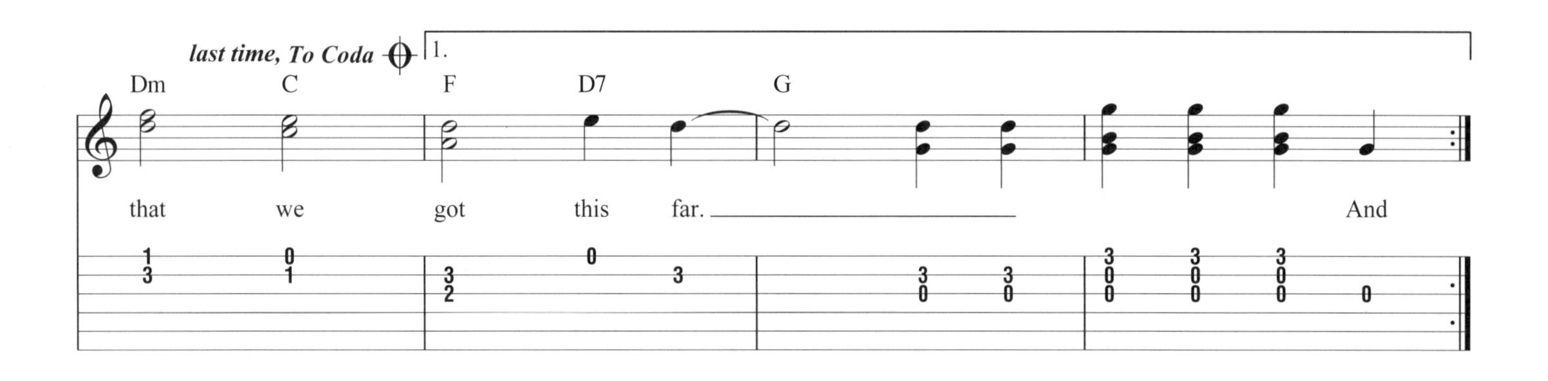
last time, To Coda
1.
Dm C F D7 G
that we got this far. And

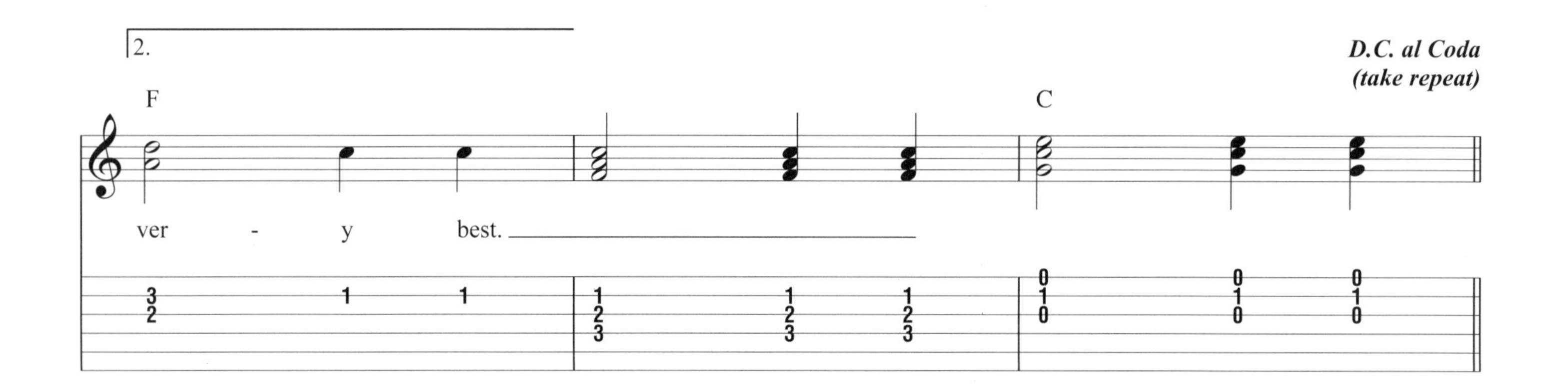

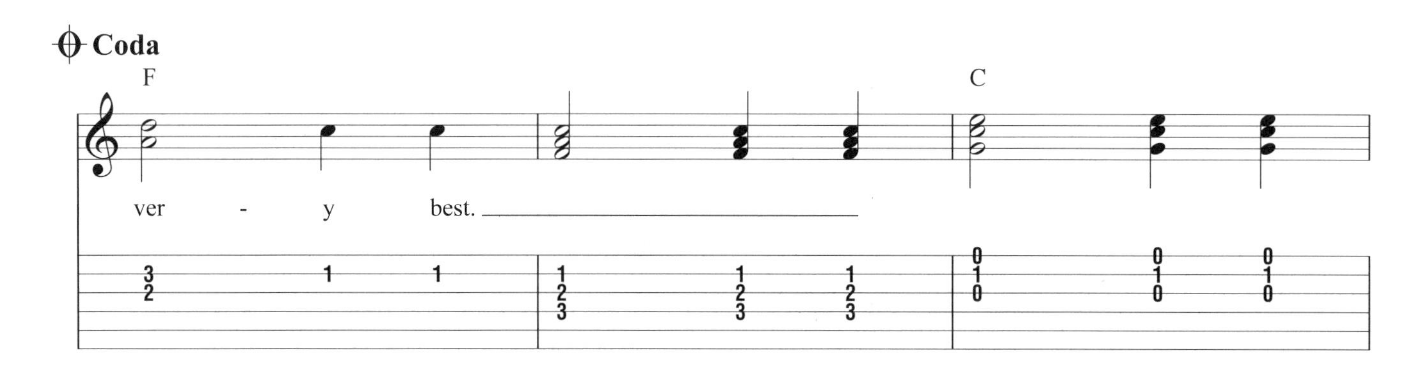

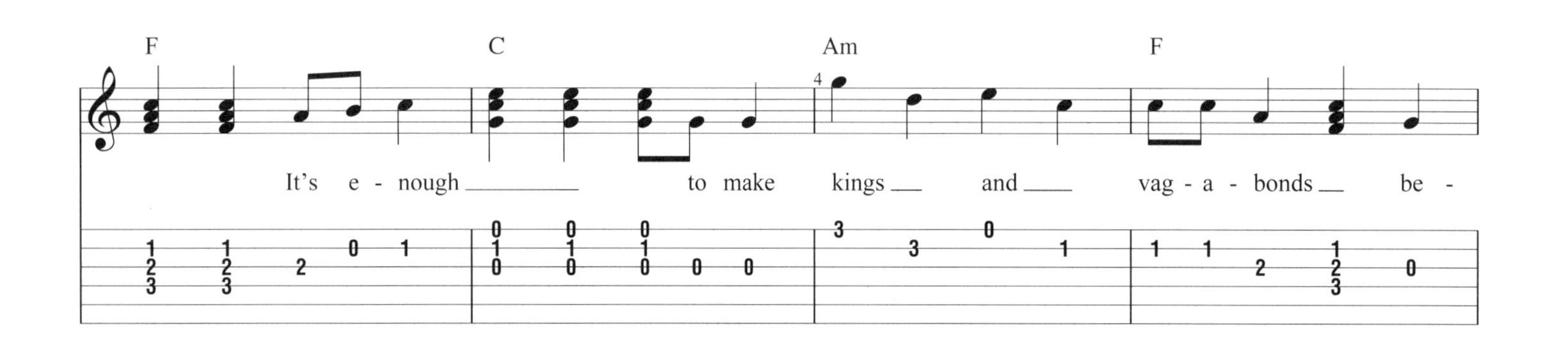

Additional Lyrics

2. There's a time for ev'ryone,
   If they only learn
   That the twisting kaleidoscope
   Moves us all in turn.
   There's a rhyme and reason
   To the wild outdoors
   When the heart of this star-crossed voyager
   Beats in time with yours.

Chorus And can you feel the love tonight.
How it's laid to rest?
It's enough to make kings and vagabonds
Believe the very best.

Do You Want to Build a Snowman?

from FROZEN

Music and Lyrics by Kristen Anderson-Lopez and Robert Lopez

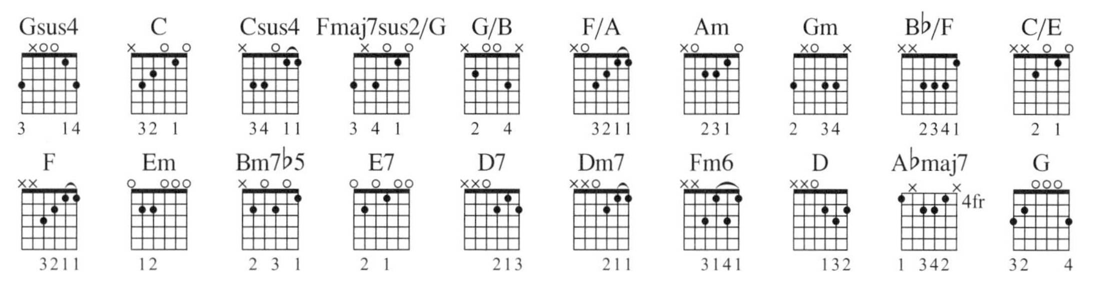

Strum Pattern: 6
Pick Pattern: 6

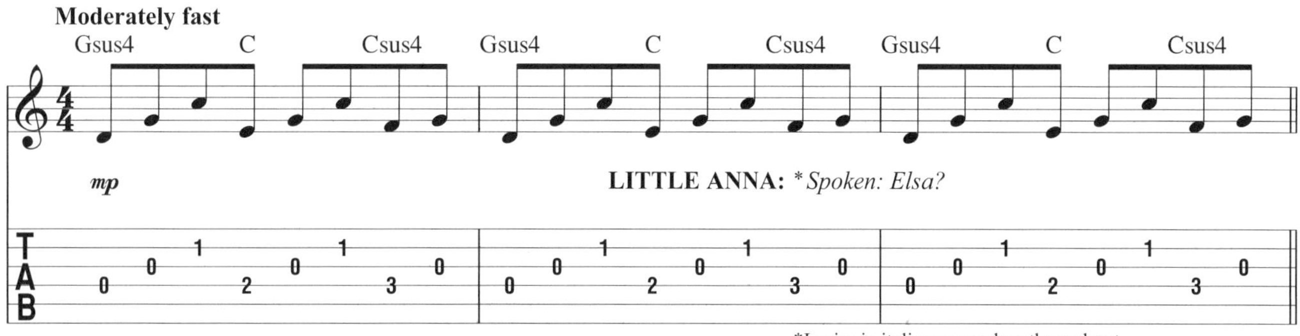

*Lyrics in italics are spoken throughout.

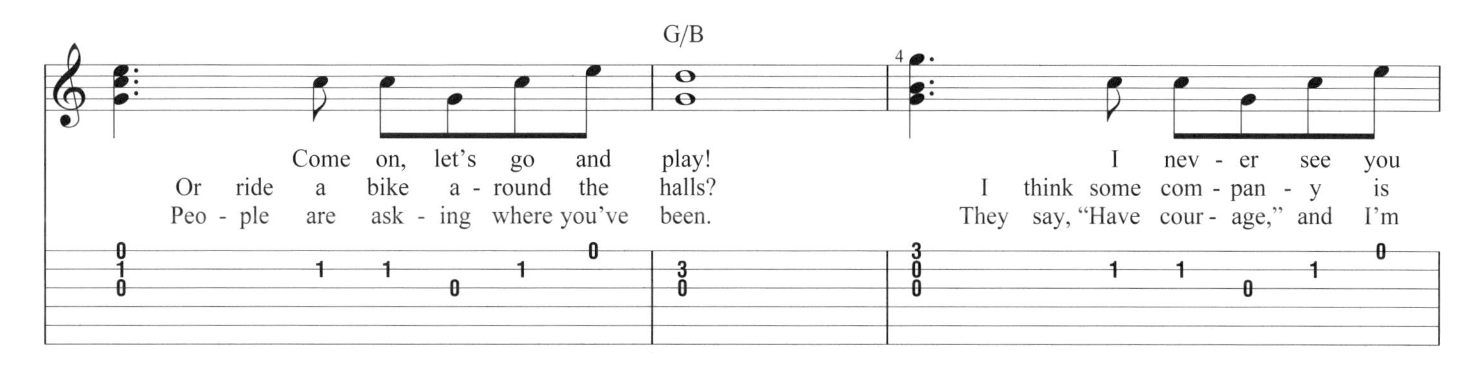

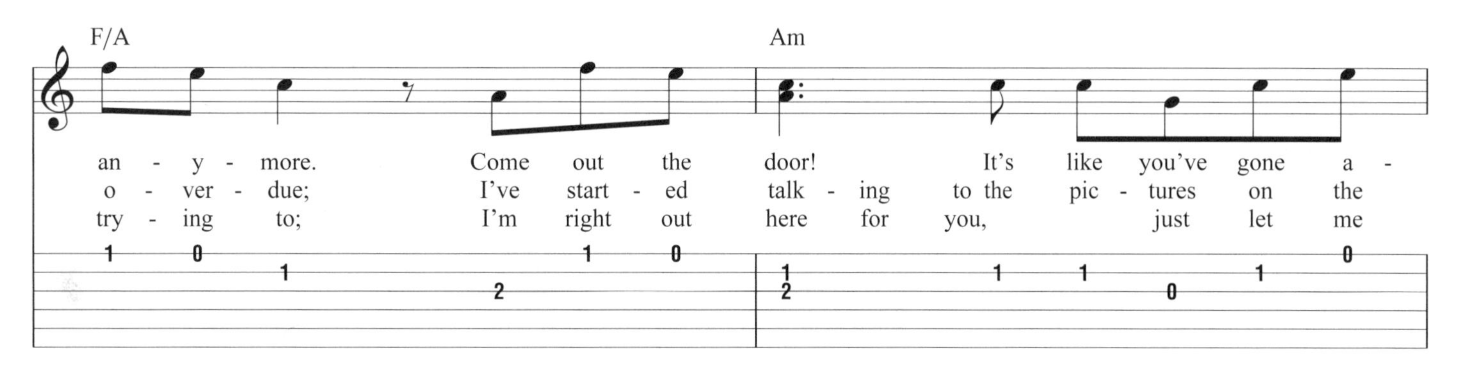

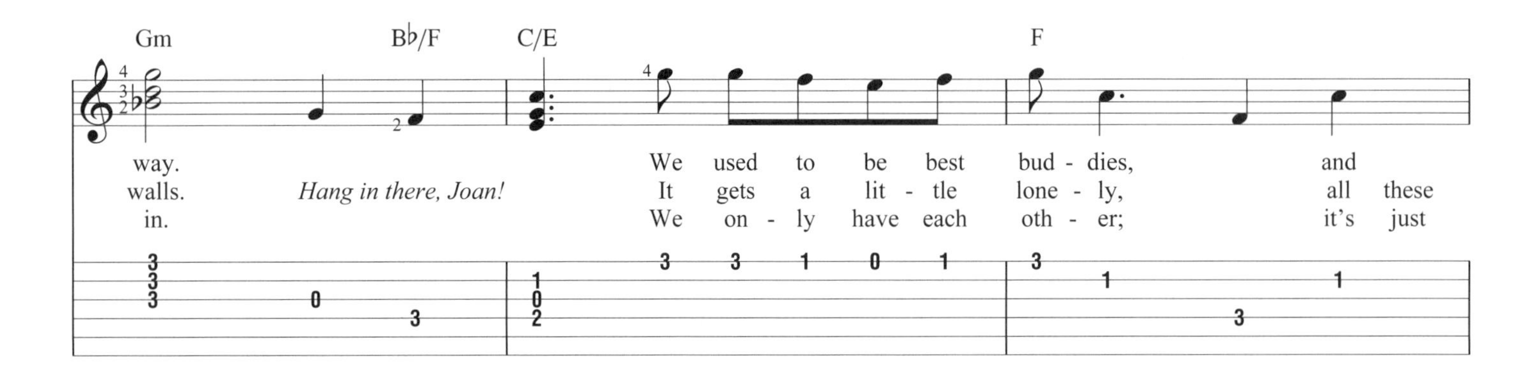

Gm B♭/F C/E F
way. We used to be best bud - dies, and
walls. Hang in there, Joan! It gets a lit - tle lone - ly, all these
in. We on - ly have each oth - er; it's just

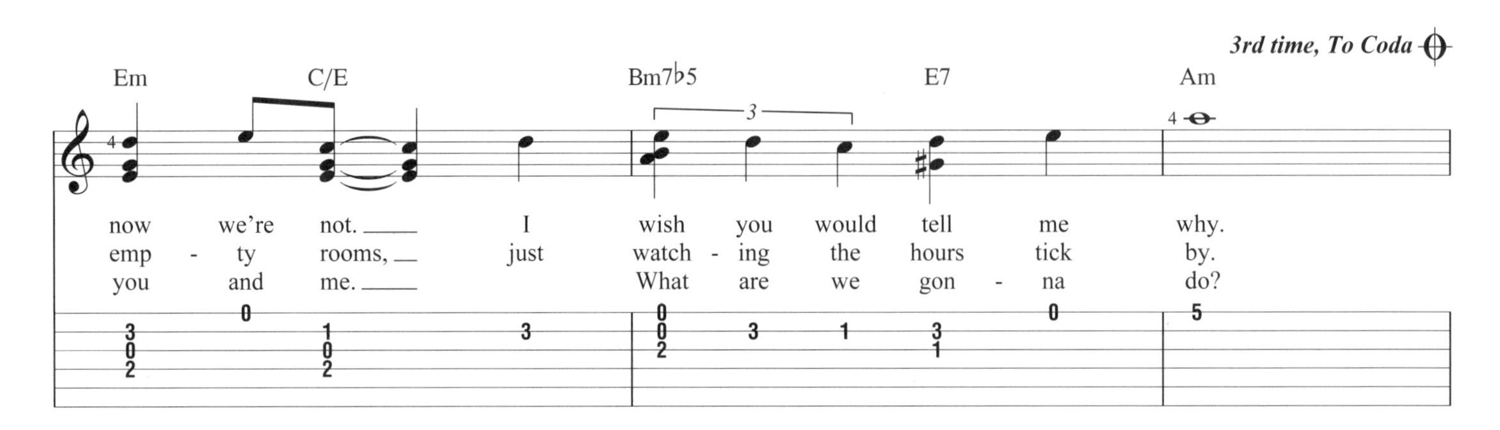

3rd time, To Coda
Em C/E Bm7♭5 E7 Am
now we're not. I wish you would tell me why.
emp - ty rooms, just watch - ing the hours tick by.
you and me. What are we gon - na do?

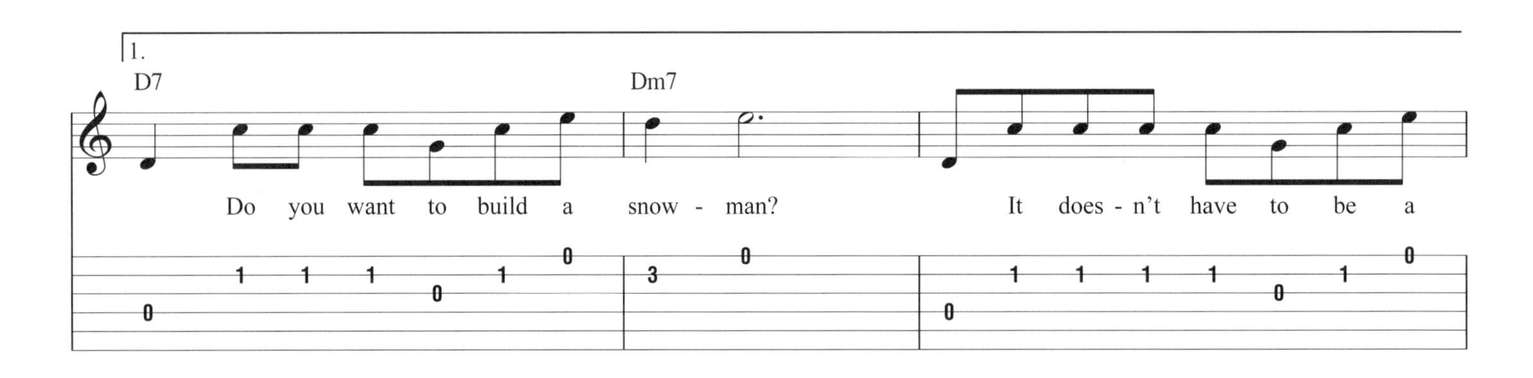

1.
D7 Dm7
Do you want to build a snow - man? It does - n't have to be a

Fm6 Gsus4 C Csus4
snow - man. LITTLE ELSA: Go away, Anna. LITTLE ANNA: O - kay, bye.

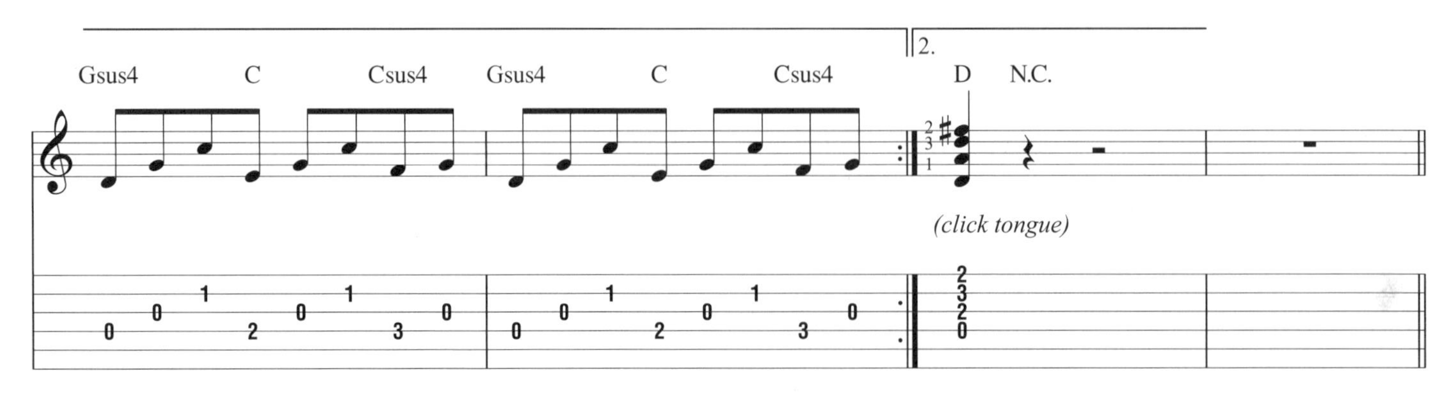

Gsus4 C Csus4 Gsus4 C Csus4
2.
D N.C.
(click tongue)

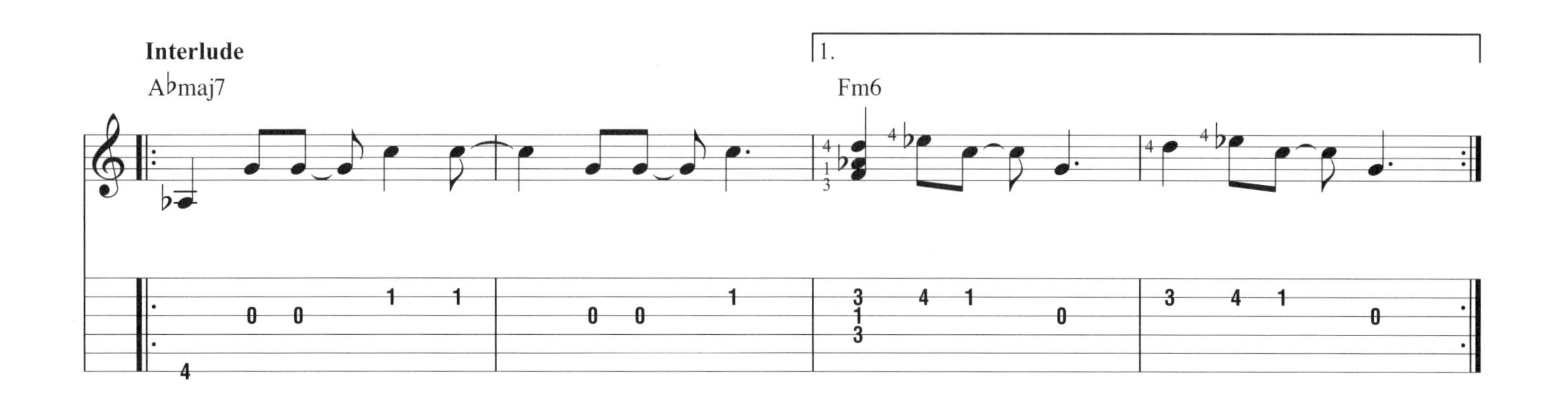
Interlude
A♭maj7
1.
Fm6

2.
N.C.

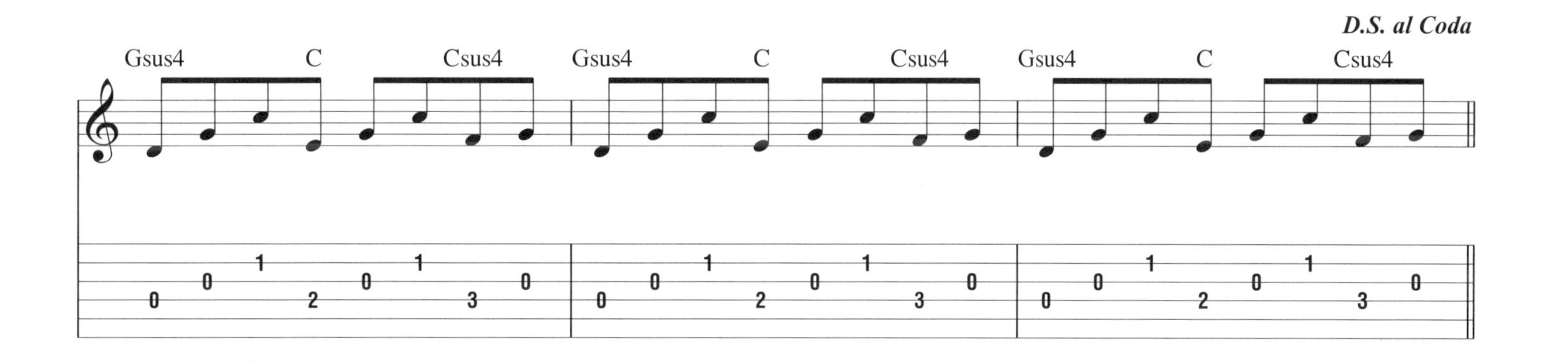
D.S. al Coda
Gsus4 C Csus4
Gsus4 C Csus4
Gsus4 C Csus4

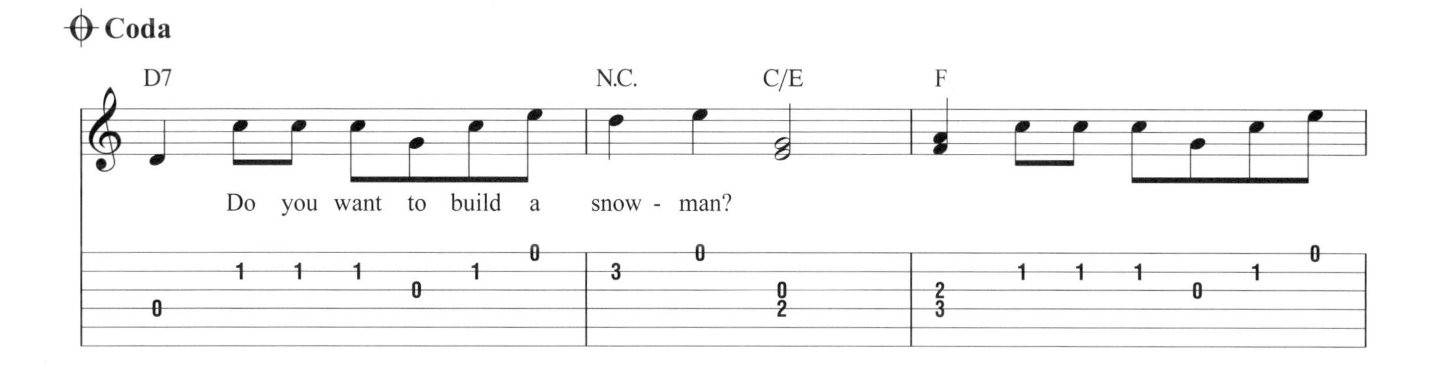
Coda
D7
N.C.
C/E
F
Do you want to build a snow - man?

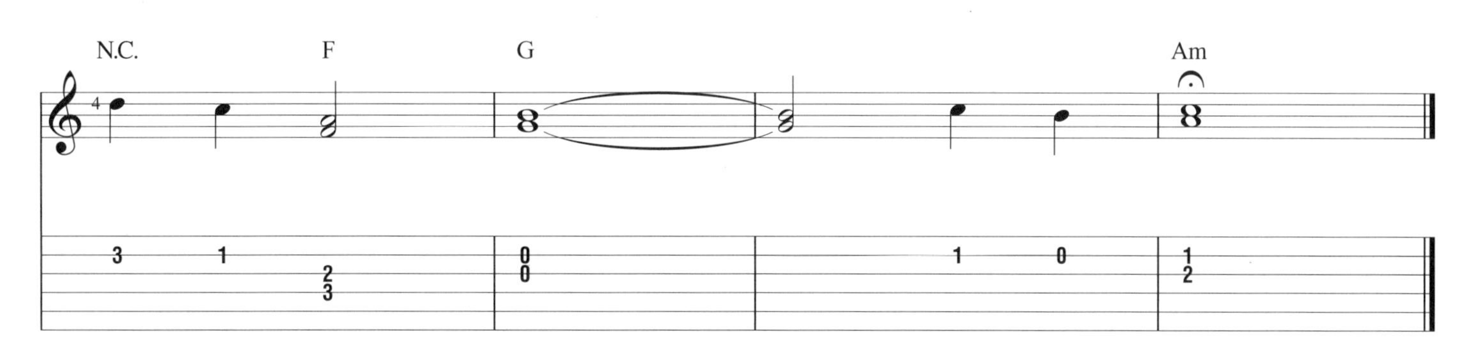
N.C.
F
G
Am

Circle of Life

from THE LION KING

Music by Elton John
Lyrics by Tim Rice

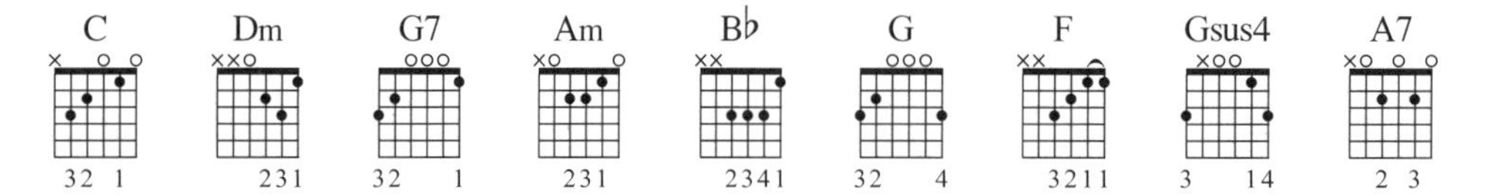

*Tune down 1 step:
(low to high) D-G-C-F-A-D

Strum Pattern: 2
Pick Pattern: 2

*Optional: To match recording, tune down 1 step.

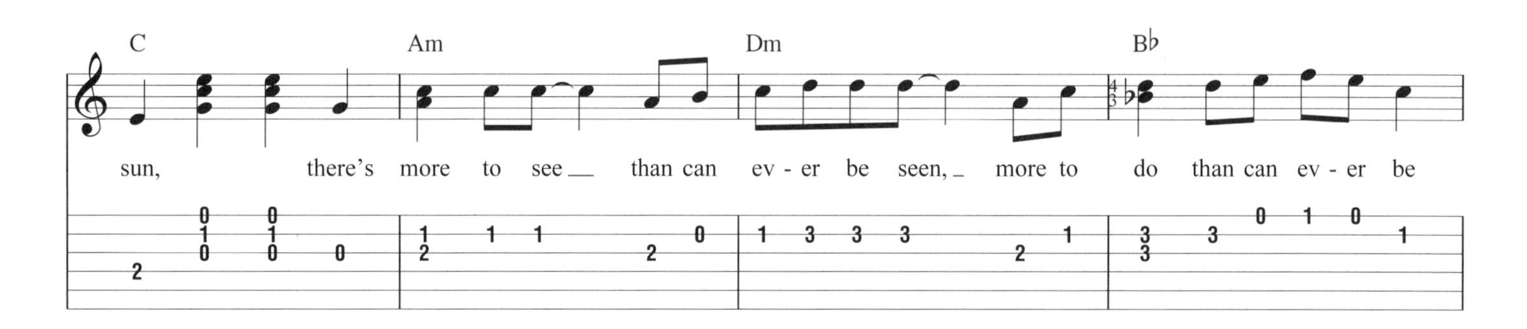

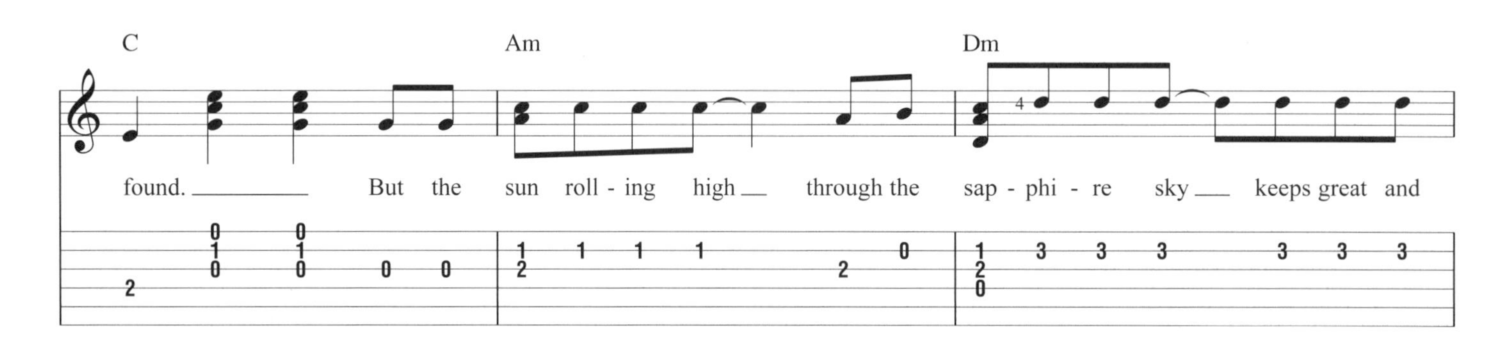

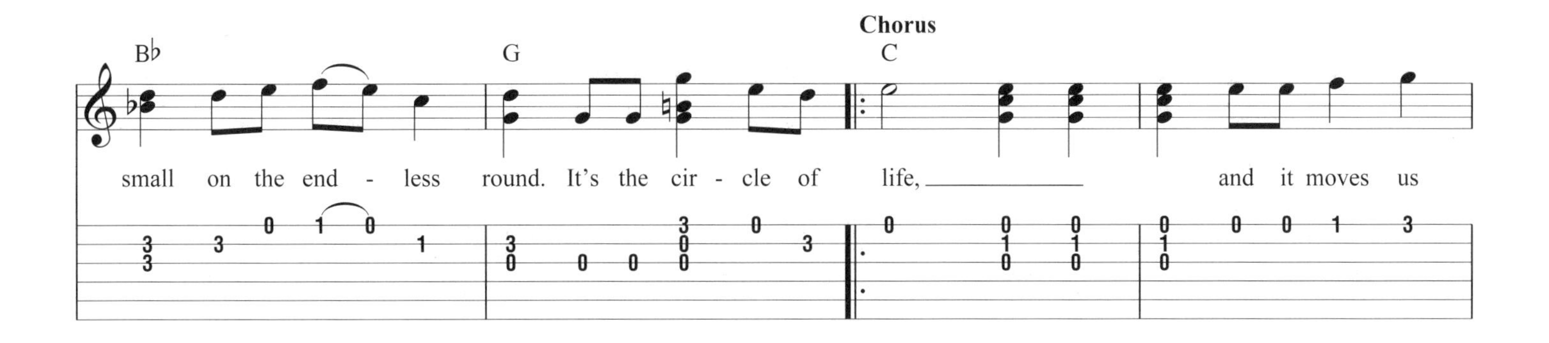
Chorus
B♭
G
C
small on the end - less round. It's the cir - cle of life, and it moves us

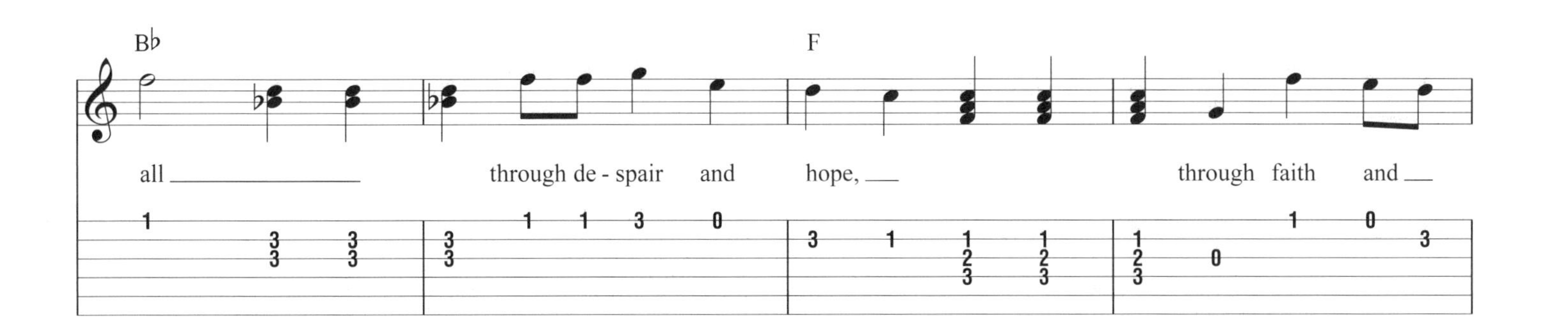
B♭
F
all through de - spair and hope, through faith and

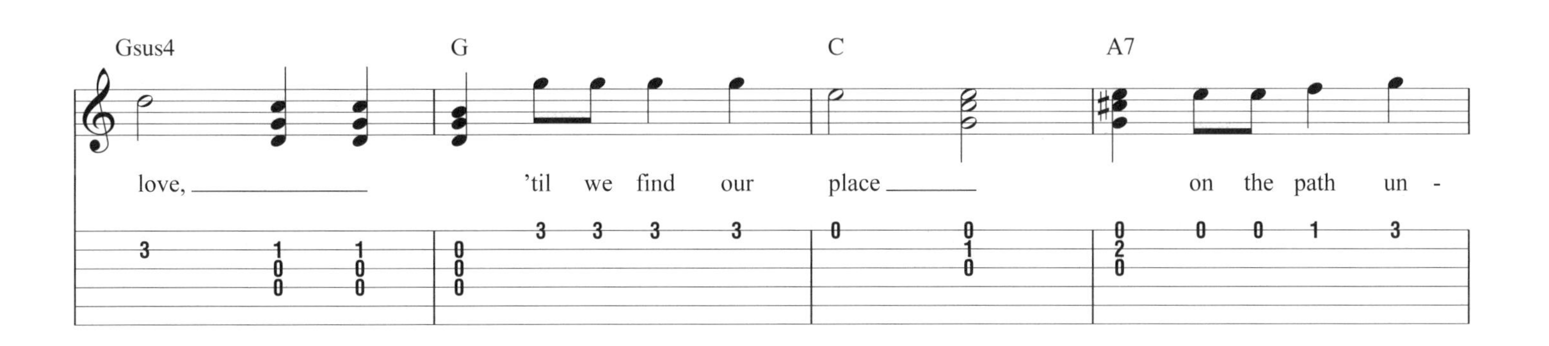
Gsus4
G
C
A7
love, 'til we find our place on the path un -

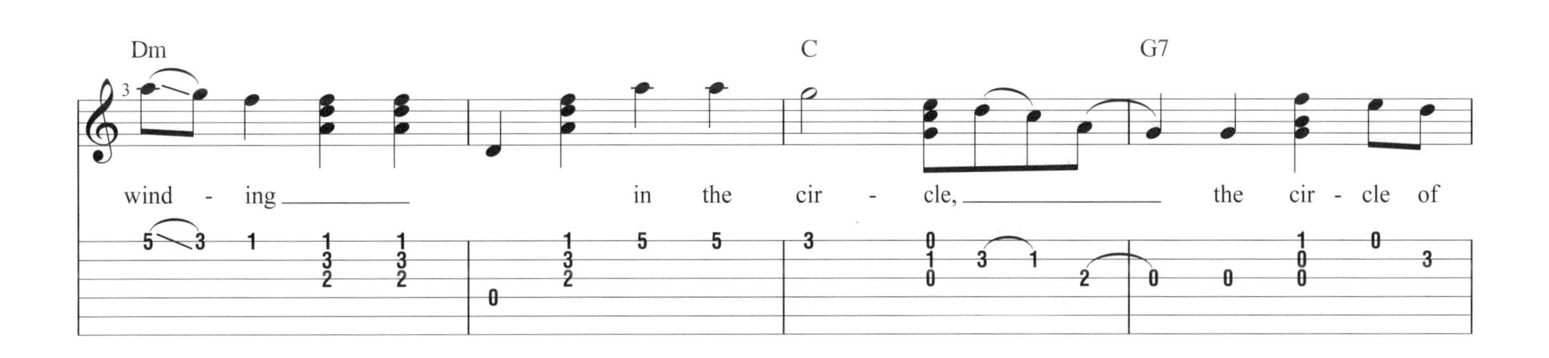
Dm
C
G7
wind - ing in the cir - cle, the cir - cle of

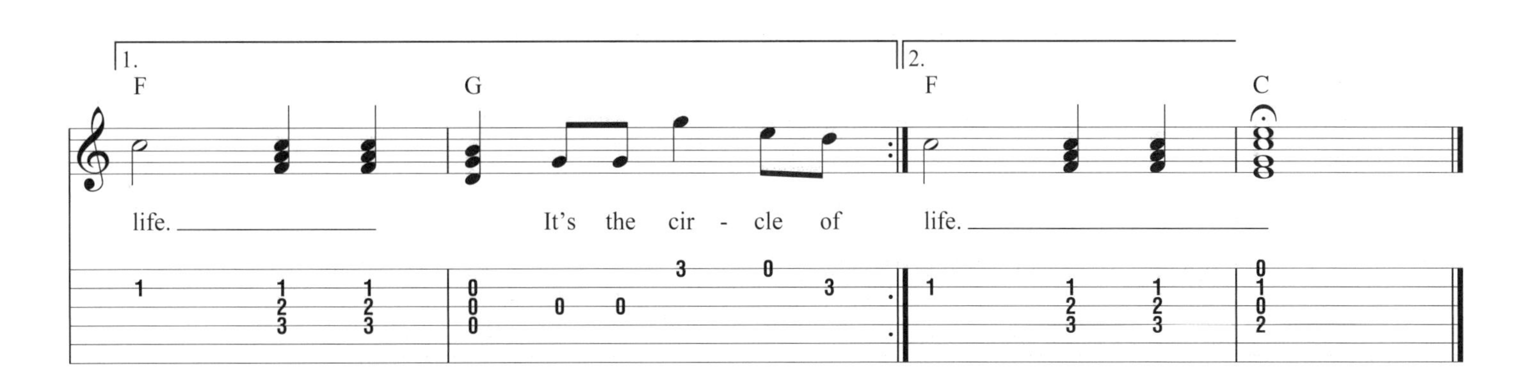
1.
2.
F
G
F
C
life. It's the cir - cle of life.

Colors of the Wind

from POCAHONTAS

Music by Alan Menken
Lyrics by Stephen Schwartz

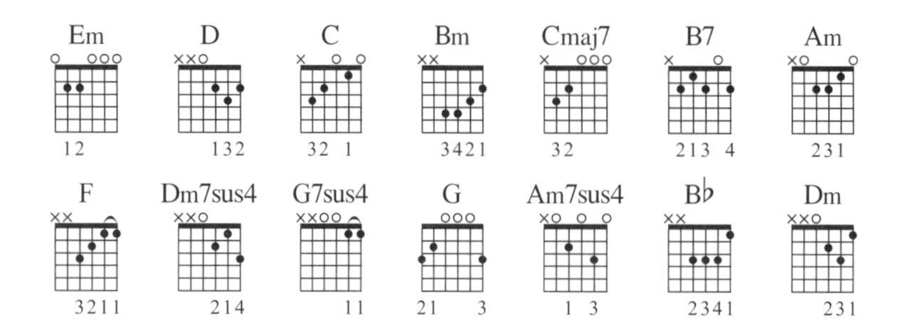

Strum Pattern: 2
Pick Pattern: 2

Intro

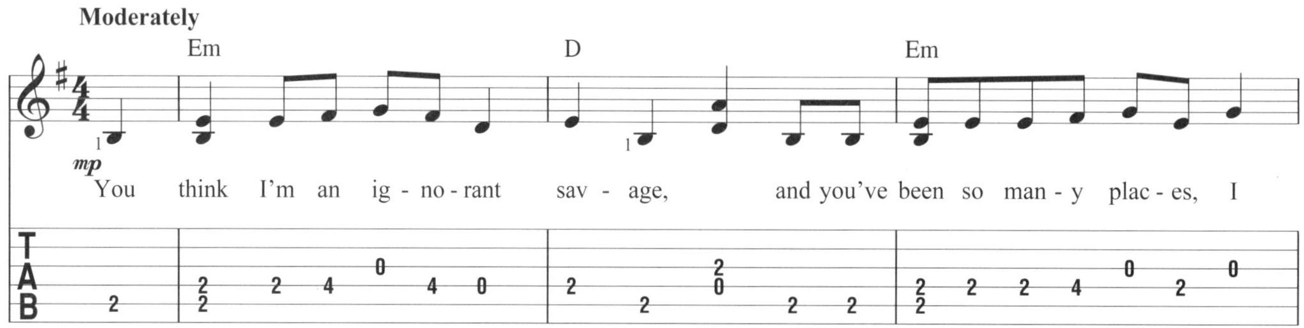

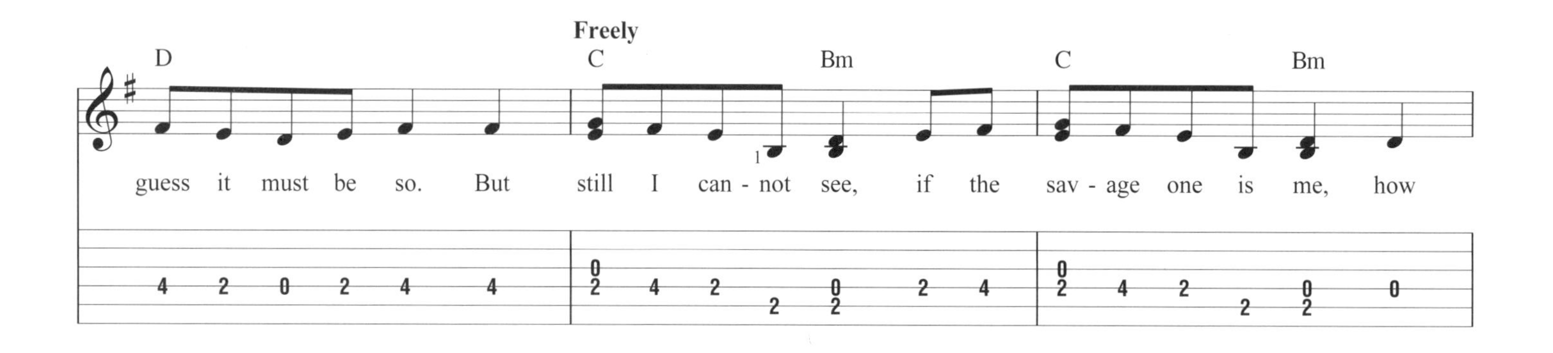

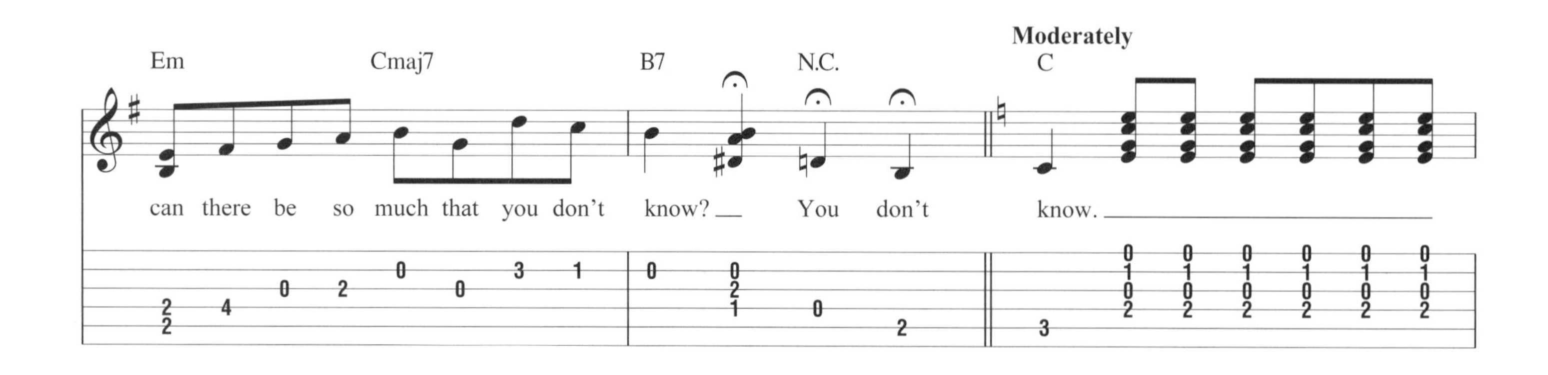

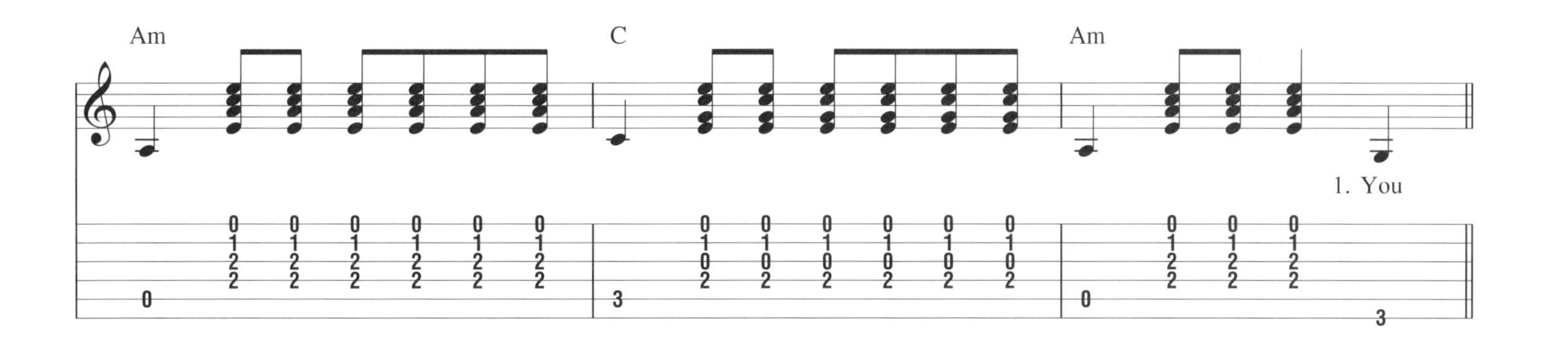
Am
C
Am
1. You

Verse
C
Am
C
think you own what - ev - er land you land on; the earth is just a dead thing you can
2., 3., 4. See additional lyrics

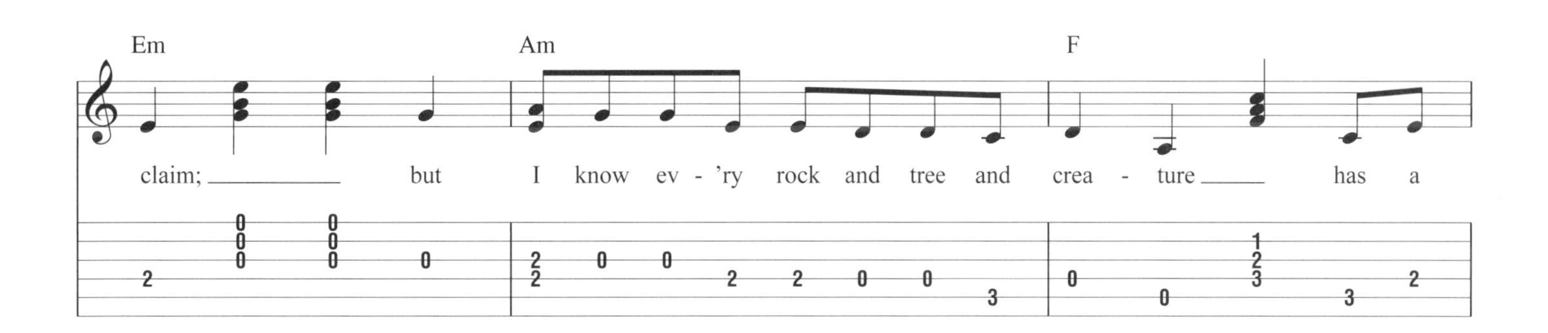
Em
Am
F
claim; but I know ev - 'ry rock and tree and crea - ture has a

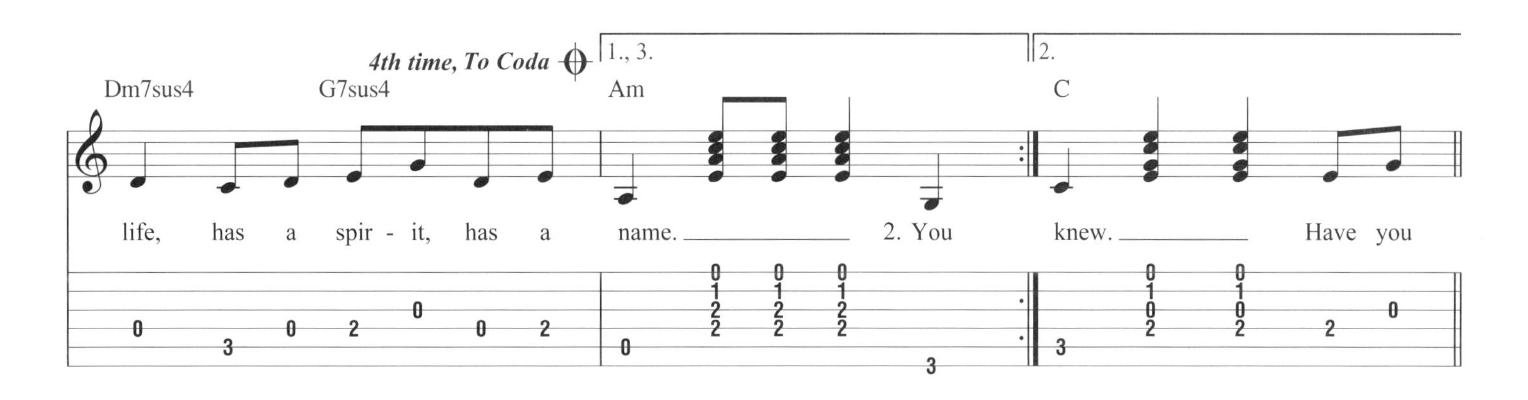
4th time, To Coda
1., 3.
2.
Dm7sus4
G7sus4
Am
C
life, has a spir - it, has a name. 2. You knew. Have you

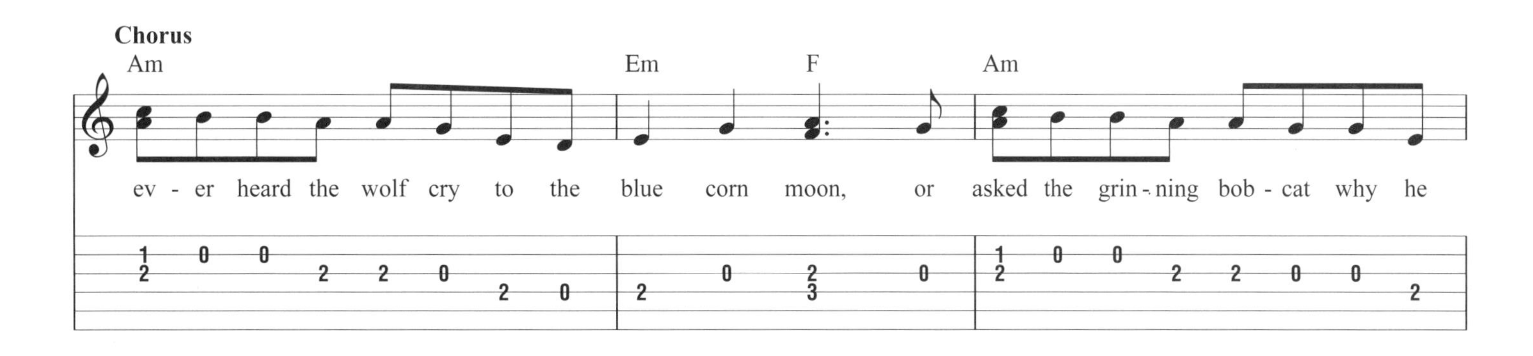
Chorus
Am
Em
F
Am
ev - er heard the wolf cry to the blue corn moon, or asked the grin - ning bob - cat why he

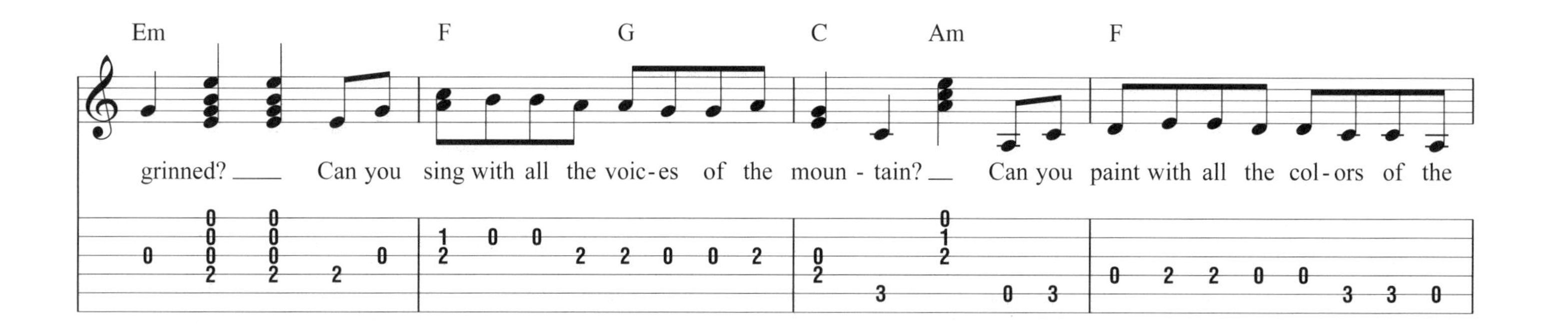
Em F G C Am F
grinned? Can you sing with all the voic-es of the moun - tain? Can you paint with all the col-ors of the

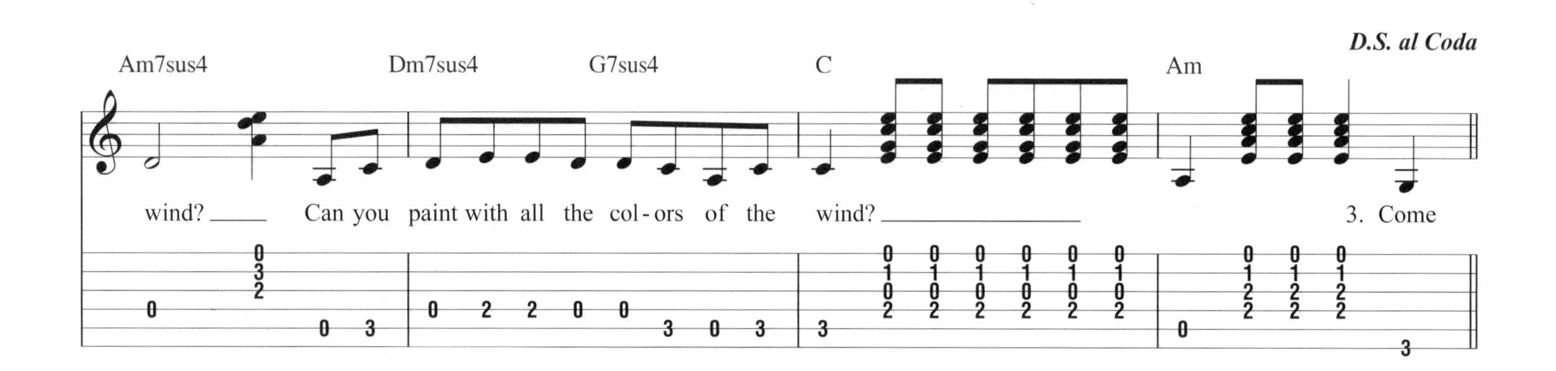
D.S. al Coda
Am7sus4 Dm7sus4 G7sus4 C Am
wind? Can you paint with all the col-ors of the wind? 3. Come

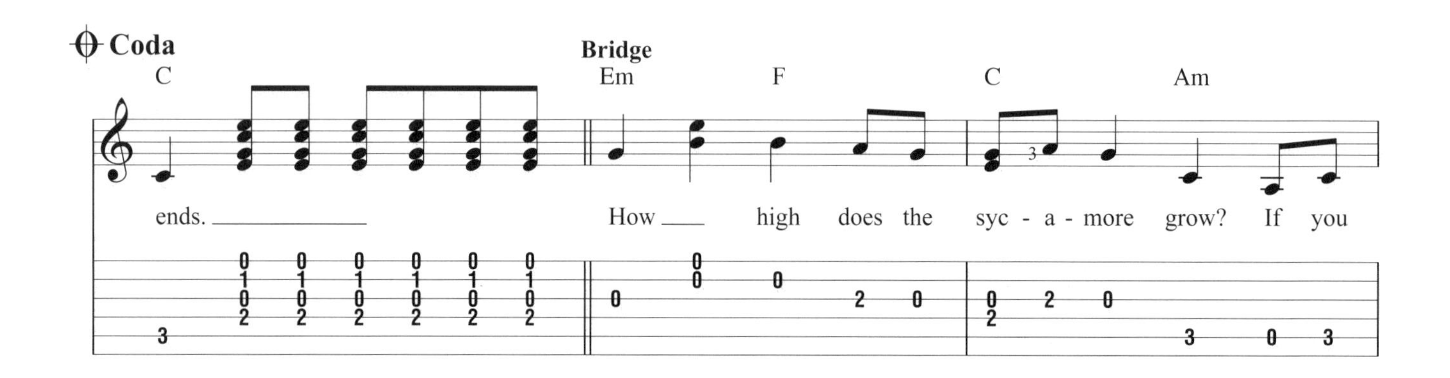
Coda
Bridge
C Em F C Am
ends. How high does the syc - a - more grow? If you

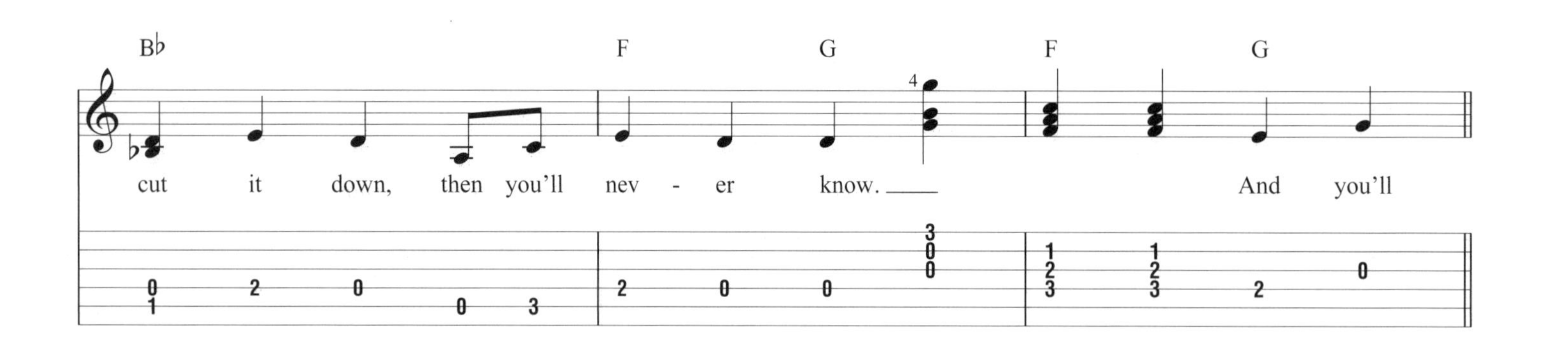
B♭ F G F G
cut it down, then you'll nev - er know. And you'll

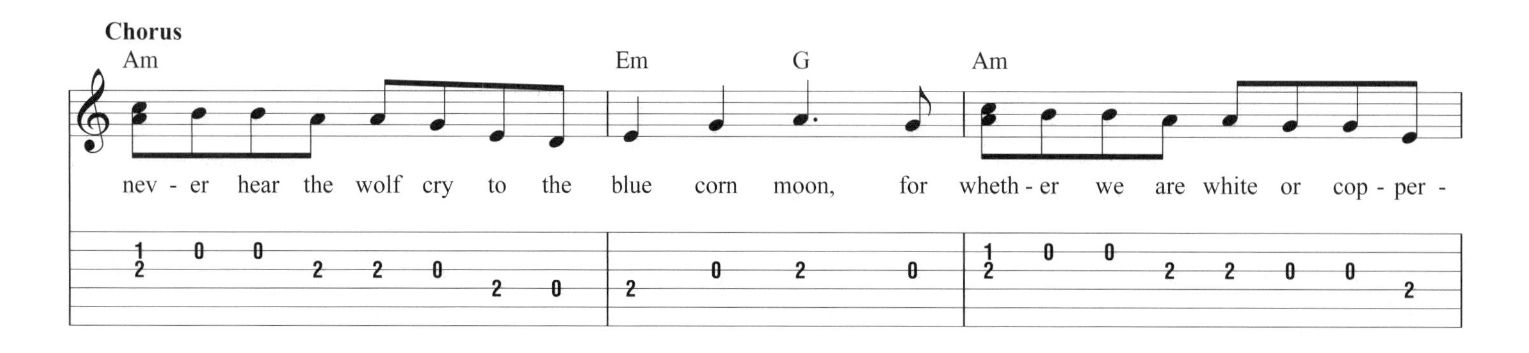
Chorus
Am Em G Am
nev - er hear the wolf cry to the blue corn moon, for wheth - er we are white or cop - per -

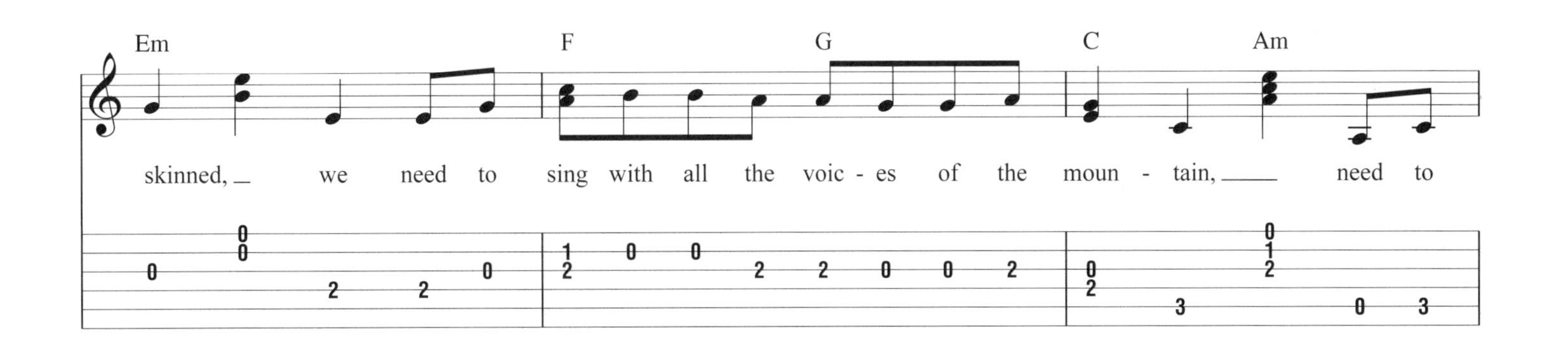

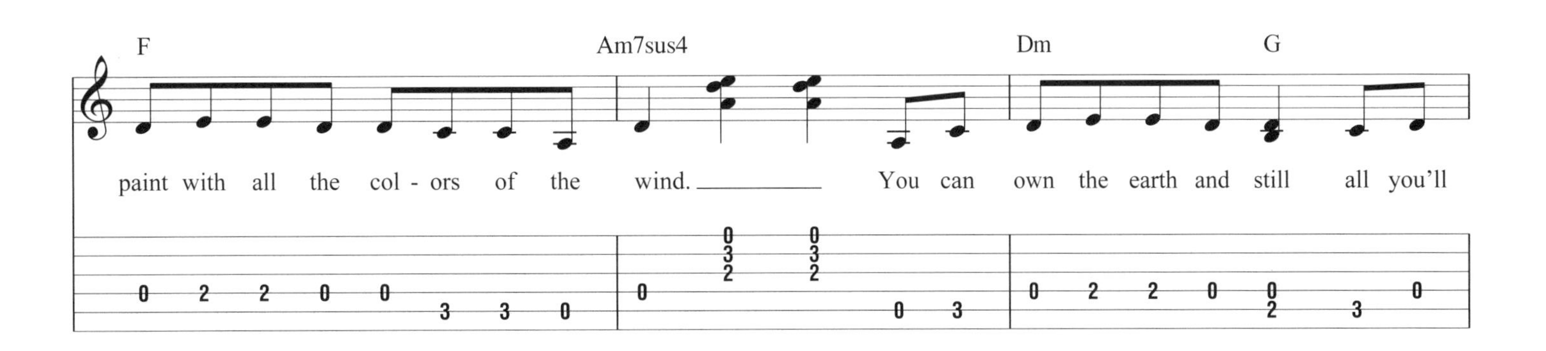

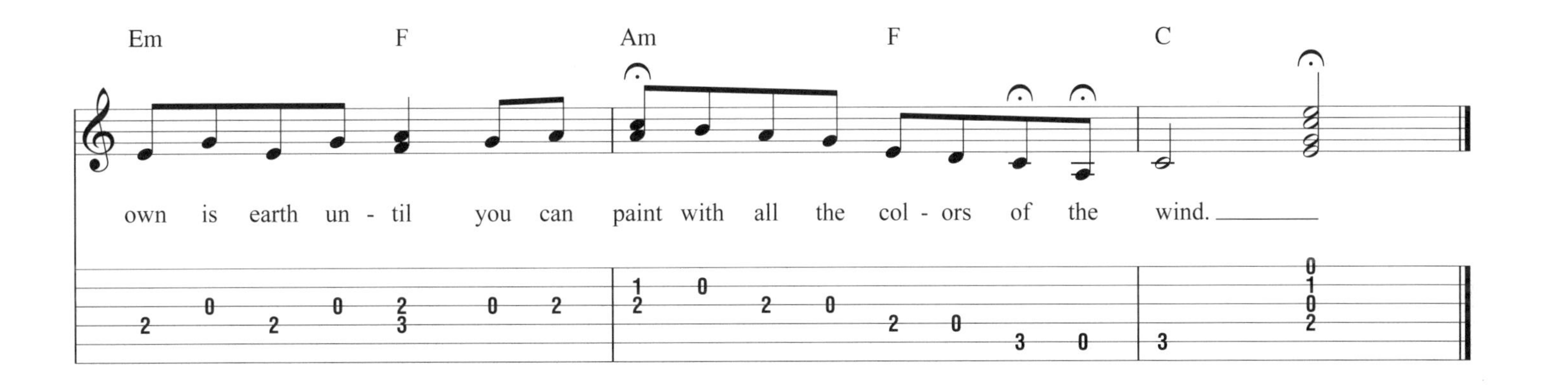

Additional Lyrics

2. You think the only people who are people
   Are the people who look and think like you,
   But if you walk the footsteps of a stranger
   You'll learn things you never knew you never knew.

3. Come run the hidden pine trails of the forest,
   Come taste the sunsweet berries of the earth;
   Come roll in all the riches all around you,
   And for once never wonder what they're worth.

4. The rainstorm and the river are my brothers;
   The heron and the otter are my frineds;
   And we are all connected to each other
   In a circle, in a hoop that never ends.

Fixer Upper

from FROZEN

Music and Lyrics by Kristen Anderson-Lopez and Robert Lopez

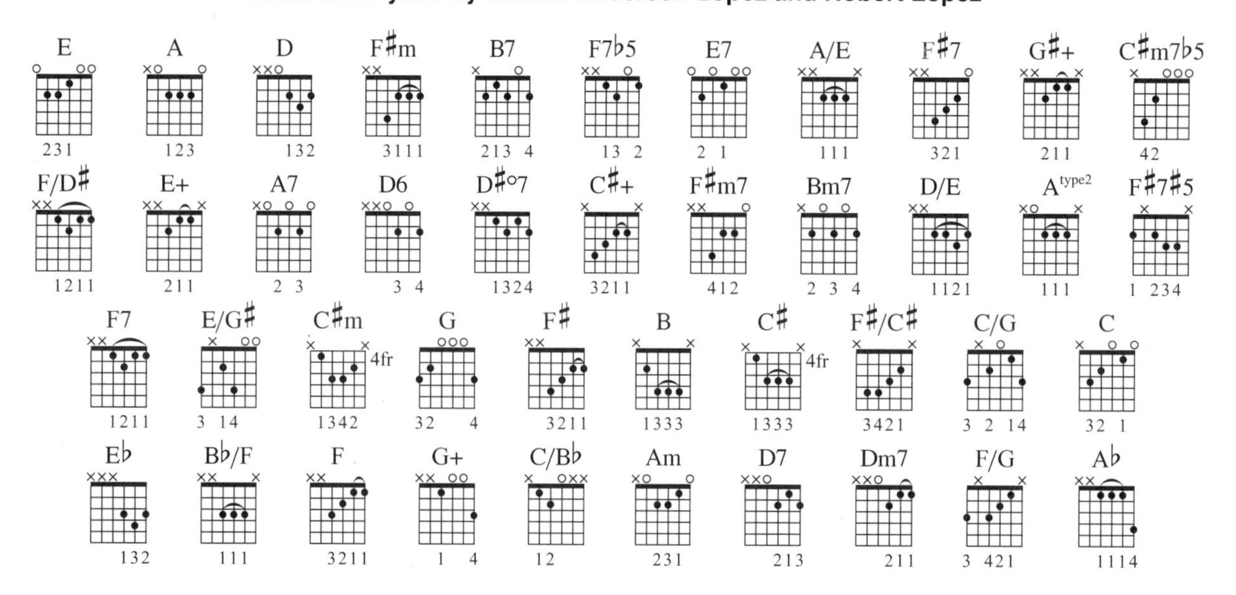

Strum Pattern: 3
Pick Pattern: 3

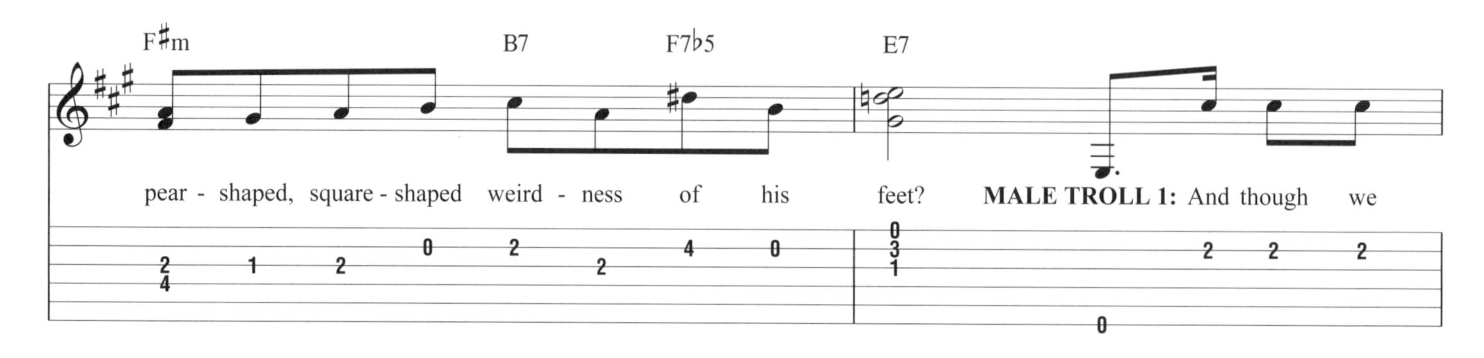

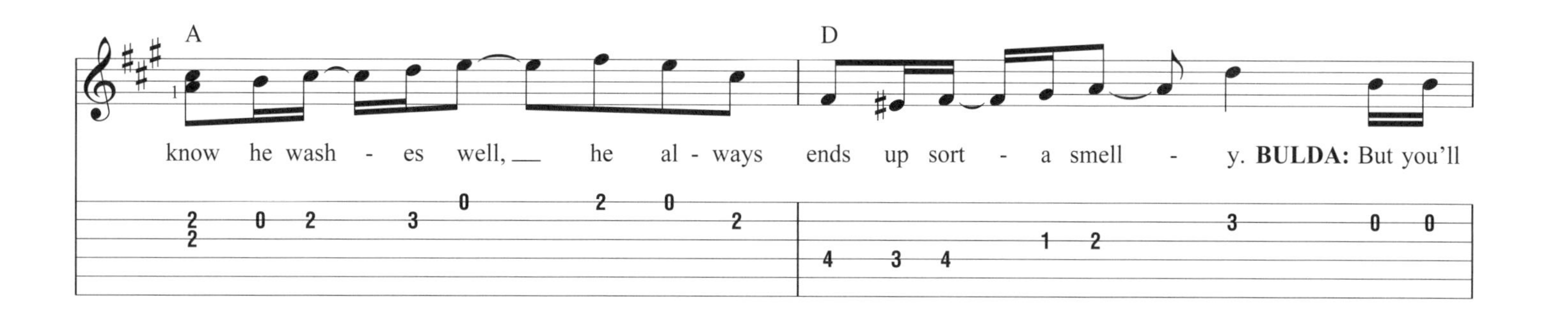
A
D
know he wash - es well, he al - ways ends up sort - a smell - y. BULDA: But you'll

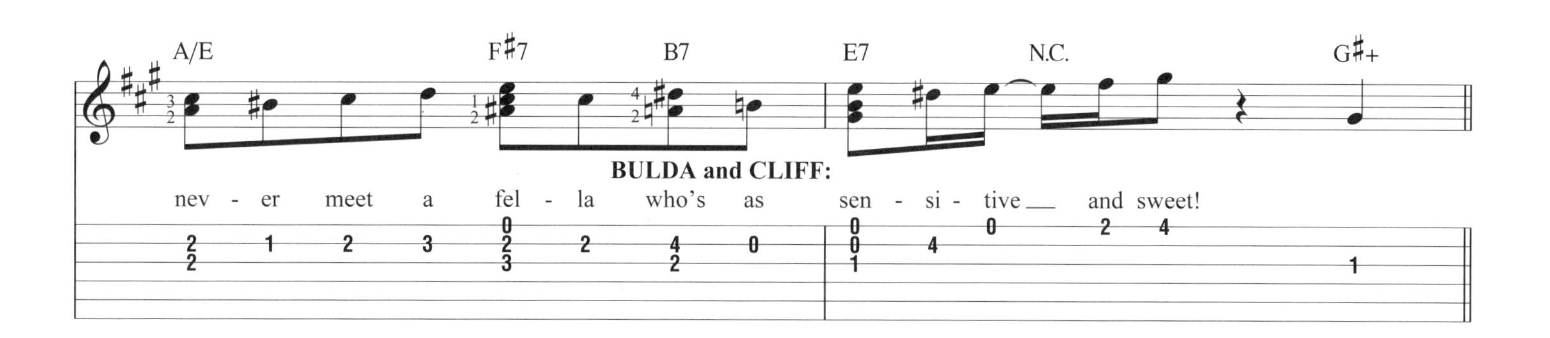
A/E
F♯7
B7
E7
N.C.
G♯+
BULDA and CLIFF:
nev - er meet a fel - la who's as sen - si - tive and sweet!

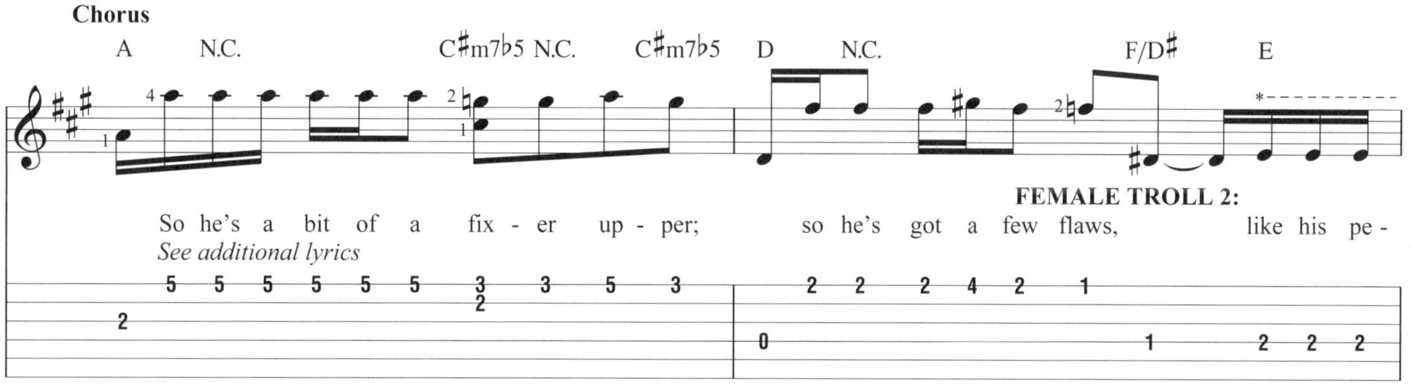
Chorus
A N.C. C♯m7♭5 N.C. C♯m7♭5
D N.C. F/D♯ E
FEMALE TROLL 2:
So he's a bit of a fix - er up - per; so he's got a few flaws, like his pe -
See additional lyrics
*Sung one octave higher.

A N.C. C♯m7♭5 N.C.
D N.C. B7 E7 N.C. E+
MALE TROLL 2:
TROLL DUET:
cu - liar brain, dear, his thing with the rein - deer... that's a lit - tle out - side of na - ture's laws!

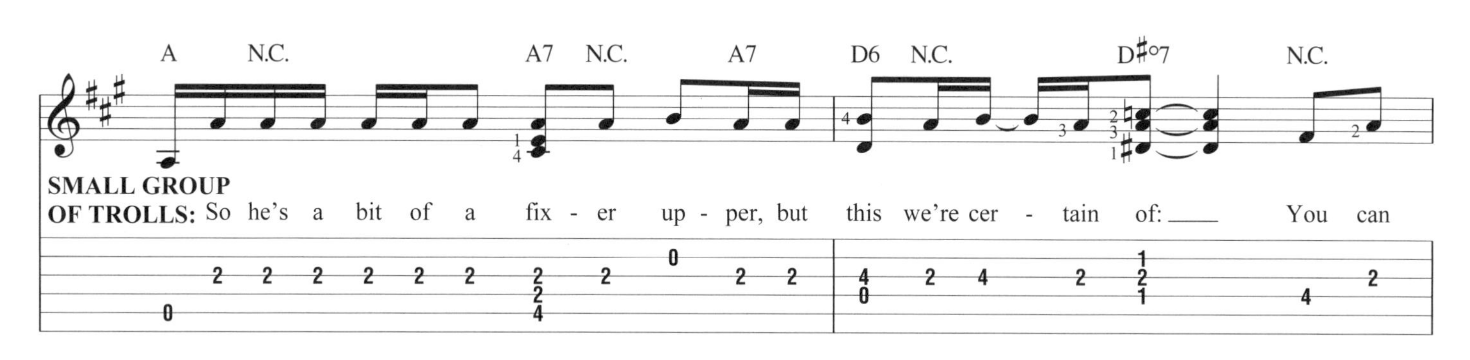
A N.C. A7 N.C. A7
D6 N.C. D♯°7 N.C.
SMALL GROUP
OF TROLLS: So he's a bit of a fix - er up - per, but this we're cer - tain of: You can

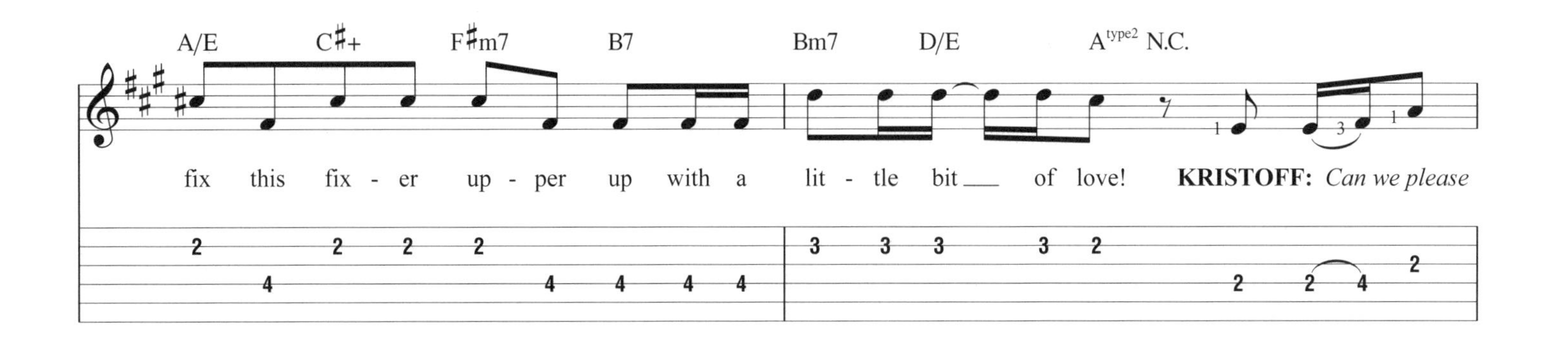
A/E C♯+ F♯m7 B7 Bm7 D/E A type2 N.C.
fix this fix - er up - per up with a lit - tle bit of love! KRISTOFF: Can we please

F♯7♯5 B7 E7 A A7 D F/D♯
just stop talking about this? We've got a real actual problem here. BULDA: I'll say!

1. 2.
E7 E7
So tell me, dear... 2. Is it the okay?

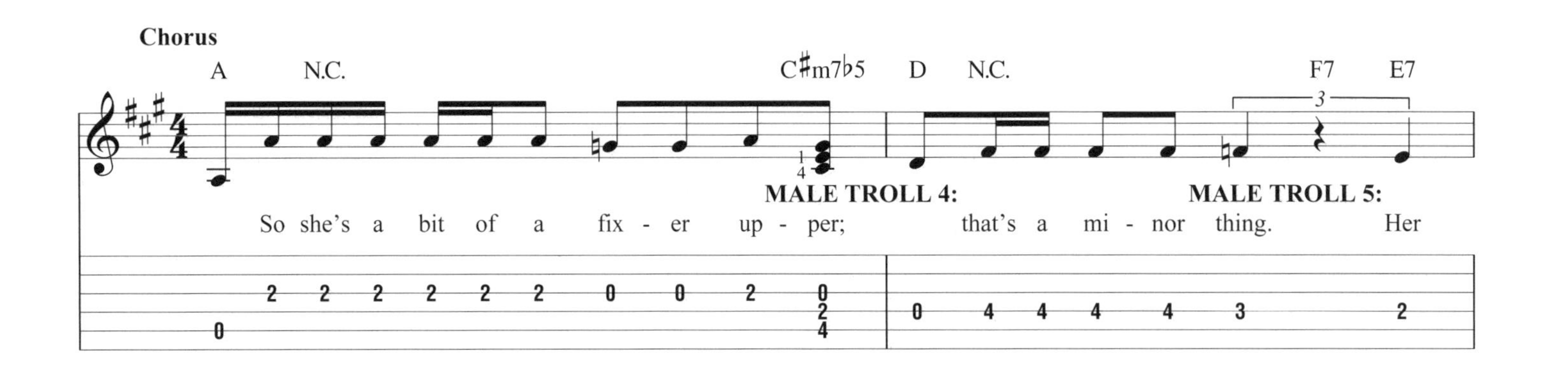
Chorus
A N.C. C♯m7♭5 D N.C. F7 E7
MALE TROLL 4: MALE TROLL 5:
So she's a bit of a fix - er up - per; that's a mi - nor thing. Her

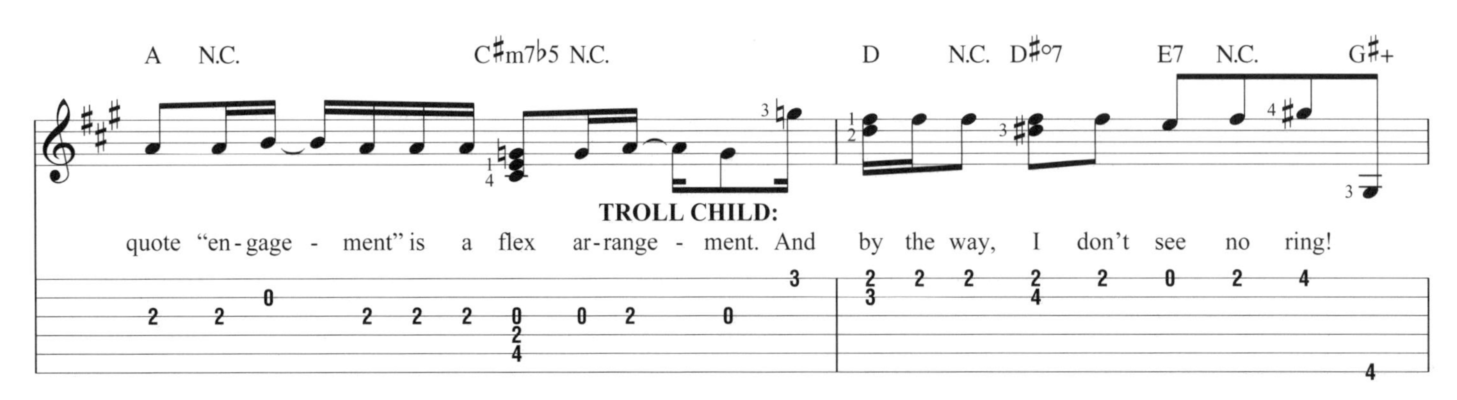
A N.C. C♯m7♭5 N.C. D N.C. D♯°7 E7 N.C. G♯+
TROLL CHILD:
quote "en-gage - ment" is a flex ar-range - ment. And by the way, I don't see no ring!

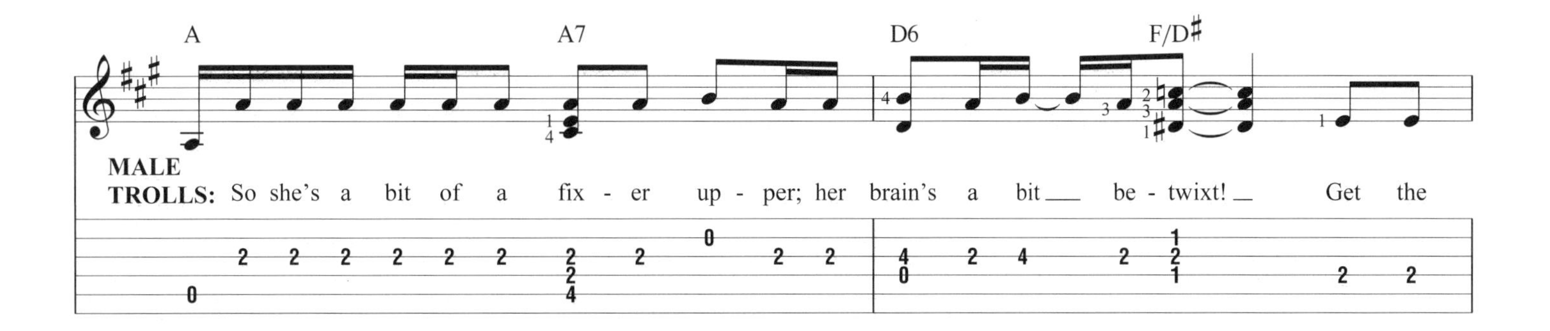

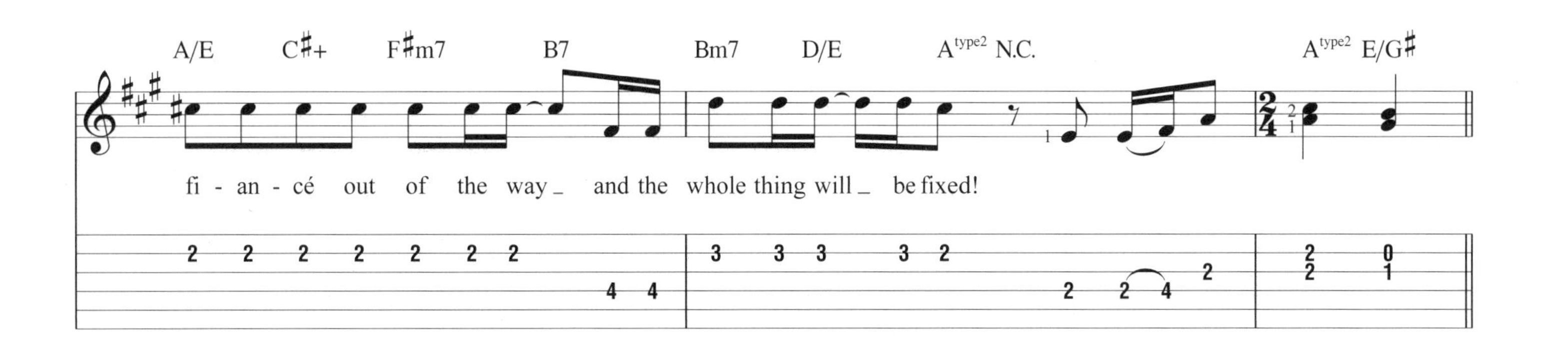

*Sung one octave higher throughout Bridge.

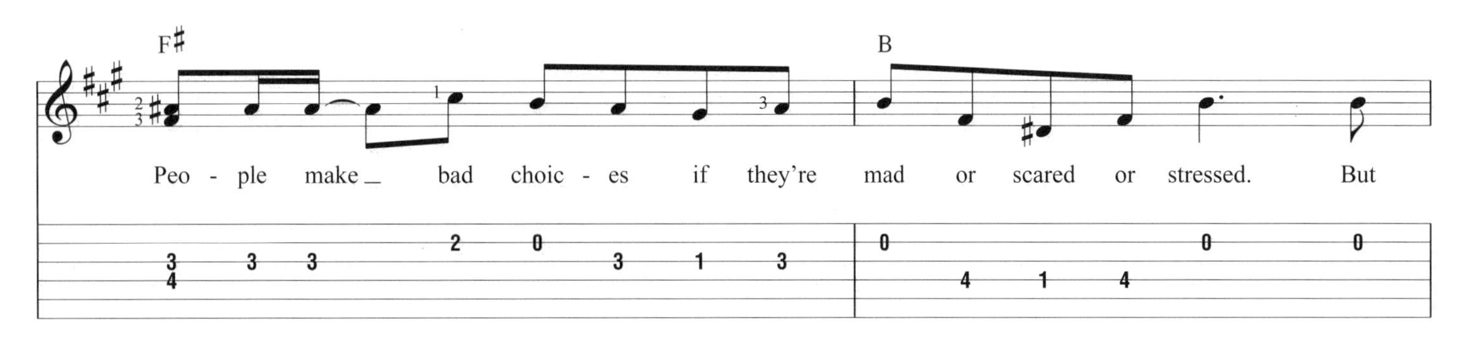

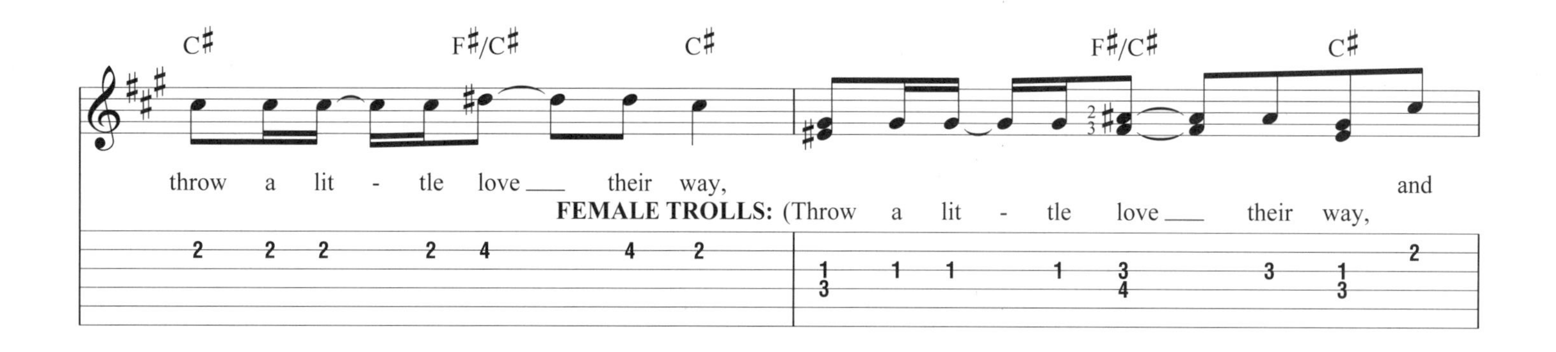
C♯ F♯/C♯ C♯ F♯/C♯ C♯
throw a lit - tle love their way, and
FEMALE TROLLS: (Throw a lit - tle love their way,

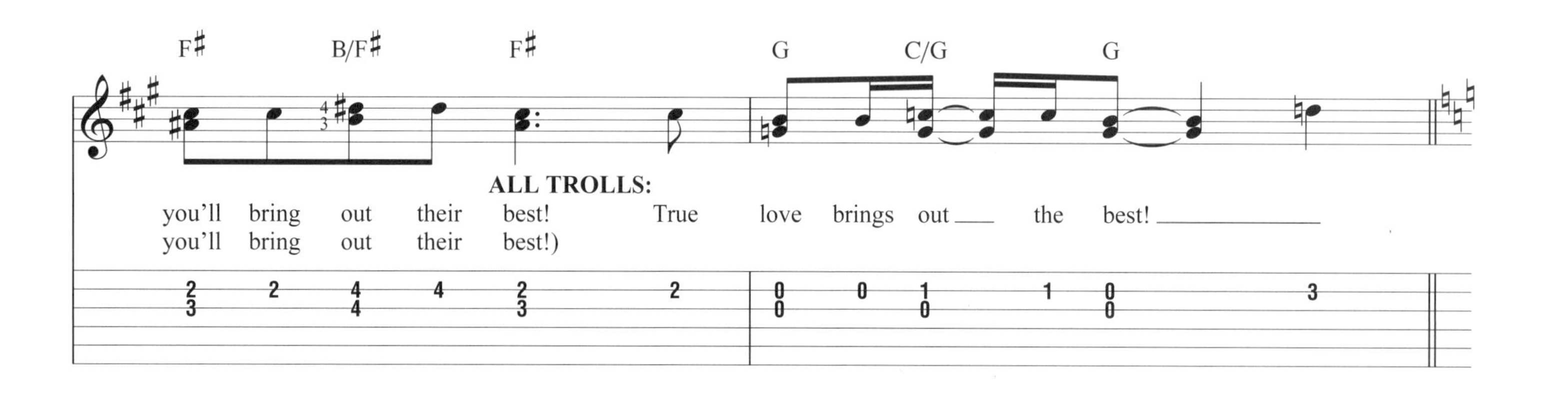
F♯ B/F♯ F♯ G C/G G
ALL TROLLS:
you'll bring out their best! True love brings out the best!
you'll bring out their best!)

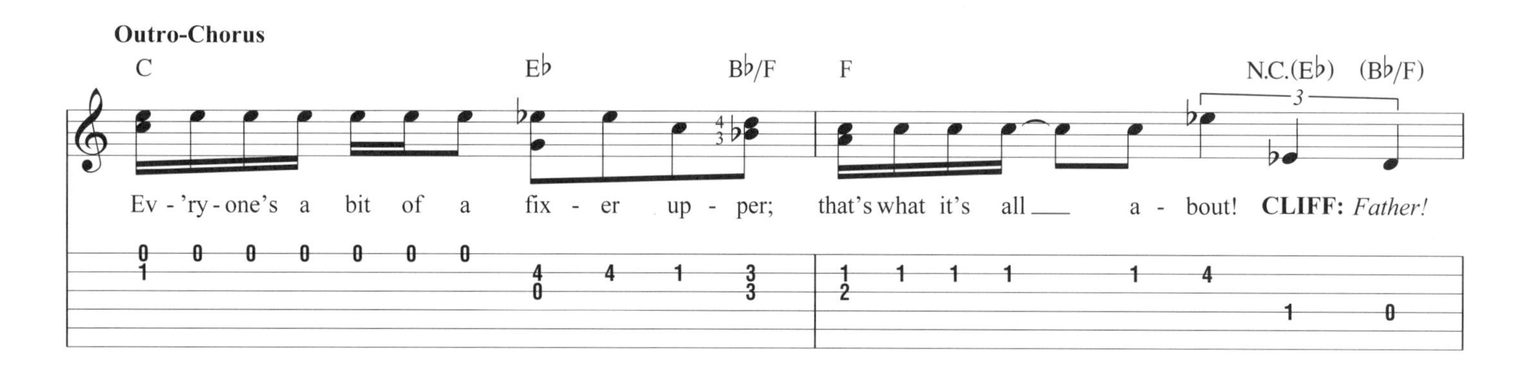
Outro-Chorus
C E♭ B♭/F F N.C.(E♭) (B♭/F)
Ev - 'ry - one's a bit of a fix - er up - per; that's what it's all a - bout! CLIFF: *Father!*

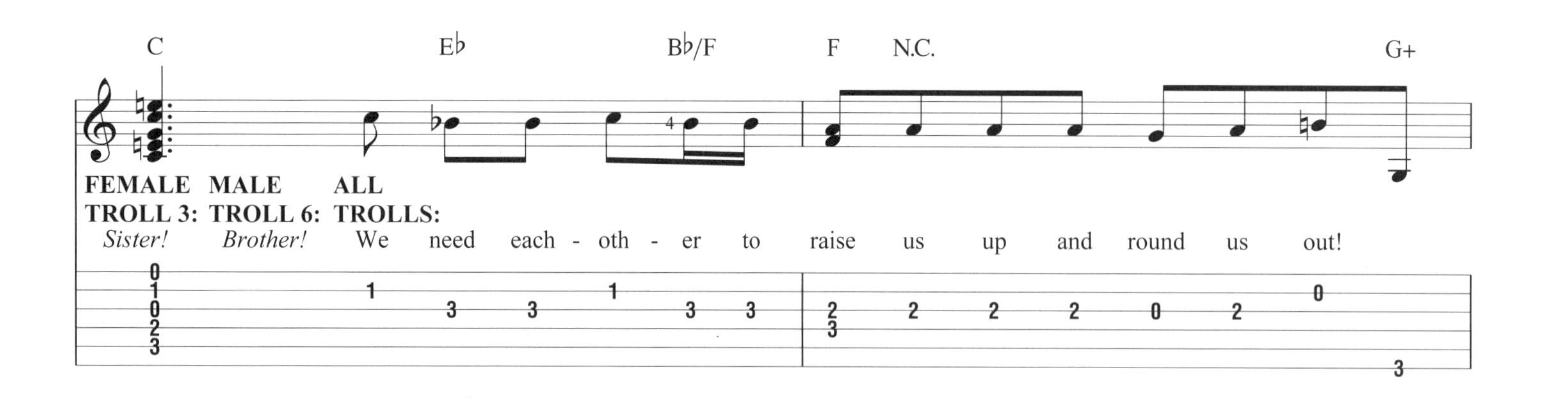
C E♭ B♭/F F N.C. G+
FEMALE TROLL 3: MALE TROLL 6: ALL TROLLS:
Sister! *Brother!* We need each - oth - er to raise us up and round us out!

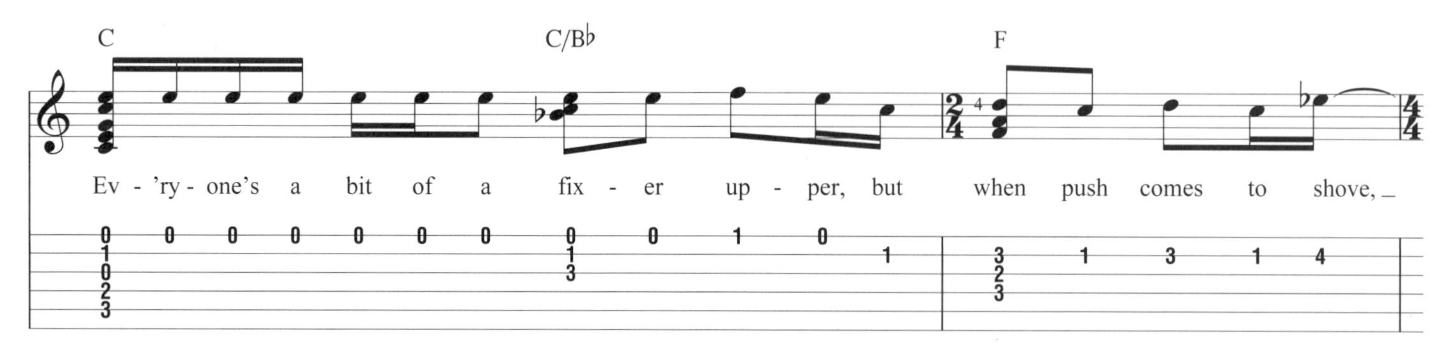
C C/B♭ F
Ev - 'ry - one's a bit of a fix - er up - per, but when push comes to shove,

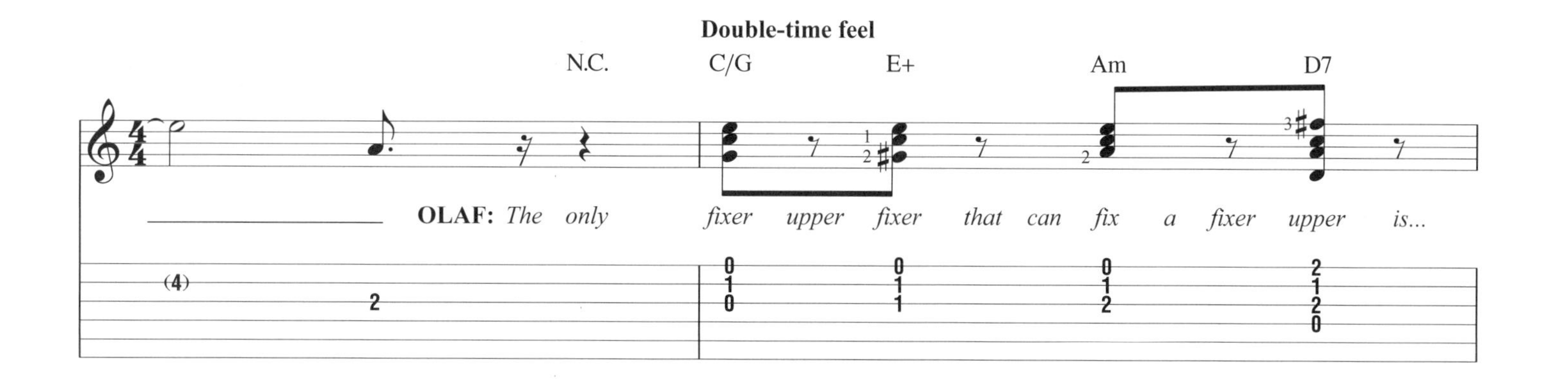

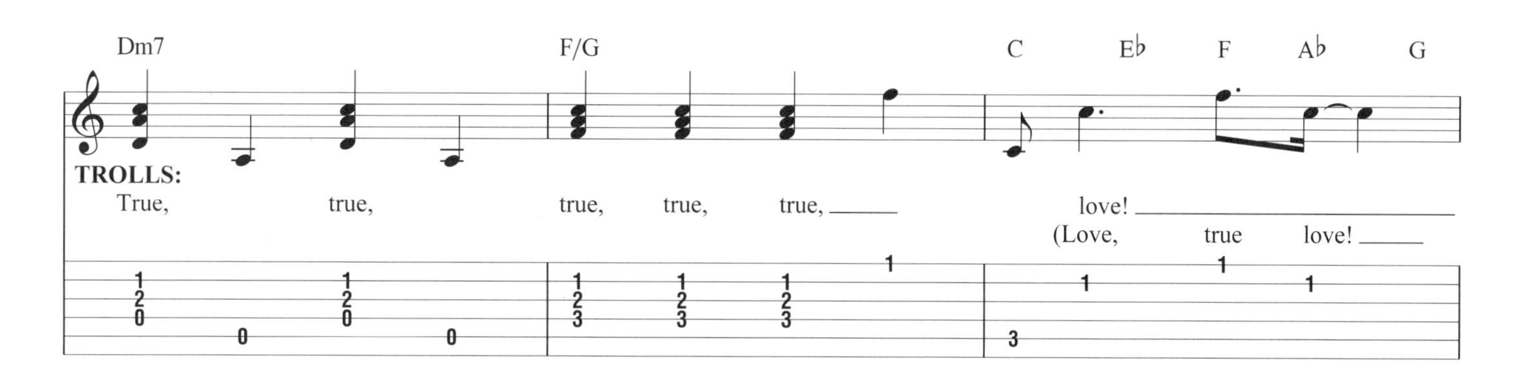

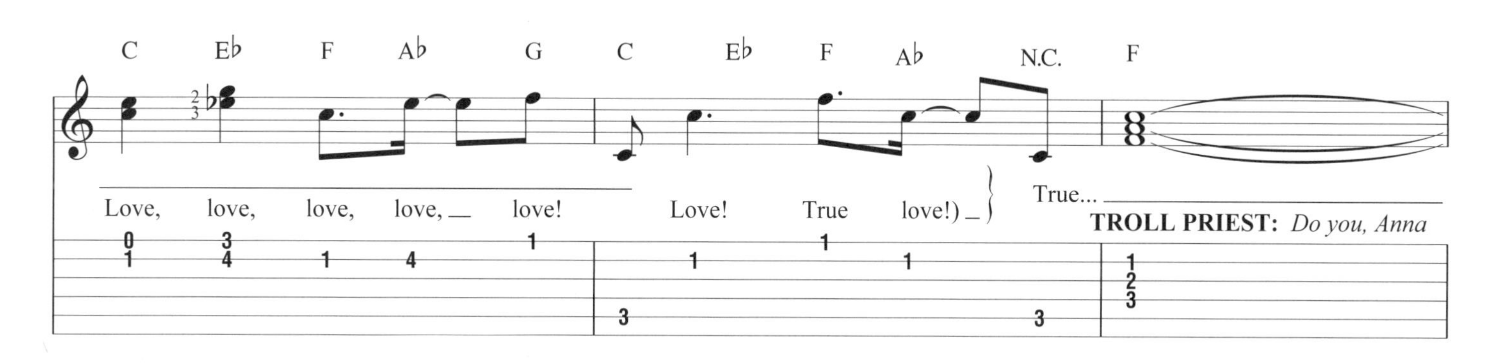

Additional Lyrics

2. Is it the way that he runs scared?
MALE TROLL 3: Or that he's socially impaired?
TROLL CHILD: Or that he only likes to tinkle in the woods? *What?*
CLIFF: Are you holding back your fondness due to his unmanly blondeness?
FEMALE TROLLS: Or the way he covers up that he's the honest goods?

Chorus **ALL TROLLS:** He's just a bit of a fixer upper; he's got a couple 'a bugs.
His isolation is confirmation of his desperation for healing hugs!
So he's a bit of a fixer upper, but we know what to do:
The way to fix up this fixer upper is to fix him up with you!
KRISTOFF: *ENOUGH! She is engaged to someone else, okay?*

For the First Time in Forever

from FROZEN

Music and Lyrics by Kristen Anderson-Lopez and Robert Lopez

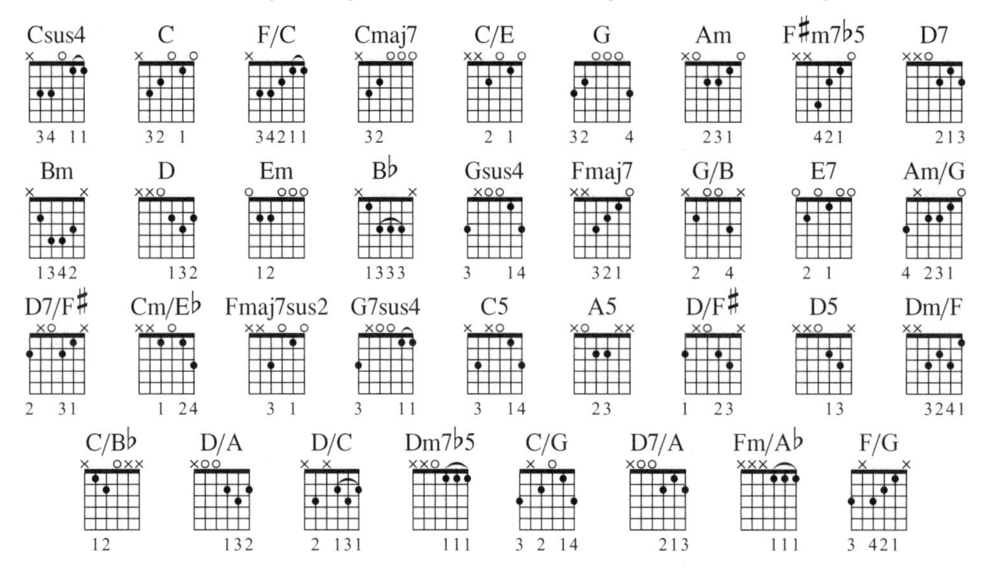

*Strum Pattern: 3
*Pick Pattern: 3

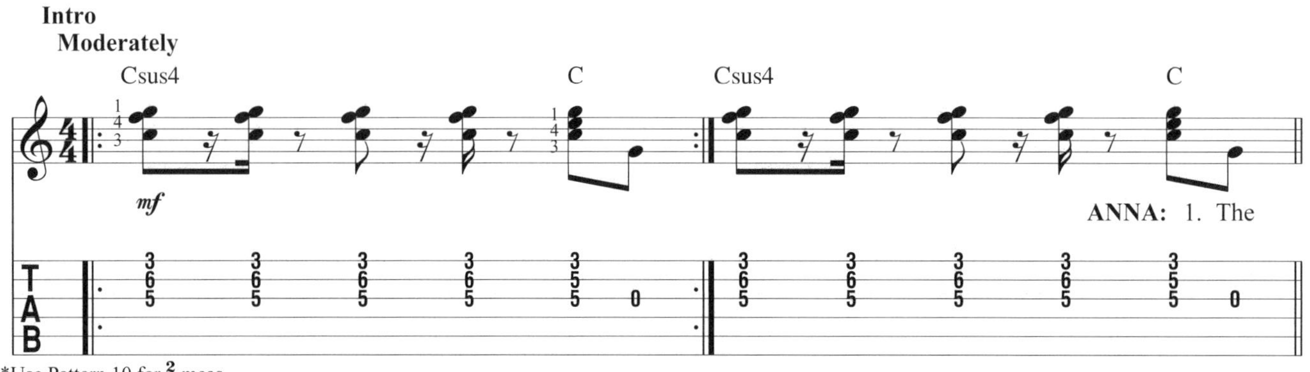

*Use Pattern 10 for $\frac{2}{4}$ meas.

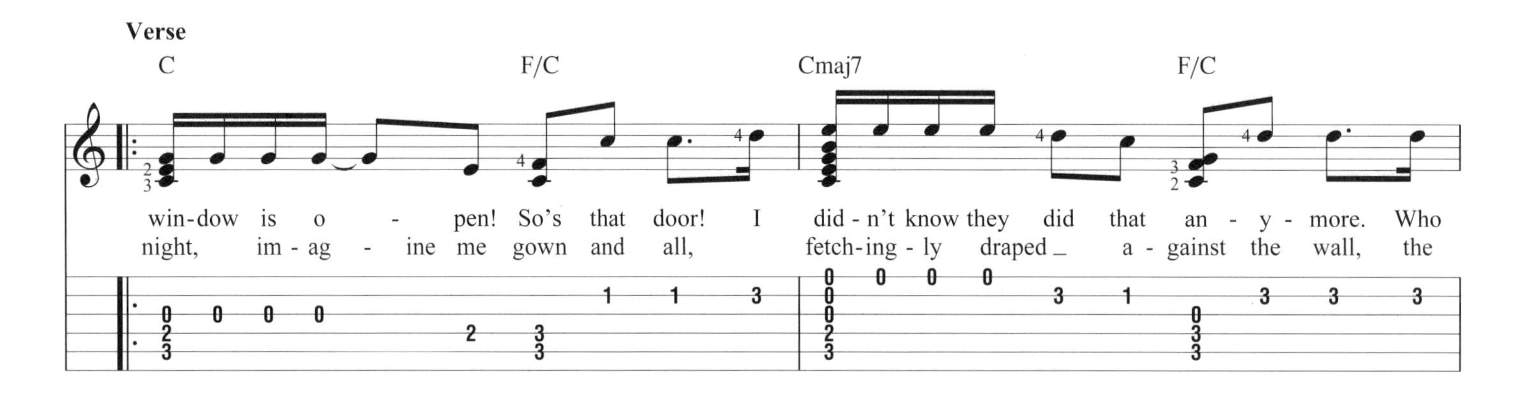

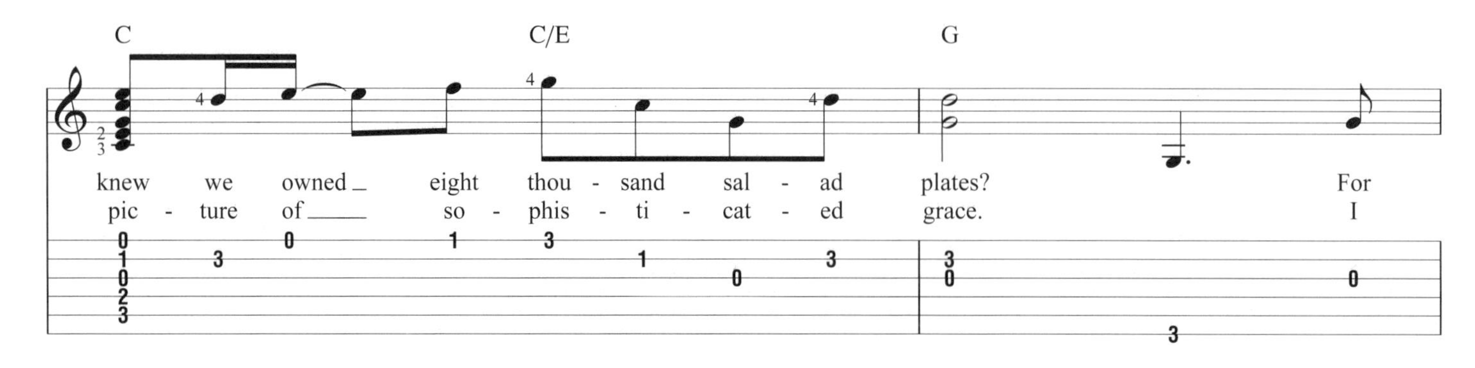

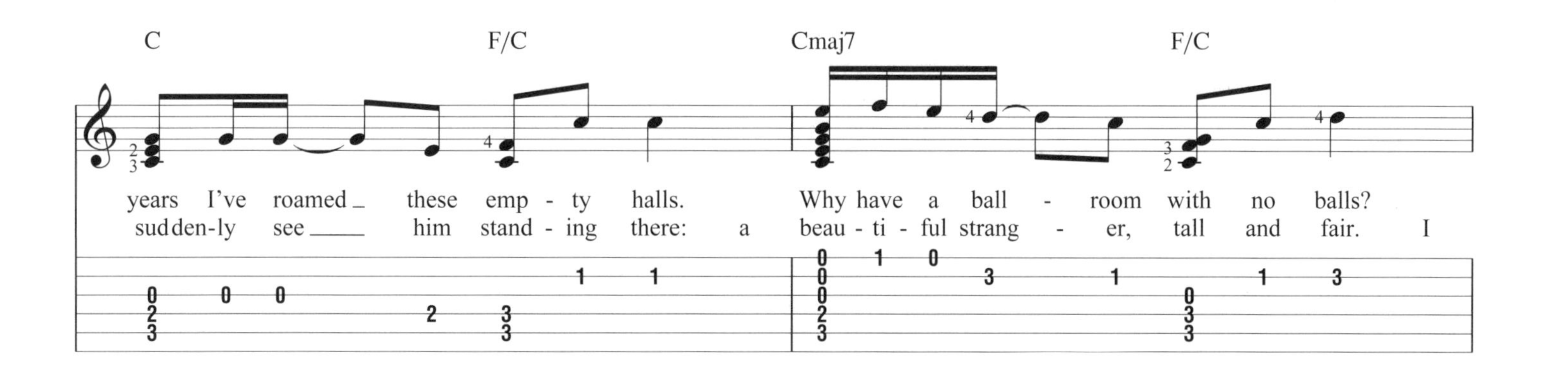
C F/C Cmaj7 F/C
years I've roamed these emp - ty halls. Why have a ball - room with no balls?
sud den-ly see him stand - ing there: a beau - ti - ful strang - er, tall and fair. I

Am F♯m7♭5 D7
Fi - nal - ly, they're o - p'ning up the gates! There'll be
wan - na stuff some choc - 'late in my face! Then we

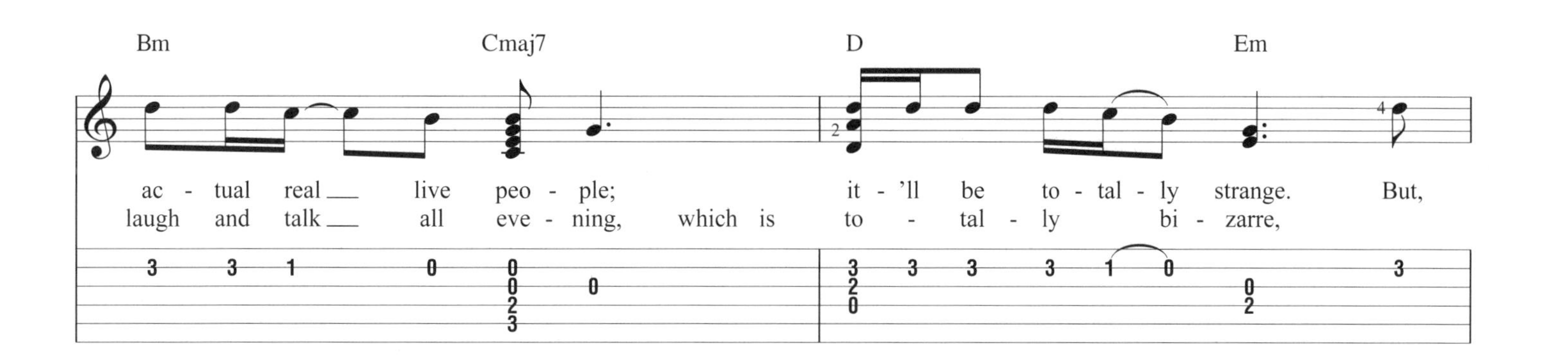
Bm Cmaj7 D Em
ac - tual real live peo - ple; it - 'll be to - tal - ly strange. But,
laugh and talk all eve - ning, which is to - tal - ly bi - zarre,

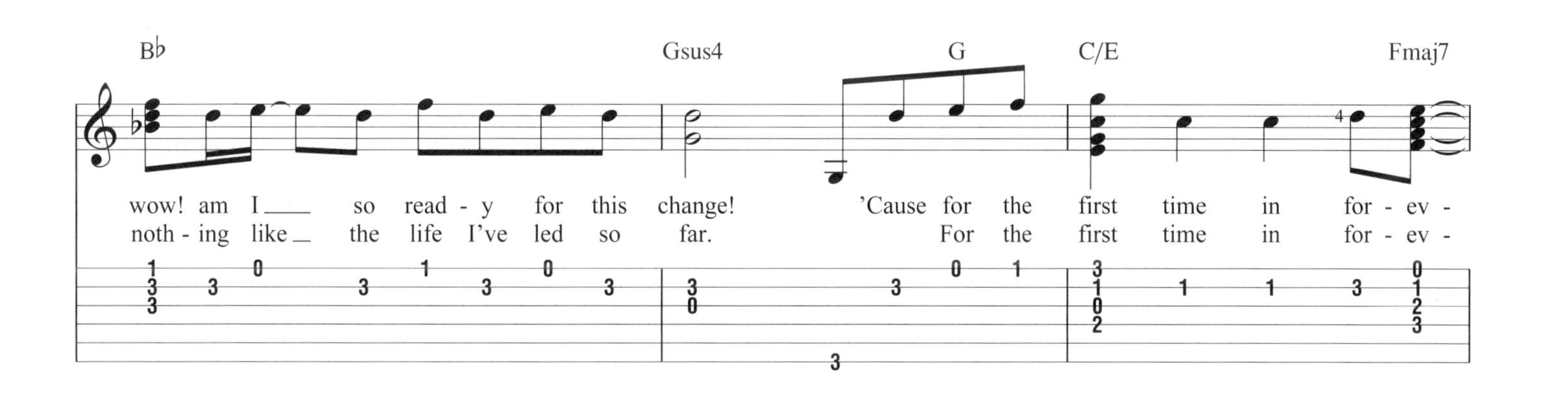
B♭ Gsus4 G C/E Fmaj7
wow! am I so read - y for this change! 'Cause for the first time in for - ev -
noth - ing like the life I've led so far. For the first time in for - ev -

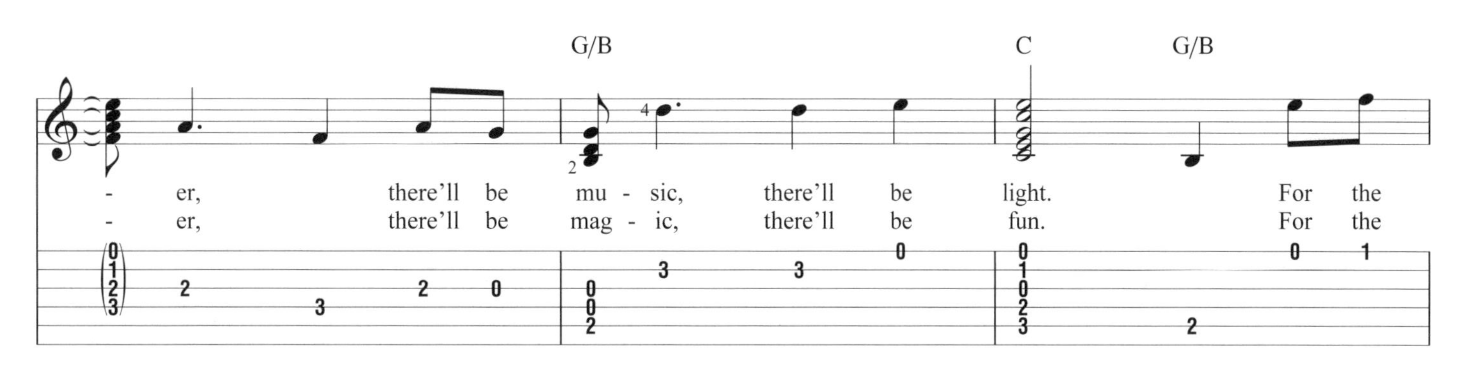
G/B C G/B
- er, there'll be mu - sic, there'll be light. For the
- er, there'll be mag - ic, there'll be fun. For the

Am Em B♭
first time in for - ev - er, I'll be danc - ing through the
first time in for - ev - er, I could be no - ticed by some -

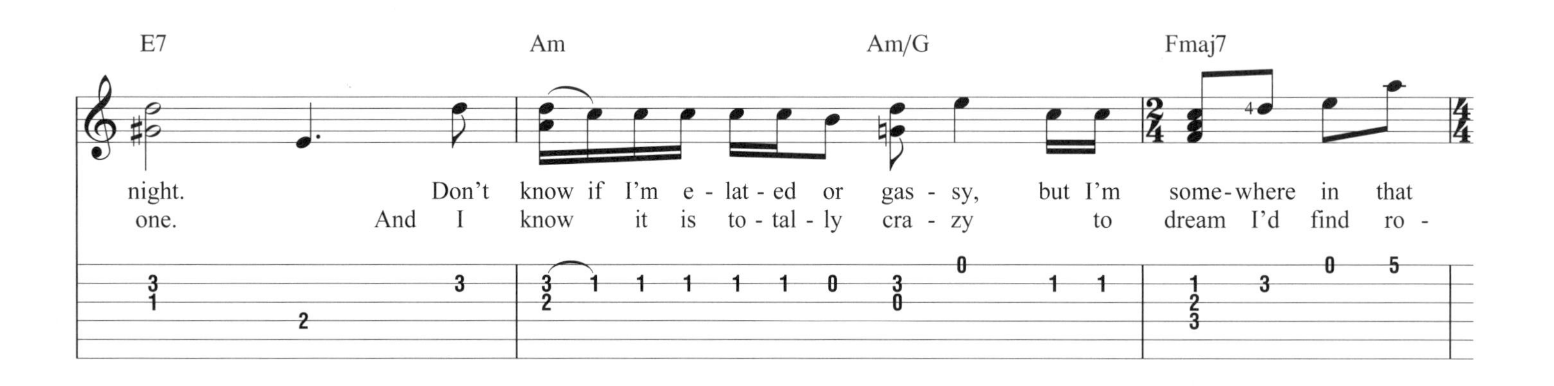
E7 Am Am/G Fmaj7
night. Don't know if I'm e - lat - ed or gas - sy, but I'm some - where in that
one. And I know it is to - tal - ly cra - zy to dream I'd find ro -

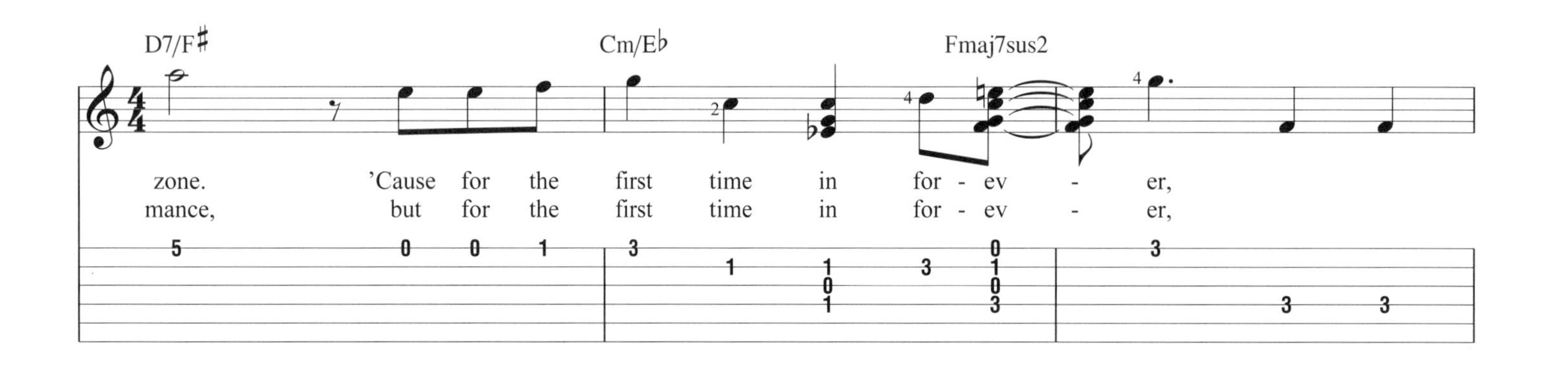
D7/F♯ Cm/E♭ Fmaj7sus2
zone. 'Cause for the first time in for - ev - er,
mance, but for the first time in for - ev - er,

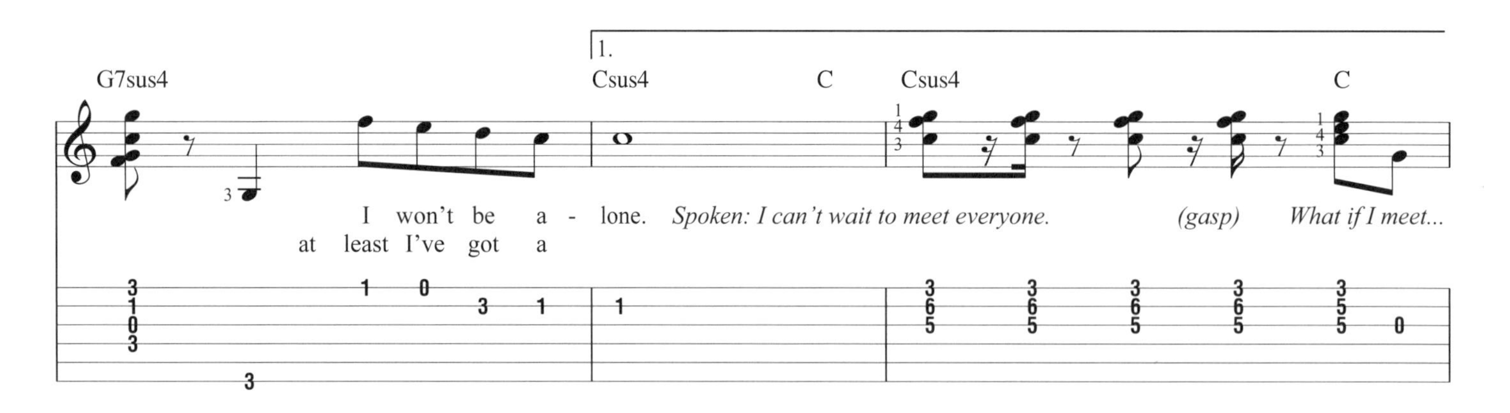
1.
G7sus4 Csus4 C Csus4 C
I won't be a - lone. Spoken: I can't wait to meet everyone. (gasp) What if I meet...
at least I've got a

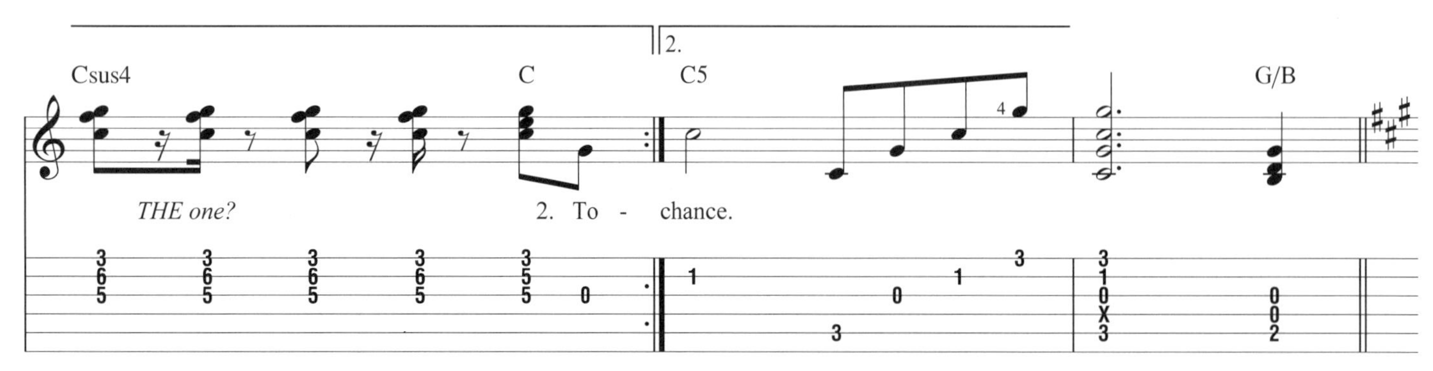
2.
Csus4 C C5 G/B
THE one? 2. To - chance.

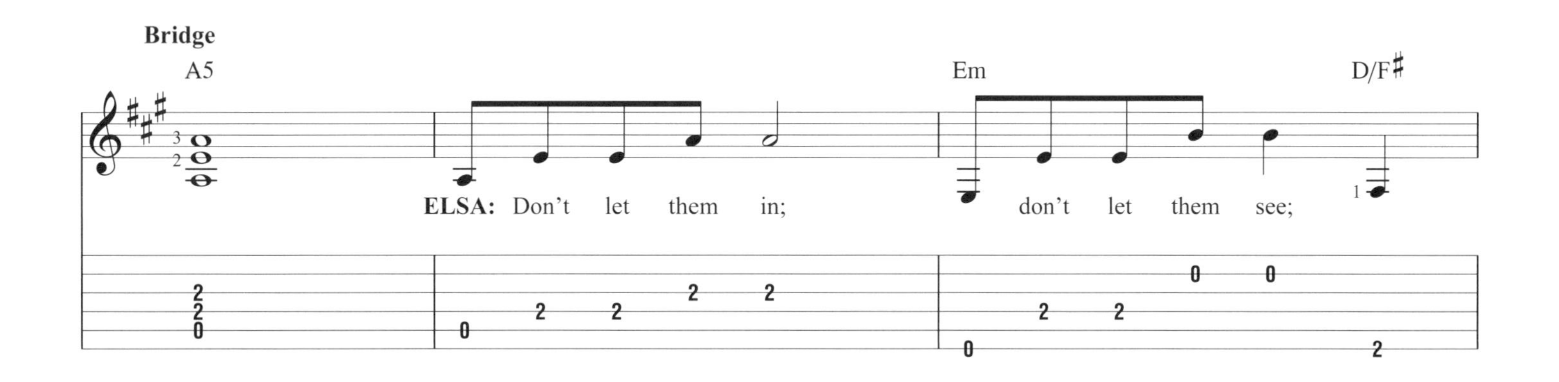
Bridge
A5
Em
D/F♯
ELSA: Don't let them in;
don't let them see;

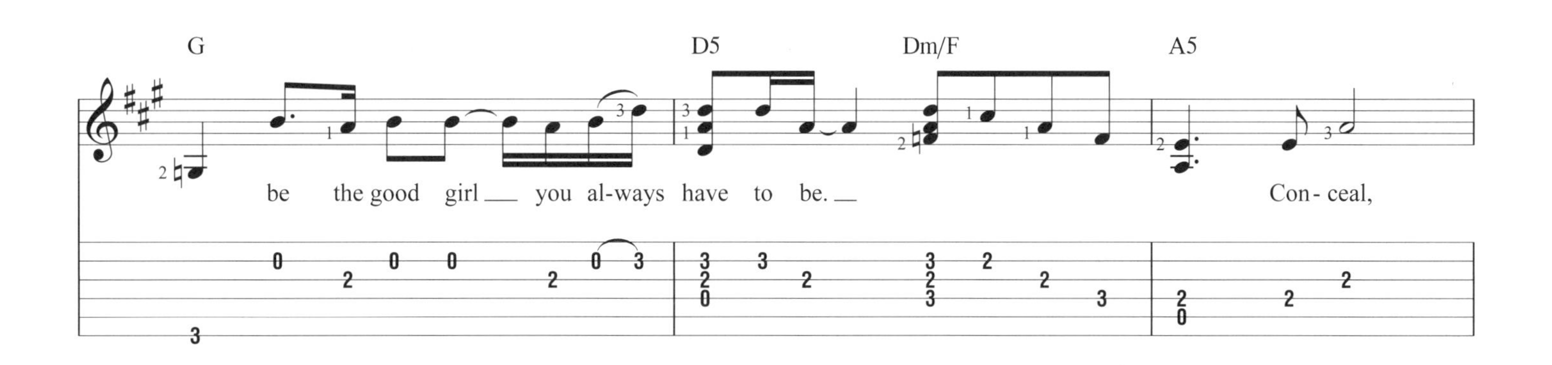
G
D5
Dm/F
A5
be the good girl you al-ways have to be.
Con-ceal,

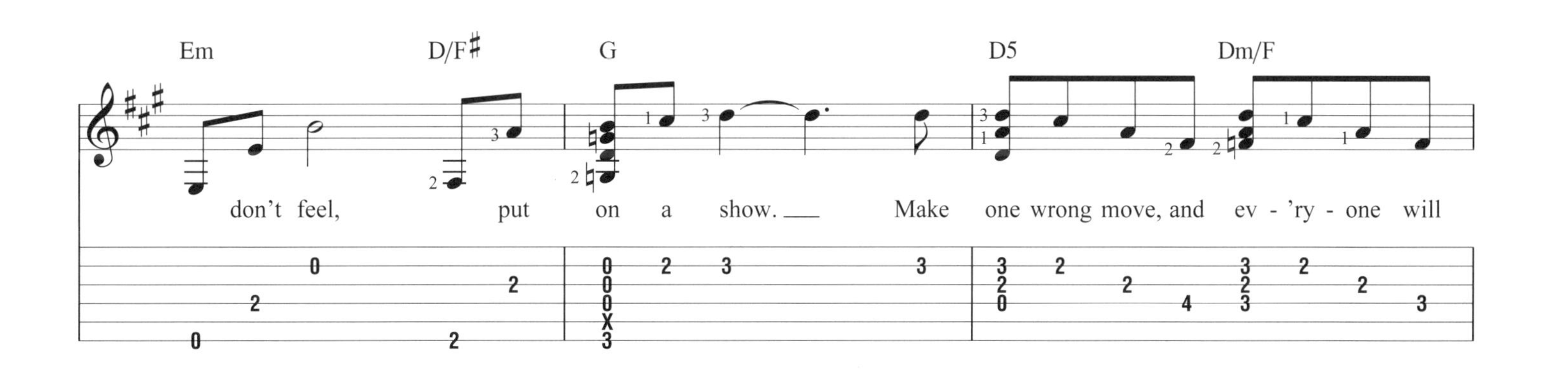
Em
D/F♯
G
D5
Dm/F
don't feel, put on a show.
Make one wrong move, and ev-'ry-one will

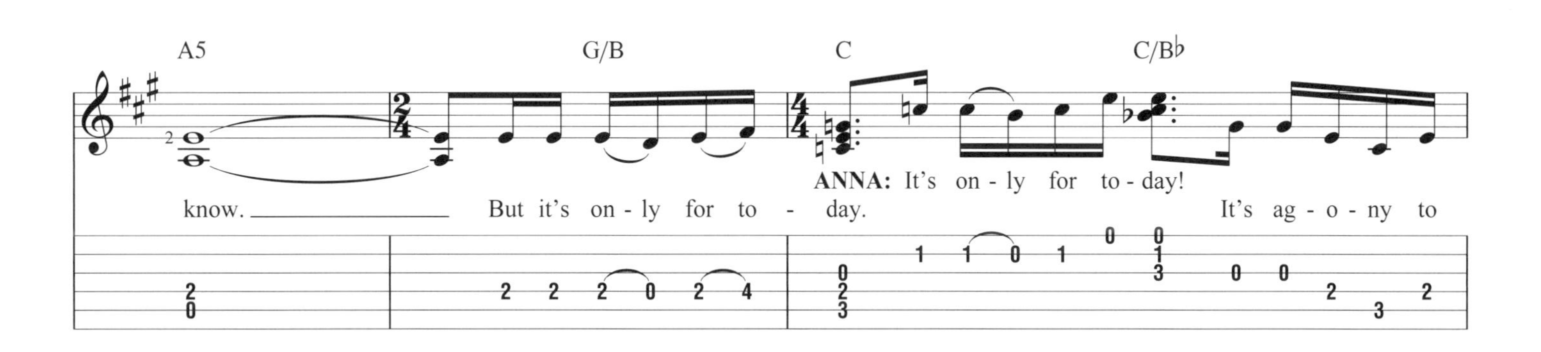
A5
G/B
C
C/B♭
know. But it's on-ly for to-day.
ANNA: It's on-ly for to-day!
It's ag-o-ny to

Slightly slower
D/A
D/C
Dm7♭5
rit.
N.C.
B♭
It's ag-o-ny to wait!
The
wait! Tell the guards to o-pen up the gate!

Outro
C/E
Fmaj7
gate! For the first time in for - ev - er, I'm get - ting
G/B
C
G/B
Am
what I'm dream - ing of: a chance to change my lone -
Em
B♭
E7
- ly world, a chance to find true love. I
Am
Am/G
Fmaj7
D7/F♯
D
N.C.
know it all ends to - mor - row, so it has to be to - day. 'Cause for the
C/E
Fmaj7sus2
C/G
D7/A
first time in for - ev - er, for the first time in for - ev -
Fm/A♭
C/G
F/G
C
N.C.
- er, noth ing's in my way!

A Girl Worth Fighting For

from MULAN

Music by Matthew Wilder
Lyrics by David Zippel

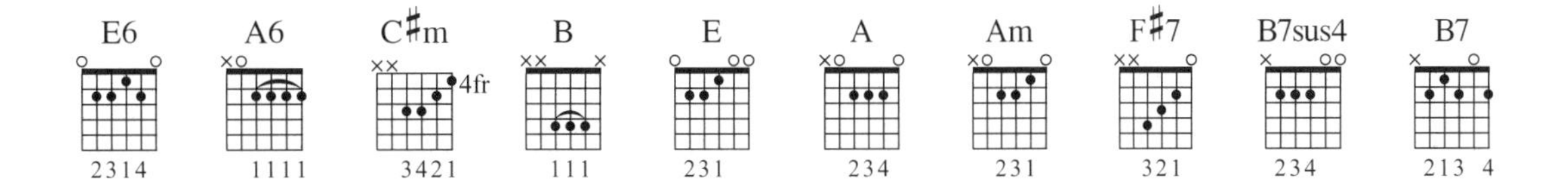

Strum Pattern: 5
Pick Pattern: 6

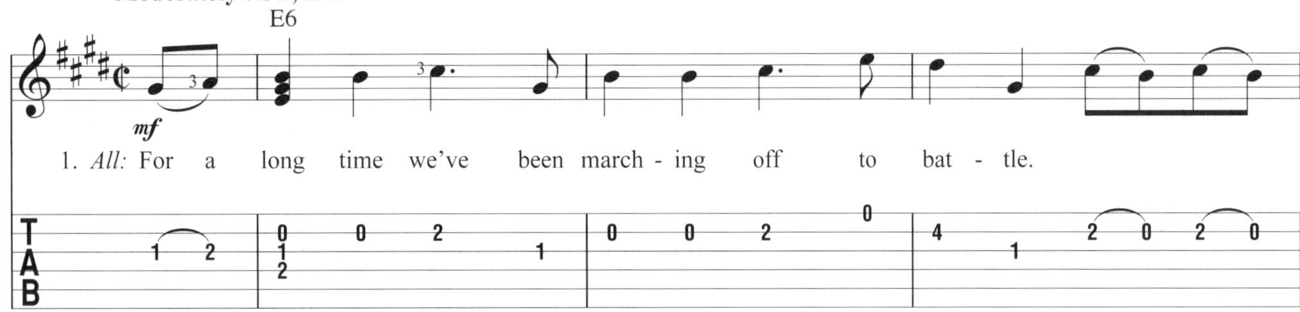

*Lyrics in italics are spoken throughout.

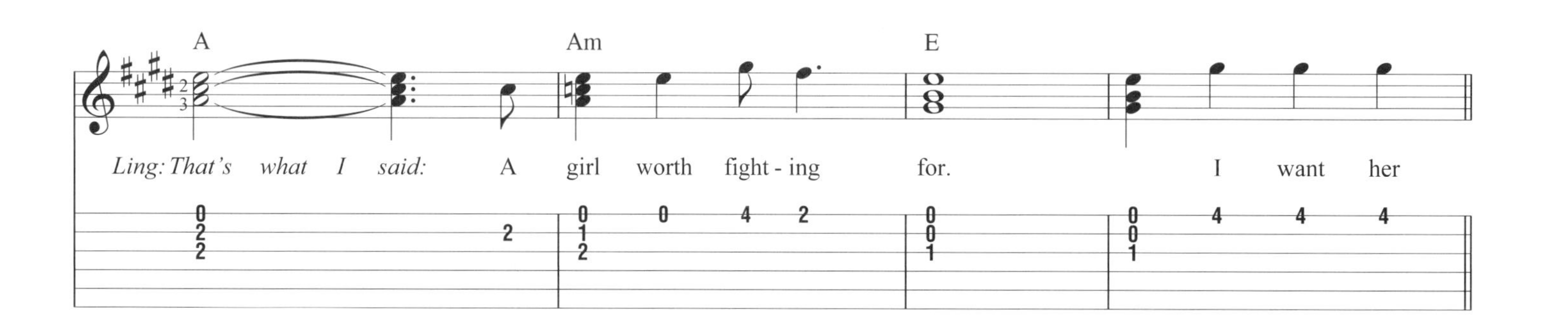

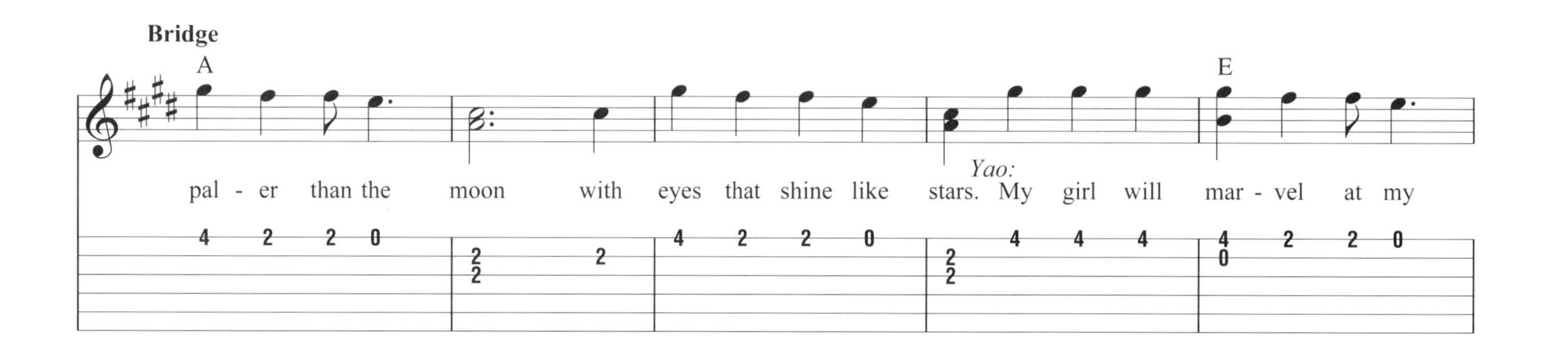

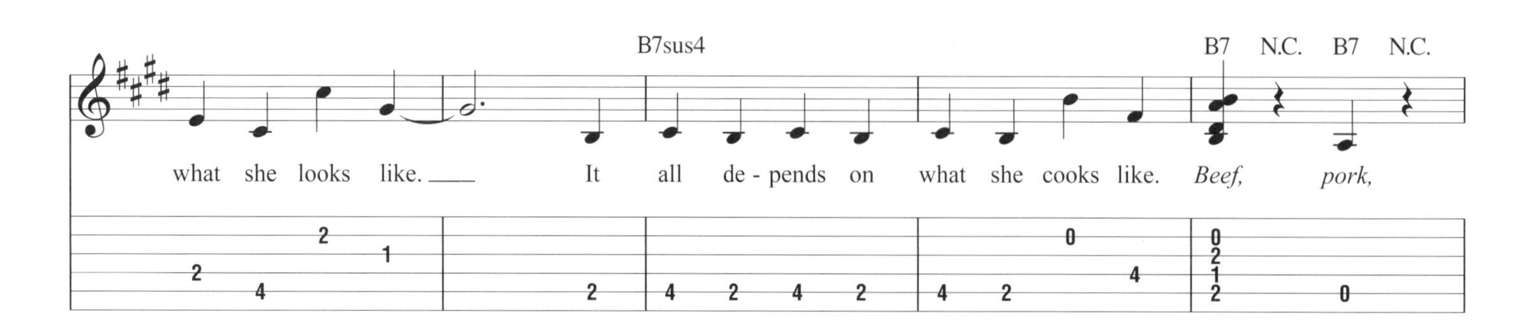

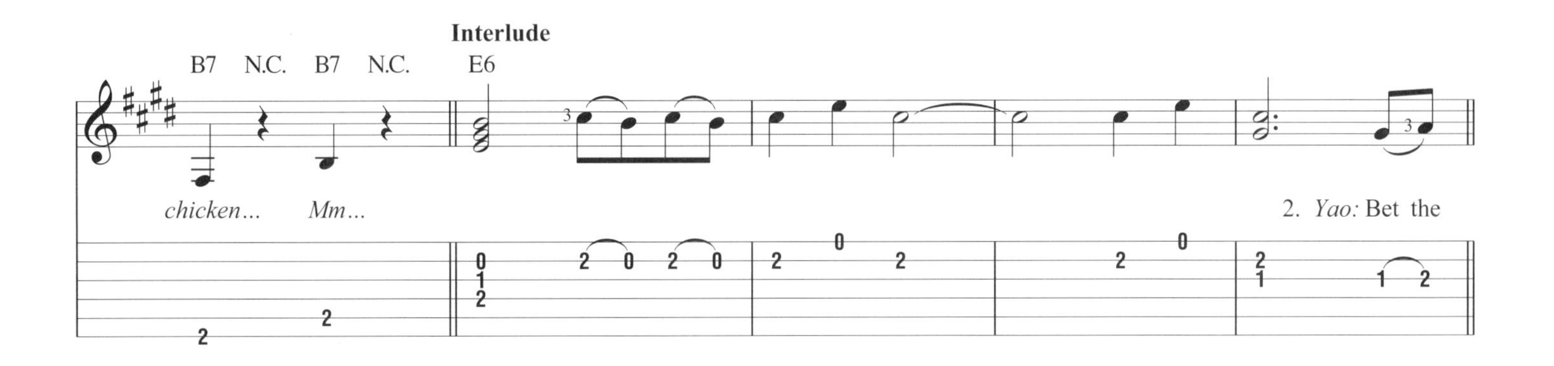
Interlude
B7 N.C. B7 N.C. E6
chicken... Mm...
2. Yao: Bet the

Verse
E6
lo - cal girls thought you were quite the charm - er.
Ling: And I'll

bet the la - dies love a man in ar - mor.
All: You can

A6 C♯m B
guess what we have missed the most since we went off to war.

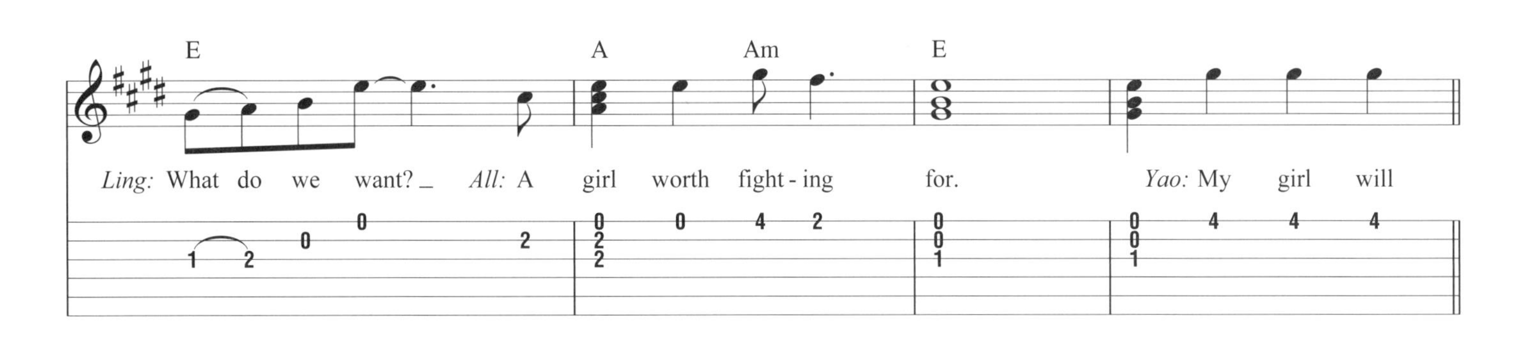
E A Am E
Ling: What do we want? _ All: A girl worth fight - ing for.
Yao: My girl will

Bridge
A
think I have no faults. Chien Po: That I'm a ma - jor find. Mulan: How 'bout a

E
N.C.
girl who's got a brain, who al - ways speaks her mind? Gang of 3: Naaaa! Ling: My

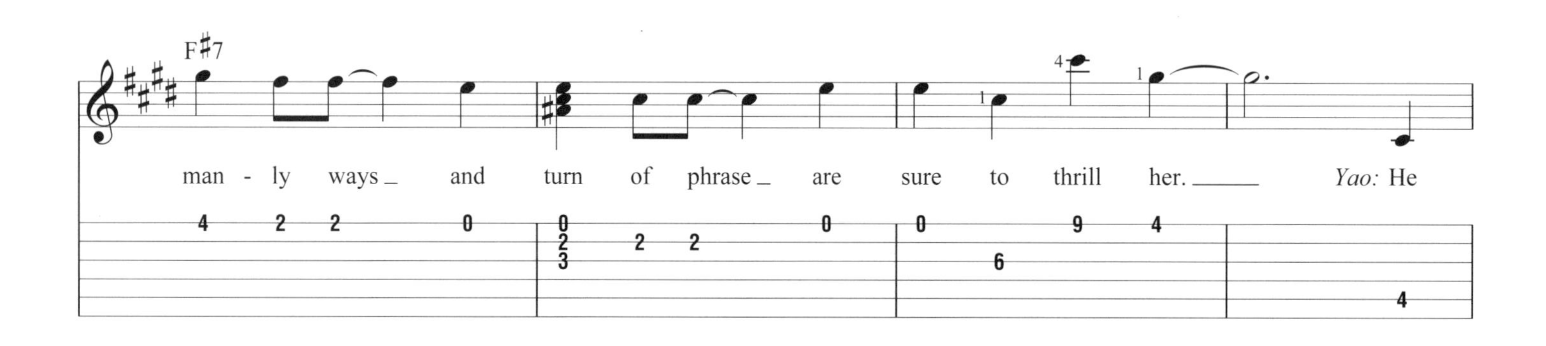
F♯7
man - ly ways and turn of phrase are sure to thrill her. Yao: He

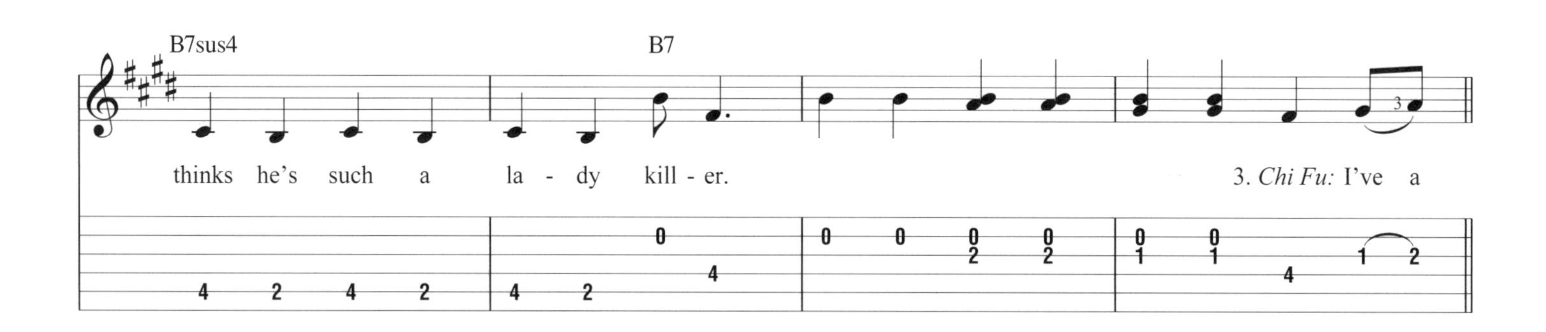
B7sus4
B7
thinks he's such a la - dy kill - er. 3. Chi Fu: I've a

Verse
E6
girl back home who's un - like an - y oth - er. Yao: Yeah, the

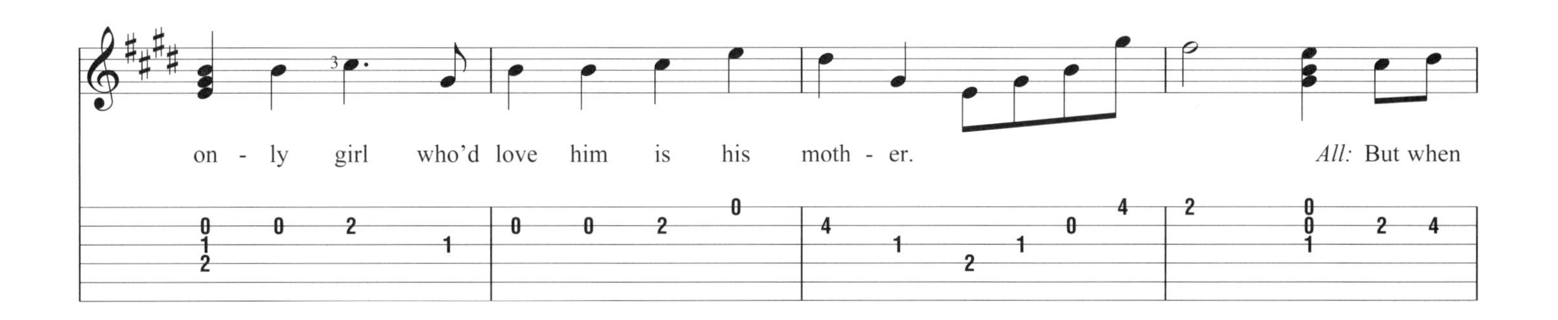
on - ly girl who'd love him is his moth - er. All: But when

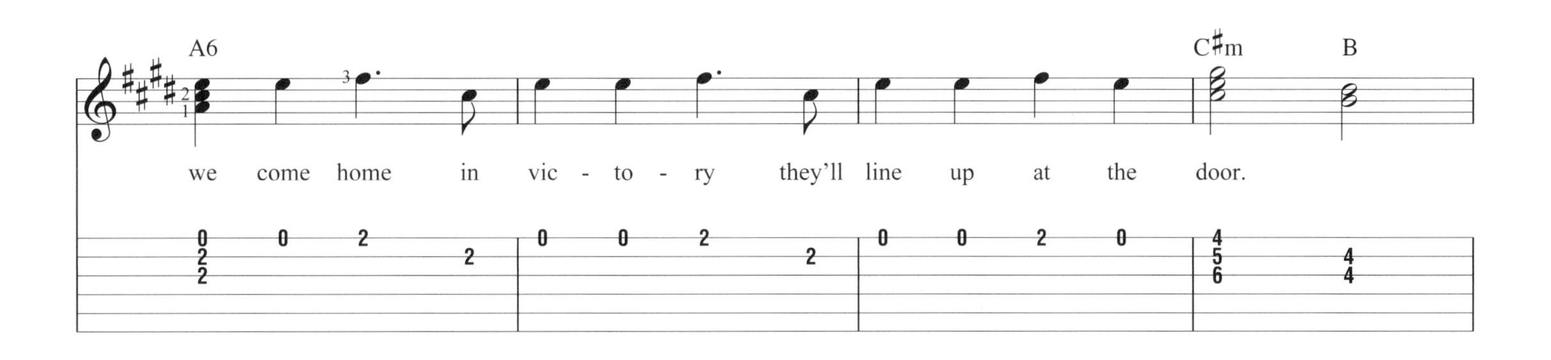
A6
C♯m
B
we come home in vic - to - ry they'll line up at the door.

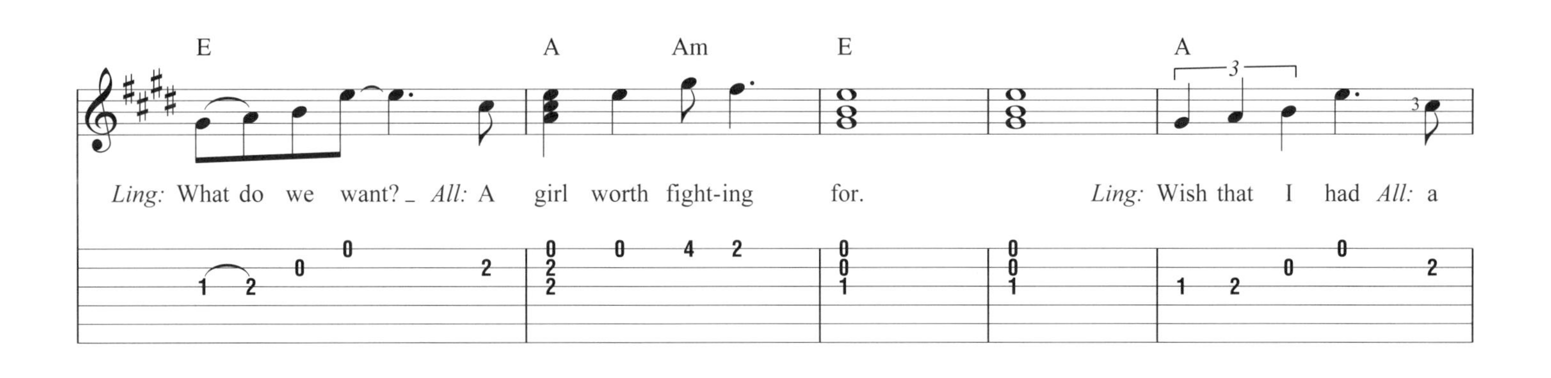
E
A
Am
E
A
Ling: What do we want? All: A girl worth fight-ing for. Ling: Wish that I had All: a

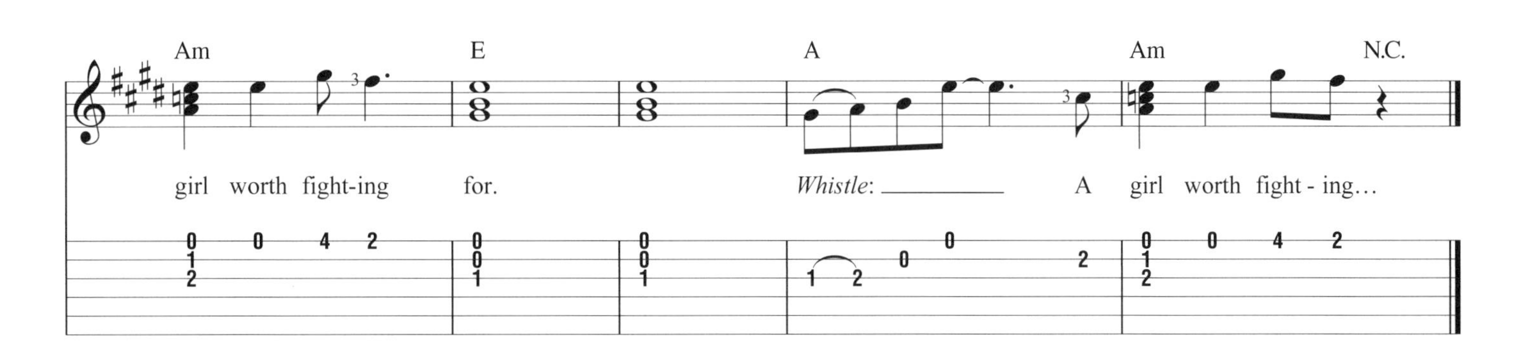
Am
E
A
Am
N.C.
girl worth fight-ing for. Whistle: A girl worth fight - ing…

Go the Distance

from HERCULES

Music by Alan Menken
Lyrics by David Zippel

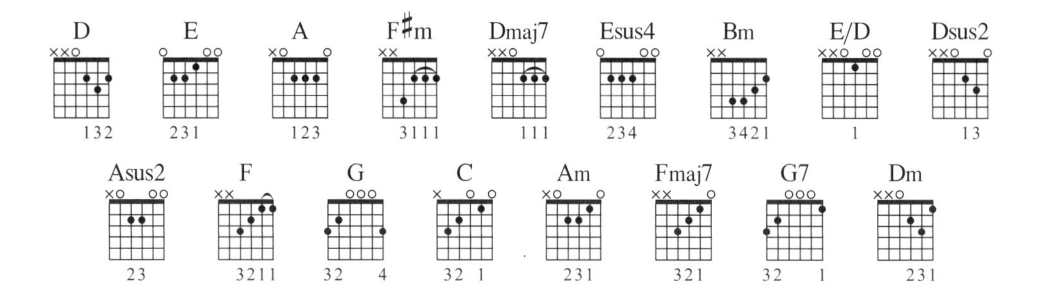

Strum Pattern: 1, 3
Pick Pattern: 2

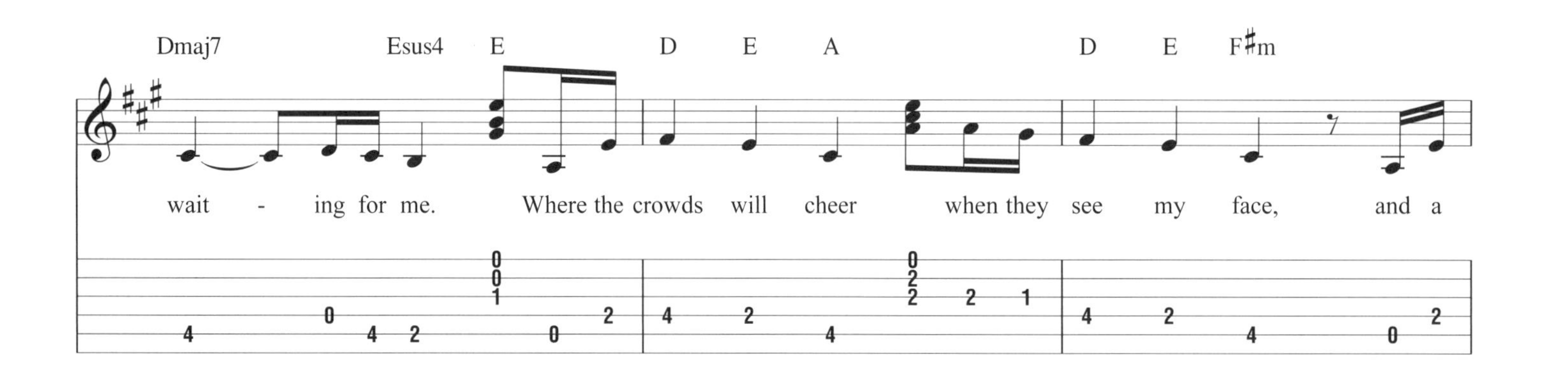

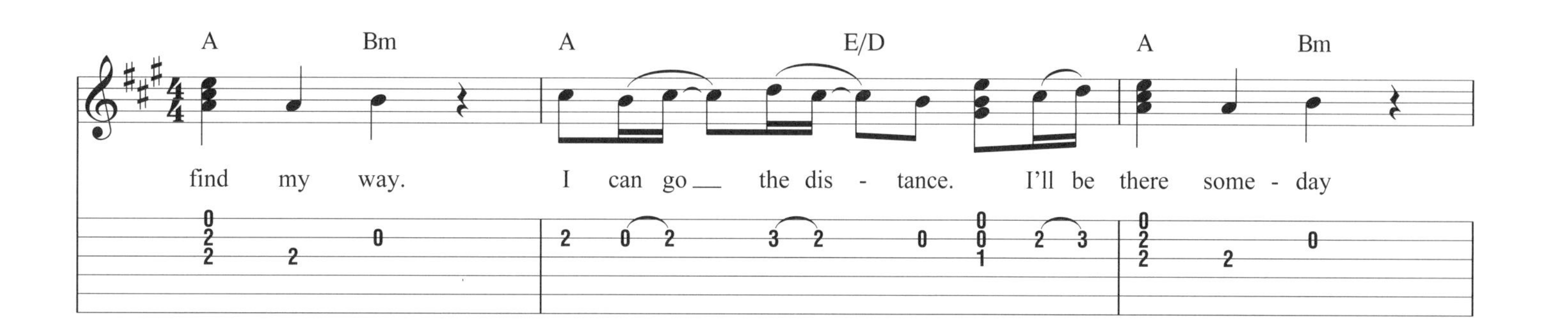
A Bm A E/D A Bm
find my way. I can go the dis - tance. I'll be there some - day

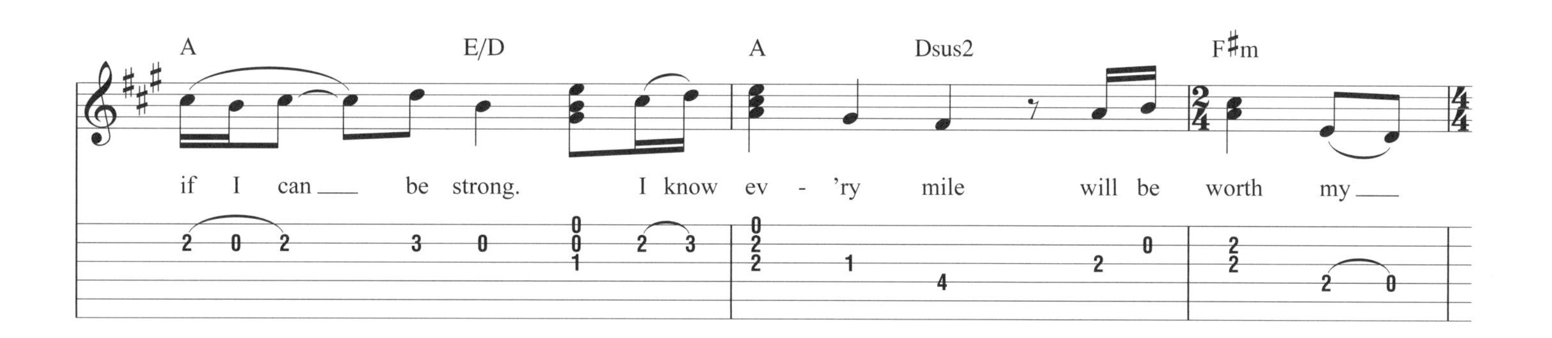
A E/D A Dsus2 F♯m
if I can be strong. I know ev - 'ry mile will be worth my

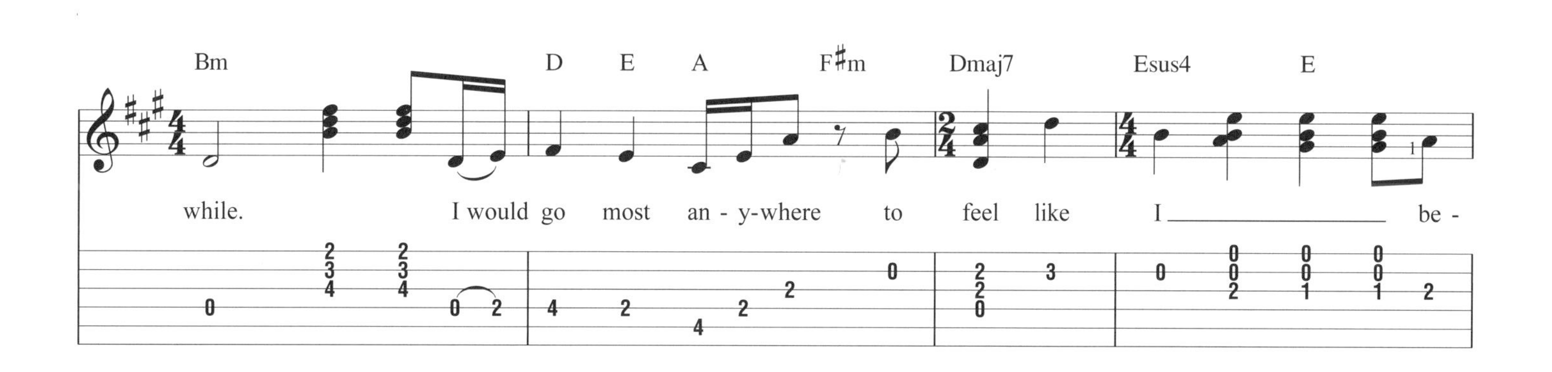
Bm D E A F♯m Dmaj7 Esus4 E
while. I would go most an - y-where to feel like I be -

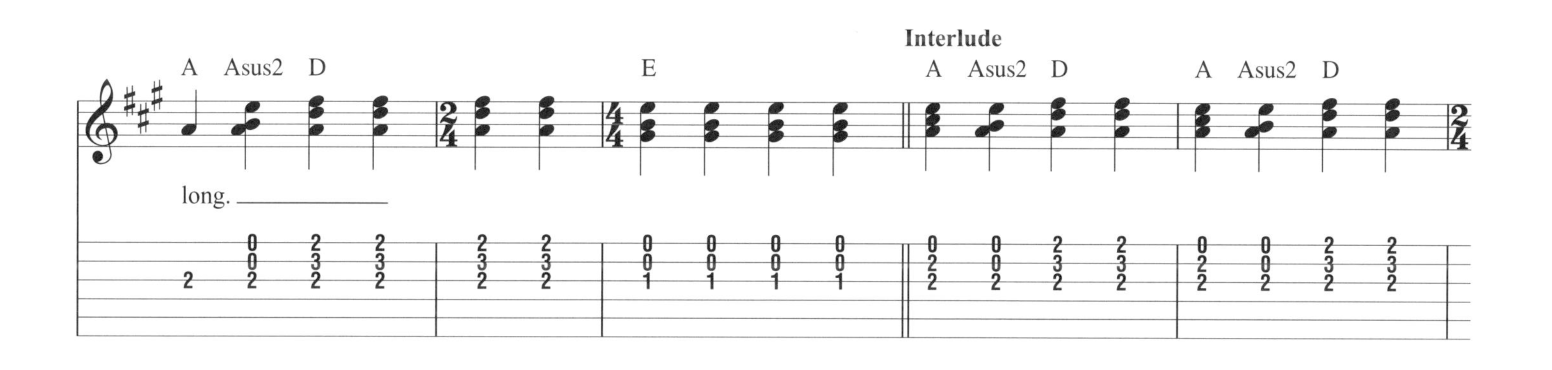
A Asus2 D E
Interlude
A Asus2 D A Asus2 D
long.

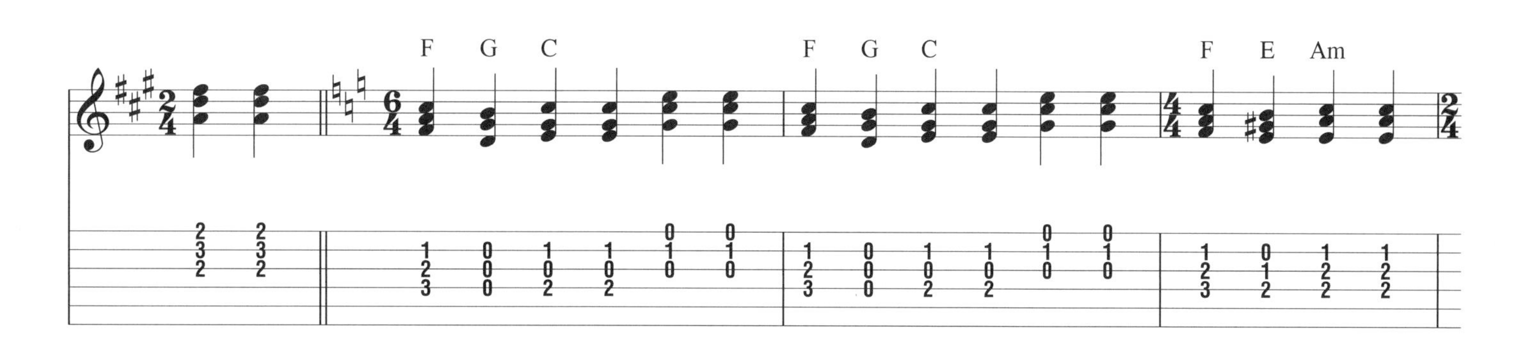
F G C F G C F E Am

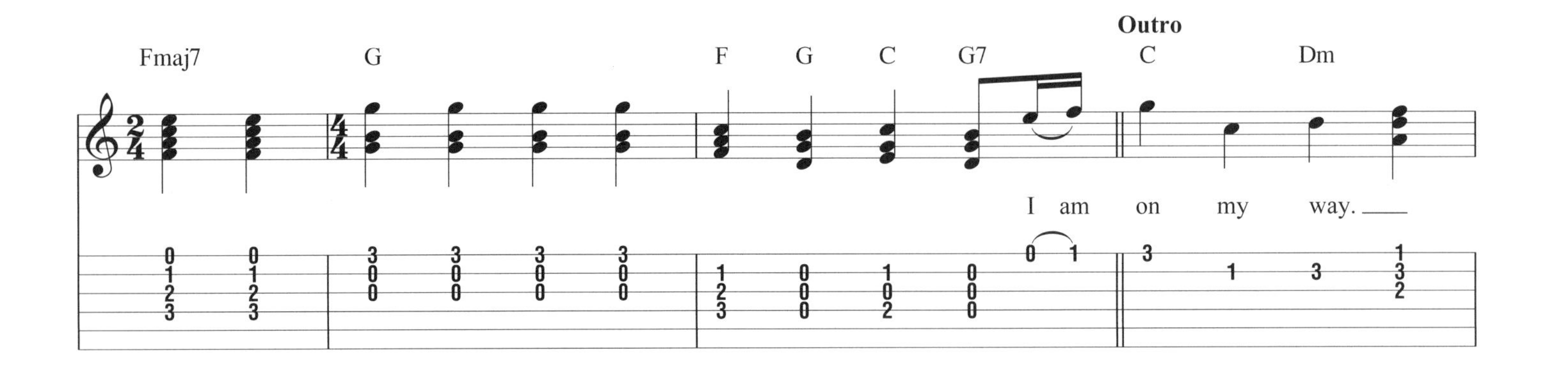
Outro
Fmaj7
G
F
G
C
G7
C
Dm
I am on my way.

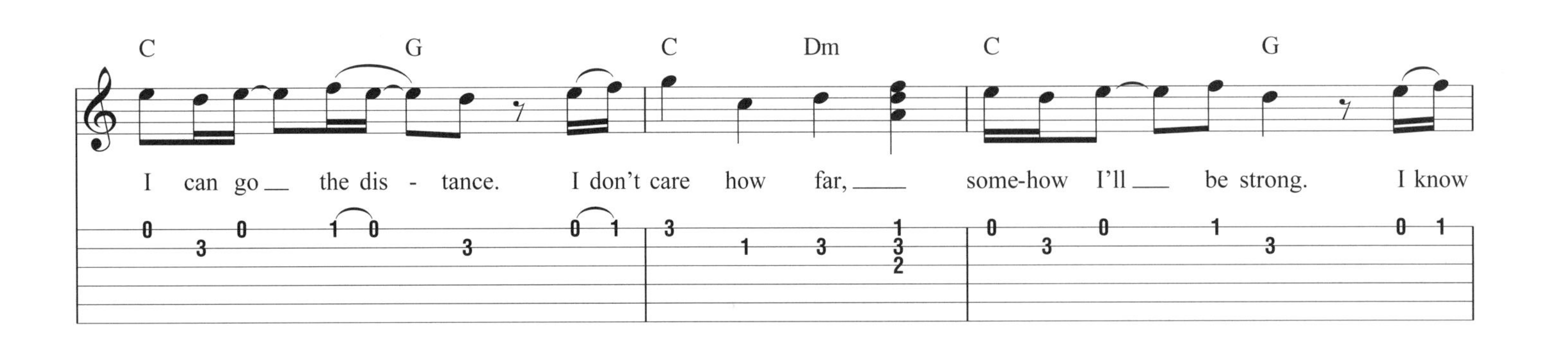
C
G
C
Dm
C
G
I can go the dis - tance. I don't care how far, some-how I'll be strong. I know

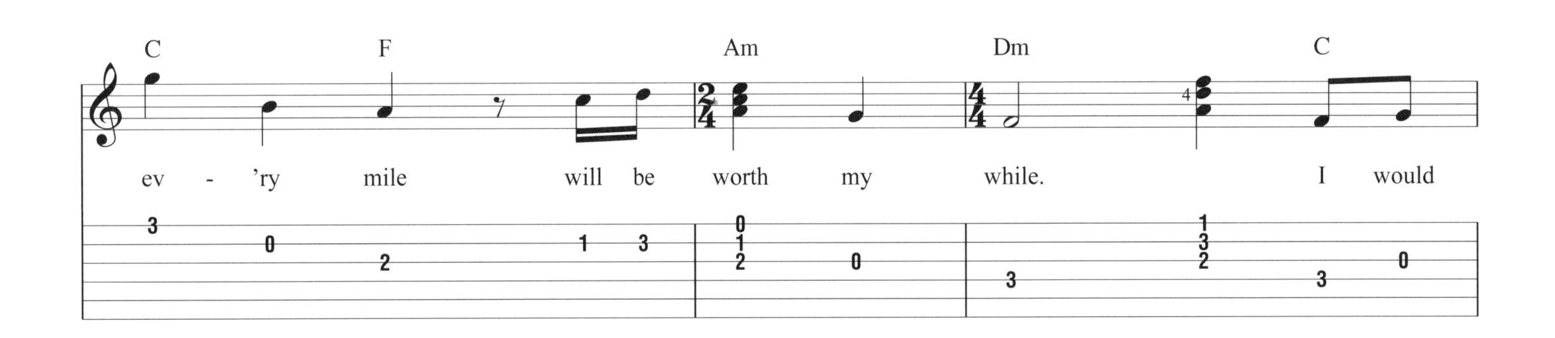
C
F
Am
Dm
C
ev - 'ry mile will be worth my while. I would

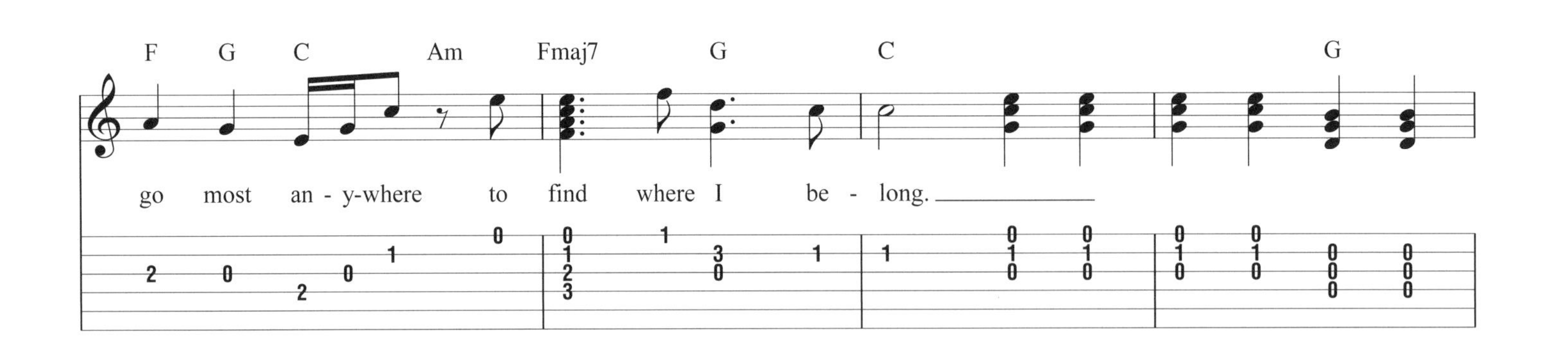
F
G
C
Am
Fmaj7
G
C
G
go most an - y-where to find where I be - long.

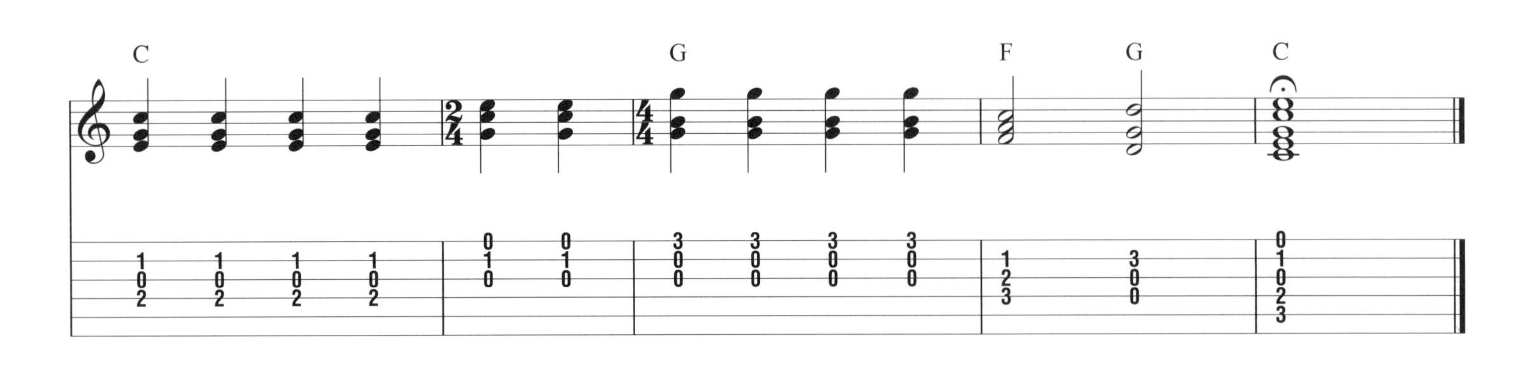
C
G
F
G
C

Hawaiian Roller Coaster Ride

from LILO & STITCH

Words and Music by Alan Silvestri and Mark Keali'i Ho'omalu

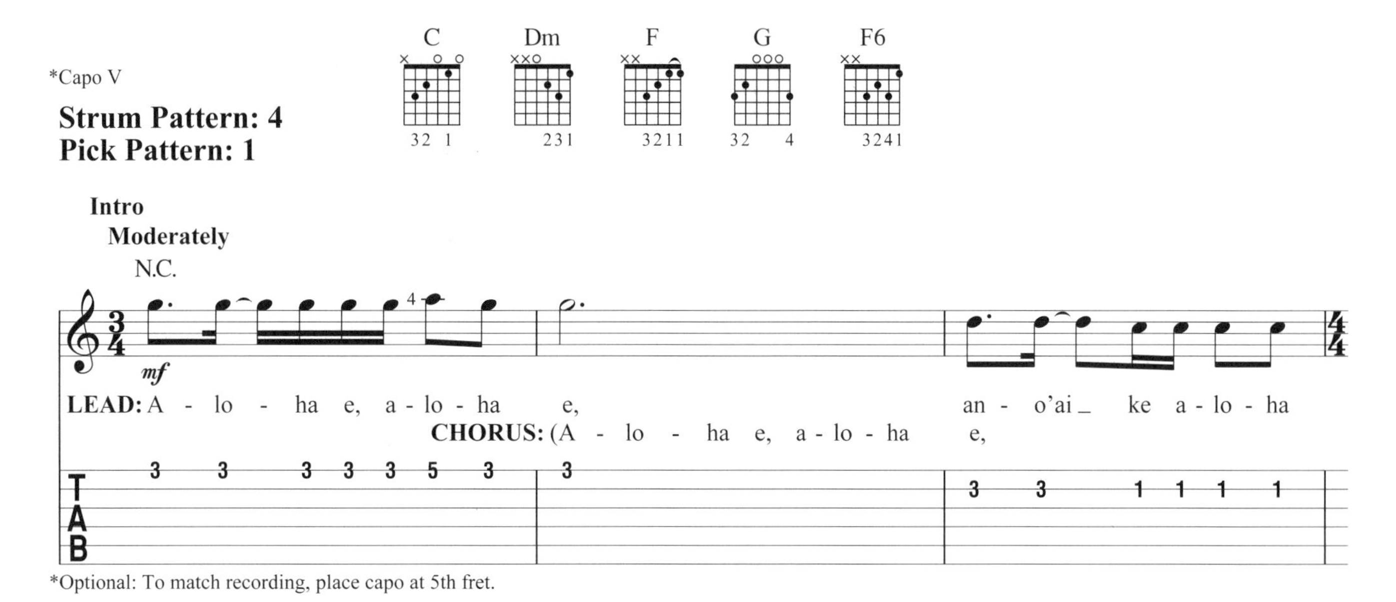

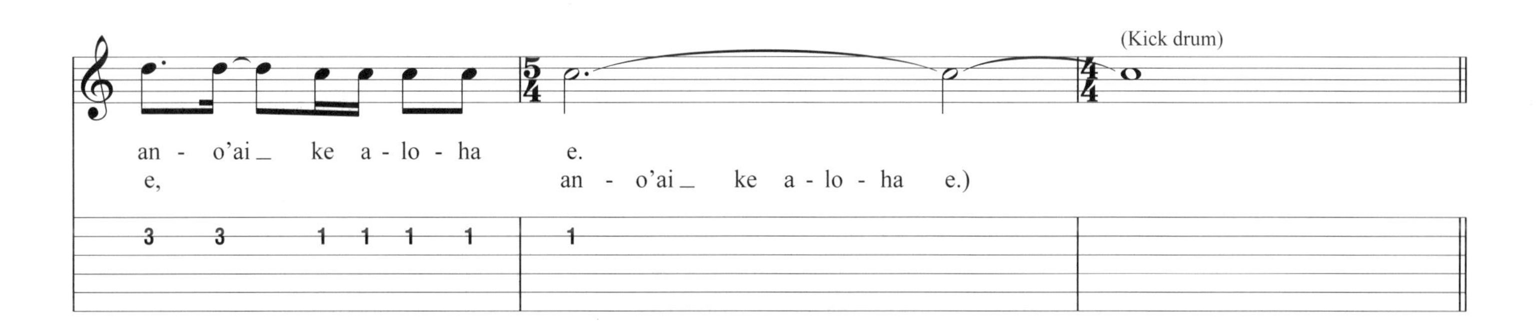

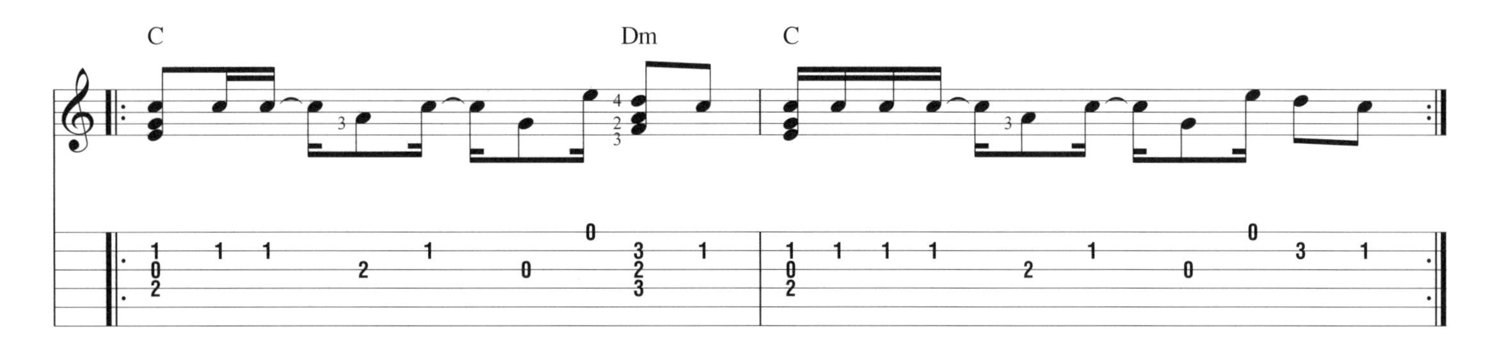

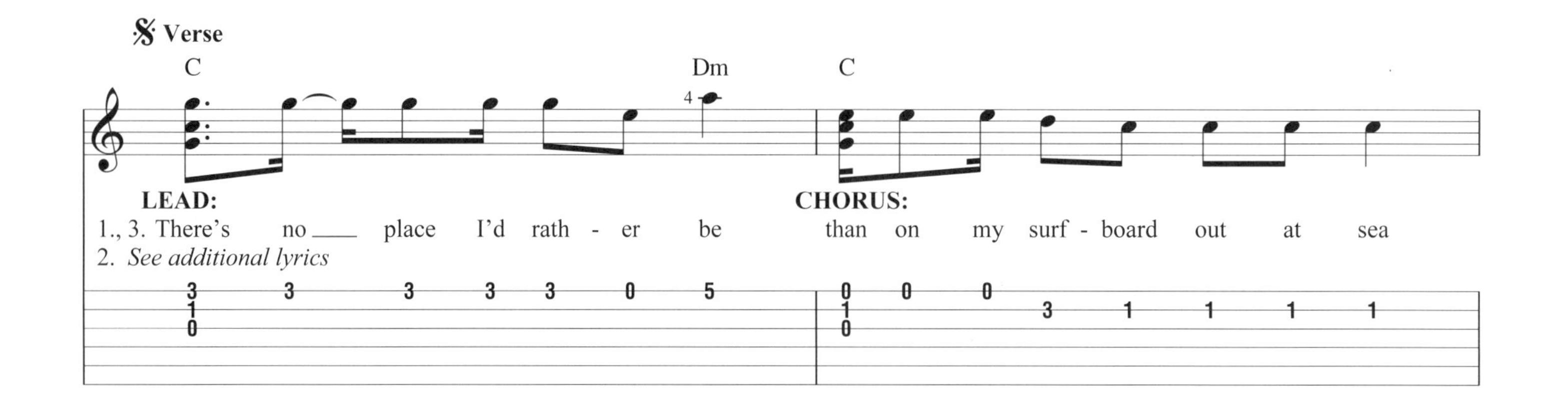
Verse
C
Dm
C
LEAD:
CHORUS:
1., 3. There's no place I'd rath - er be than on my surf - board out at sea
2. See additional lyrics

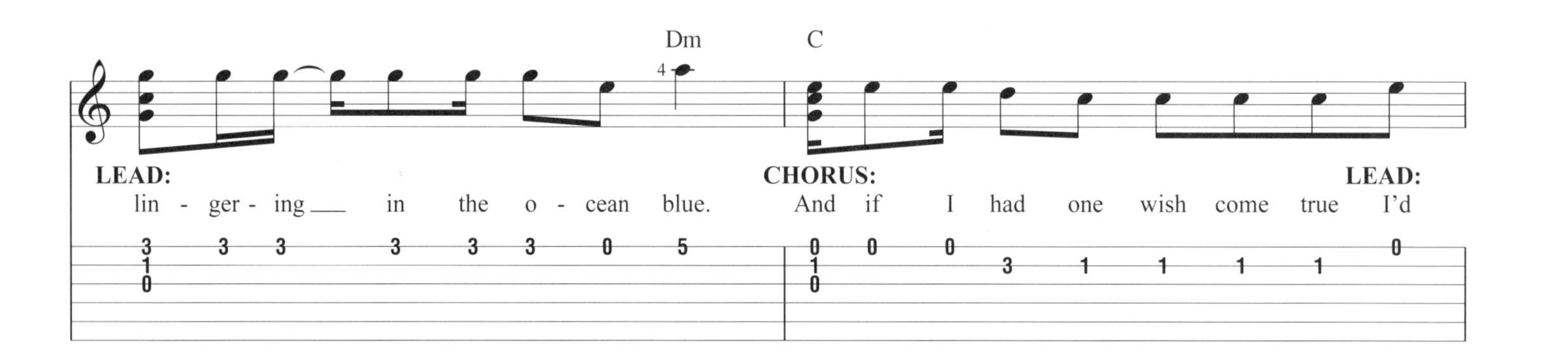
Dm
C
LEAD:
CHORUS:
LEAD:
lin - ger - ing in the o - cean blue. And if I had one wish come true I'd

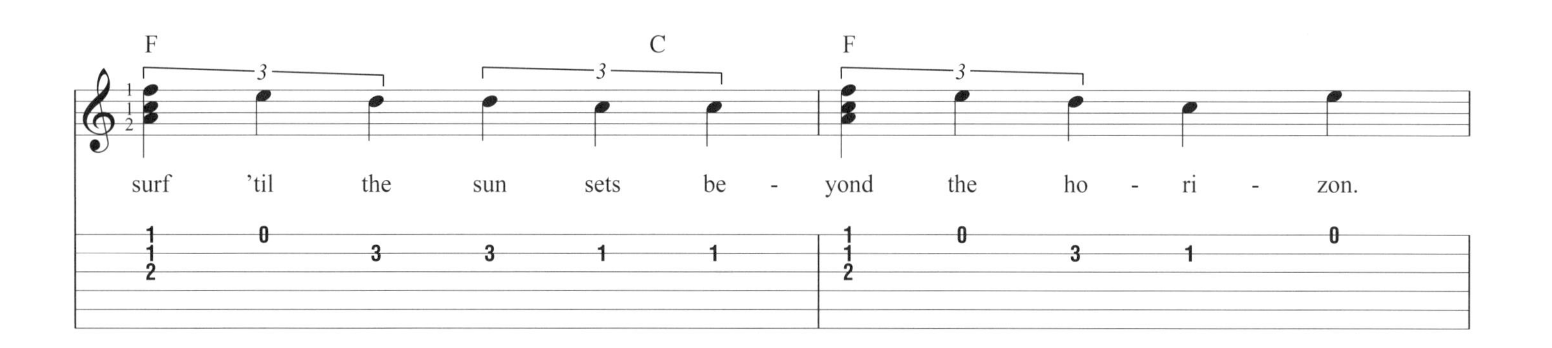
F
C
F
surf 'til the sun sets be - yond the ho - ri - zon.

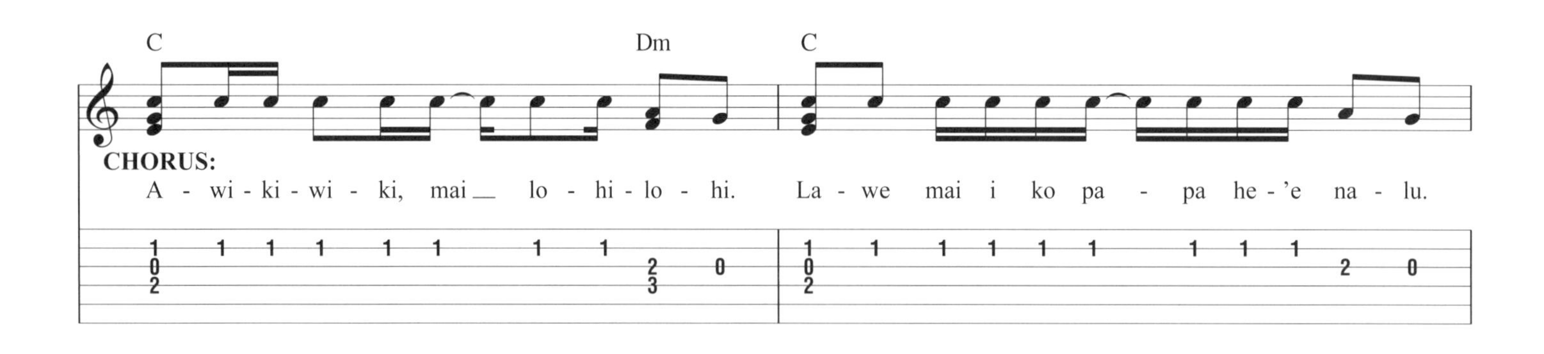
C
Dm
C
CHORUS:
A - wi - ki - wi - ki, mai lo - hi - lo - hi. La - we mai i ko pa - pa he - 'e na - lu.

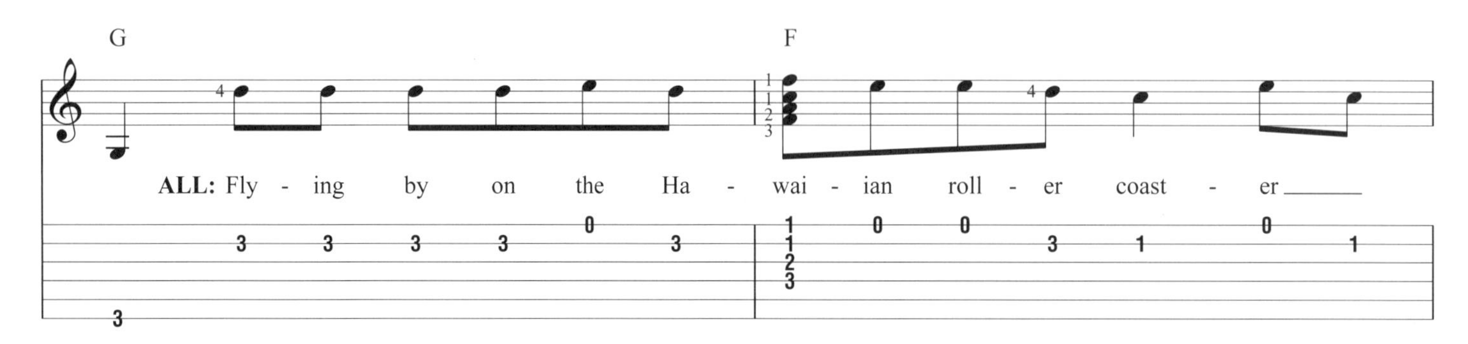
G
F
ALL: Fly - ing by on the Ha - wai - ian roll - er coast - er

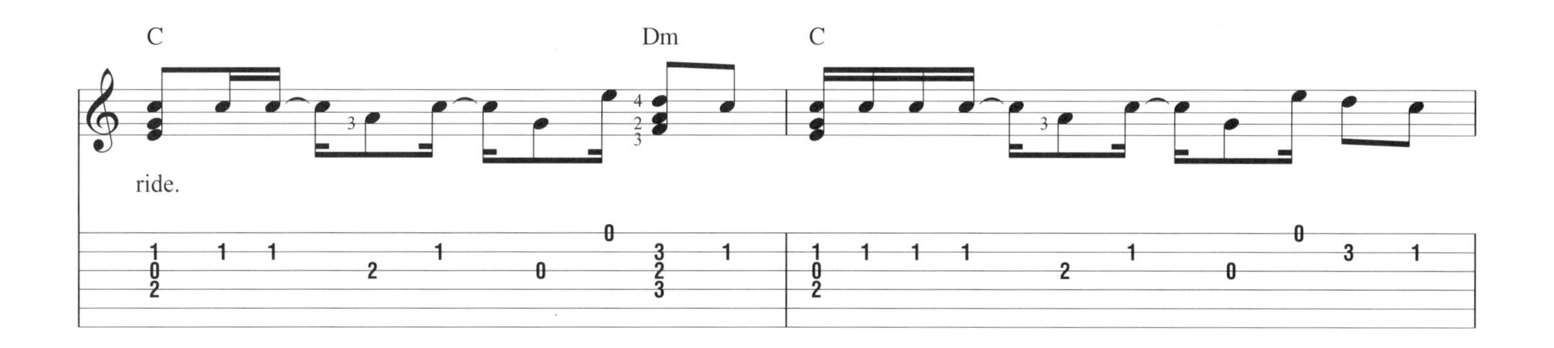
C
Dm
C
ride.

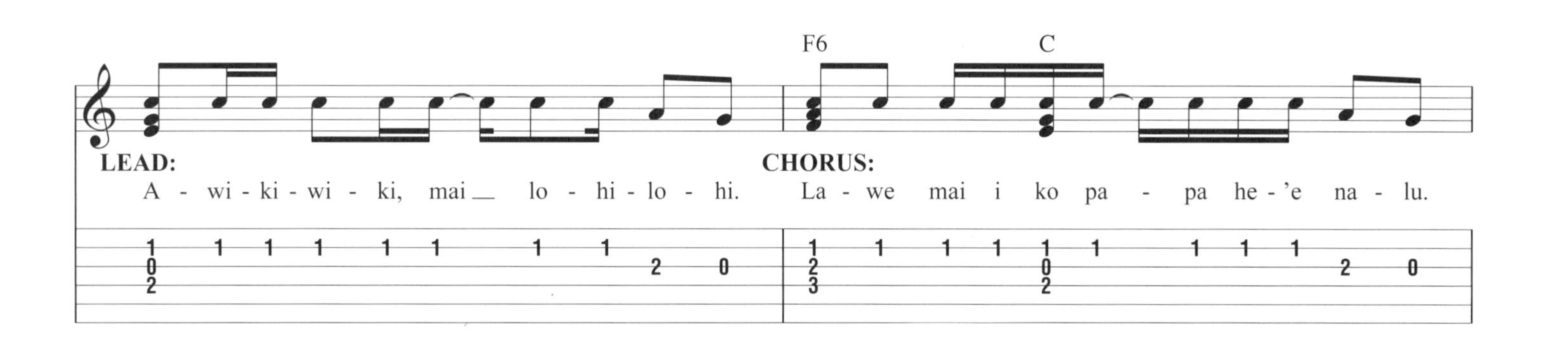
F6
C
LEAD:
A - wi - ki - wi - ki, mai lo - hi - lo - hi.
CHORUS:
La - we mai i ko pa - pa he - 'e na - lu.

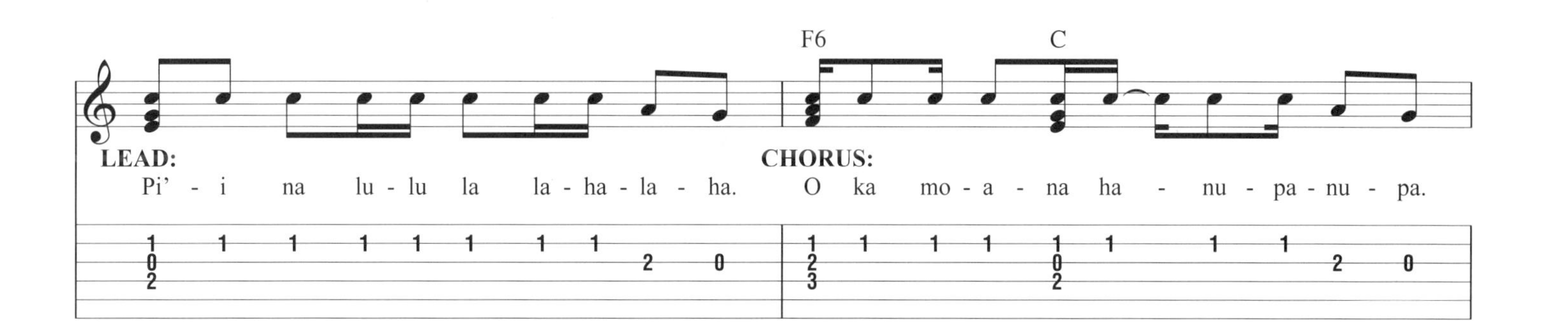
F6
C
LEAD:
Pi' - i na lu - lu la la - ha - la - ha.
CHORUS:
O ka mo - a - na ha - nu - pa - nu - pa.

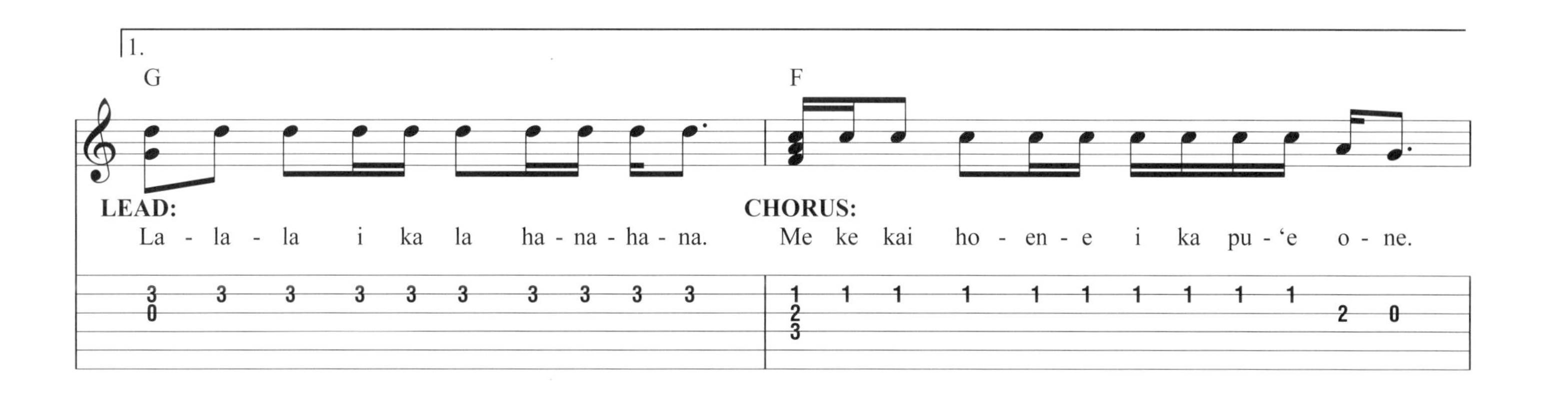
1.
G
F
LEAD:
La - la - la i ka la ha - na - ha - na.
CHORUS:
Me ke kai ho - en - e i ka pu - 'e o - ne.

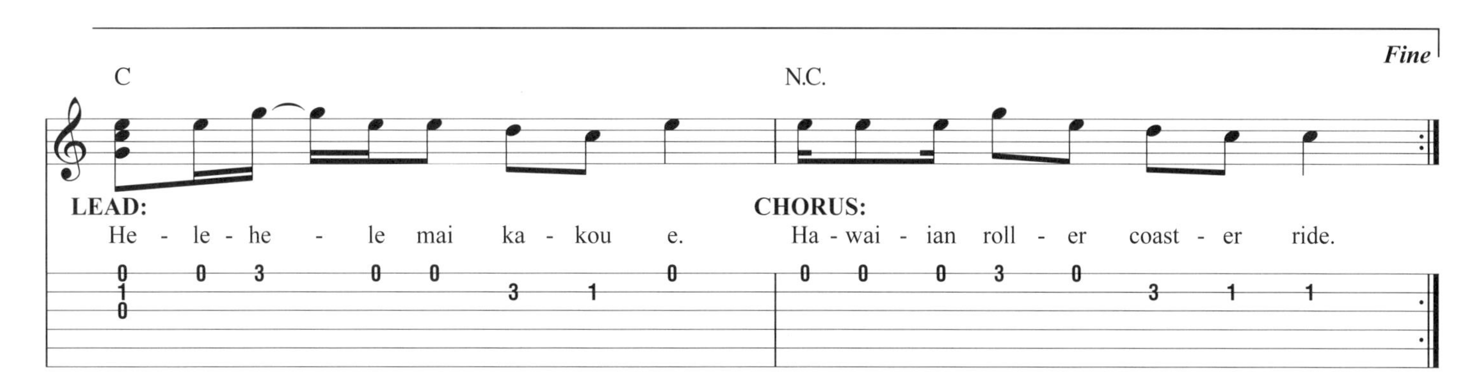
C
N.C.
Fine
LEAD:
He - le - he - le mai ka - kou e.
CHORUS:
Ha - wai - ian roll - er coast - er ride.

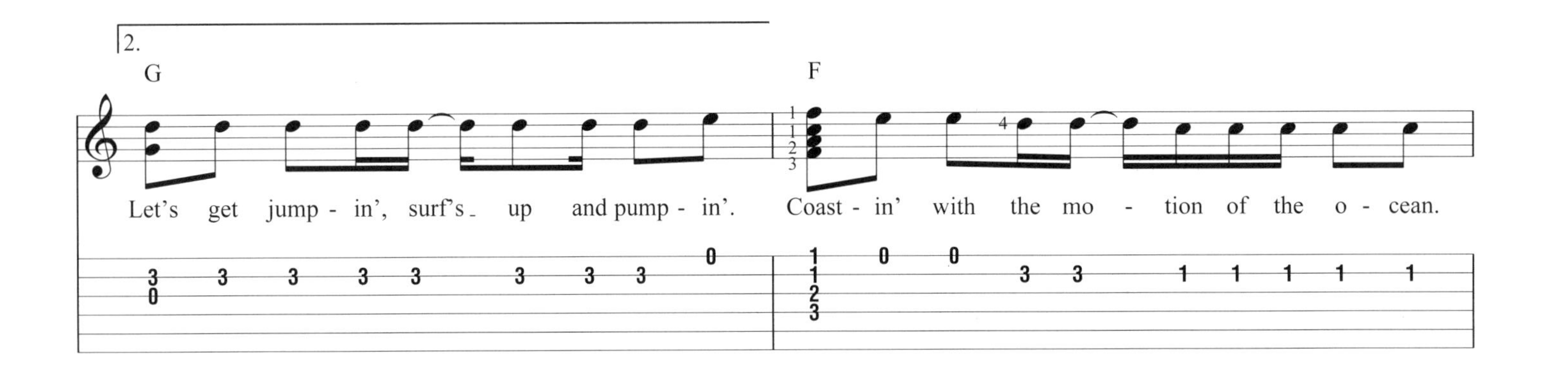
2.
G
F
Let's get jump - in', surf's up and pump - in'. Coast - in' with the mo - tion of the o - cean.

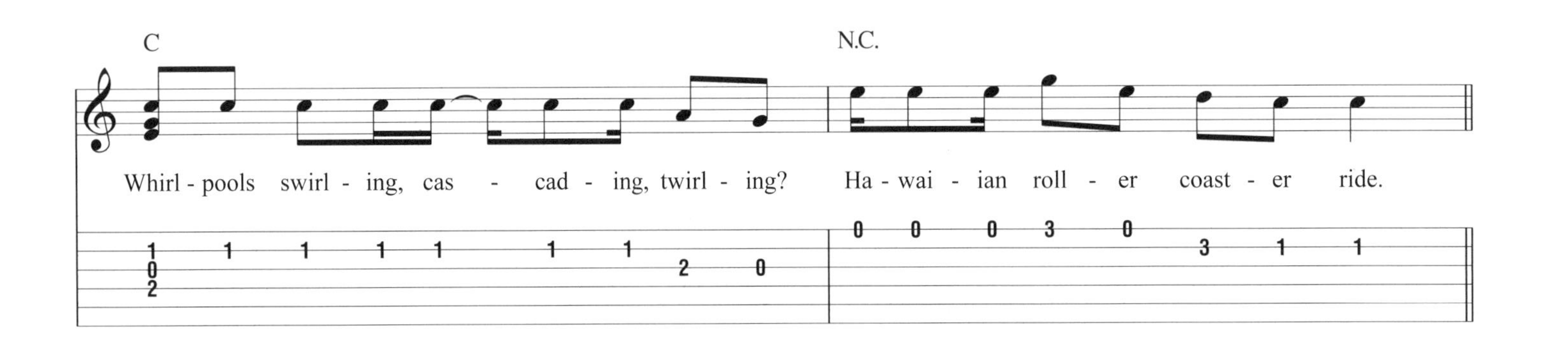
C
N.C.
Whirl - pools swirl - ing, cas - cad - ing, twirl - ing? Ha - wai - ian roll - er coast - er ride.

Instrumental
C
Dm
C

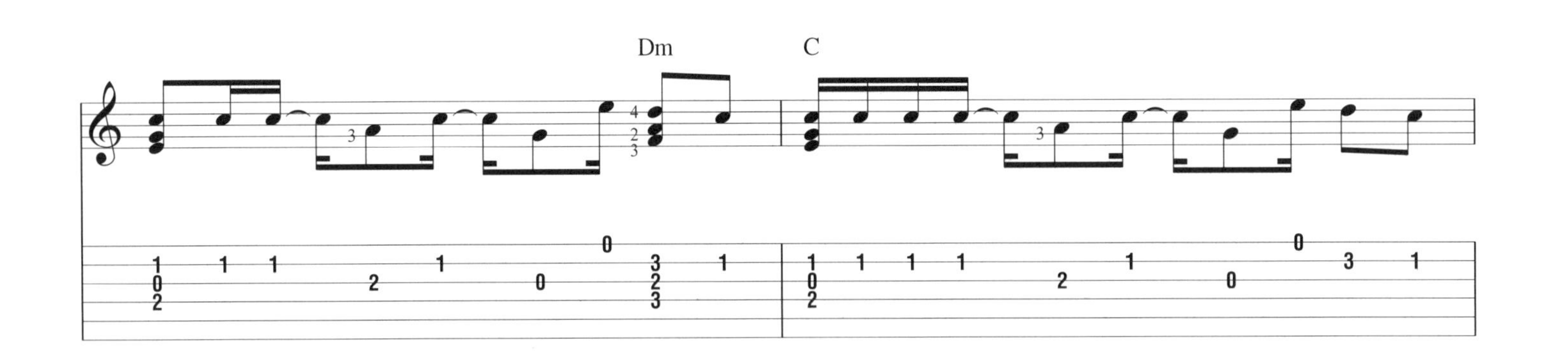
Dm
C

F
C
F

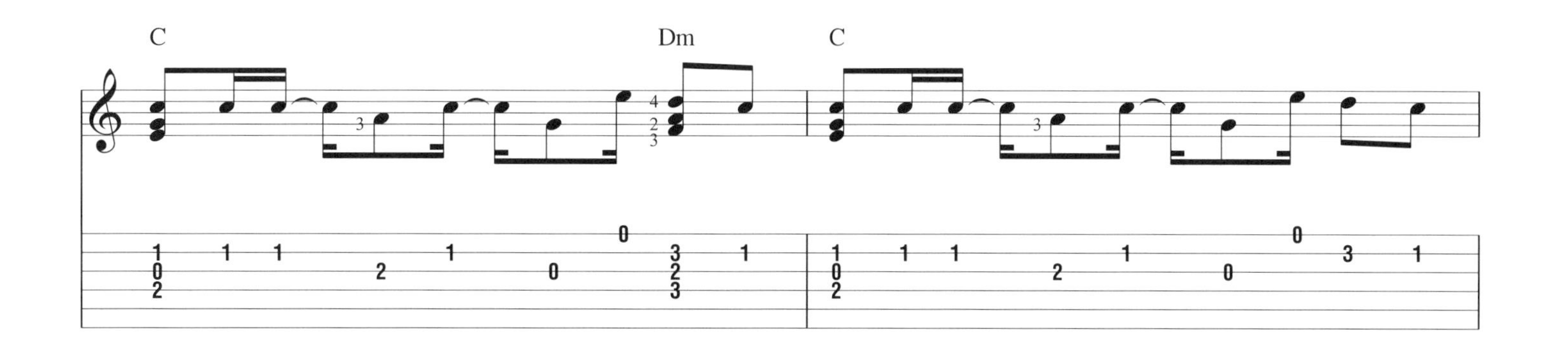

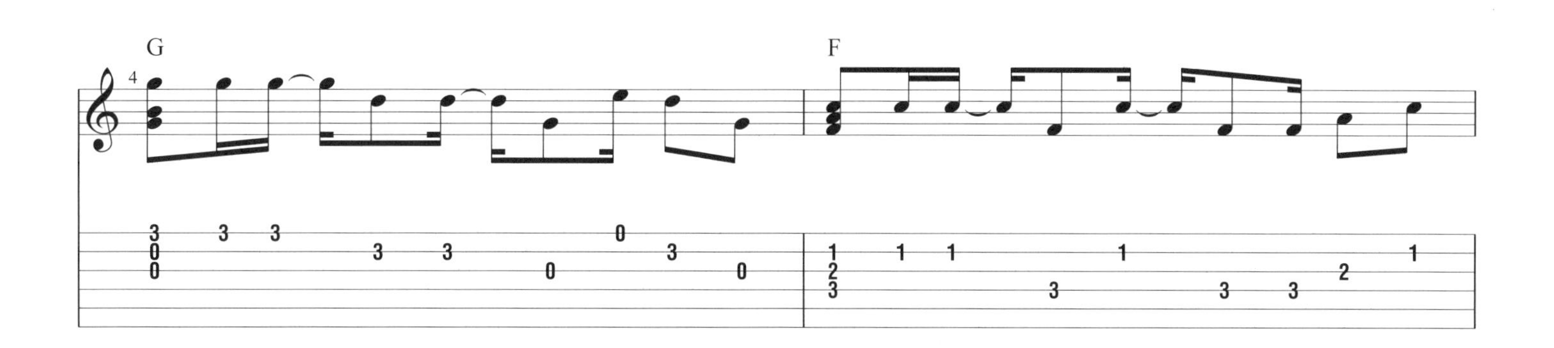

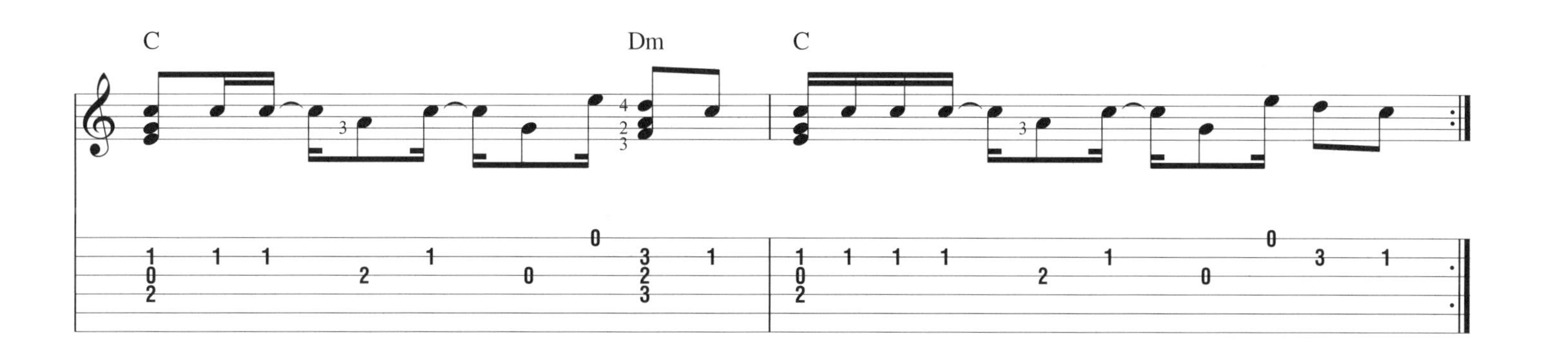

Additional Lyrics

ALL:	2. There's no place I'd rather be
CHORUS:	Than on the seashore dry, wet, free.
ALL:	On golden sand is where I'd lay
CHORUS:	And if I only had my way
ALL:	I'd play 'til the sun sets beyond the horizon.
CHORUS:	Lalala i ka la hanahana.
	Me ke kai hoene i ka pu'e one.
ALL:	It's time to try the Hawaiian roller coaster ride.
	Hang loose, hang ten, how's it shake-a-shaka.
	No worry, no fear, ain't no biggy, brahda.
	Puttin' in, cuttin' up, cuttin' back, cuttin' out.
	Front side, back side, goofy-footed wipe out.
	Let's get jumpin', surf's up and pumpin'.
	Coastin' with the motion of the ocean.
	Whirlpools swirling, cascading, twirling.
CHORUS:	Hawaiian roller coaster ride.

Hakuna Matata

from THE LION KING

Music by Elton John

Lyrics by Tim Rice

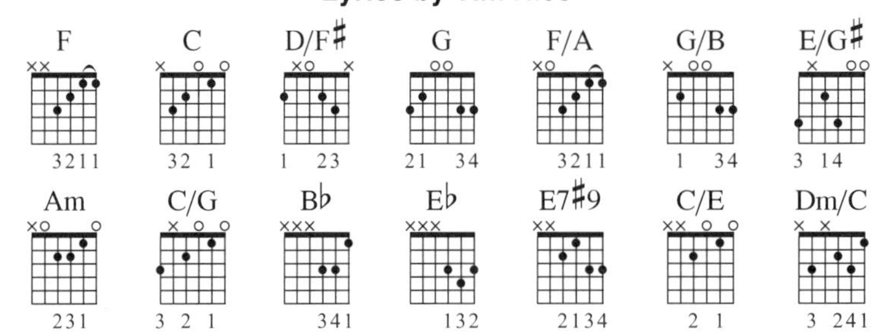

Strum Pattern: 6
Pick Pattern: 6

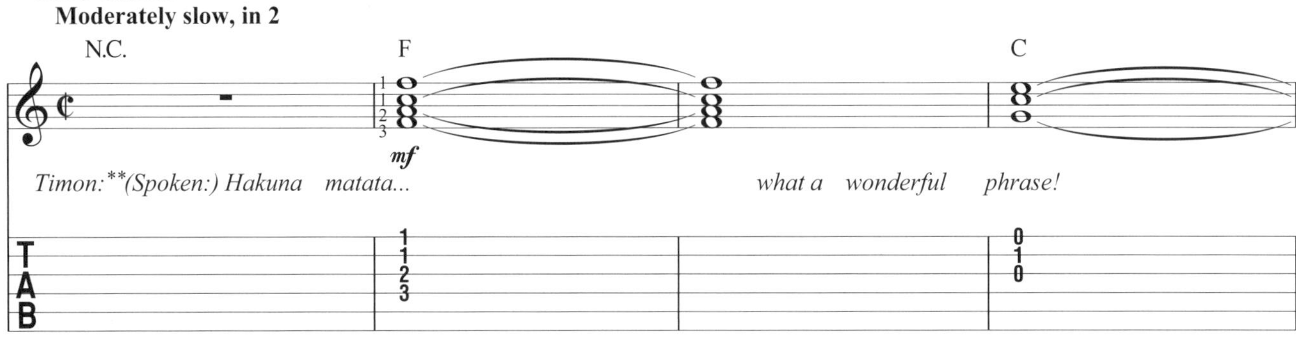

**Lyrics in italics are spoken throughout.
*Optional: To match recording, tune down 1/2 step.

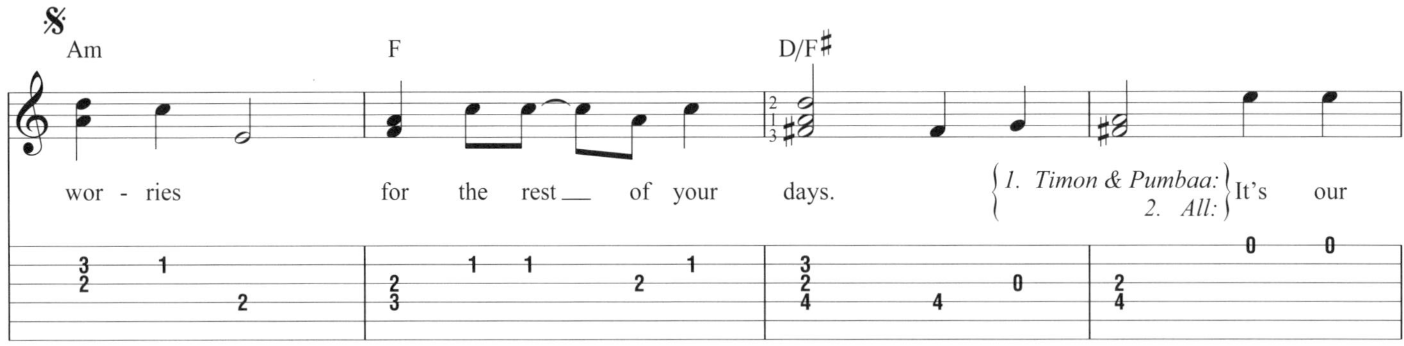

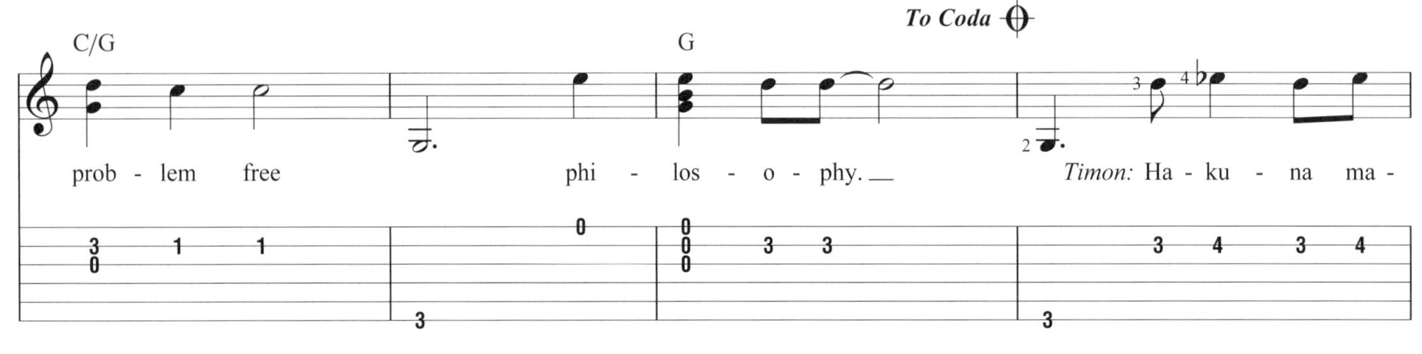

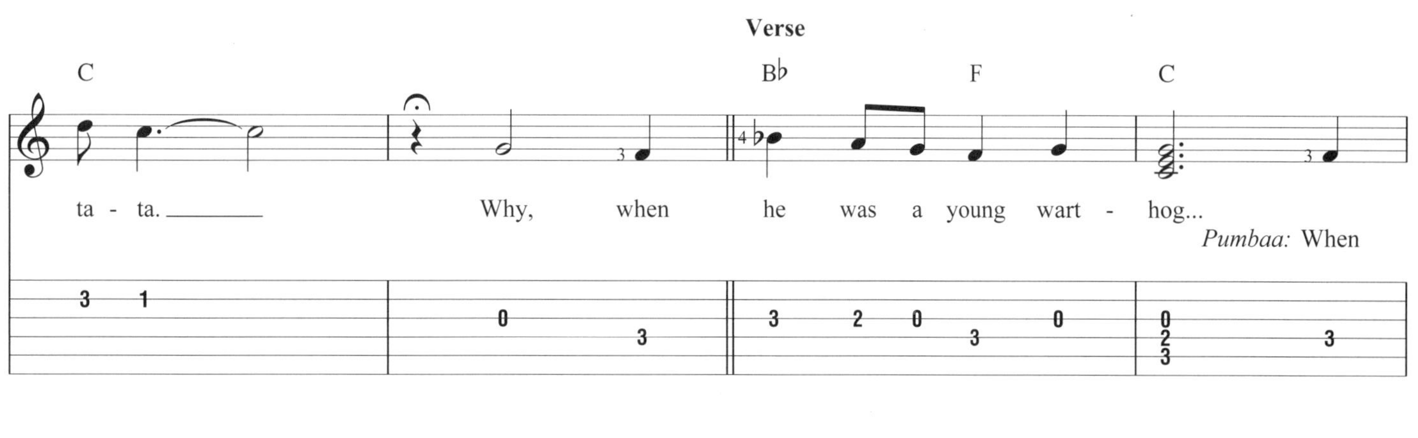
Verse
C
Bb
F
C
ta - ta. Why, when he was a young wart - hog...
Pumbaa: When

Bb
F
C
Eb
Very nice. He found his a - ro - ma lacked a
I was a young wart - hog! Thanks.

F
C
G
cer - tain ap - peal. He could clear the sa - van - nah af - ter ev - 'ry meal!
I'm a

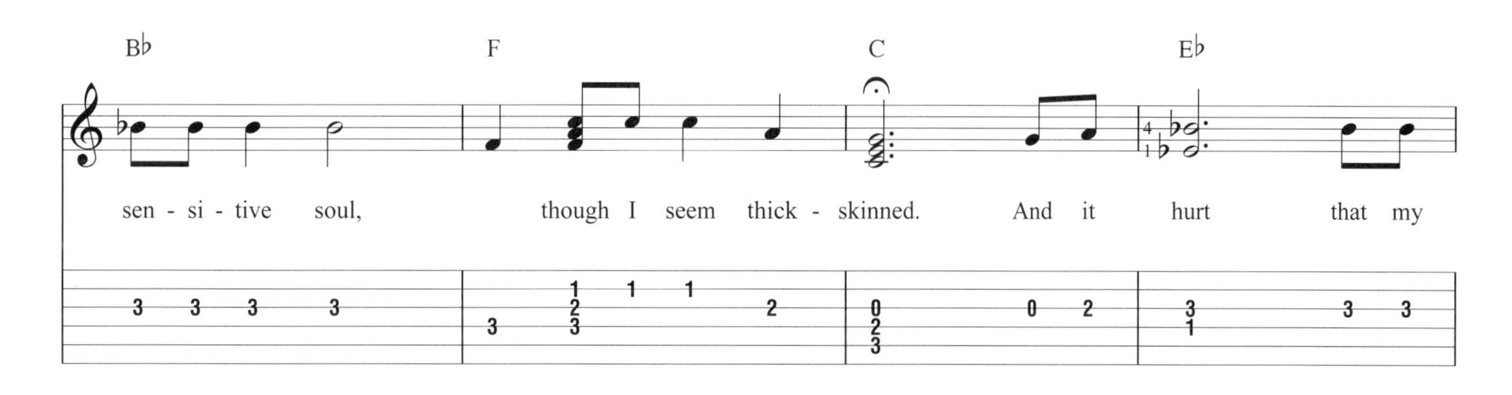
Bb
F
C
Eb
sen - si - tive soul, though I seem thick - skinned. And it hurt that my

F
G
C
It was a
friends nev - er stood down wind! And oh, the shame!

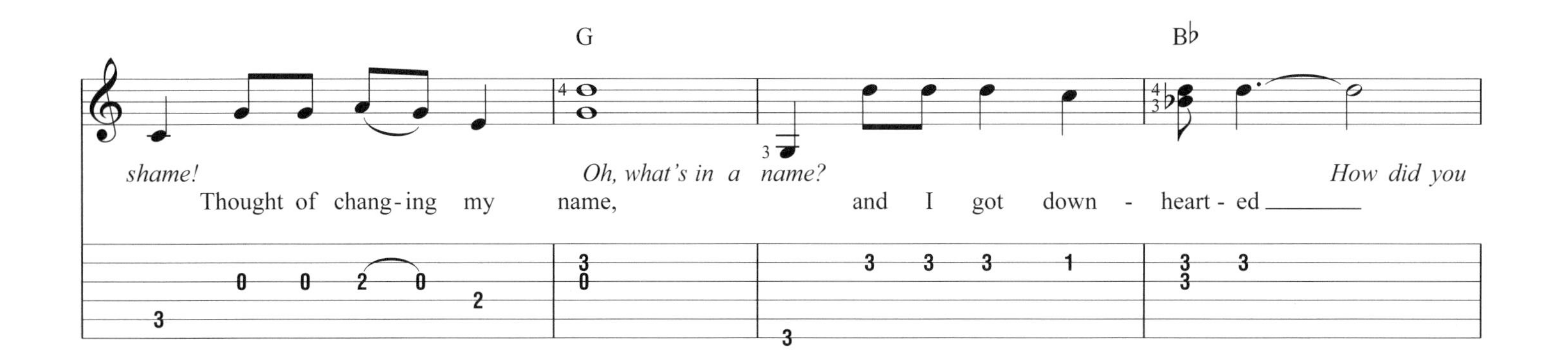
G
B♭
shame!
Oh, what's in a name?
How did you
Thought of chang-ing my name,
and I got down - heart - ed

N.C.
feel?
Hey, Pumbaa, not in front of the kids.
ev - 'ry time that I...
Oh, sorry.
Timon & Pumbaa: Ha - ku - na ma -

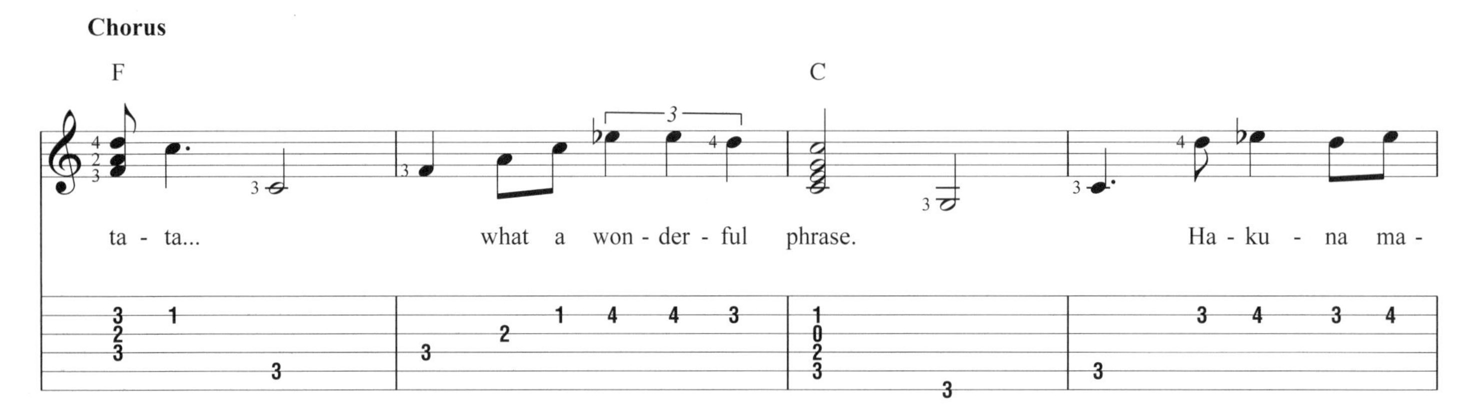
Chorus
F
C
ta - ta...
what a won - der - ful phrase.
Ha - ku - na ma -

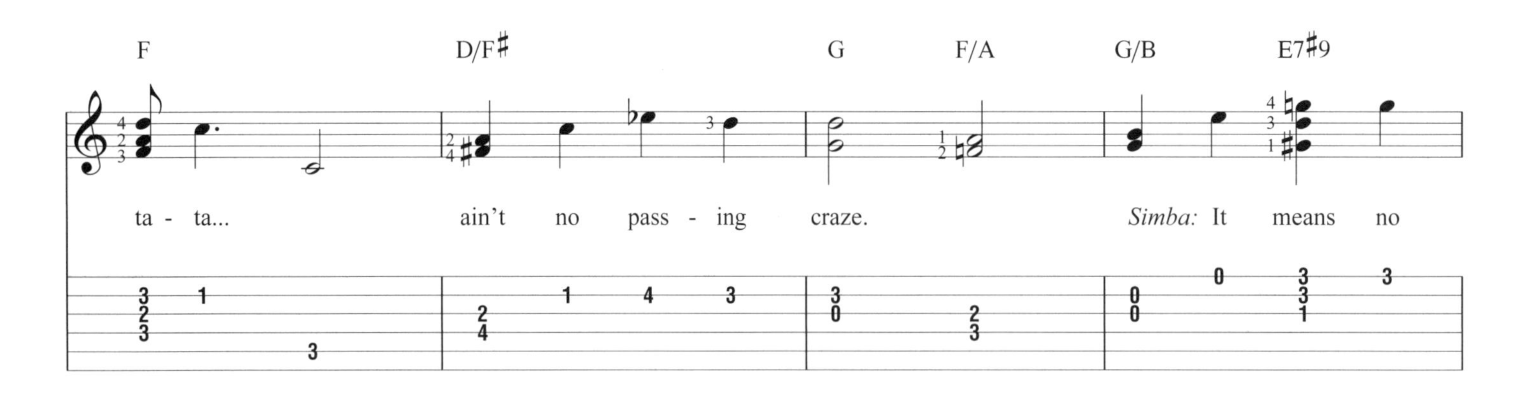
F
D/F♯
G
F/A
G/B
E7♯9
ta - ta...
ain't no pass - ing craze.
Simba: It means no

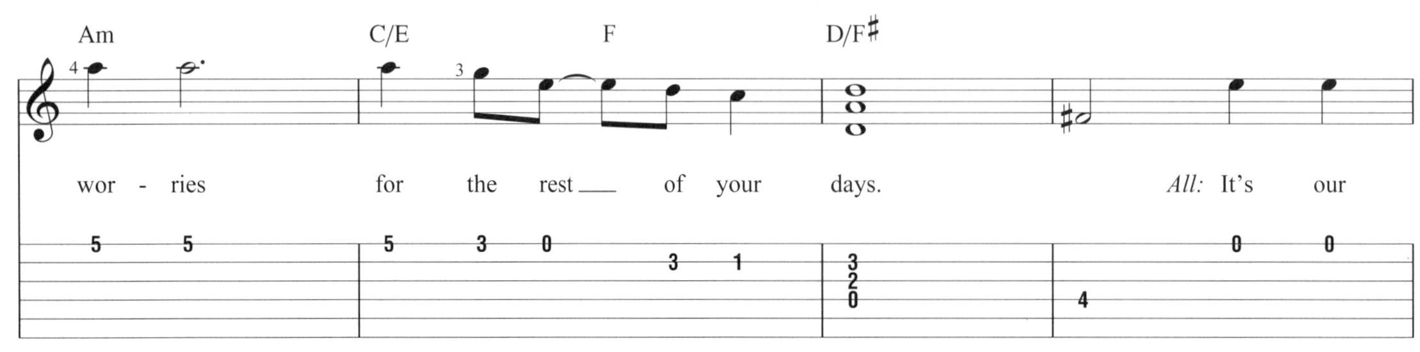
Am
C/E
F
D/F♯
wor - ries for the rest of your days.
All: It's our

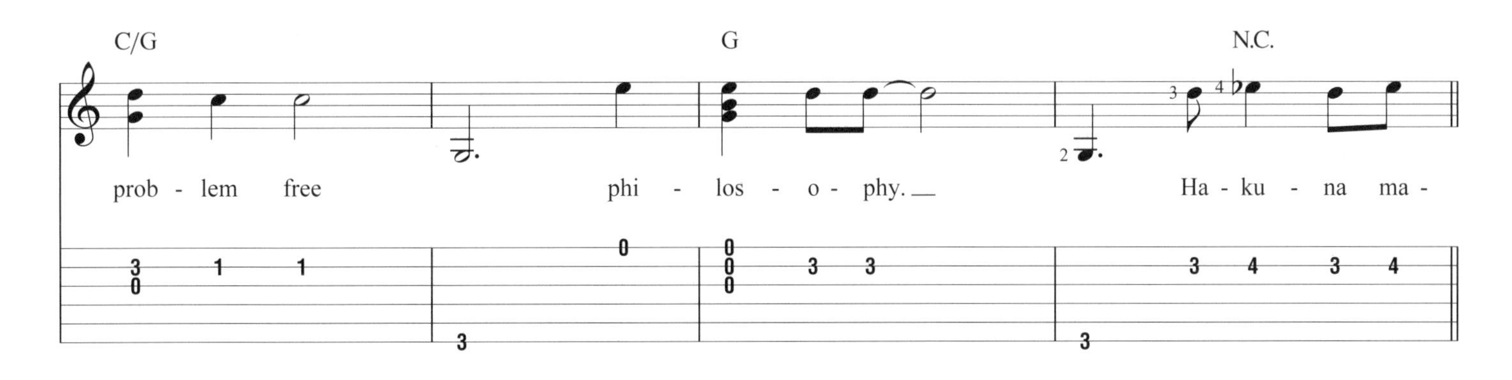

Interlude

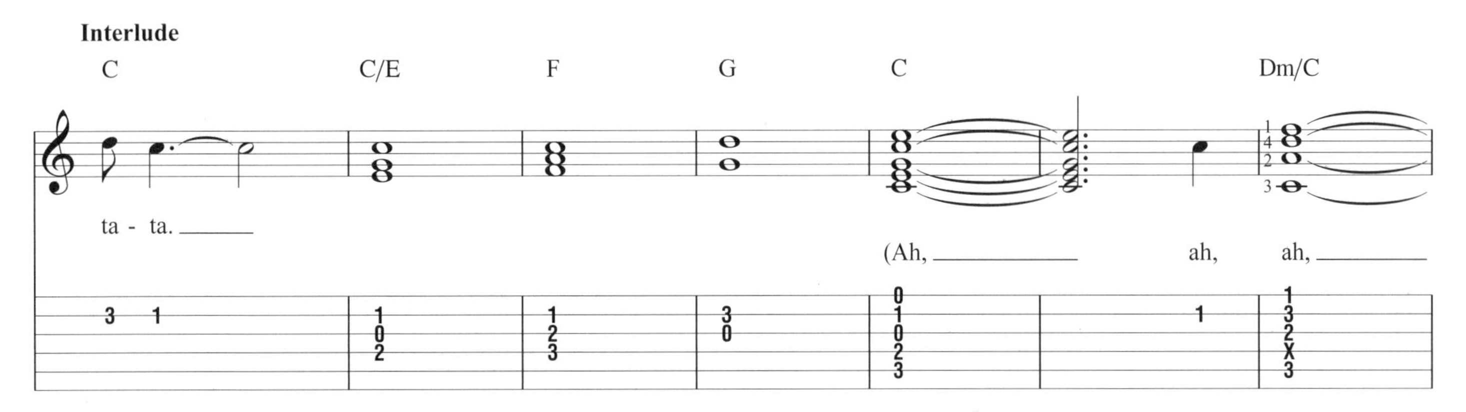

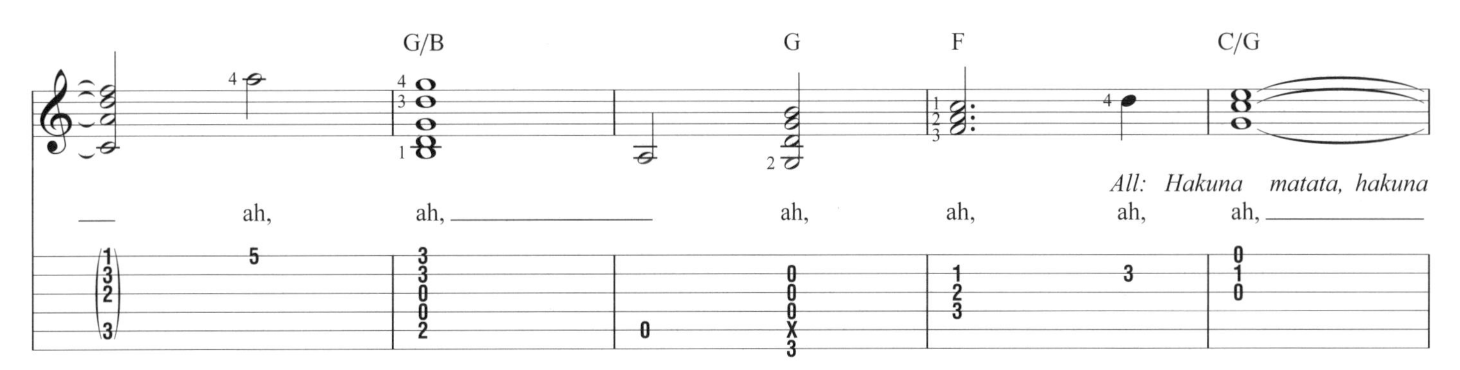

D.S. al Coda

Coda

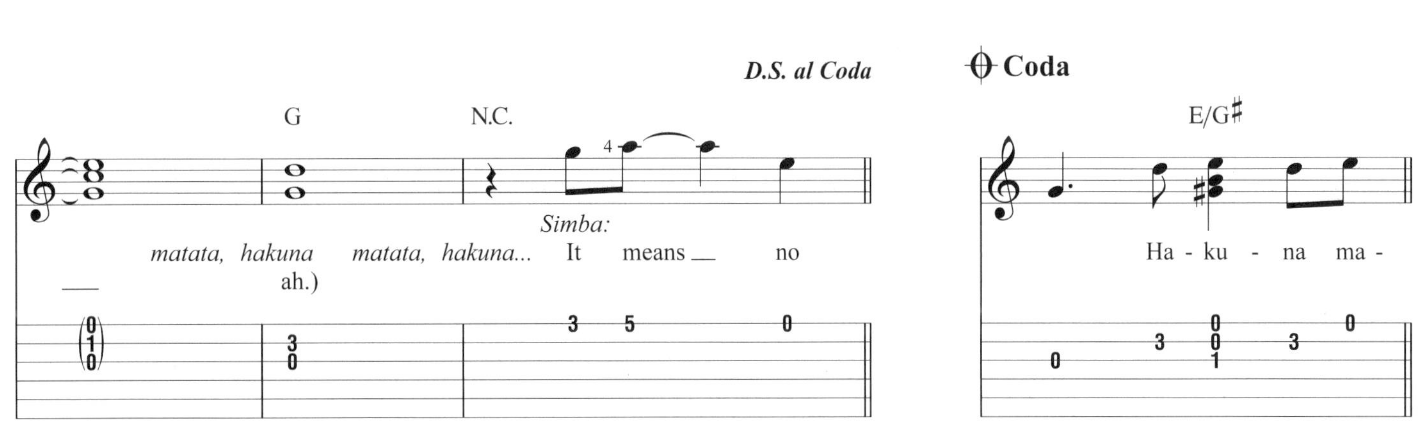

Outro

Repeat and fade

How Far I'll Go

from MOANA

Music and Lyrics by Lin-Manuel Miranda

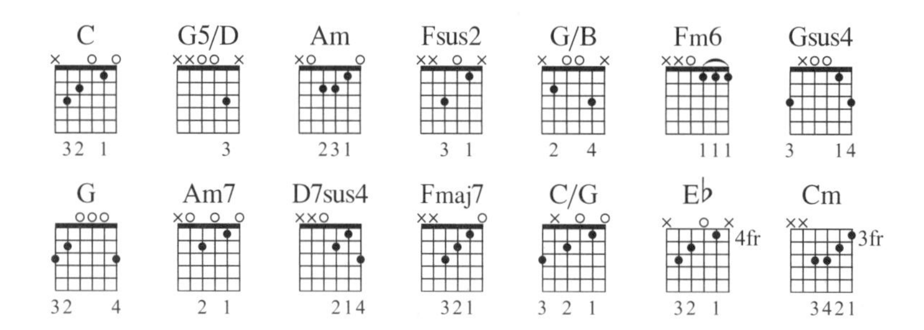

*Capo IV

Strum Pattern: 6
Pick Pattern: 4

Verse

Moderately slow

C G5/D

mp

1. I've been_ star - ing at the edge of the wa - ter_ long_ as I can re -

*Optional: To match recording, place capo at 4th fret.

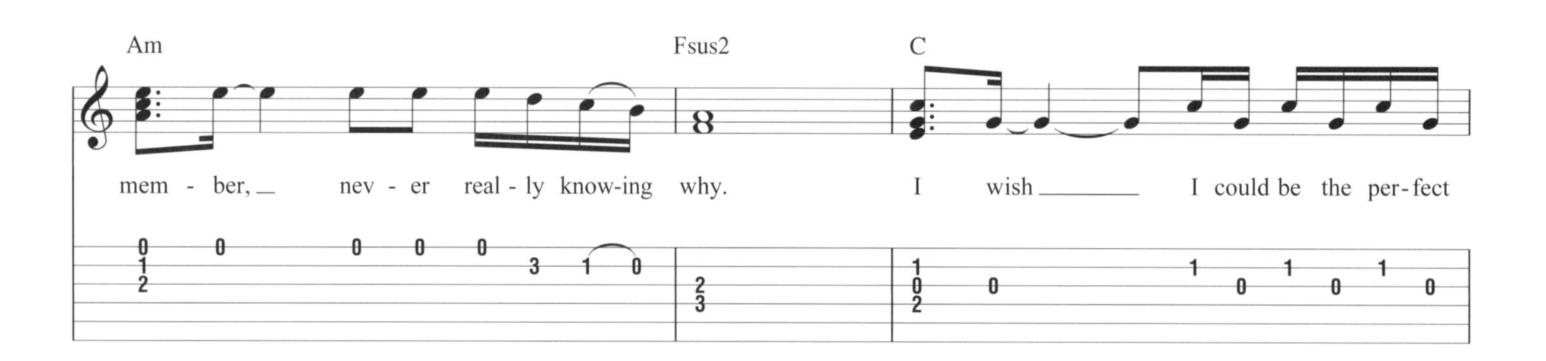

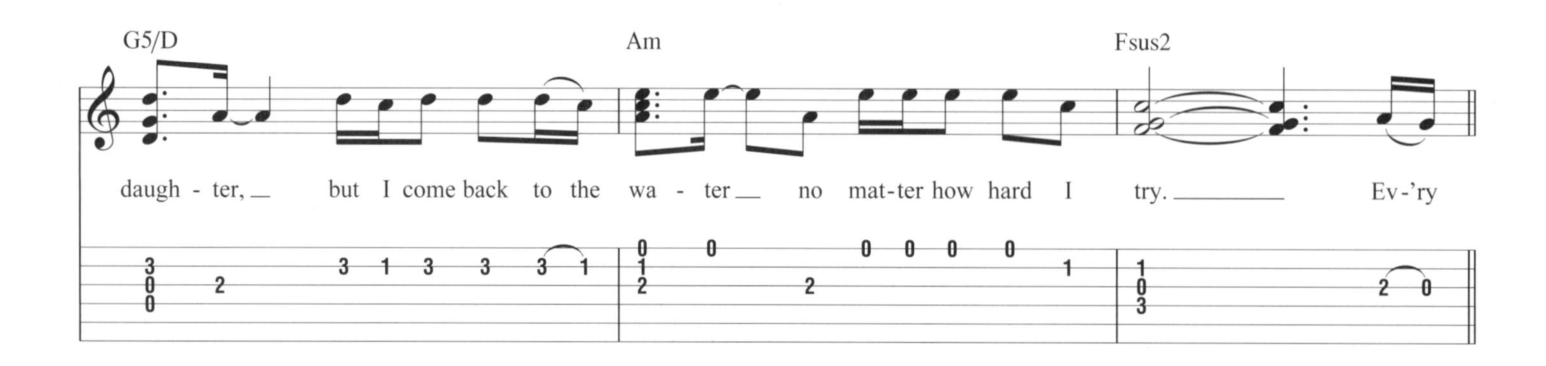

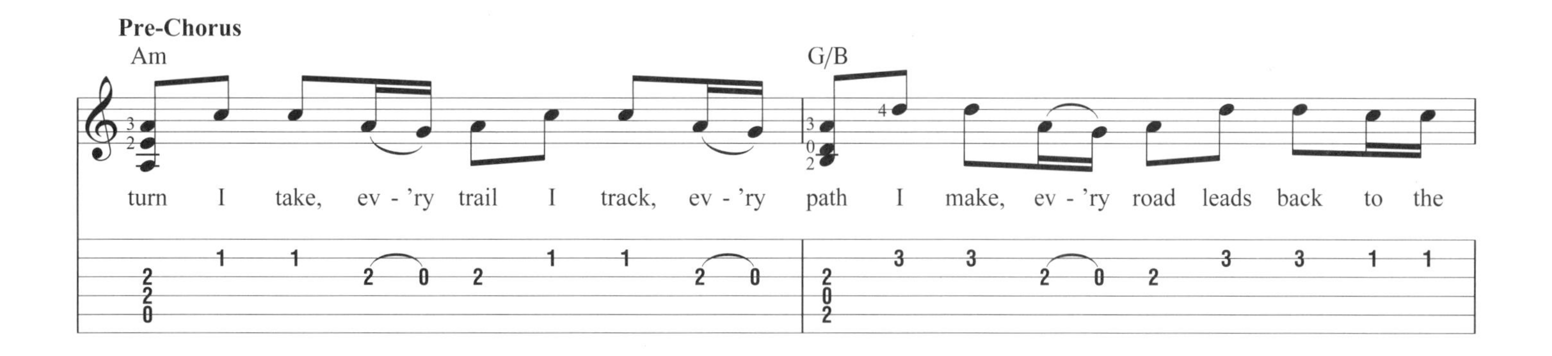

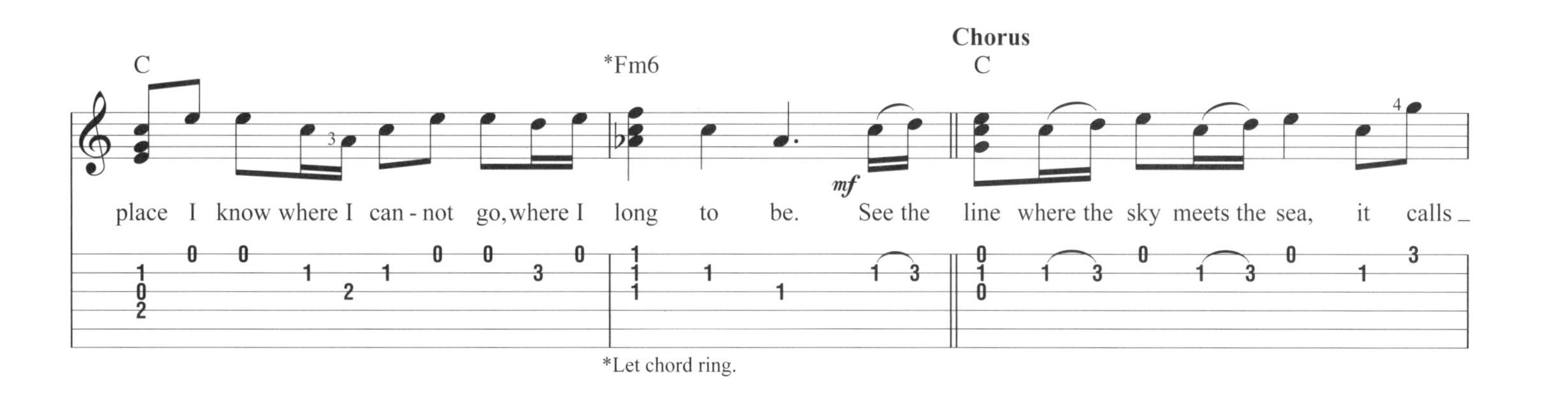

*Let chord ring.

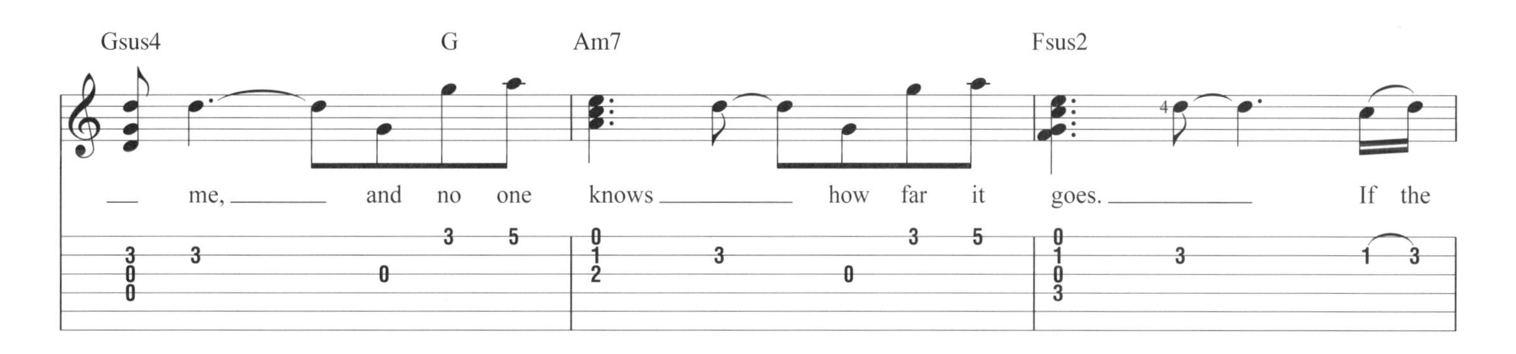

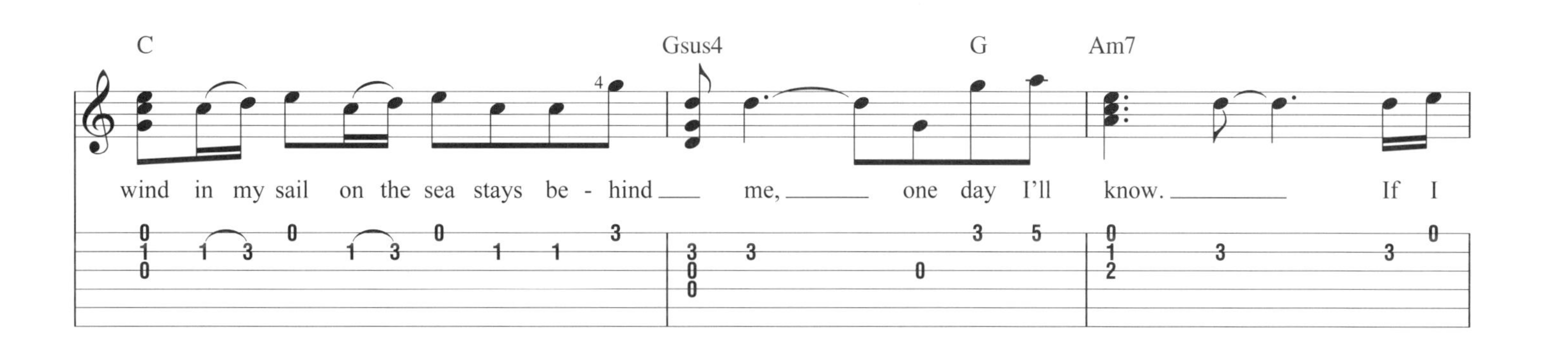

**As before

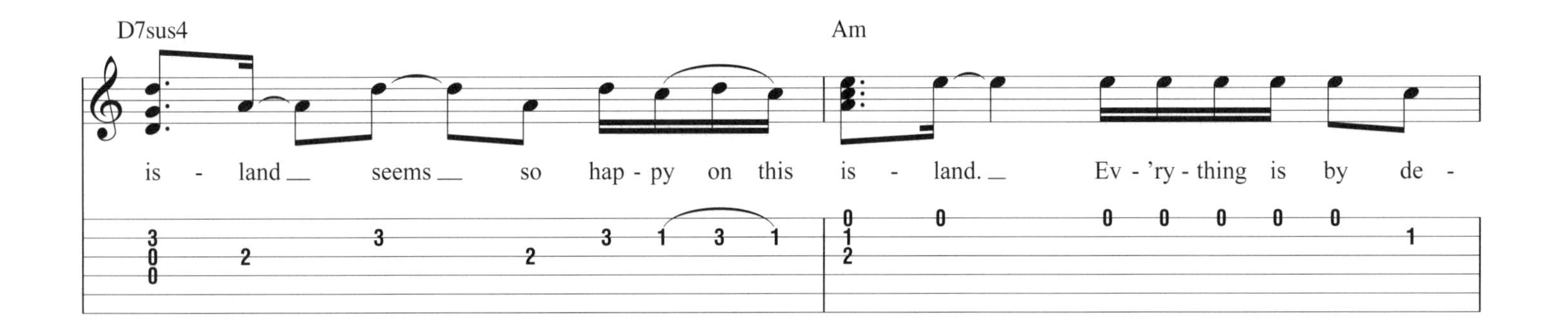
D7sus4
Am
is - land seems so hap - py on this is - land. Ev - 'ry - thing is by de -

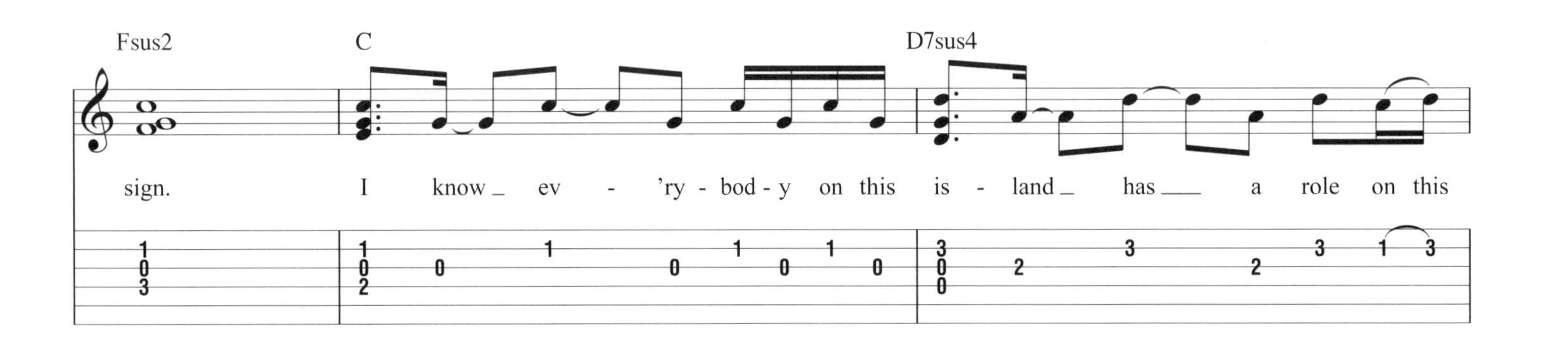
Fsus2
C
D7sus4
sign. I know ev - 'ry - bod - y on this is - land has a role on this

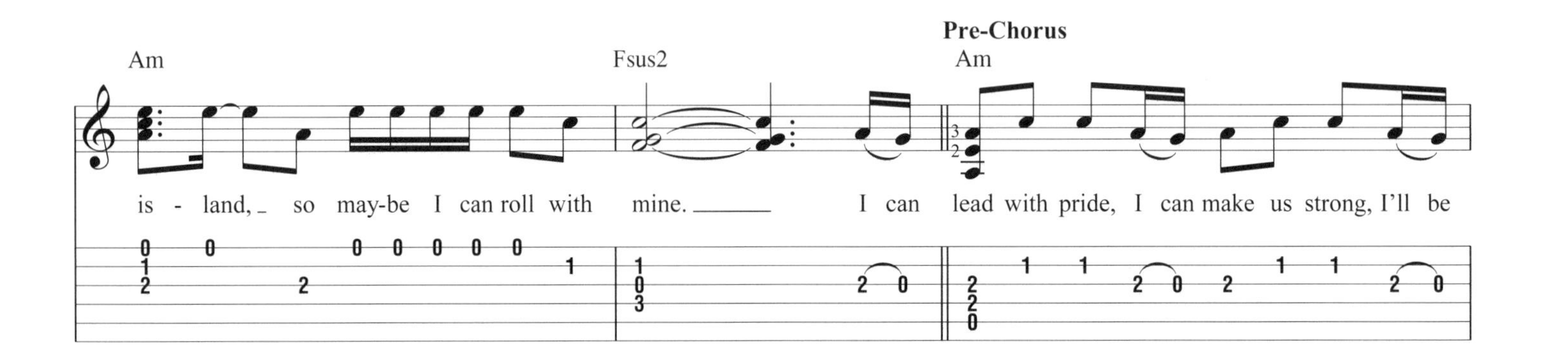
Pre-Chorus
Am
Fsus2
Am
is - land, so may-be I can roll with mine. I can lead with pride, I can make us strong, I'll be

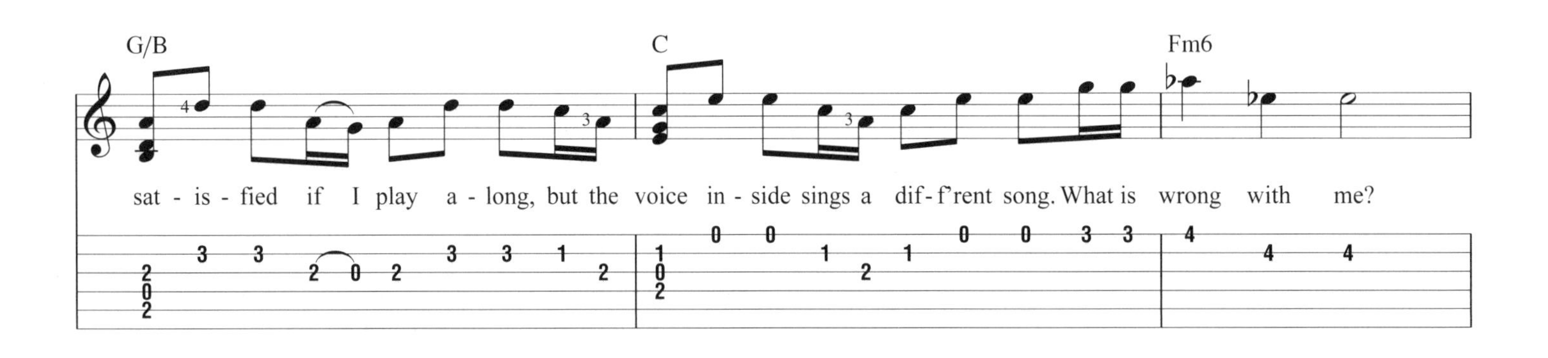
G/B
C
Fm6
sat - is - fied if I play a - long, but the voice in - side sings a dif - f'rent song. What is wrong with me?

Chorus
C
Gsus4
See the light as it shines on the sea: it's blind - ing, but no one

Am7
Fsus2
C
knows ___ how deep it goes. ___ And it seems like it's call-ing out to me, so come find

Gsus4
G
Am7
Fm6
___ me ___ and let me know. ___ What's be - yond that line? Will I cross that line? The

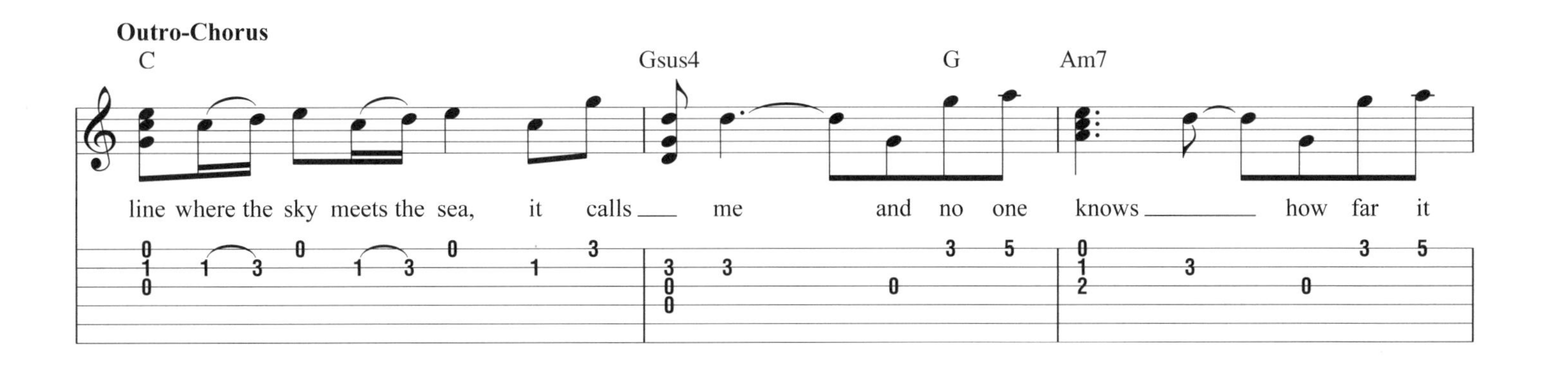
Outro-Chorus
C
Gsus4
G
Am7
line where the sky meets the sea, it calls ___ me and no one knows ___ how far it

Fmaj7
C
Gsus4
G
goes. ___ If the wind in my sail on the sea stays be - hind ___ me, ___ one day I'll

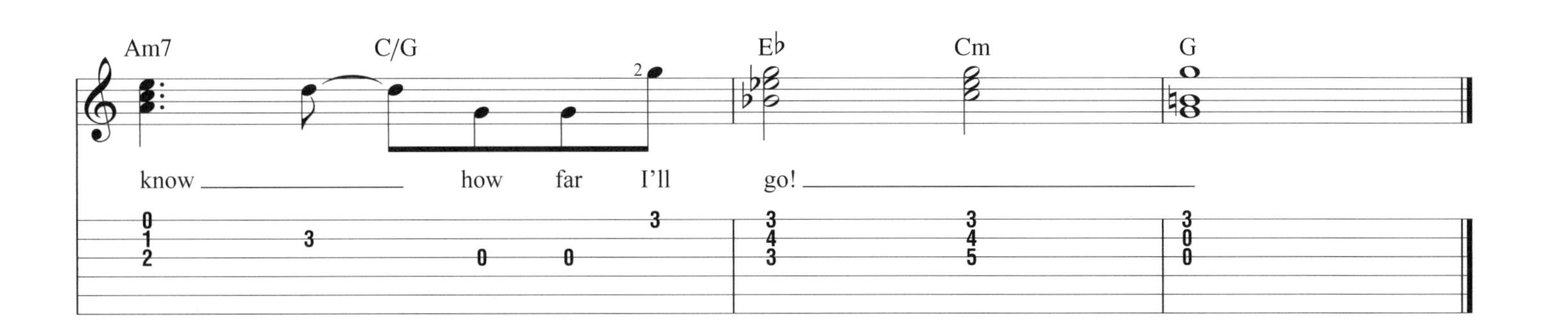
Am7
C/G
E♭
Cm
G
know ___ how far I'll go! ___

I Just Can't Wait to Be King

from THE LION KING

Music by Elton John
Lyrics by Tim Rice

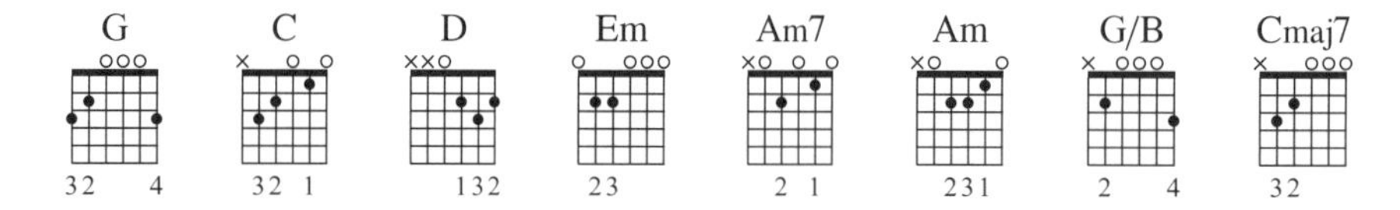

*Tune down 1/2 step:
(low to high) E♭-A♭-D♭-G♭-B♭-E♭

Strum Pattern: 3
Pick Pattern: 3

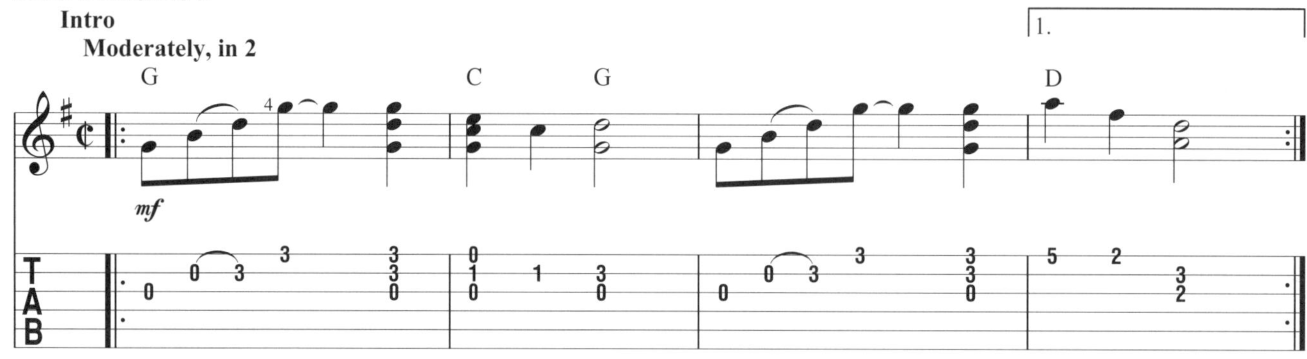

*Optional: To match recording, tune down 1/2 step.

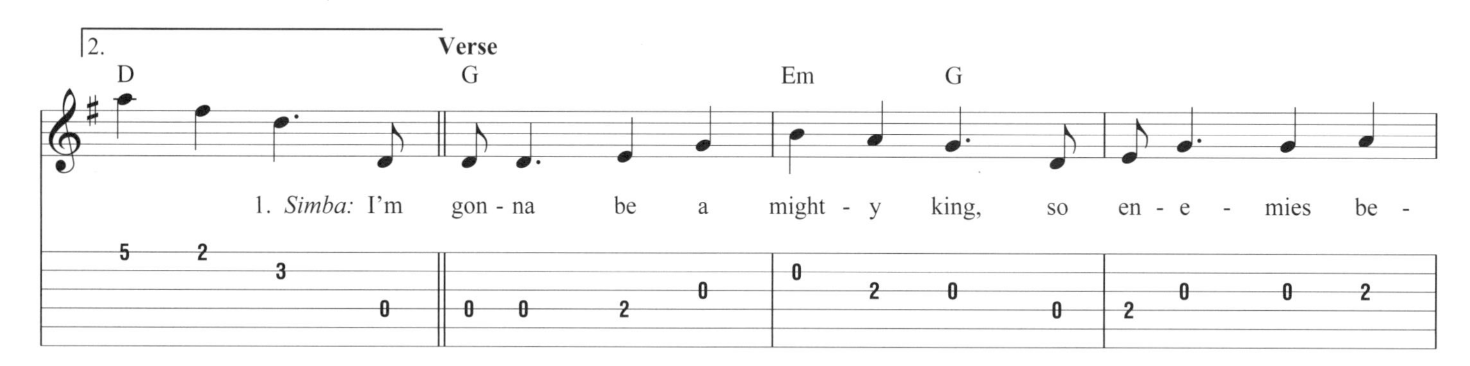

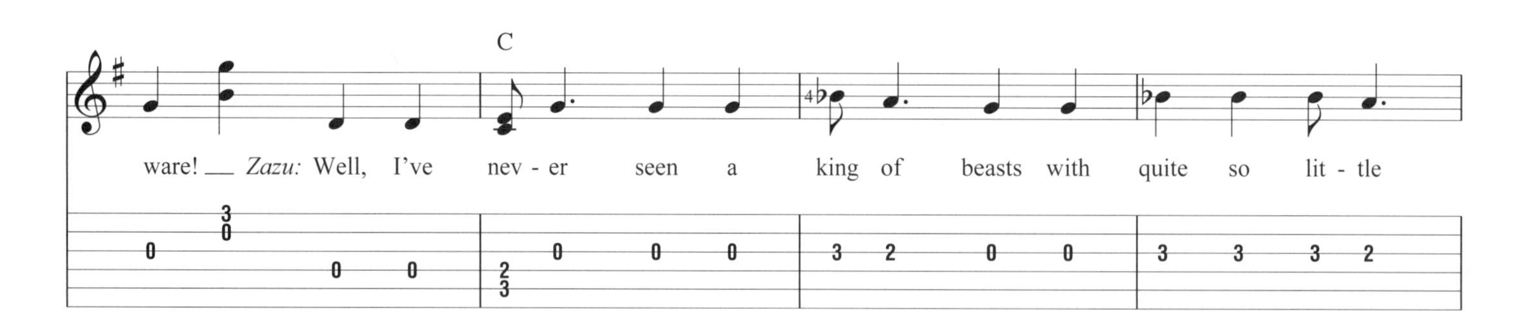

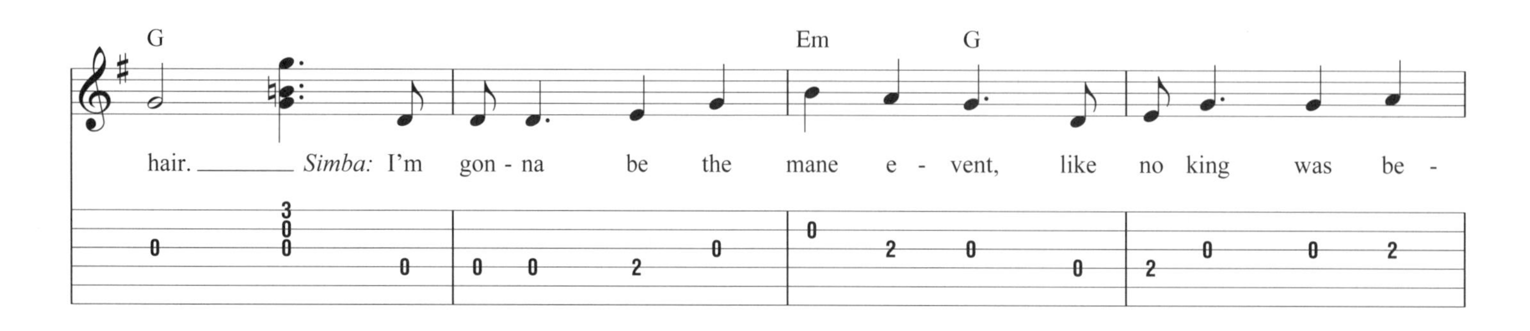

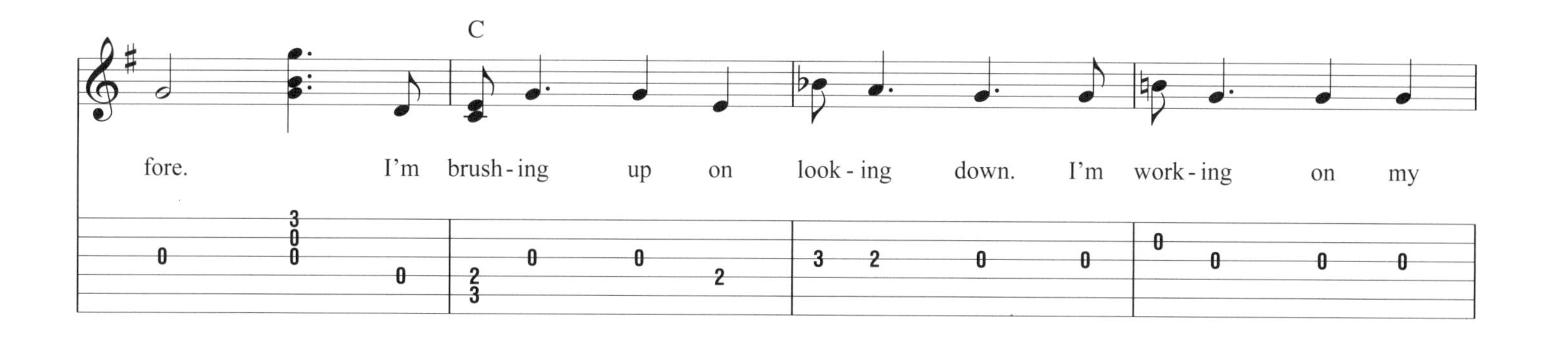
C
fore. I'm brush-ing up on look-ing down. I'm work-ing on my

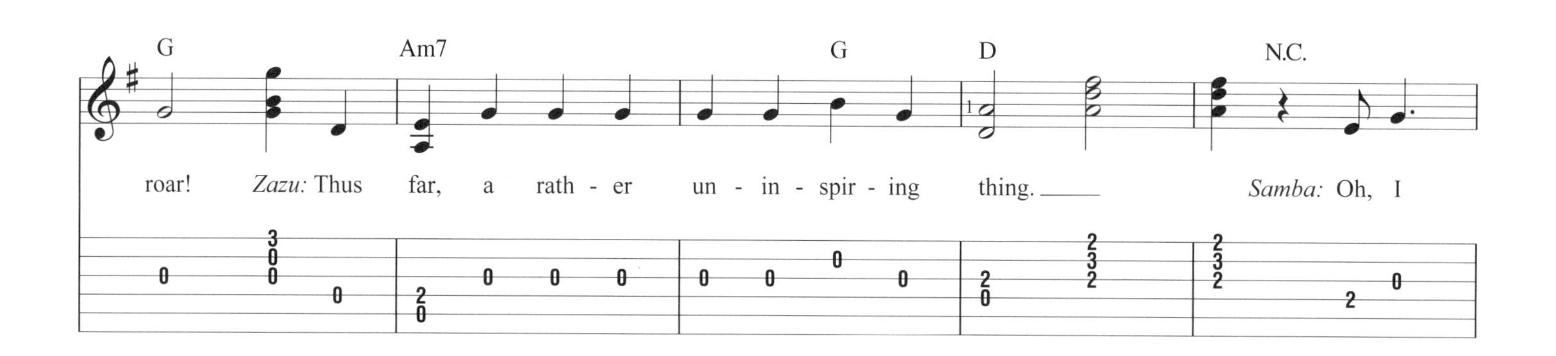
G Am7 G D N.C.
roar! Zazu: Thus far, a rath-er un-in-spir-ing thing. Samba: Oh, I

C D G
just can't wait to be king!
Zazu: You've

C G N.C.
rather a long way to go, young Master! If you think...
Samba: No one say-ing

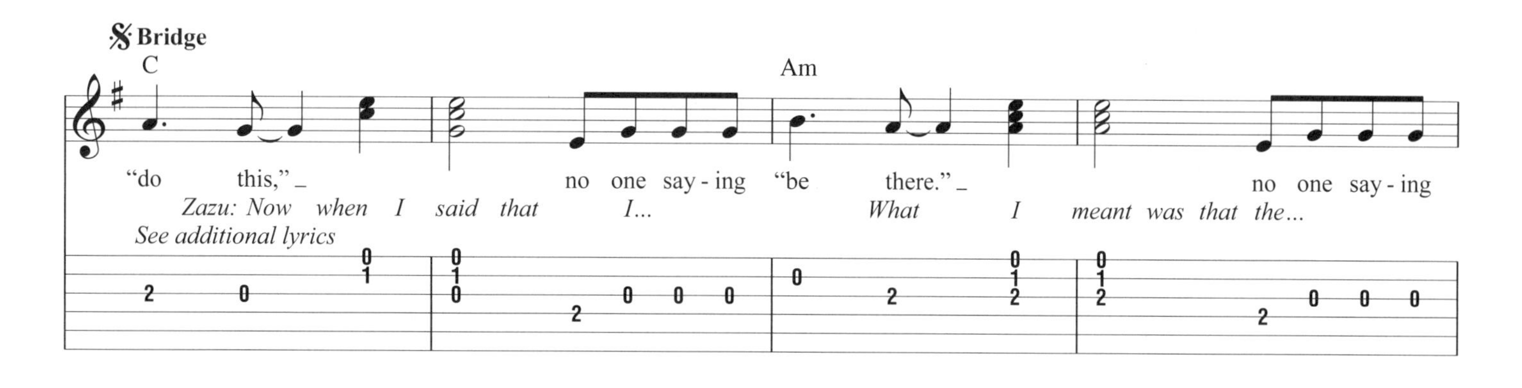
Bridge
C Am
"do this," no one say-ing "be there." no one say-ing
Zazu: Now when I said that I... What I meant was that the...
See additional lyrics

D
G
"stop that," no one say - ing "see here."
But what you don't realize...
Now see here!

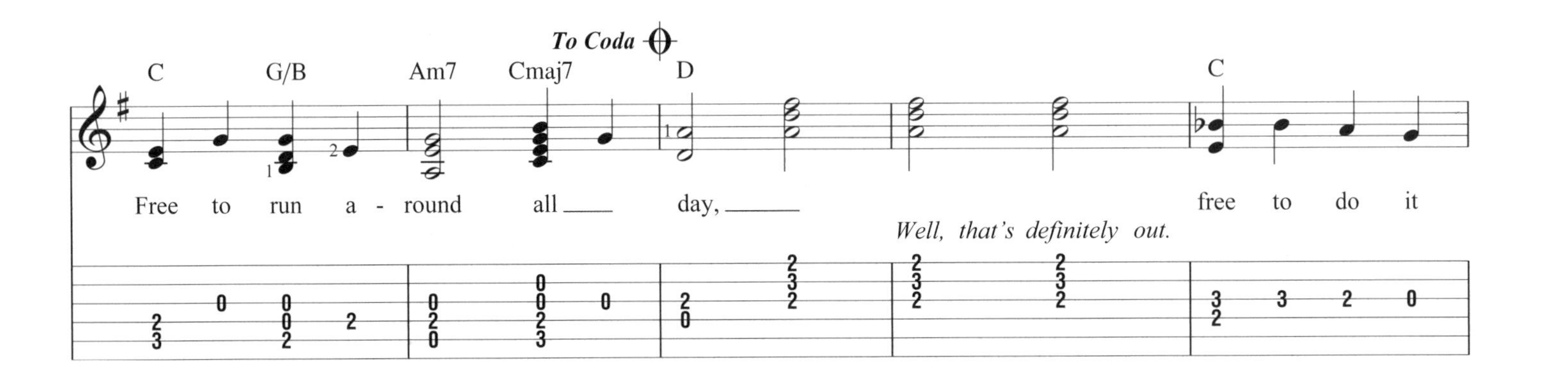
To Coda
C G/B Am7 Cmaj7 D C
Free to run a - round all day, free to do it
Well, that's definitely out.

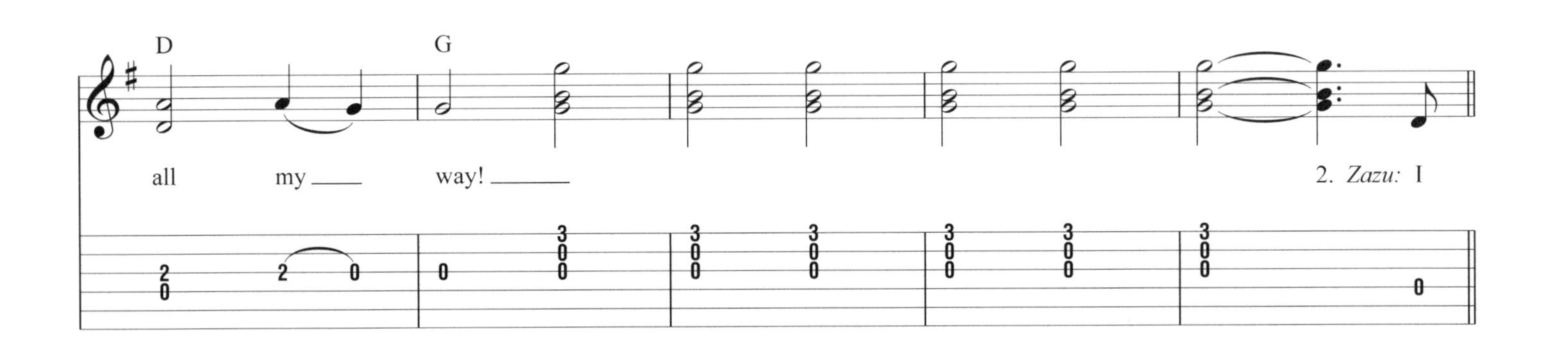
D G
all my way!
2. Zazu: I

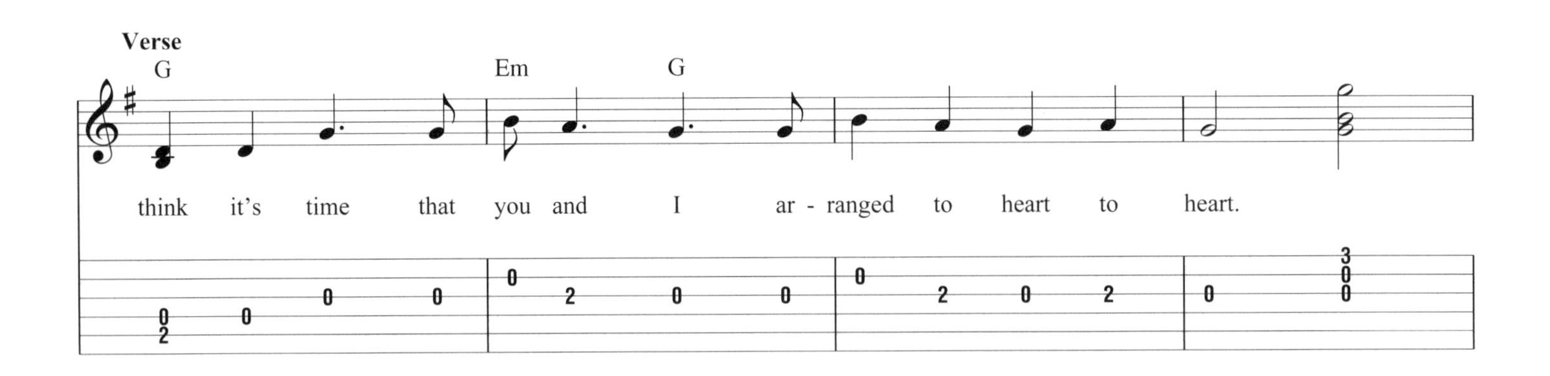
Verse
G Em G
think it's time that you and I ar - ranged to heart to heart.

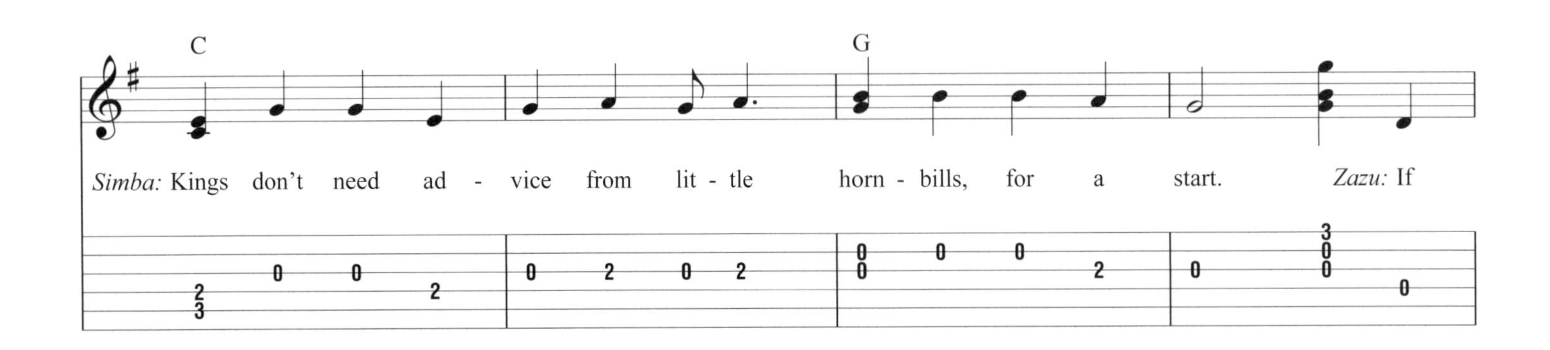
C G
Simba: Kings don't need ad - vice from lit - tle horn - bills, for a start.
Zazu: If

this is where the mon - ar - chy is head - ed, count me out! Out of
C G
ser - vice, out of Af - ri - ca. I would - n't hang a - bout. This
Am7 D N.C.
child is get - ting wild - ly out of wing! Simba: Oh, I
C D G
just can't wait to be King!
Interlude
G C G
1.
D G
2.
D.S. al Coda
D G
Ev - 'ry - bod - y
Coda
D C G/B
sing. Let's hear it in the

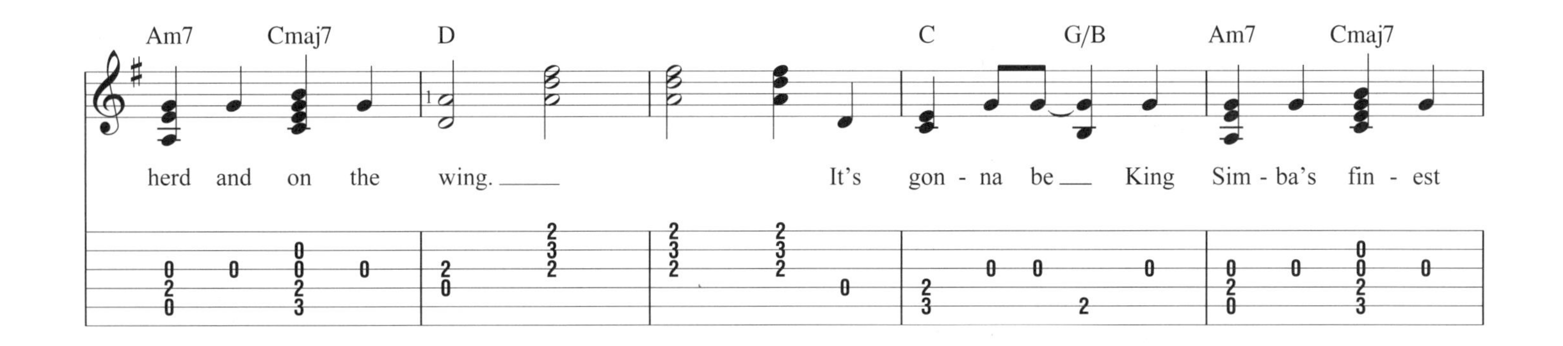

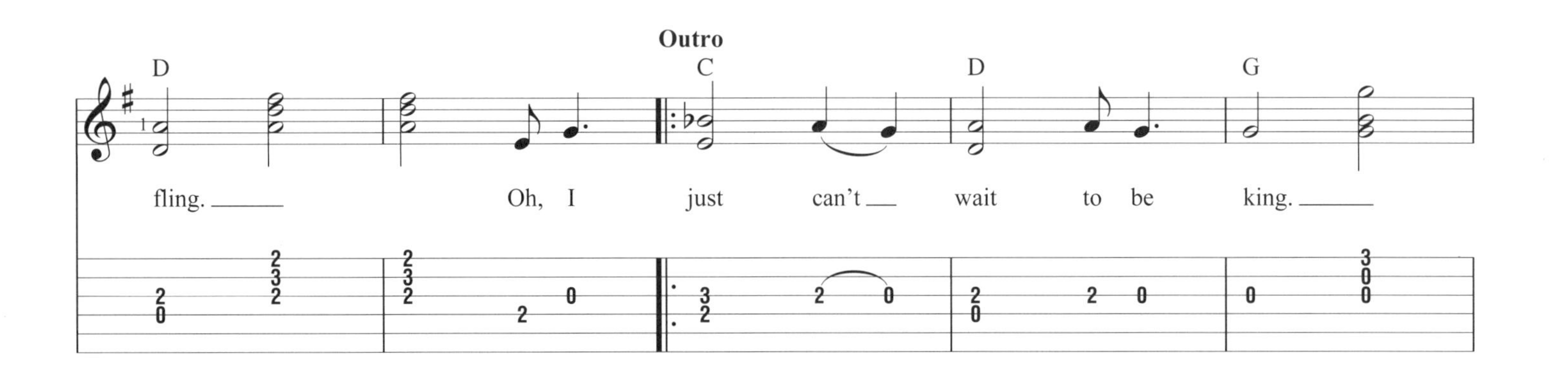

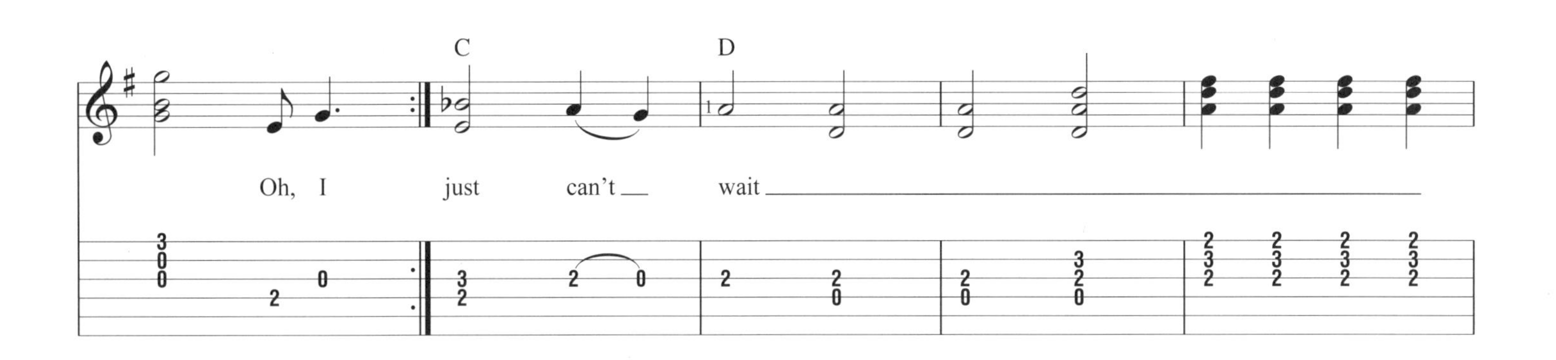

Additional Lyrics

Bridge Ev'rybody look left,
Ev'rybody look right.
Everywhere you look,
I'm standing in the spotlight.
Let every creature go for broke and sing.
Let's hear it in the herd and on the wing.
It's gonna be King Simba's finest fling.

I See the Light

from TANGLED

Music by Alan Menken
Lyrics by Glenn Slater

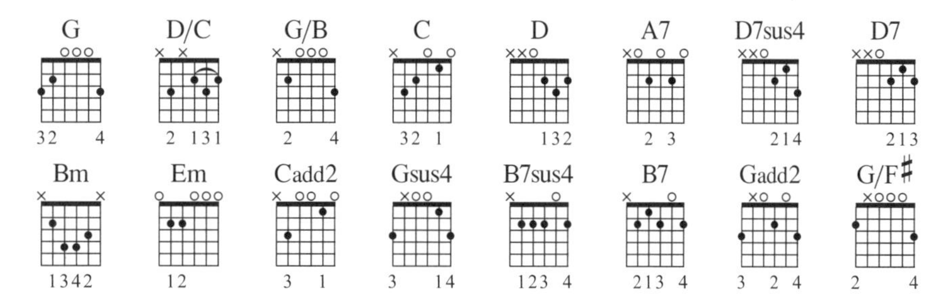

*Capo V

Strum Pattern: 3
Pick Pattern: 5

Intro
Moderately

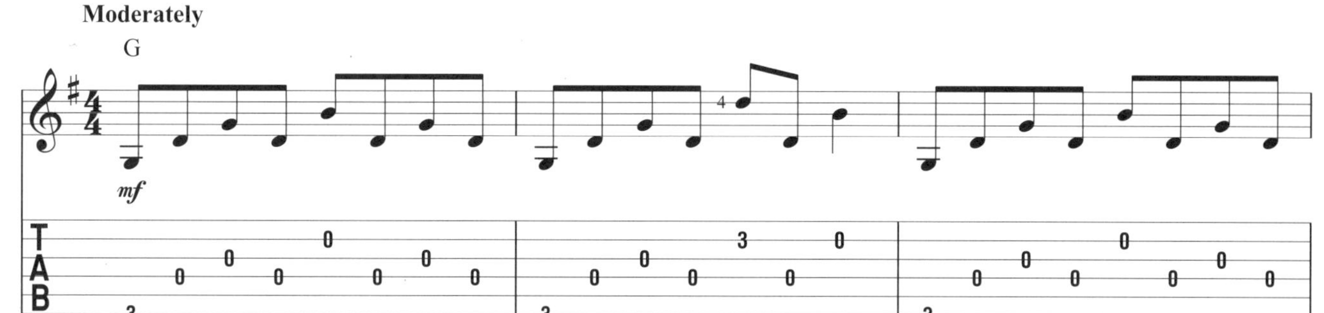

*Optional: To match recording, place capo at 5th fret.

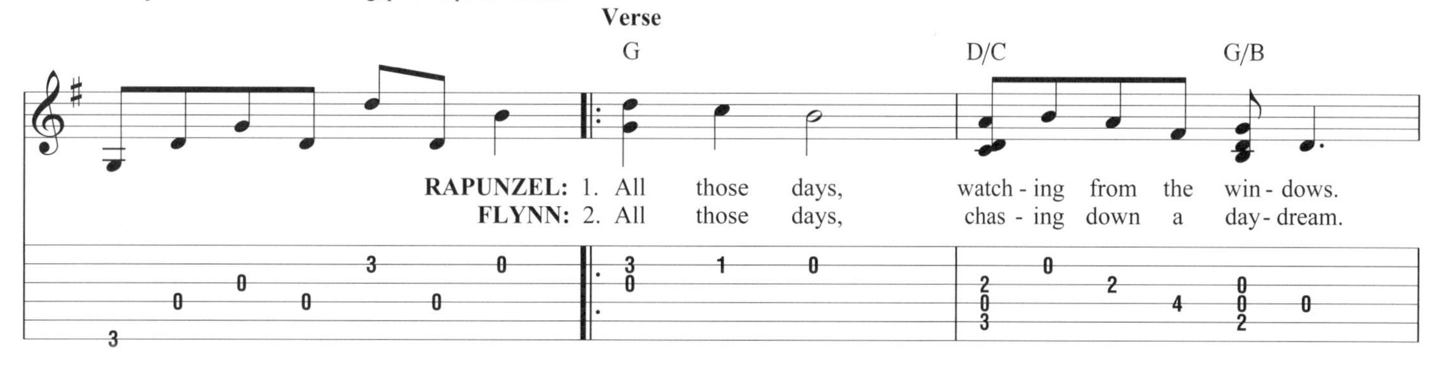

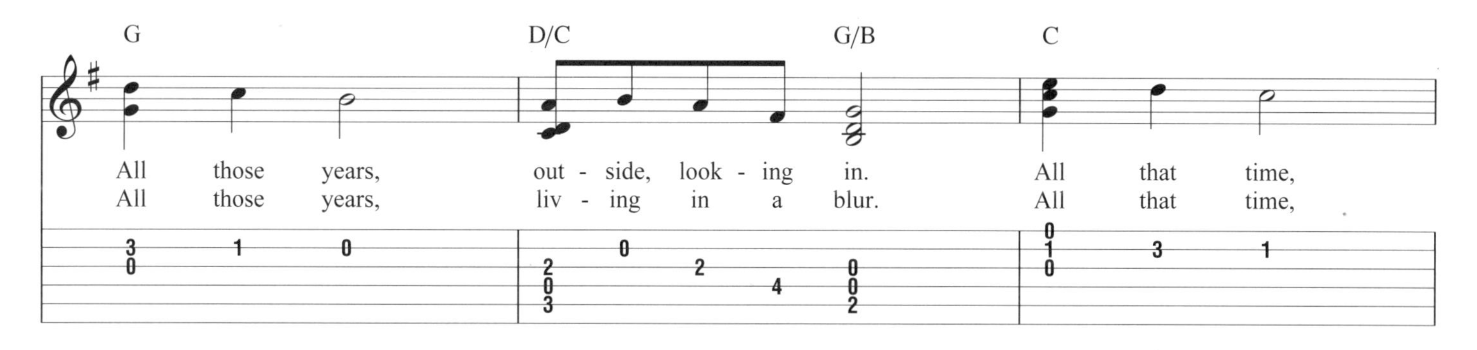

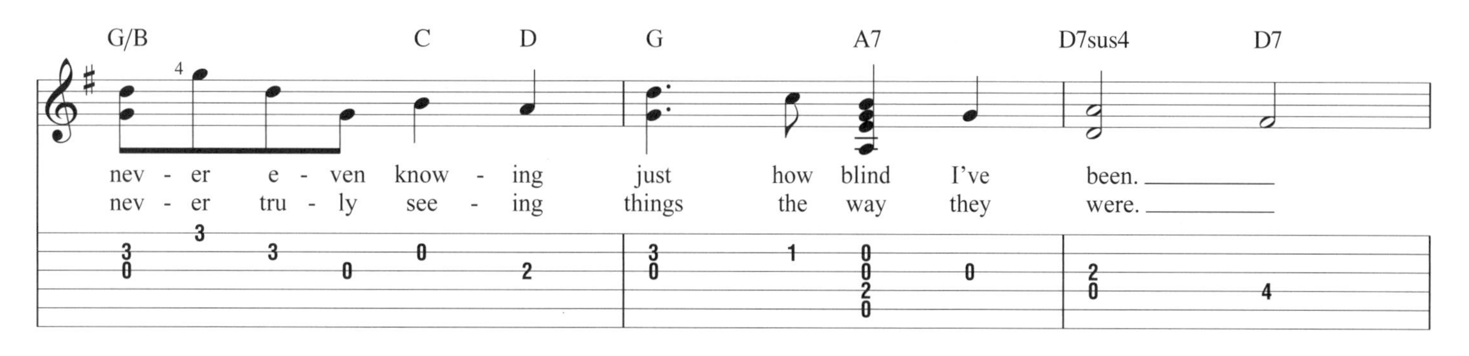

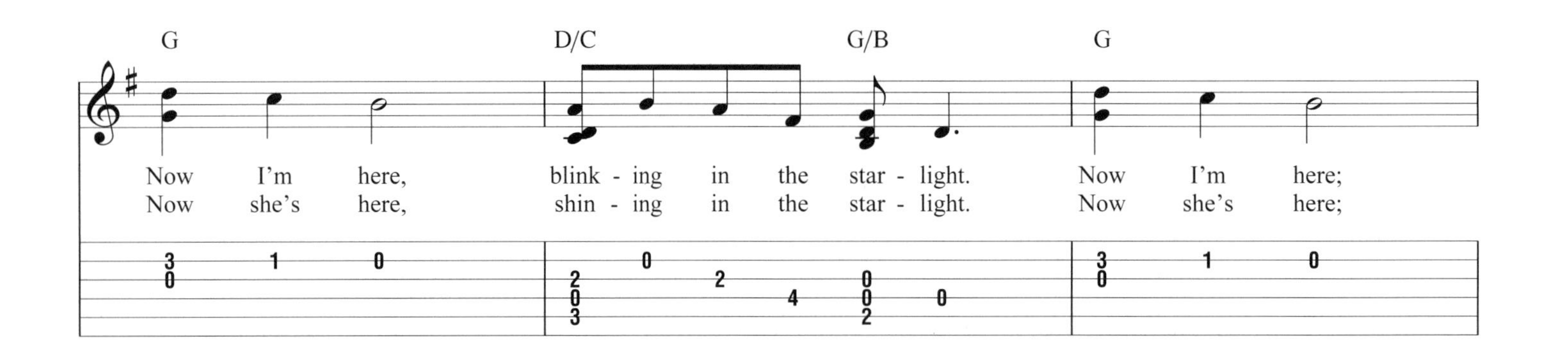
G D/C G/B G
Now I'm here, blink - ing in the star - light. Now I'm here;
Now she's here, shin - ing in the star - light. Now she's here;

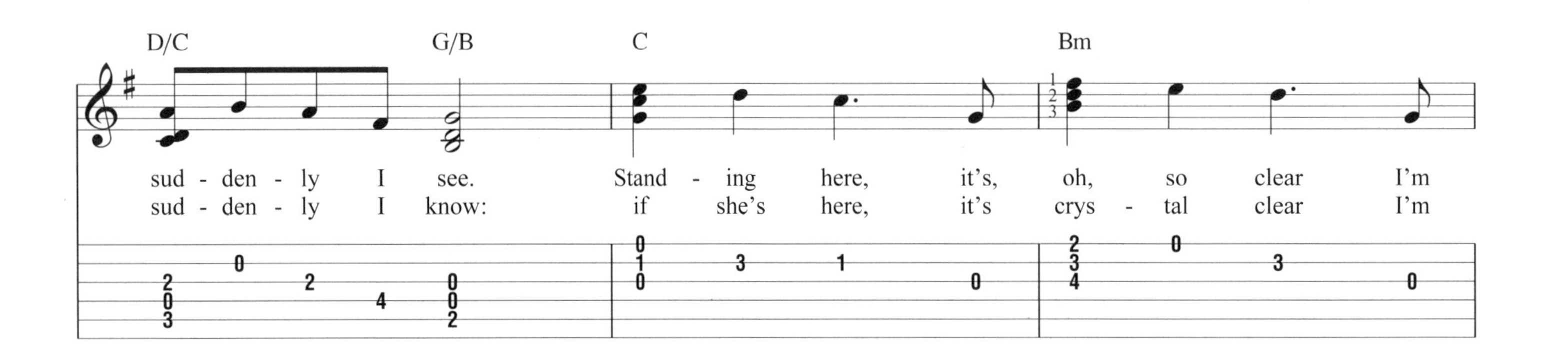
D/C G/B C Bm
sud - den - ly I see. Stand - ing here, it's, oh, so clear I'm
sud - den - ly I know: if she's here, it's crys - tal clear I'm

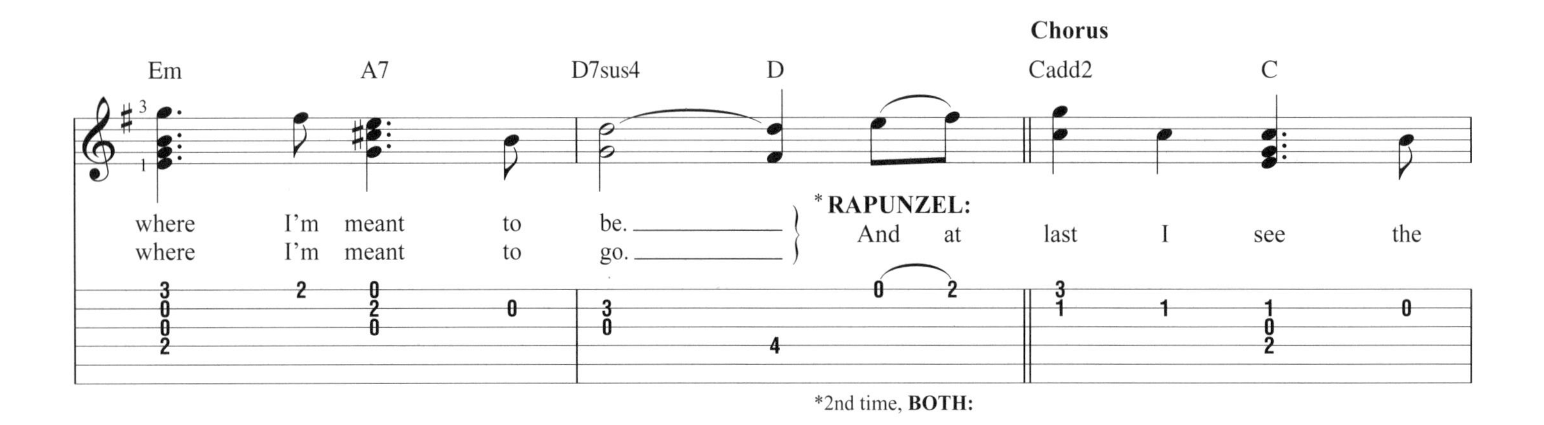
Chorus
Em A7 D7sus4 D Cadd2 C
where I'm meant to be.
where I'm meant to go.
*RAPUNZEL:
And at last I see the
*2nd time, BOTH:

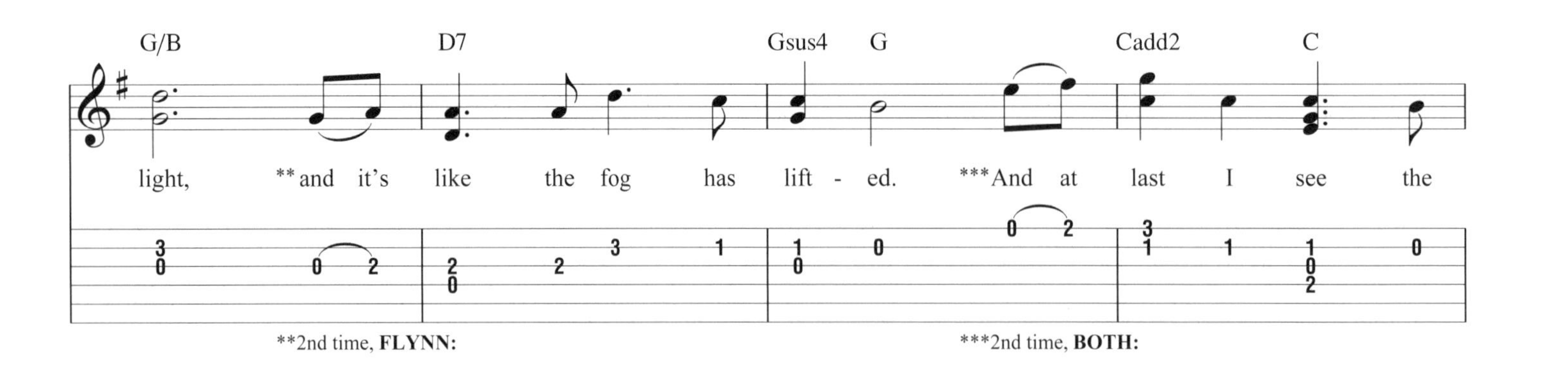
G/B D7 Gsus4 G Cadd2 C
light, **and it's like the fog has lift - ed. ***And at last I see the
**2nd time, FLYNN:
***2nd time, BOTH:

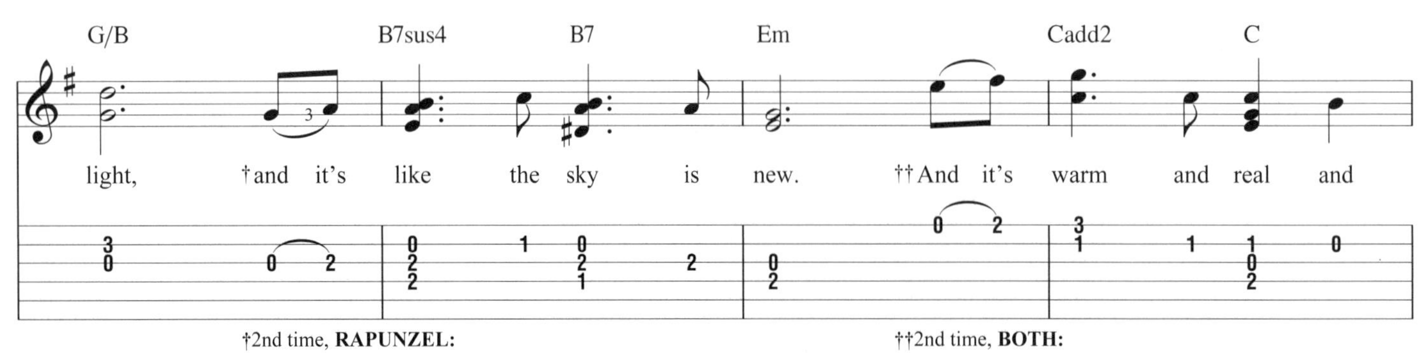
G/B B7sus4 B7 Em Cadd2 C
light, †and it's like the sky is new. ††And it's warm and real and
†2nd time, RAPUNZEL:
††2nd time, BOTH:

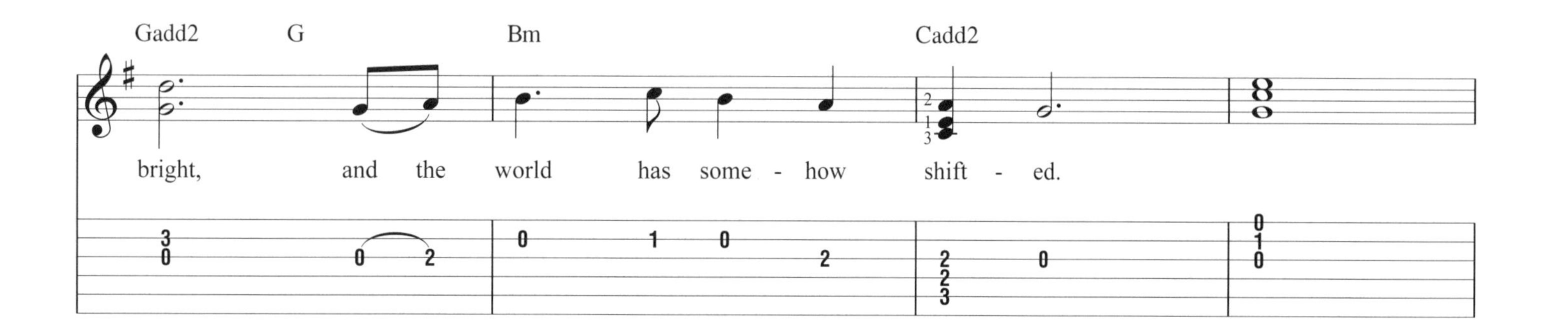
Gadd2 G Bm Cadd2
bright, and the world has some - how shift - ed.

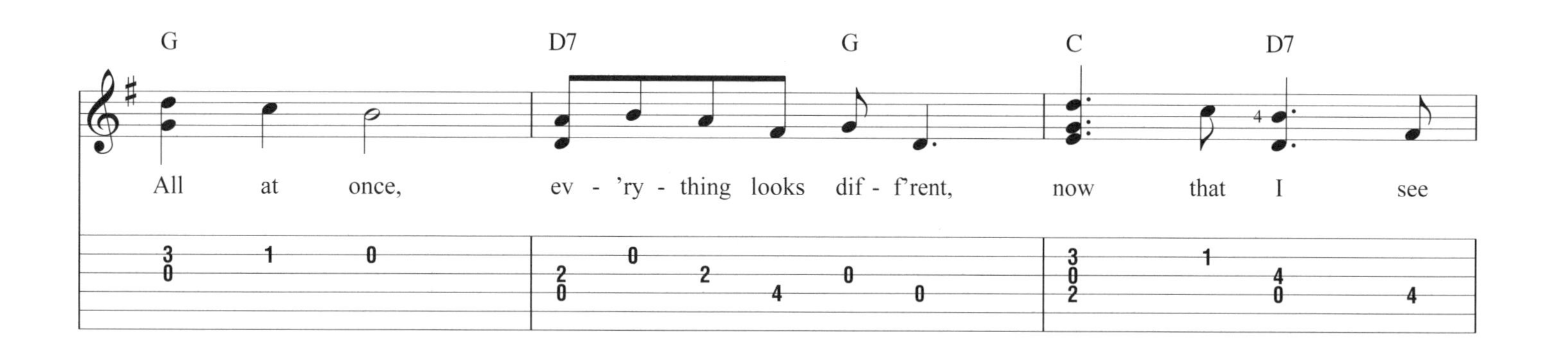
G D7 G C D7
All at once, ev - 'ry - thing looks dif - f'rent, now that I see

1.
G
you.

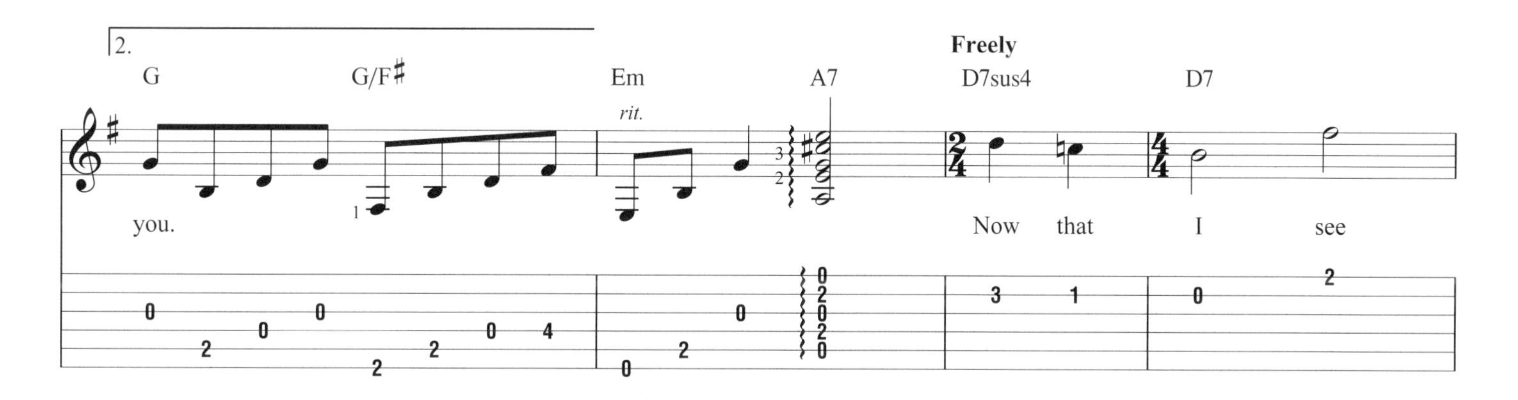
2.
G G/F♯ Em A7 D7sus4 D7
rit.
Freely
you.
Now that I see

G
rit.
you.

I Won't Say (I'm in Love)

from HERCULES

Music by Alan Menken
Lyrics by David Zippel

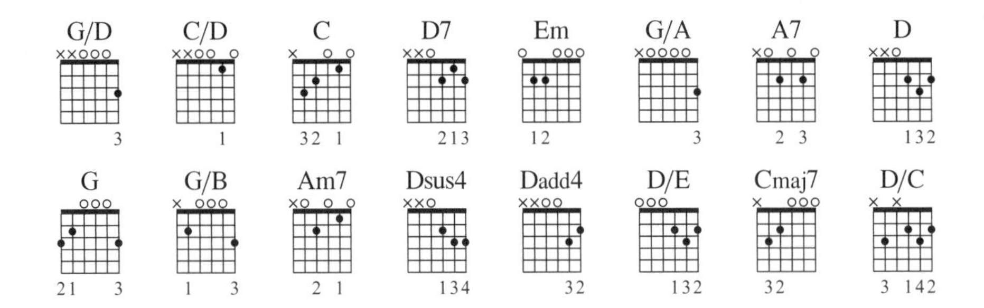

*Capo V

Strum Pattern: 3
Pick Pattern: 3

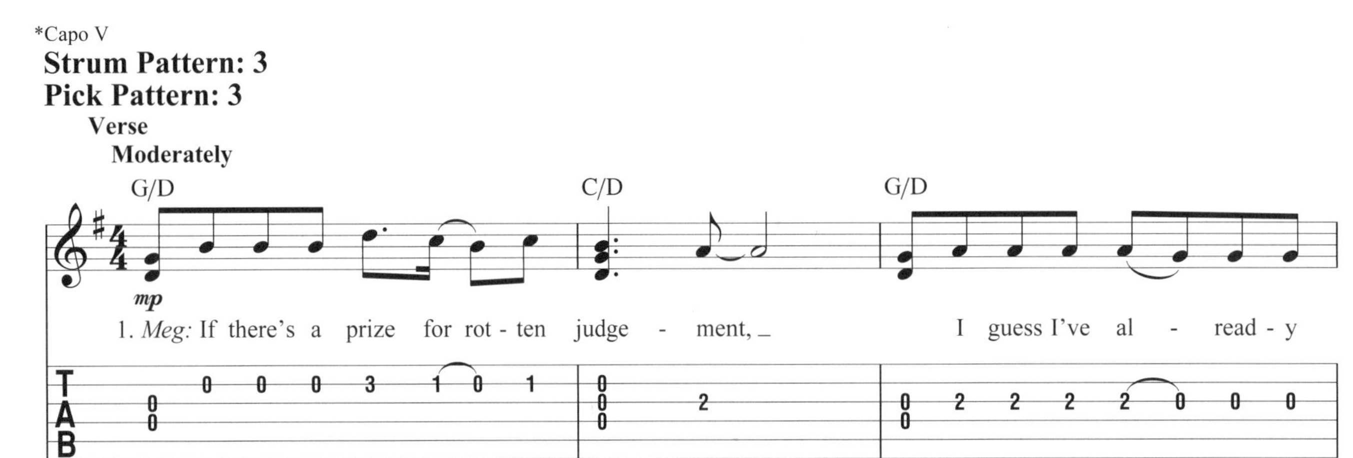

*Optional: To match recording, place capo at 5th fret.

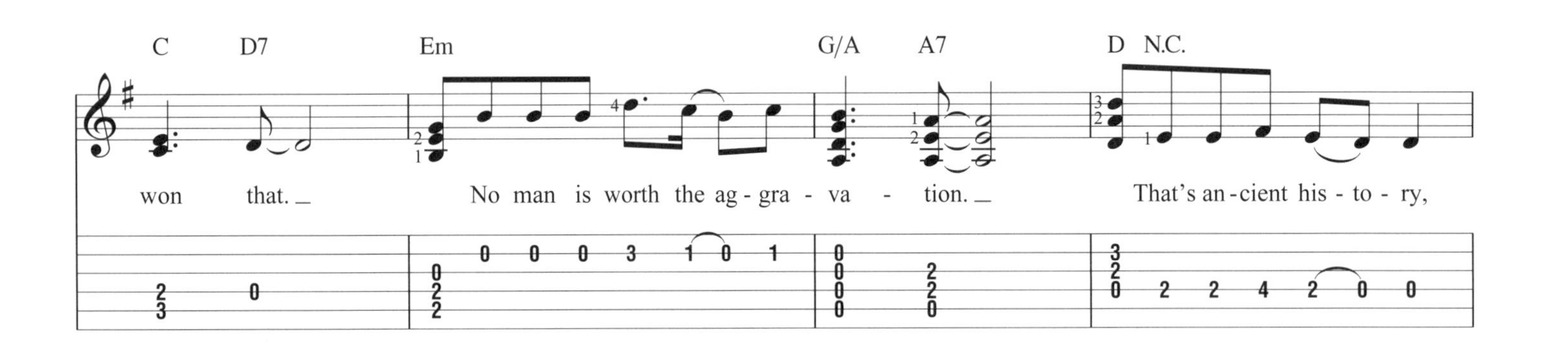

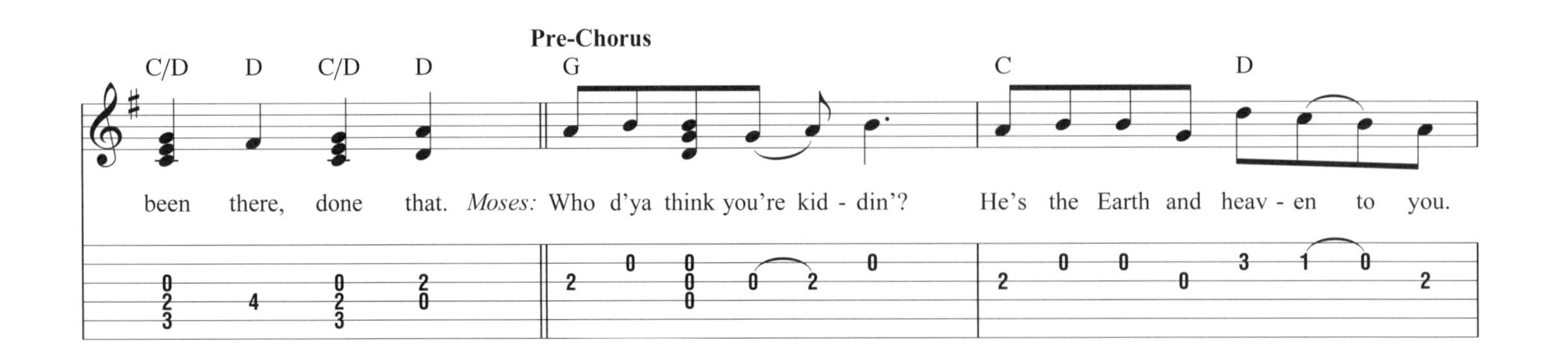

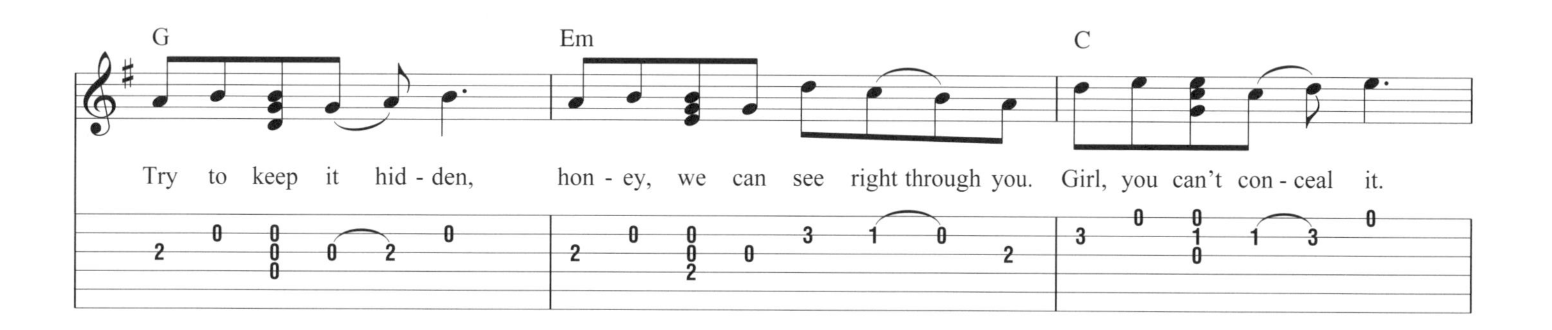
G
Em
C
Try to keep it hid - den, hon - ey, we can see right through you. Girl, you can't con - ceal it.

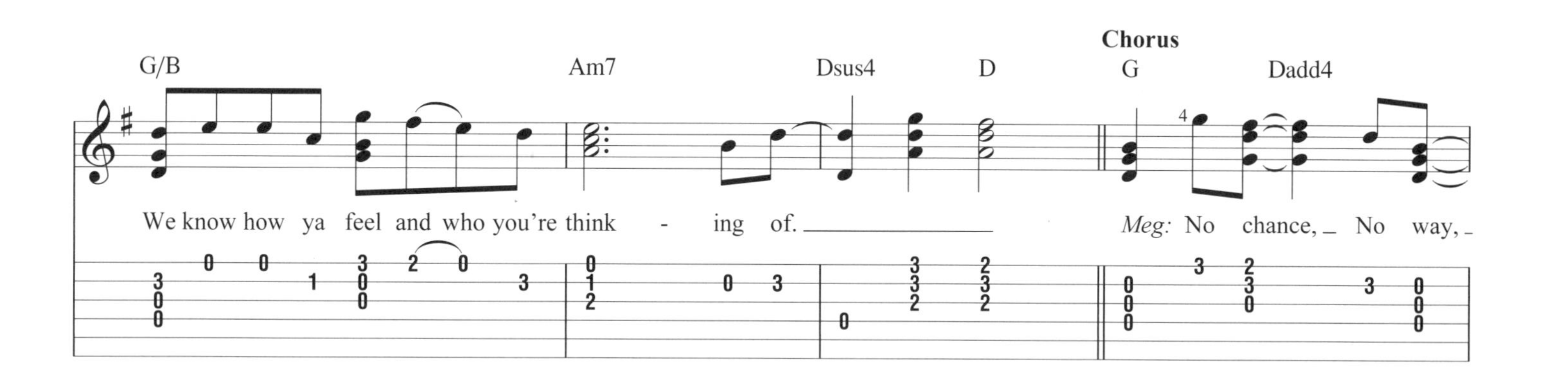
Chorus
G/B
Am7
Dsus4
D
G
Dadd4
We know how ya feel and who you're think - ing of.
Meg: No chance, No way,

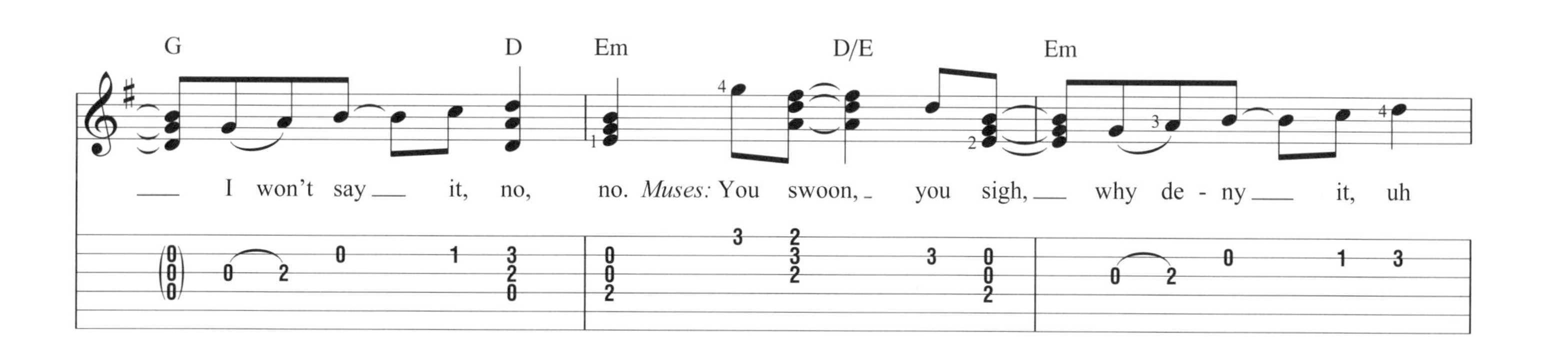
G
D
Em
D/E
Em
I won't say it, no, no. Muses: You swoon, you sigh, why de - ny it, uh

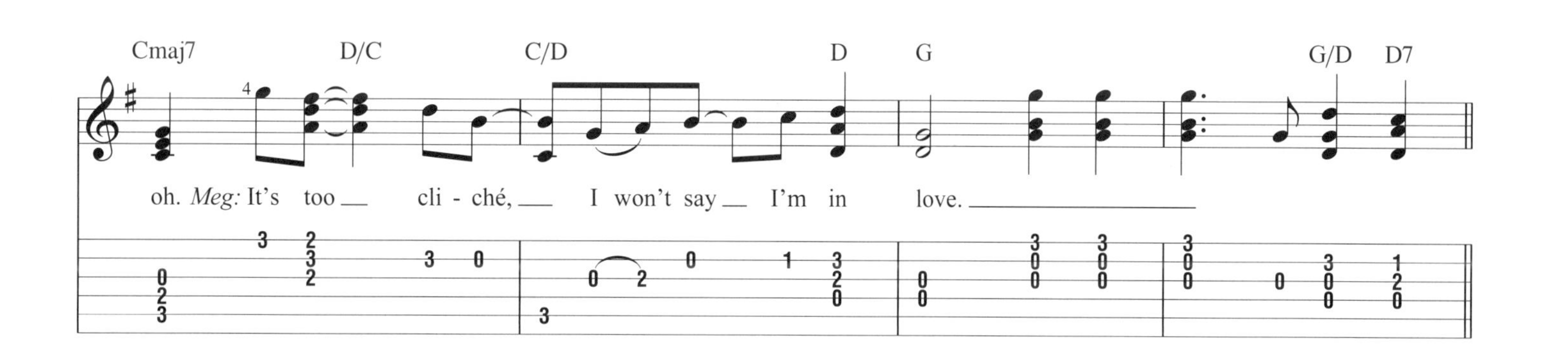
Cmaj7
D/C
C/D
D
G
G/D
D7
oh. Meg: It's too cli - ché, I won't say I'm in love.

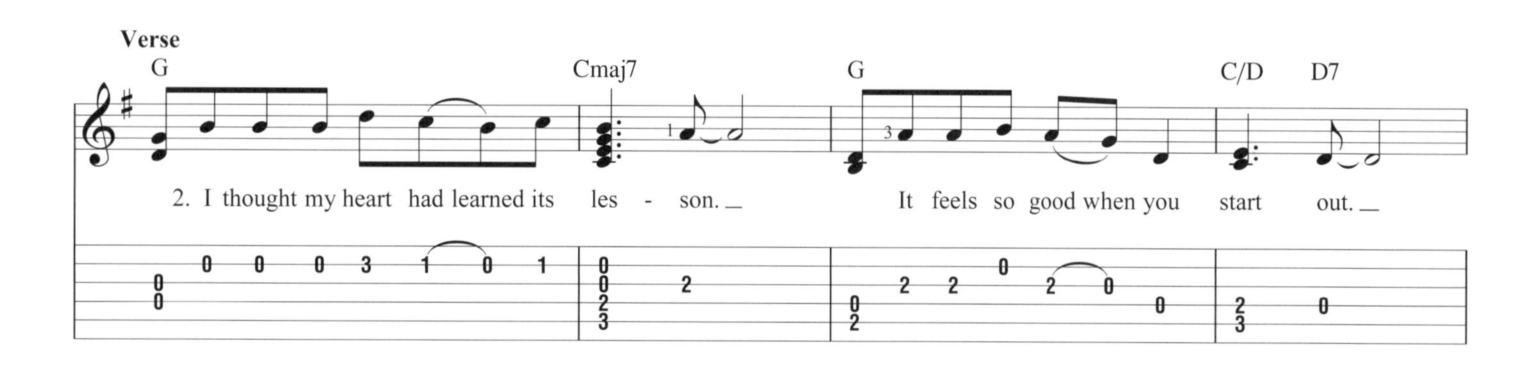
Verse
G
Cmaj7
G
C/D
D7
2. I thought my heart had learned its les - son. It feels so good when you start out.

Em G/A A7 D N.C. C/D D C/D D
My head is scream-ing, get a grip, girl, un-less you're dy-ing to cry your heart out.

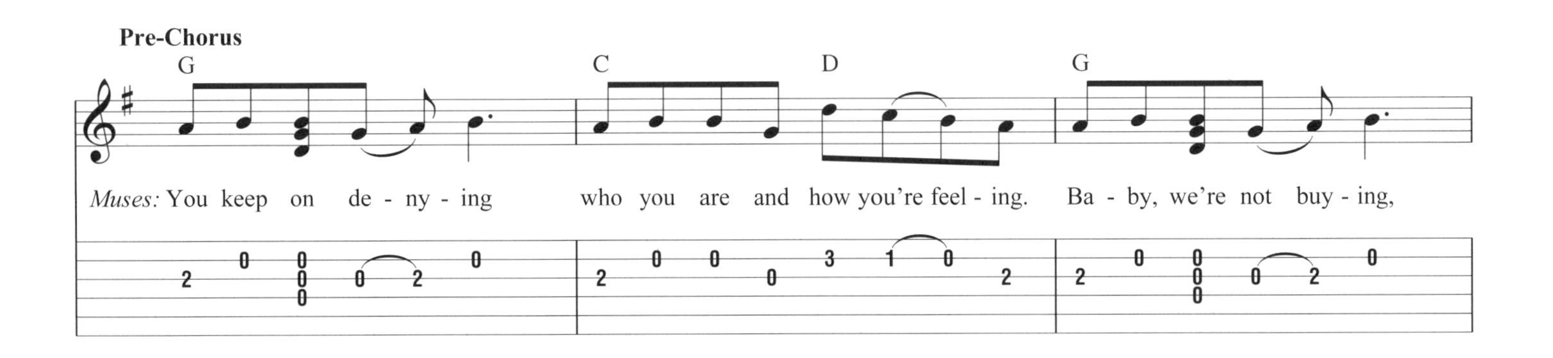
Pre-Chorus
G C D G
Muses: You keep on de-ny-ing who you are and how you're feel-ing. Ba-by, we're not buy-ing,

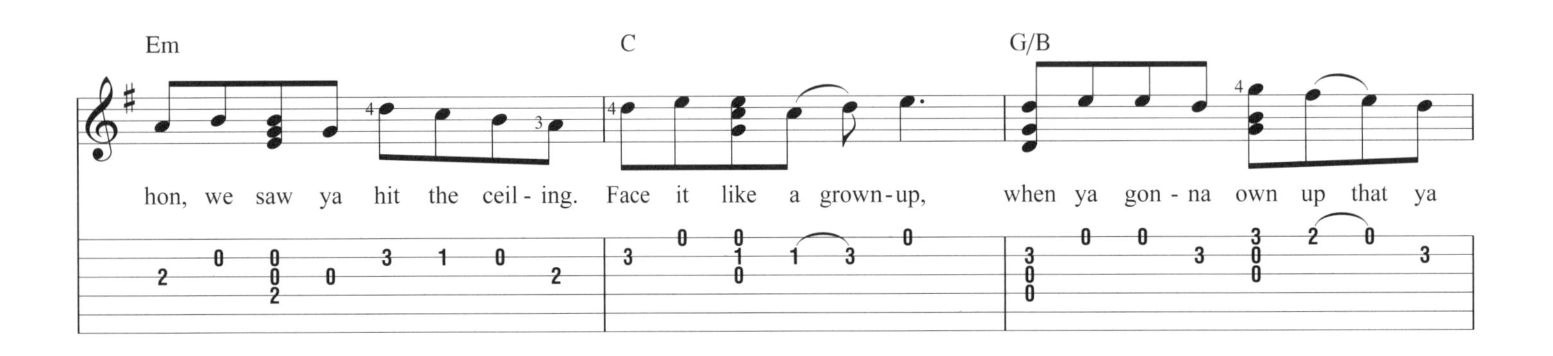
Em C G/B
hon, we saw ya hit the ceil-ing. Face it like a grown-up, when ya gon-na own up that ya

Am7 Dsus4 D Chorus G Dadd4
got, got it, got it bad. Meg: No chance, no way,

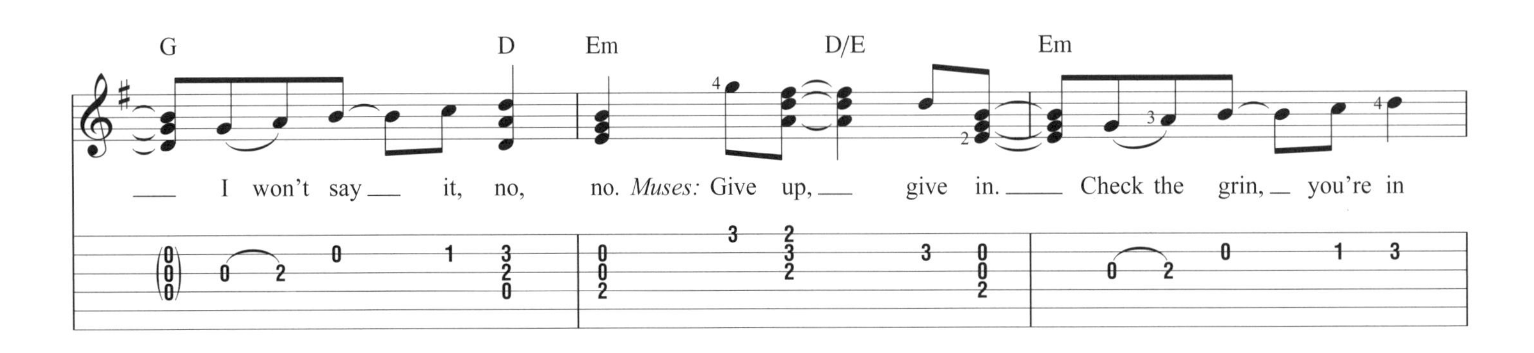
G D Em D/E Em
I won't say it, no, no. Muses: Give up, give in. Check the grin, you're in

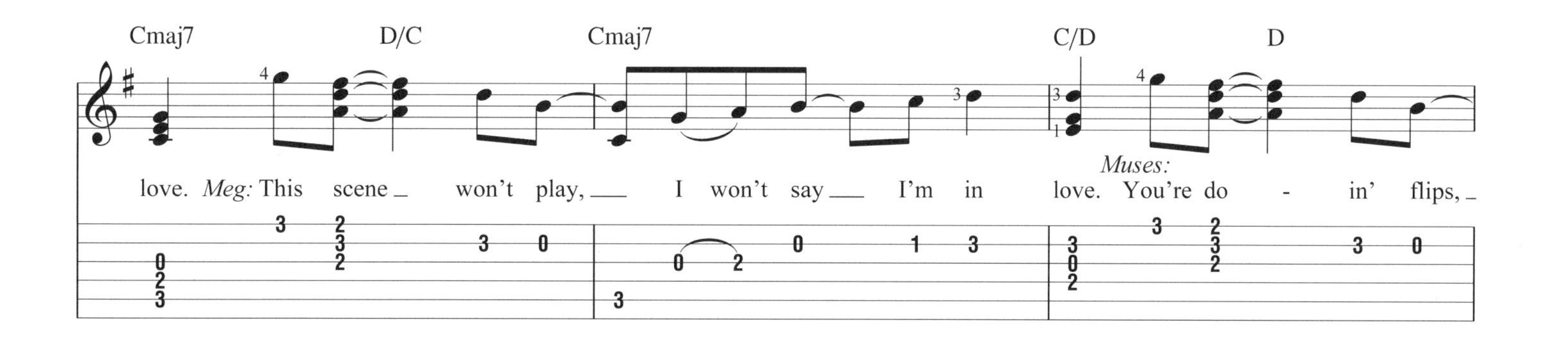
Cmaj7 D/C Cmaj7 C/D D
Muses:
love. Meg: This scene won't play, I won't say I'm in love. You're do - in' flips,

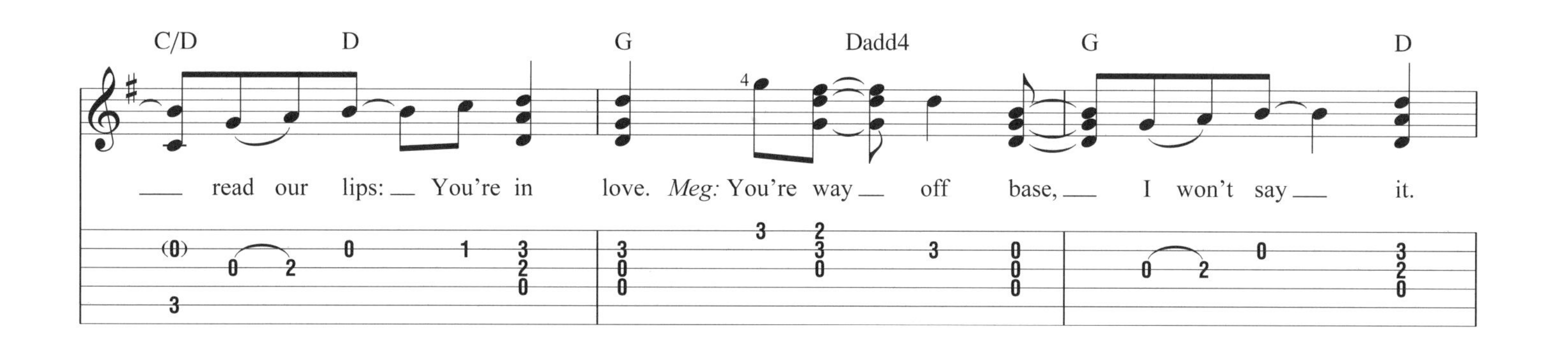
C/D D G Dadd4 G D
read our lips: You're in love. Meg: You're way off base, I won't say it.

Em D/E Em Cmaj7 D/C
Get off my case, I won't say it. Muses: Girl, don't be proud,

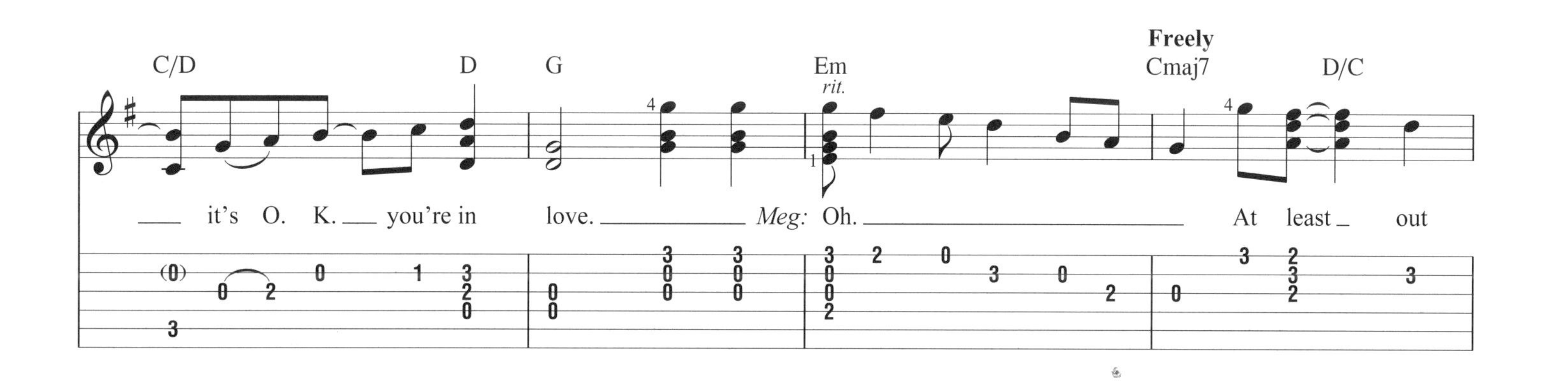
Freely
C/D D G Em Cmaj7 D/C
rit.
it's O. K. you're in love. Meg: Oh. At least out

C/D D7 G
a tempo
rit.
loud, I won't say I'm in love.

I'll Make a Man Out of You

from MULAN

Music by Matthew Wilder
Lyrics by David Zippel

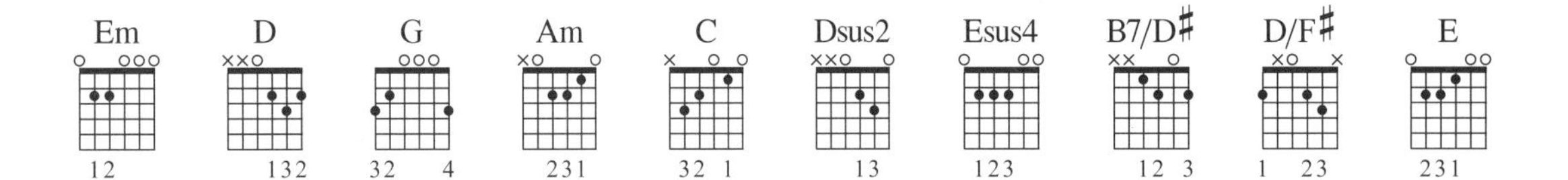

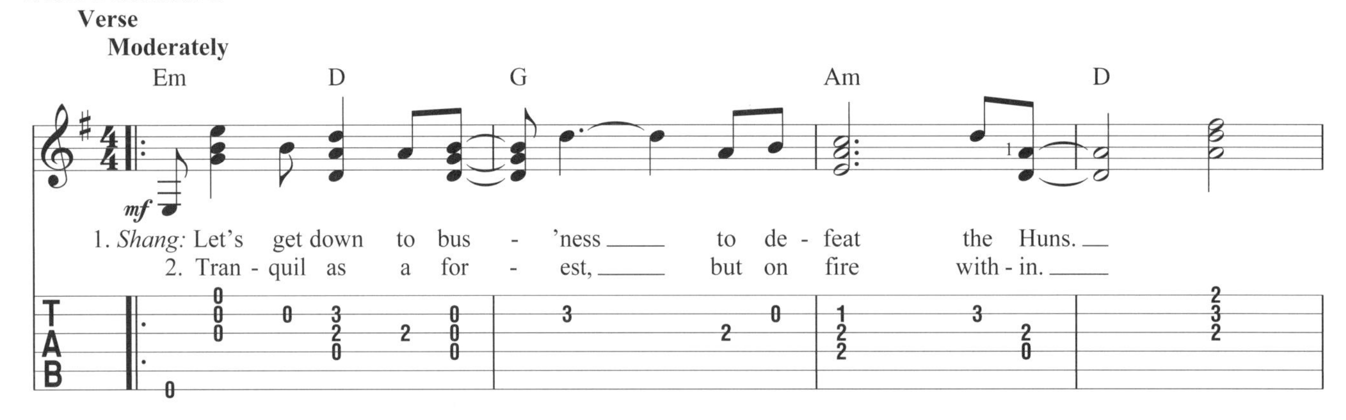

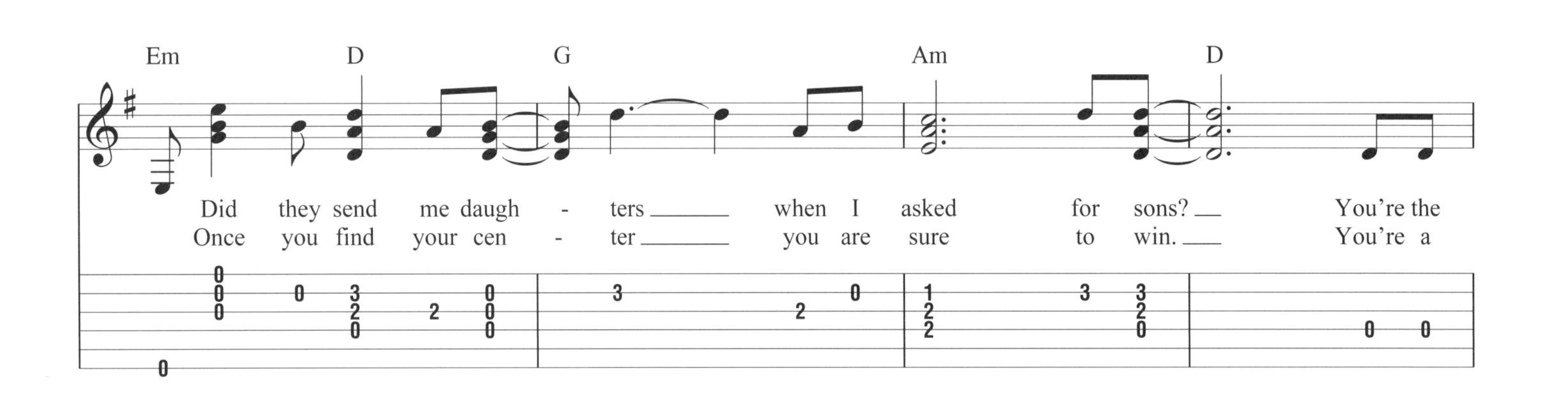

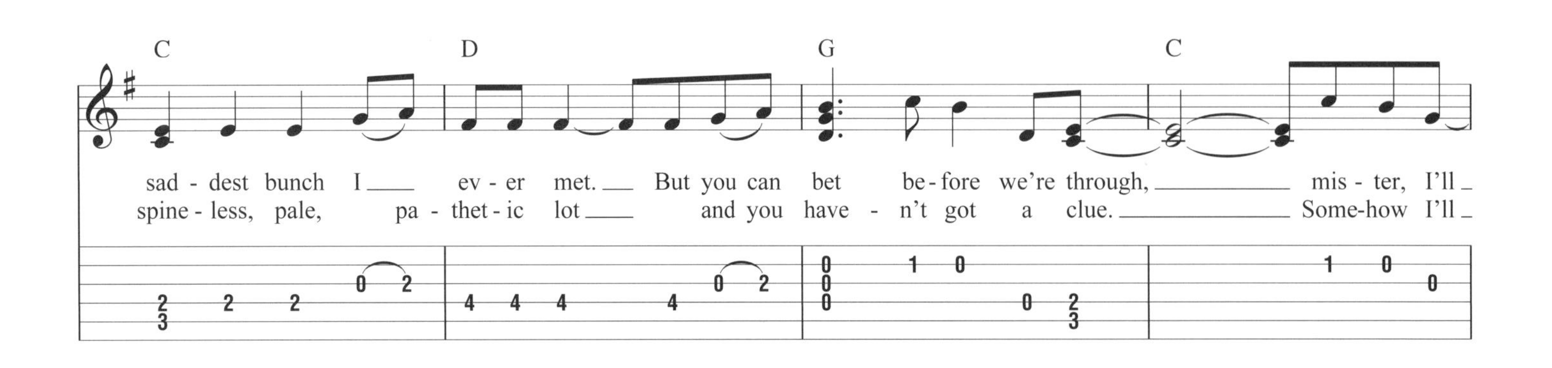

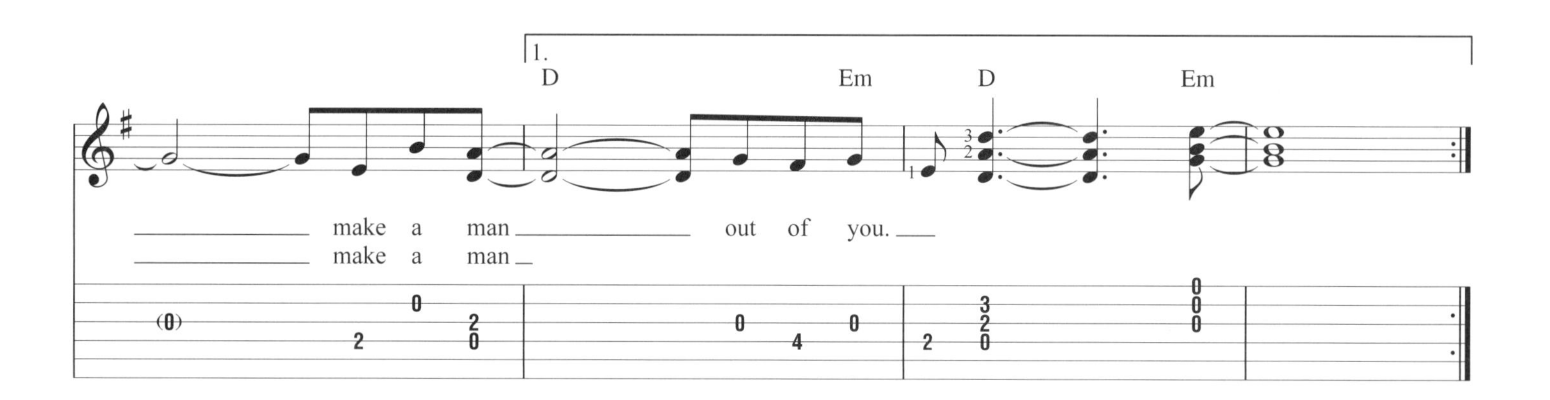
1.
D Em D Em
make a man out of you.
make a man

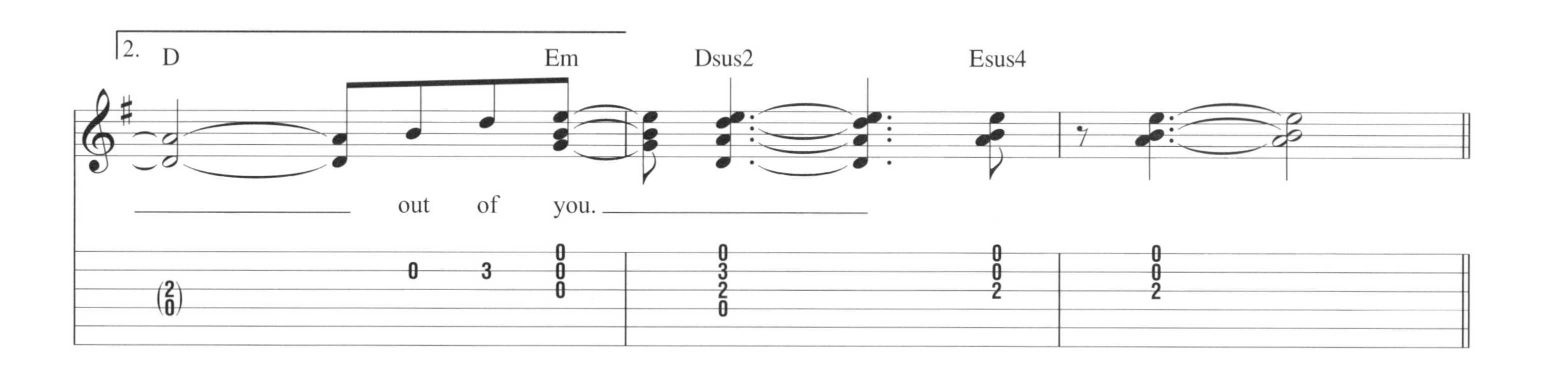
2.
D Em Dsus2 Esus4
out of you.

Pre-Chorus
C D B7/D♯ Em
Chien Po: I'm nev - er gon - na catch my breath. Yao: Say good-bye to those who knew me.

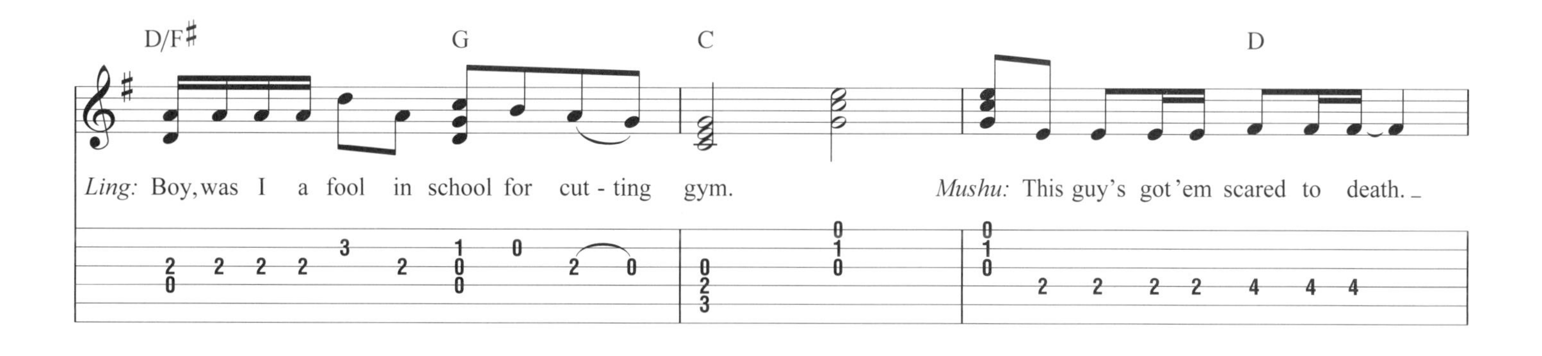
D/F♯ G C D
Ling: Boy, was I a fool in school for cut - ting gym. Mushu: This guy's got 'em scared to death.

B7/D♯ Em D/F♯ G
Mulan:
Hope he does - n't see right through me. Chien Po: Now I real - ly wish that I knew how to

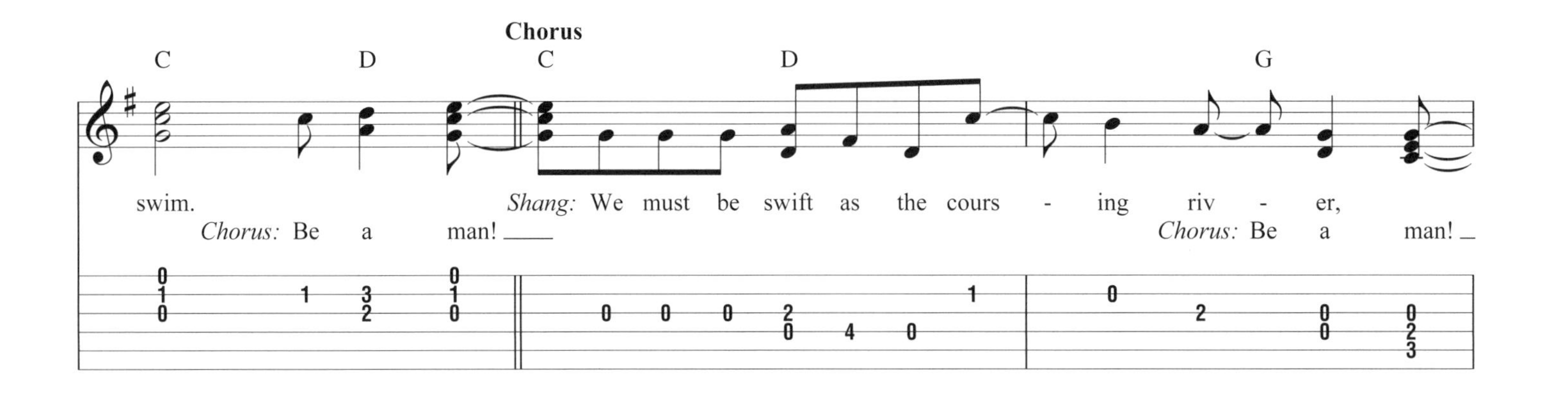
Chorus
C D C D G
swim. Shang: We must be swift as the cours - ing riv - er,
Chorus: Be a man! Chorus: Be a man!

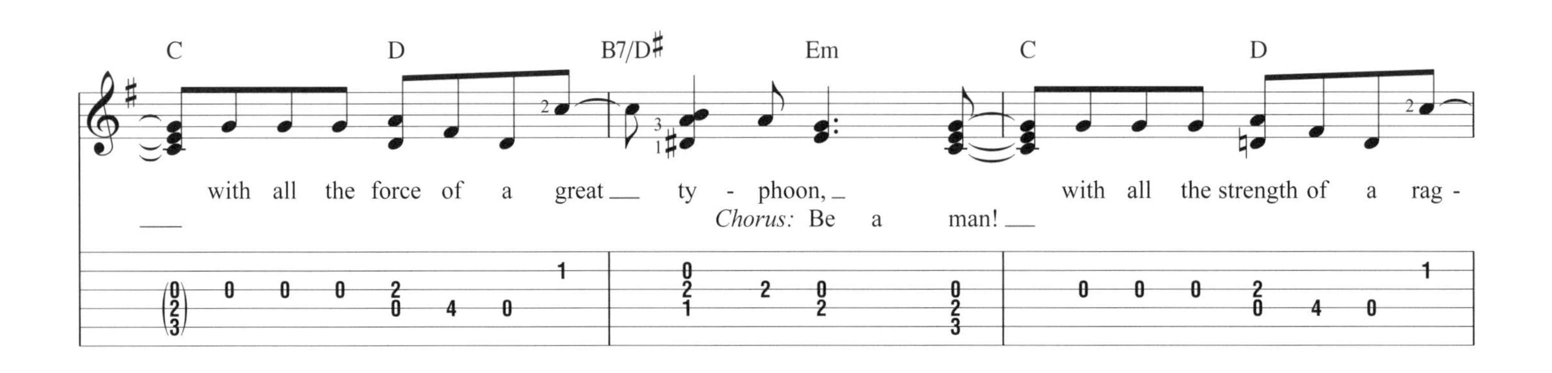
C D B7/D♯ Em C D
with all the force of a great ty - phoon,
with all the strength of a rag -
Chorus: Be a man!

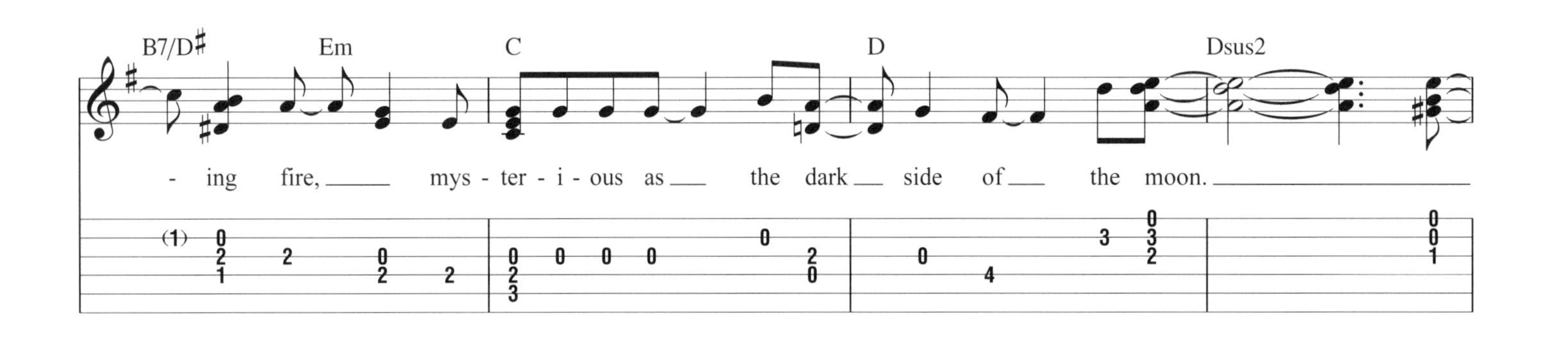
B7/D♯ Em C D Dsus2
- ing fire, mys - ter - i - ous as the dark side of the moon.

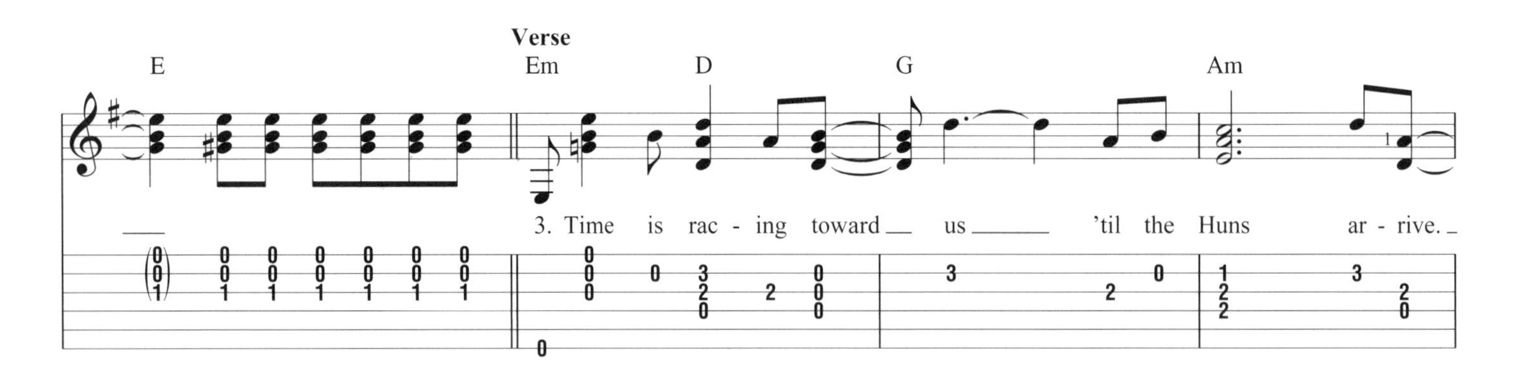
Verse
E Em D G Am
3. Time is rac - ing toward us 'til the Huns ar - rive.

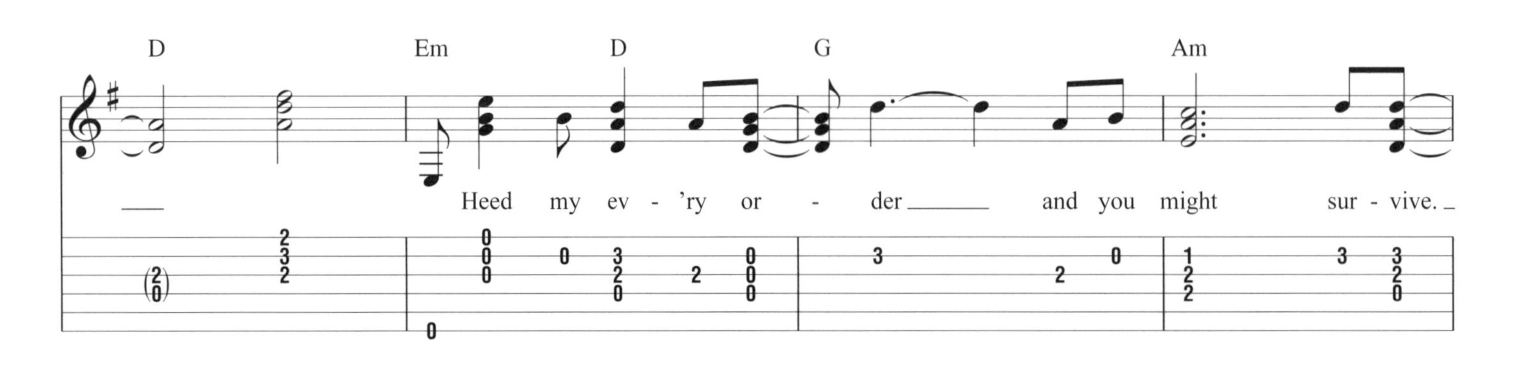
D Em D G Am
Heed my ev - 'ry or - der and you might sur - vive.

D C D G
You're un - suit - ed for the rage of war. So pack up, go home, you're through.

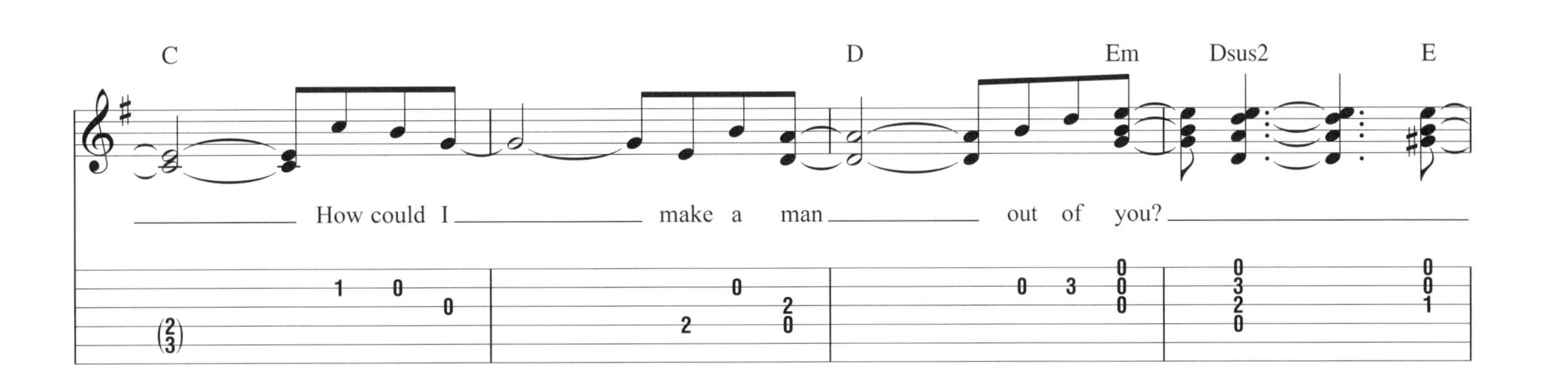

C D Em Dsus2 E
How could I make a man out of you?

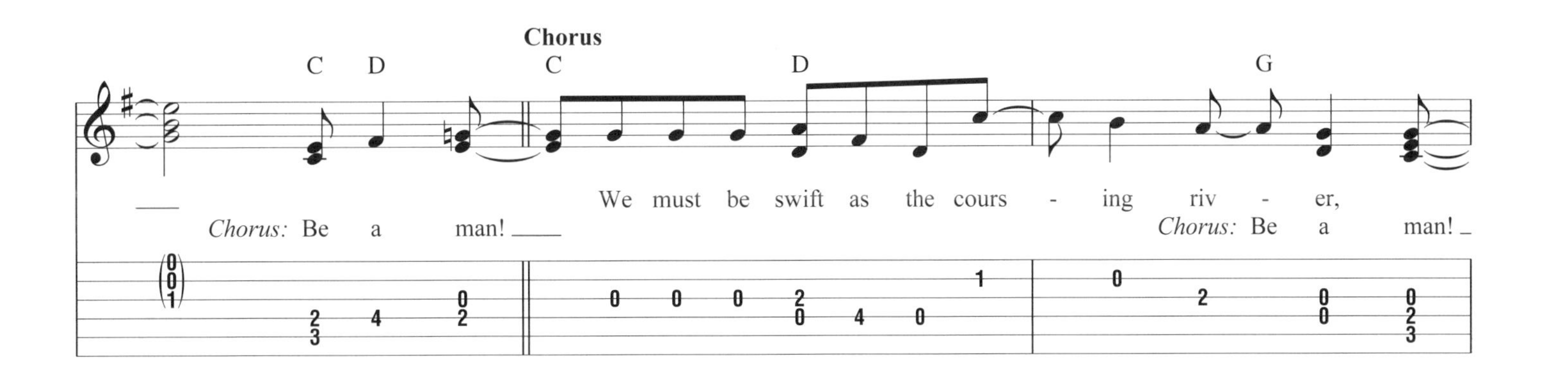

Chorus
C D C D G
We must be swift as the cours - ing riv - er,
Chorus: Be a man! Chorus: Be a man!

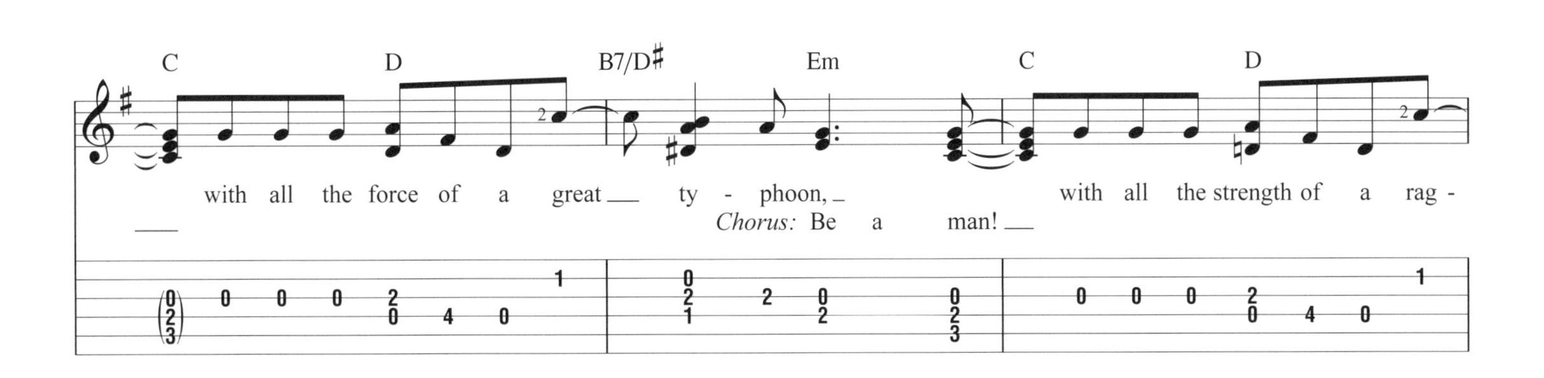

C D B7/D♯ Em C D
with all the force of a great ty - phoon, with all the strength of a rag -
Chorus: Be a man!

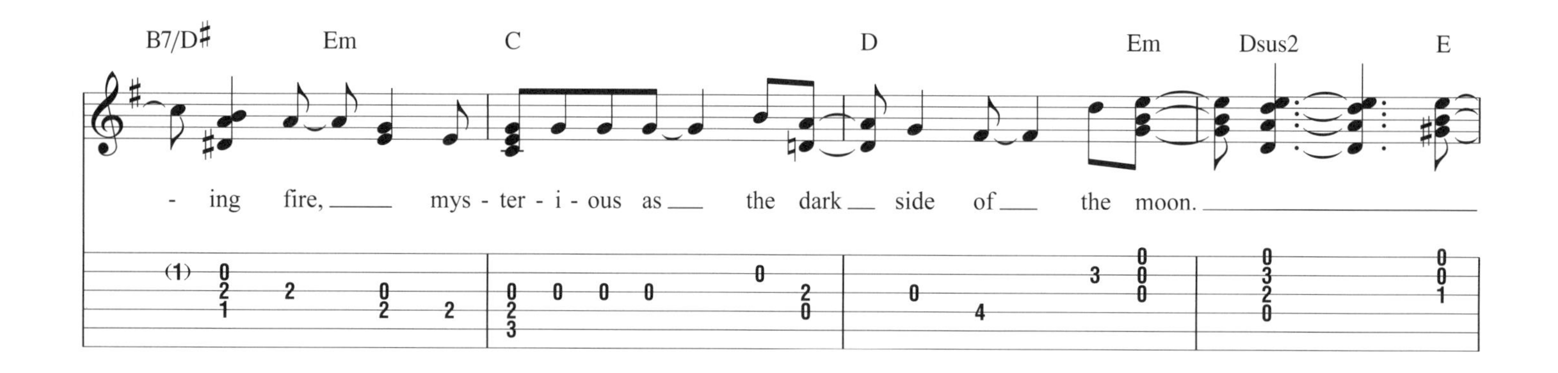
B7/D♯ Em C D Em Dsus2 E
- ing fire, mys - ter - i - ous as the dark side of the moon.

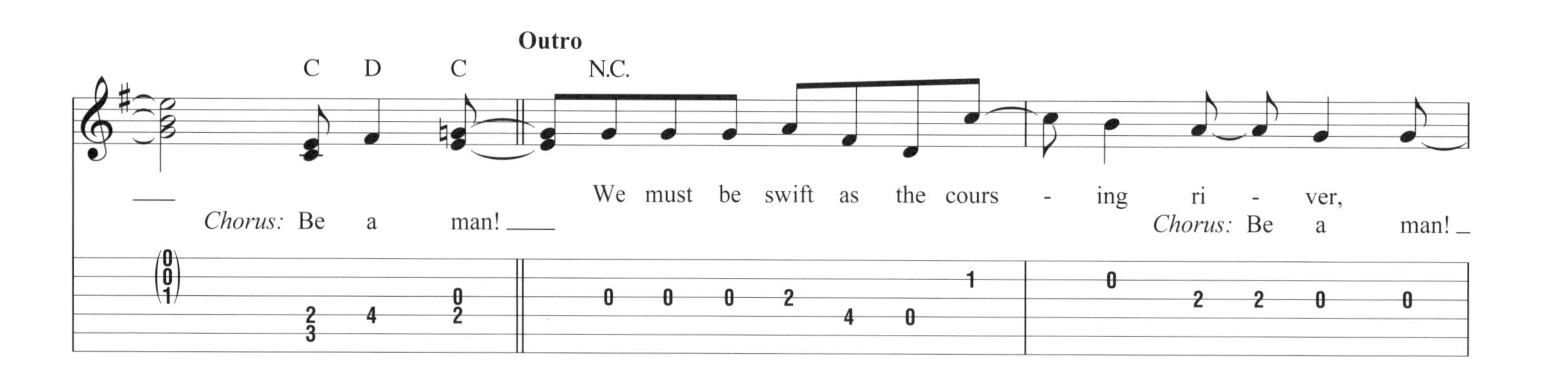
Outro
C D C N.C.
We must be swift as the cours - ing ri - ver,
Chorus: Be a man! Chorus: Be a man!

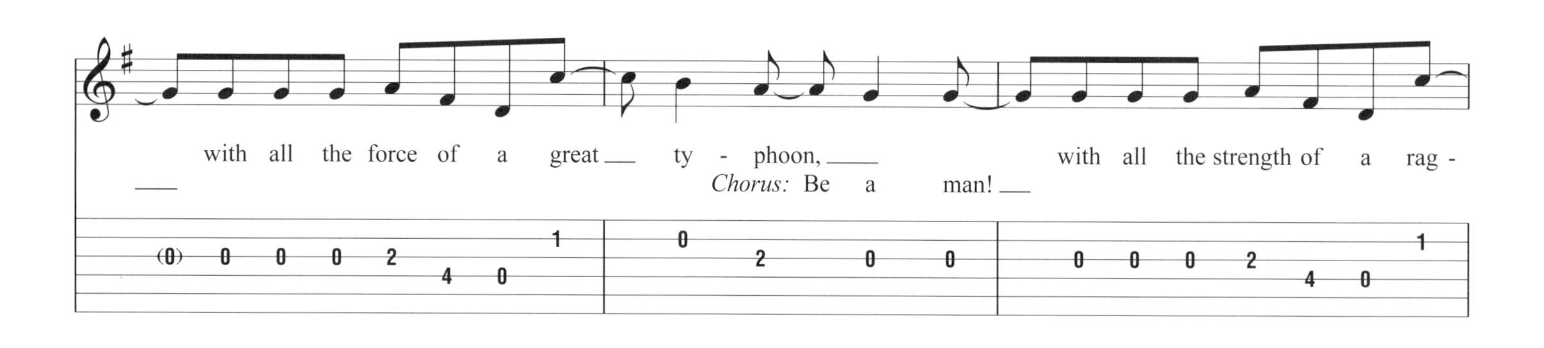
with all the force of a great ty - phoon, with all the strength of a rag -
Chorus: Be a man!

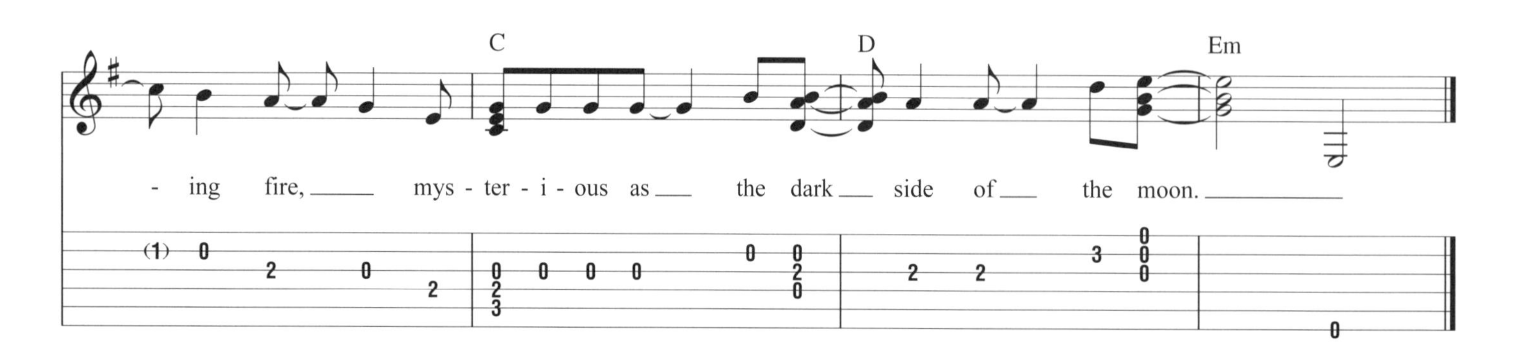
C D Em
- ing fire, mys - ter - i - ous as the dark side of the moon.

Know Who You Are

from MOANA

Music by Opetaia Foa'i, Lin-Manuel Miranda and Mark Mancina
Lyrics by Opetaia Foa'i and Lin-Manuel Miranda

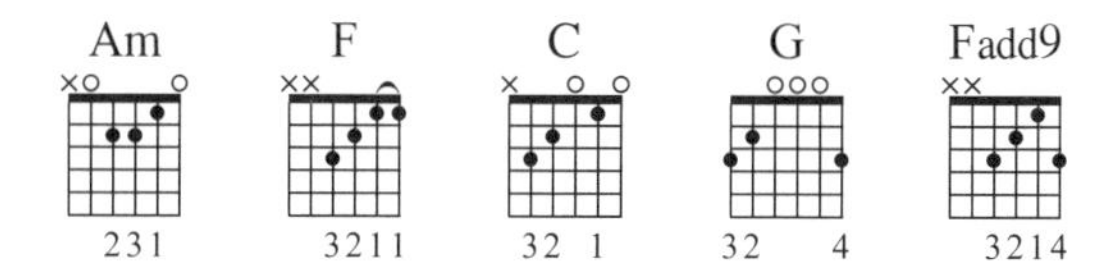

*Capo II

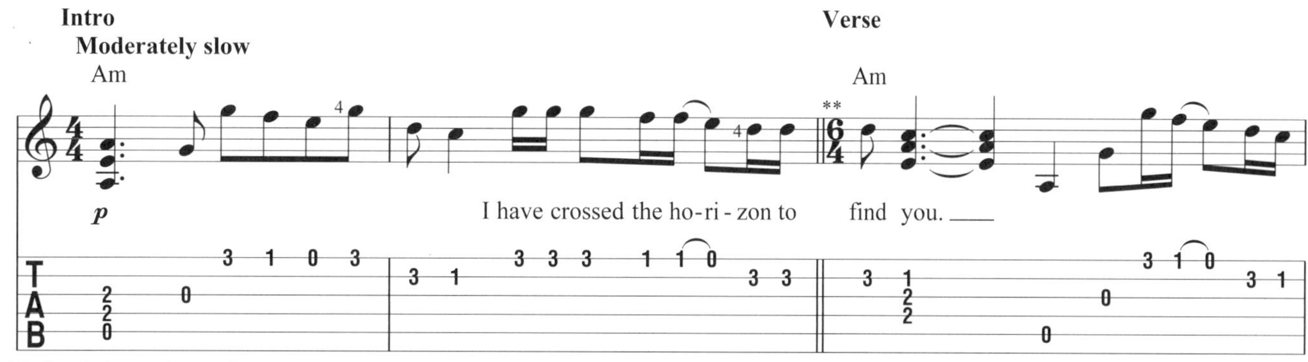

*Optional: To match recording, place capo at 2nd fret.

**Combine Patterns 4 & 10.

***Combine Patterns 8 & 10.

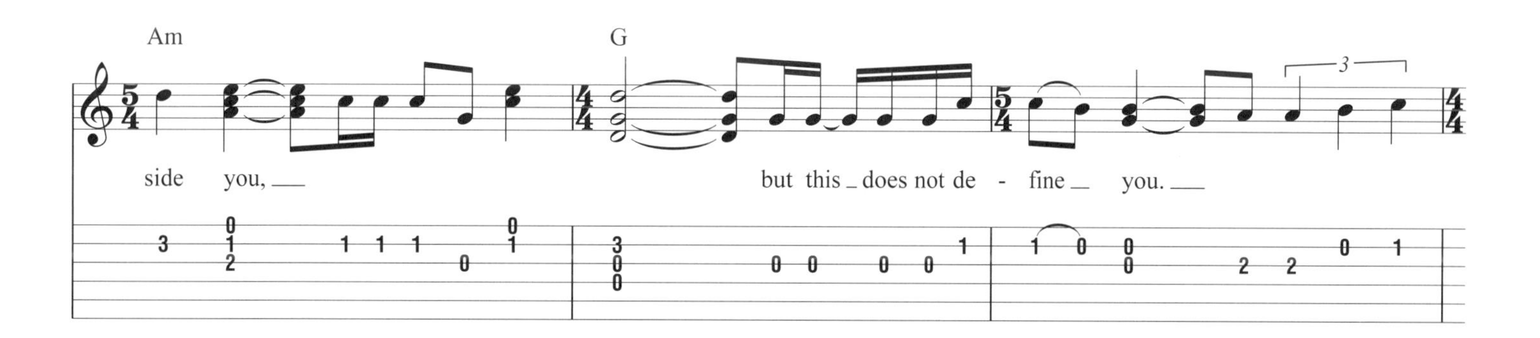

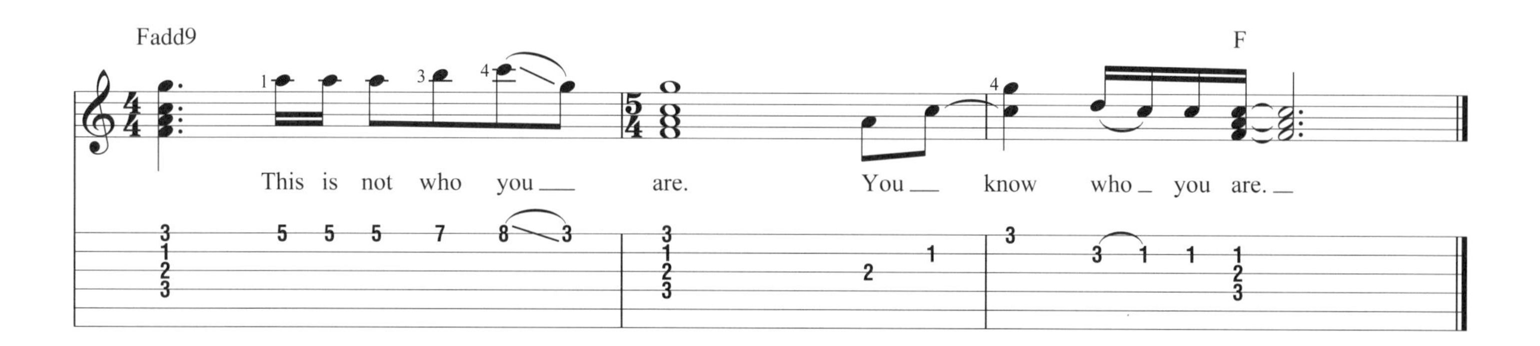

I've Got a Dream

from TANGLED

Music by Alan Menken
Lyrics by Glenn Slater

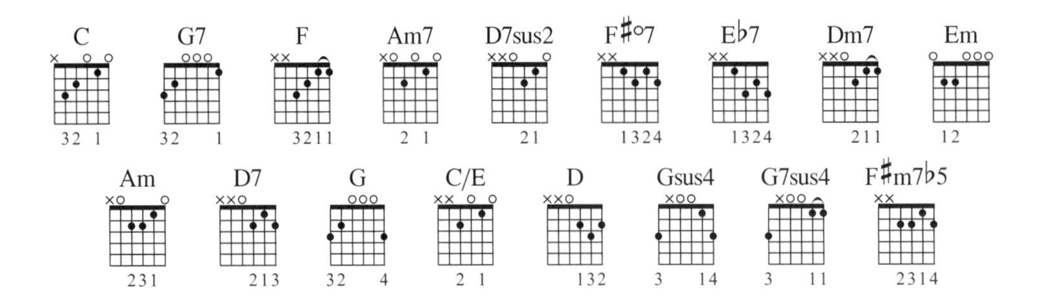

*Capo IV

Strum Pattern: 4
Pick Pattern: 4

*Optional: To match recording, place capo at 4th fret.

**Sung one octave lower.

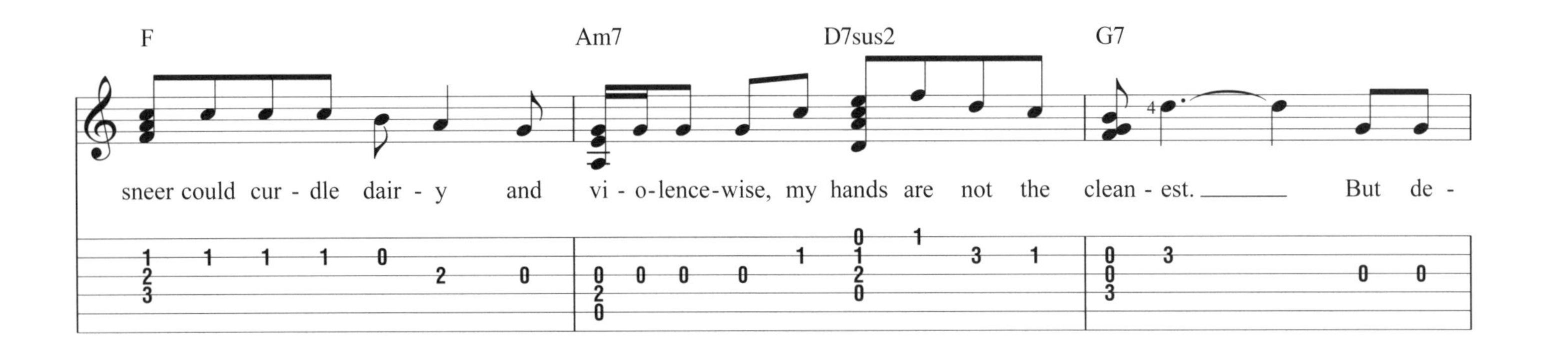

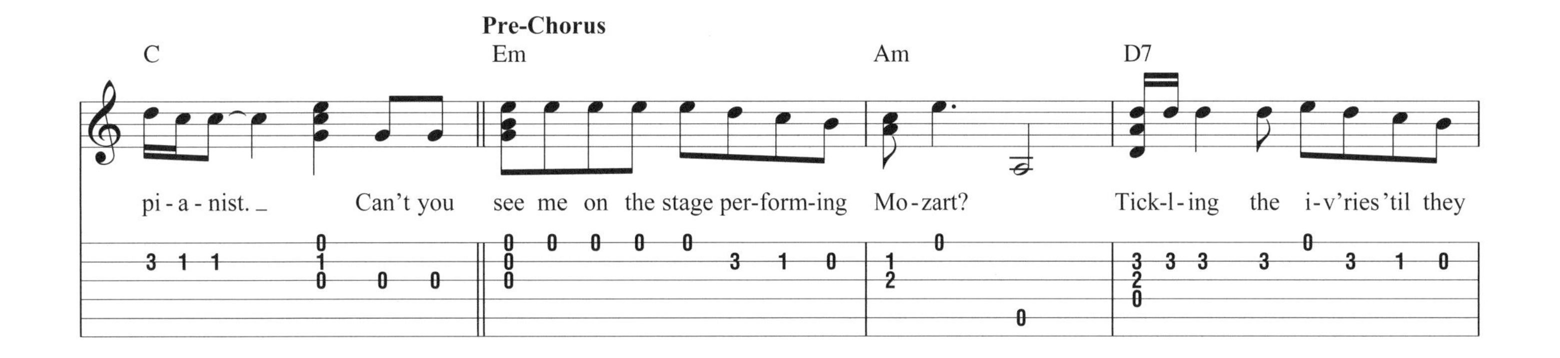
Pre-Chorus
C
Em
Am
D7
pi - a - nist. Can't you see me on the stage per-form-ing Mo-zart? Tick-l-ing the i-v'ries 'til they

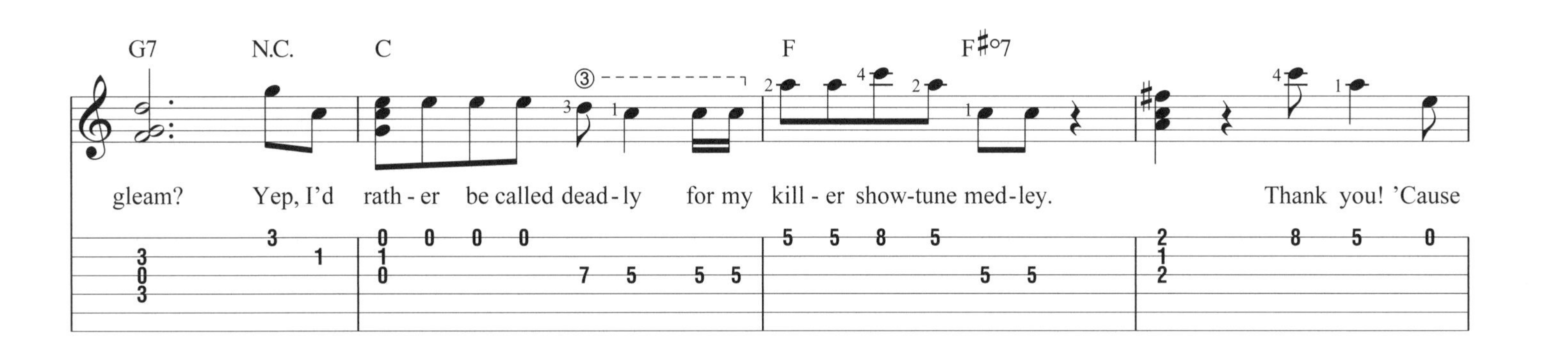
G7
N.C.
C
F
F♯°7
gleam? Yep, I'd rath - er be called dead - ly for my kill - er show-tune med-ley. Thank you! 'Cause

E♭7
Dm7
G7
C
Chorus
F
Thug Chorus:
way down deep in - side, I've got a dream. He's got a dream. He's got a

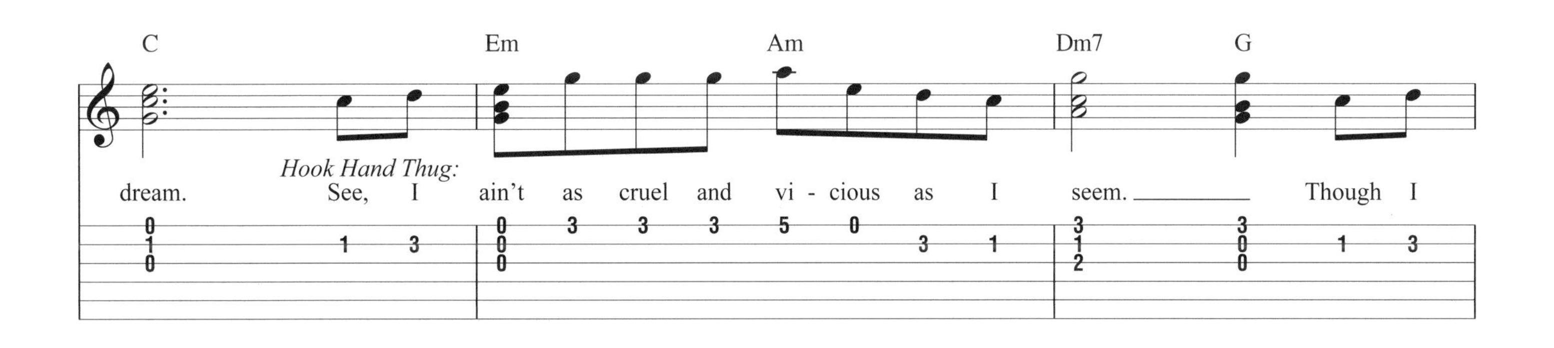
C
Em
Am
Dm7
G
Hook Hand Thug:
dream. See, I ain't as cruel and vi - cious as I seem. Though I

C
F
F♯°7
E♭7
Dm7
G7
do like break-ing fe - murs, you could count me with the dream-ers. Like ev - 'ry - bod - y else, I've got a

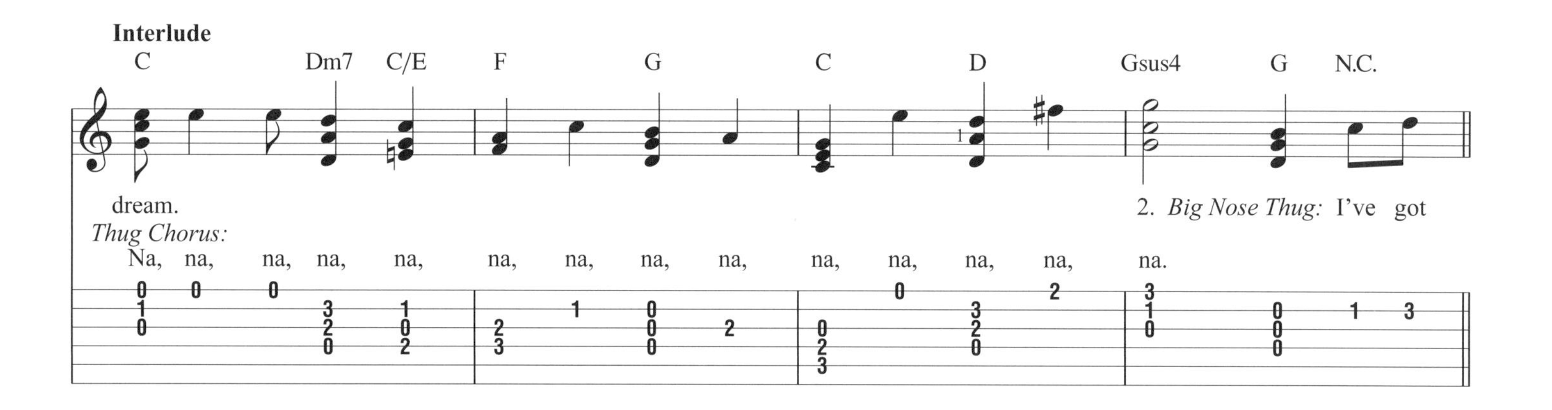

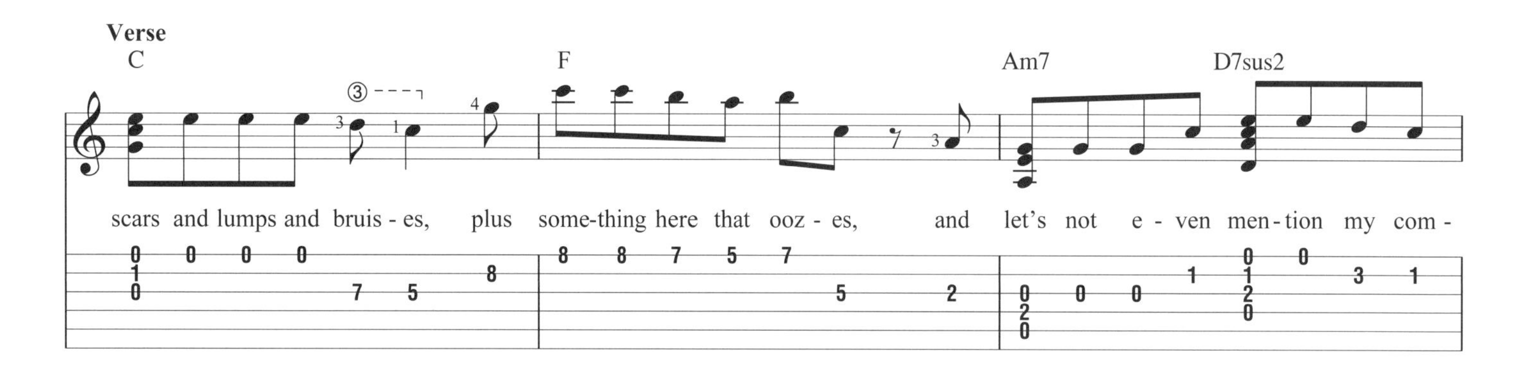

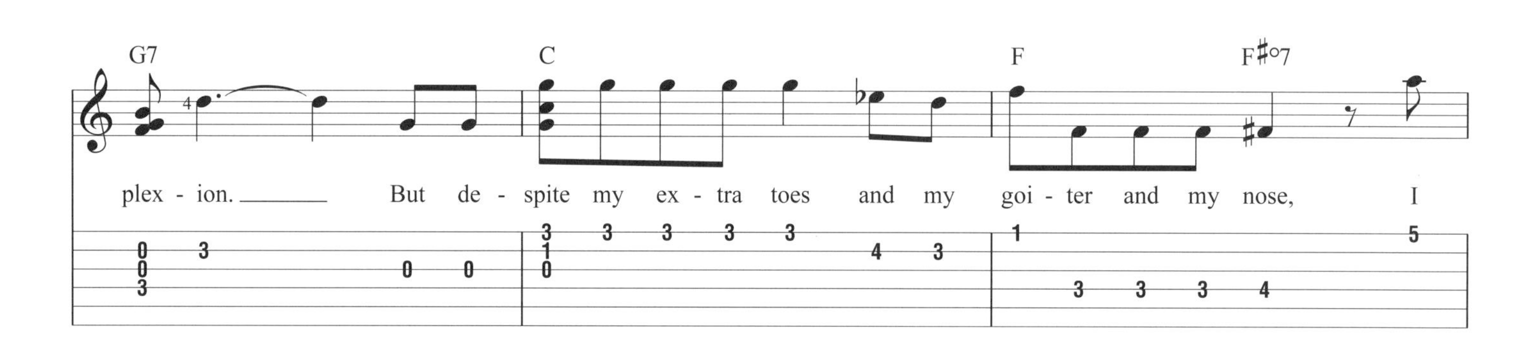

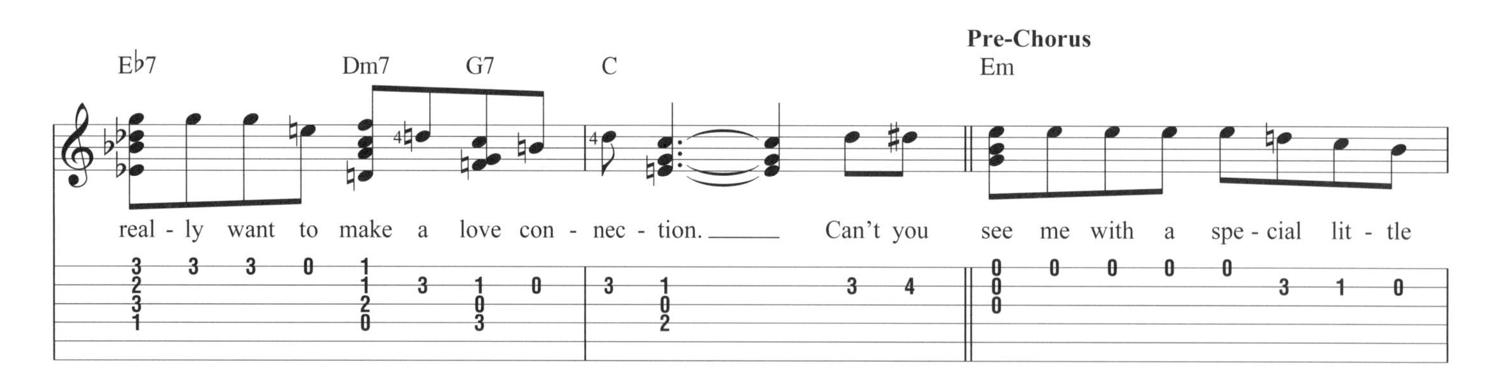

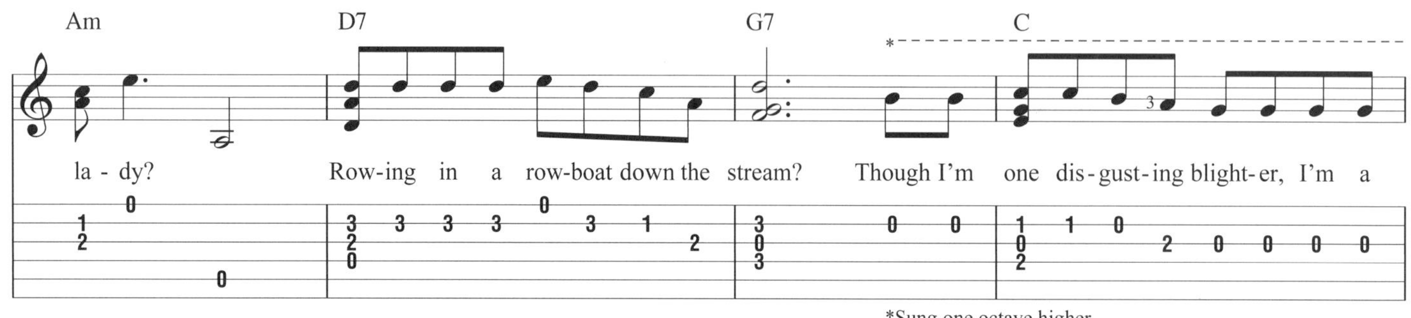

*Sung one octave higher.

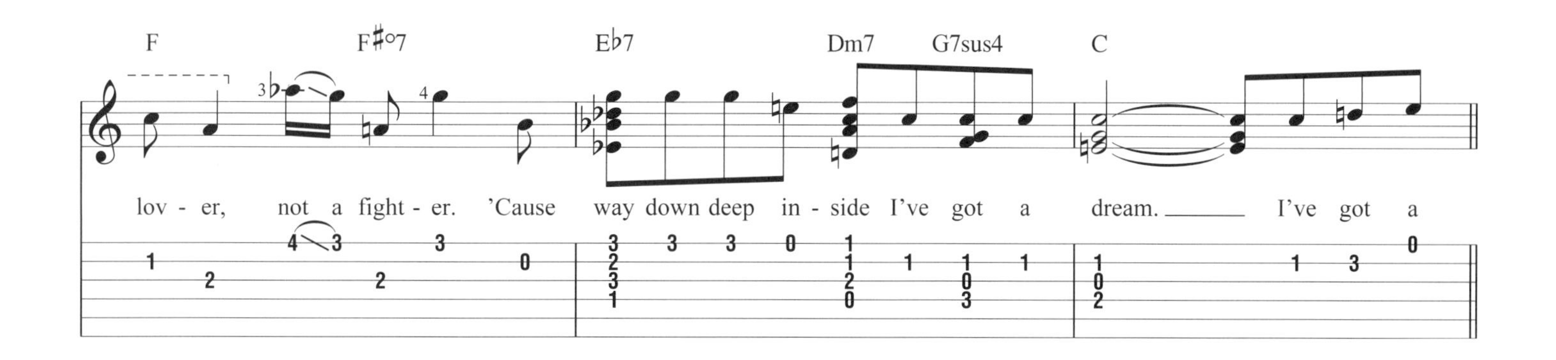

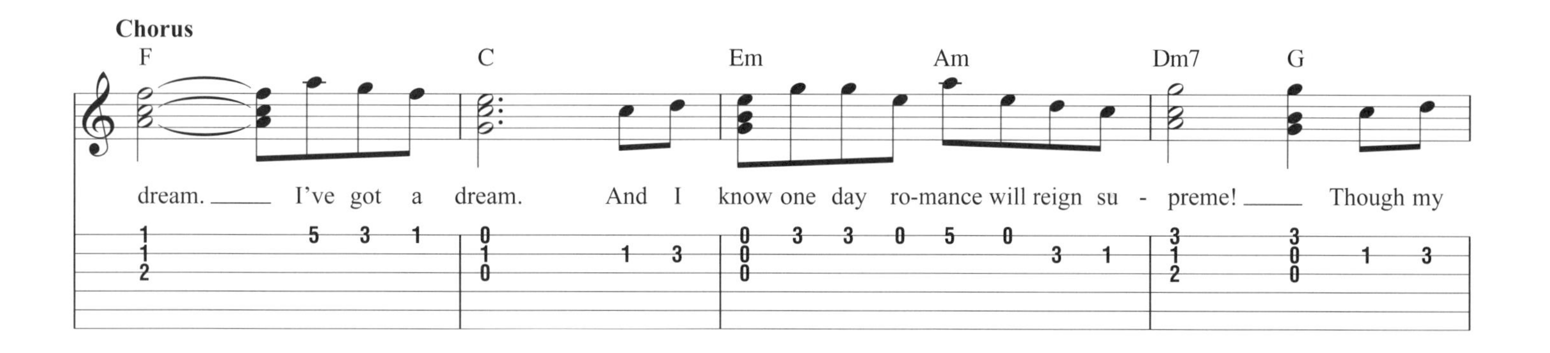

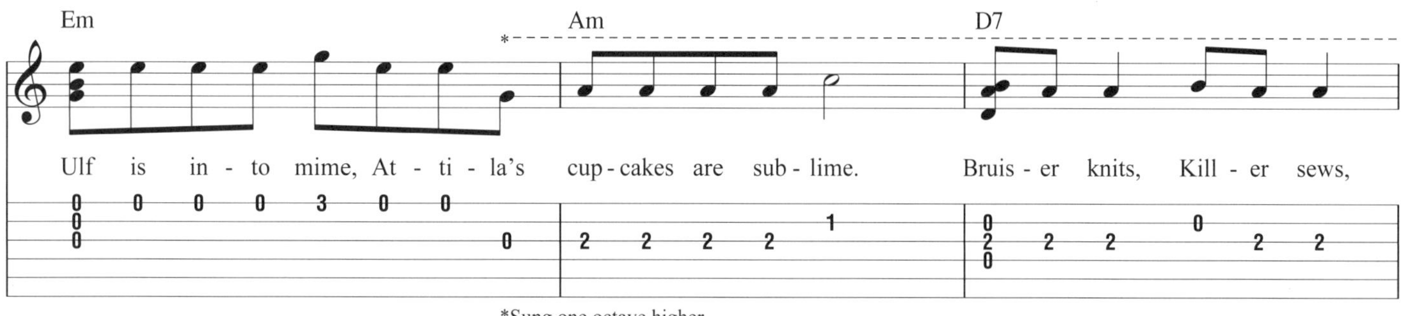

*Sung one octave higher.

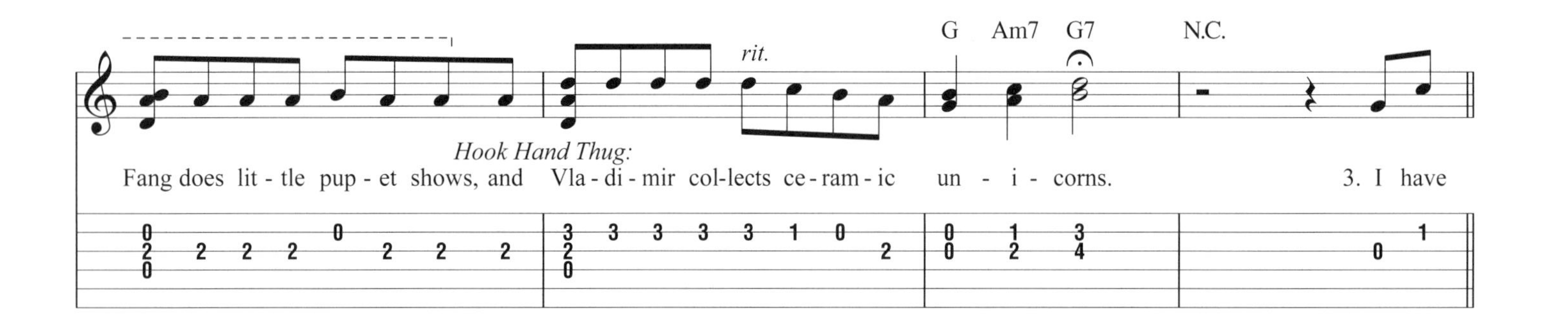
G Am7 G7 N.C.
rit.
Hook Hand Thug:
Fang does lit - tle pup - et shows, and Vla - di - mir col-lects ce - ram - ic un - i - corns. 3. I have

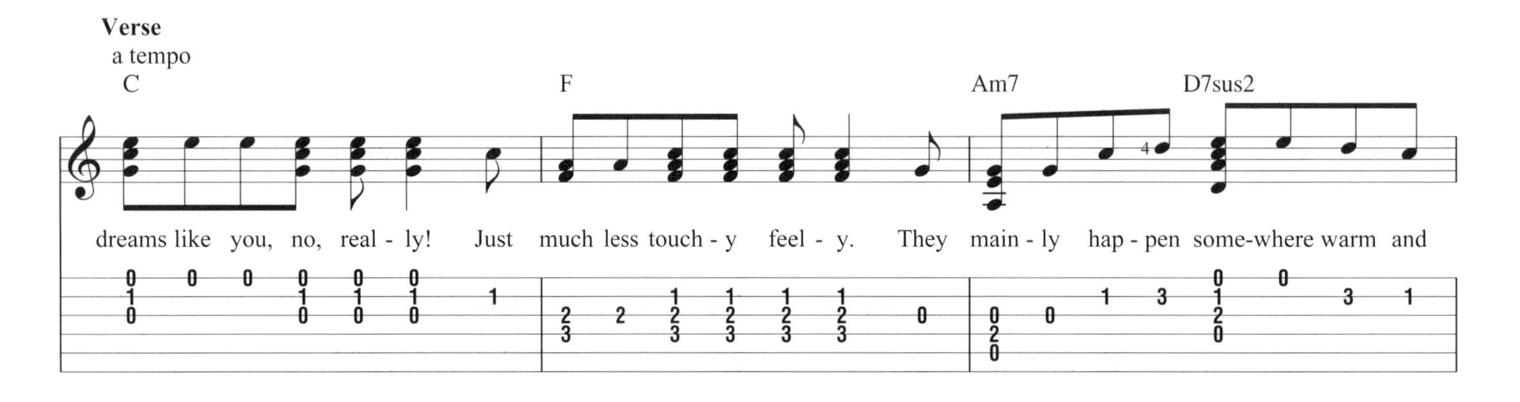
Verse
a tempo
C F Am7 D7sus2
dreams like you, no, real - ly! Just much less touch - y feel - y. They main - ly hap - pen some-where warm and

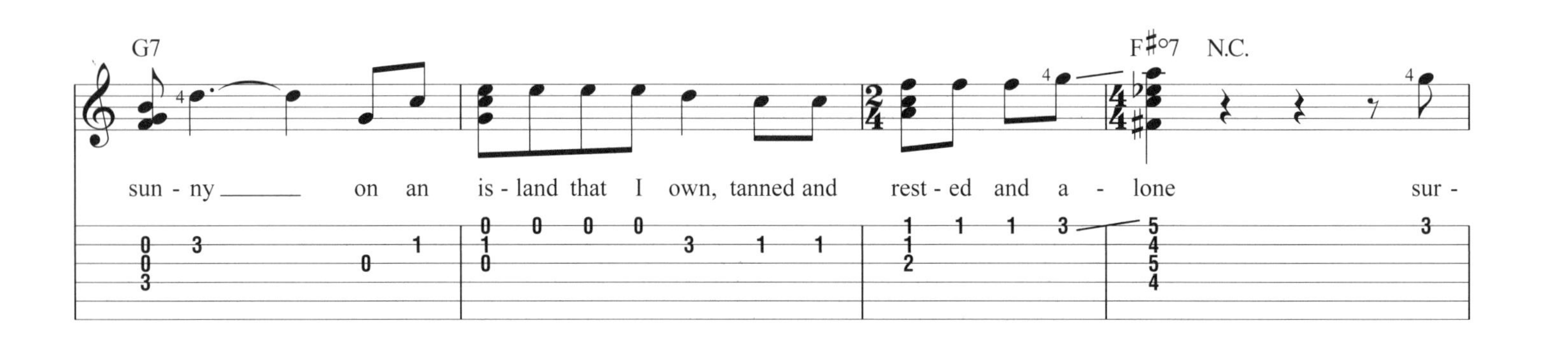
G7 F♯°7 N.C.
sun - ny on an is - land that I own, tanned and rest - ed and a - lone sur -

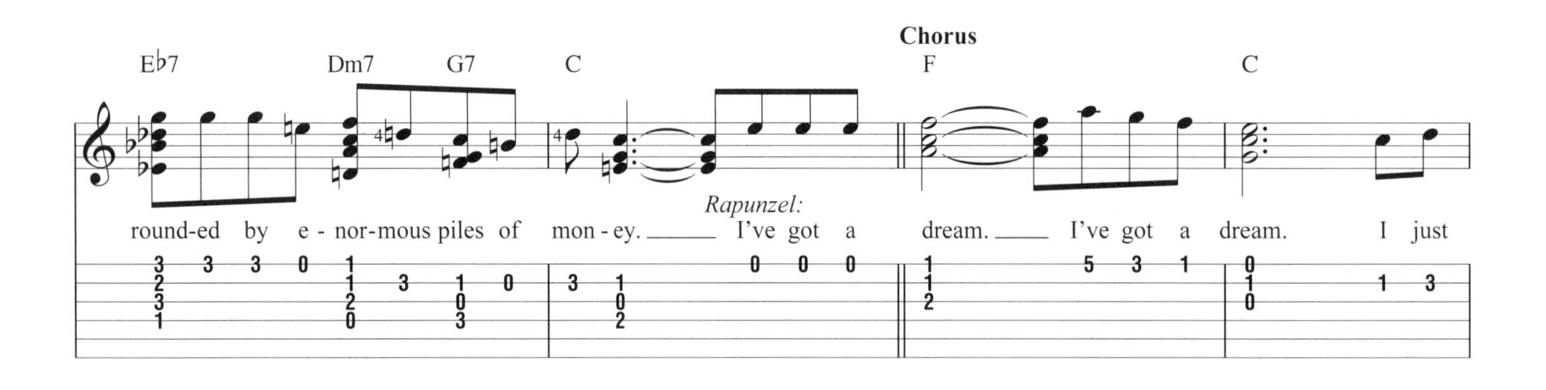
Chorus
E♭7 Dm7 G7 C F C
Rapunzel:
round-ed by e - nor-mous piles of mon - ey. I've got a dream. I've got a dream. I just

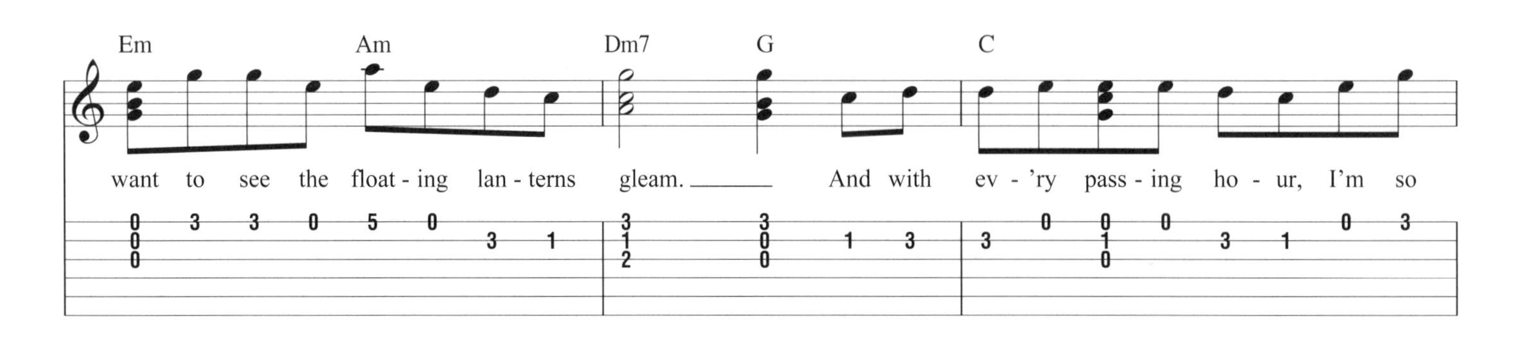
Em Am Dm7 G C
want to see the float - ing lan - terns gleam. And with ev - 'ry pass - ing ho - ur, I'm so

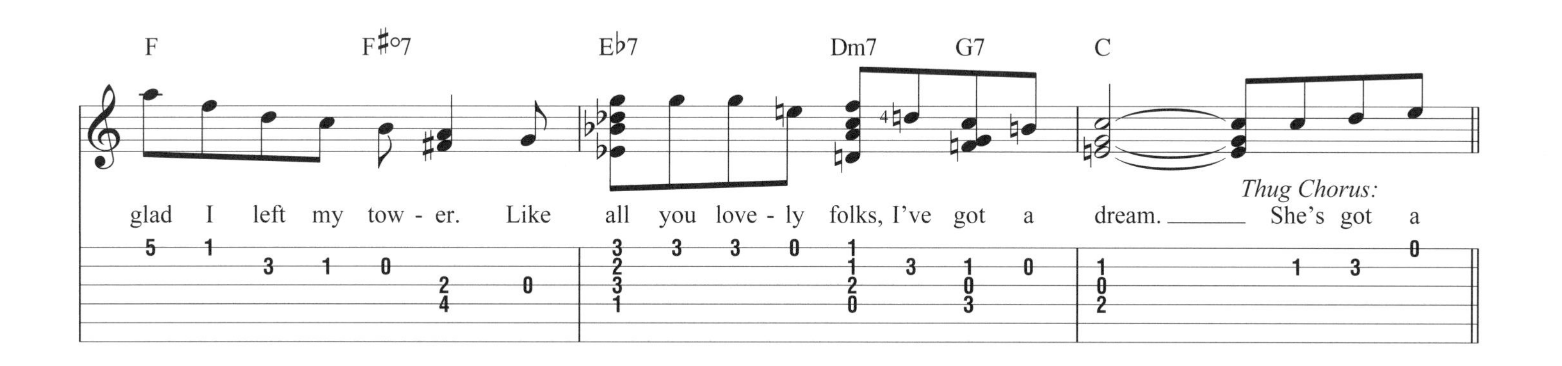
F F♯°7 E♭7 Dm7 G7 C
glad I left my tow - er. Like all you love - ly folks, I've got a dream.
Thug Chorus:
She's got a

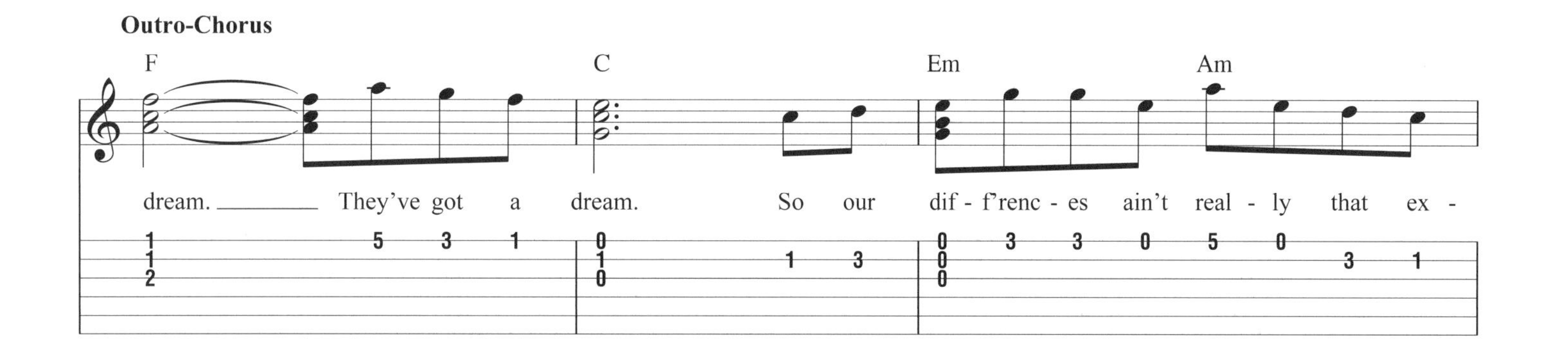
Outro-Chorus
F C Em Am
dream. They've got a dream. So our dif - f'renc - es ain't real - ly that ex -

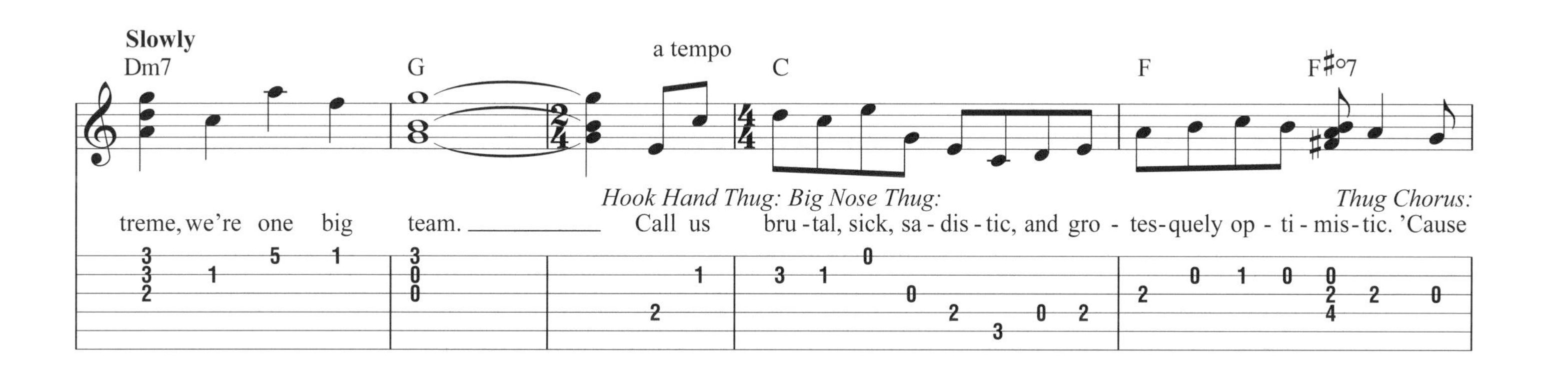
Slowly
a tempo
Dm7 G C F F♯°7
treme, we're one big team.
Hook Hand Thug:
Call us
Big Nose Thug:
bru - tal, sick, sa - dis - tic, and gro - tes-quely op - ti - mis - tic.
Thug Chorus:
'Cause

E♭7 Dm7 G7 Am Am7
way down deep in - side, we've got a
Hook Hand Thug:
dream. I've got a
Big Nose Thug:
dream. I've got a
Thug Chorus:
dream. I've got a dream. I've got a

F♯m7♭5 D C Dm7 G7 C
dream. I've got a
Rapunzel:
dream. I've got a dream. Yes, way down deep in - side, I've got a dream.

In Summer

from FROZEN

Music and Lyrics by Kristen Anderson-Lopez and Robert Lopez

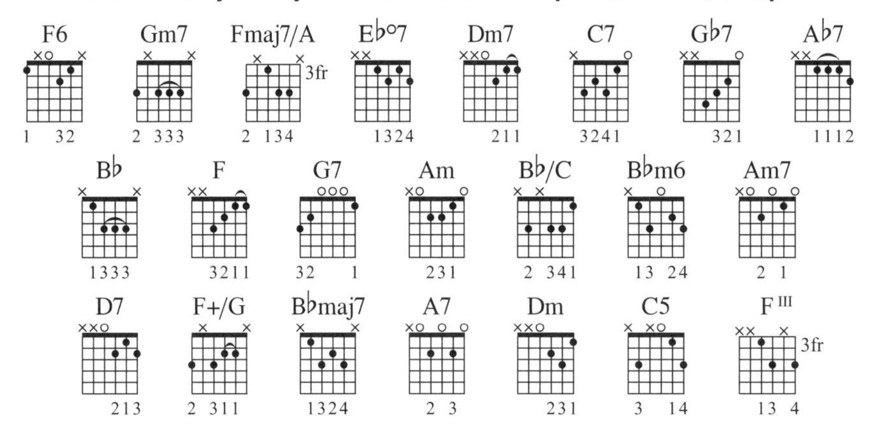

Strum Pattern: 3
Pick Pattern: 3

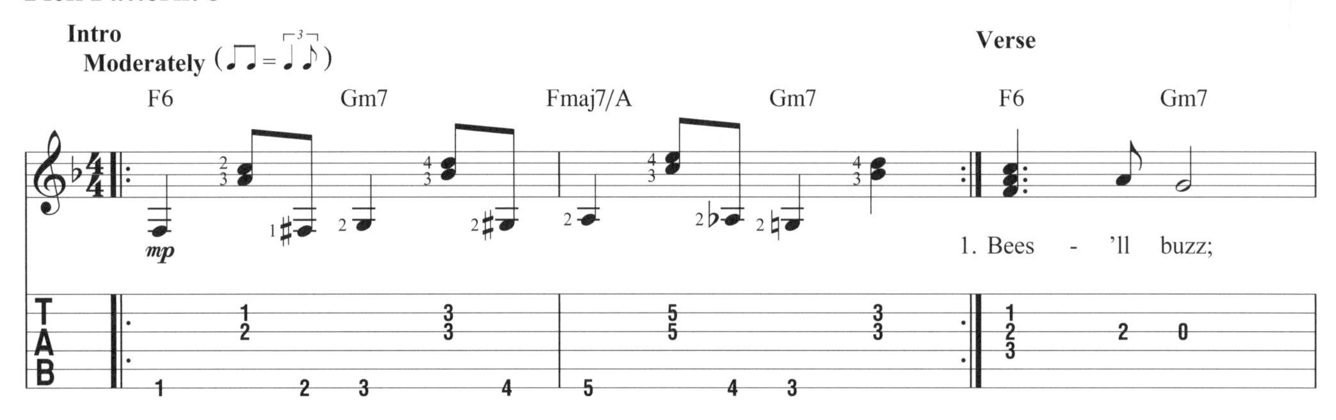

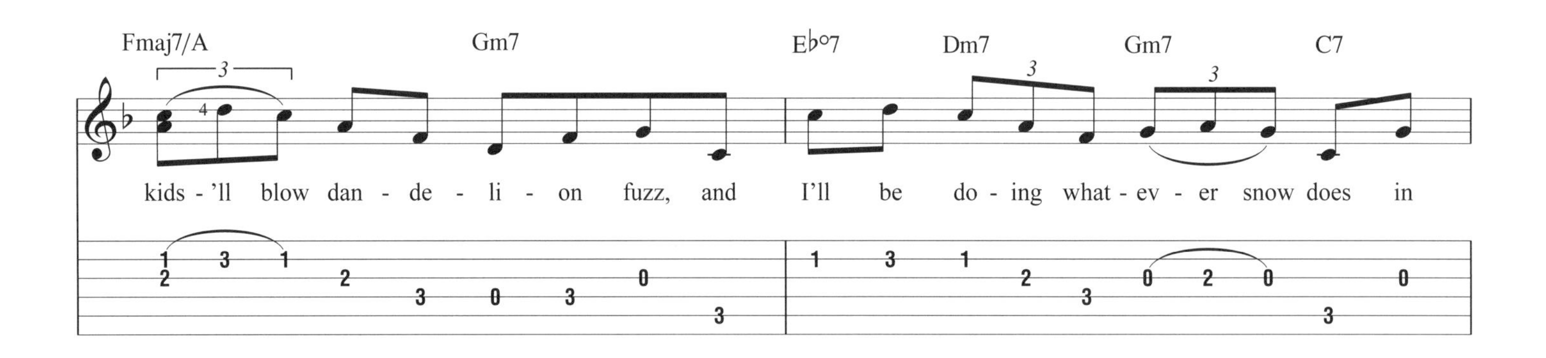

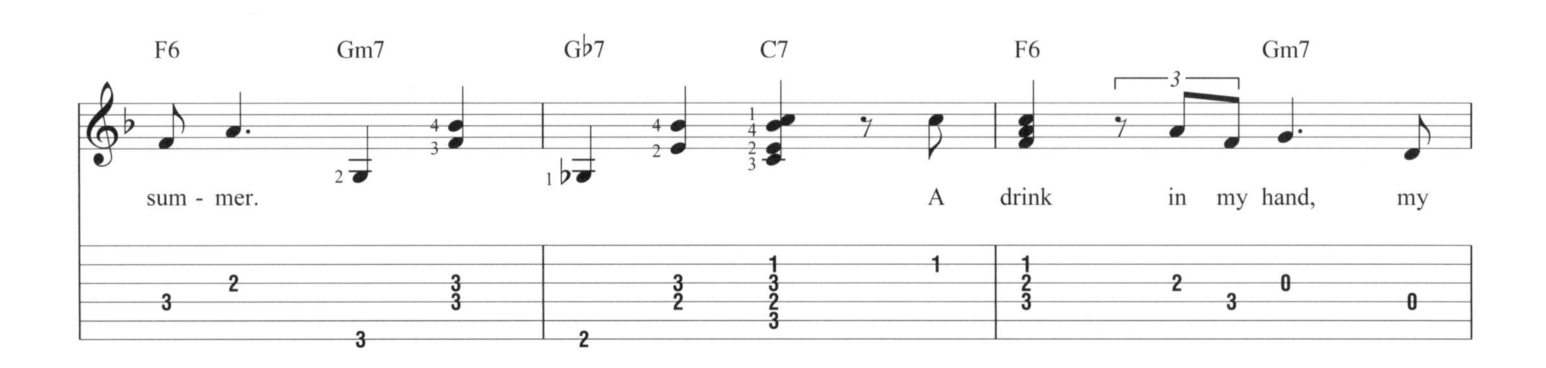

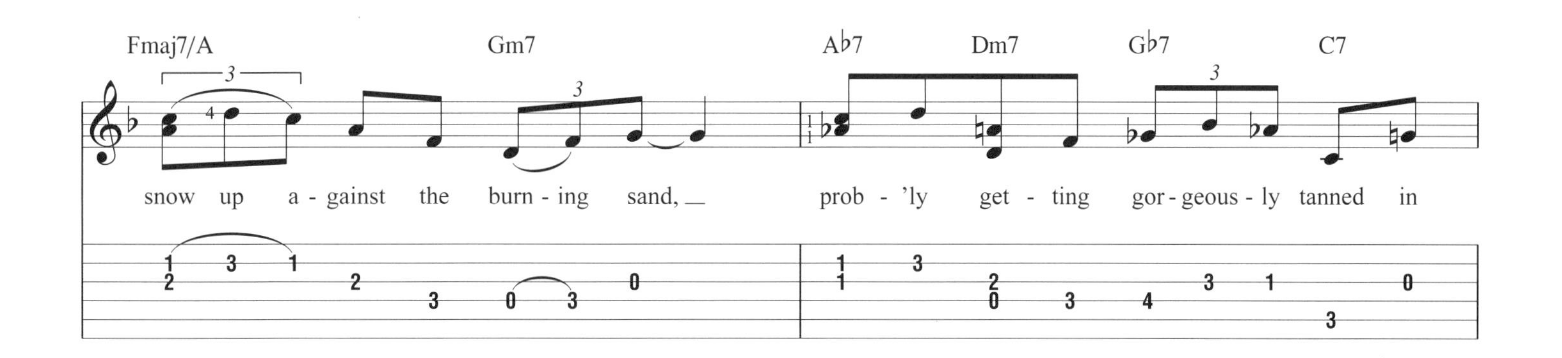
Fmaj7/A Gm7 A♭7 Dm7 G♭7 C7
snow up a - gainst the burn - ing sand, prob - 'ly get - ting gor - geous - ly tanned in

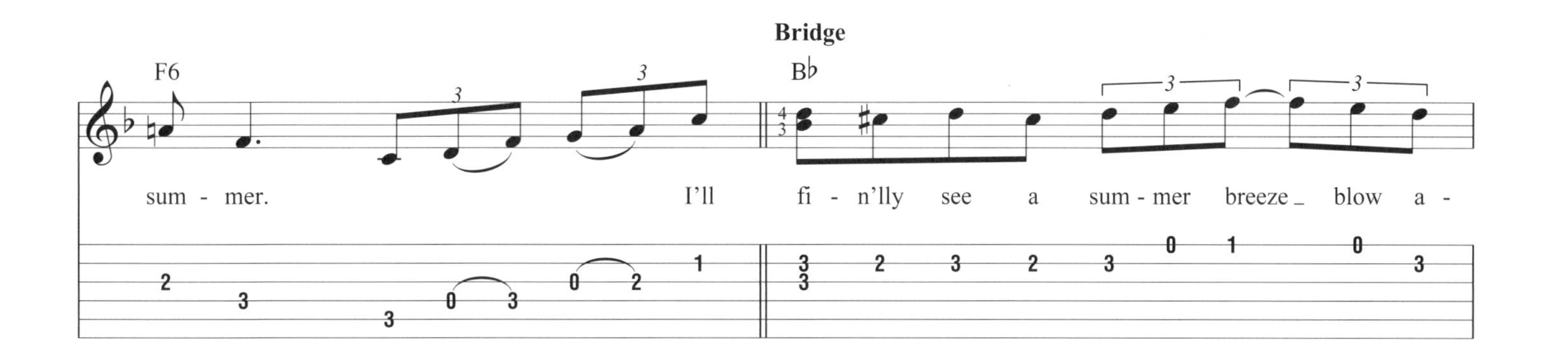
Bridge
F6 B♭
sum - mer. I'll fi - n'lly see a sum - mer breeze blow a -

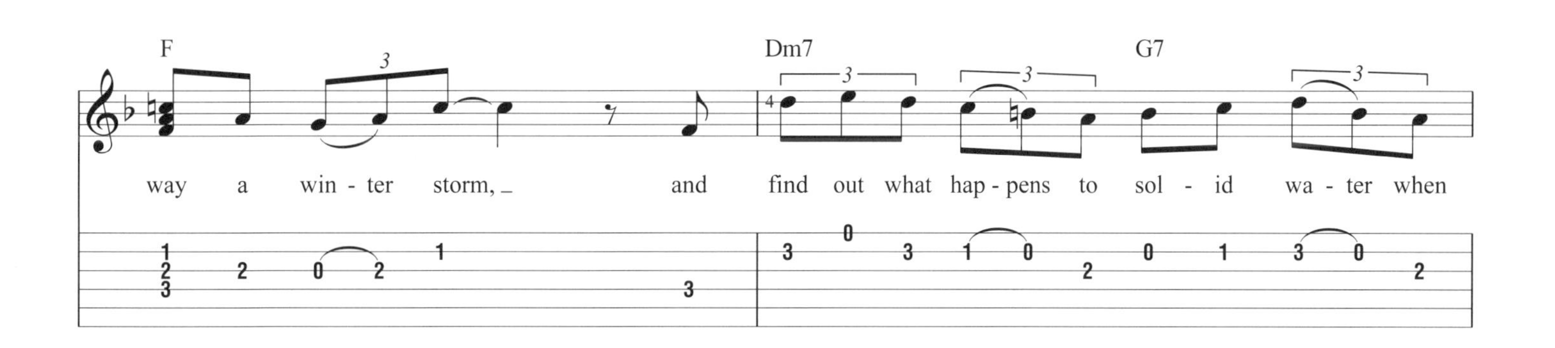
F Dm7 G7
way a win - ter storm, and find out what hap - pens to sol - id wa - ter when

Verse
B♭ Am Gm7 B♭/C F6 Gm7
it gets warm. 2. And I can't wait to see what my

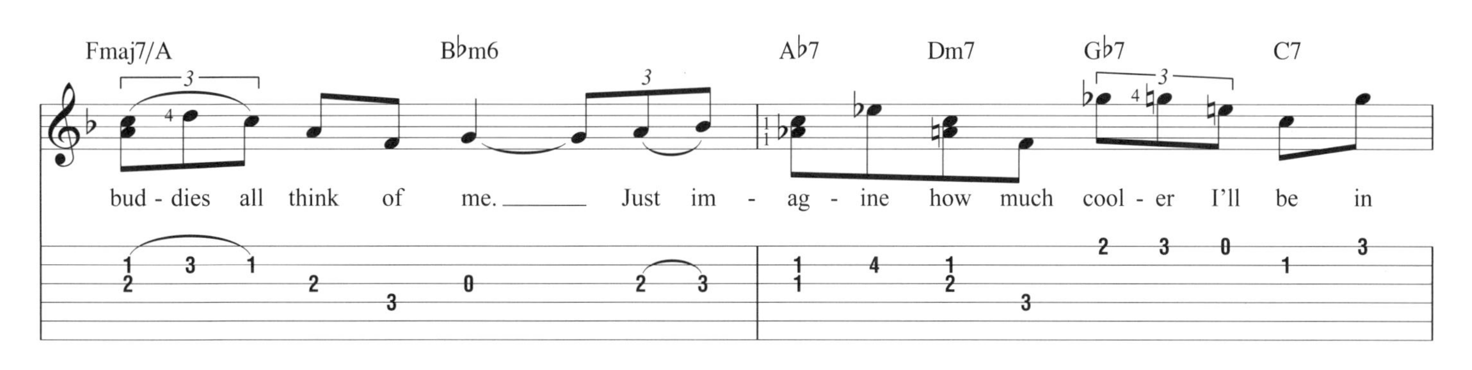
Fmaj7/A B♭m6 A♭7 Dm7 G♭7 C7
bud - dies all think of me. Just im - ag - ine how much cool - er I'll be in

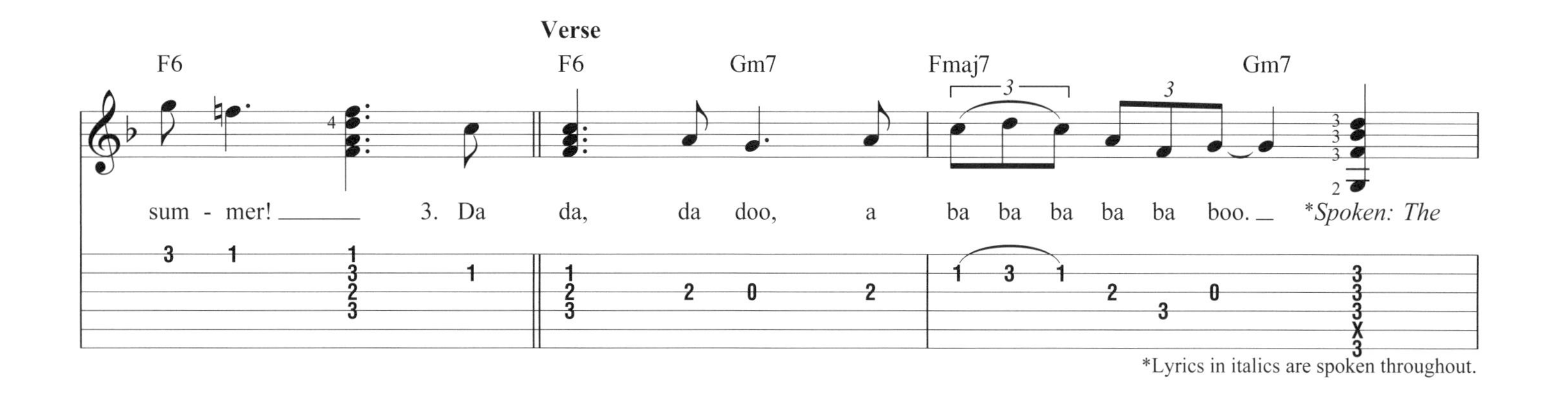

*Lyrics in italics are spoken throughout.

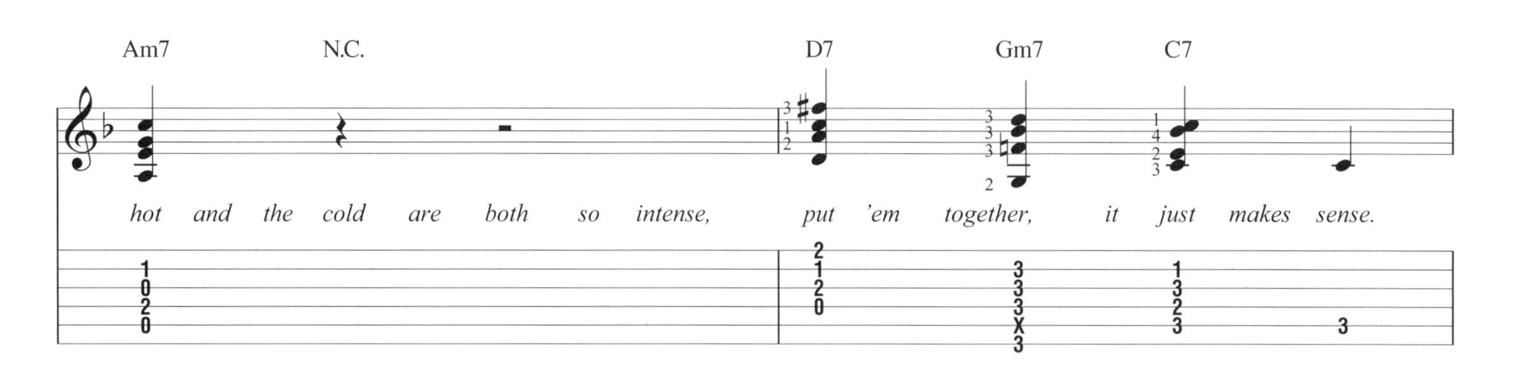

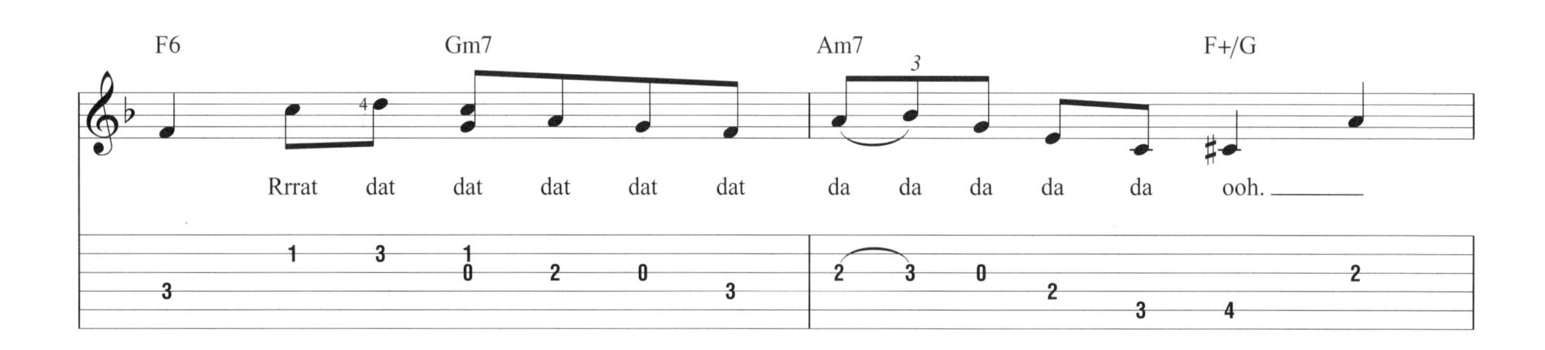

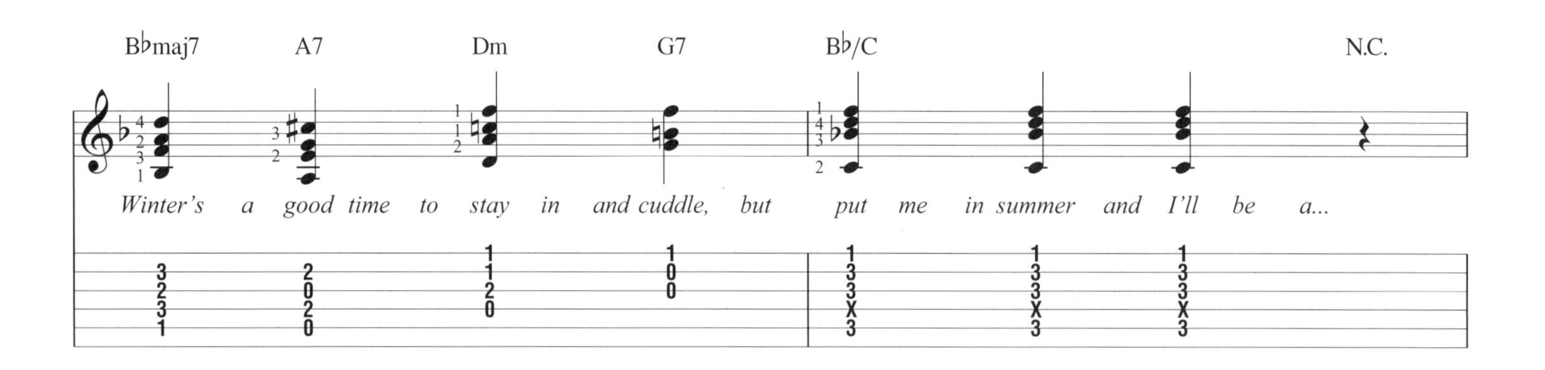

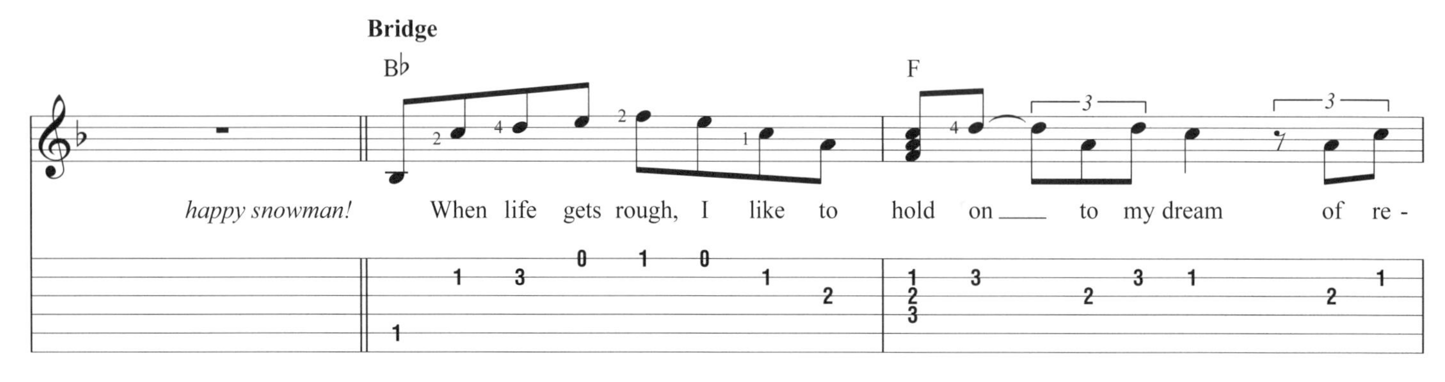

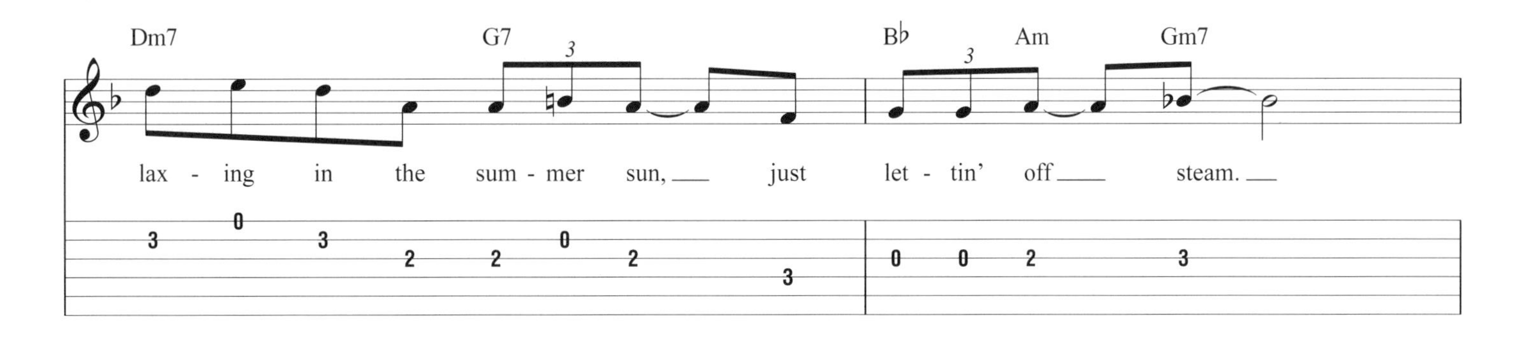
Dm7
G7
B♭
Am
Gm7
lax - ing in the sum - mer sun, just let - tin' off steam.

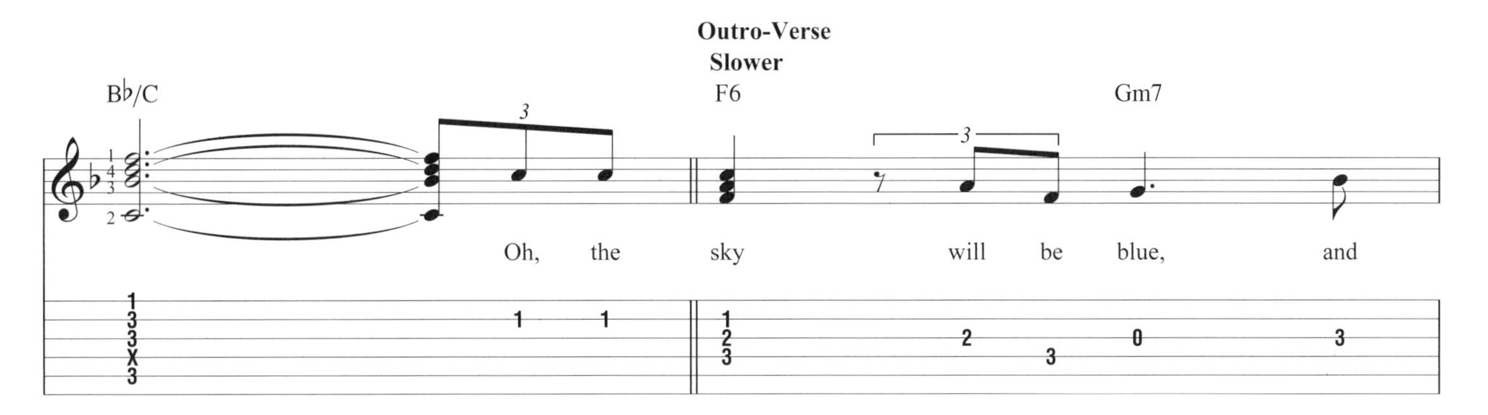
Outro-Verse
Slower
B♭/C
F6
Gm7
Oh, the sky will be blue, and

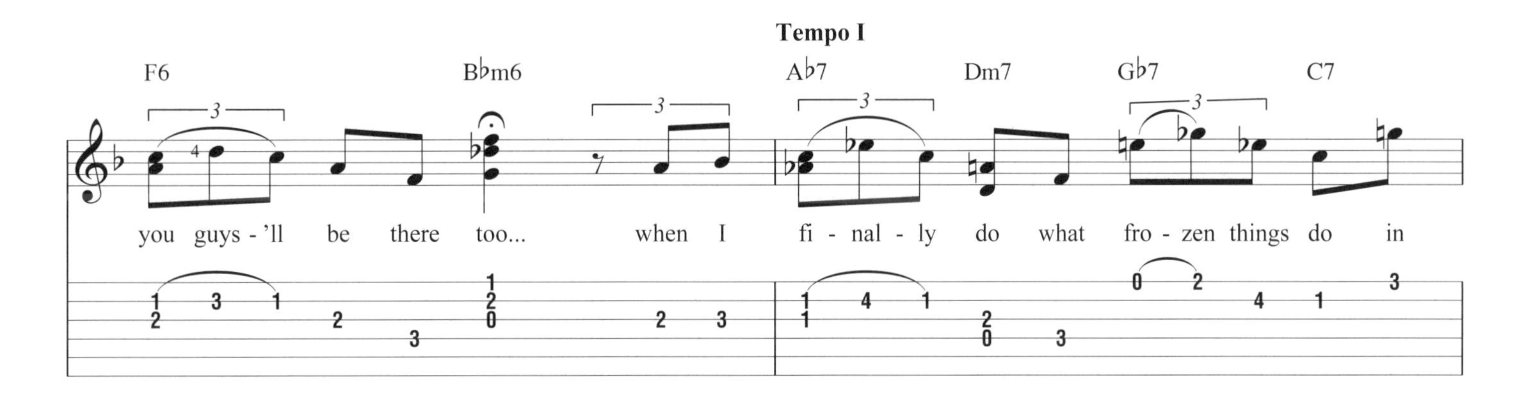
Tempo I
F6
B♭m6
A♭7
Dm7
G♭7
C7
you guys - 'll be there too... when I fi - nal - ly do what fro - zen things do in

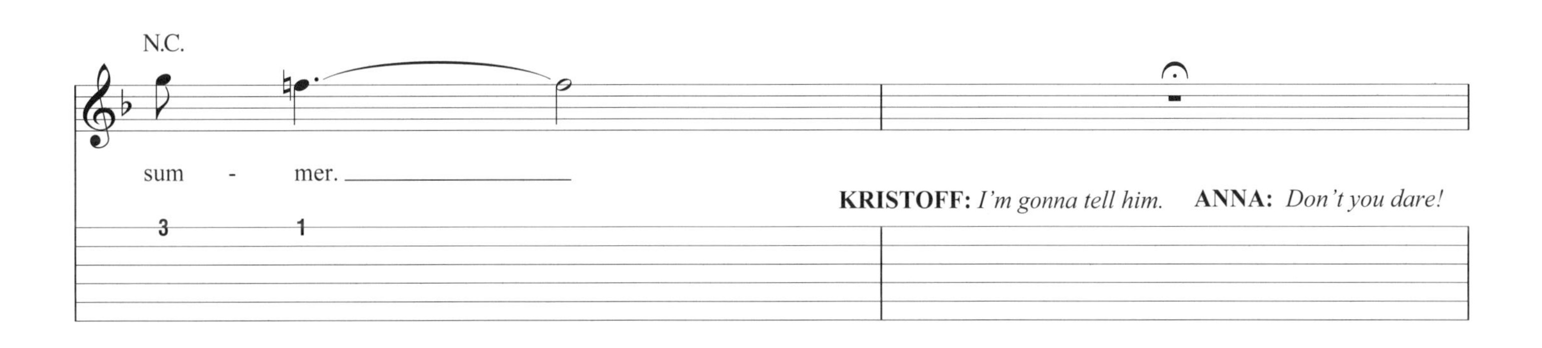
N.C.
sum - mer.
KRISTOFF: I'm gonna tell him. ANNA: Don't you dare!

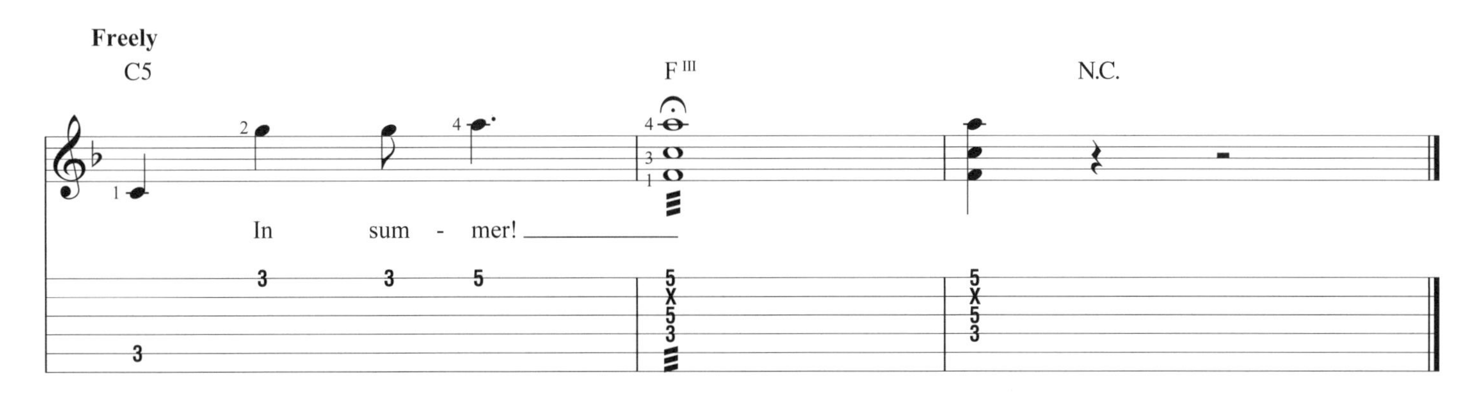
Freely
C5
F III
N.C.
In sum - mer!

An Innocent Warrior

from MOANA

By Opetaia Foa'i

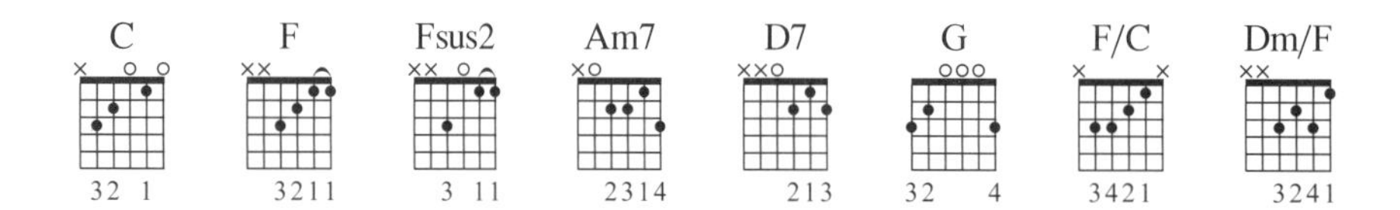

*Capo II

Strum Pattern: 4
Pick Pattern: 4

*Optional: To match recording, place capo at 2nd fret.

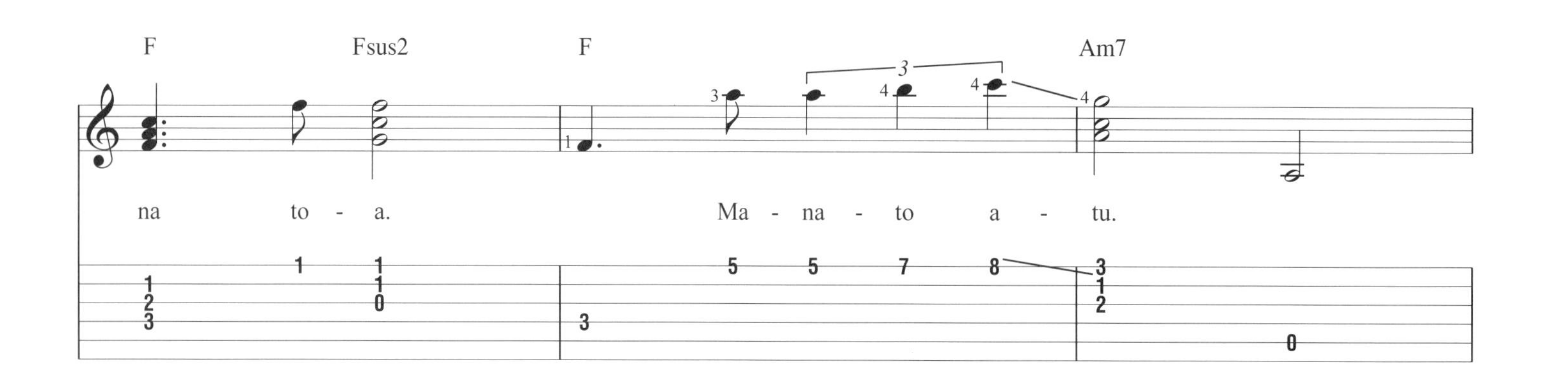

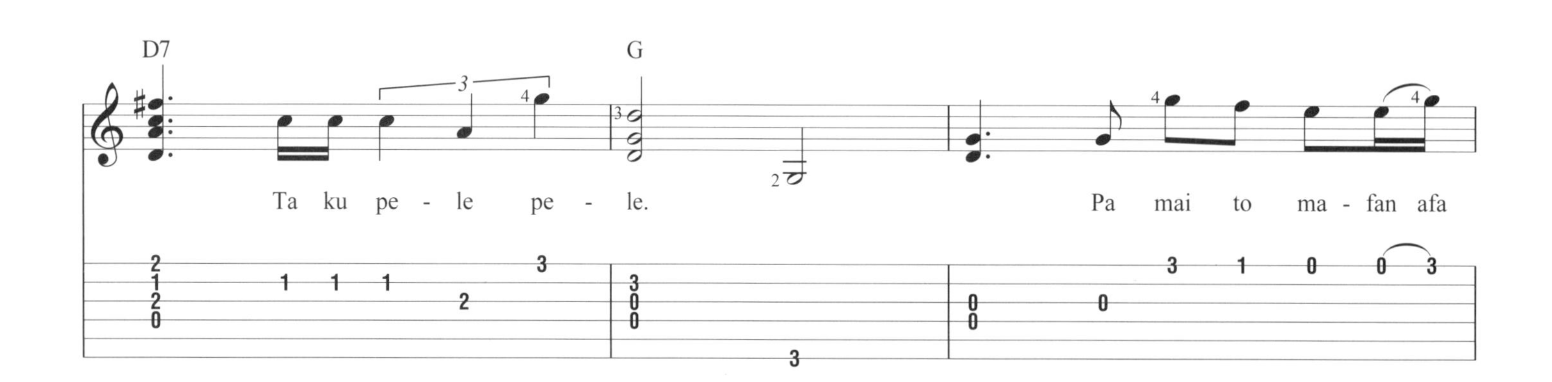

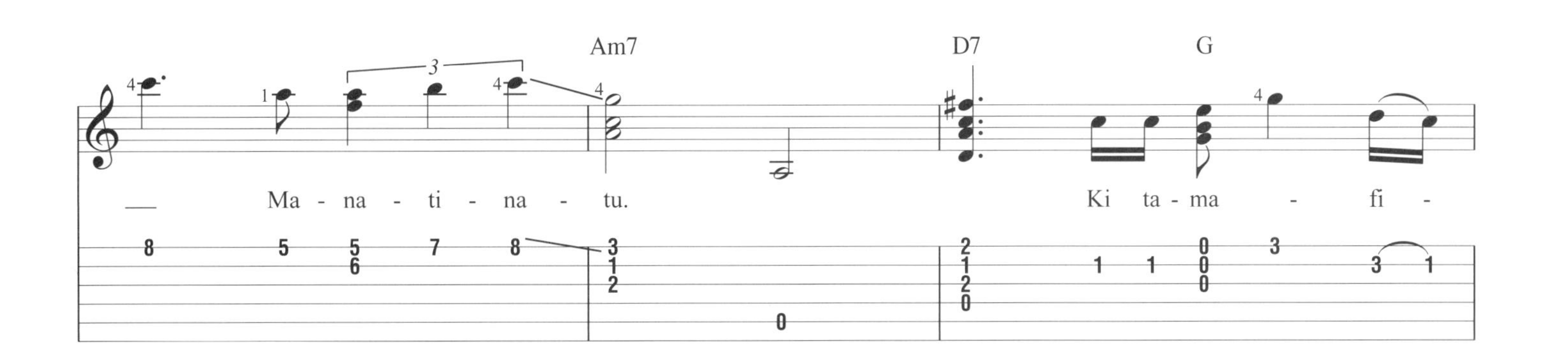

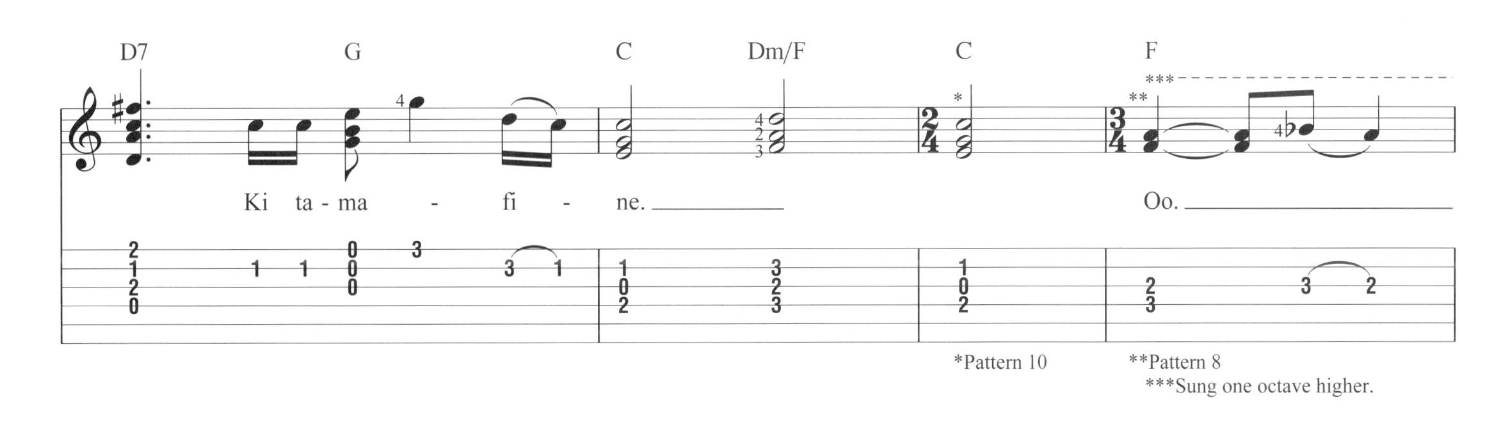

*Pattern 10

**Pattern 8

***Sung one octave higher.

Just Around the Riverbend

from POCAHONTAS

Music by Alan Menken
Lyrics by Stephen Schwartz

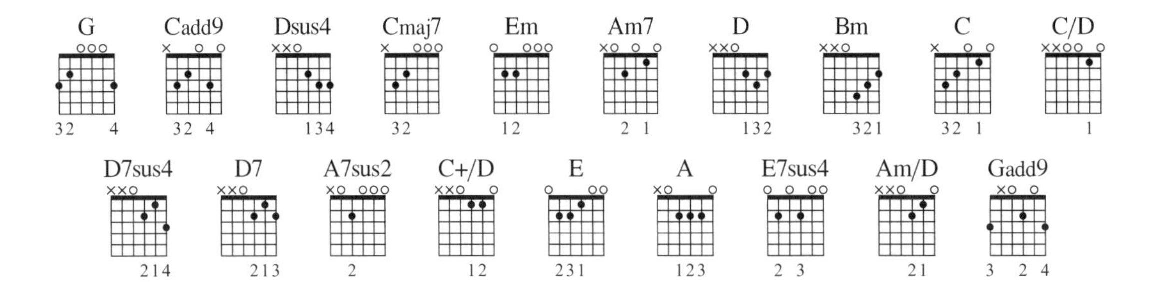

*Capo V

Strum Pattern: 4
Pick Pattern: 3

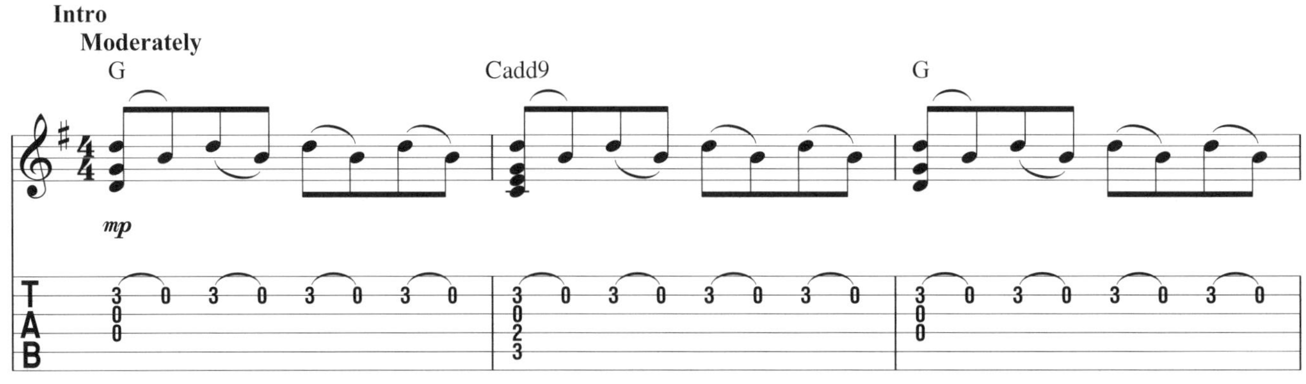

*Optional: To match recording, place capo at 5th fret.

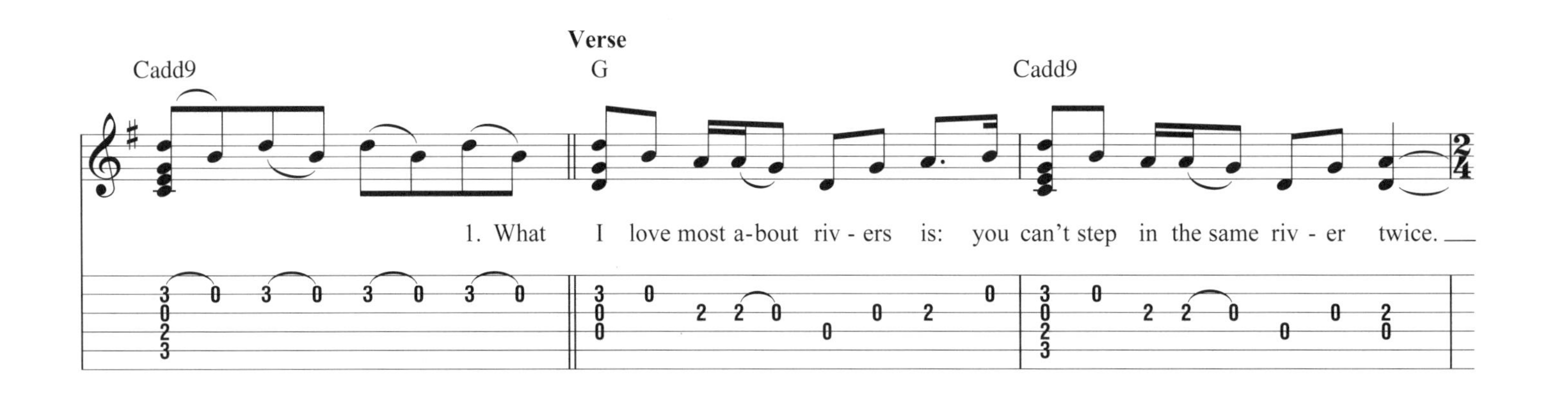

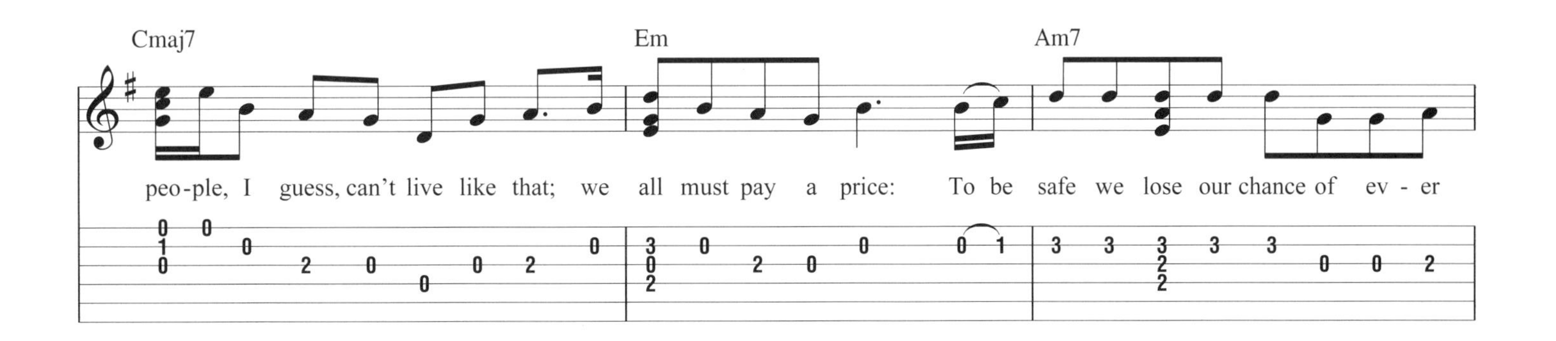
Cmaj7 Em Am7
peo-ple, I guess, can't live like that; we all must pay a price: To be safe we lose our chance of ev - er

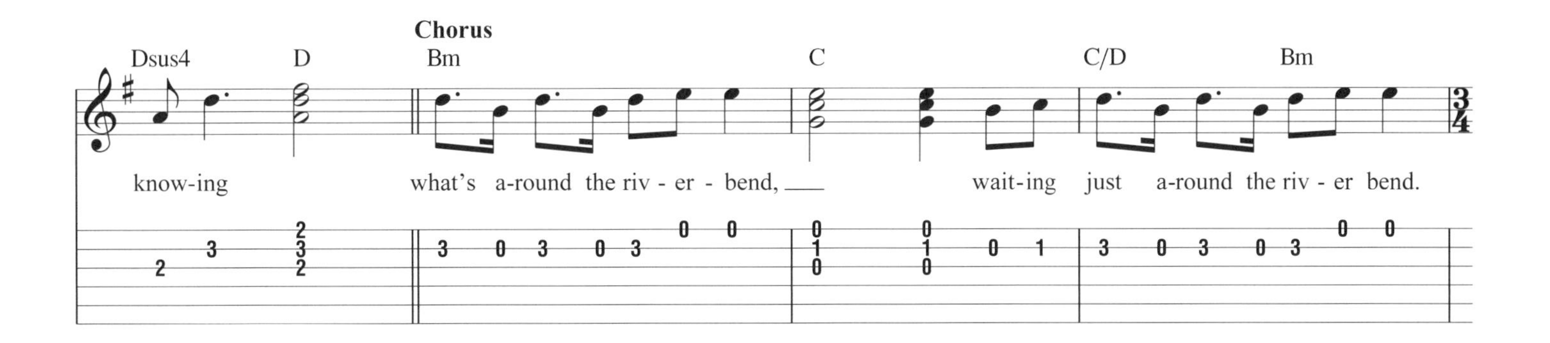
Chorus
Dsus4 D Bm C C/D Bm
know-ing what's a-round the riv - er - bend, wait-ing just a-round the riv - er bend.

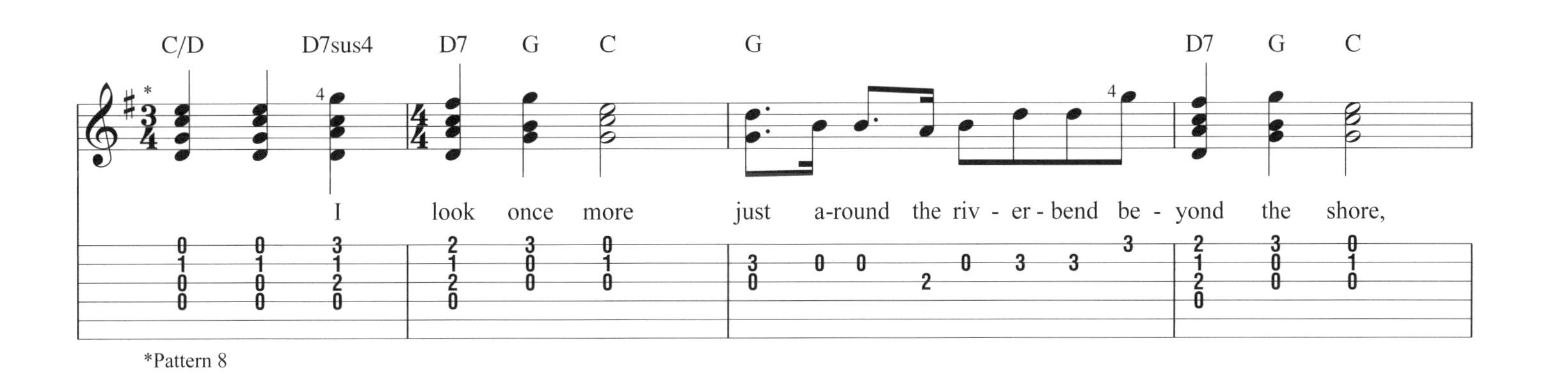
C/D D7sus4 D7 G C G D7 G C
I look once more just a-round the riv - er - bend be - yond the shore,
*Pattern 8

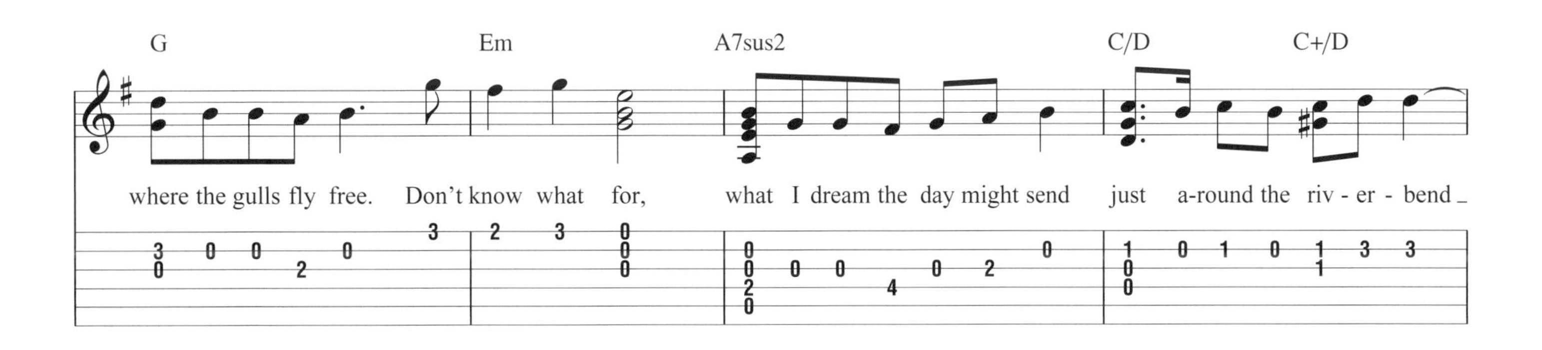
G Em A7sus2 C/D C+/D
where the gulls fly free. Don't know what for, what I dream the day might send just a-round the riv - er - bend

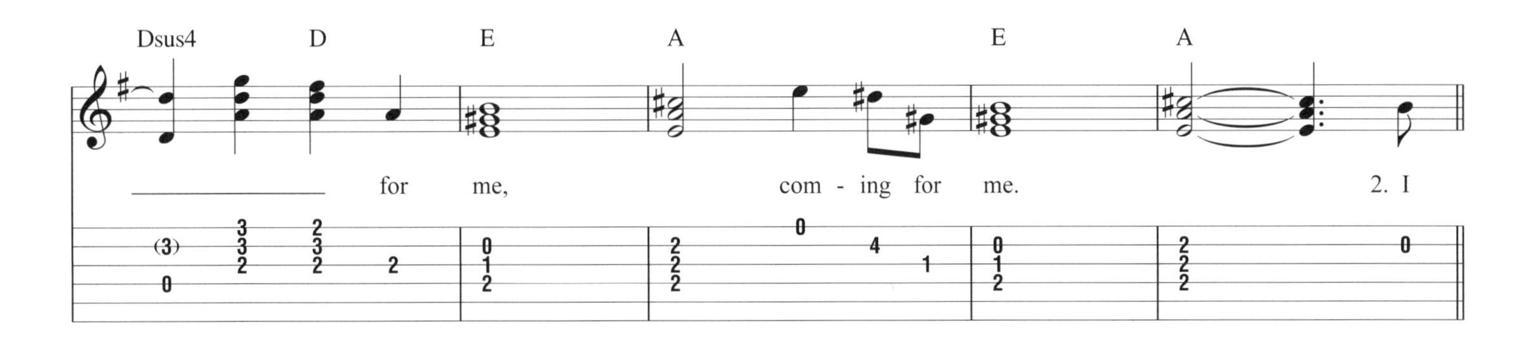
Dsus4 D E A E A
for me, com - ing for me. 2. I

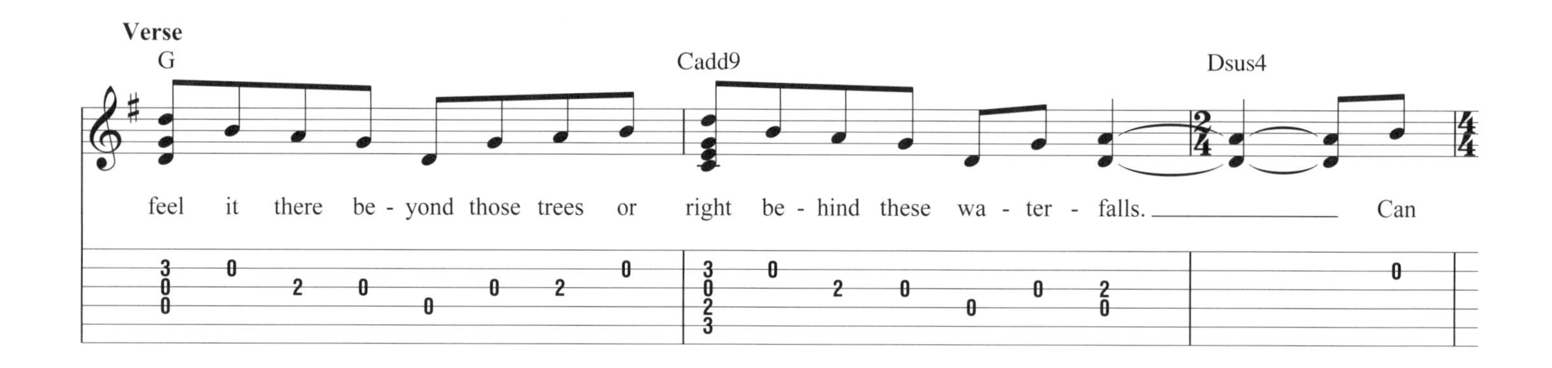
Verse
G
Cadd9
Dsus4
feel it there be - yond those trees or right be - hind these wa - ter - falls. Can

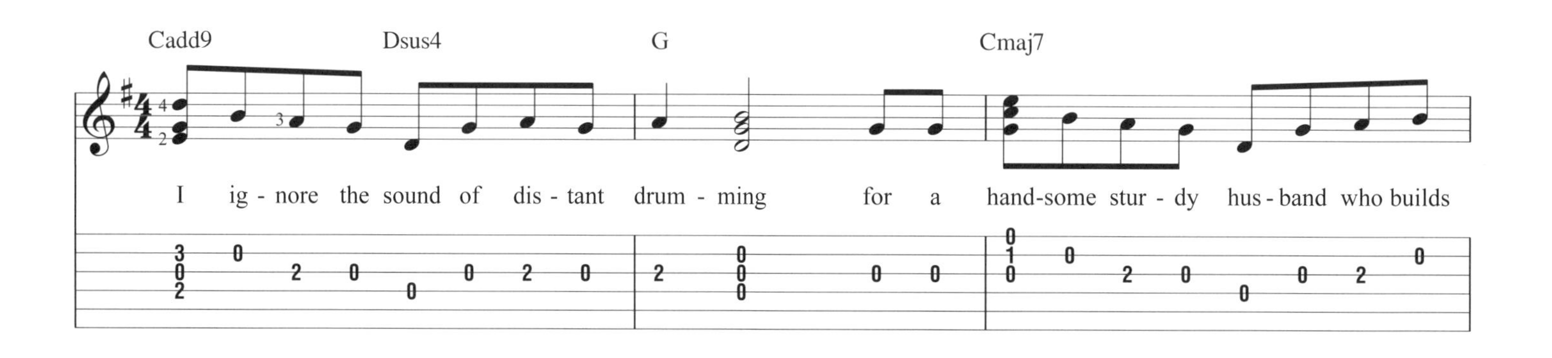
Cadd9
Dsus4
G
Cmaj7
I ig - nore the sound of dis - tant drum - ming for a hand-some stur - dy hus - band who builds

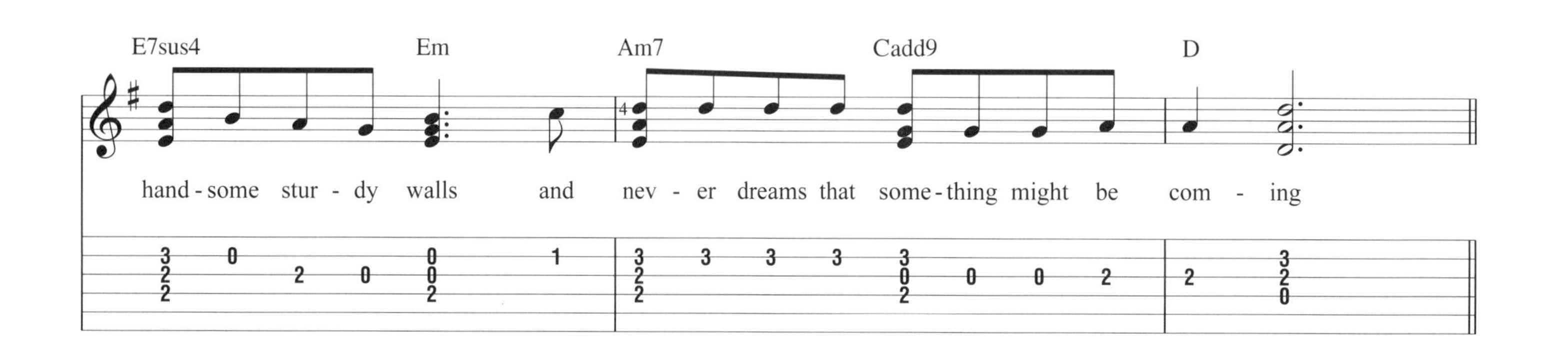
E7sus4
Em
Am7
Cadd9
D
hand - some stur - dy walls and nev - er dreams that some - thing might be com - ing

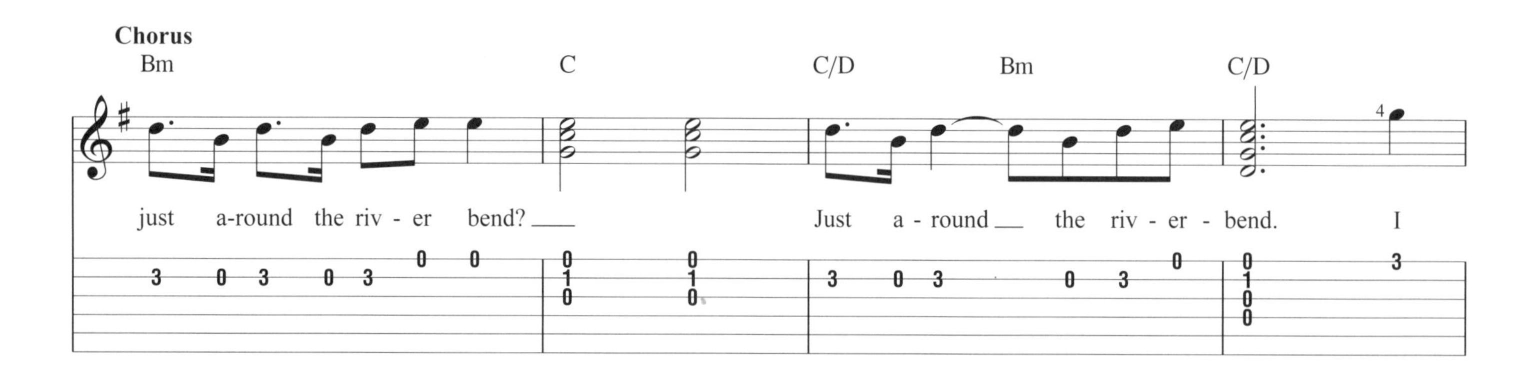
Chorus
Bm
C
C/D
Bm
C/D
just a-round the riv - er bend? Just a - round the riv - er - bend. I

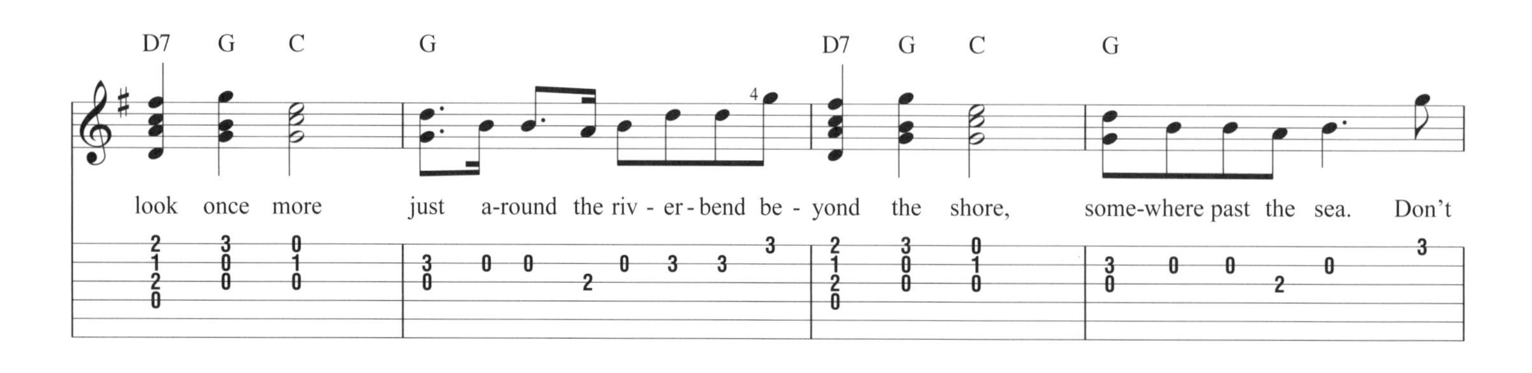
D7
G
C
G
D7
G
C
G
look once more just a-round the riv - er - bend be - yond the shore, some-where past the sea. Don't

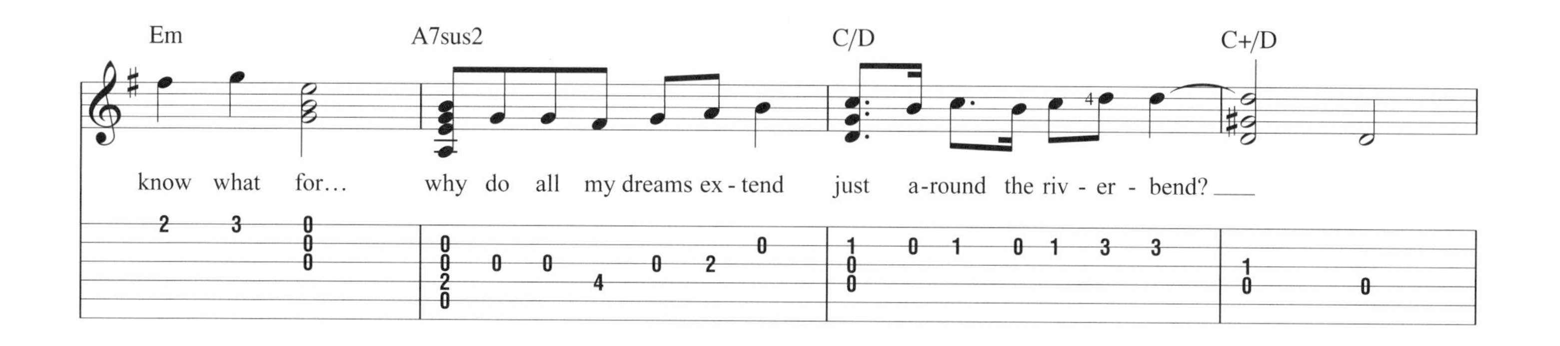
Em
A7sus2
C/D
C+/D
know what for… why do all my dreams ex - tend just a-round the riv - er - bend?

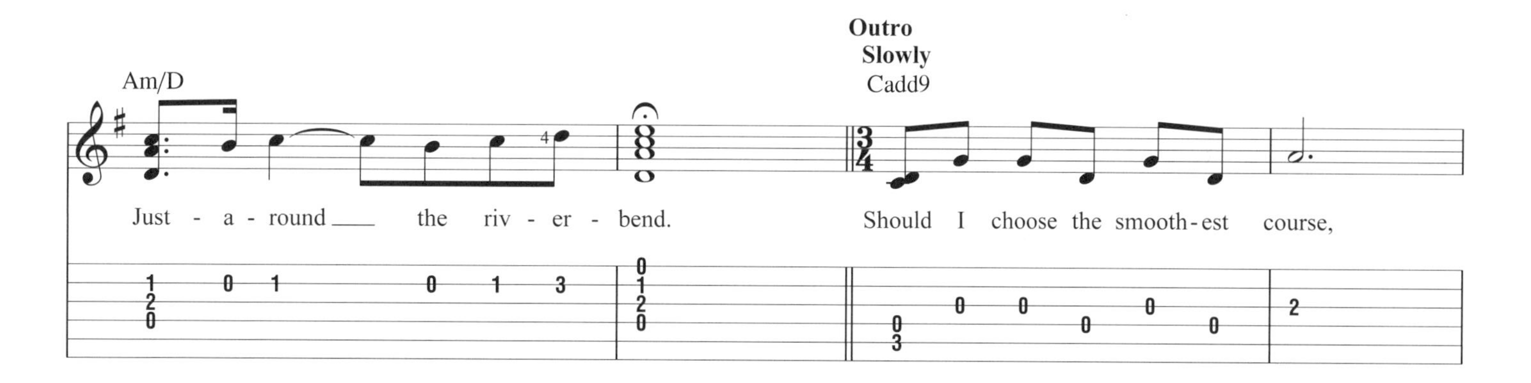
Am/D
Outro
Slowly
Cadd9
Just - a - round the riv - er - bend. Should I choose the smooth-est course,

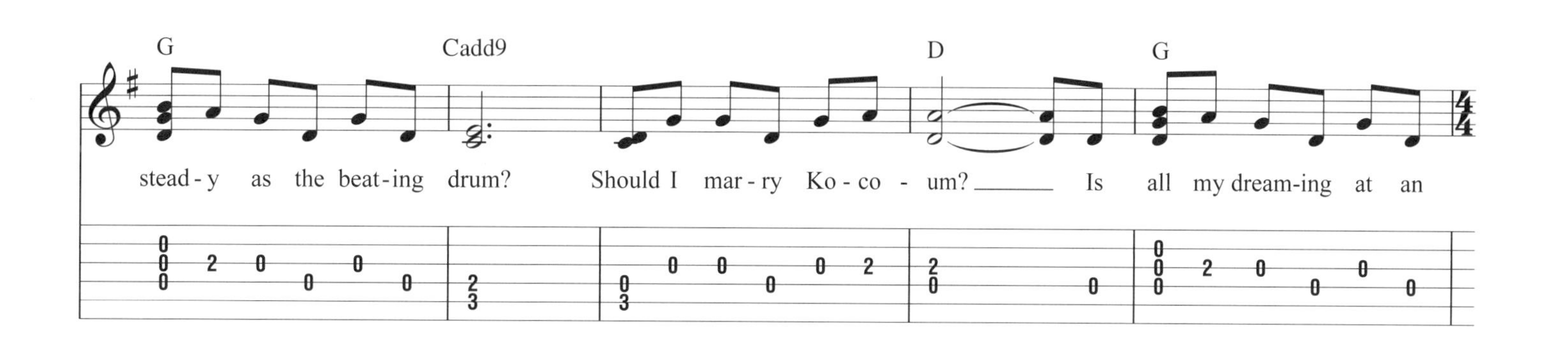
G
Cadd9
D
G
stead - y as the beat-ing drum? Should I mar - ry Ko - co - um? Is all my dream-ing at an

Cadd9
E7sus4
Em
E7sus4
Em
Am7
end? Or do you still wait for me, Dream Giv - er just a - round the

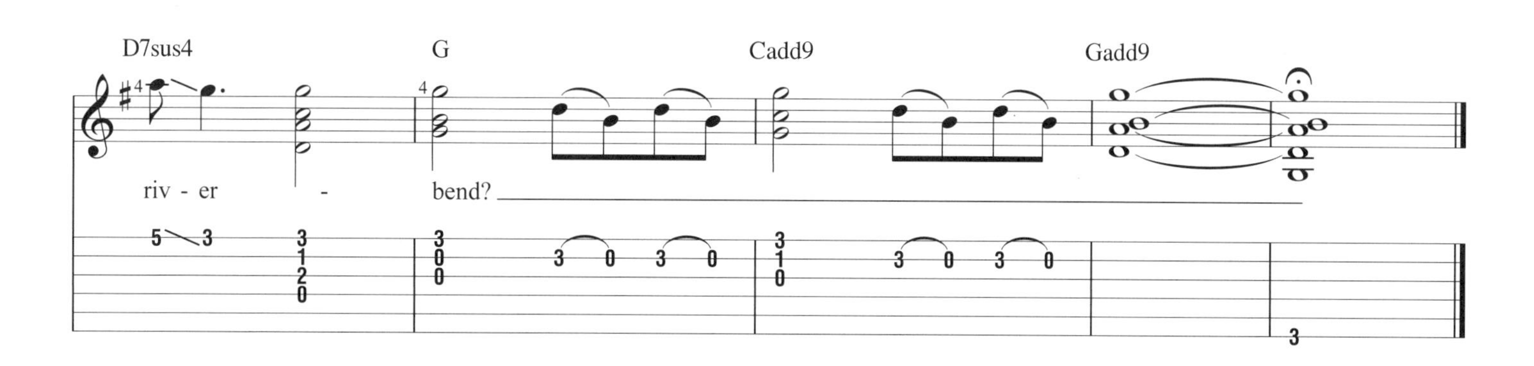
D7sus4
G
Cadd9
Gadd9
riv - er - bend?

Kiss the Girl

from THE LITTLE MERMAID

Music by Alan Menken
Lyrics by Howard Ashman

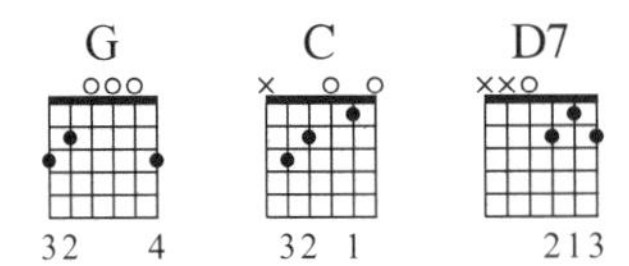

*Capo V

Strum Pattern: 6
Pick Pattern: 4

Verse
Moderately fast

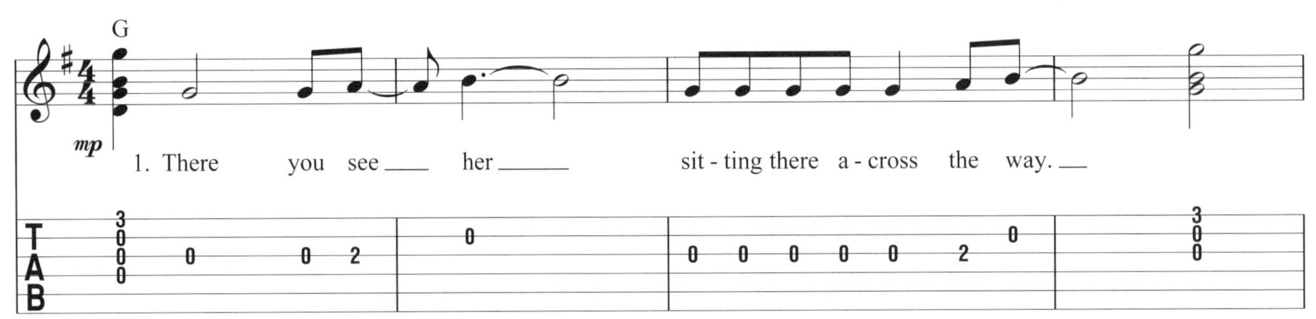

*Optional: To match recording, place capo at 5th fret.

Verse
G
2. Yes, you want her. Look at her, you know you do.

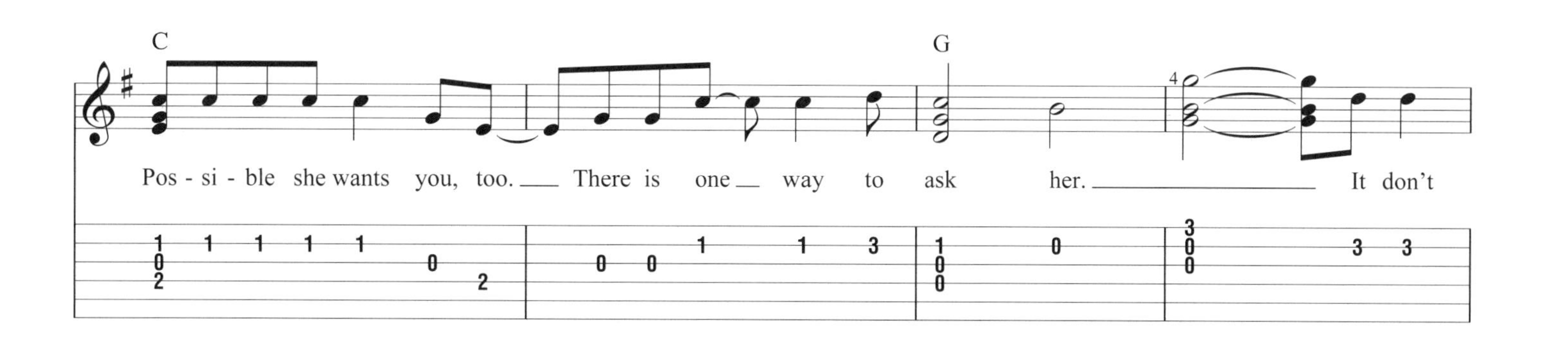
C
G
Pos - si - ble she wants you, too. There is one way to ask her. It don't

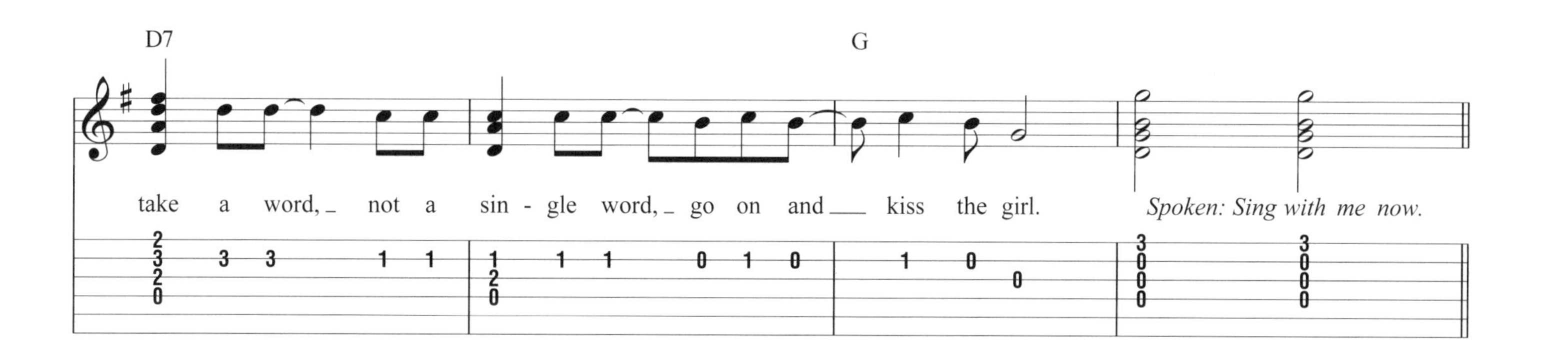
D7
G
take a word, not a sin - gle word, go on and kiss the girl.
Spoken: Sing with me now.

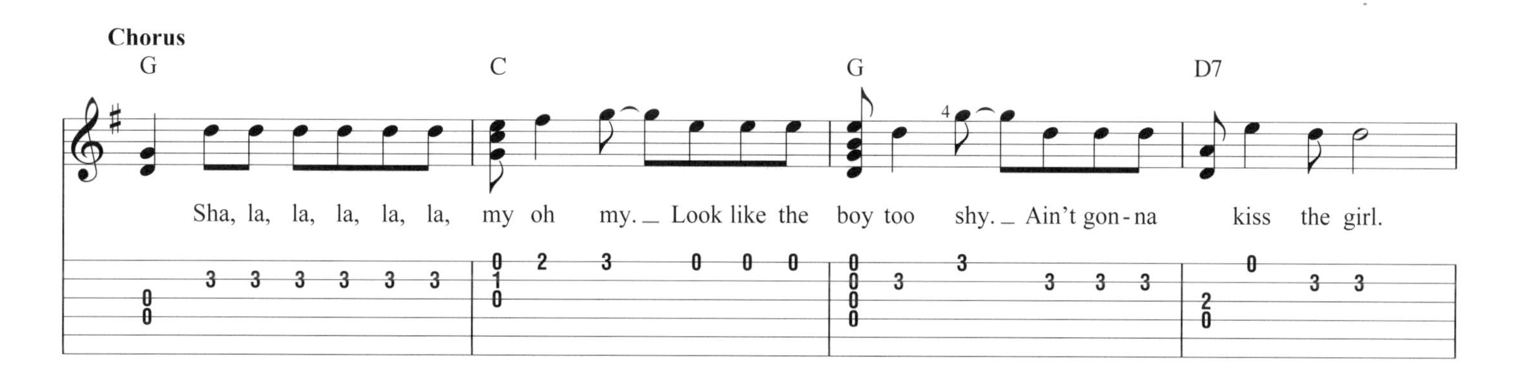
Chorus
G
C
G
D7
Sha, la, la, la, la, la, my oh my. Look like the boy too shy. Ain't gon - na kiss the girl.

G
C
D7
G
Sha, la, la, la, la, la, ain't that sad. Ain't it a shame, too bad. He gon - na miss the girl.

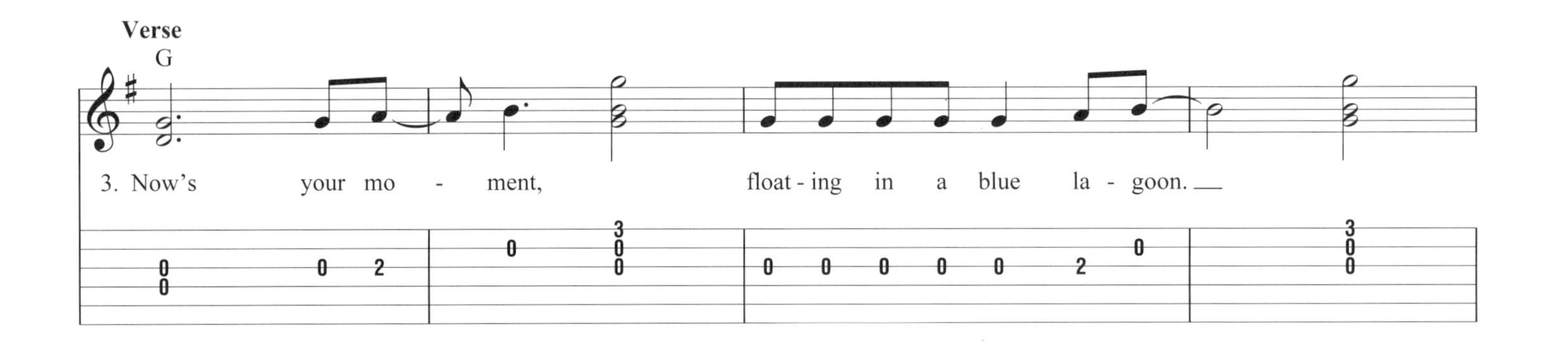
Verse
G
3. Now's your mo - ment, float - ing in a blue la - goon.

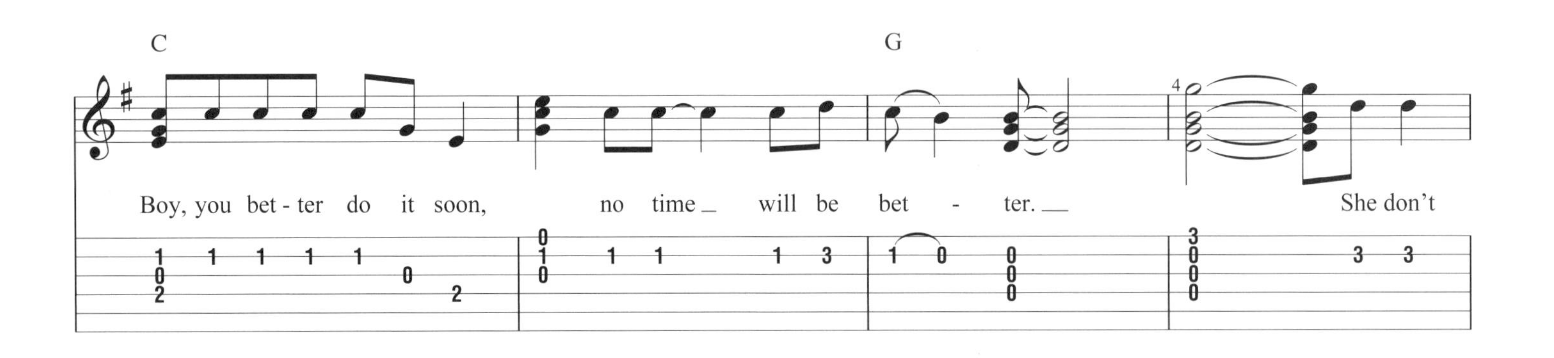
C
G
Boy, you bet - ter do it soon, no time will be bet - ter. She don't

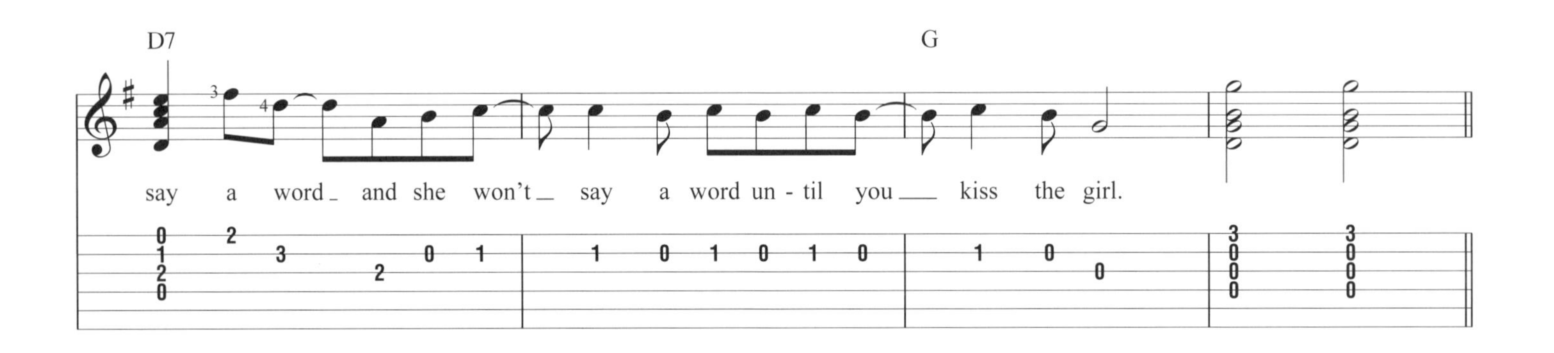
D7
G
say a word and she won't say a word un - til you kiss the girl.

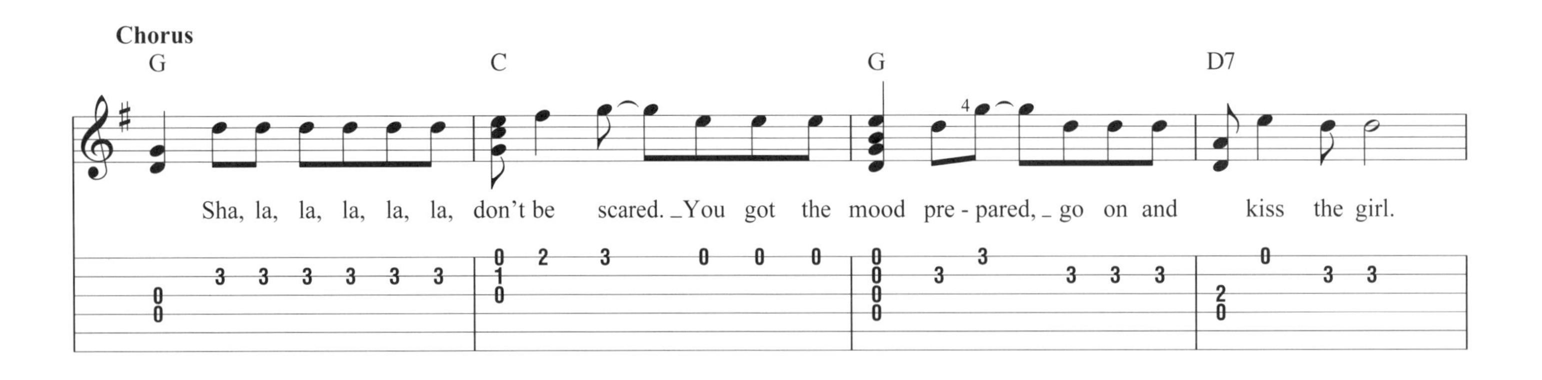
Chorus
G
C
G
D7
Sha, la, la, la, la, la, don't be scared. You got the mood pre - pared, go on and kiss the girl.

G
C
D7
G
Sha, la, la, la, la, la, don't stop now. Don't try to hide it how you wan-na kiss the girl.

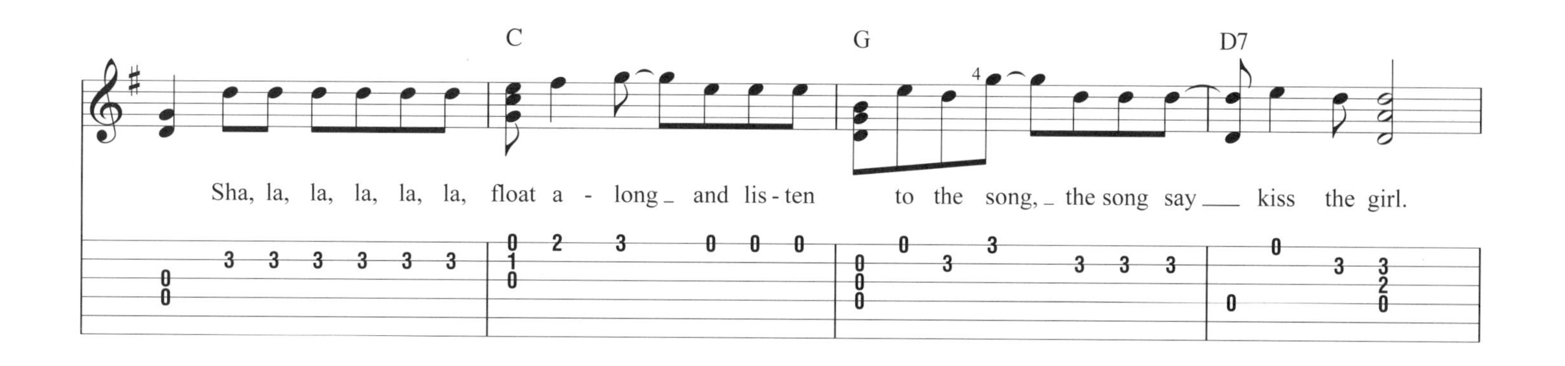
C
G
D7
Sha, la, la, la, la, la, float a - long and lis - ten to the song, the song say kiss the girl.

G
C
D7
G
Sha, la, la, la, la, la, mu - sic play. Do what the mu - sic say. You got - ta kiss the girl.

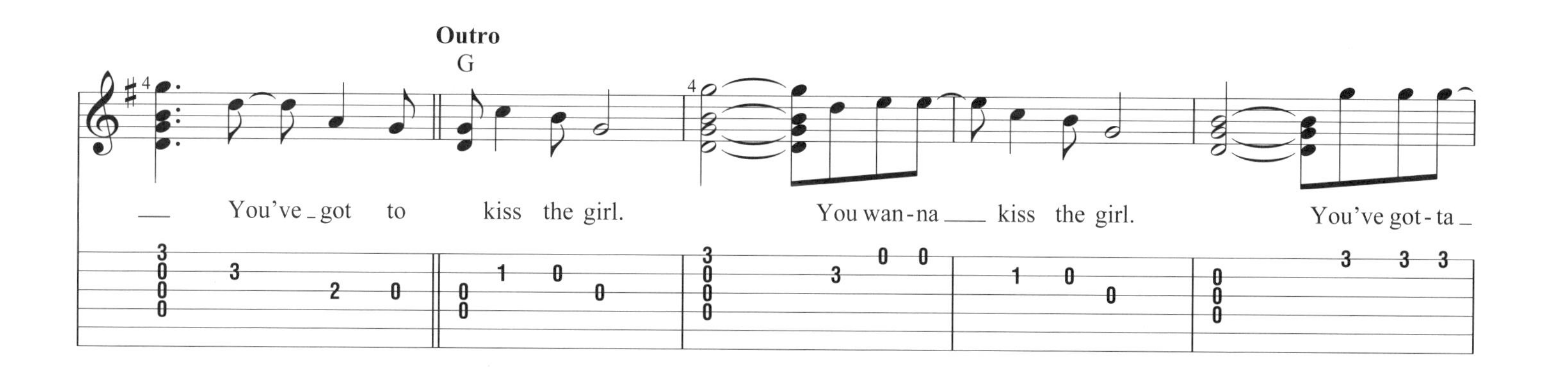
Outro
G
You've got to kiss the girl. You wan - na kiss the girl. You've got - ta

N.C.
kiss the girl. Go on and kiss the girl.

Let It Go

from FROZEN

Music and Lyrics by Kristen Anderson-Lopez and Robert Lopez

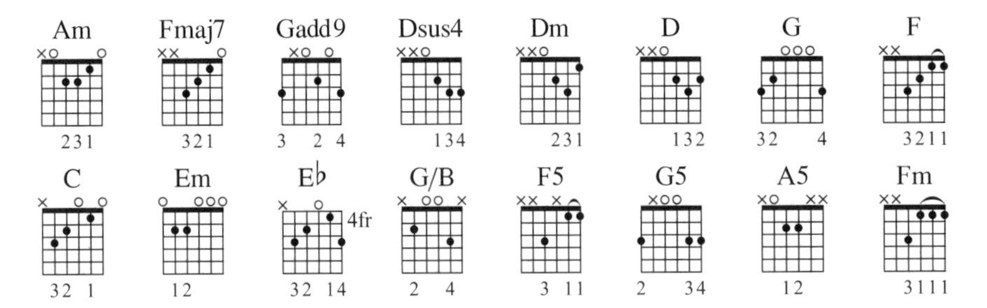

*Capo VIII

Strum Pattern: 3
Pick Pattern: 5

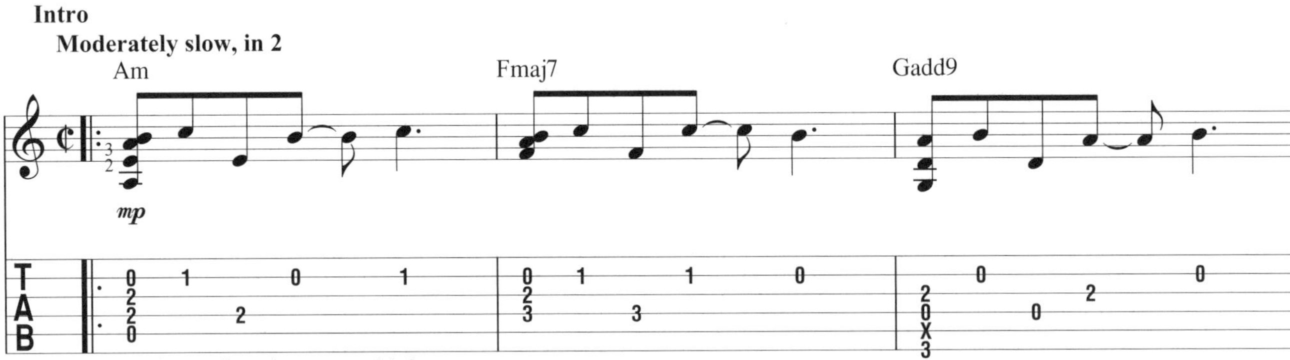

*Optional: To match recording, place capo at 8th fret.

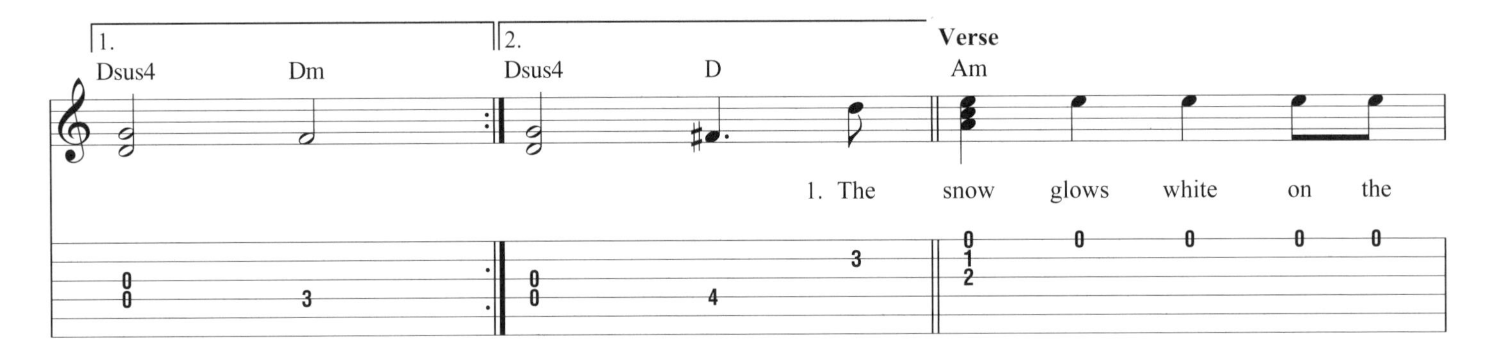

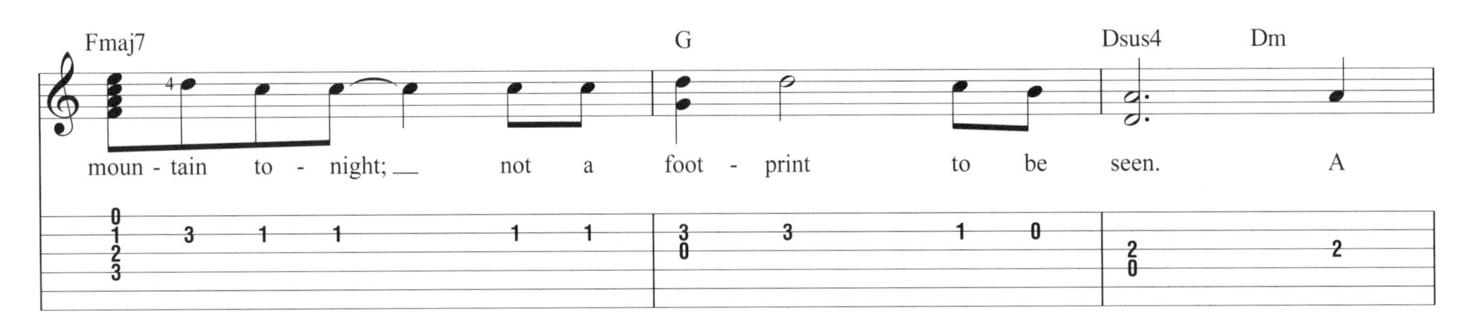

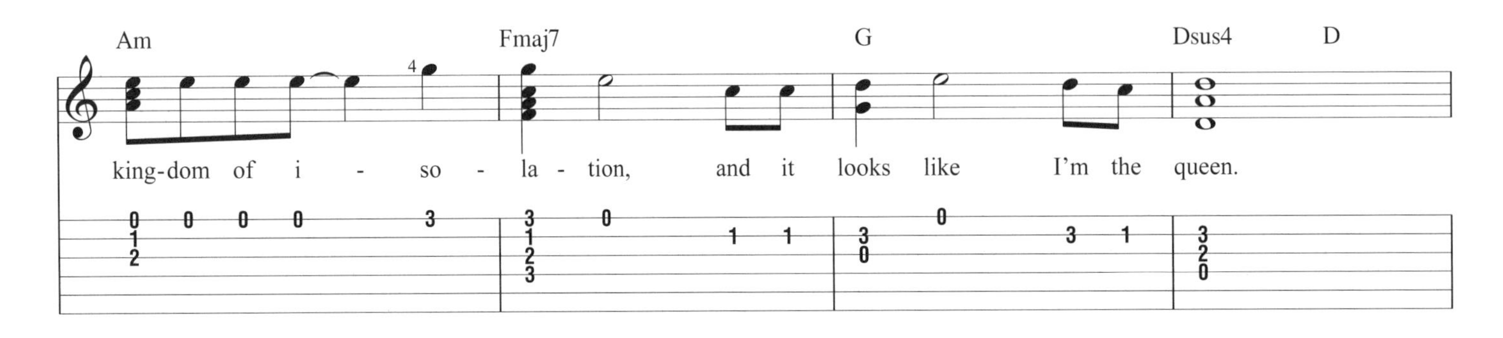

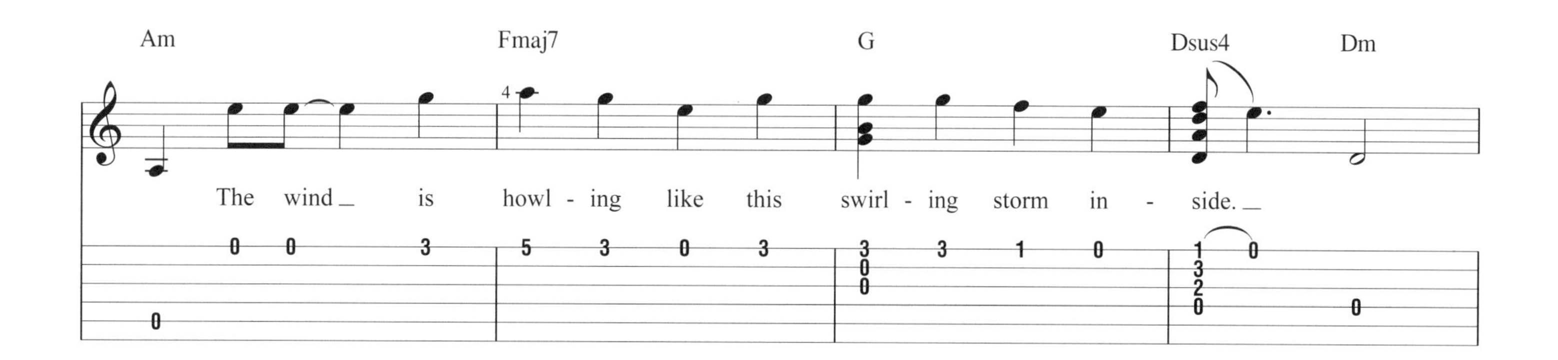
Am Fmaj7 G Dsus4 Dm
The wind _ is howl - ing like this swirl - ing storm in - side. _

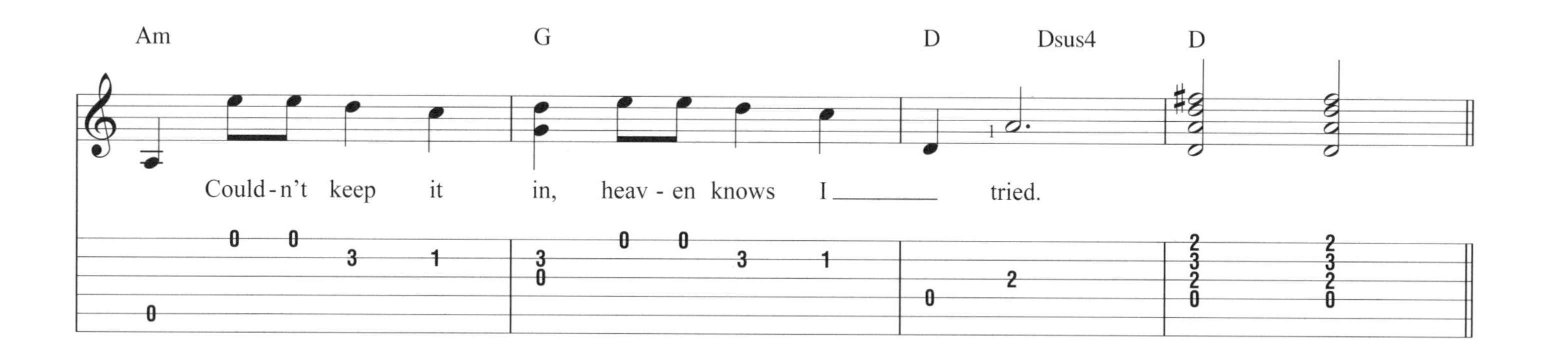
Am G D Dsus4 D
Could - n't keep it in, heav - en knows I ________ tried.

Pre-Chorus
G F
Don't let ___ them in, don't let them see; be the good girl you
*Sung one octave higher.

G
al - ways have ___ to be. Con - ceal, ___ don't feel, don't let ____ them

F
know... Well, now ___ they know. _________ Let it

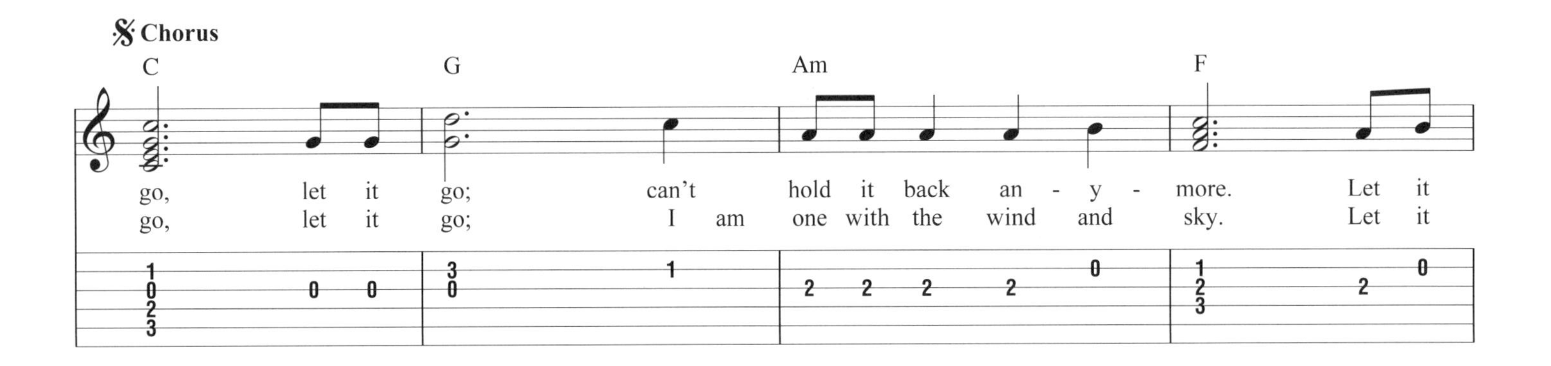

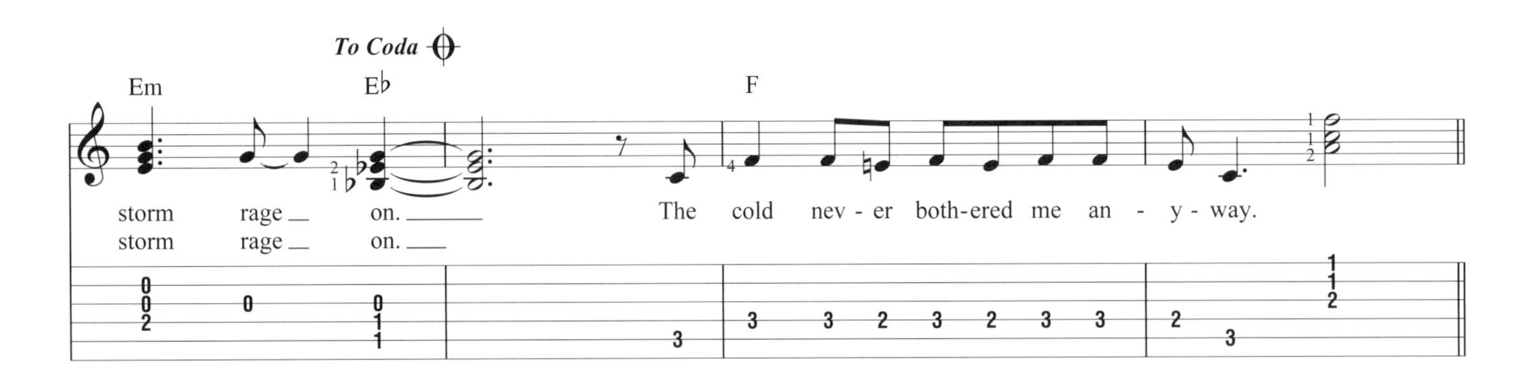

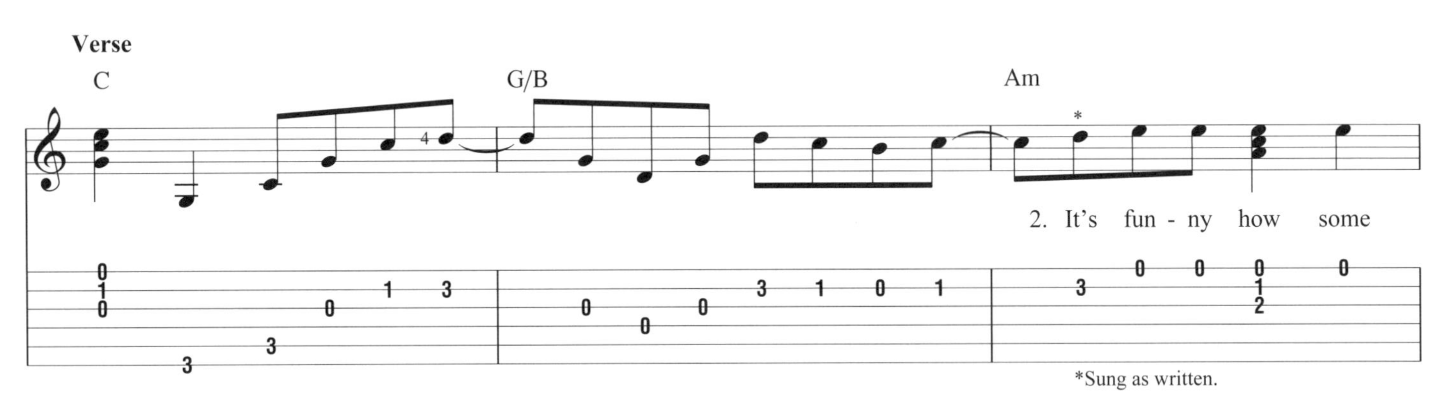

*Sung as written.

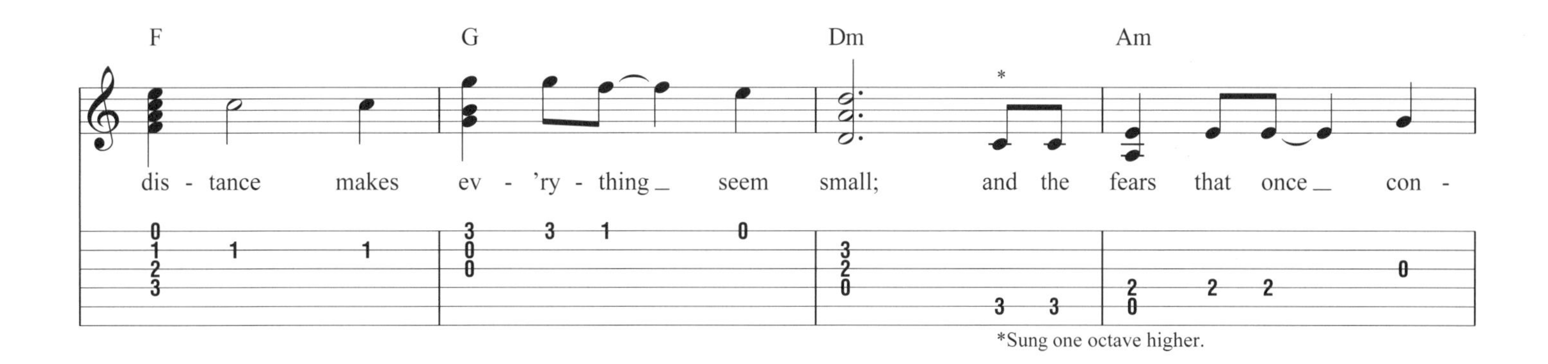
F G Dm Am
dis - tance makes ev - 'ry - thing seem small; and the fears that once con -
*Sung one octave higher.

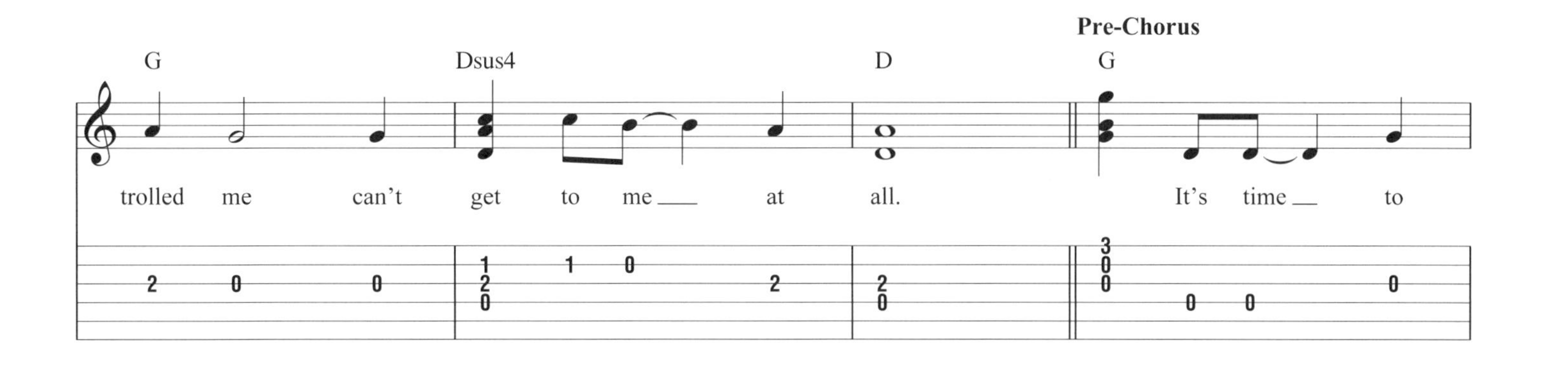
Pre-Chorus
G Dsus4 D G
trolled me can't get to me at all. It's time to

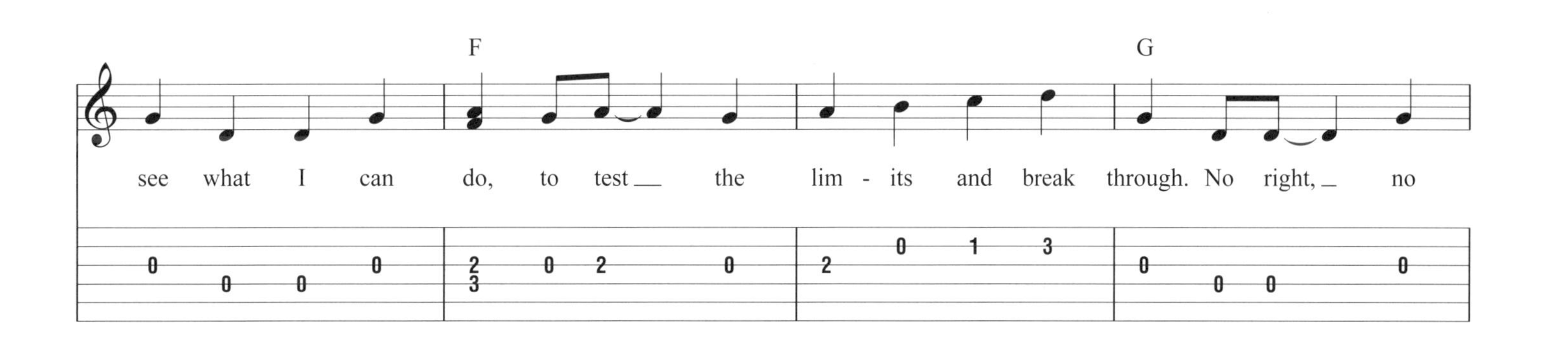
F G
see what I can do, to test the lim - its and break through. No right, no

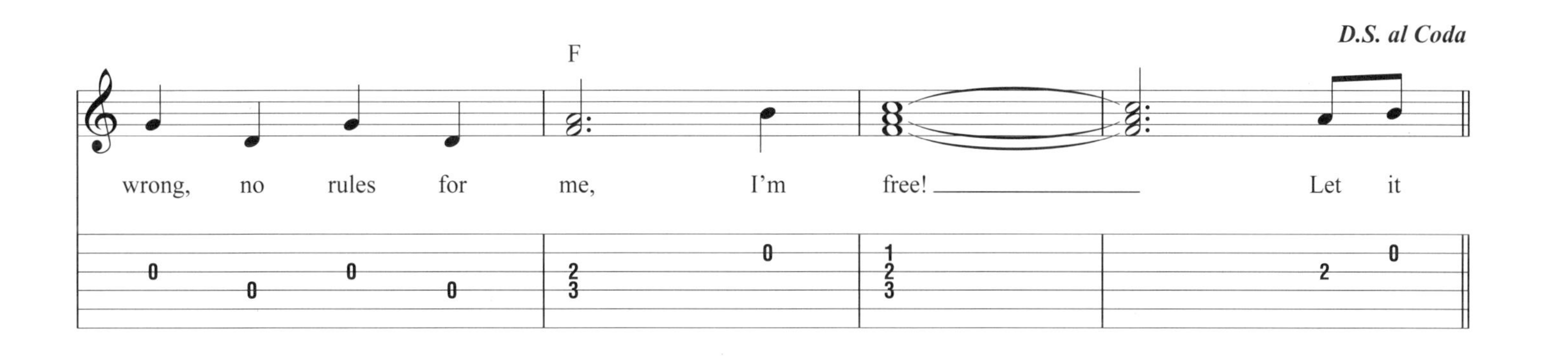
D.S. al Coda
F
wrong, no rules for me, I'm free! Let it

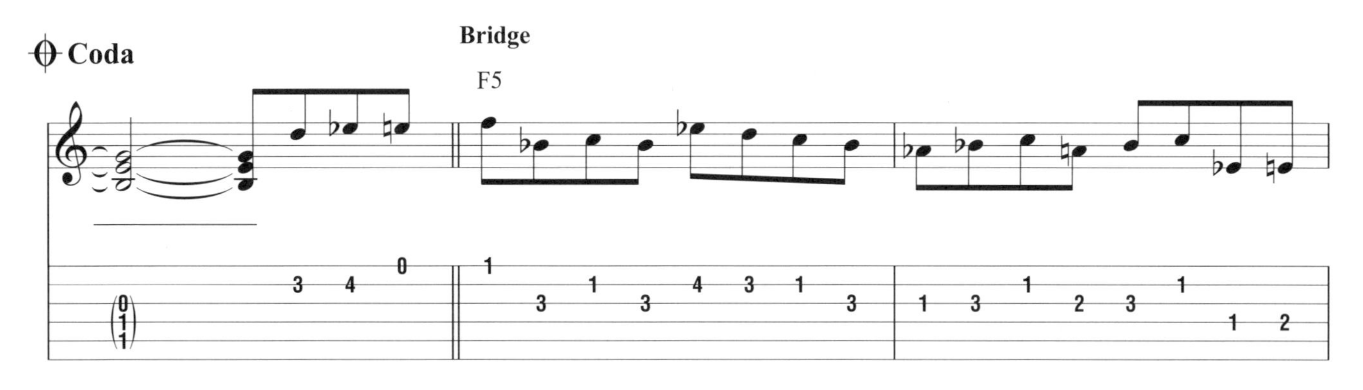
Coda
Bridge
F5

My pow - er

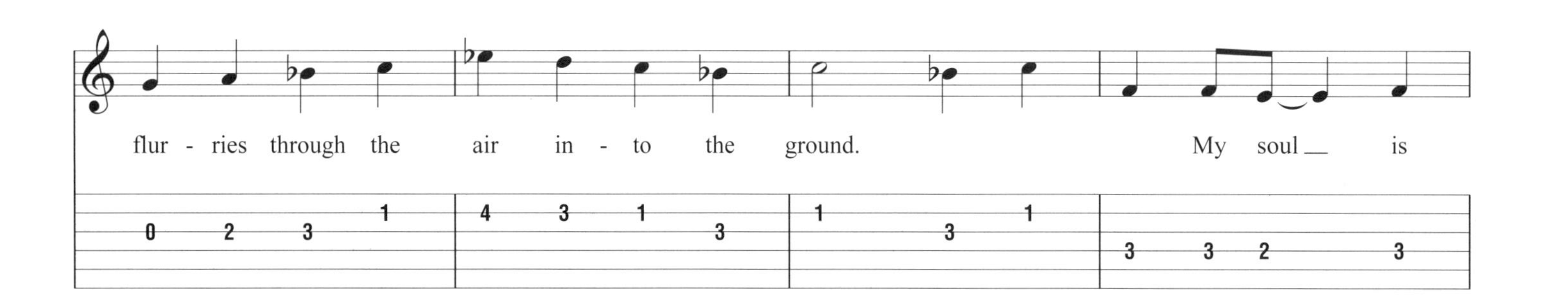
flur - ries through the air in - to the ground. My soul is

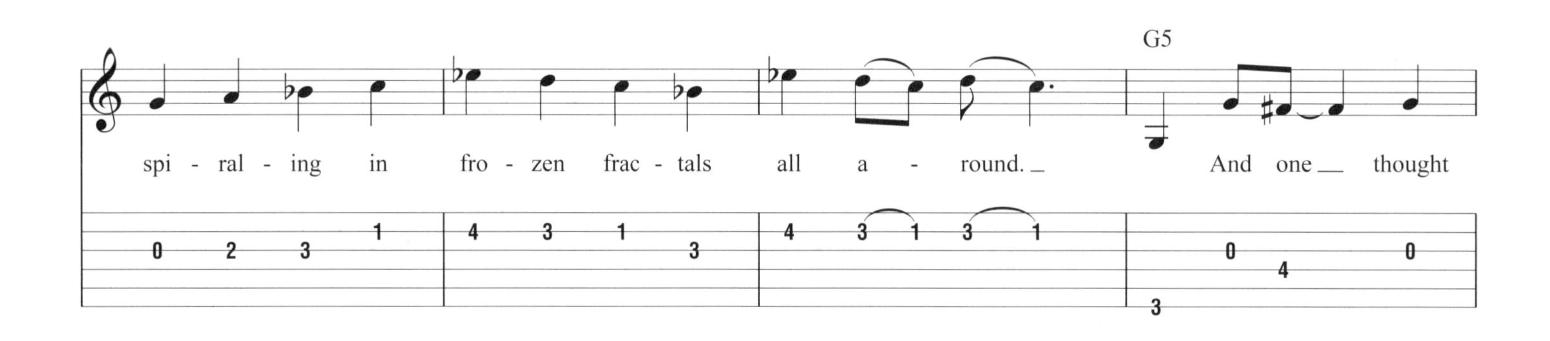
G5
spi - ral - ing in fro - zen frac - tals all a - round. And one thought

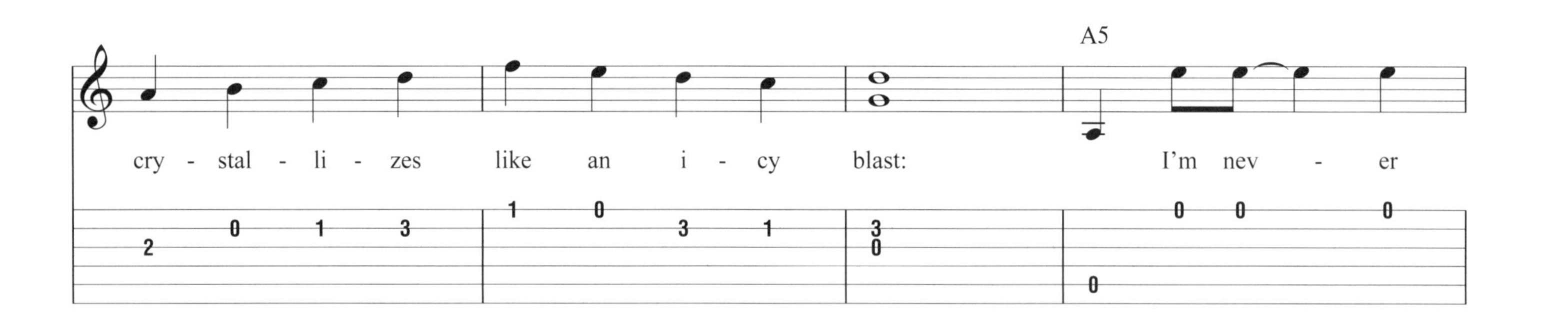
A5
cry - stal - li - zes like an i - cy blast: I'm nev - er

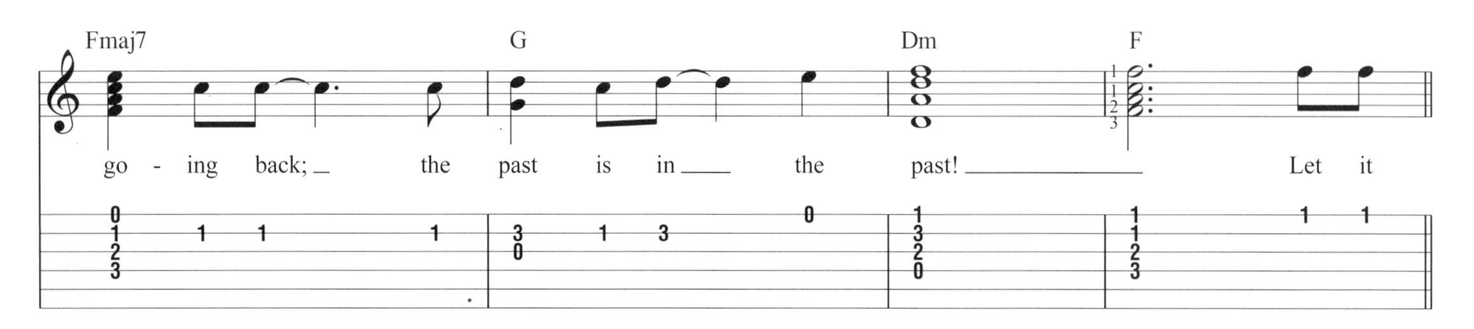
Fmaj7
G
Dm
F
go - ing back; the past is in the past! Let it

Outro-Chorus

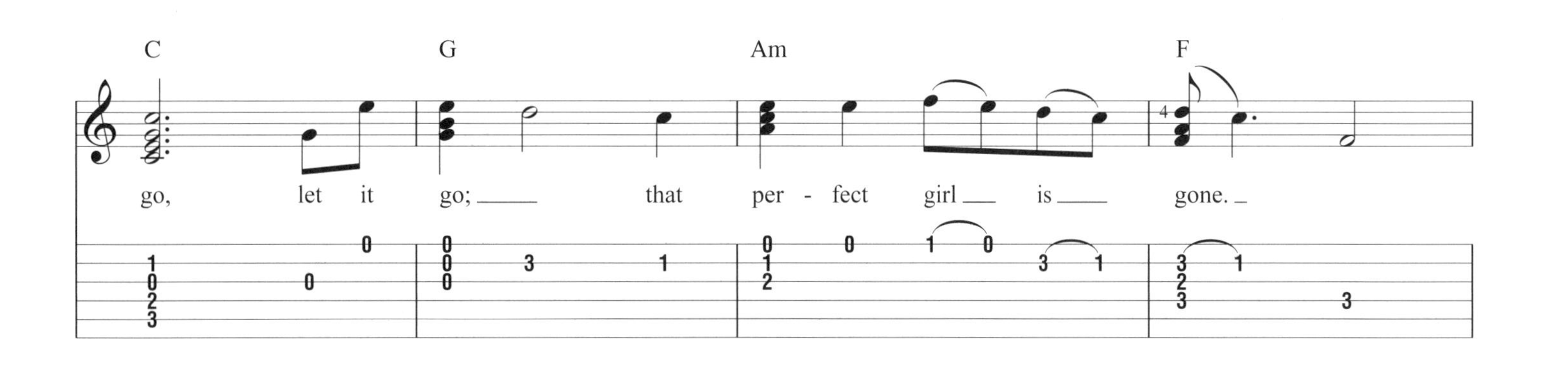

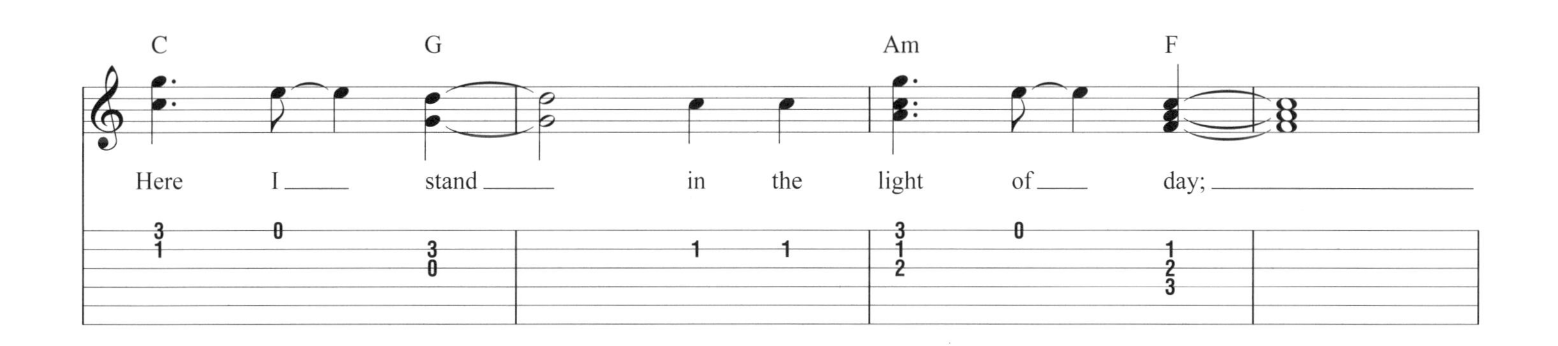

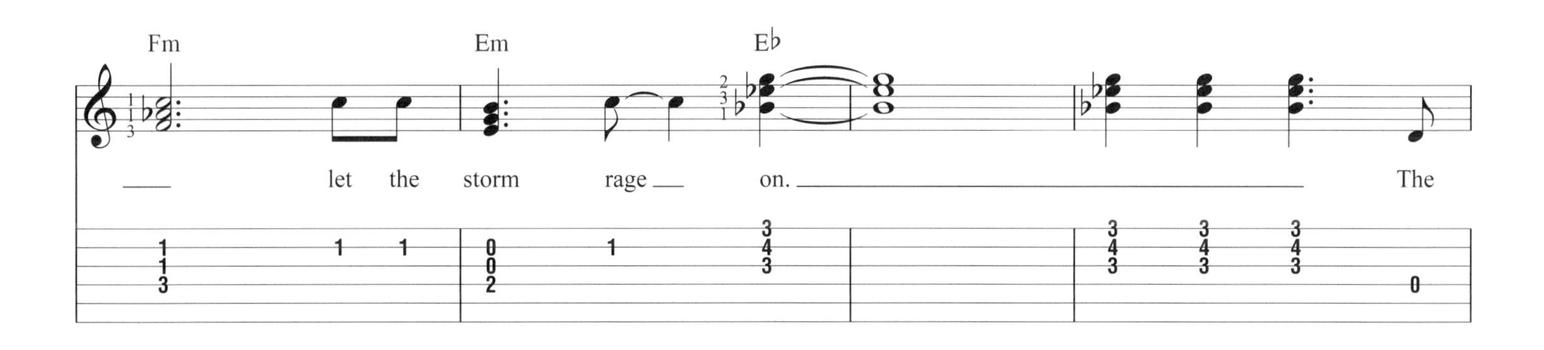

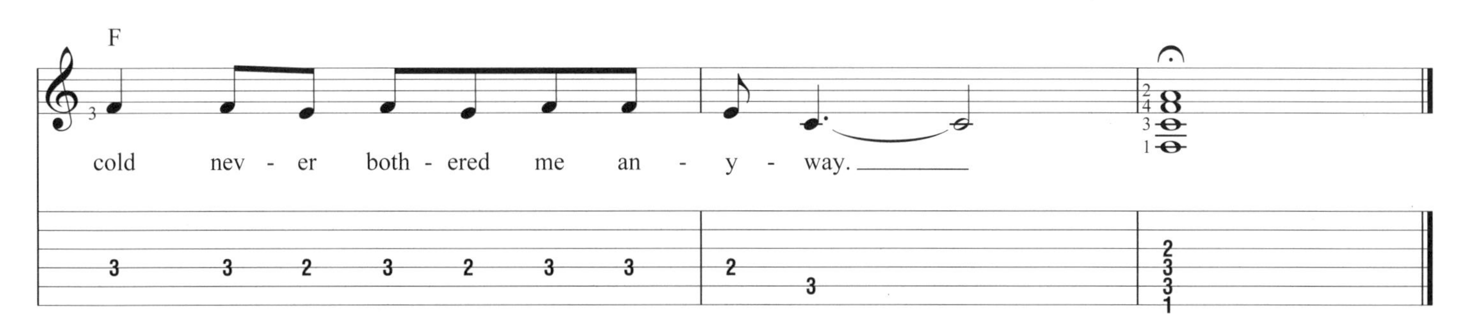

Logo Te Pate

from MOANA

By Opetaia Foa‘i

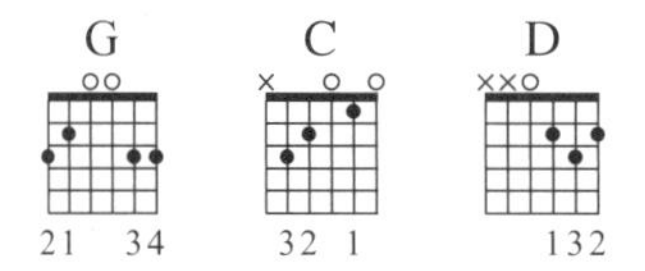

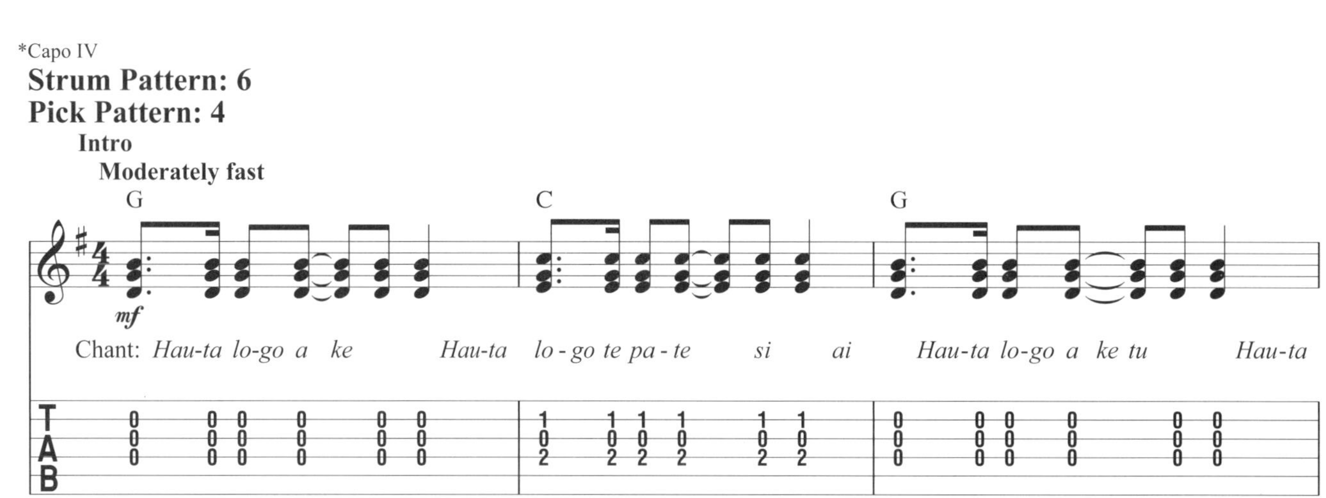

*Optional: To match recording, place capo at 4th fret.

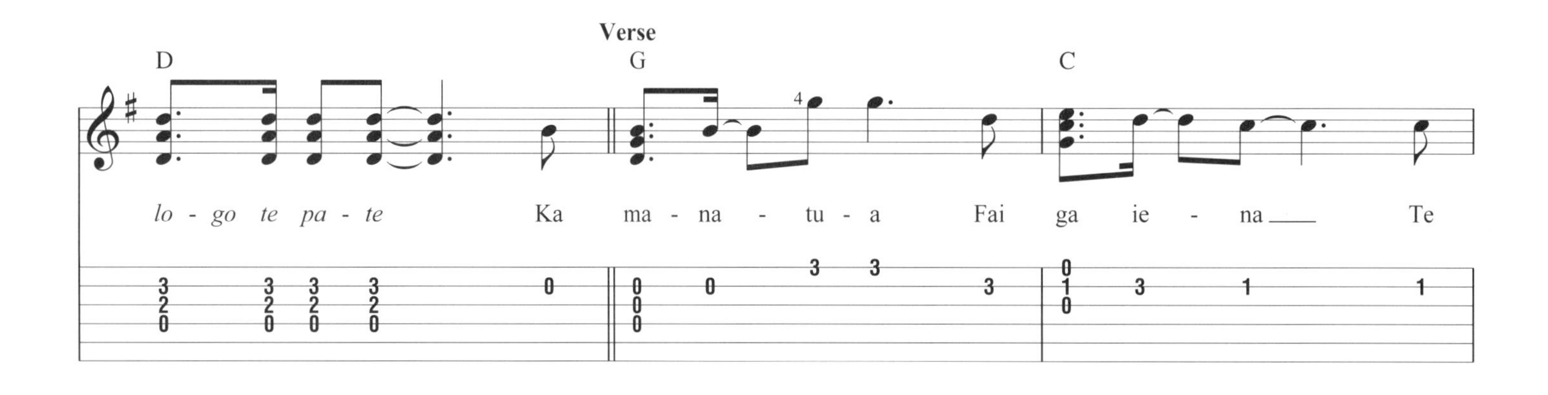

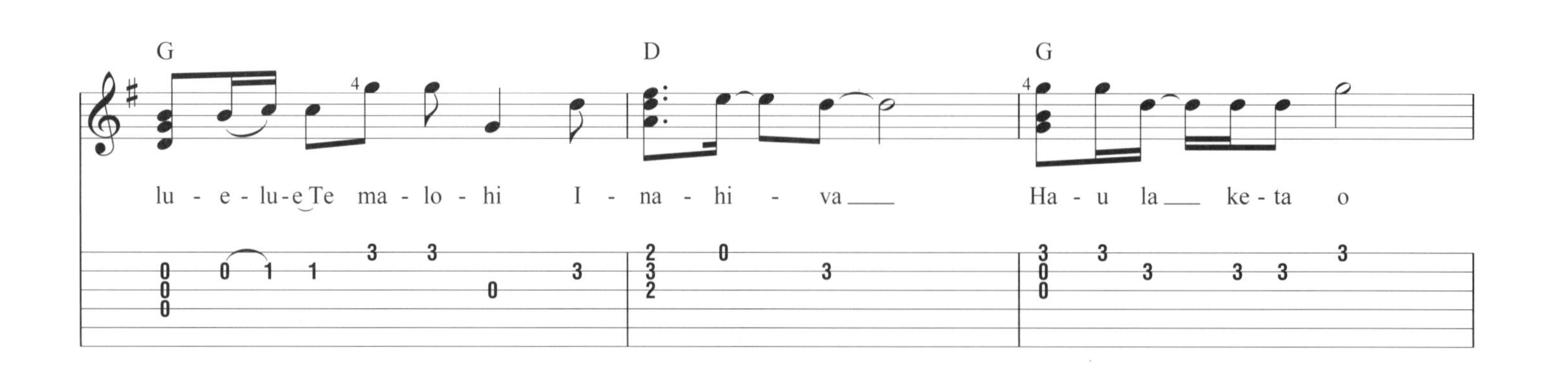

C
G
D
Hi - ki mai to li - ma
Ha - u la ke - ta o
Ha - u ta hau - ni - ga

G
C
G
Ha - u la ke - ta o
Hi - ki mai to li - ma
Ha - u la ke - ta o

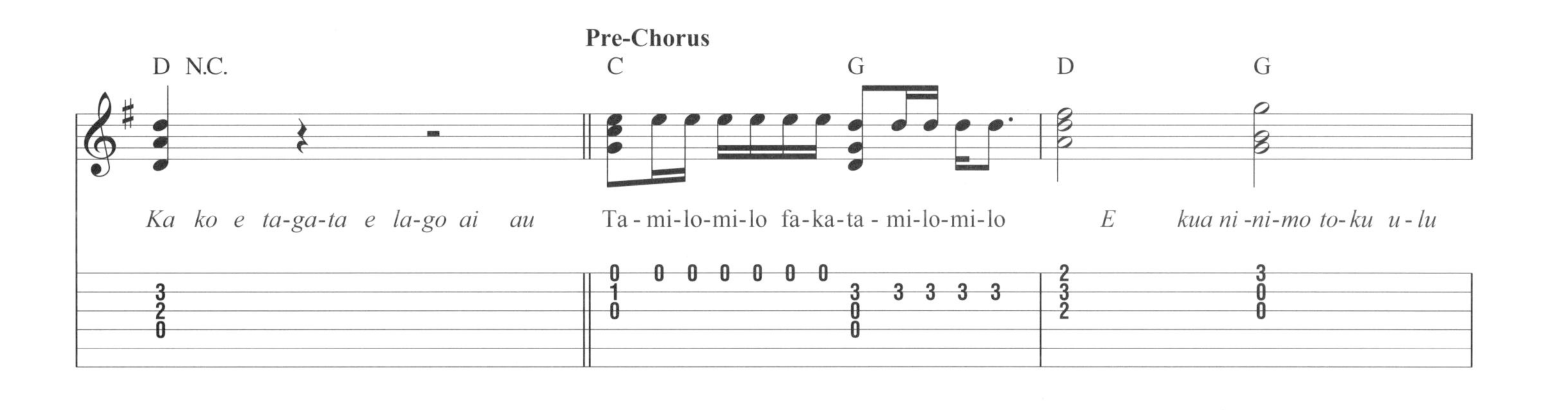
Pre-Chorus
D N.C.
C
G
D
G
Ka ko e ta-ga-ta e la-go ai au
Ta - mi-lo-mi-lo fa-ka-ta - mi-lo-mi-lo
E kua ni -ni-mo to-ku u-lu

Chorus
C
G
D N.C.
C
Ta - mi-lo-mi-lo fa-ka-ta - mi-lo-mi-lo
To - e fai mai la-ua ke ma-ni no
Ka - ta - ka - ta mai Hi -

G D G
hi - va mai Fa - ka - lo - go kite pa - te Ma te lu - e - lu - e

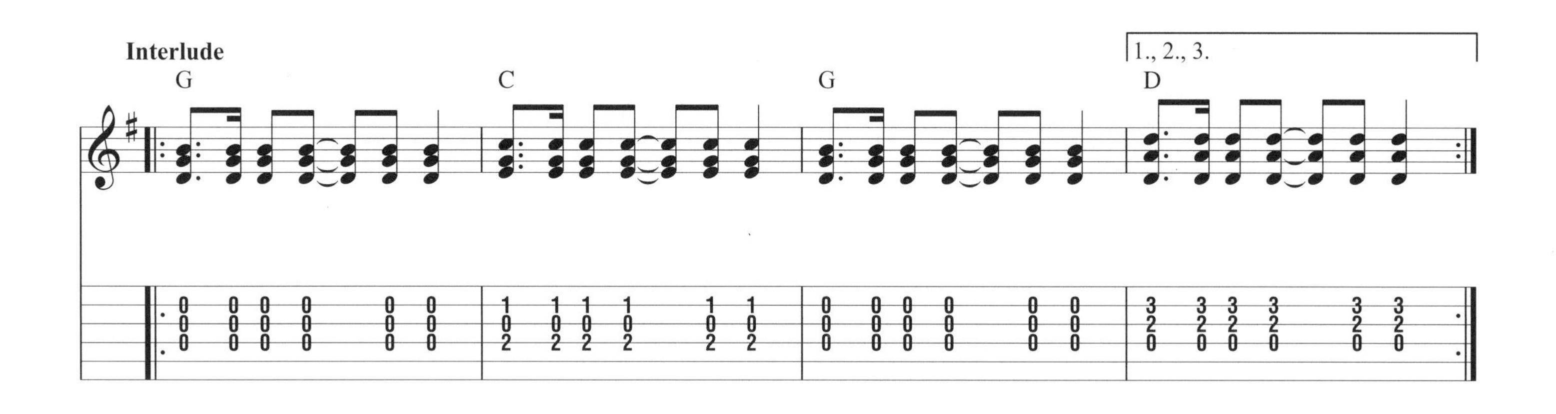
Interlude
1., 2., 3.
G C G D

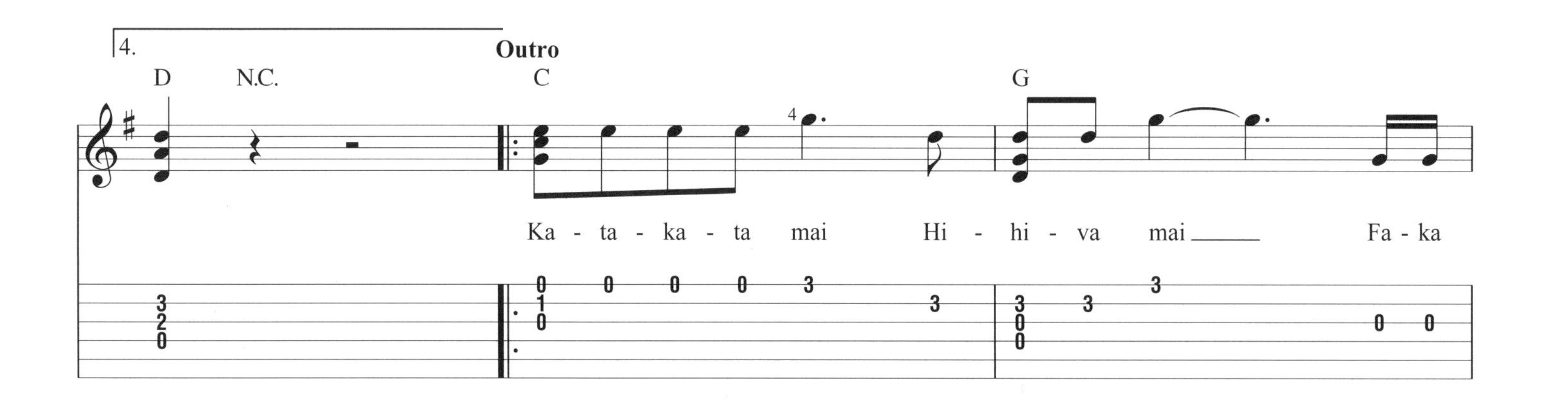
4.
Outro
D N.C. C G
Ka - ta - ka - ta mai Hi - hi - va mai Fa - ka

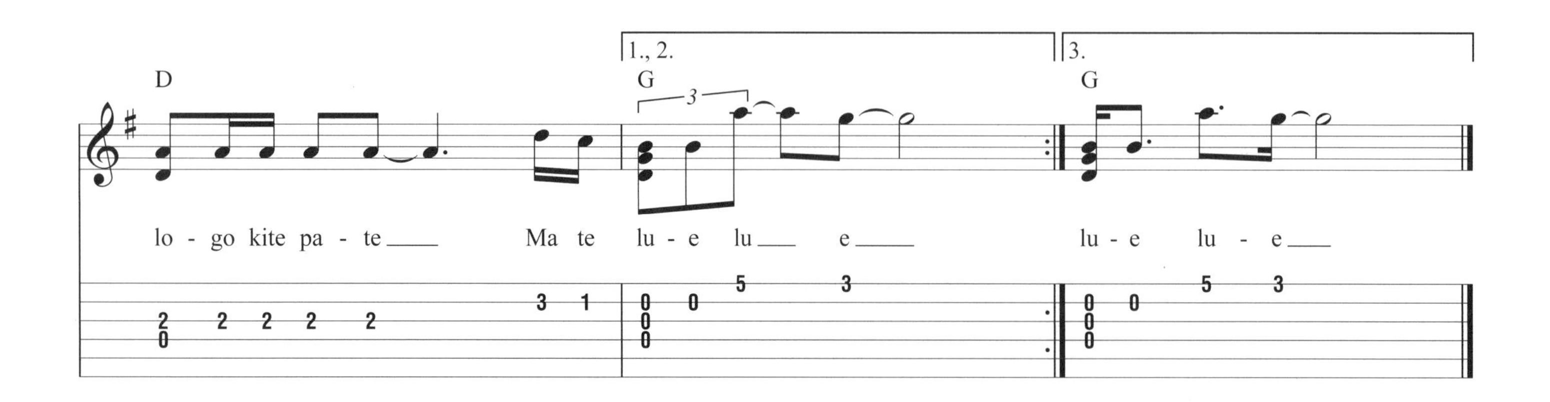
1., 2.
3.
D G G
lo - go kite pa - te Ma te lu - e lu e lu - e lu - e

Love Is an Open Door

from FROZEN

Music and Lyrics by Kristen Anderson-Lopez and Robert Lopez

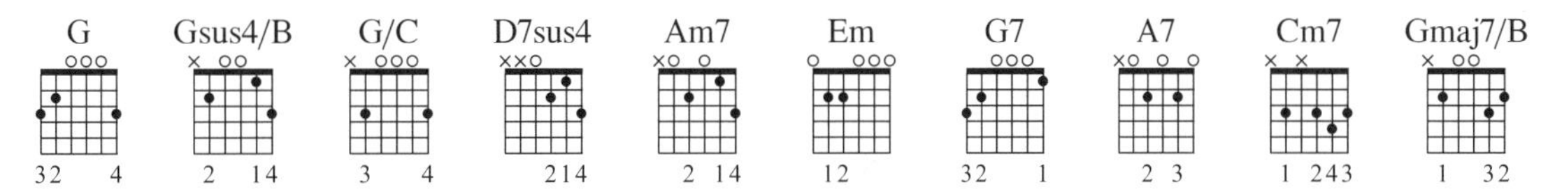

*Capo VII

Strum Pattern: 3
Pick Pattern: 3

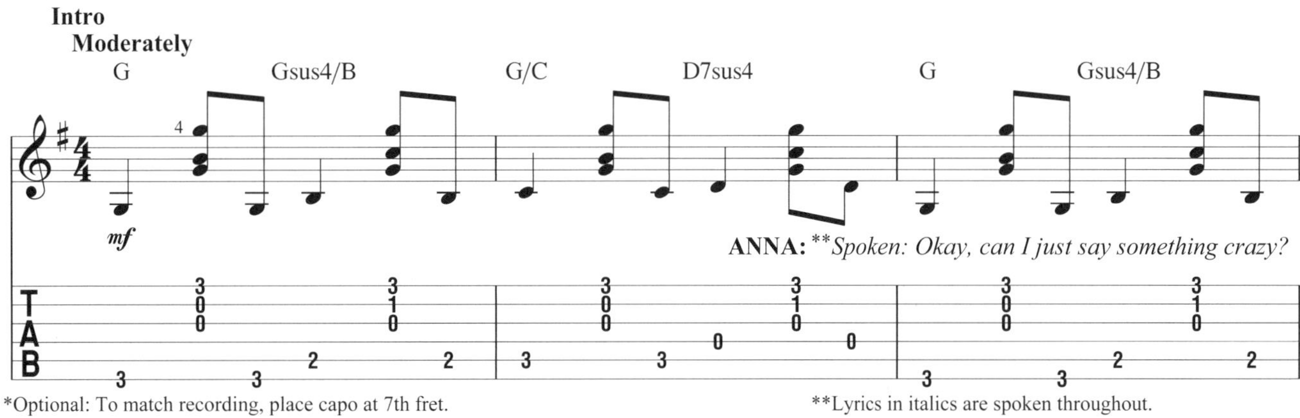

*Optional: To match recording, place capo at 7th fret.

**Lyrics in italics are spoken throughout.

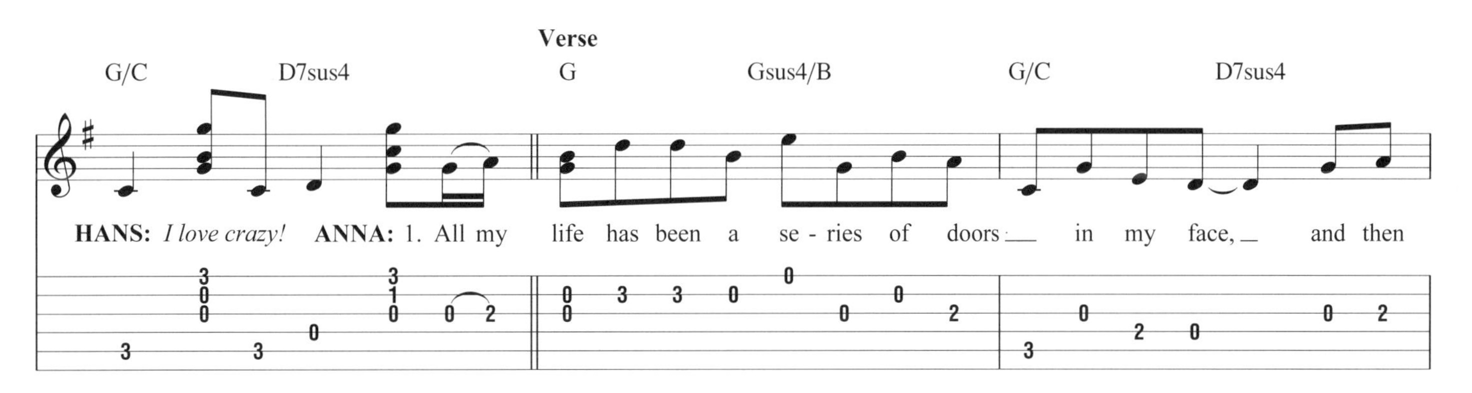

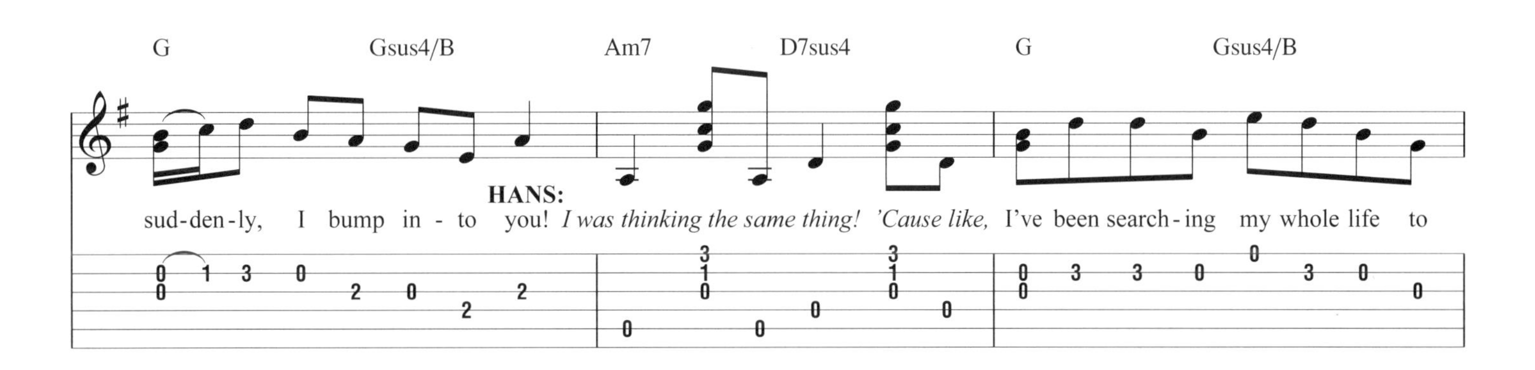

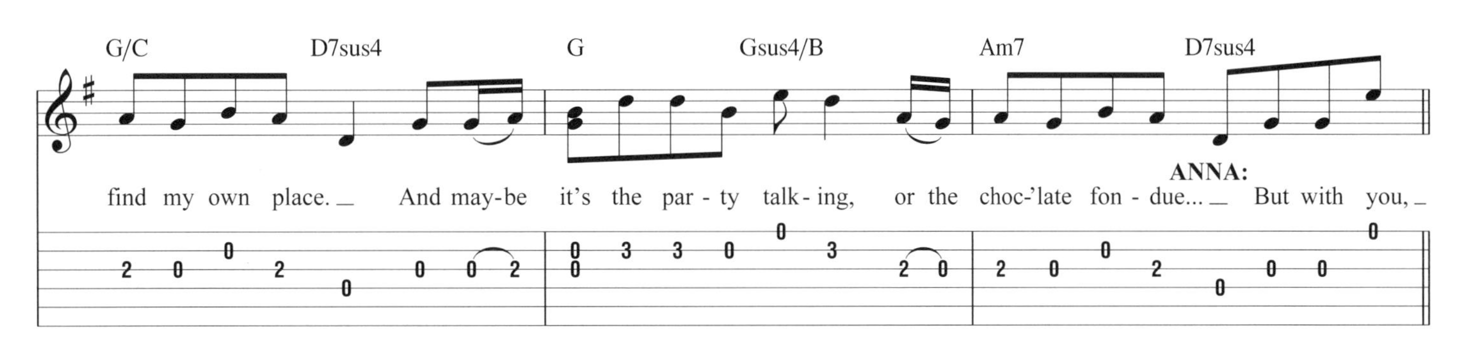

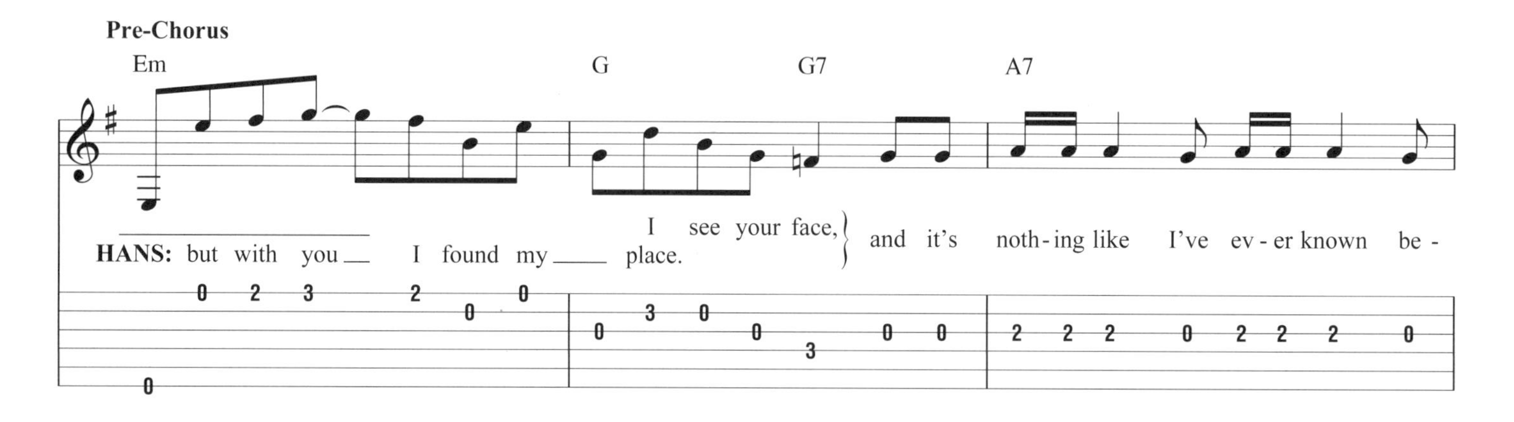
Pre-Chorus
Em
G
G7
A7
HANS: but with you I found my place.
I see your face,
and it's noth-ing like I've ev-er known be-

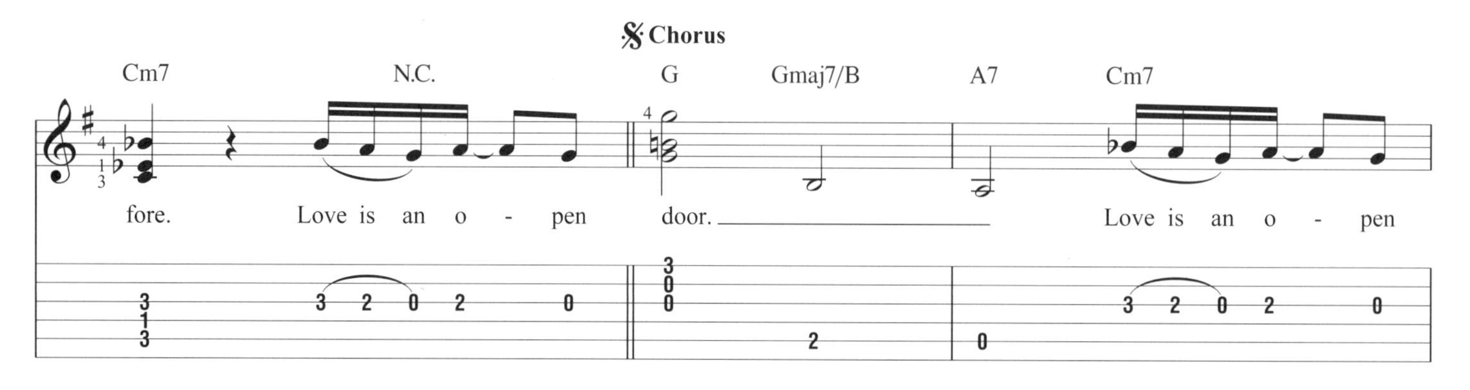
Chorus
Cm7
N.C.
G
Gmaj7/B
A7
Cm7
fore. Love is an o - pen door.
Love is an o - pen

G
Gmaj7/B
A7
Cm7
G
Gmaj7/B
door.
Love is an o - pen door
Life can be so much more
with you, with

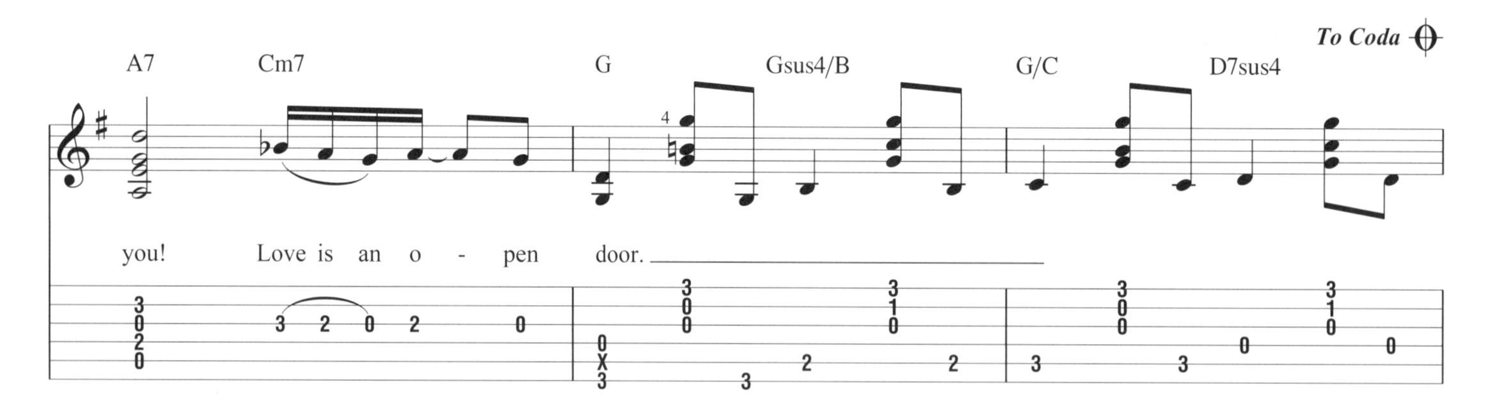
To Coda
A7
Cm7
G
Gsus4/B
G/C
D7sus4
you! Love is an o - pen door.

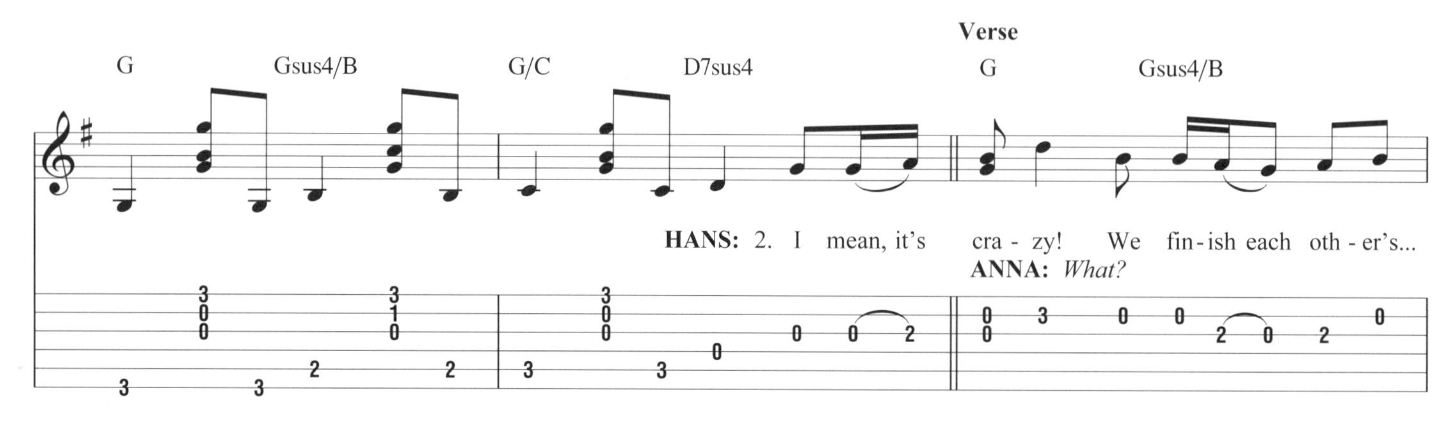
Verse
G
Gsus4/B
G/C
D7sus4
G
Gsus4/B
HANS: 2. I mean, it's cra - zy! We fin-ish each oth-er's...
ANNA: What?

G/C D7sus4 G Gsus4/B Am7 D7sus4
That's what I was gonna say!
...sand-wich-es! I nev-er met some-one
who thinks so much like me. Jinx! Jinx again! Our

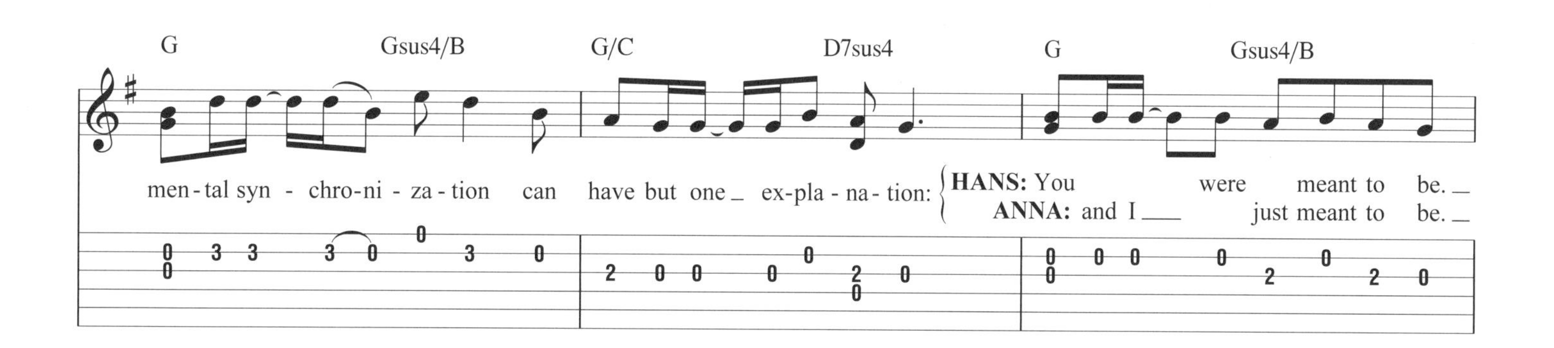
G Gsus4/B G/C D7sus4 G Gsus4/B
men-tal syn-chro-ni-za-tion can have but one ex-pla-na-tion:
HANS: You were meant to be.
ANNA: and I just meant to be.

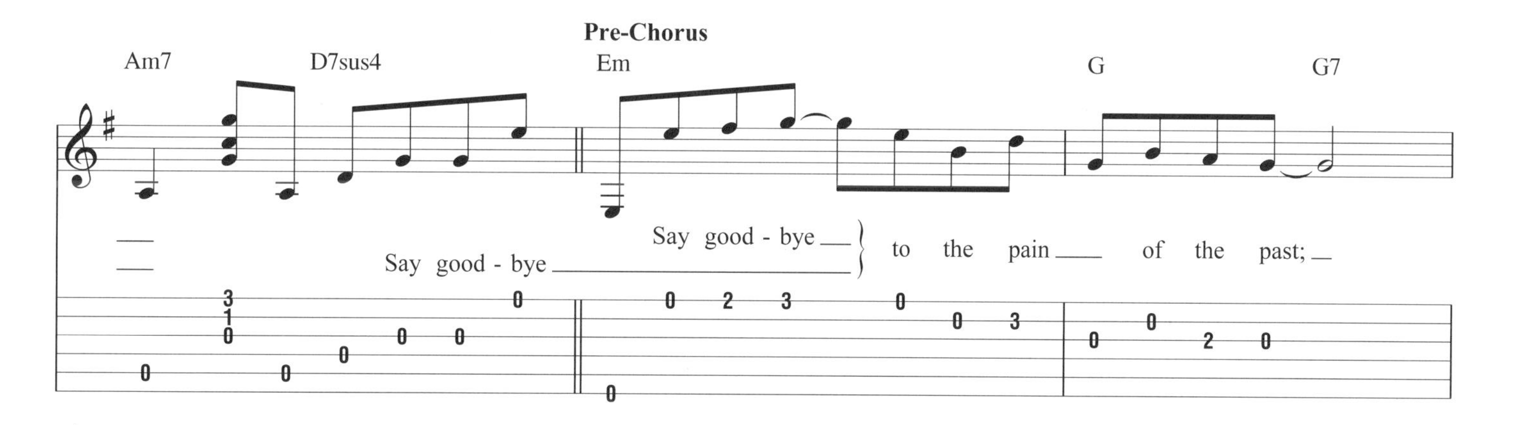
Pre-Chorus
Am7 D7sus4 Em G G7
Say good-bye
Say good-bye
to the pain of the past;

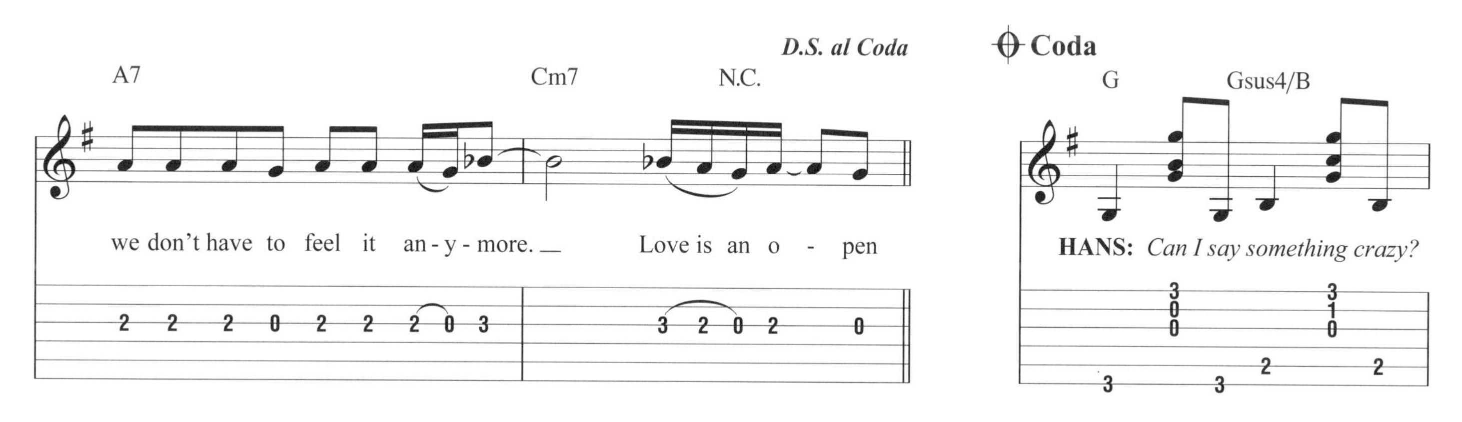
D.S. al Coda
Coda
A7 Cm7 N.C. G Gsus4/B
we don't have to feel it an-y-more. Love is an o-pen
HANS: Can I say something crazy?

G/C D7sus4 N.C. G
Will you marry me? ANNA: Can I say something even crazier? Yes!

One Jump Ahead

from ALADDIN

Music by Alan Menken
Lyrics by Tim Rice

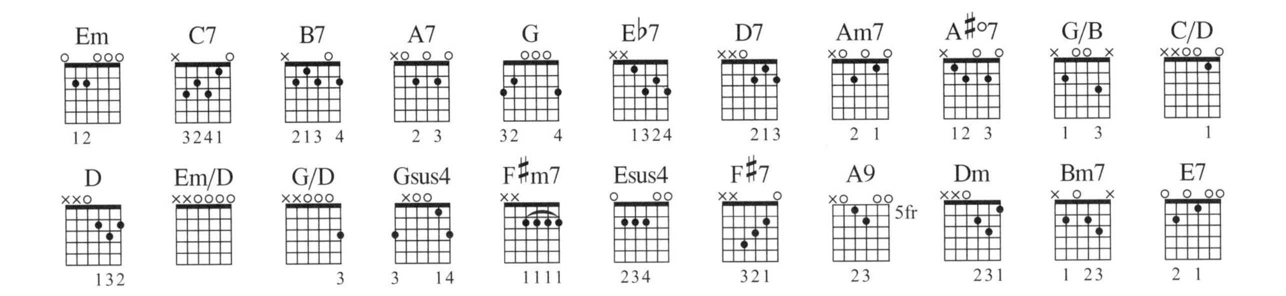

Strum Pattern: 4
Pick Pattern: 3

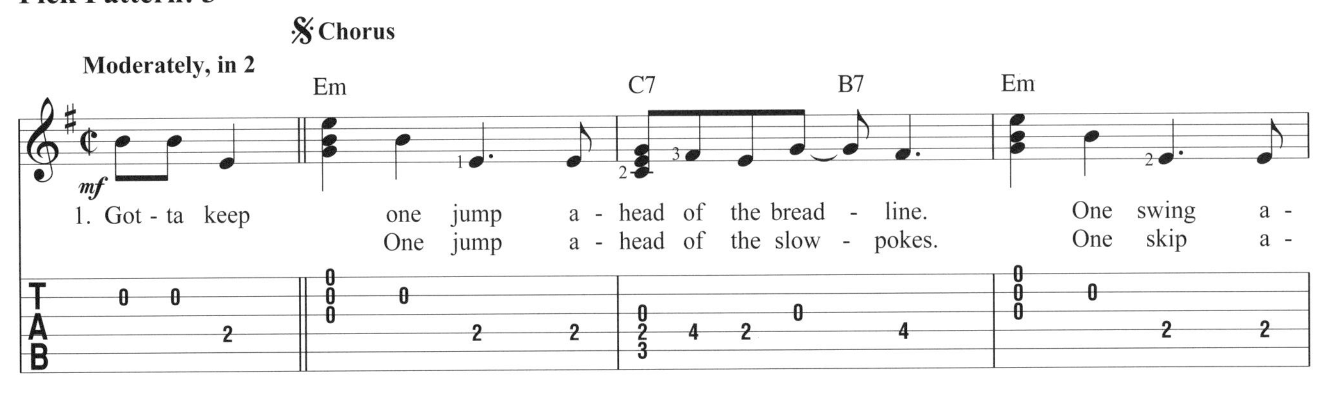

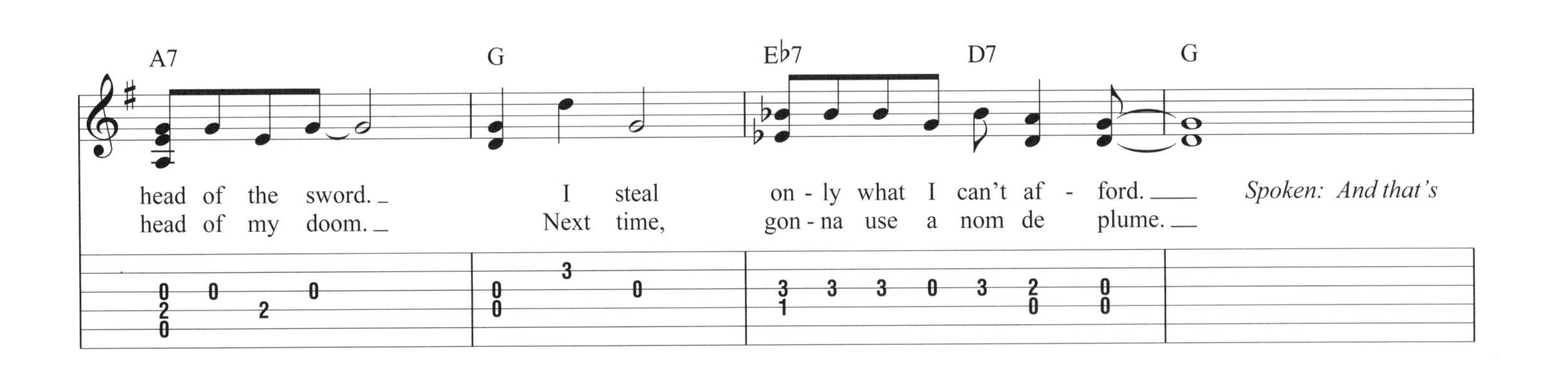

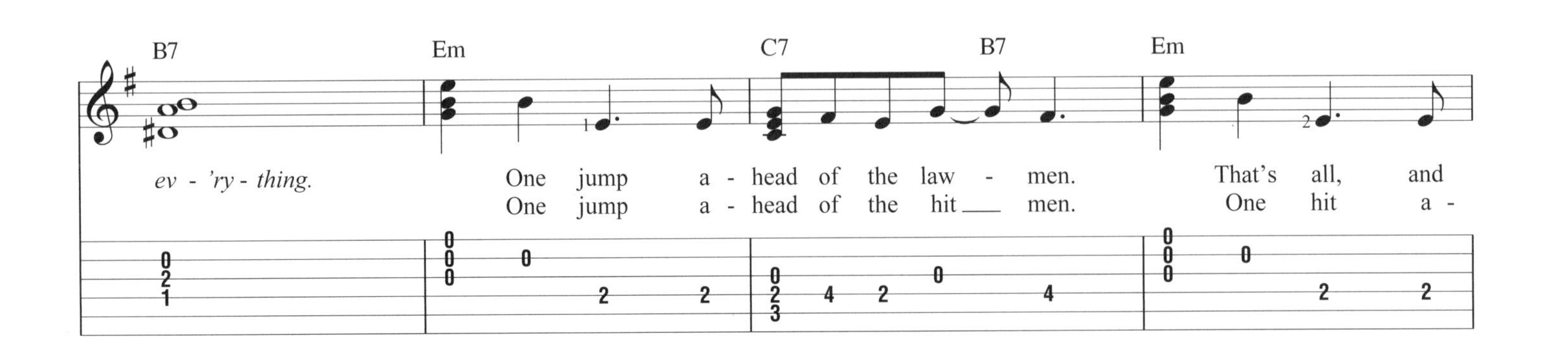

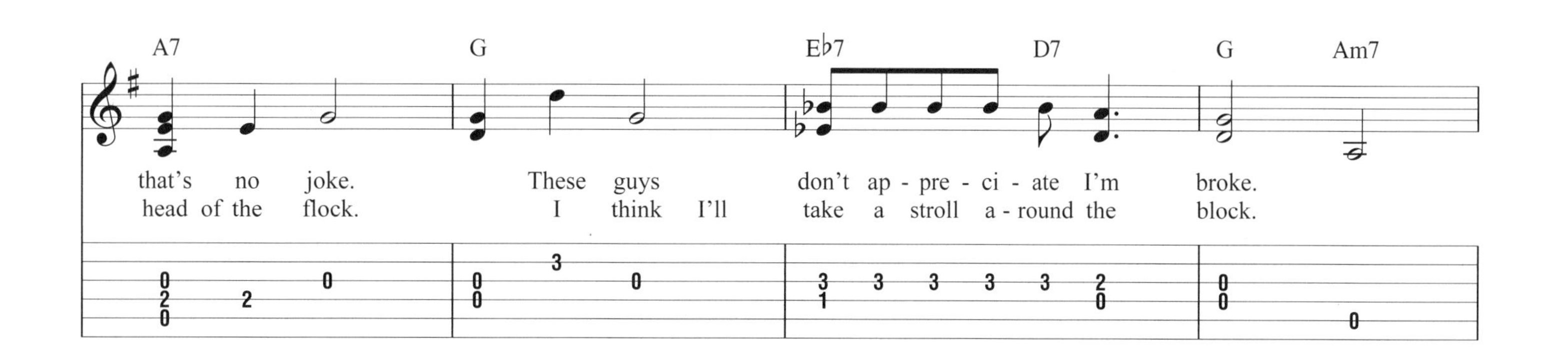
A7
G
E♭7
D7
G
Am7
that's no joke. These guys don't ap - pre - ci - ate I'm broke.
head of the flock. I think I'll take a stroll a - round the block.

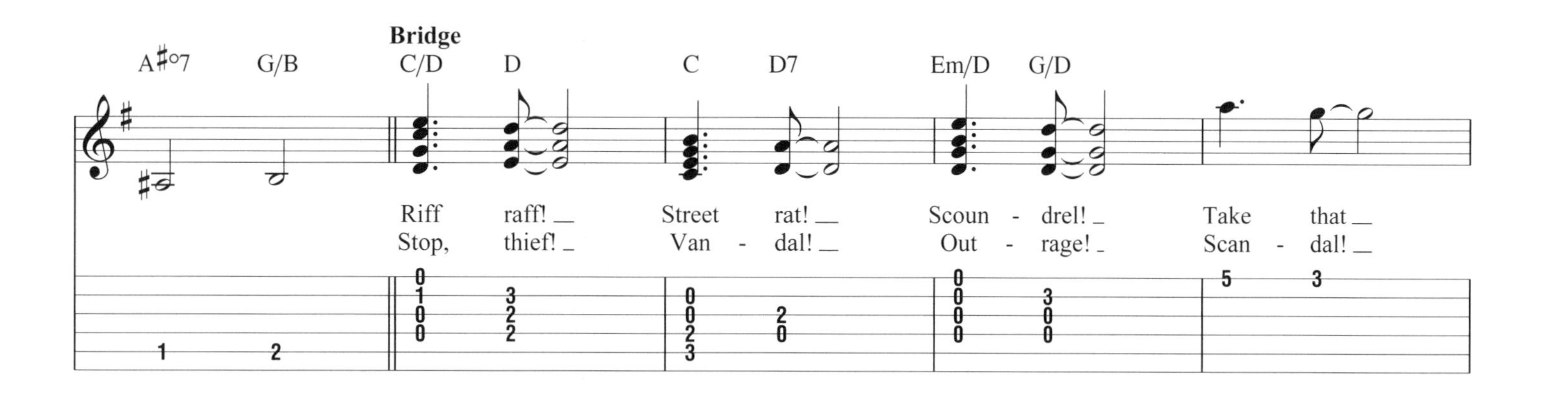
Bridge
A♯o7
G/B
C/D
D
C
D7
Em/D
G/D
Riff raff! Street rat! Scoun - drel! Take that
Stop, thief! Van - dal! Out - rage! Scan - dal!

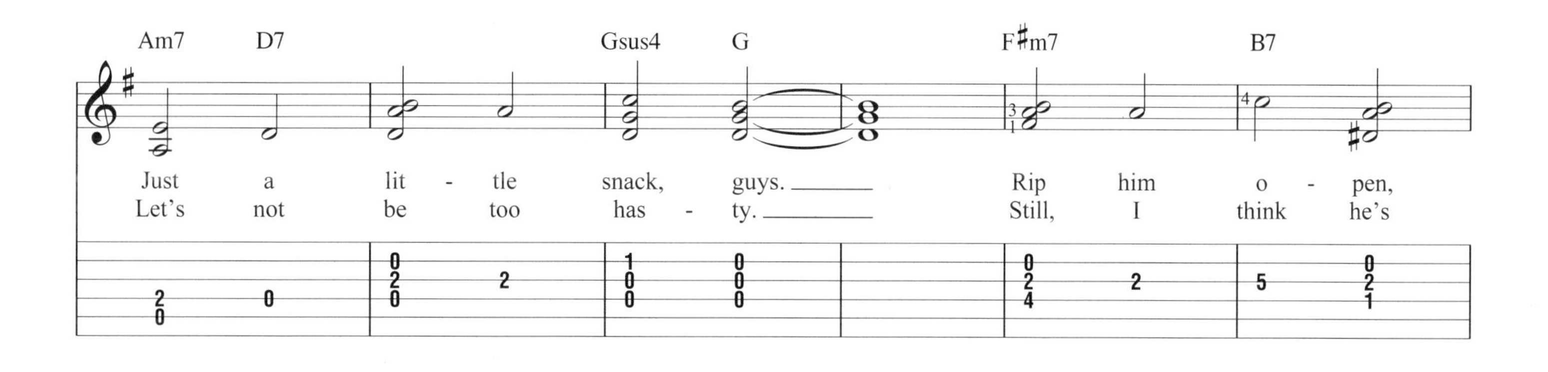
Am7
D7
Gsus4
G
F♯m7
B7
Just a lit - tle snack, guys. Rip him o - pen,
Let's not be too has - ty. Still, I think he's

To Coda
Esus4
Em
B7
Em
C7
take it back, guys. I can take a hint, got - ta face the facts.
rath - er tas - ty. Got - ta eat to live, got - ta steal to eat.

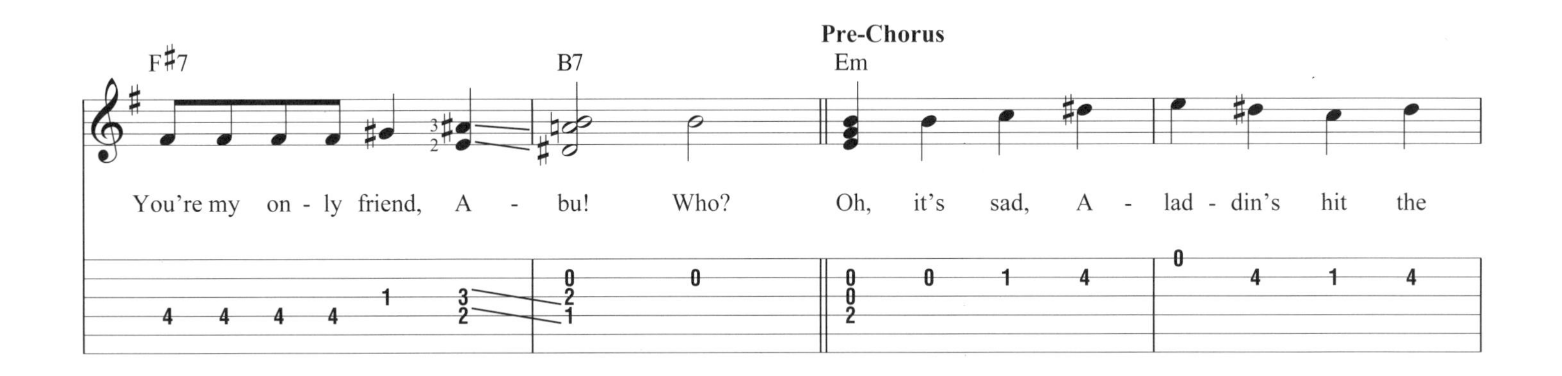
Pre-Chorus
F♯7
B7
Em
You're my on - ly friend, A - bu! Who? Oh, it's sad, A - lad - din's hit the

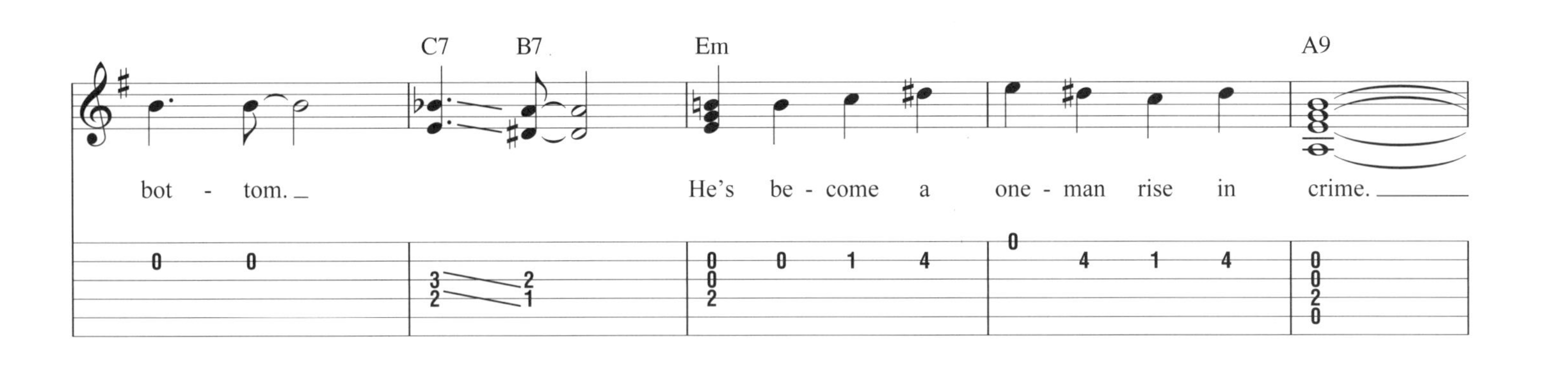
C7
B7
Em
A9
bot - tom. He's be - come a one - man rise in crime.

Dm
I'd blame par - ents ex - cept he has - n't got 'em.

D.S. al Coda
F♯7
B7
Got - ta eat to live, got - ta steal to eat. Tell you all a - bout it when I got the time.

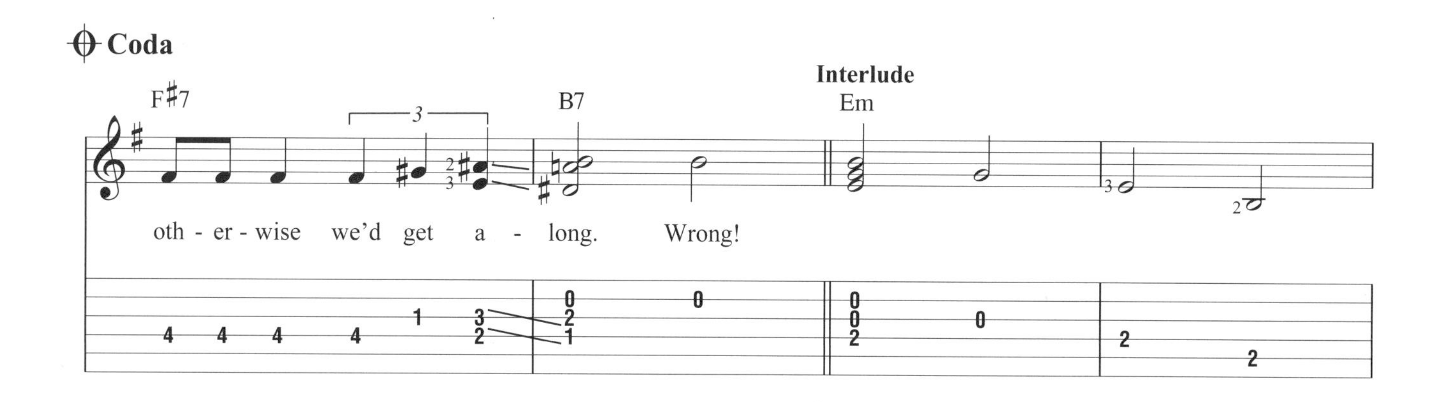
Coda
Interlude
F♯7
B7
Em
oth - er - wise we'd get a - long. Wrong!

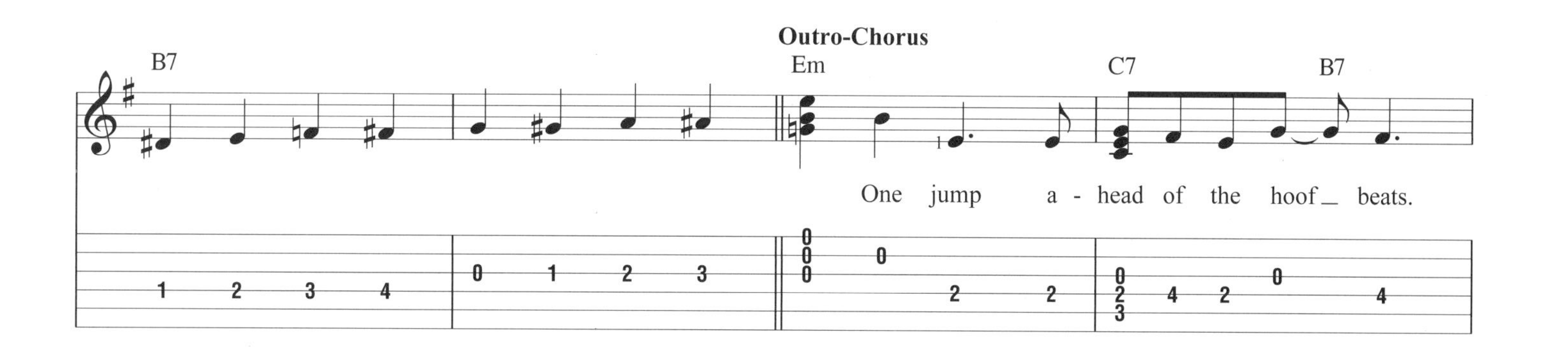
Outro-Chorus
B7
Em
C7
B7
One jump a - head of the hoof_ beats.

Em
A7
G
E♭7
D7
One hop a - head of the hump._ One trick a - head of dis - as - ter.

Bm7
E7
Am7
C/D
They're quick, but I'm much fast - er. Here goes, bet - ter throw my hand in,

N.C.
wish me hap - py land - in'. All I got - ta do is jump.

Part of Your World

from THE LITTLE MERMAID

Music by Alan Menken
Lyrics by Howard Ashman

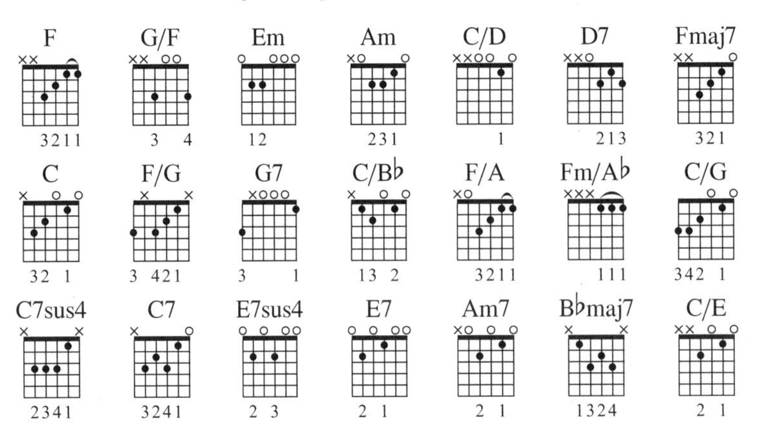

Strum Pattern: 5
Pick Pattern: 5

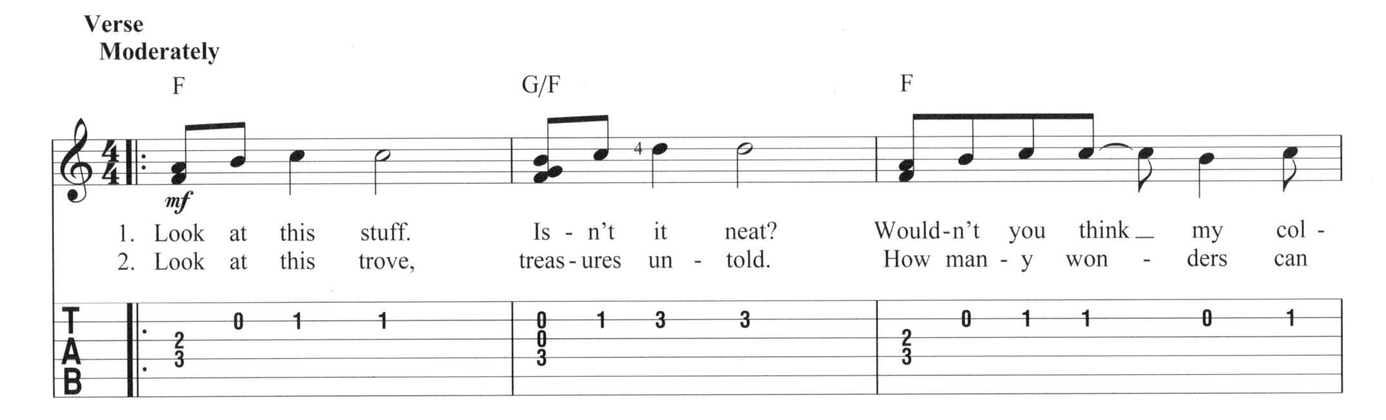

Pre-Chorus
Fmaj7
Em
C
Am
gad - gets and giz - mos a - plen - ty. I've got who - zits and what - zits ga -
C/D
D7
Fmaj7
Em
C
lore. You want thing - a - ma - bobs, I've got twen - ty. But who

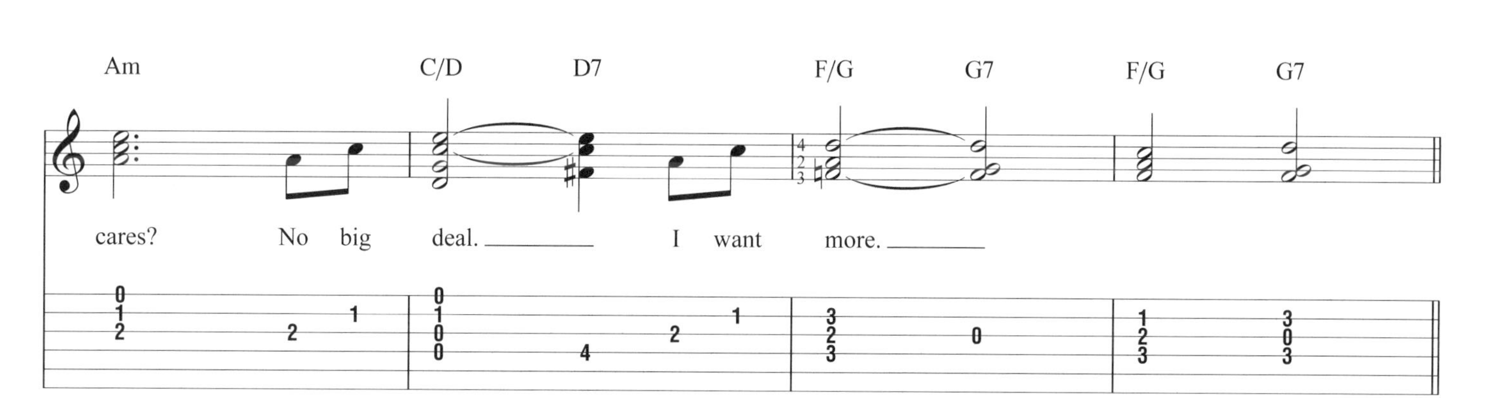
Am
C/D
D7
F/G
G7
F/G
G7
cares? No big deal. I want more.

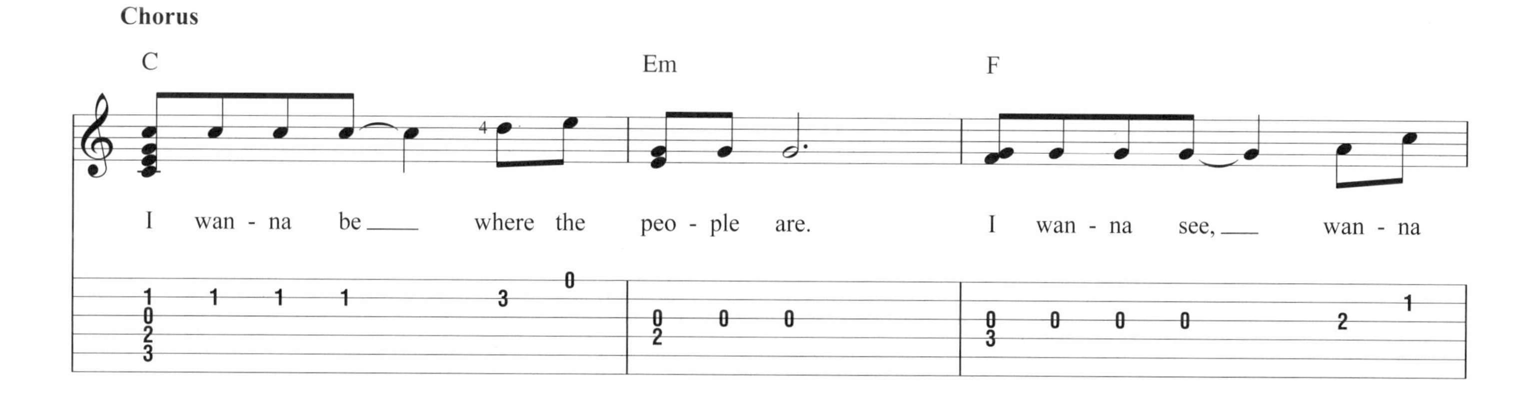
Chorus
C
Em
F
I wan - na be where the peo - ple are. I wan - na see, wan - na

F/G
G7
Am
Em
see 'em danc - in', walk - in' a - round on those, what do you call 'em,

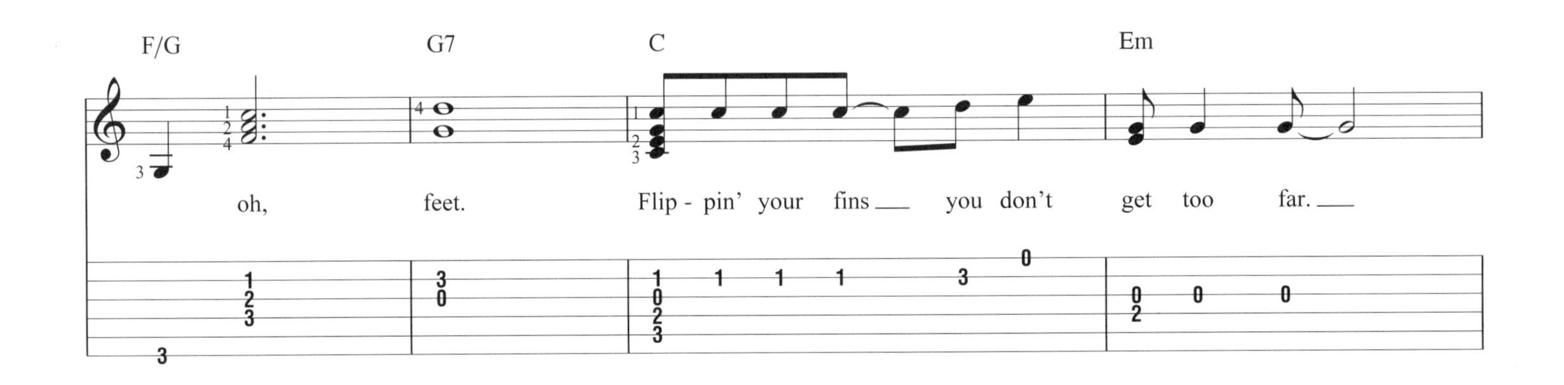
F/G G7 C Em
oh, feet. Flip - pin' your fins you don't get too far.

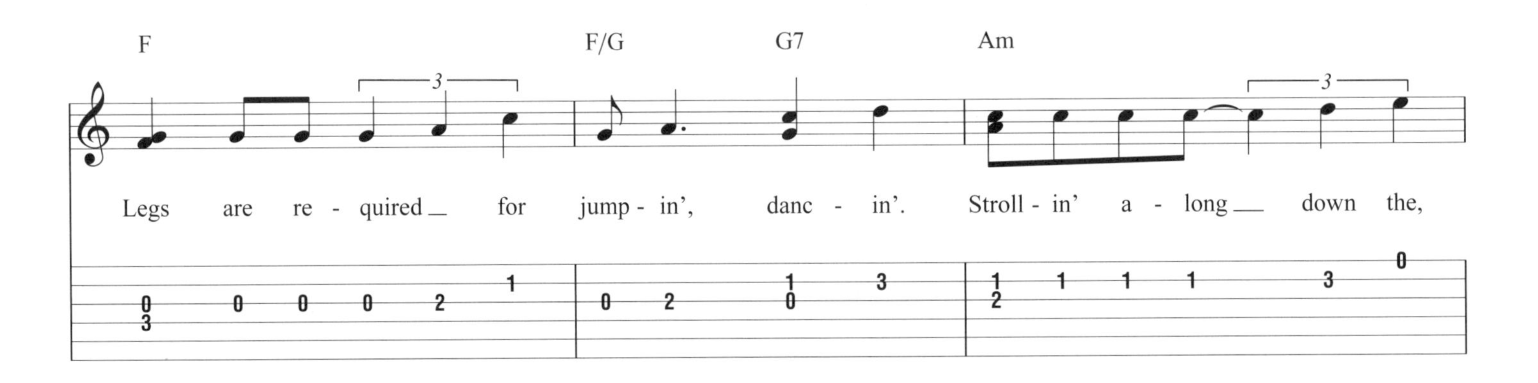
F F/G G7 Am
Legs are re - quired for jump - in', danc - in'. Stroll - in' a - long down the,

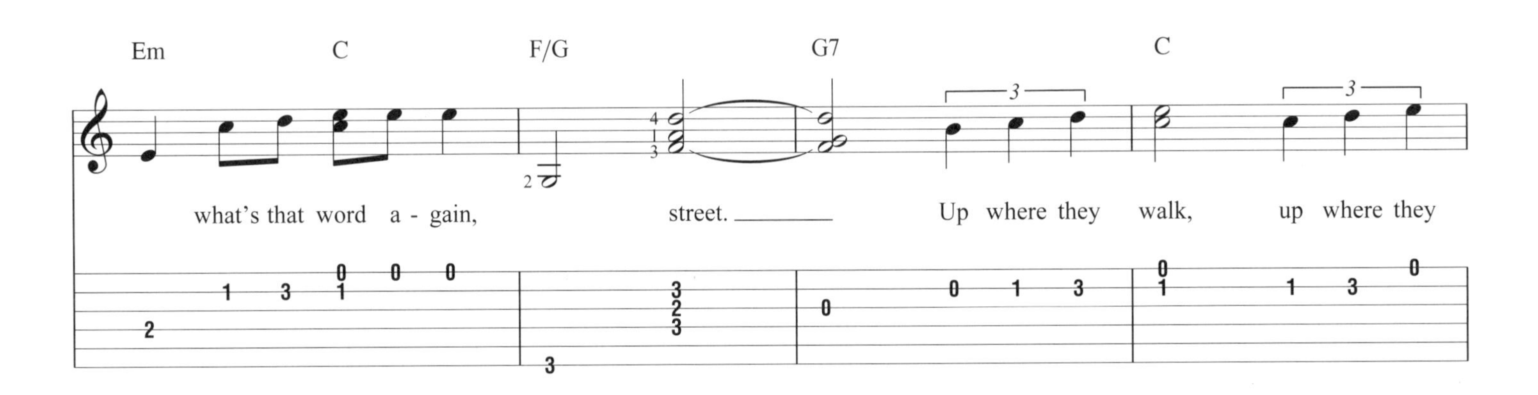
Em C F/G G7 C
what's that word a - gain, street. Up where they walk, up where they

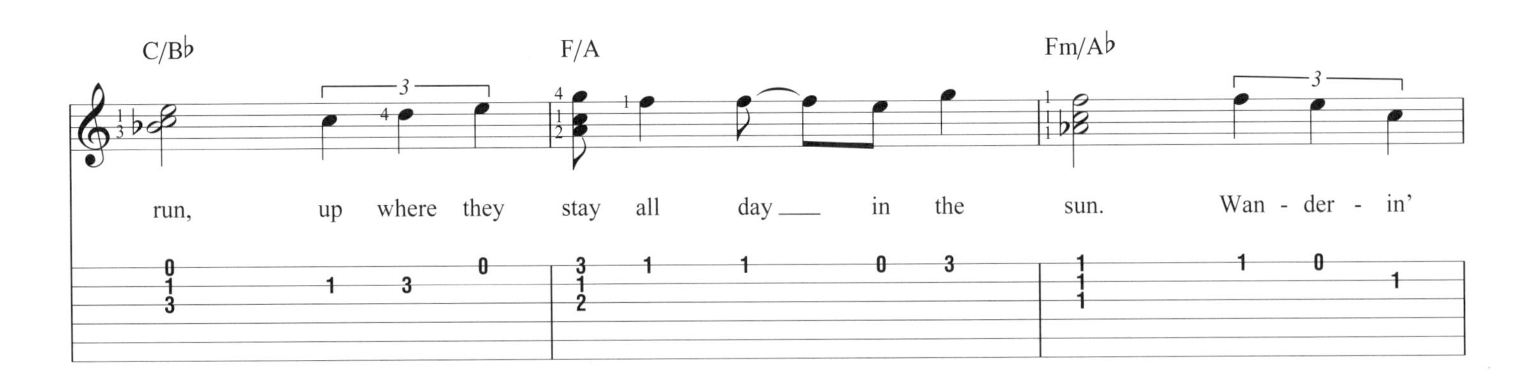
C/B♭ F/A Fm/A♭
run, up where they stay all day in the sun. Wan - der - in'

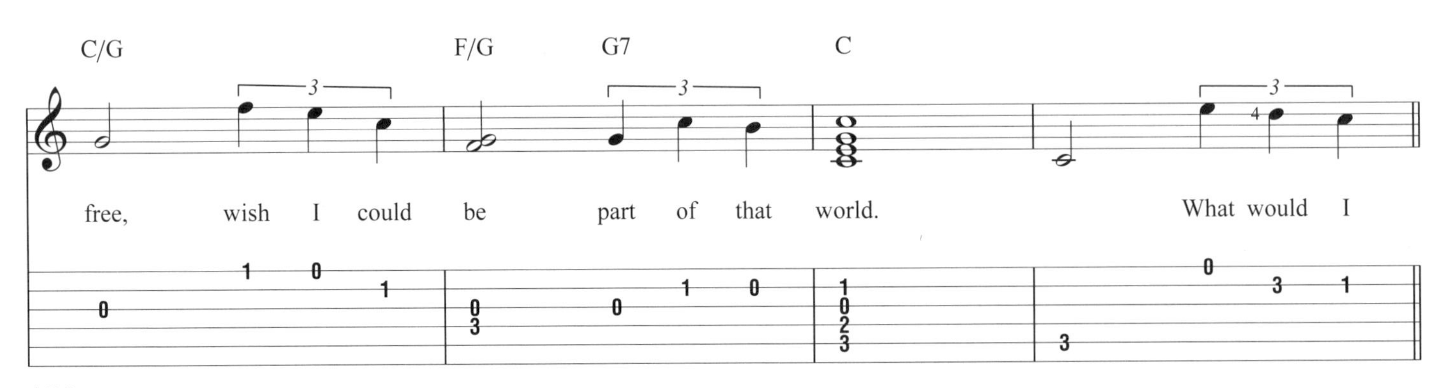
C/G F/G G7 C
free, wish I could be part of that world. What would I

Bridge
F G/F Em
give if I could live out of these wa - ters.
Am F G/F Em
What would I pay to spend a day warm on the sand?
C7sus4 C7 F G/F
Bet ya on land they un - der - stand. Bet they don't
E7sus4 E7 Am Am7 C/D D7
rep - ri - mand their daugh - ters. Bright young wom - en, sick of

C/D D7 B♭maj7 F/G G7
swim - min', read - y to stand. And

Outro-Chorus

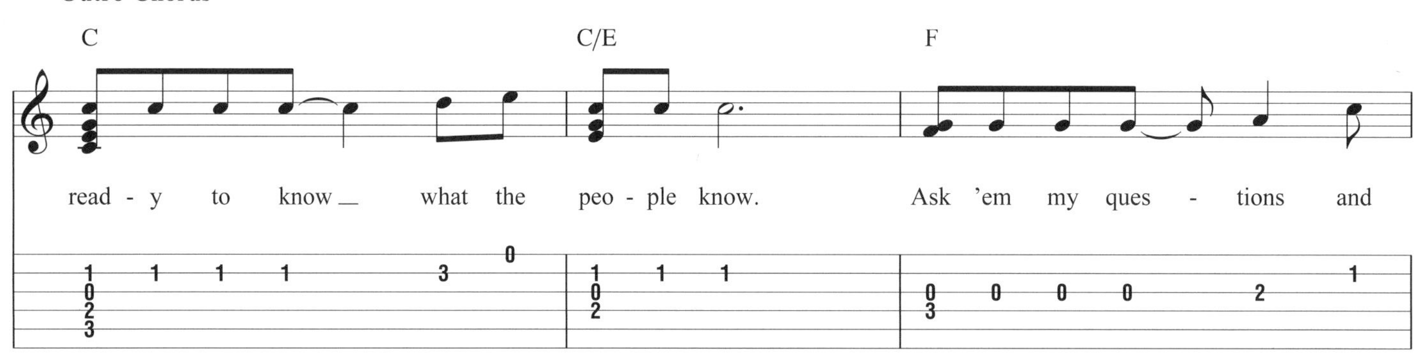
C
C/E
F
read - y to know what the peo - ple know. Ask 'em my ques - tions and

F/G
G7
Am
Em
C
get some an - swers. What's a fire, and why does it, what's the word,

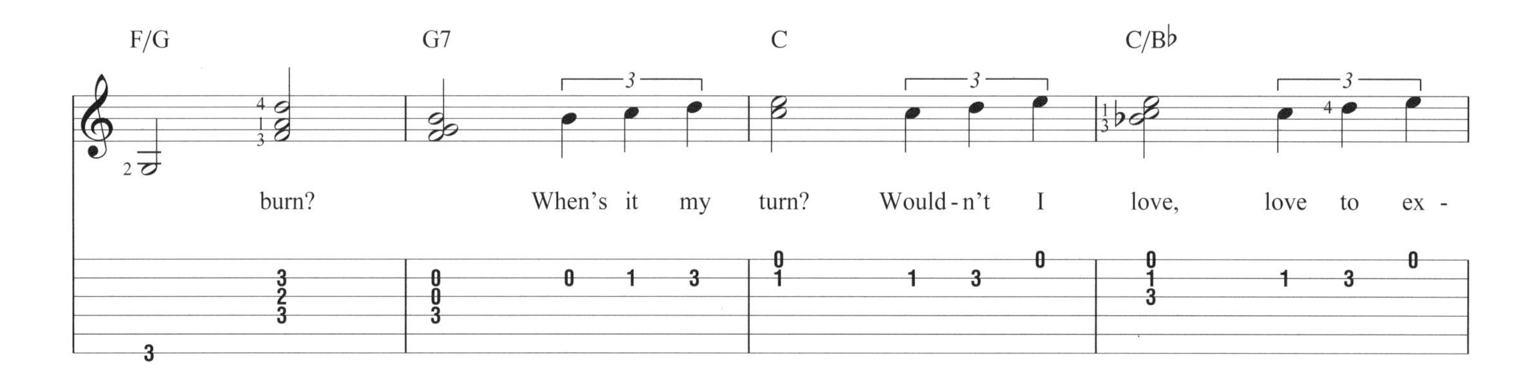
F/G
G7
C
C/B♭
burn? When's it my turn? Would-n't I love, love to ex -

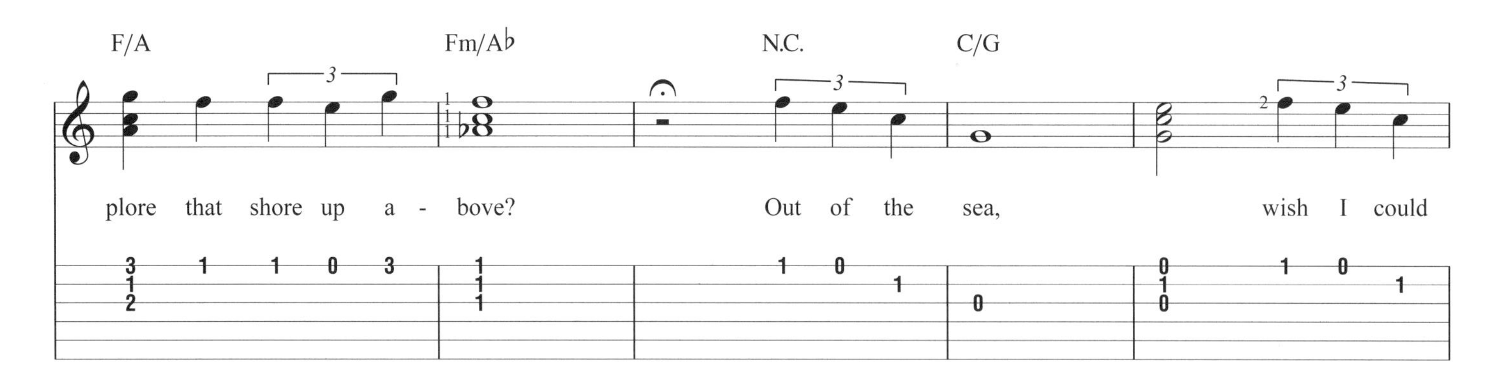
F/A
Fm/A♭
N.C.
C/G
plore that shore up a - bove? Out of the sea, wish I could

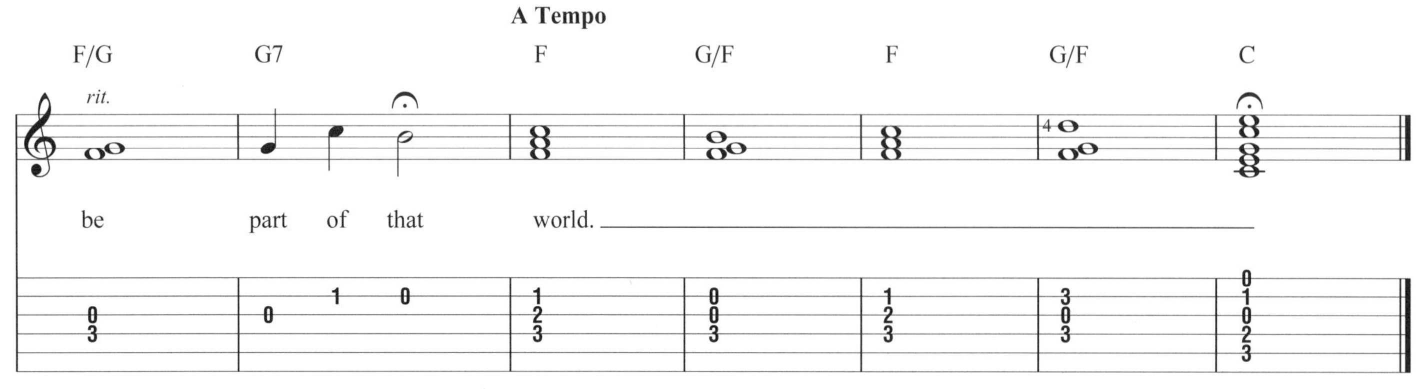
A Tempo
F/G
G7
F
G/F
F
G/F
C
rit.
be part of that world.

from MOANA

Music by Lin-Manuel Miranda and Mark Mancina
Lyrics by Lin-Manuel Miranda

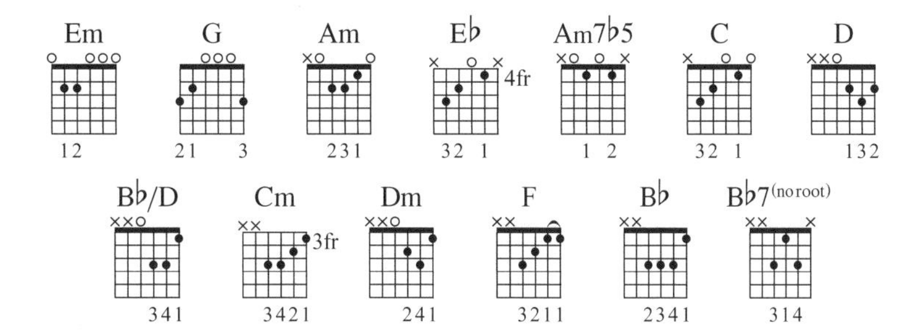

Strum Pattern: 3
Pick Pattern: 3

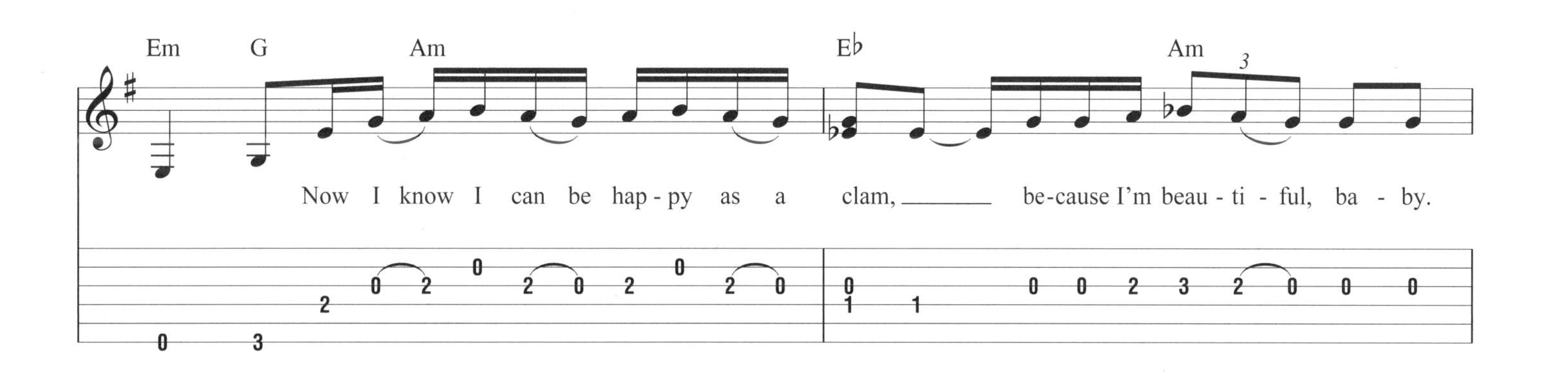

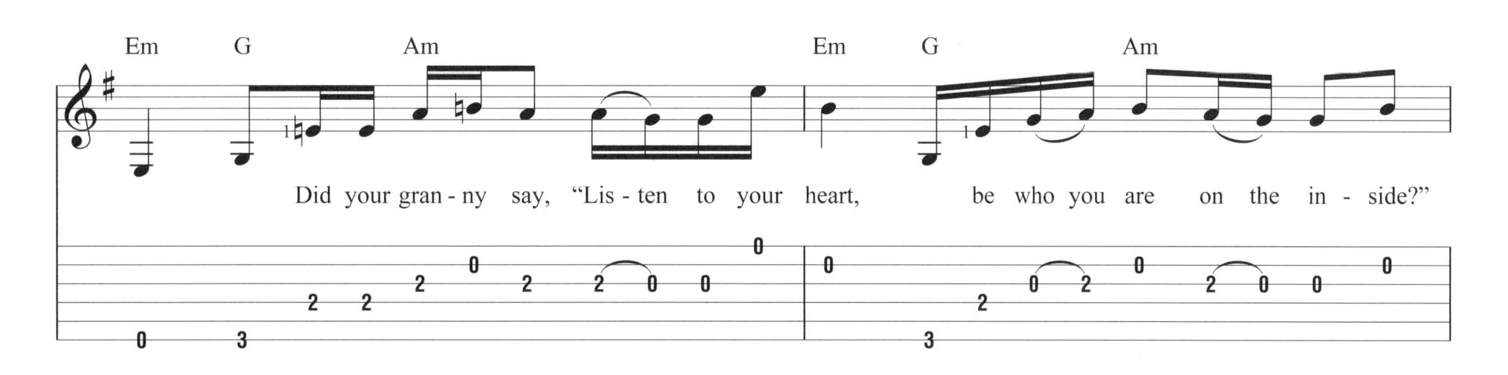

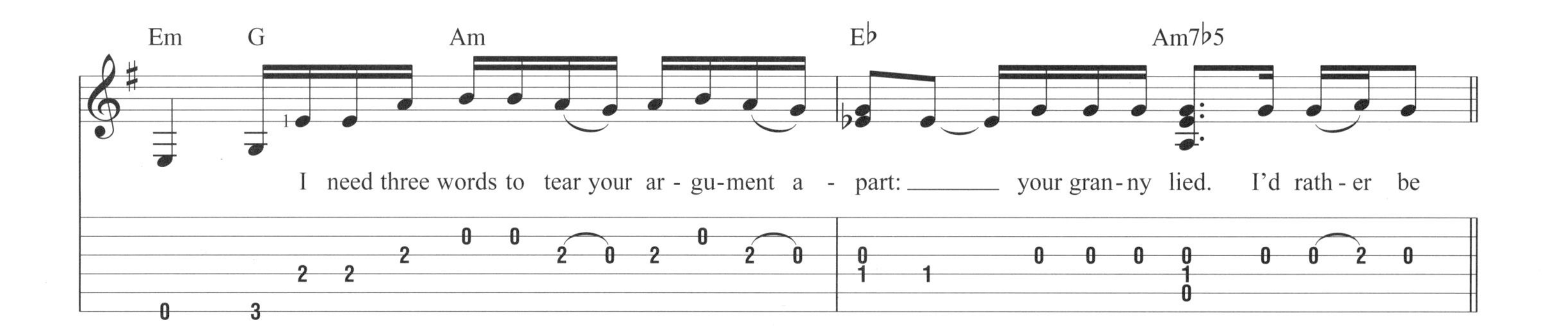
Em G Am Eb Am7b5
I need three words to tear your ar - gu-ment a - part: your gran-ny lied. I'd rath - er be

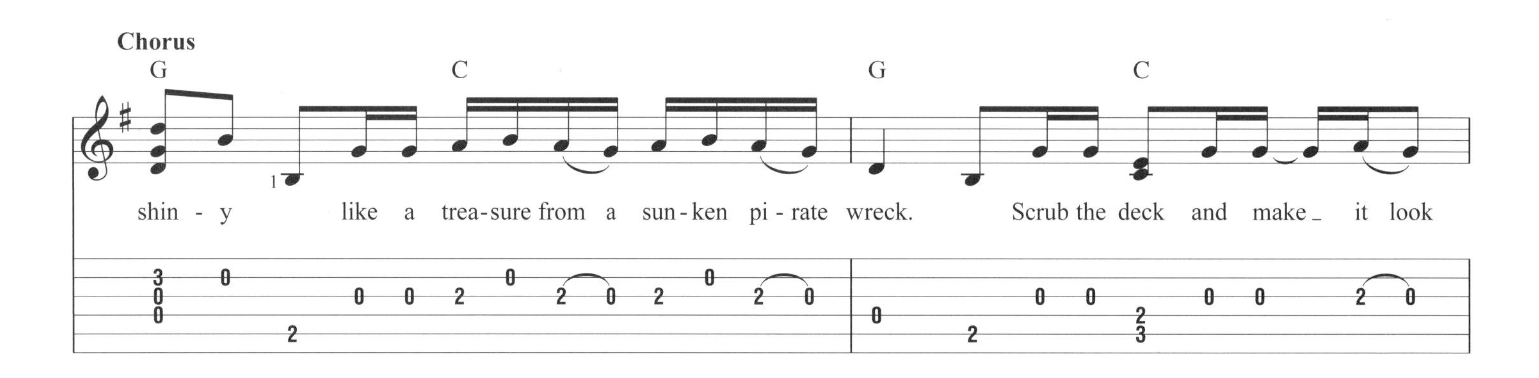
Chorus
G C G C
shin - y like a trea-sure from a sun-ken pi-rate wreck. Scrub the deck and make it look

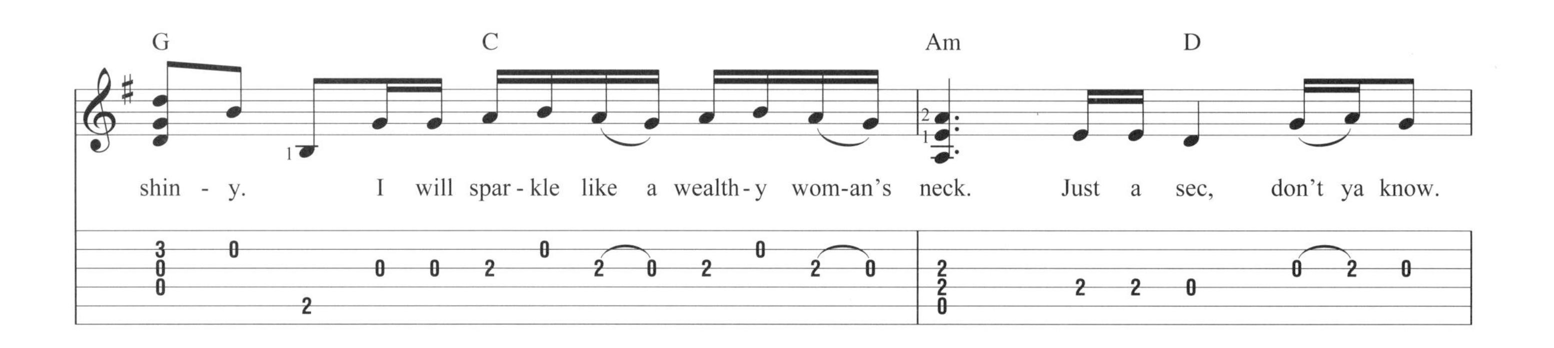
G C Am D
shin - y. I will spar-kle like a wealth-y wom-an's neck. Just a sec, don't ya know.

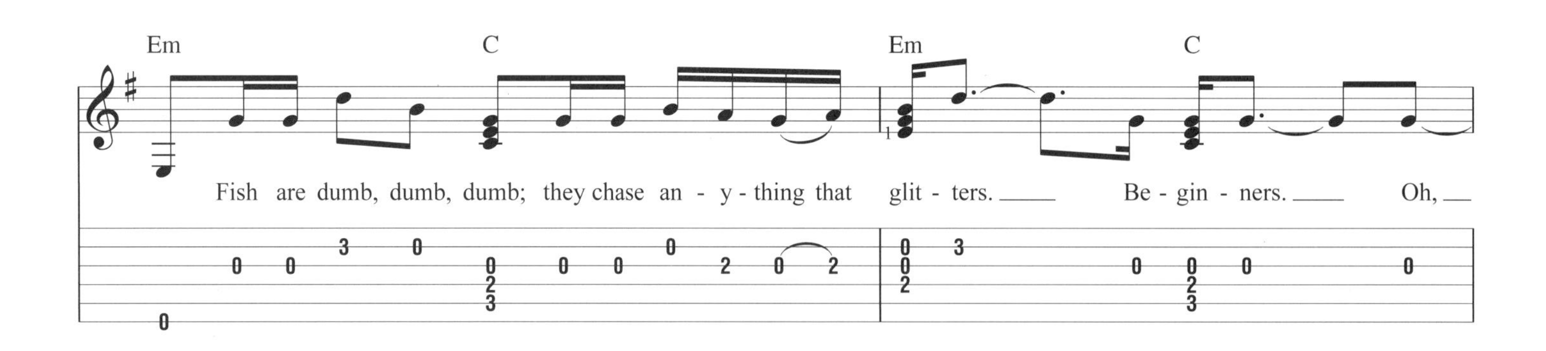
Em C Em C
Fish are dumb, dumb, dumb; they chase an - y-thing that glit - ters. Be - gin - ners. Oh,

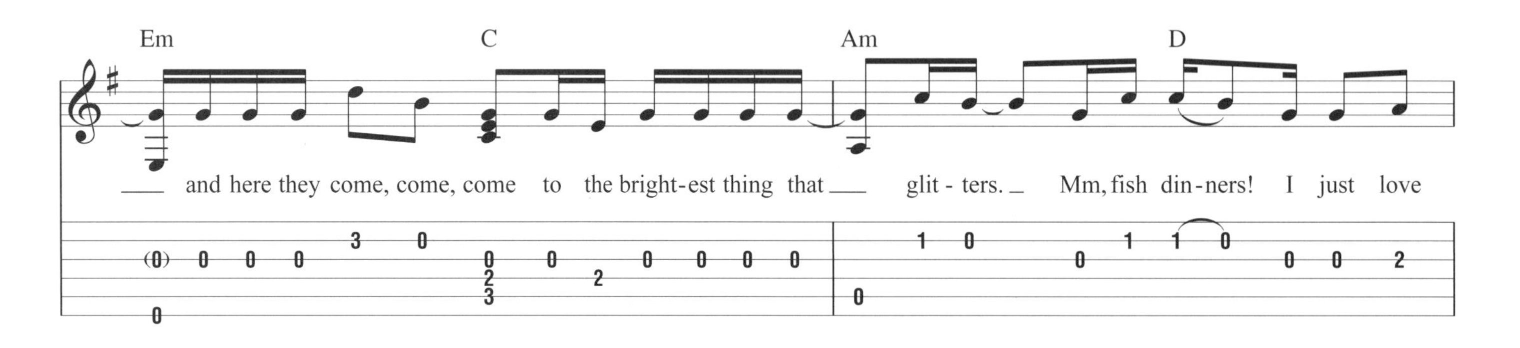
Em C Am D
and here they come, come, come to the bright-est thing that glit - ters. Mm, fish din-ners! I just love

*Lyrics in italics are spoken throughout.

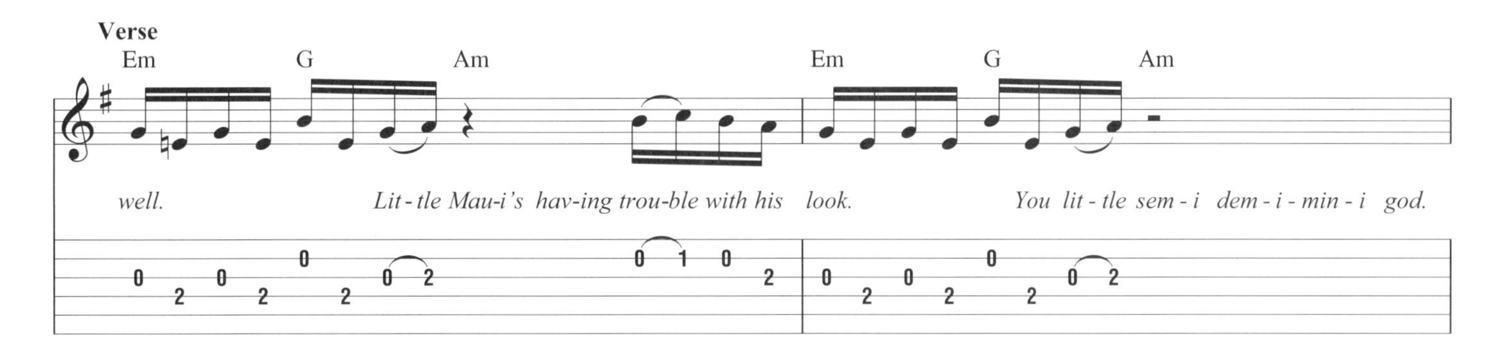

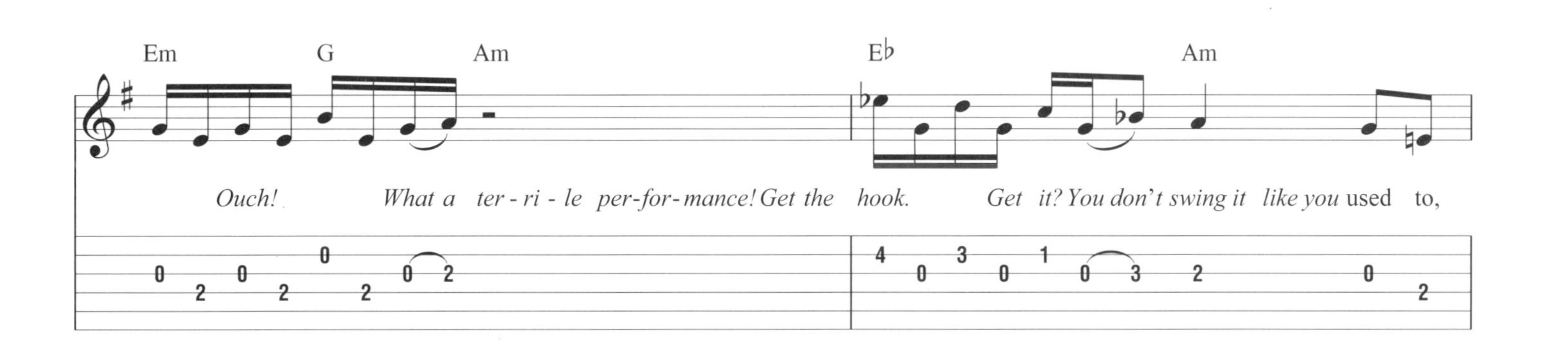

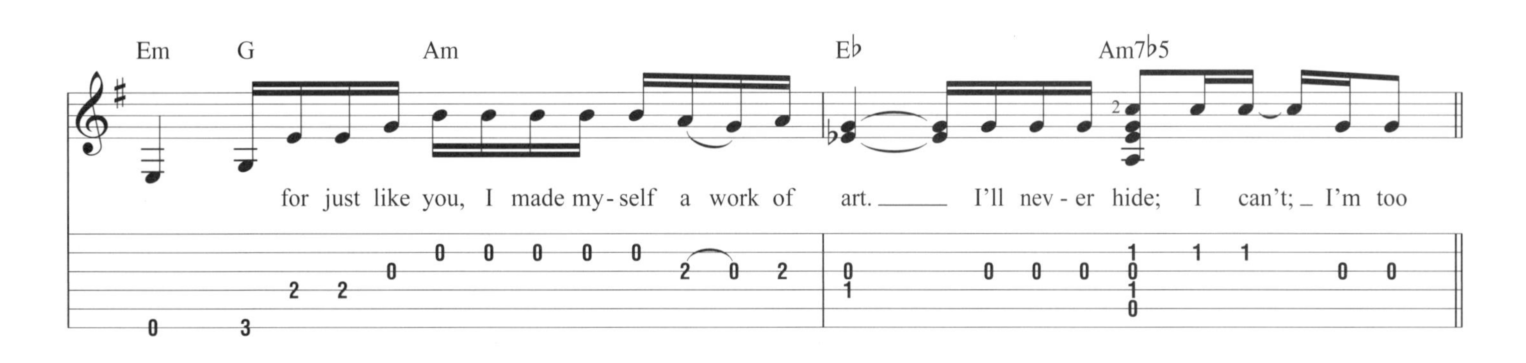

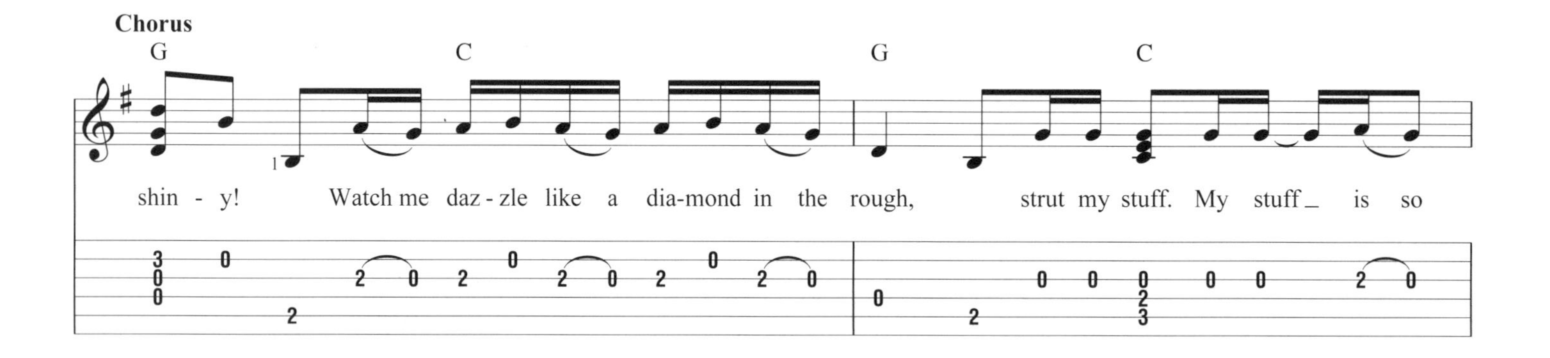
Chorus
G C G C
shin - y! Watch me daz - zle like a dia-mond in the rough, strut my stuff. My stuff _ is so

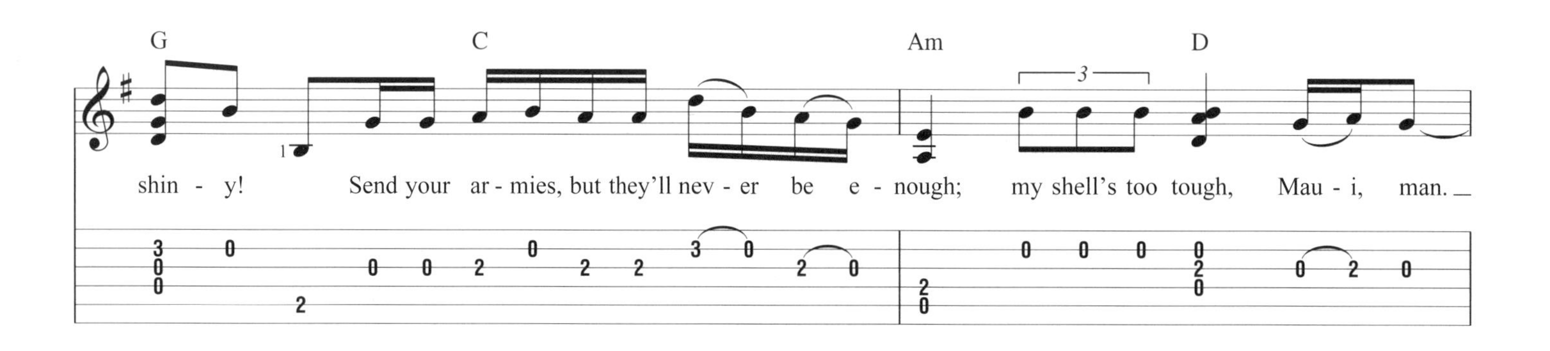
G C Am D
shin - y! Send your ar - mies, but they'll nev - er be e - nough; my shell's too tough, Mau - i, man. _

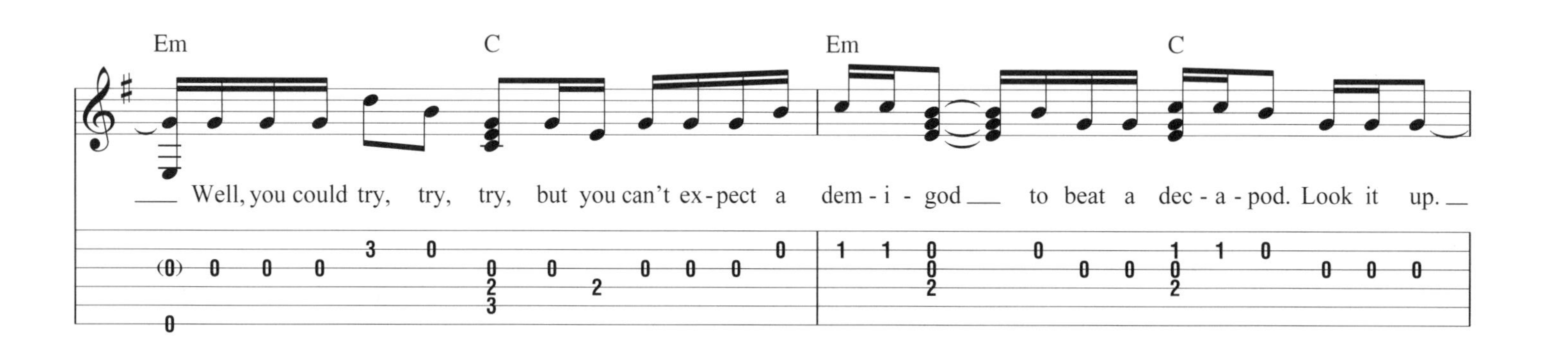
Em C Em C
_ Well, you could try, try, try, but you can't ex - pect a dem - i - god _ to beat a dec - a - pod. Look it up. _

Em C Am D
_ You will die, die, die; now it's time for me to take a - part _ your ach - ing heart.

Bridge
E♭ B♭/D
Far from _ the ones who _ a - ban - doned _ you, chas - ing _ the love of _ these hu - mans _ who

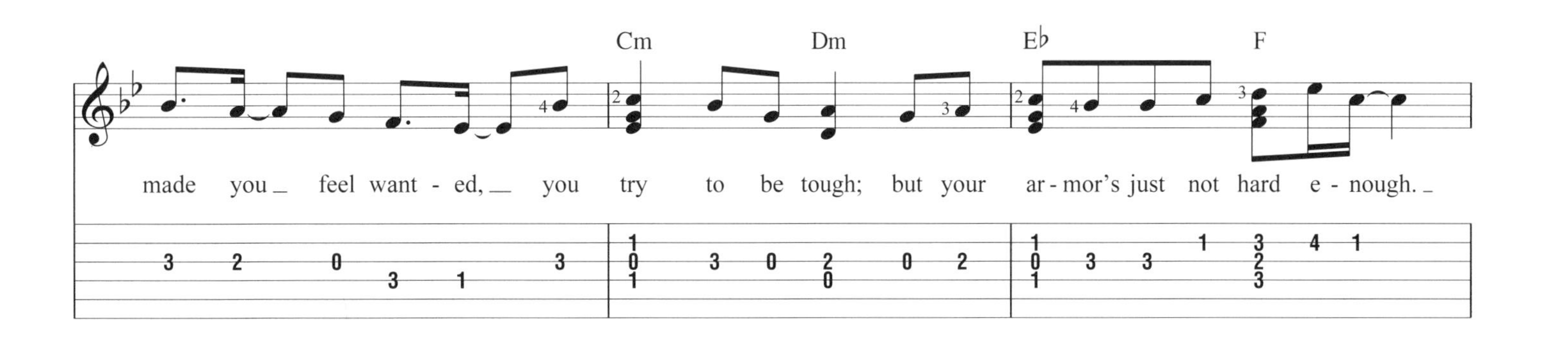
Cm Dm E♭ F
made you feel want - ed, you try to be tough; but your ar - mor's just not hard e - nough.

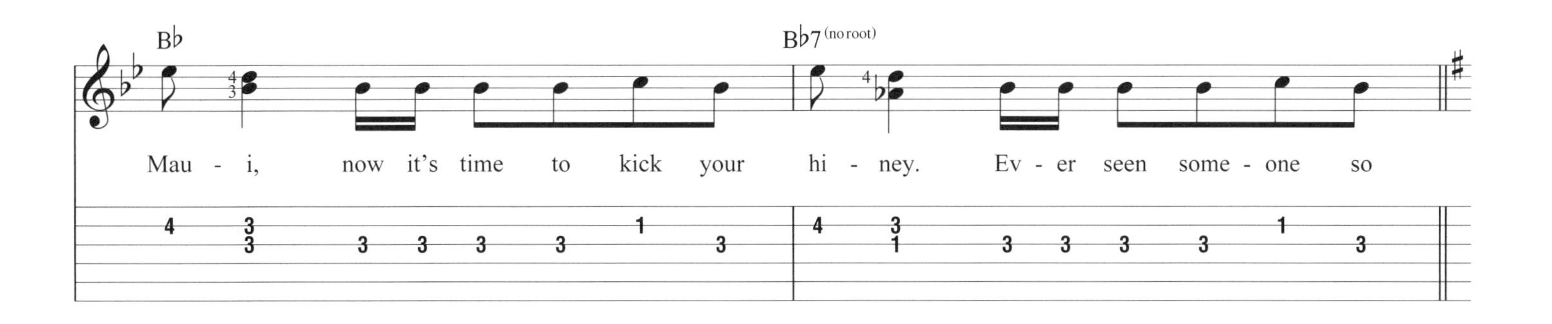
B♭ B♭7 (no root)
Mau - i, now it's time to kick your hi - ney. Ev - er seen some - one so

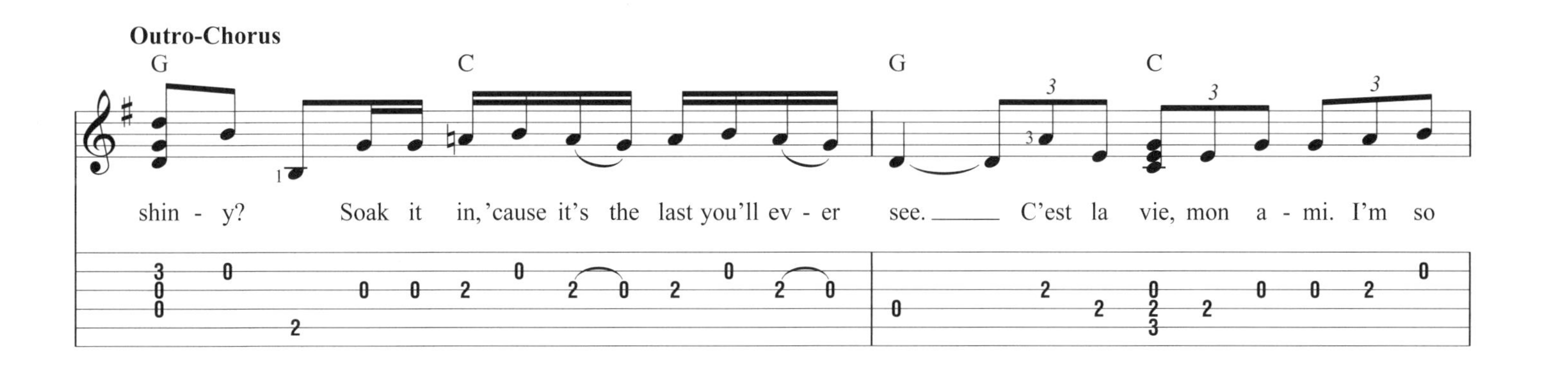
Outro-Chorus
G C G C
shin - y? Soak it in, 'cause it's the last you'll ev - er see. C'est la vie, mon a - mi. I'm so

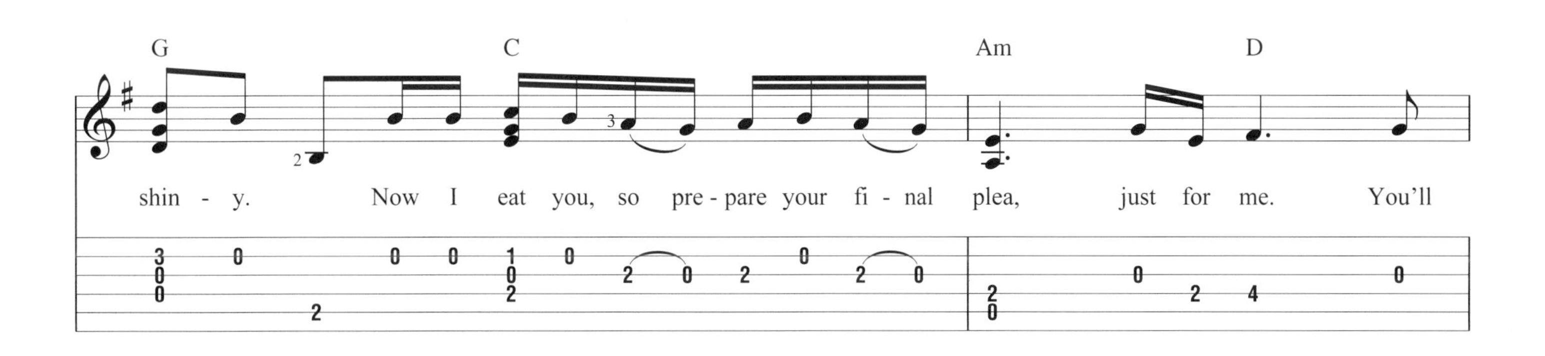
G C Am D
shin - y. Now I eat you, so pre - pare your fi - nal plea, just for me. You'll

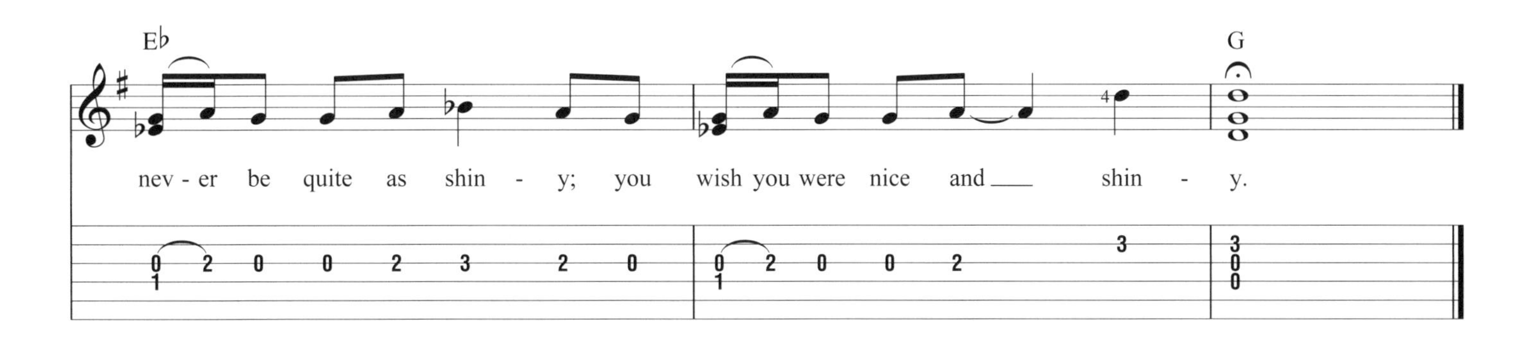
E♭ G
nev - er be quite as shin - y; you wish you were nice and shin - y.

Reflection

from MULAN
Music by Matthew Wilder
Lyrics by David Zippel

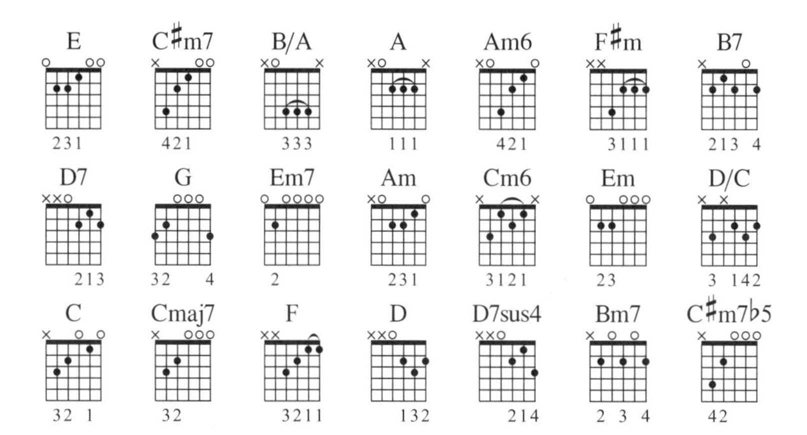

*Capo I

Strum Pattern: 3
Pick Pattern: 3

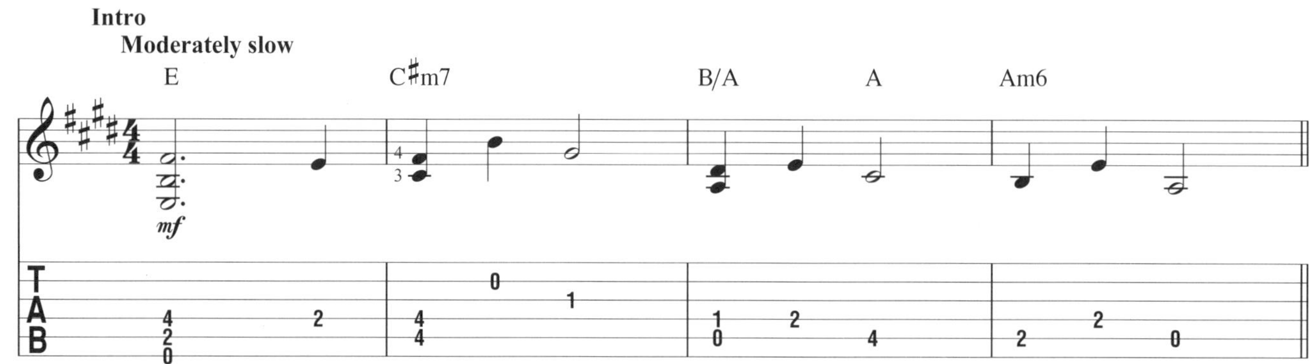

*Optional: To match recording, place capo at 1st fret.

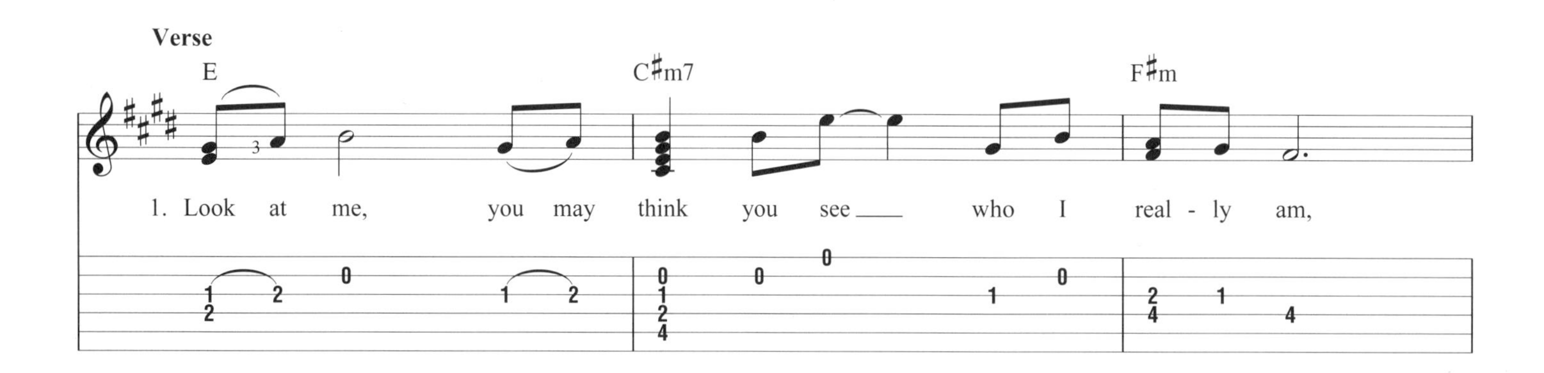

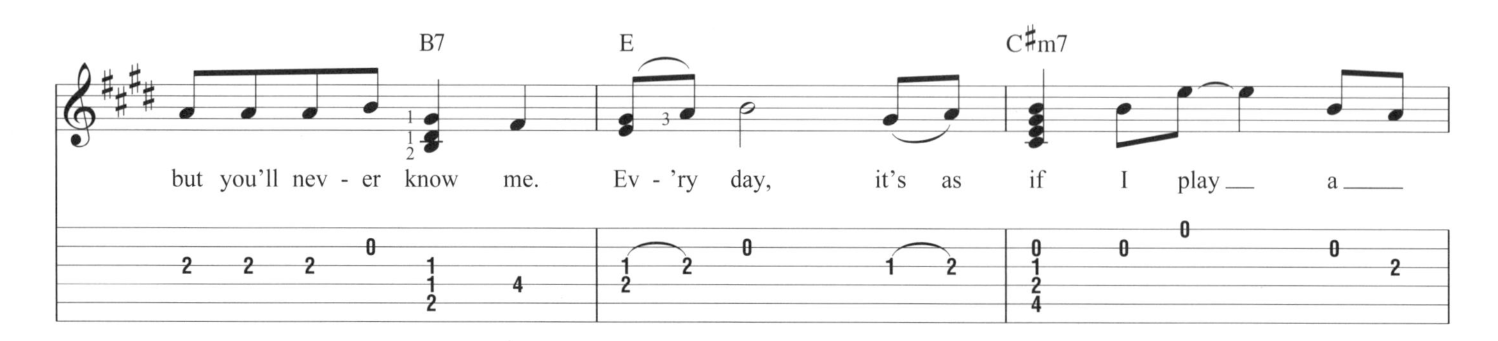

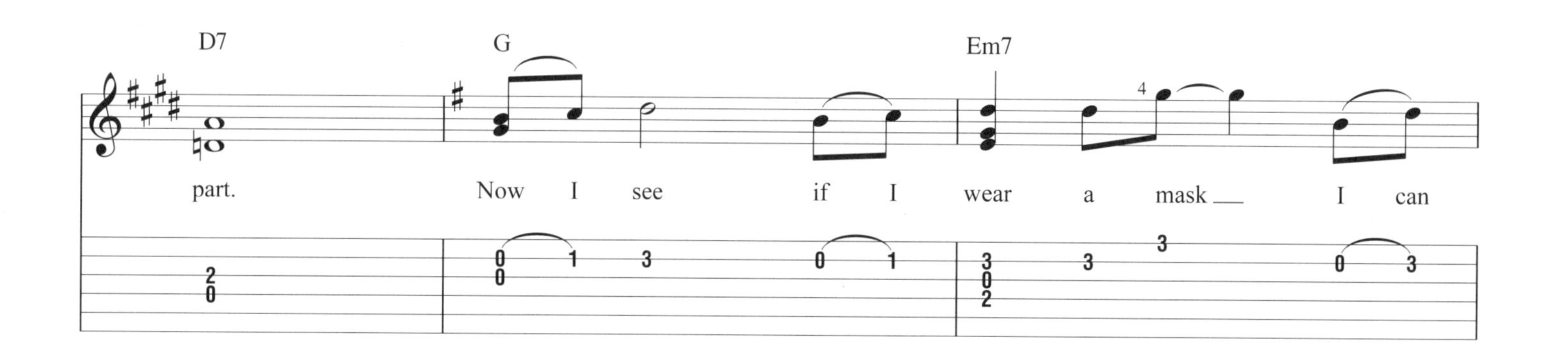
D7
G
Em7
part. Now I see if I wear a mask I can

Am
Cm6
G
fool the world, but I can - not fool my heart.

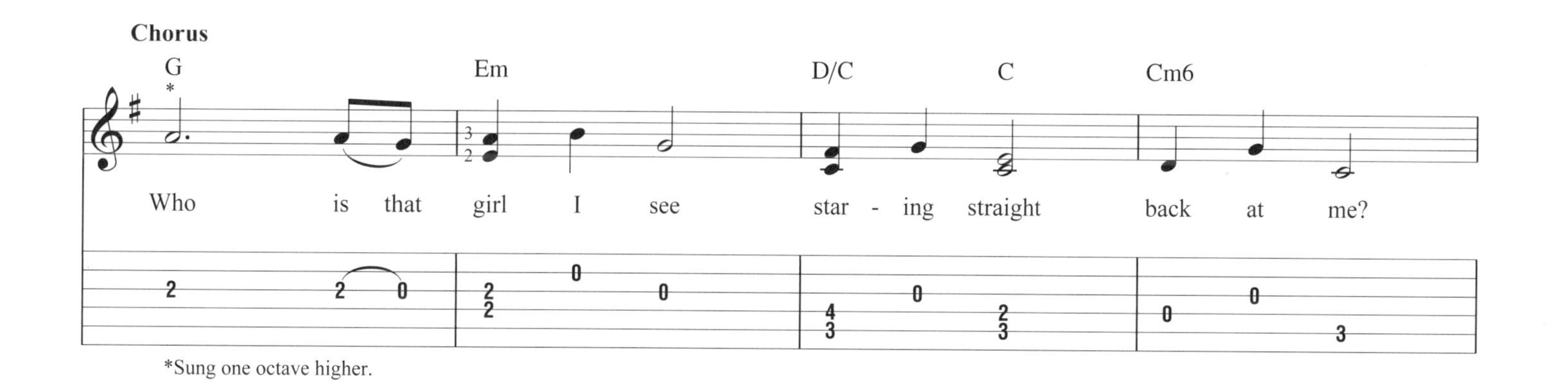
Chorus
G
Em
D/C
C
Cm6
Who is that girl I see star - ing straight back at me?
*Sung one octave higher.

G
Em
Cmaj7
Cm6
G
When will my re - flec - tion show who I am in - side?

Em7
Verse
E
C♯m7
F♯m
2. I am now in a world where I have to hide my heart
**Sung as written.

B7 G Em7
and what I be - lieve in. But some-how I will show the world _ what's in -

Am Cm6 G
side my heart, _ and be loved for who _ I ___ am.

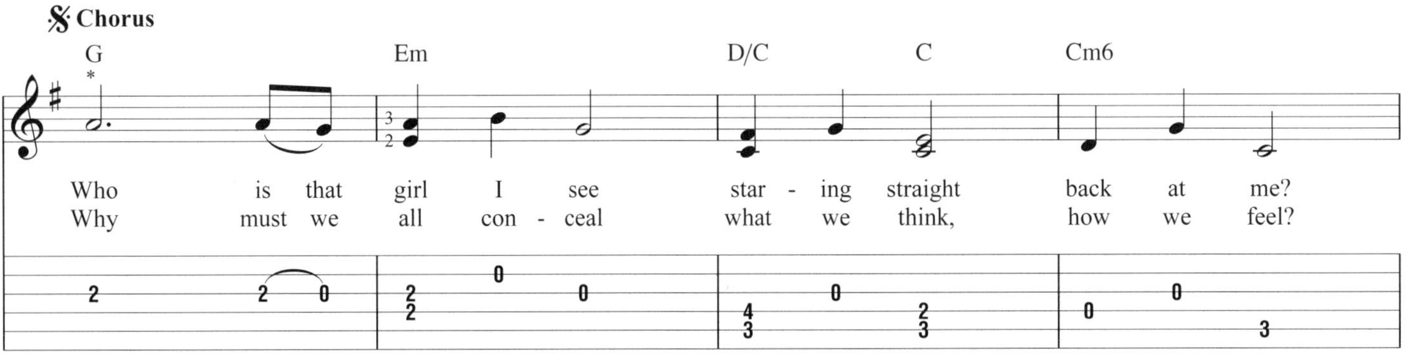
Chorus
G Em D/C C Cm6
Who is that girl I see star - ing straight back at me?
Why must we all con - ceal what we think, how we feel?
*Sung one octave higher.

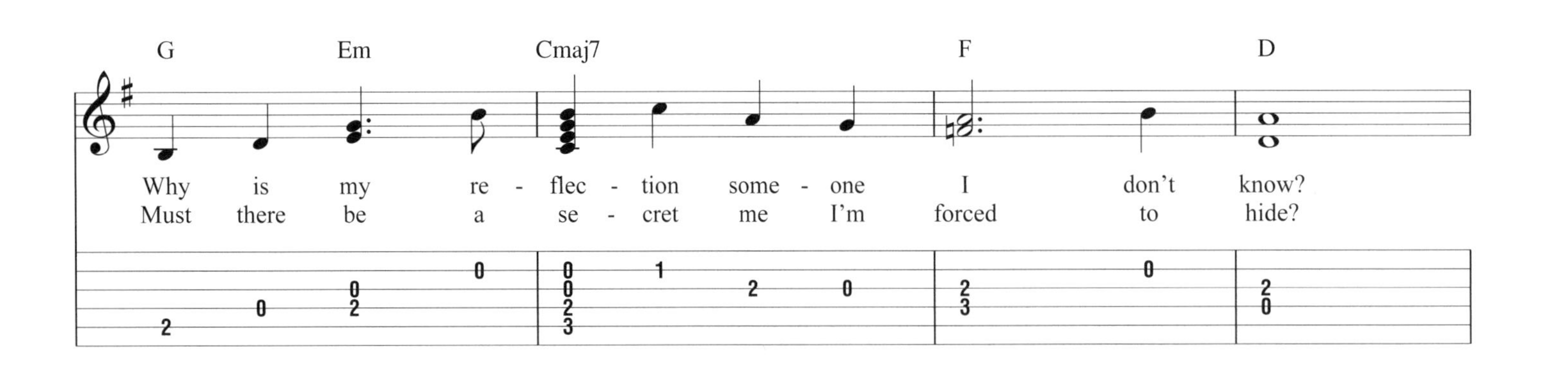
G Em Cmaj7 F D
Why is my re - flec - tion some - one I don't know?
Must there be a se - cret me I'm forced to hide?

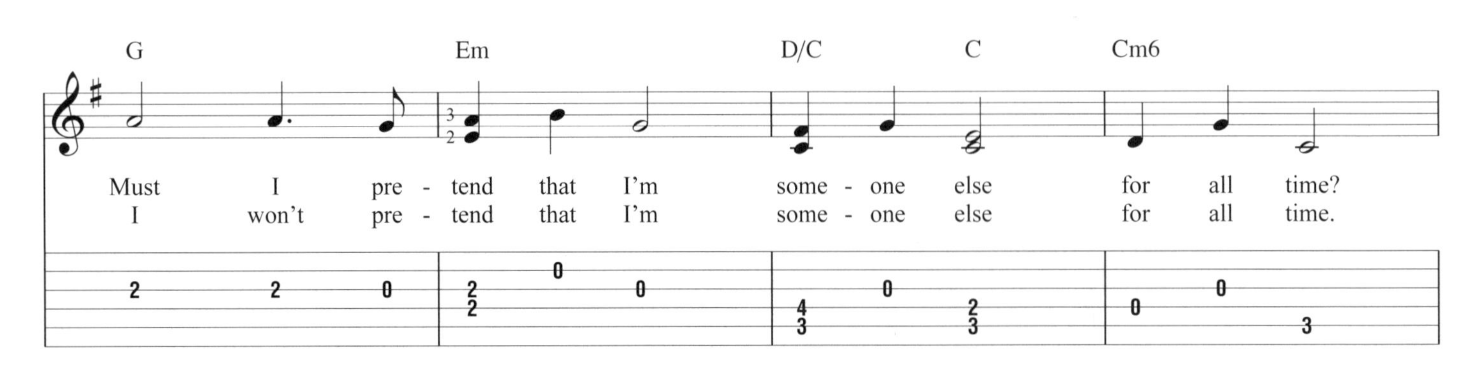
G Em D/C C Cm6
Must I pre - tend that I'm some - one else for all time?
I won't pre - tend that I'm some - one else for all time.

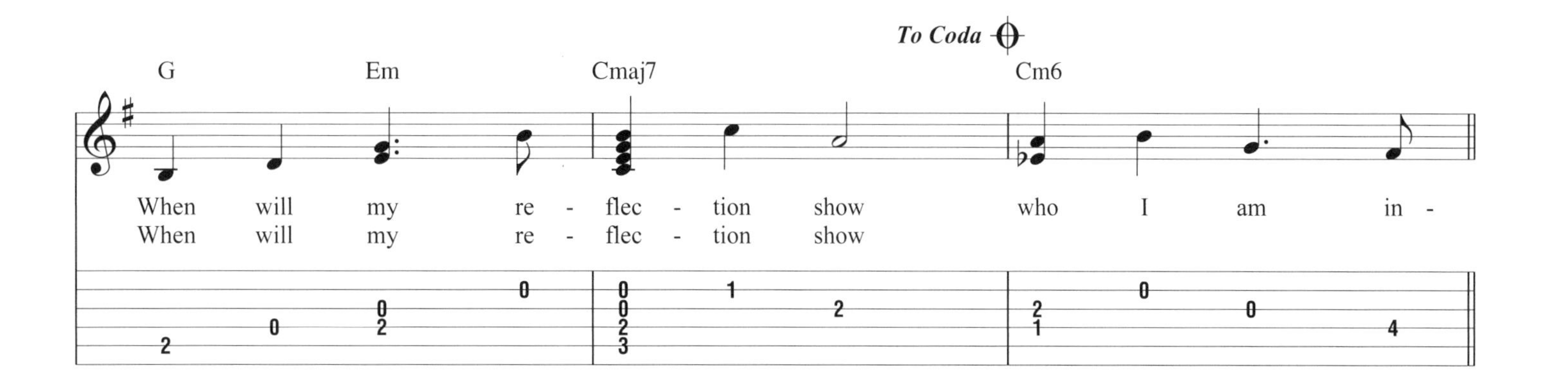
To Coda
G Em Cmaj7 Cm6
When will my re - flec - tion show who I am in -
When will my re - flec - tion show

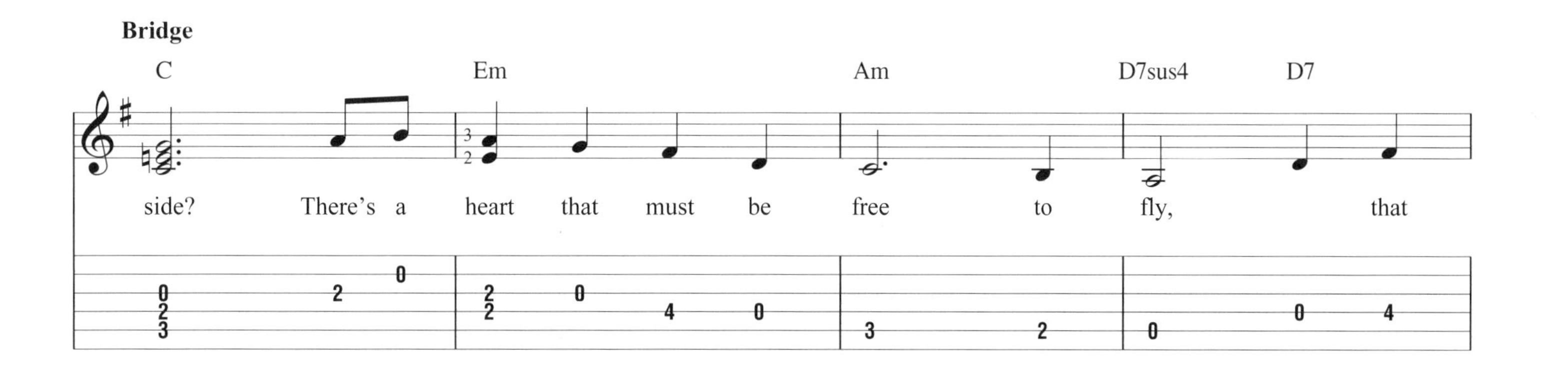
Bridge
C Em Am D7sus4 D7
side? There's a heart that must be free to fly, that

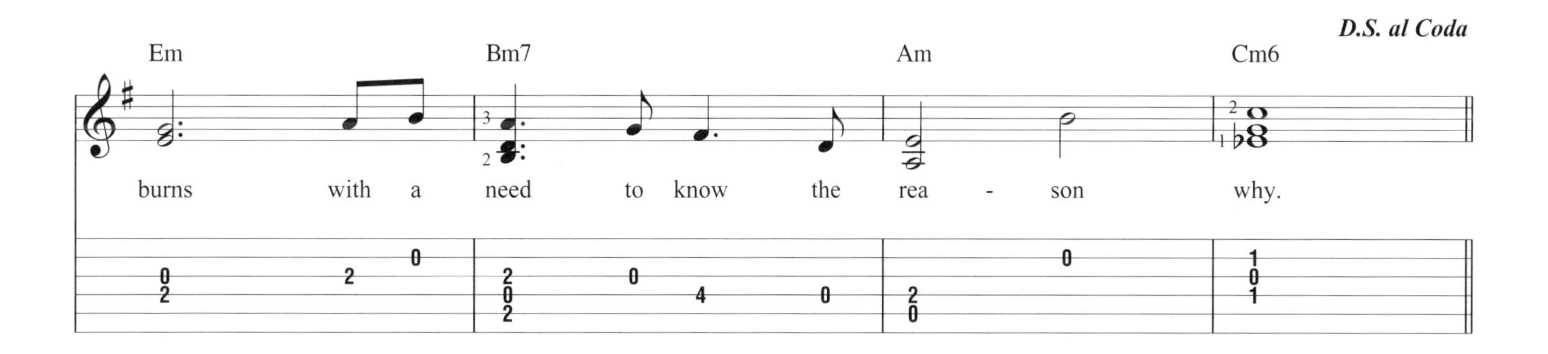
D.S. al Coda
Em Bm7 Am Cm6
burns with a need to know the rea - son why.

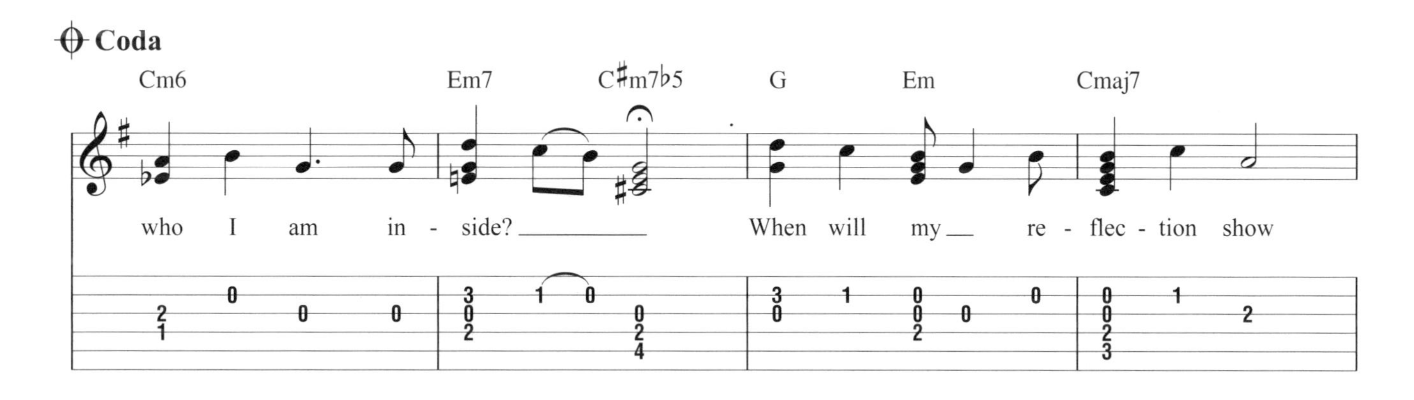
Coda
Cm6 Em7 C♯m7♭5 G Em Cmaj7
who I am in - side? When will my re - flec - tion show

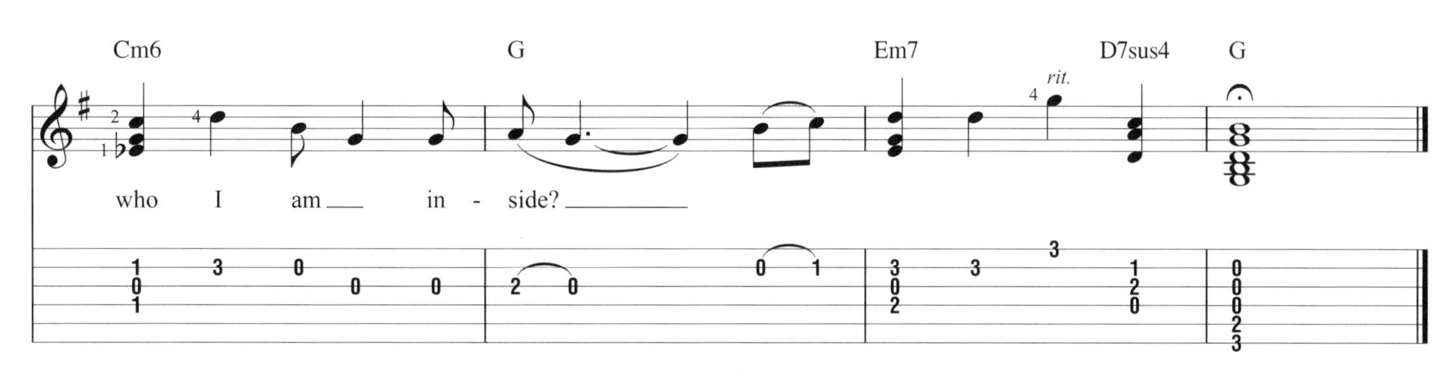
Cm6 G Em7 D7sus4 G
rit.
who I am in - side?

Strangers Like Me®

from TARZAN®

Words and Music by Phil Collins

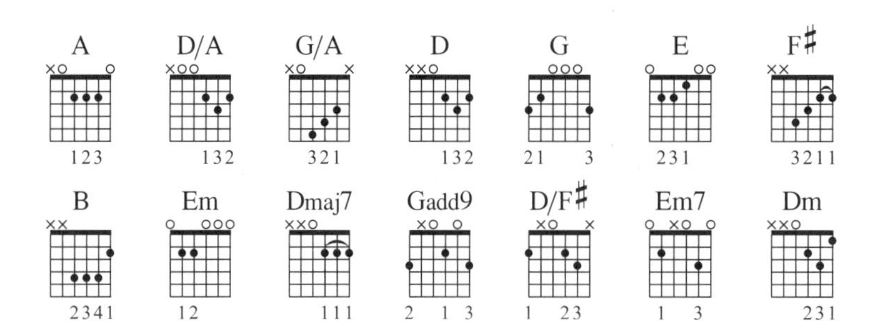

*Capo I

Strum Pattern: 2
Pick Pattern: 4

Intro

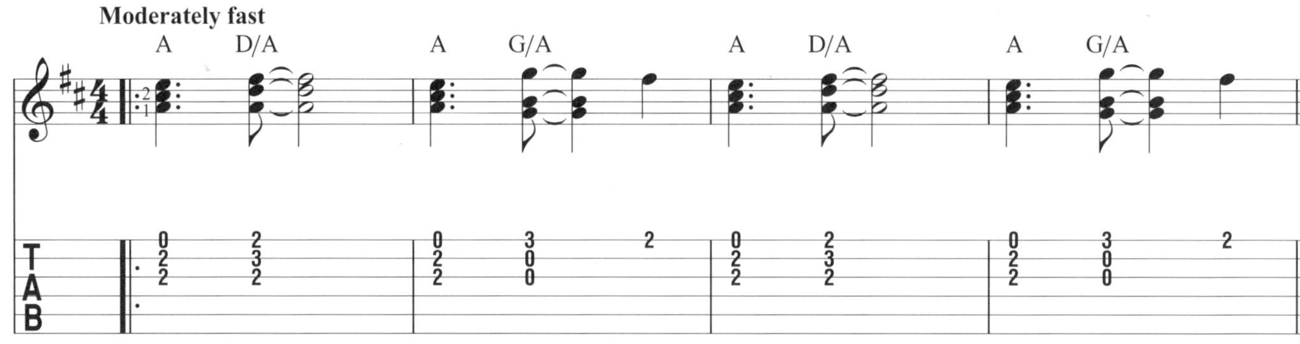

*Optional: To match recording, place capo at 1st fret.

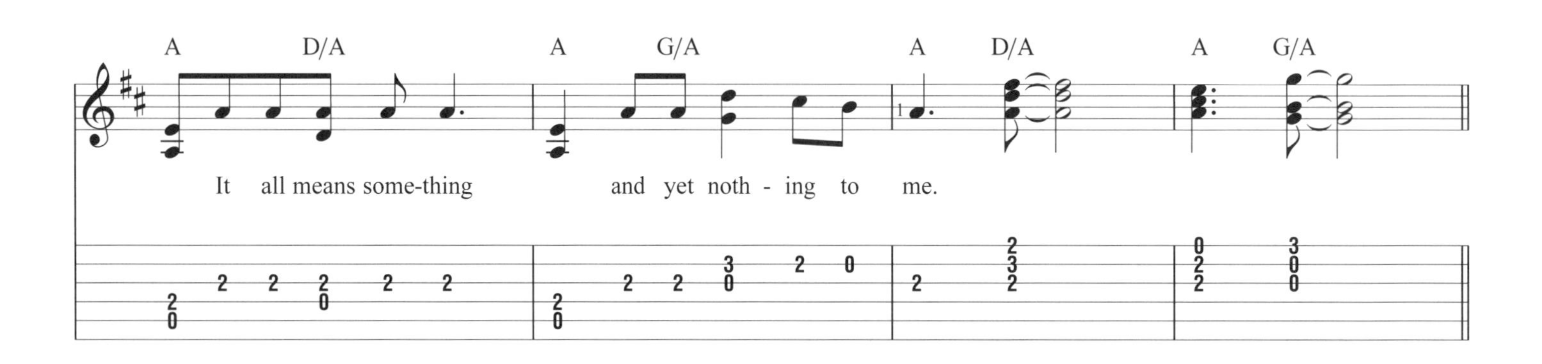

Pre-Chorus
D G E A
Oh, I can see there's so much to learn; it's all so close and yet so far.
See additional lyrics

F♯ B G A
I see my-self as peo - ple see me. Oh, I just know there's some - thing big - ger out there.

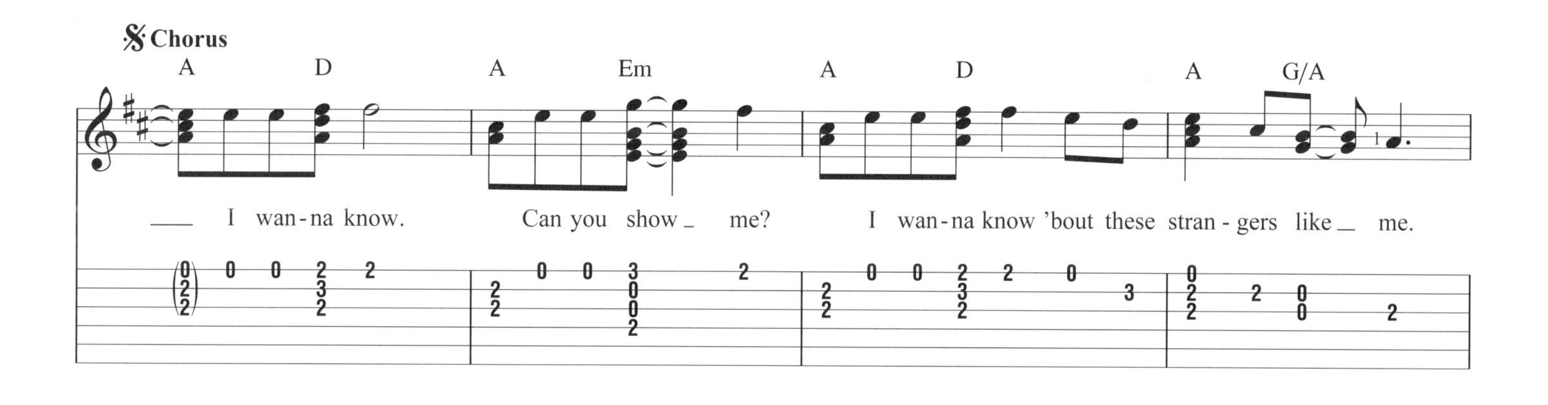
Chorus
A D A Em A D A G/A
I wan-na know. Can you show me? I wan-na know 'bout these stran - gers like me.

3rd time, To Coda
A D A Em A D A G/A
Tell me more; please show me. Some-thing's fa - mil - iar 'bout these stran-gers like me.

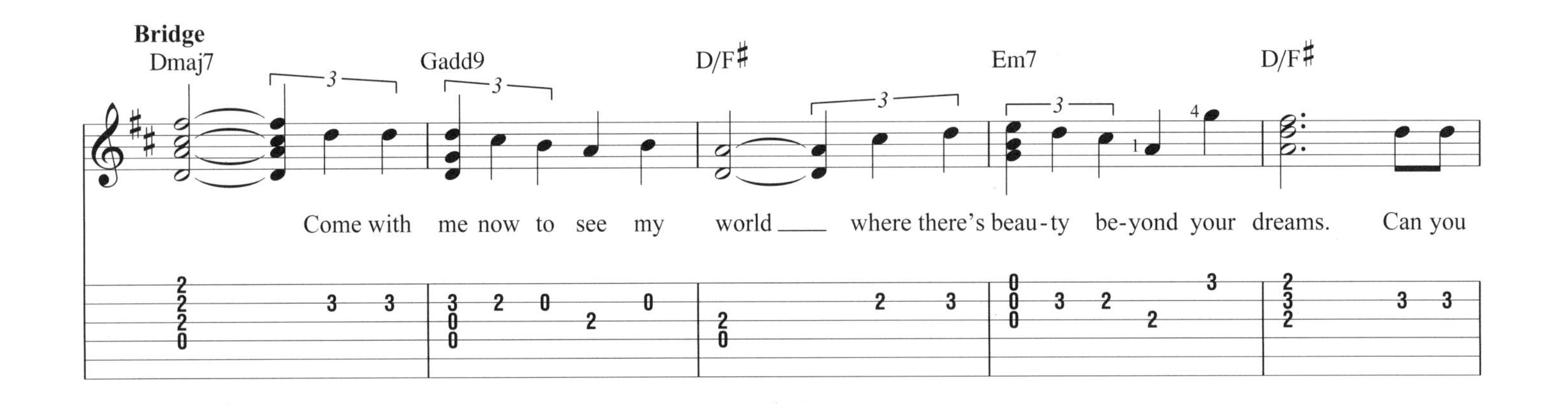

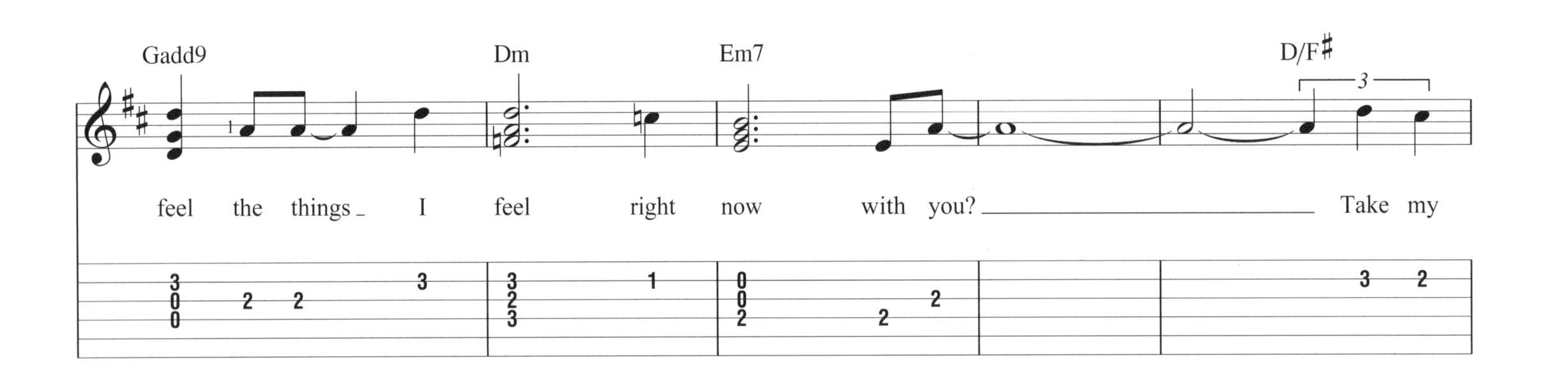

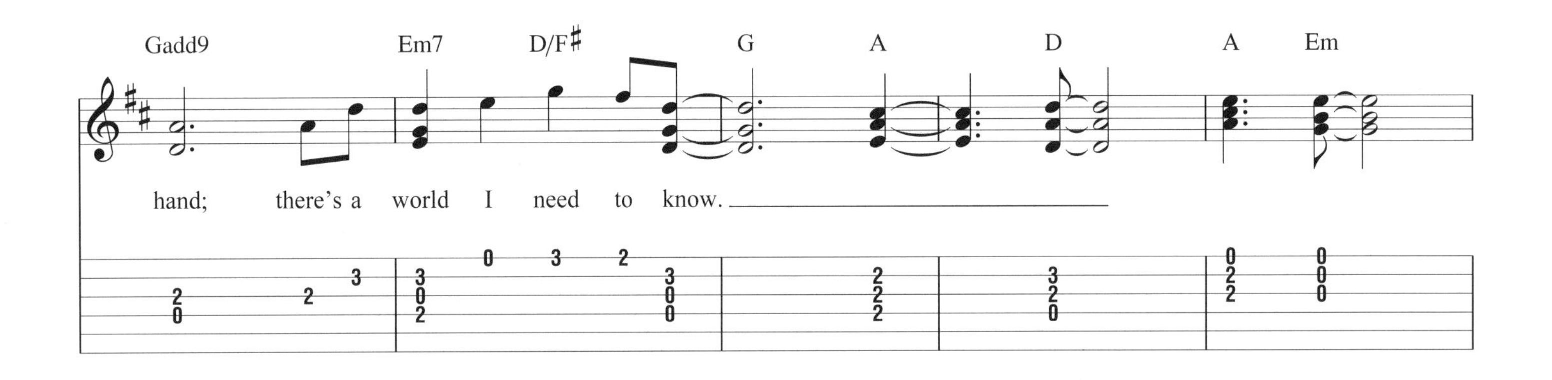

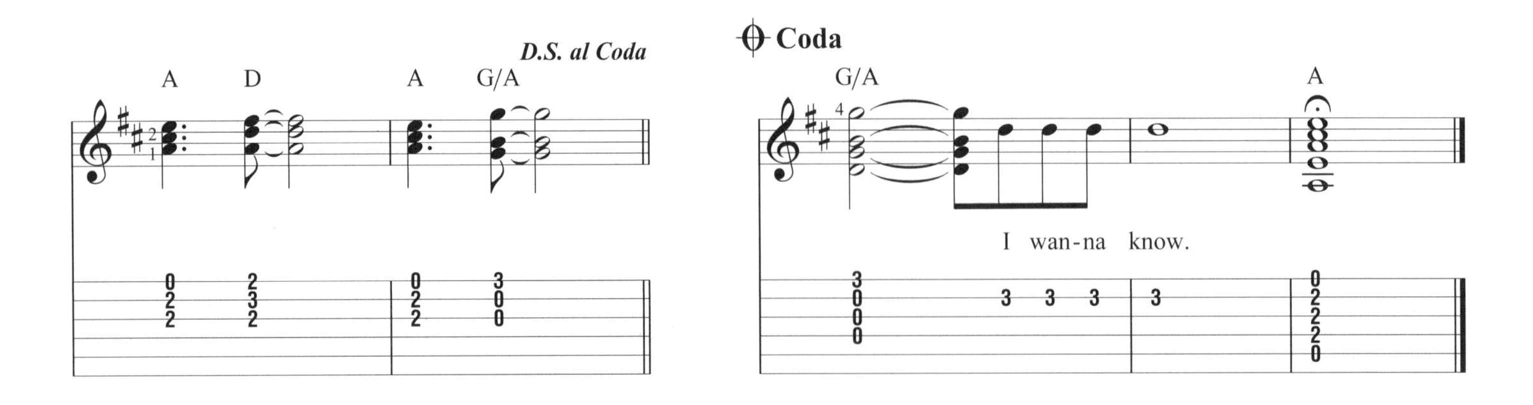

Additional Lyrics

2. Ev'ry gesture, ev'ry move that she makes
   Makes me feel like never before.
   Why do I have this growing need
   To be beside her?

Pre-Chorus Oh, these emotions I never knew,
Of some other world far beyond this place.
Beyond the trees, above the clouds.
Oh, I see before me a new horizon.

Under the Sea

from THE LITTLE MERMAID

Music by Alan Menken
Lyrics by Howard Ashman

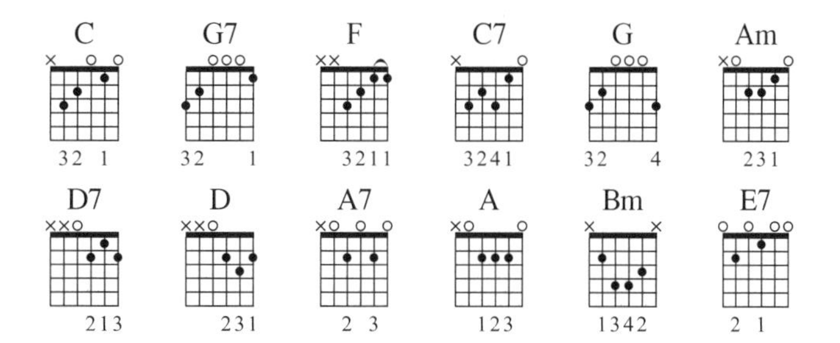

Strum Pattern: 3
Pick Pattern: 3

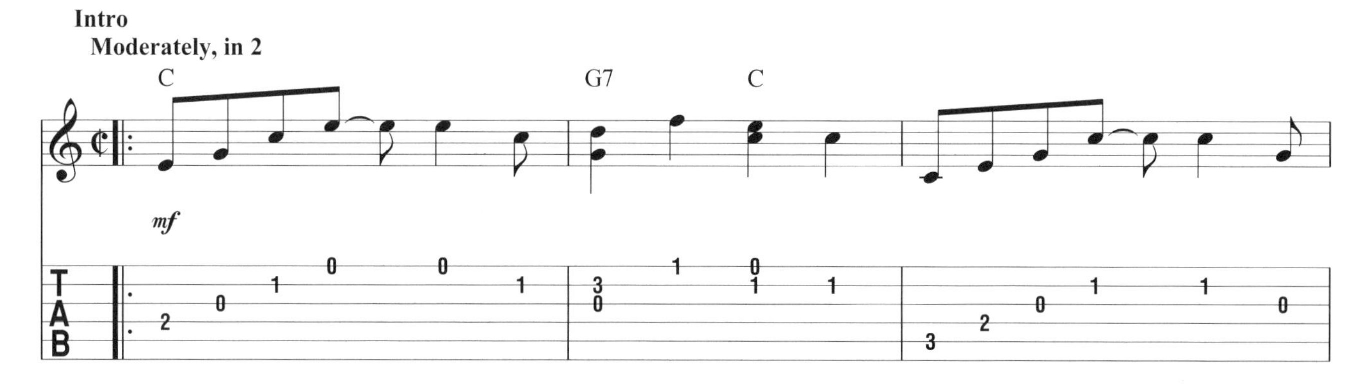

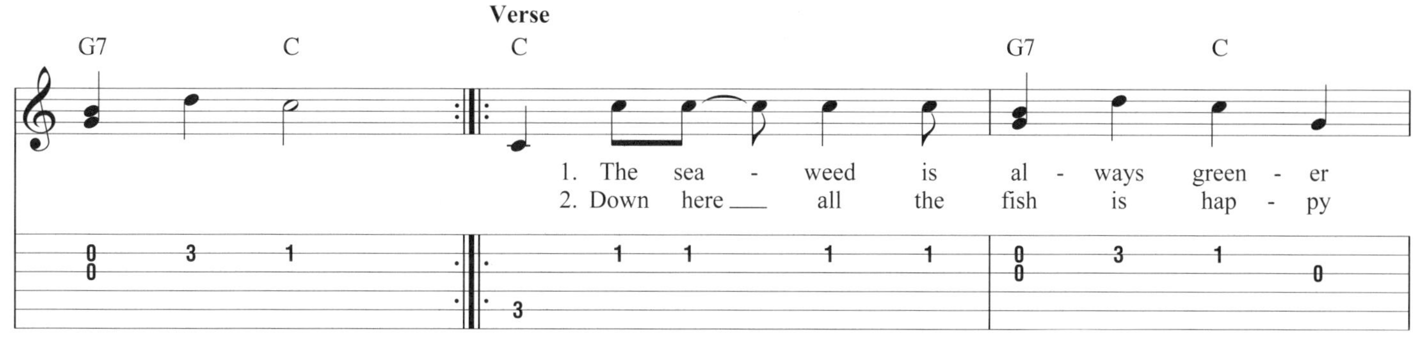

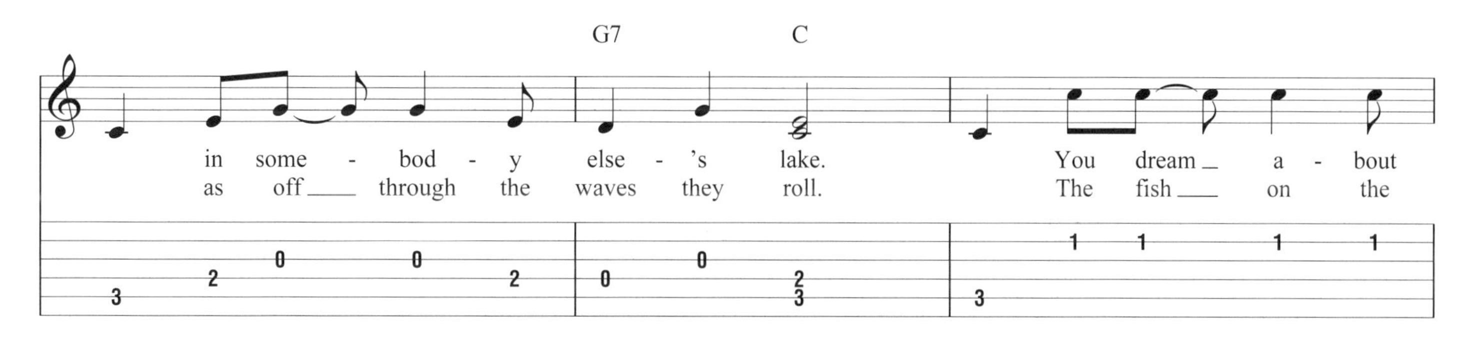

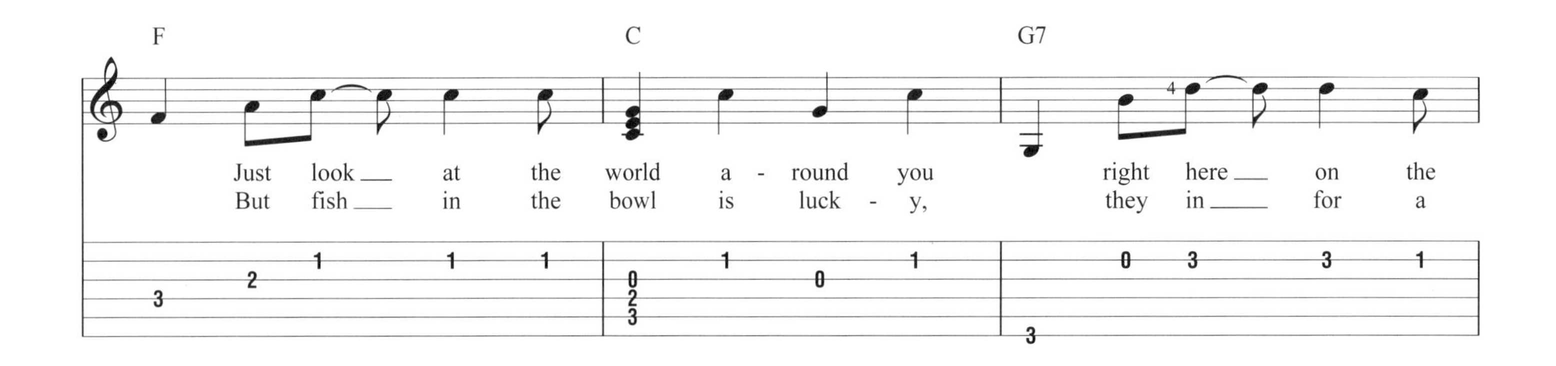
F C G7
Just look at the world a - round you right here on the
But fish in the bowl is luck - y, they in for a

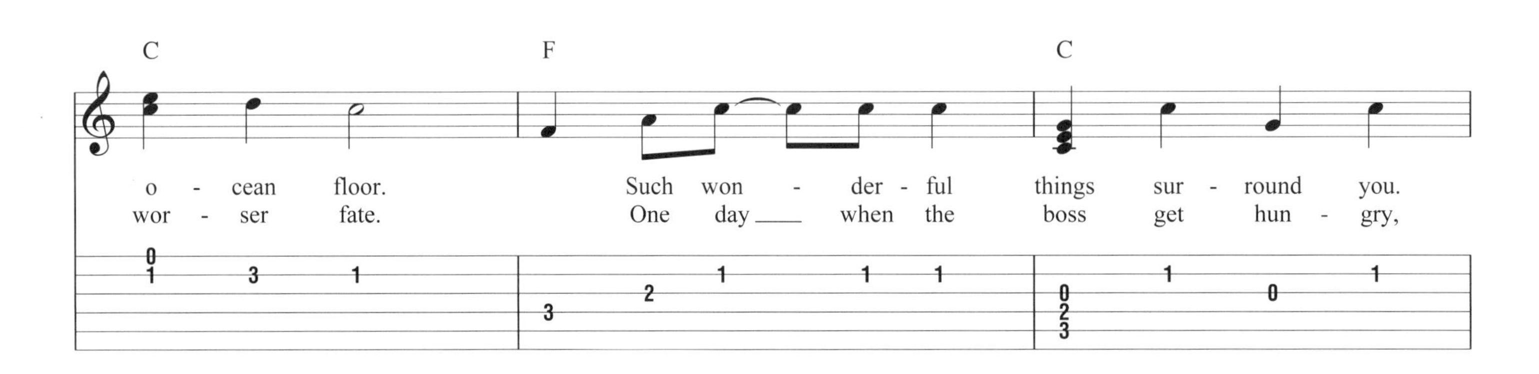
C F C
o - cean floor. Such won - der - ful things sur - round you.
wor - ser fate. One day when the boss get hun - gry,

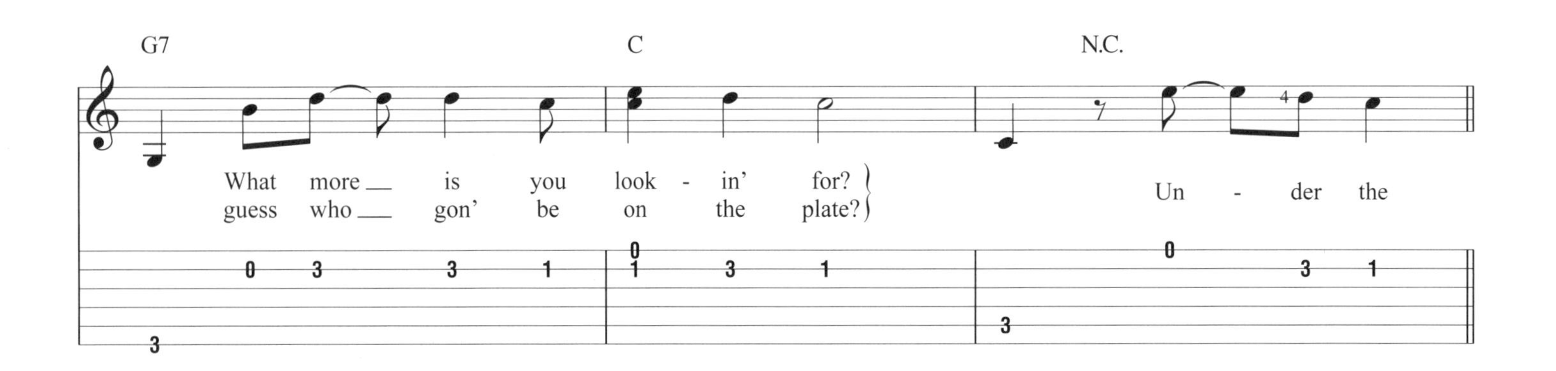
G7 C N.C.
What more is you look - in' for?
guess who gon' be on the plate?
Un - der the

Chorus

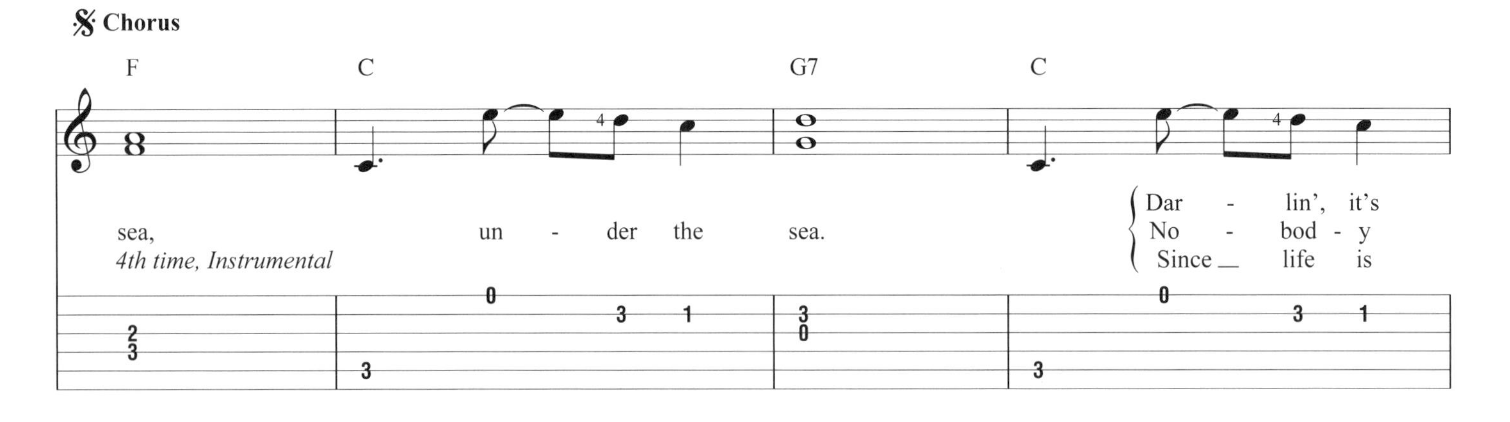
F C G7 C
sea, un - der the sea.
4th time, Instrumental
Dar - lin', it's
No - bod - y
Since life is

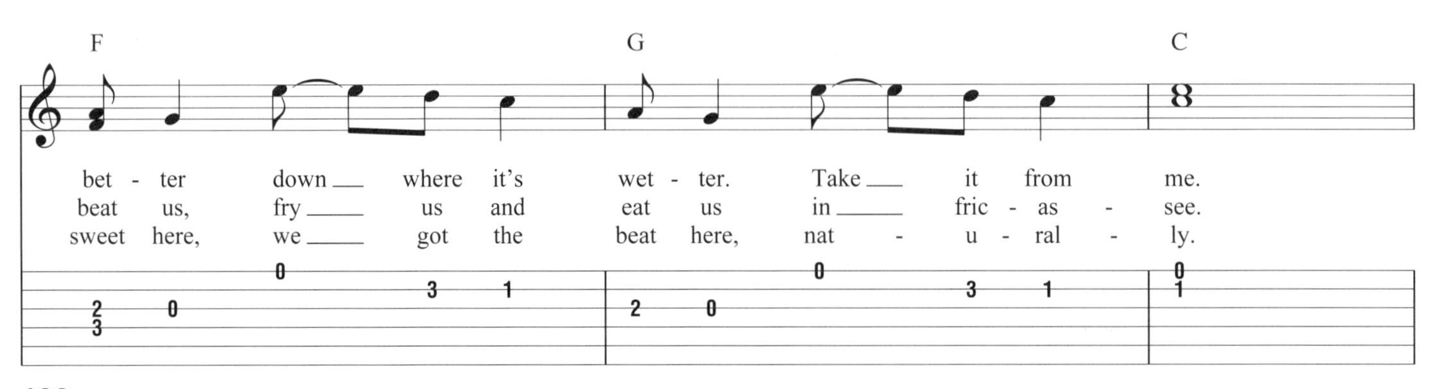
F G C
bet - ter down where it's wet - ter. Take it from me.
beat us, fry us and eat us in fric - as - see.
sweet here, we got the beat here, nat - u - ral - ly.

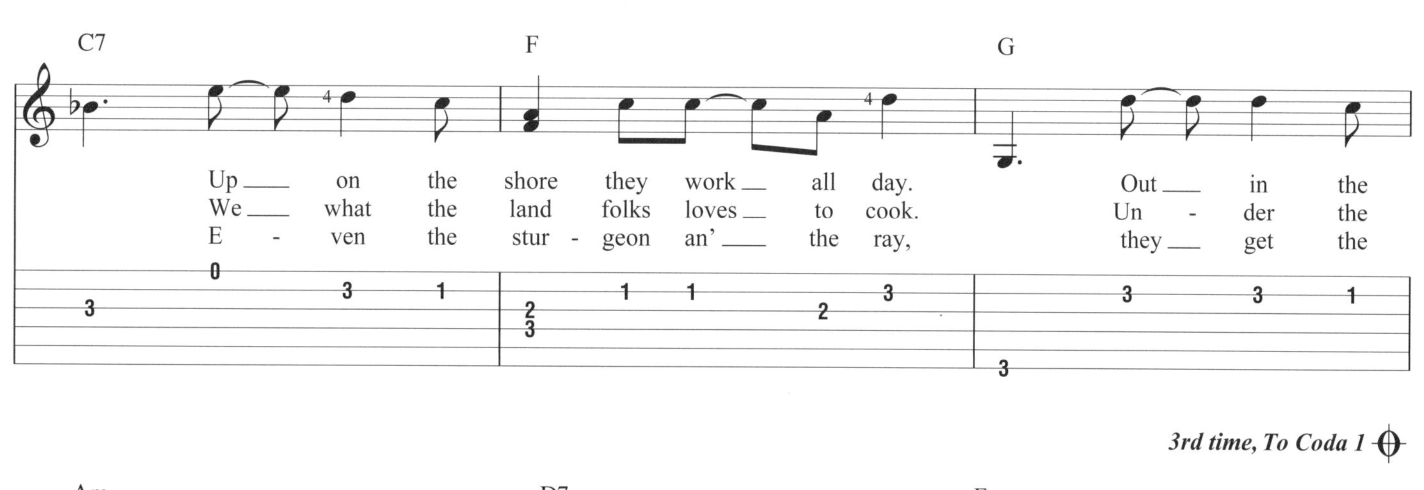

C7
F
G
Up on the shore they work all day. Out in the
We what the land folks loves to cook. Un - der the
E - ven the stur - geon an' the ray, they get the
3rd time, To Coda 1

Am
D7
F
sun, they slave a - way while we de - vot - in' full time to
sea, we off the hook. We got no trou - bles, life is the
urge 'n' start to play. We got the spir - it, you got to

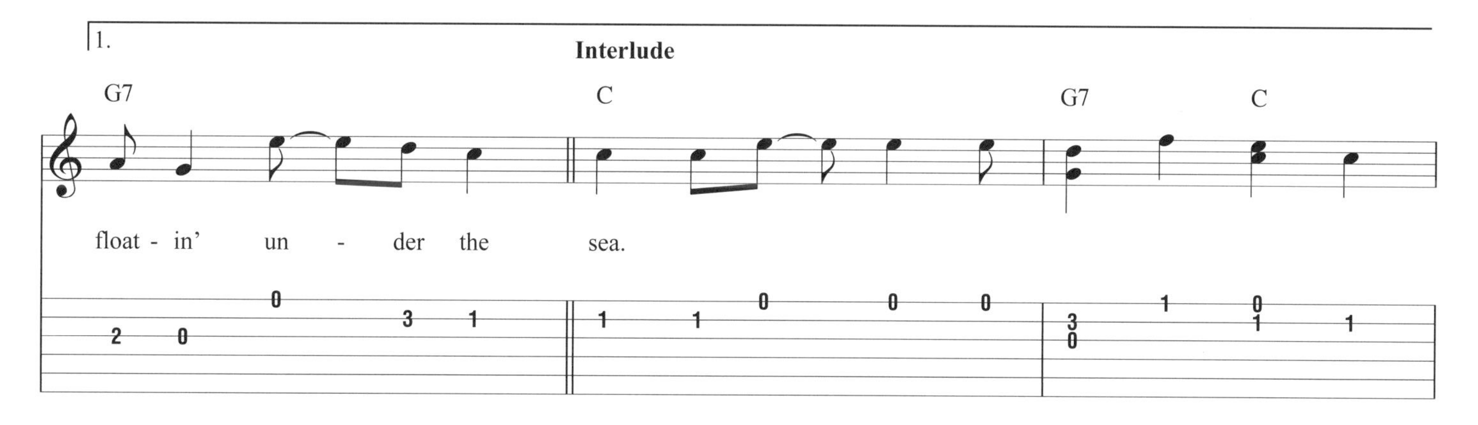

1.
Interlude
G7
C
G7
C
float - in' un - der the sea.

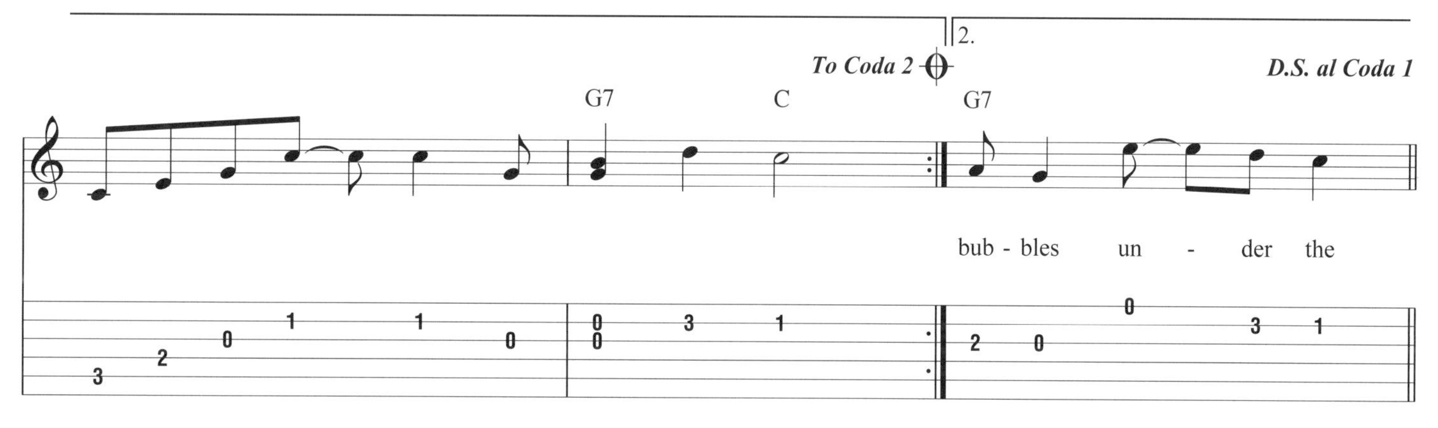

To Coda 2
2.
D.S. al Coda 1
G7
C
G7
bub - bles un - der the

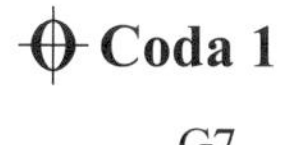

Coda 1

G7
C
G7
C
hear it un - der the sea. The newt

Bridge

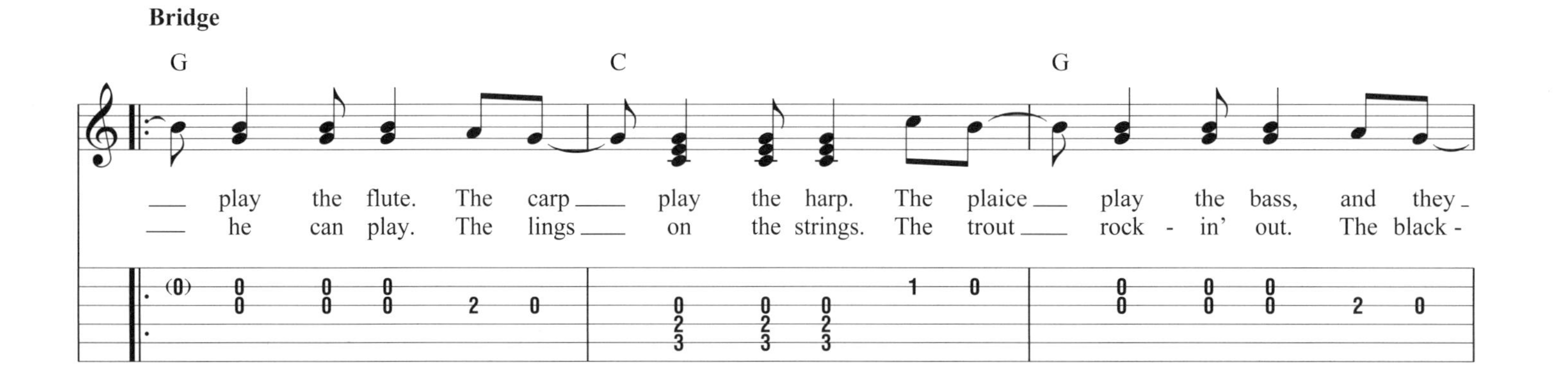
G
C
G
play the flute. The carp play the harp. The plaice play the bass, and they
he can play. The lings on the strings. The trout rock - in' out. The black -

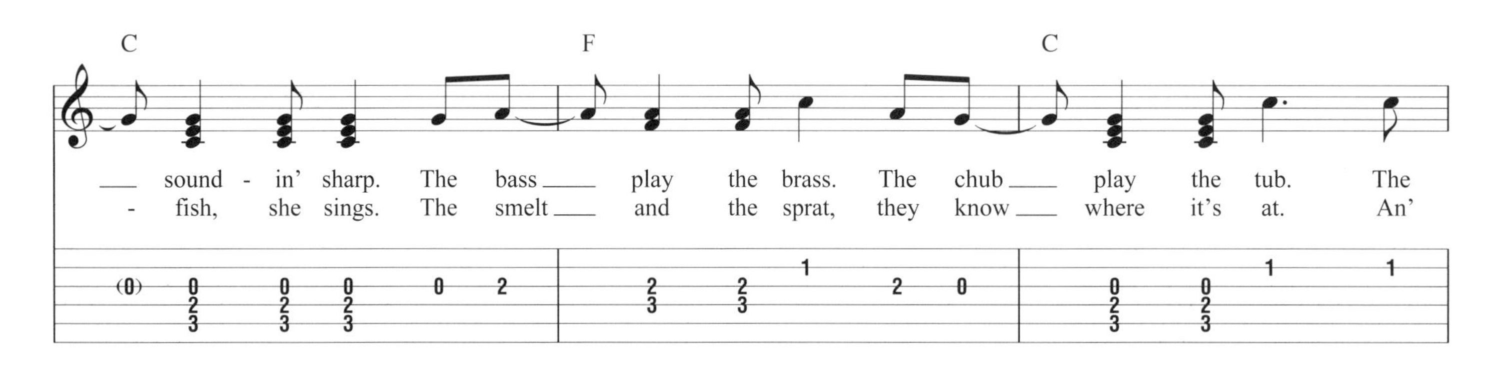
C
F
C
sound - in' sharp. The bass play the brass. The chub play the tub. The
- fish, she sings. The smelt and the sprat, they know where it's at. An'

1.
2.
D.S. al Coda 2
(take 1st ending)
G
G7
C
C
fluke is the duke of soul. (Yeah.) The ray, blow.
oh, that blow - fish

Coda 2

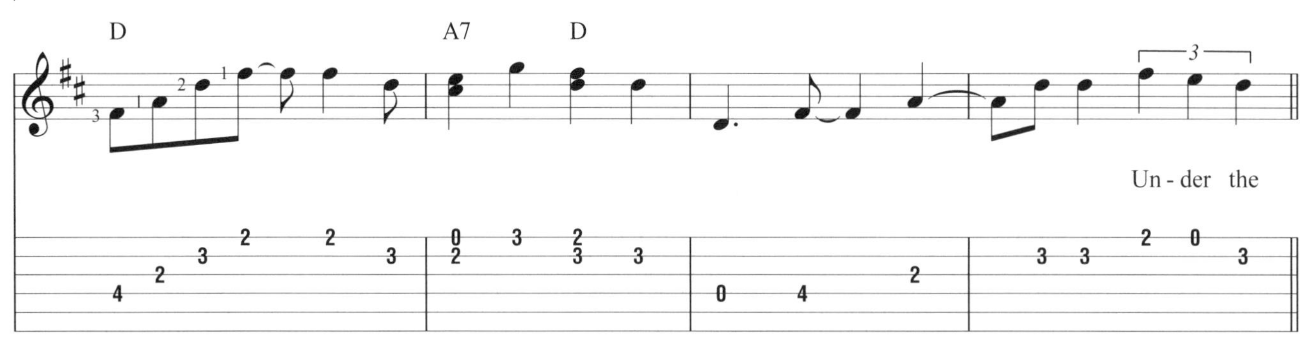
D
A7
D
Un - der the

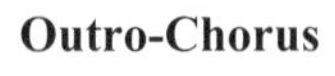
Outro-Chorus

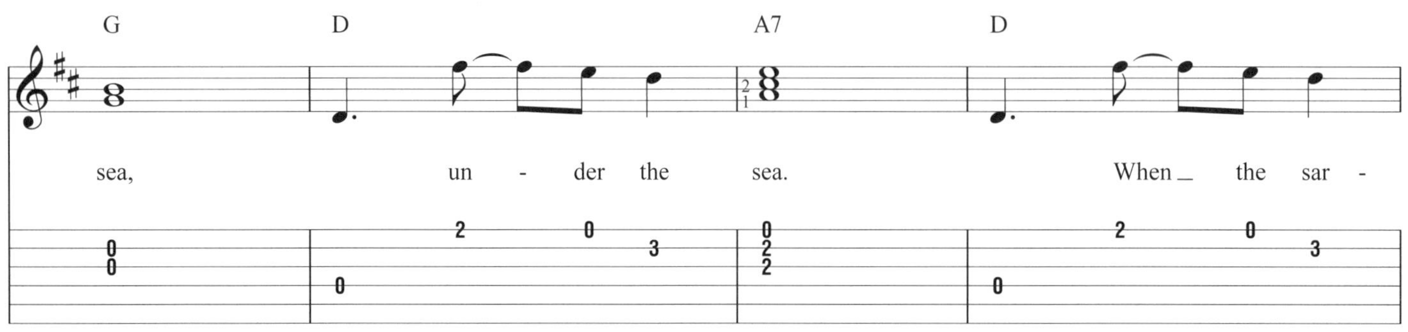
G
D
A7
D
sea, un - der the sea. When the sar -

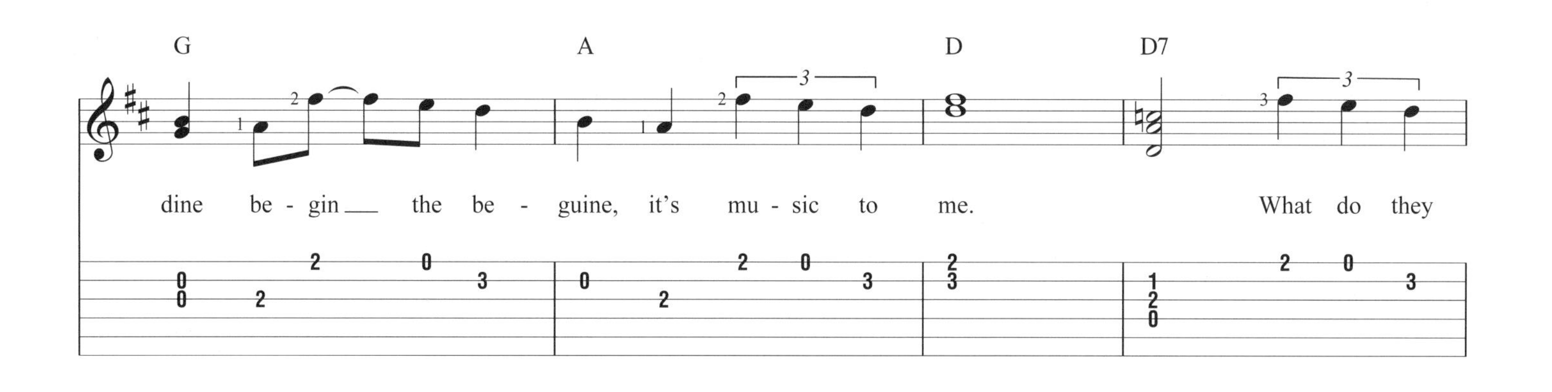
G
A
D
D7
dine be - gin the be - guine, it's mu - sic to me. What do they

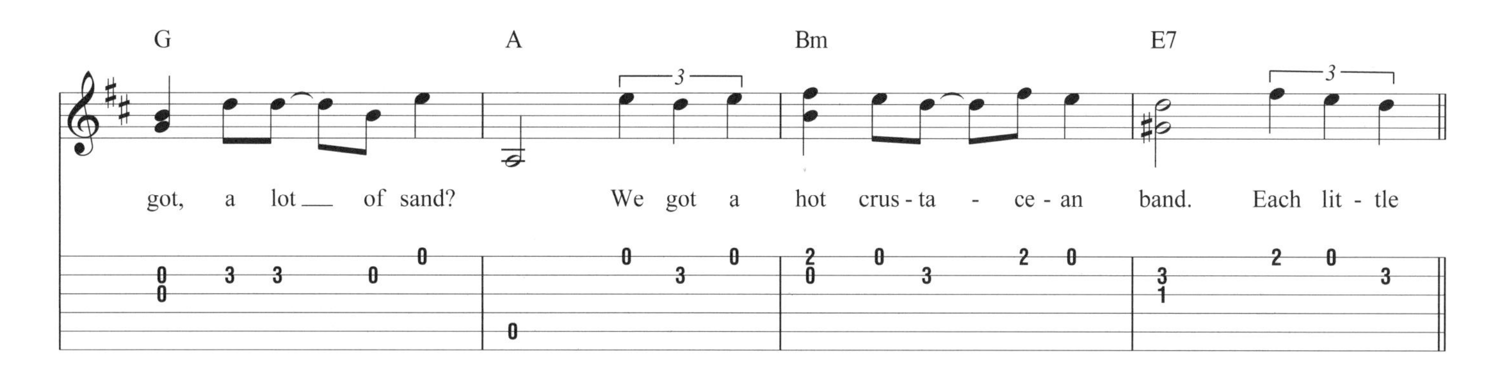
G
A
Bm
E7
got, a lot of sand? We got a hot crus - ta - ce - an band. Each lit - tle

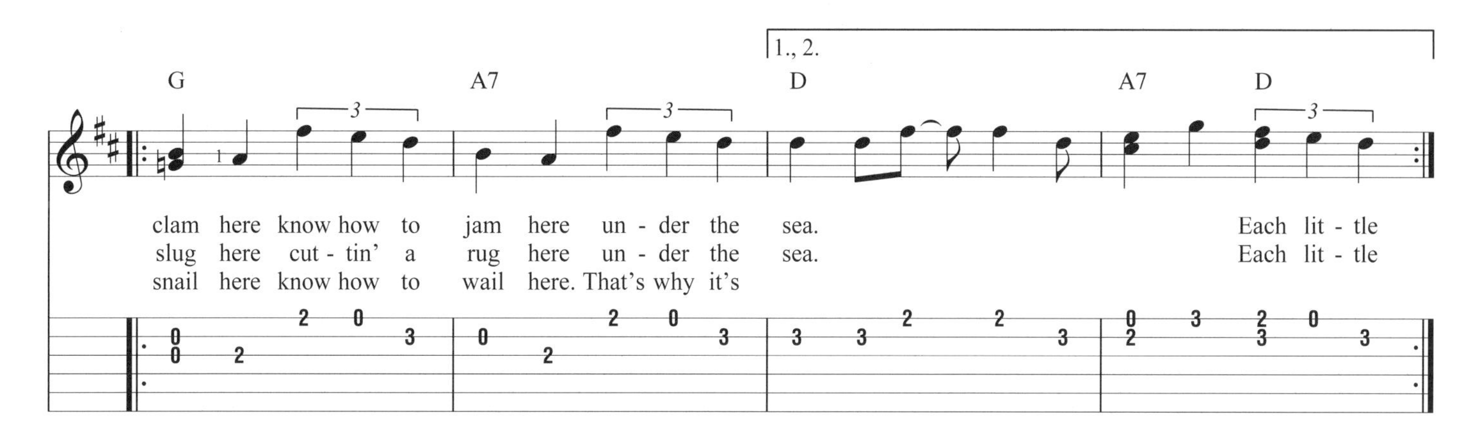
1., 2.
G
A7
D
A7
D
clam here know how to jam here un - der the sea. Each lit - tle
slug here cut - tin' a rug here un - der the sea. Each lit - tle
snail here know how to wail here. That's why it's

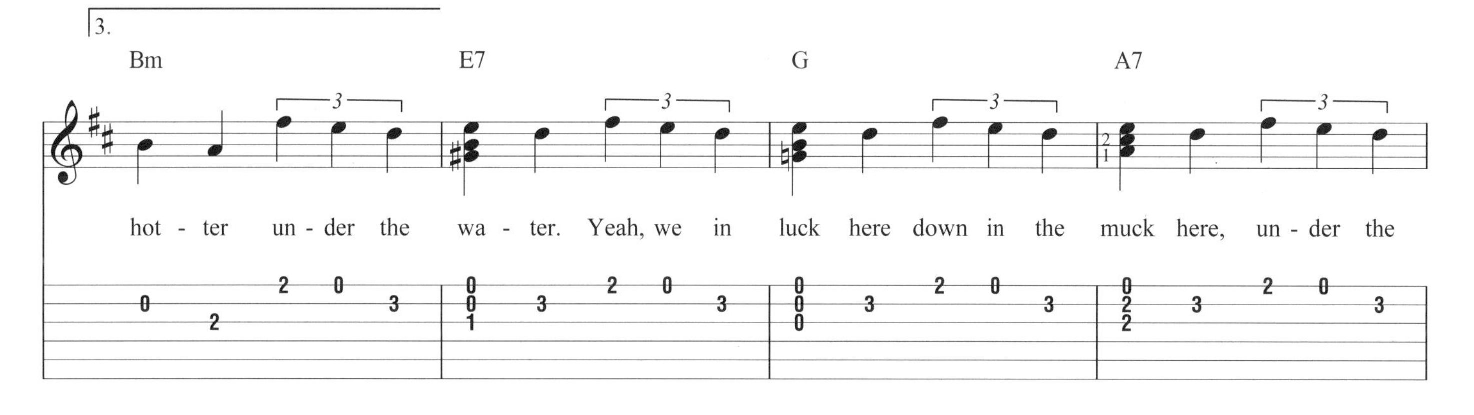
3.
Bm
E7
G
A7
hot - ter un - der the wa - ter. Yeah, we in luck here down in the muck here, un - der the

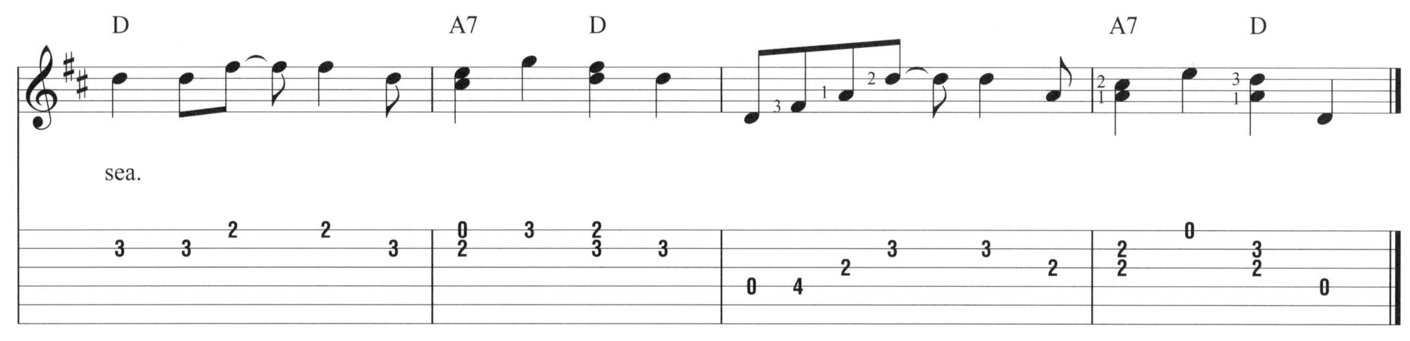
D
A7
D
A7
D
sea.

We Know the Way

from MOANA

Music by Opetaia Foa'i
Lyrics by Opetaia Foa'i and Lin-Manuel Miranda

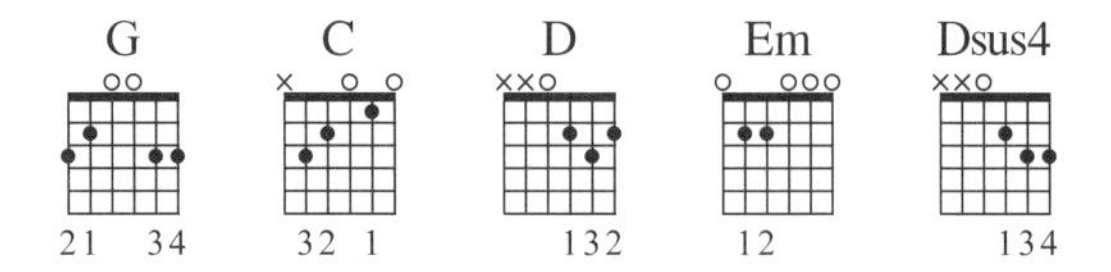

*Capo II

Strum Pattern: 6
Pick Pattern: 4

*Optional: To match recording, place capo at 2nd fret.

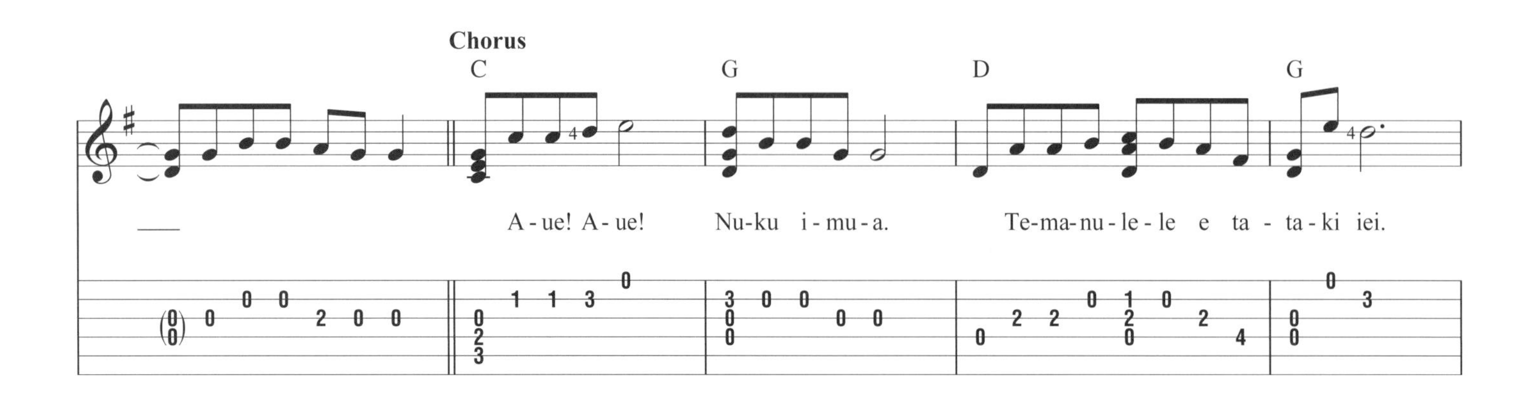

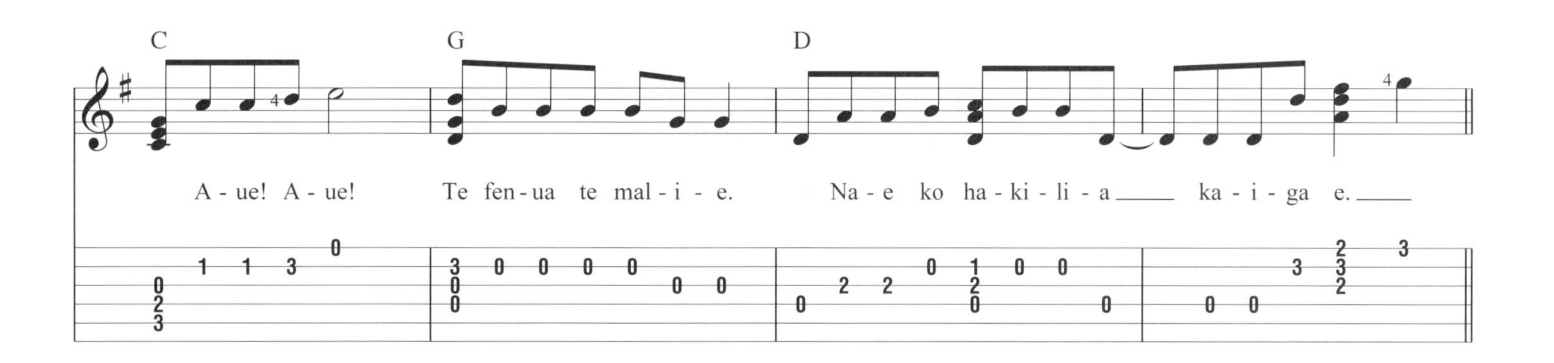
C G D
A - ue! A - ue! Te fen - ua te mal - i - e. Na - e ko ha - ki - li - a ka - i - ga e.

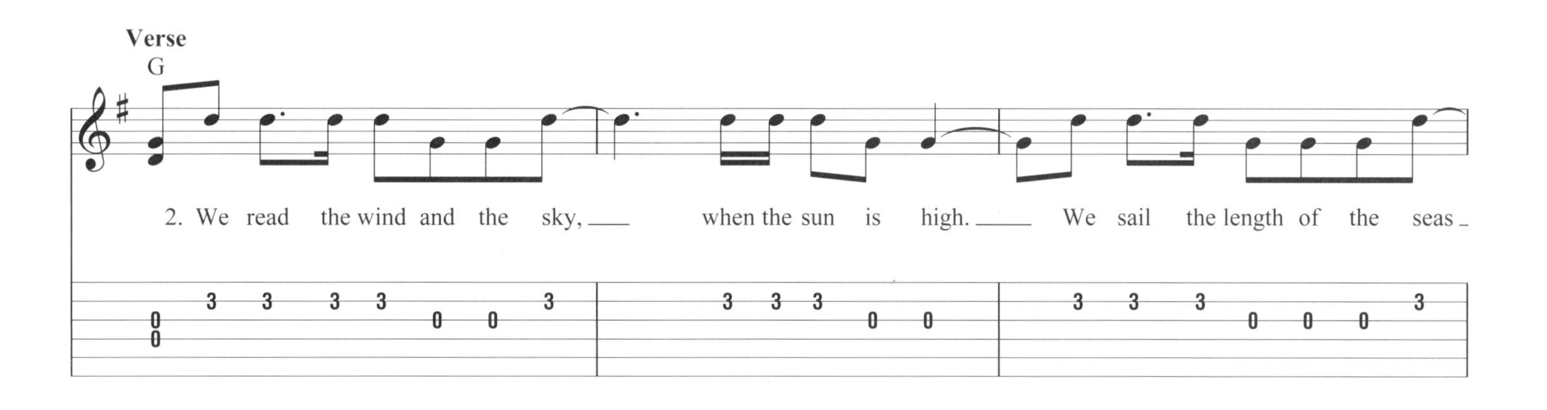
Verse
G
2. We read the wind and the sky, when the sun is high. We sail the length of the seas

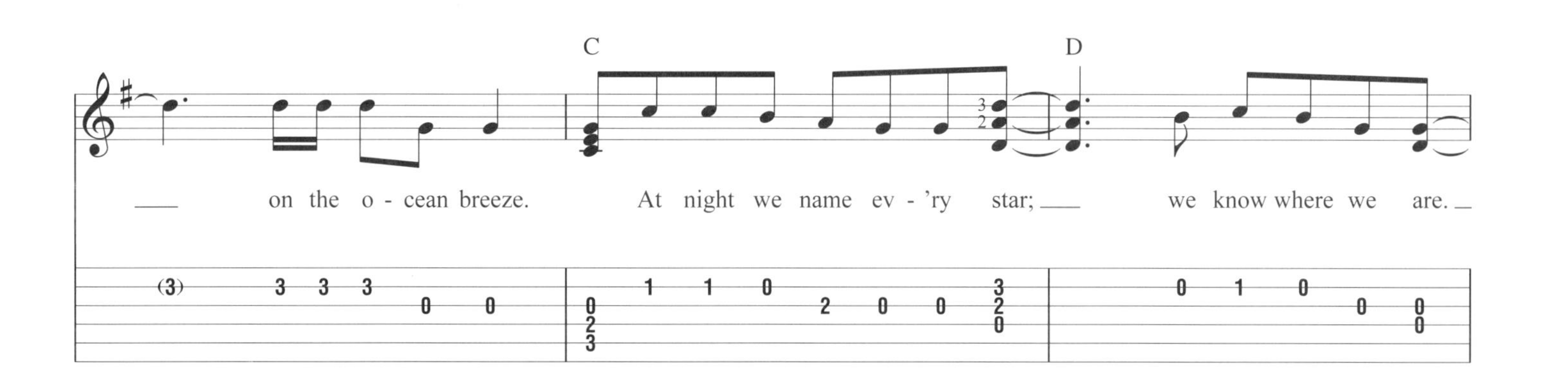
C D
on the o - cean breeze. At night we name ev - 'ry star; we know where we are.

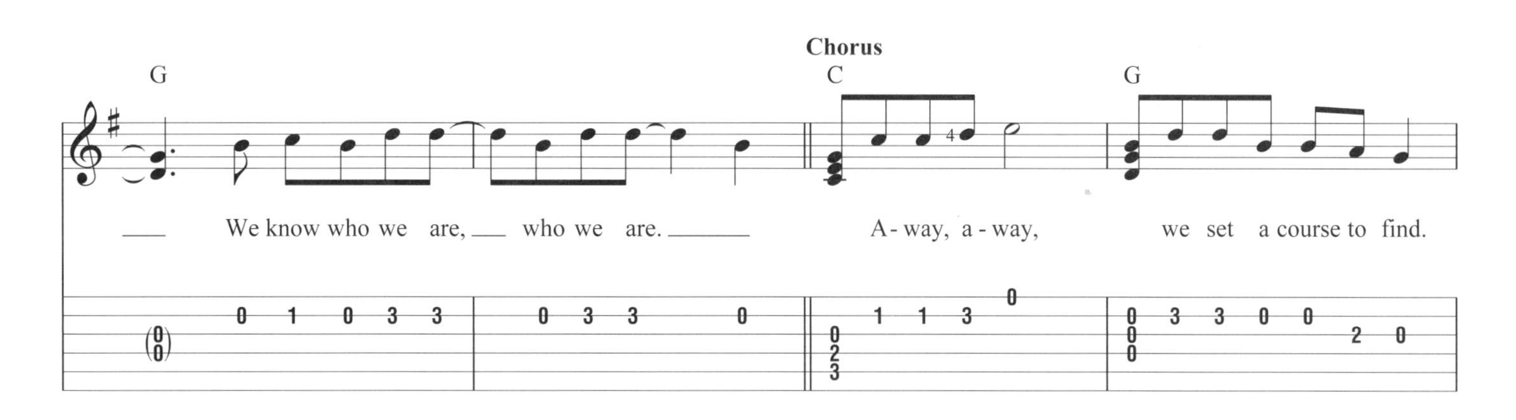
Chorus
G C G
We know who we are, who we are. A - way, a - way, we set a course to find.

D
G
C
G
A brand new is-land ev-'ry-where we roam.
A-way, a-way, we keep our is-land in our mind;

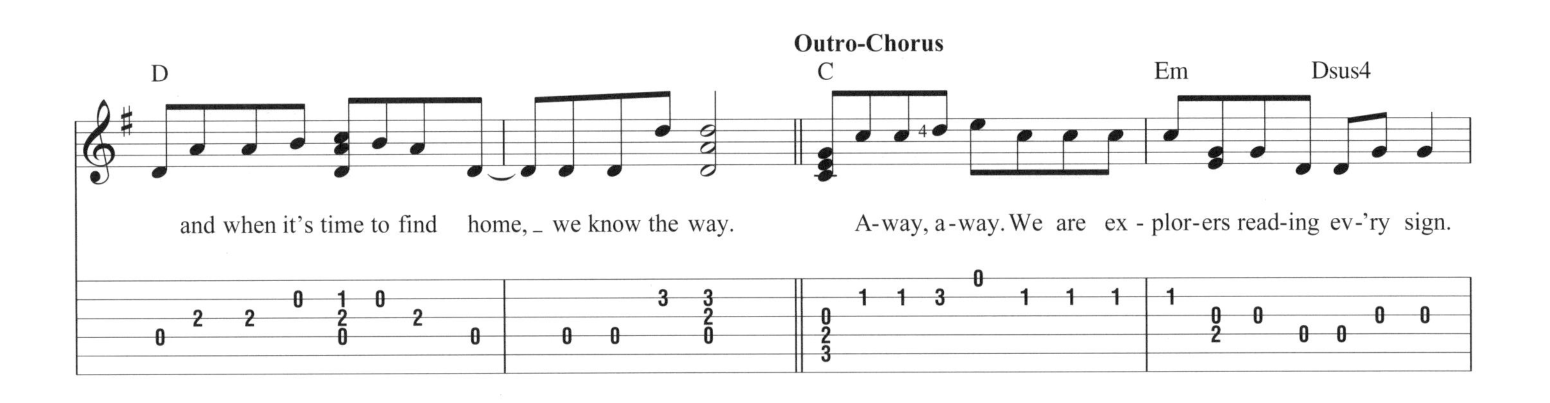
D
Outro-Chorus
C
Em
Dsus4
and when it's time to find home, we know the way.
A-way, a-way. We are ex-plor-ers read-ing ev-'ry sign.

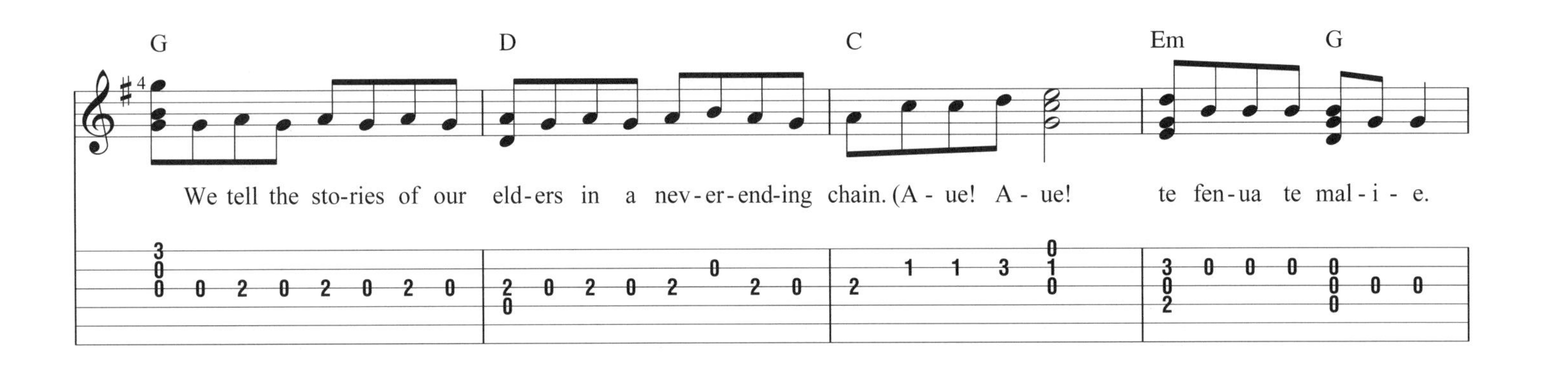
G
D
C
Em
G
We tell the sto-ries of our eld-ers in a nev-er-end-ing chain. (A-ue! A-ue! te fen-ua te mal-i-e.

D
Dsus4
G
Na-e ko ha-ki-li-a.) We know the way!

When Will My Life Begin?

from TANGLED

Music by Alan Menken
Lyrics by Glenn Slater

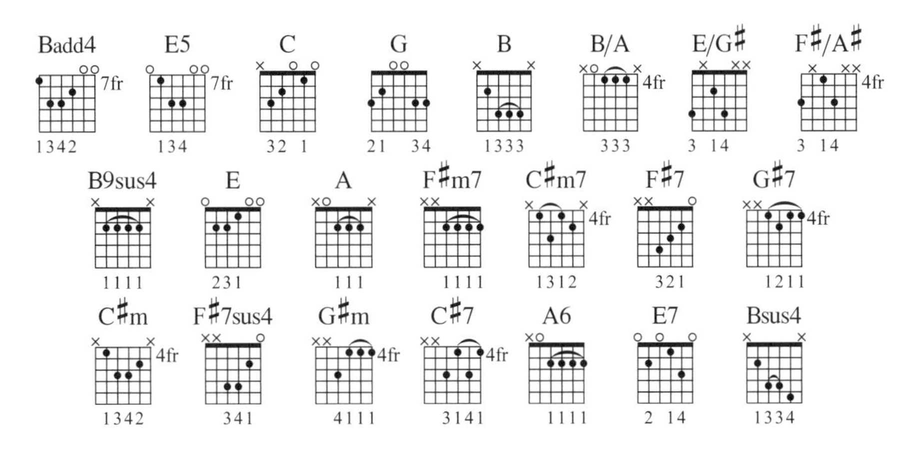

Strum Pattern: 6
Pick Pattern: 6

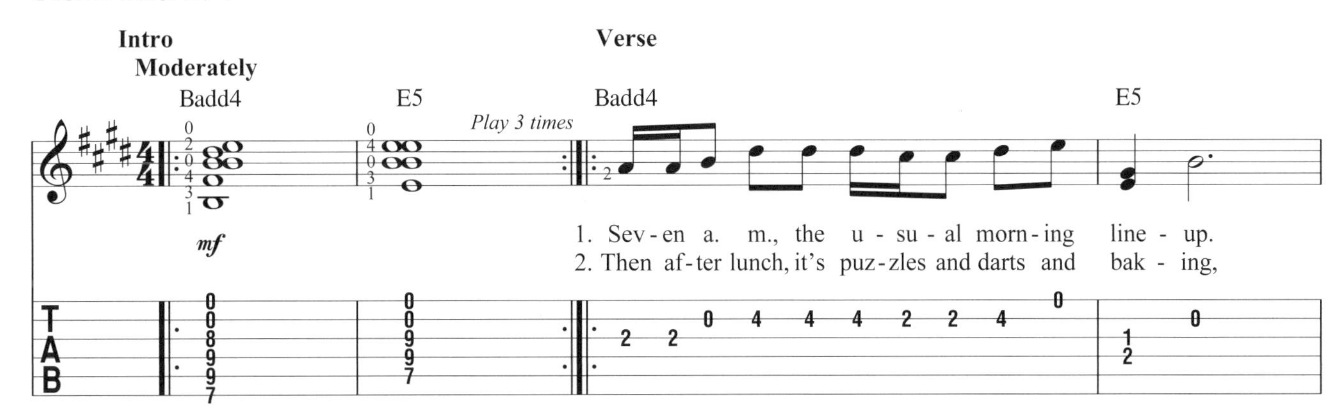

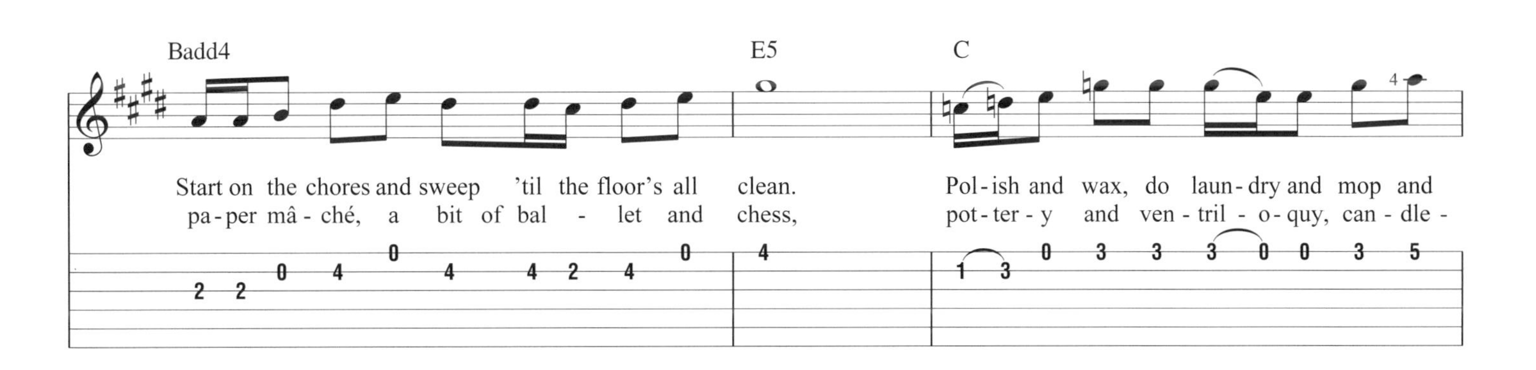

*Sung one octave higher.

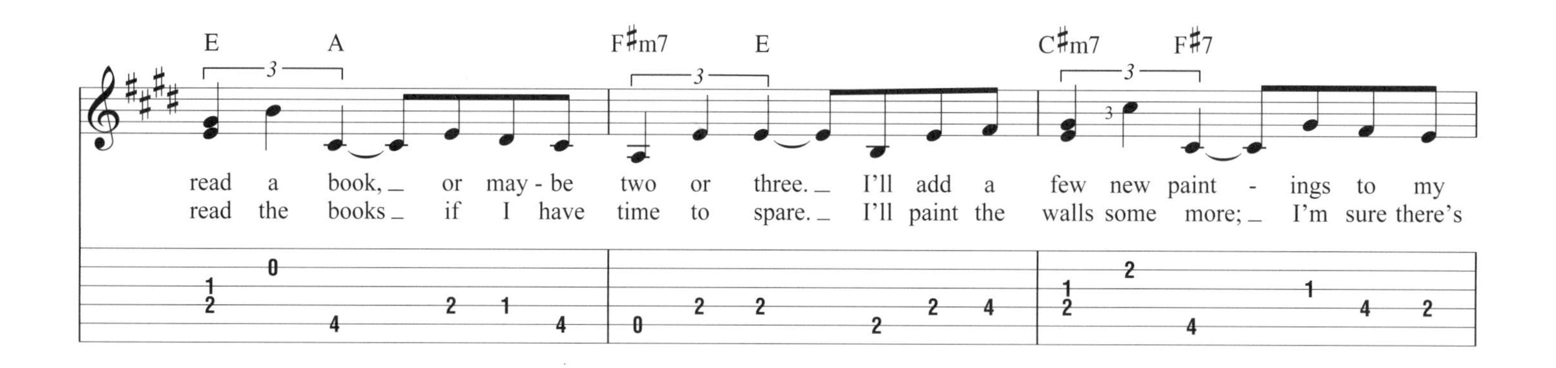
E A F♯m7 E C♯m7 F♯7
read a book, or may - be two or three. I'll add a few new paint - ings to my
read the books if I have time to spare. I'll paint the walls some more; I'm sure there's

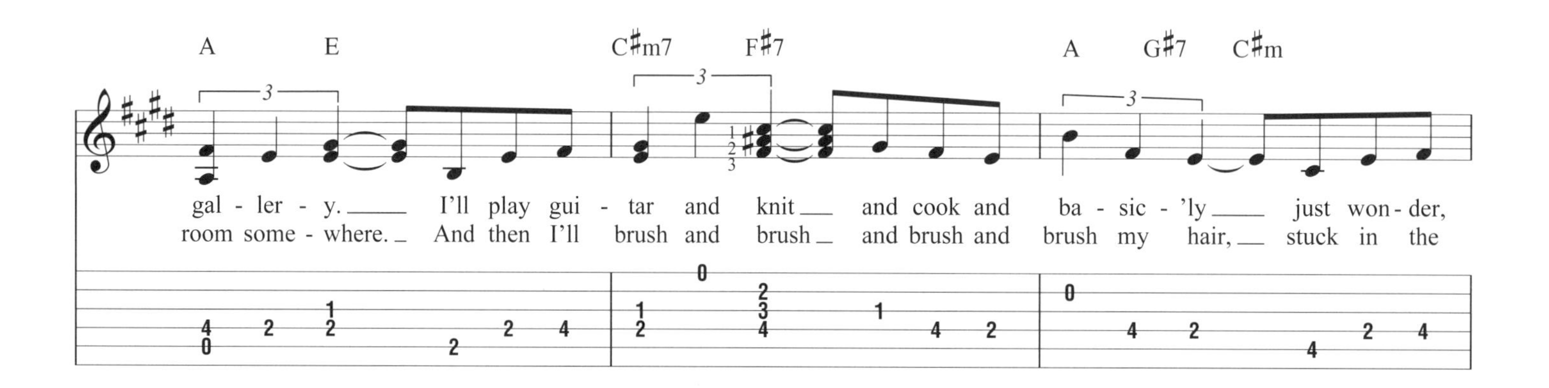
A E C♯m7 F♯7 A G♯7 C♯m
gal - ler - y. I'll play gui - tar and knit and cook and ba - sic - 'ly just won - der,
room some - where. And then I'll brush and brush and brush and brush my hair, stuck in the

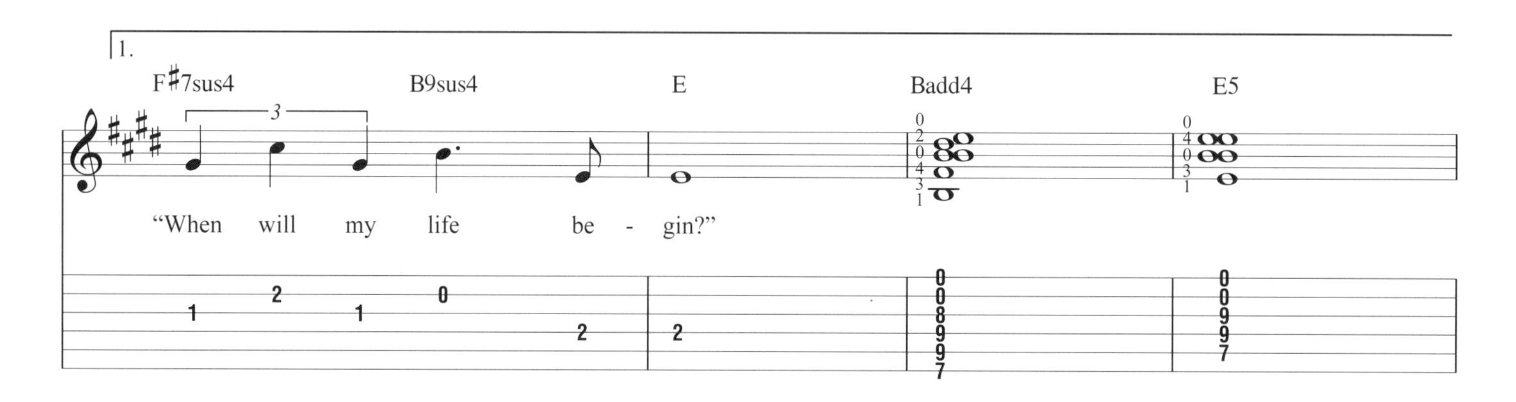
1.
F♯7sus4 B9sus4 E Badd4 E5
"When will my life be - gin?"

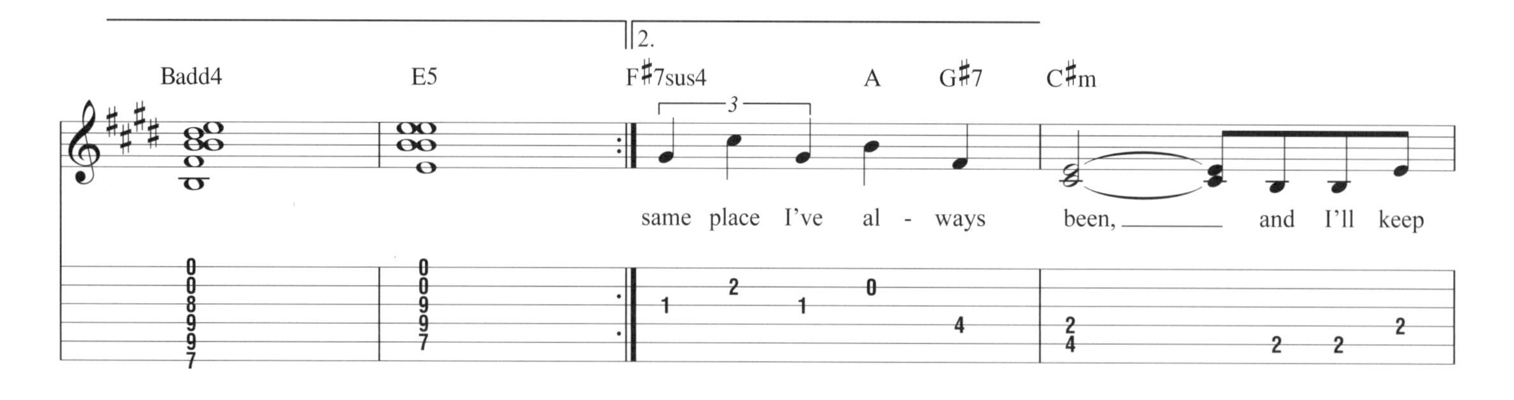
Badd4 E5
2.
F♯7sus4 A G♯7 C♯m
same place I've al - ways been, and I'll keep

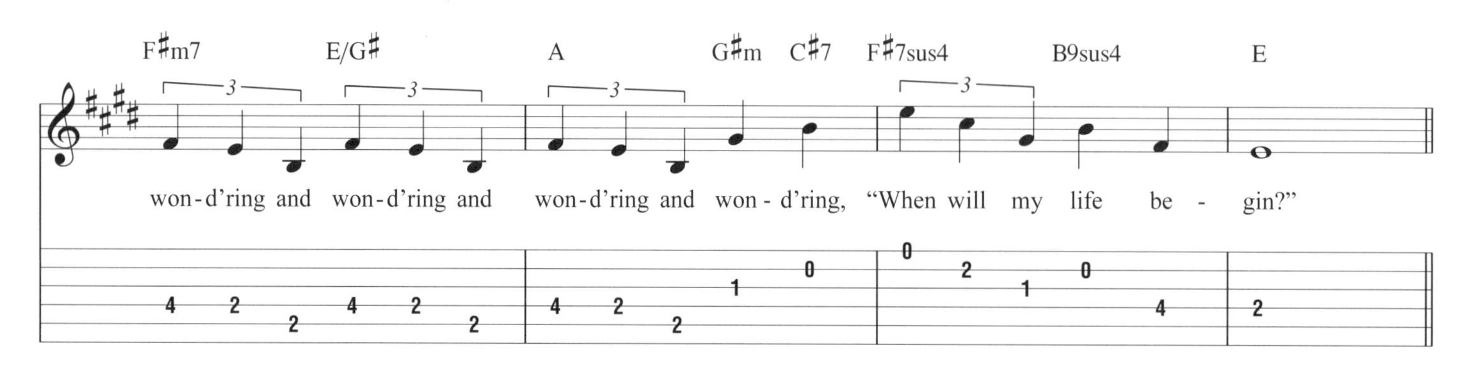
F♯m7 E/G♯ A G♯m C♯7 F♯7sus4 B9sus4 E
won - d'ring and won - d'ring and won - d'ring and won - d'ring, "When will my life be - gin?"

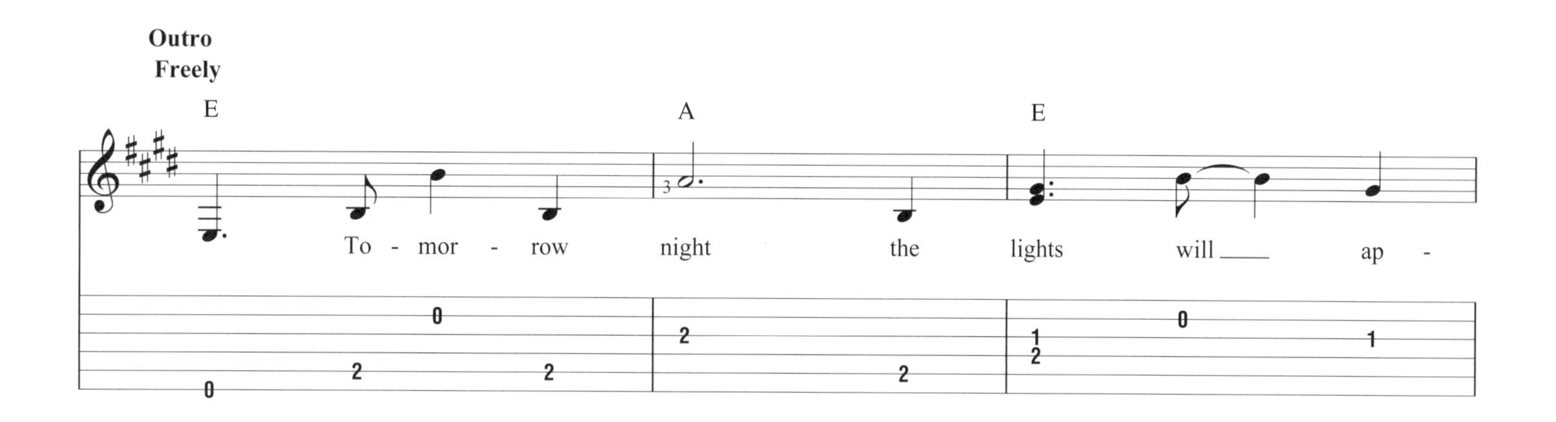

Outro
Freely
E
A
E
To - mor - row night the lights will ___ ap -

A
E
A6
pear, just like they do on ___ my

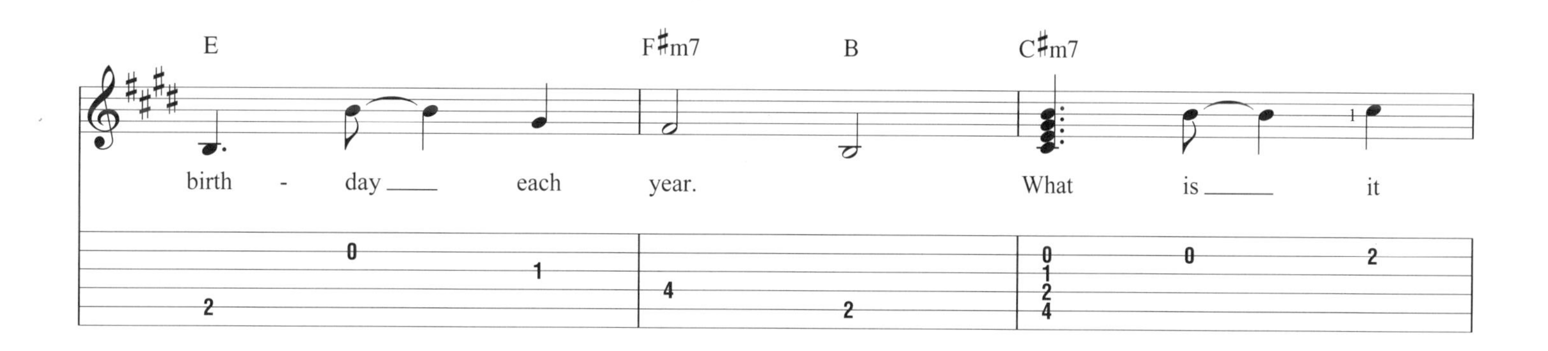

E
F♯m7
B
C♯m7
birth - day ___ each year. What is ___ it

F♯7
B9sus4
E7
like out there where they glow?

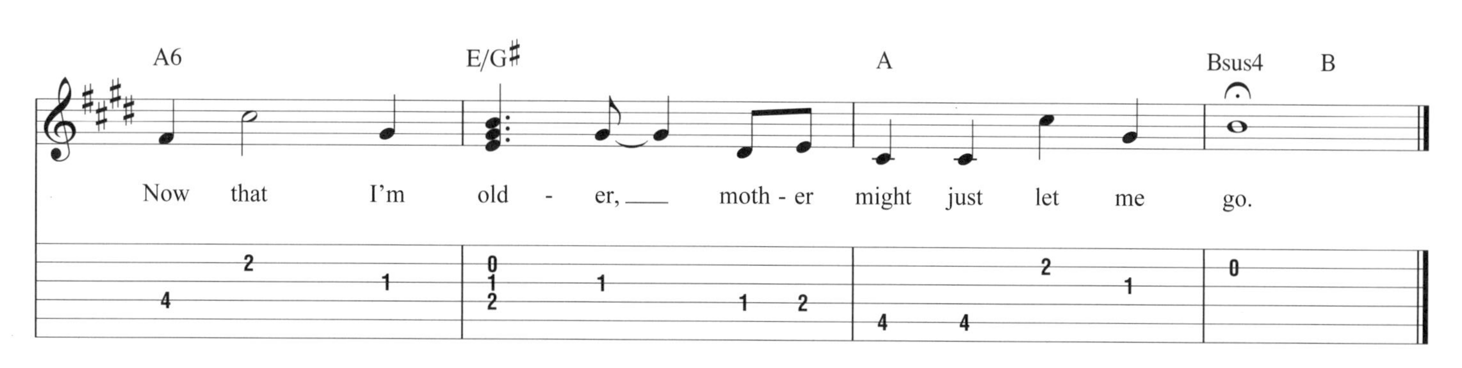

A6
E/G♯
A
Bsus4
B
Now that I'm old - er, ___ moth - er might just let me go.

A Whole New World

from ALADDIN

Music by Alan Menken
Lyrics by Tim Rice

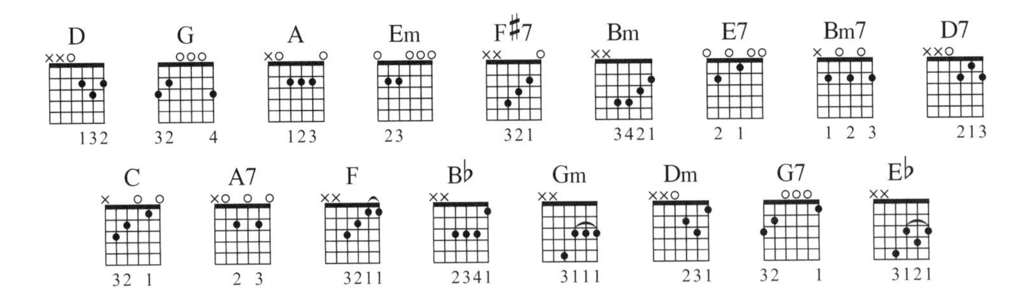

Strum Pattern: 4
Pick Pattern: 1

Verse
Moderately

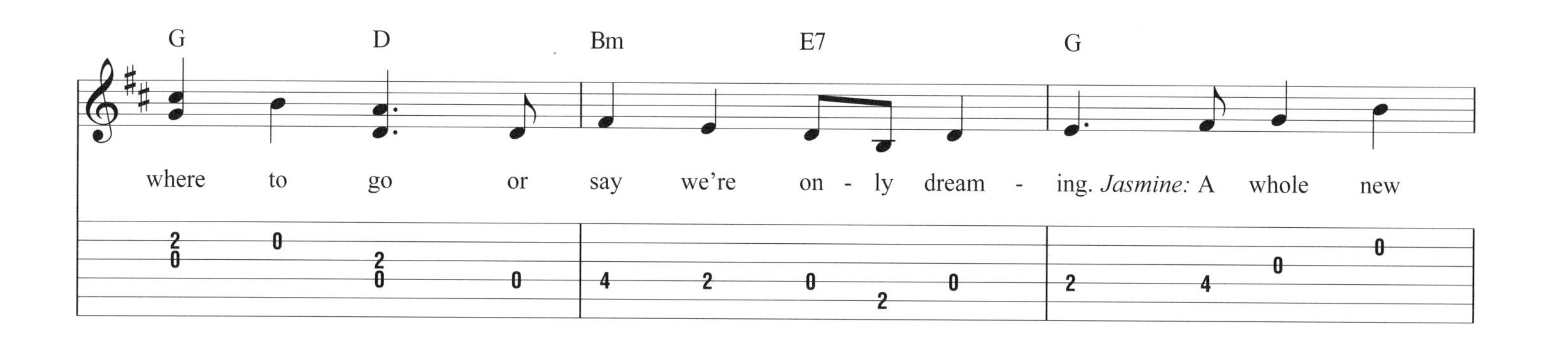
G D Bm E7 G
where to go or say we're on - ly dream - ing. Jasmine: A whole new

A D A
world, a daz - zling place I nev - er knew.

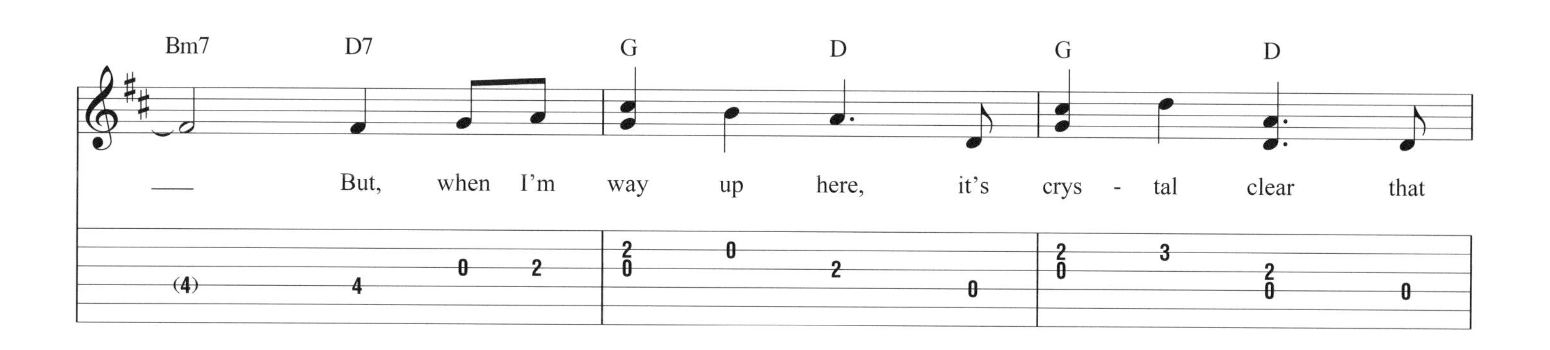
Bm7 D7 G D G D
But, when I'm way up here, it's crys - tal clear that

Bm7 E7 C A7 D
now I'm in a whole new world with you.
Jasmine:
Aladdin: Now I'm in a whole new world with

Verse
F Bb C
Jasmine: 3. Un - be - liev - a - ble sights, in - de - scrib - a - ble feel - ing.
you.

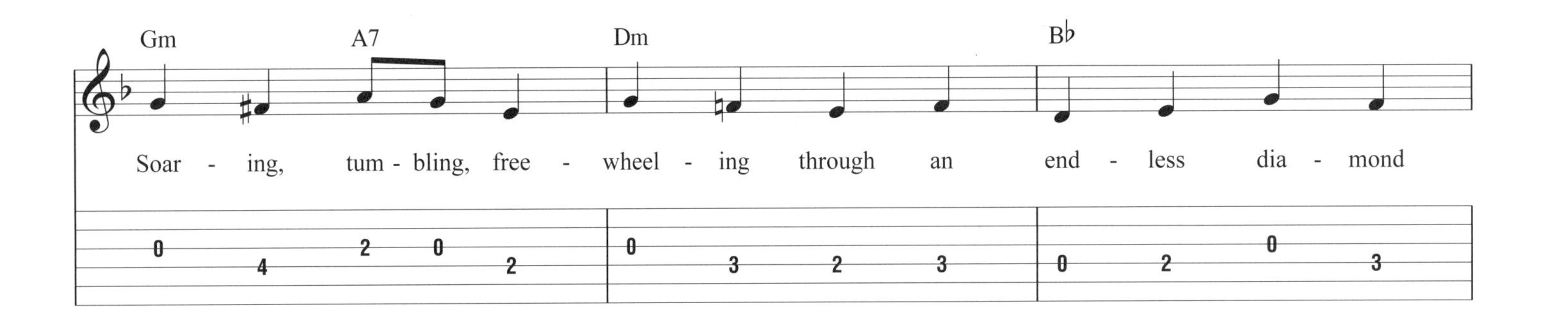
Gm A7 Dm B♭
Soar - ing, tum - bling, free - wheel - ing through an end - less dia - mond

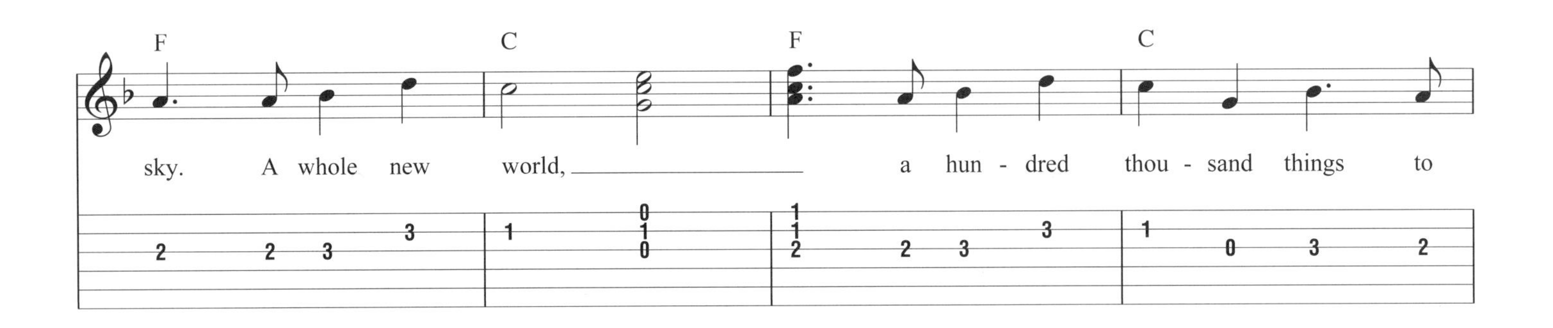
F C F C
sky. A whole new world, a hun - dred thou - sand things to

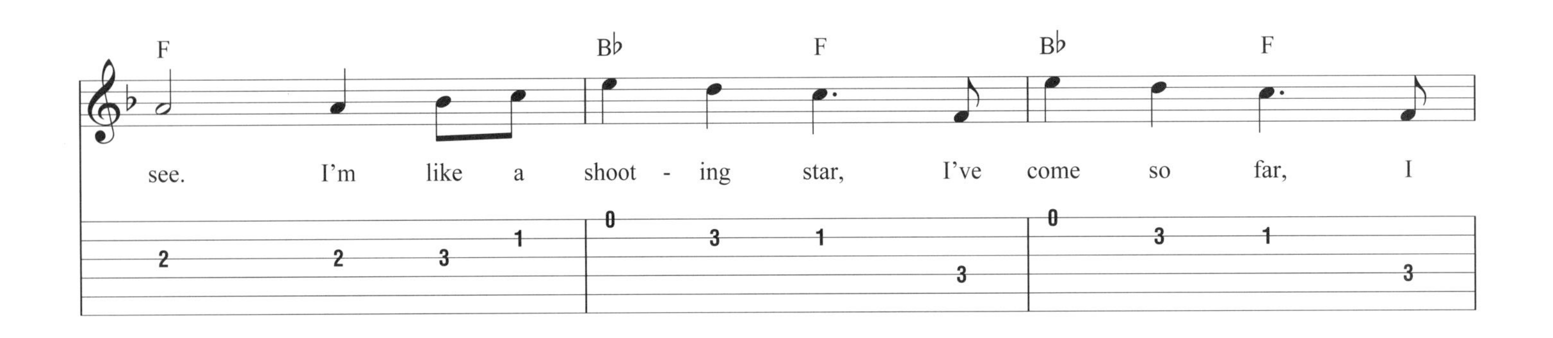
F B♭ F B♭ F
see. I'm like a shoot - ing star, I've come so far, I

Dm G7 B♭ C
can't go back to where I used to be. Ev - `ry turn a sur -

Bridge
F C Dm F B♭ F
rpise. Ev - `ry mo - ment red let - ter. I'll chase them an - y - where. There's

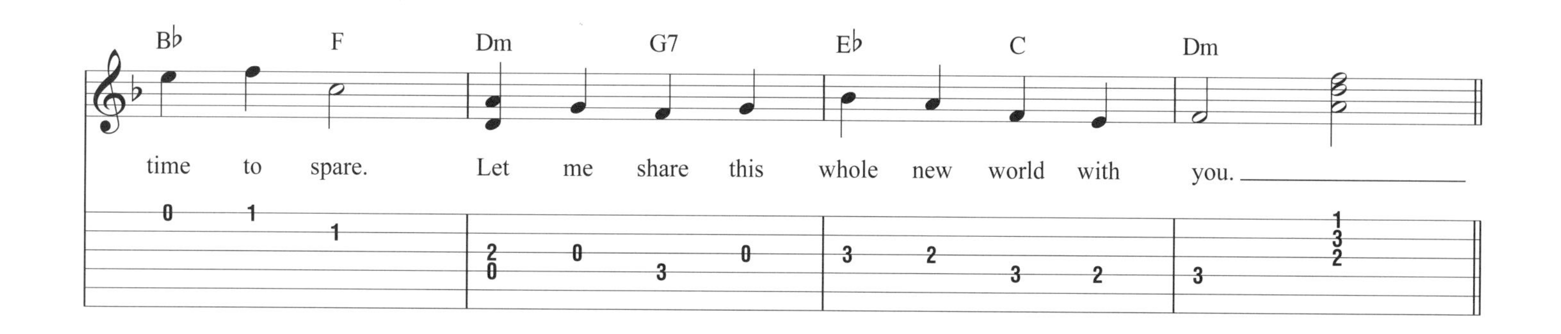

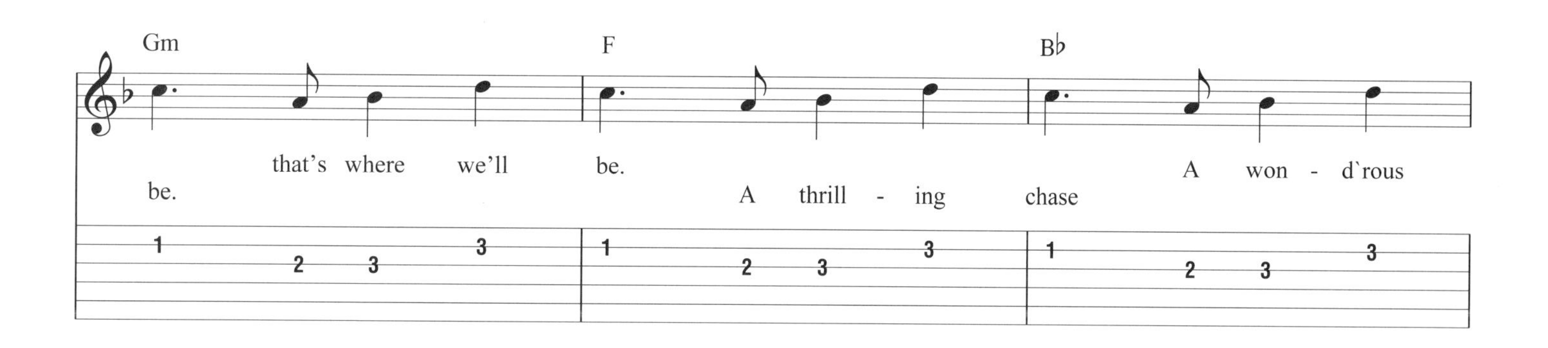

Additional Lyrics

2. I can open your eyes,
   Take you wonder by wonder.
   Over, sideways and under
   On a magic carpet ride.

You'll Be in My Heart
(Pop Version)*

from TARZAN®
Words and Music by Phil Collins

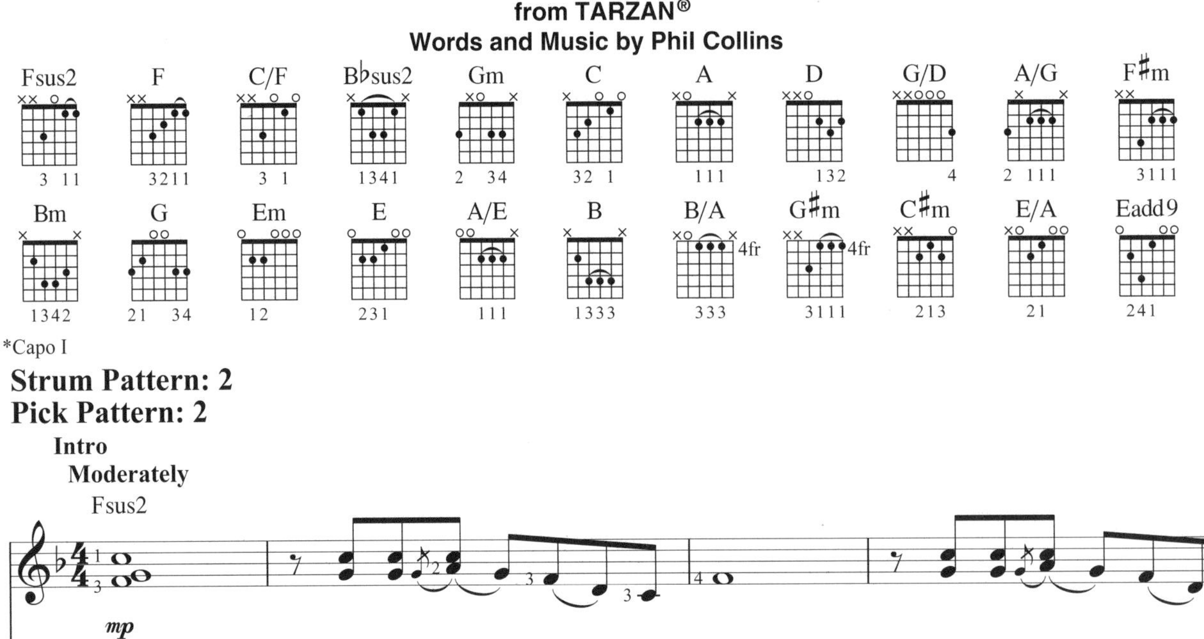

*Optional: To match recording, place capo at 1st fret.

Chorus
D G/D A A/G F♯m
you'll be in my heart, yes, you'll be in my heart from

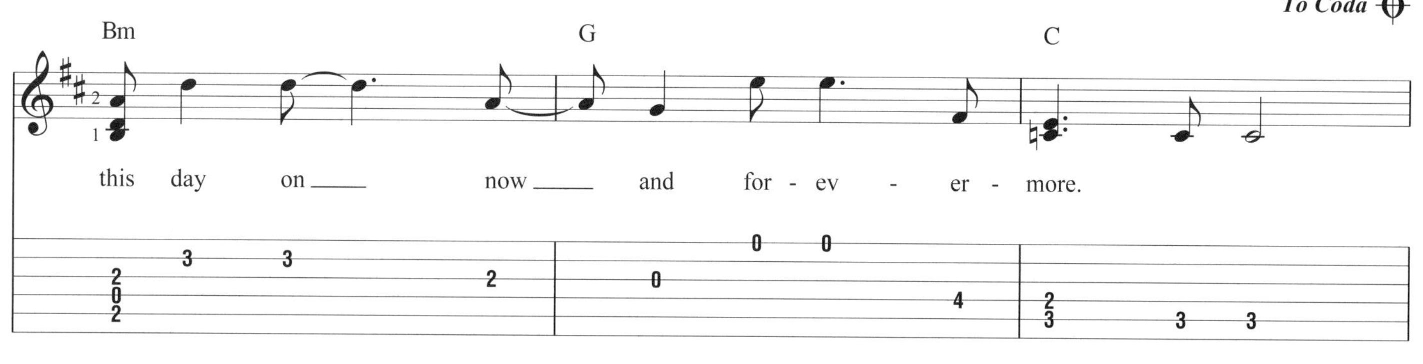
To Coda
Bm G C
this day on now and for - ev - er - more.

A D G/D A A/G
You'll be in my heart no mat - ter what they

F♯m Bm G C
say. You'll be here in my heart al - ways.

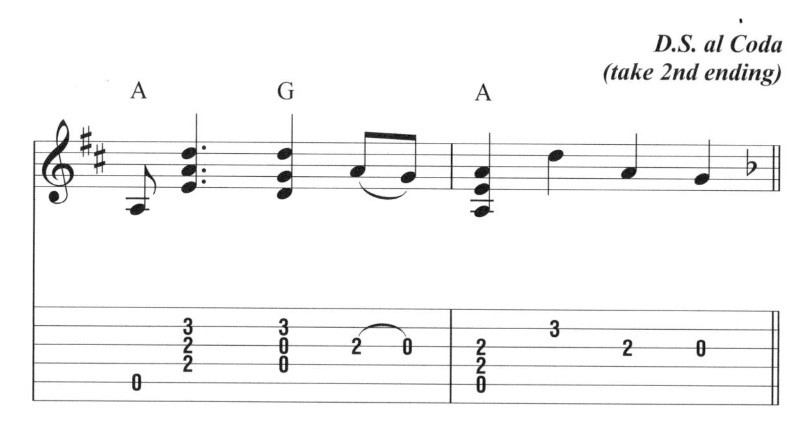
D.S. al Coda
(take 2nd ending)
A G A

Coda
A
Don't

Bridge
G
Em
lis - ten to them, ’cause what do they know? We need each oth - er to
des - tin - y calls you, you must be strong. I may not be with you, but you’ve
have, to hold.
got to hold on.
Bm
They’ll see in time,
1.
C
I know.
D
2.
C
When know.
D
A
We’ll show them to - geth - er ’cause
Chorus
E
A/E
B
B/A
G♯m
you’ll be in my heart, be-lieve me, you’ll be in my heart. I’ll be there from
You’ll be in my heart no mat - ter what they say. You’ll
1.
C♯m
A
D
B
this day on now and for - ev - er - more.

2.
C♯m
A
D
B
be here in my heart always. Al-
Outro
E/A
Eadd9
ways, I'll be with you. I'll be

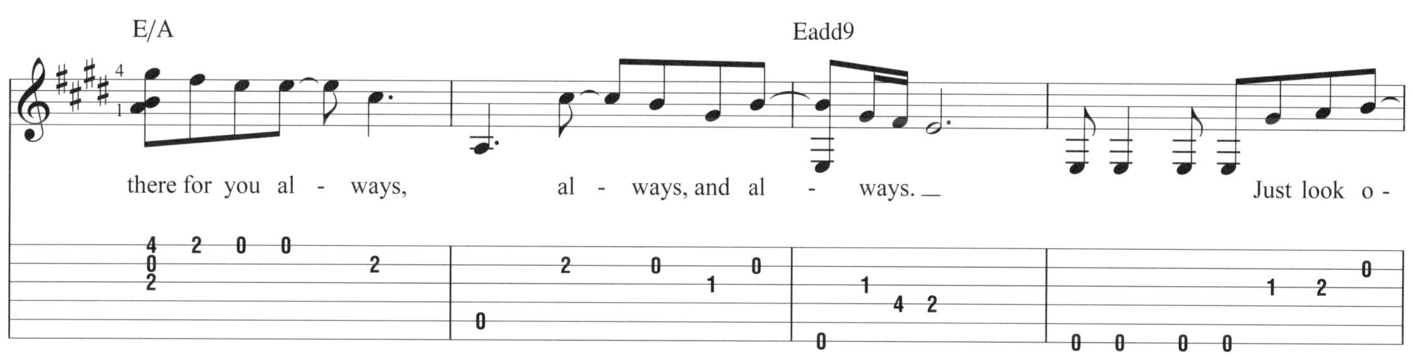
E/A
Eadd9
there for you always, always, and always. Just look o-

E/A
Eadd9
-ver your shoulder. Just look over your shoulder.

E/A
E
Just look over your shoulder; I'll be there always.

You're Welcome

from MOANA

Music and Lyrics by Lin-Manuel Miranda

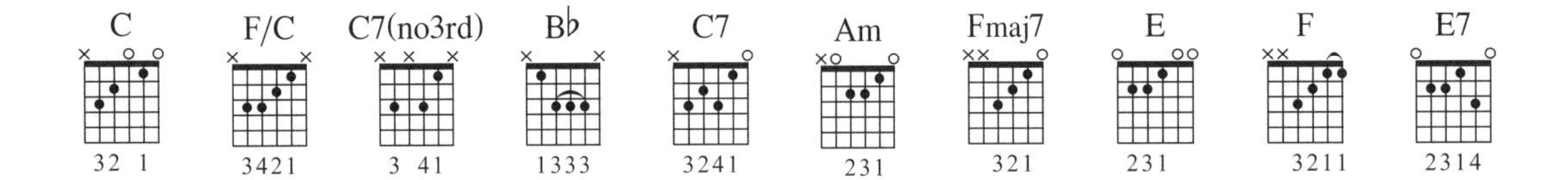

Strum Pattern: 3, 4
Pick Pattern: 3, 4

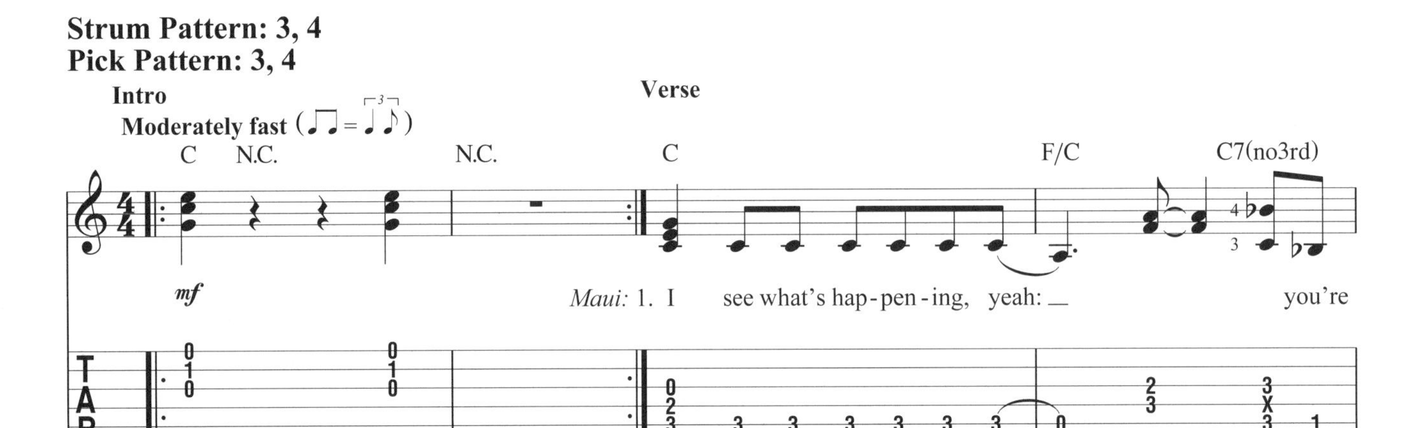

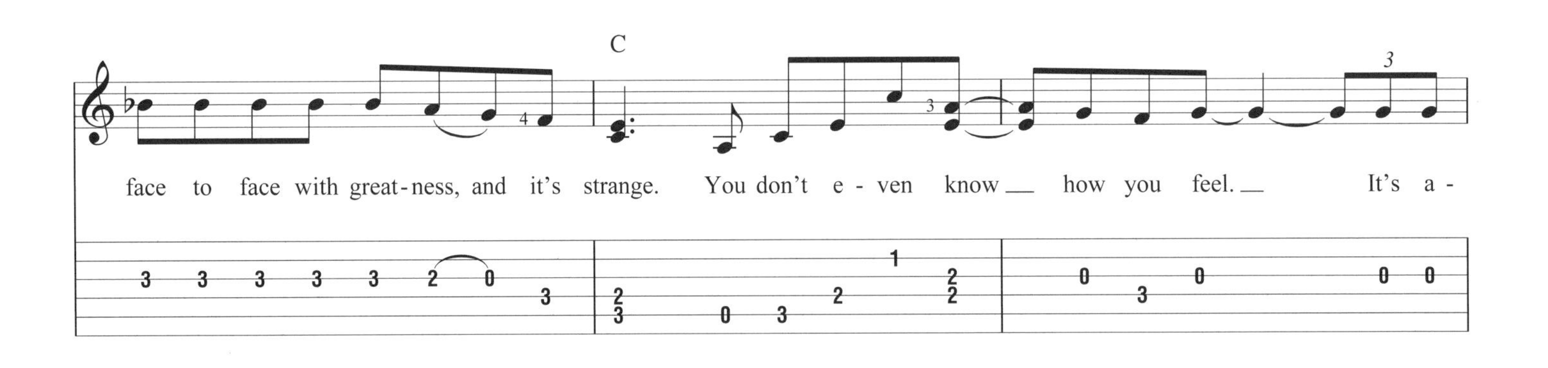

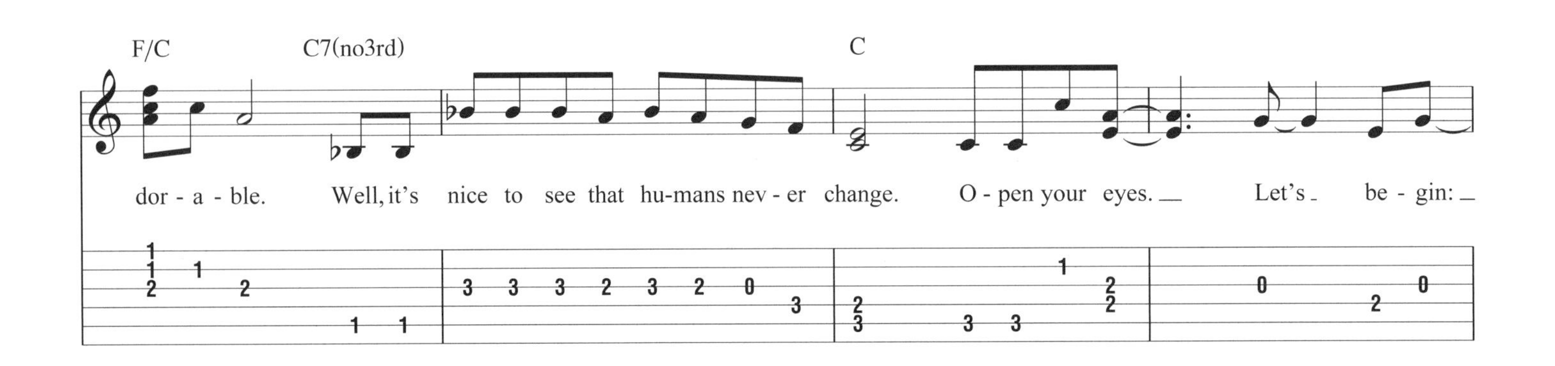

F/C
C7(no3rd)
C
Yes, it's real - ly me, it's Mau - i. Breathe it in, I know it's a lot:

F/C
B♭
C7
the hair, the bod, when you're star - ing at a dem - i - god.

Chorus
Am
Fmaj7
C
E
What can I say ex - cept, "You're wel - come for the tides, the sun, the sky?"

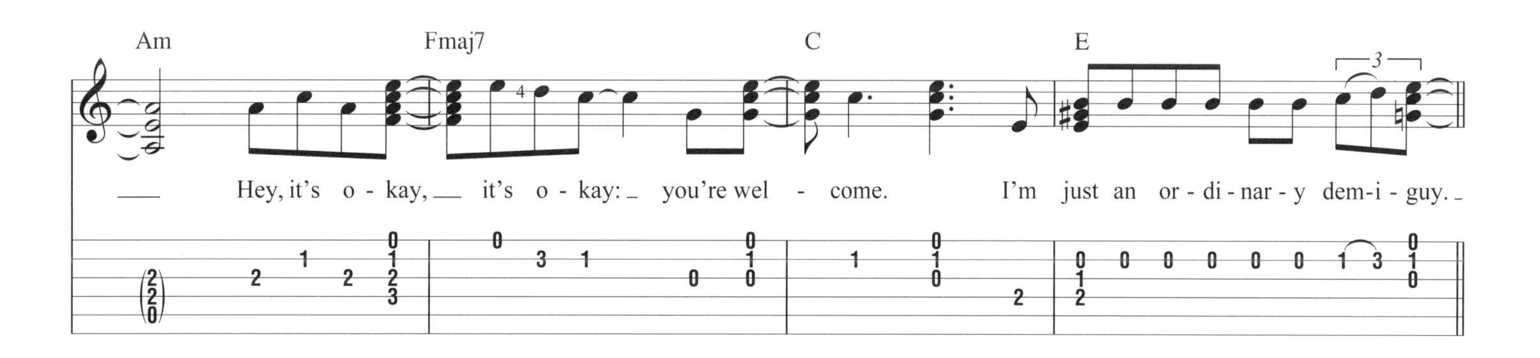
Am
Fmaj7
C
E
Hey, it's o - kay, it's o - kay: you're wel - come. I'm just an or - di - nar - y dem - i - guy.

Verse
C
F/C
C7(no3rd)
2. Hey, what has two thumbs and pulled up the sky when you were wad-dl-ing yea high? This guy!

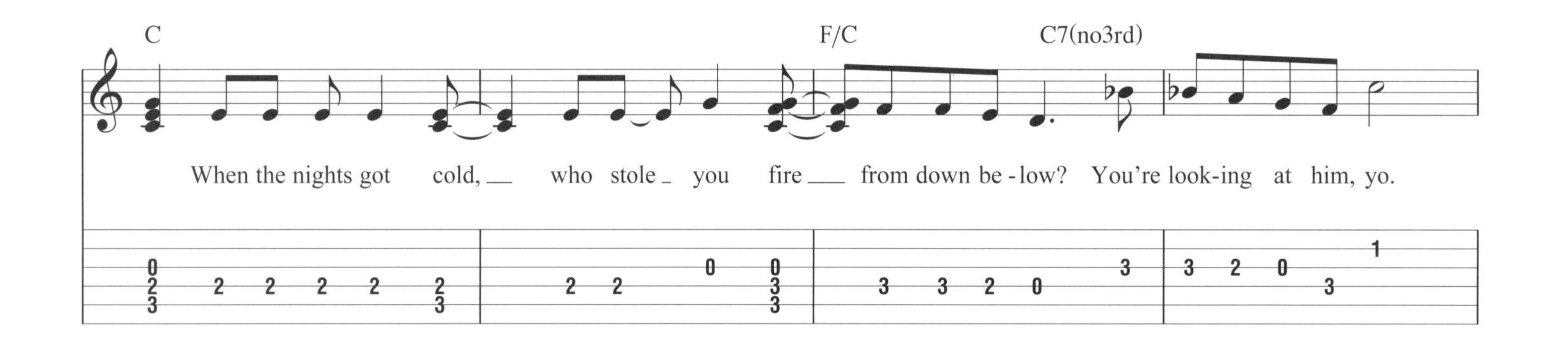
C F/C C7(no3rd)
When the nights got cold, who stole you fire from down be-low? You're look-ing at him, yo.

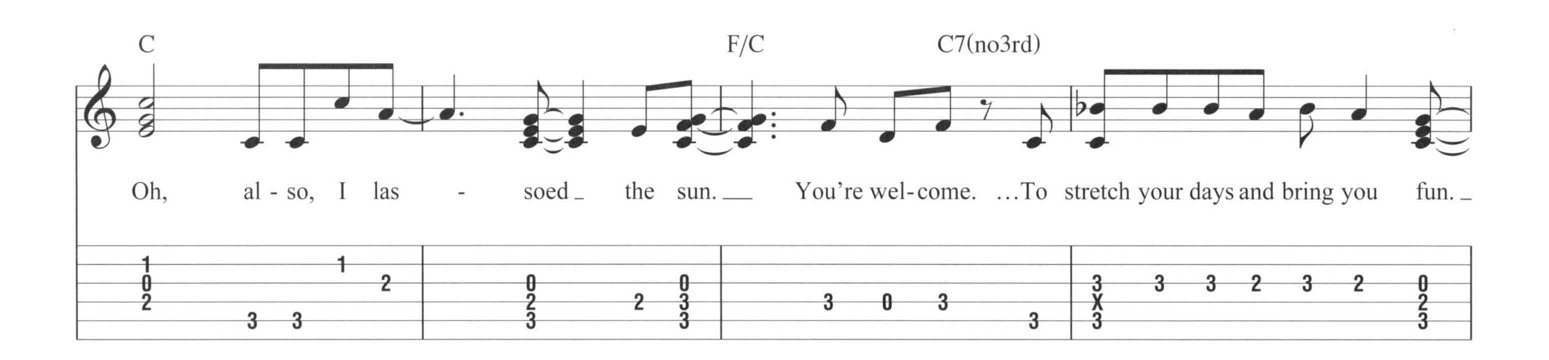
C F/C C7(no3rd)
Oh, al-so, I las-soed the sun. You're wel-come. …To stretch your days and bring you fun.

C F/C B♭ C7
Al-so, I har-nessed the breeze. You're wel-come. …To fill your sails and shake your trees.

Chorus
Am Fmaj7 C E
So what can I say ex-cept, "You're wel-come, for the is-lands I pulled from the sea"?

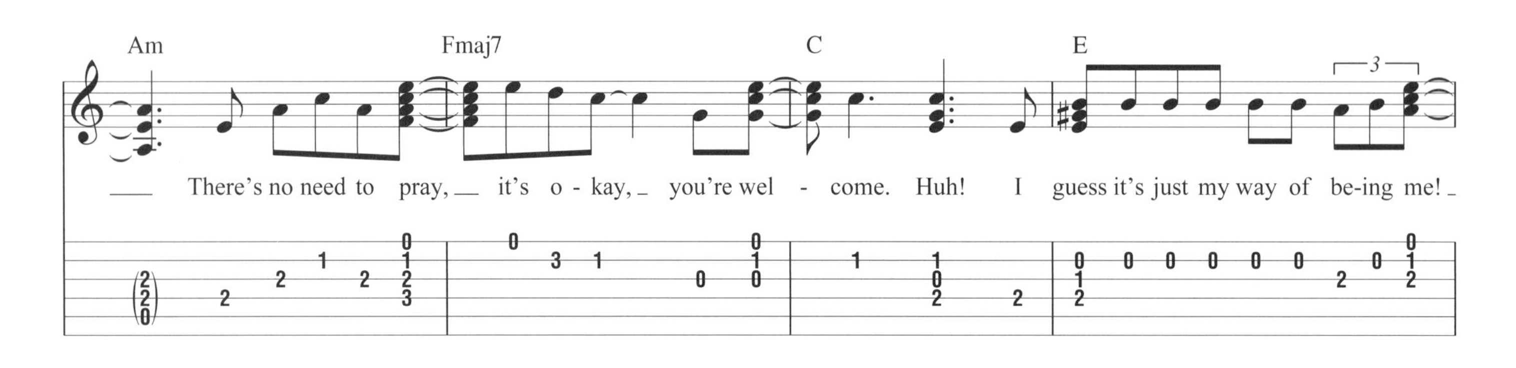
Am Fmaj7 C E
There's no need to pray, it's o-kay, you're wel-come. Huh! I guess it's just my way of be-ing me!

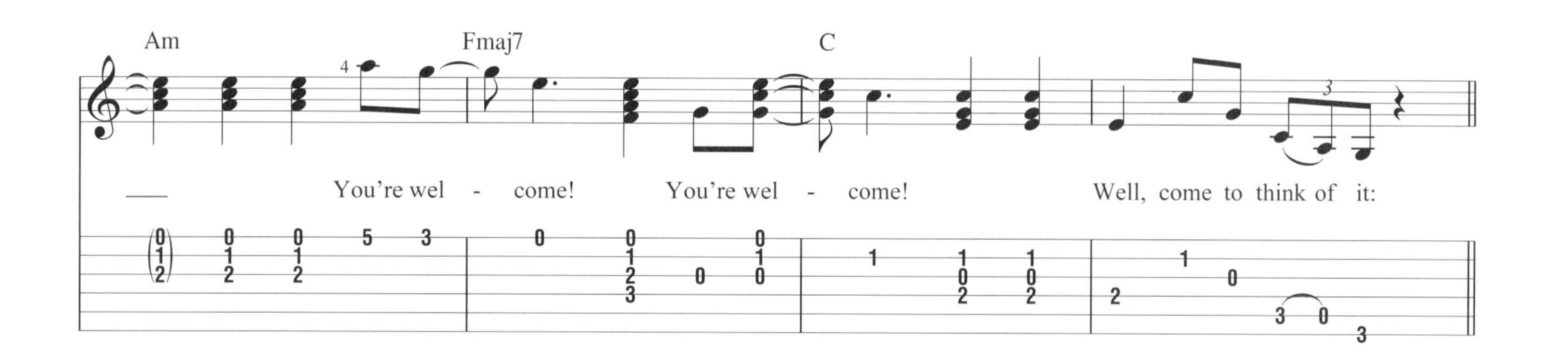
Am
Fmaj7
C
You're wel - come! You're wel - come! Well, come to think of it:

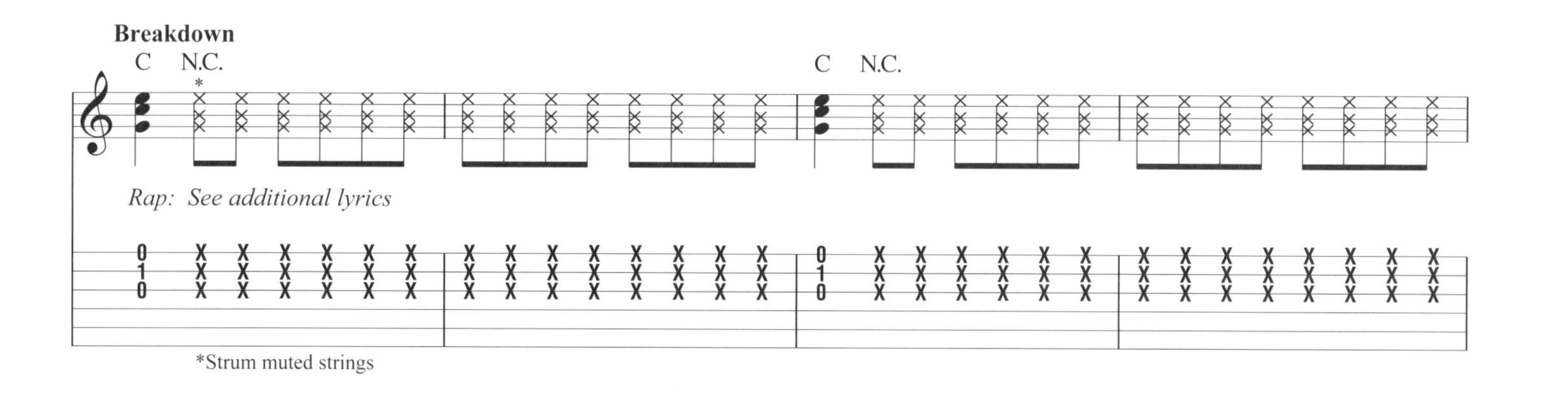
Breakdown
C N.C.
C N.C.
Rap: See additional lyrics
*Strum muted strings

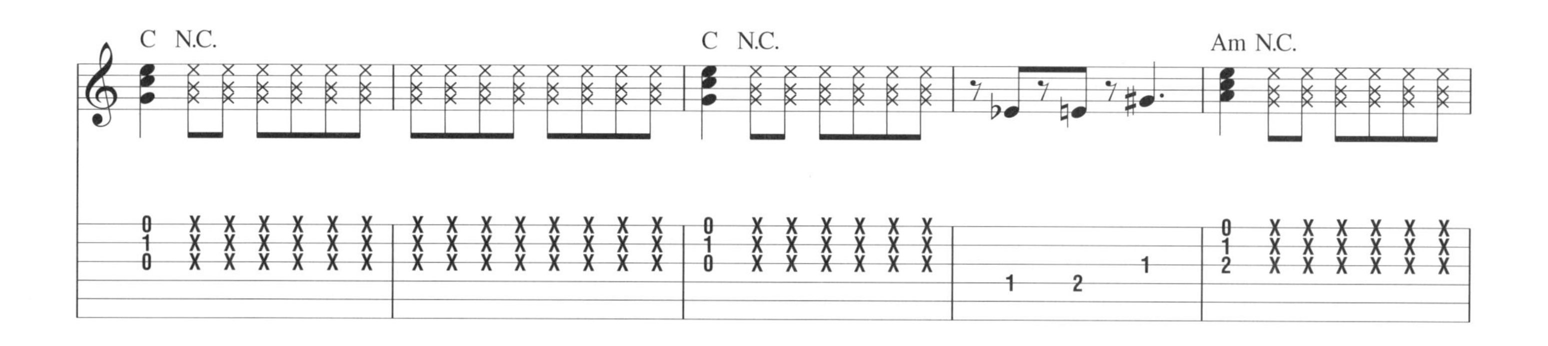
C N.C.
C N.C.
Am N.C.

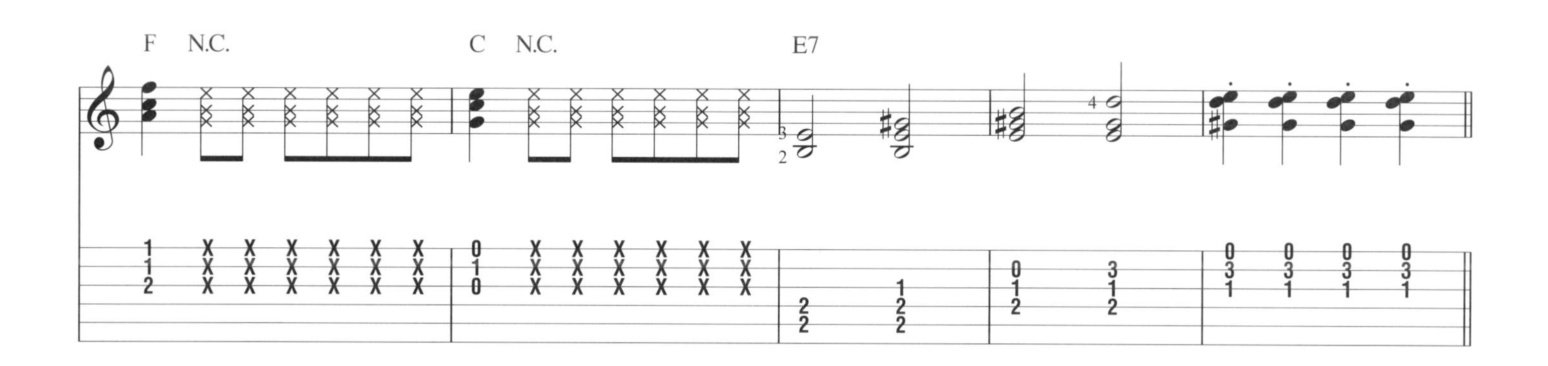
F N.C.
C N.C.
E7

Outro-Chorus
Am
Fmaj7
C
E
Well, an - y - way, let me say, "You're wel - come, for the won - der - ful world you know."

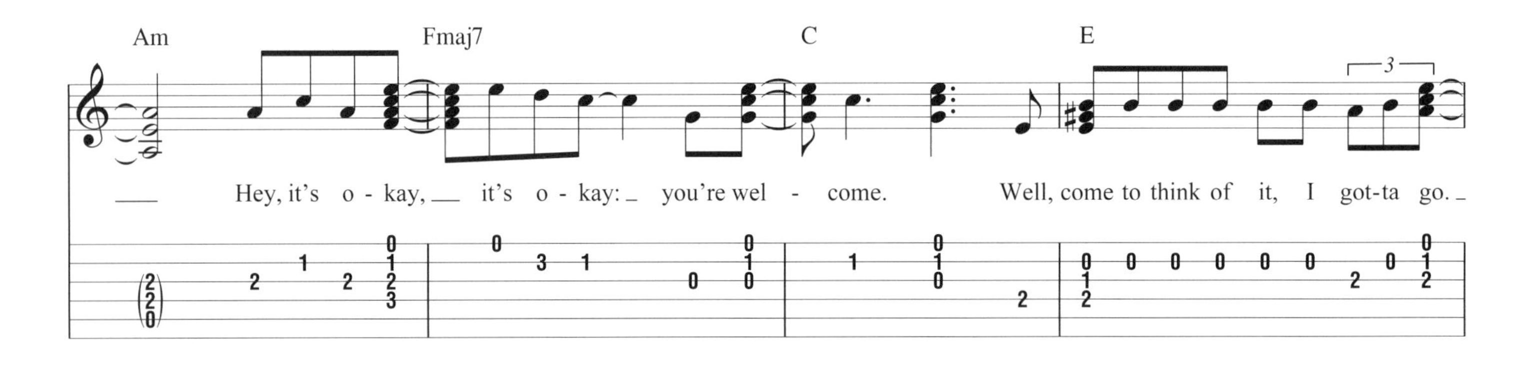

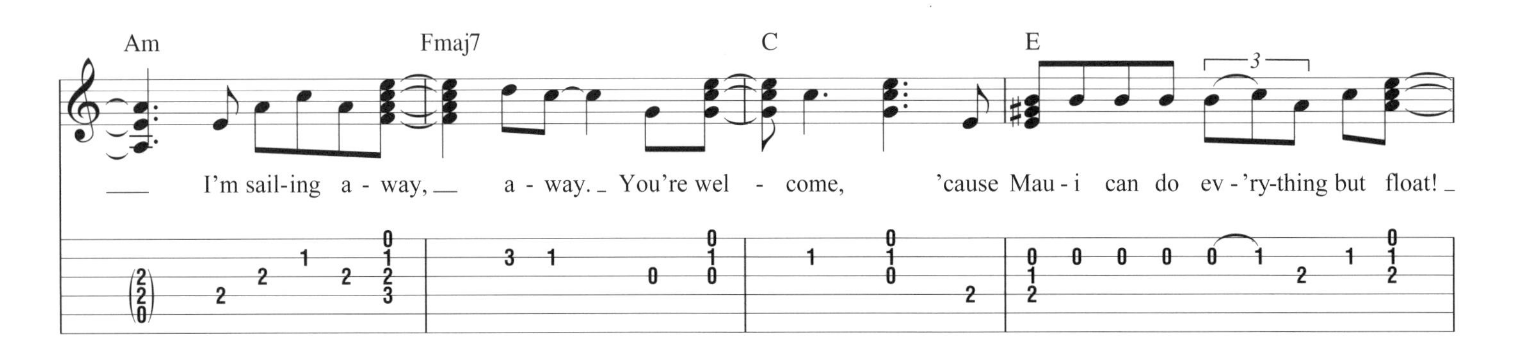

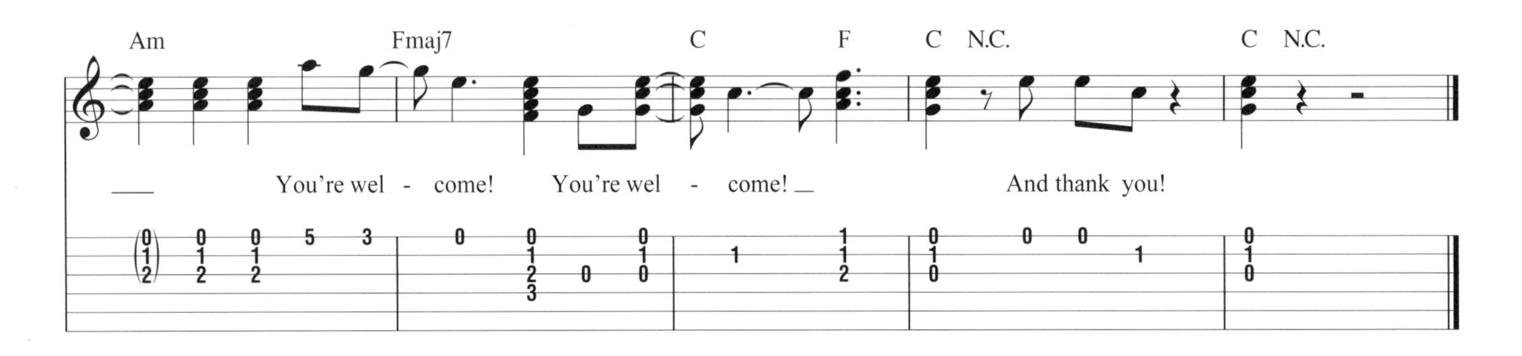

Additional Lyrics

Rap: Kid, honestly, I could go on and on.
I could explain ev'ry nat'ral phenomenon.
The tide? The grass? The ground?
Oh, that was Maui, just messing around.
I killed an eel, I buried its guts,
Sprouted a tree: now you got coconuts!
What's the lesson? What is the takeaway?
Don't mess with Maui when he's on a breakaway.
And the tapestry here in my skin
Is a map of the vict'ries I win!
Look where I've been! I make ev'rything happen!
Look at that mean mini Maui, just tickety
Tappin'! Heh, heh, heh,
Heh, heh, heh, hey!

Zero to Hero

from HERCULES
Music by Alan Menken
Lyrics by David Zippel

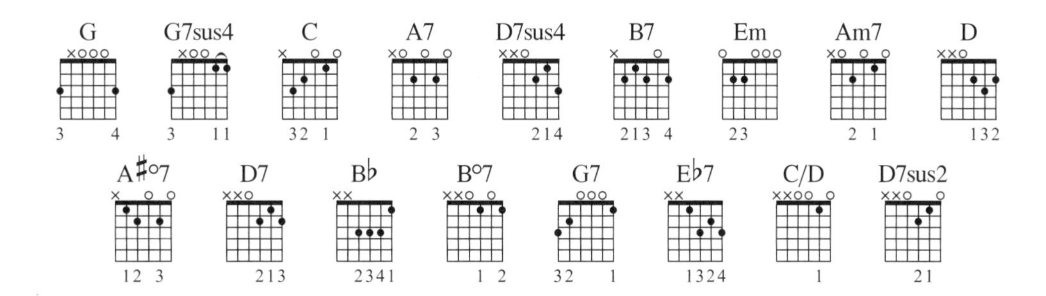

***Strum Pattern: 2**
***Pick Pattern: 5**

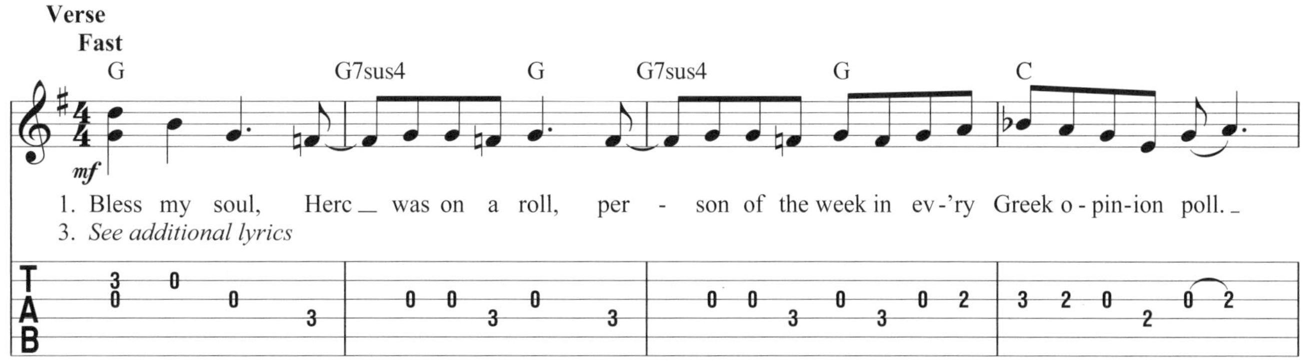

*Use Pattern 10 for $\frac{2}{4}$ measures.

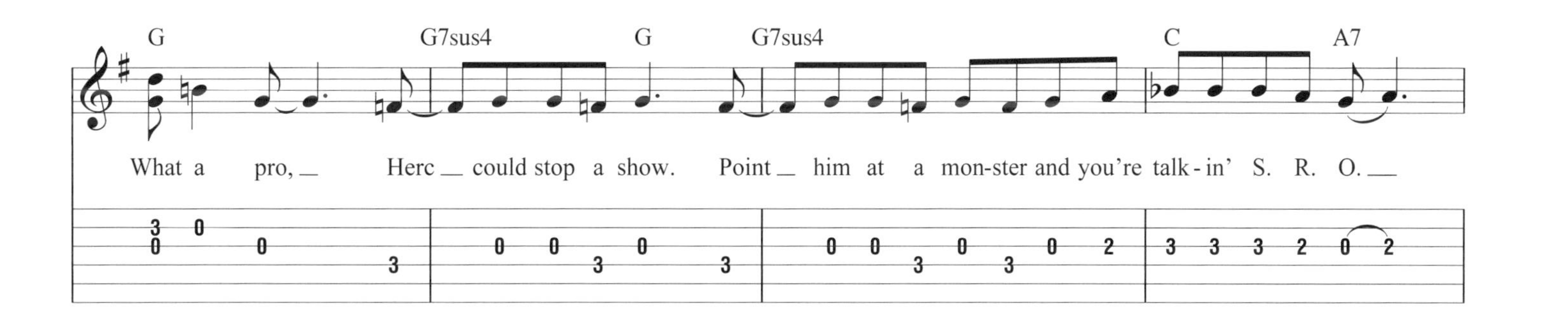

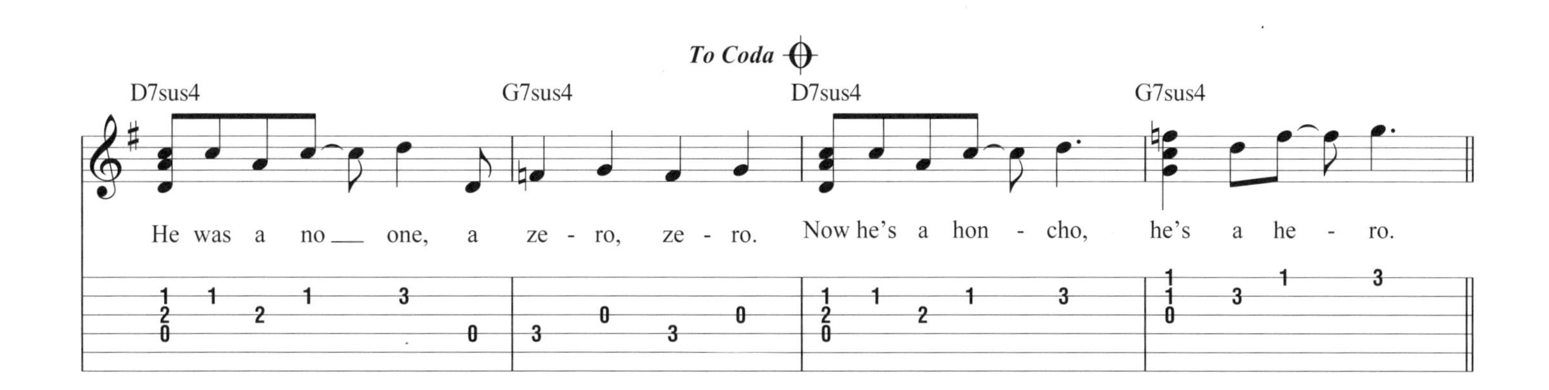

Verse

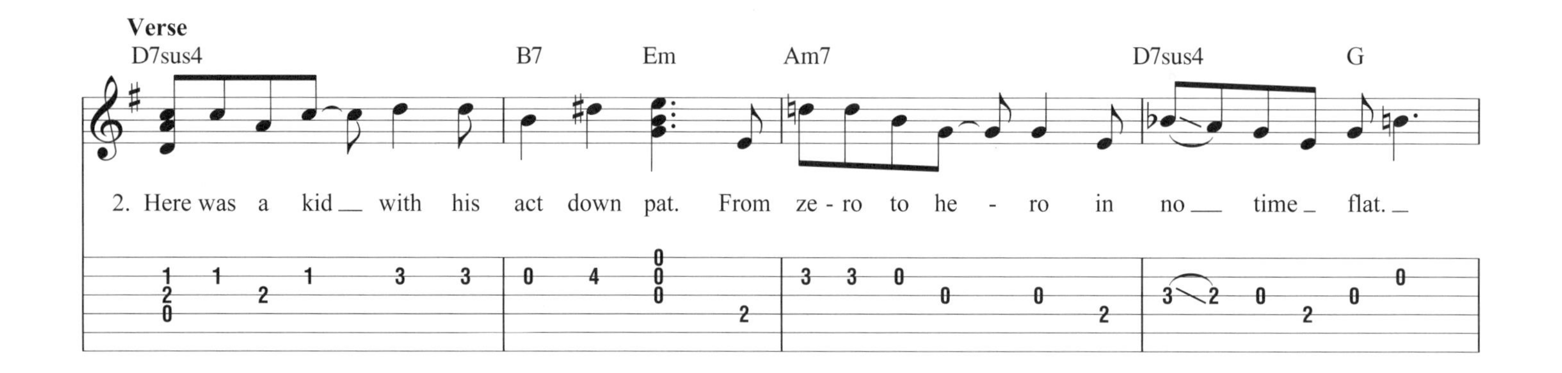
D7sus4
B7
Em
Am7
D7sus4
G
2. Here was a kid with his act down pat. From ze - ro to he - ro in no time flat.

Am7
D7sus4
G
C
D
Ze - ro to he - ro, just like that. When he smiled the girls went wild with

G
Am7
A#o7
G
C
D
oohs and ahs. And they slapped his face on ev - 'ry vase. On

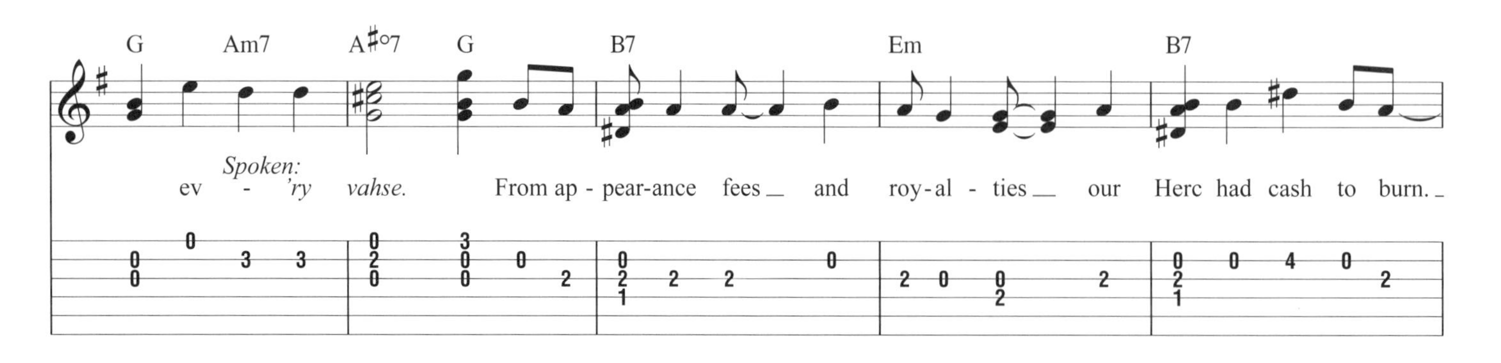
G
Am7
A#o7
G
B7
Em
B7
Spoken:
ev - 'ry vahse. From ap - pear-ance fees and roy-al - ties our Herc had cash to burn.

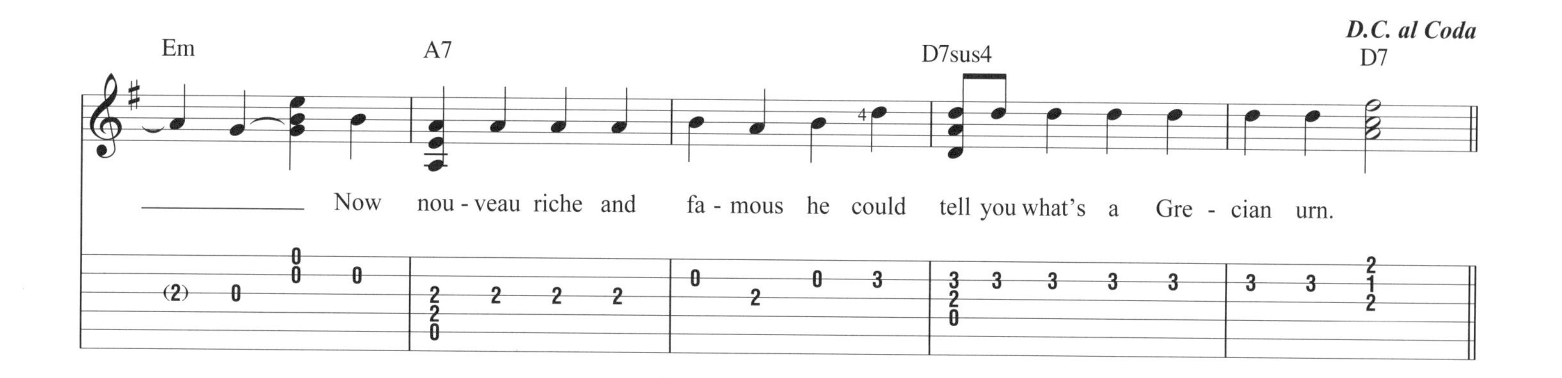
D.C. al Coda
Em A7 D7sus4 D7
Now nou - veau riche and fa - mous he could tell you what's a Gre - cian urn.

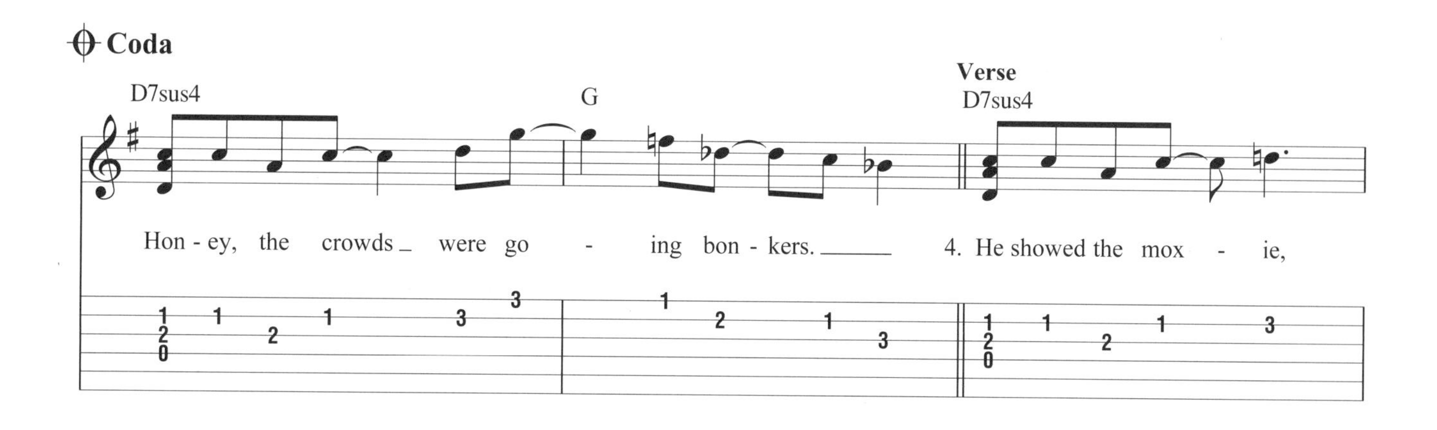
Coda
D7sus4 G
Verse
D7sus4
Hon - ey, the crowds were go - ing bon - kers. 4. He showed the mox - ie,

B7 Em Am7 C G Am7 D7sus4
brains and spunk, from ze - ro to he - ro, a ma - jor hunk. Ze - ro to he - ro
Spoken: and who'd a

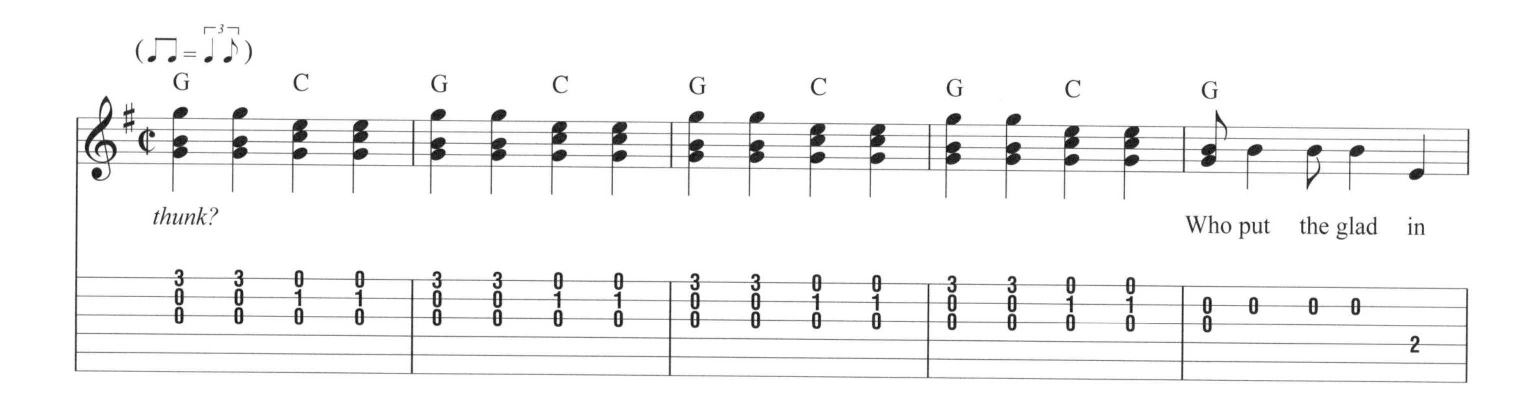
G C G C G C G C G
thunk?
Who put the glad in

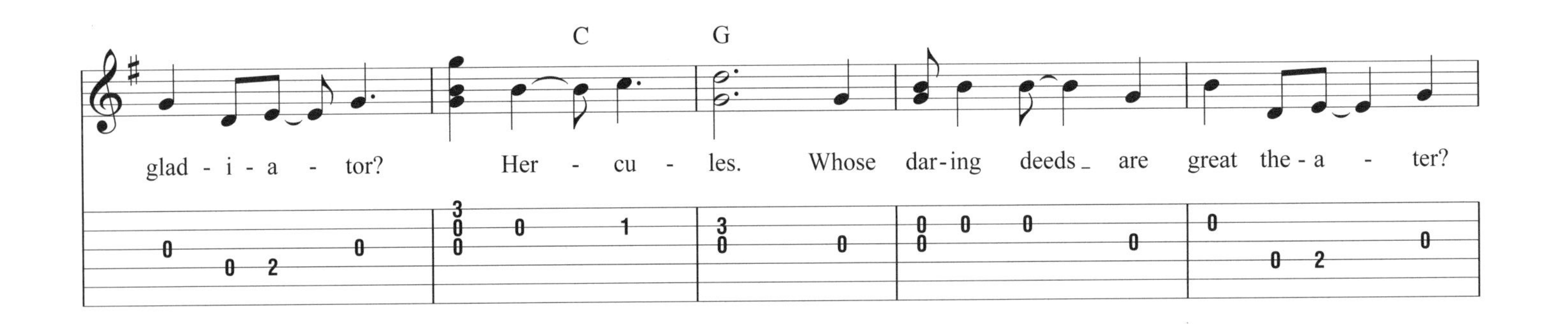
C G
glad - i - a - tor? Her - cu - les. Whose dar-ing deeds_ are great the - a - ter?

C G B♭ D7
Her - cu - les. Is he bold?_ No one brav - er. Is he sweet?_ Our

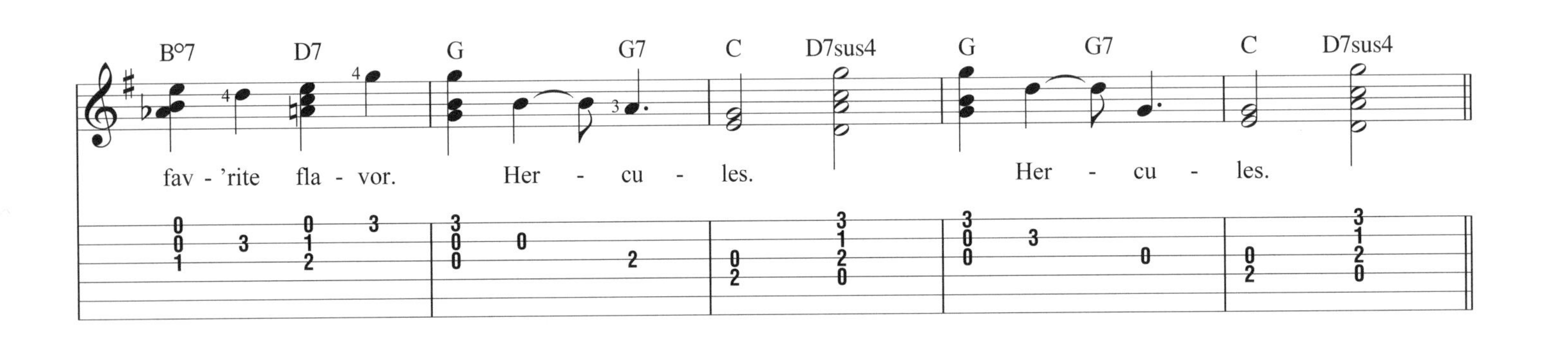
B°7 D7 G G7 C D7sus4 G G7 C D7sus4
fav - 'rite fla - vor. Her - cu - les. Her - cu - les.

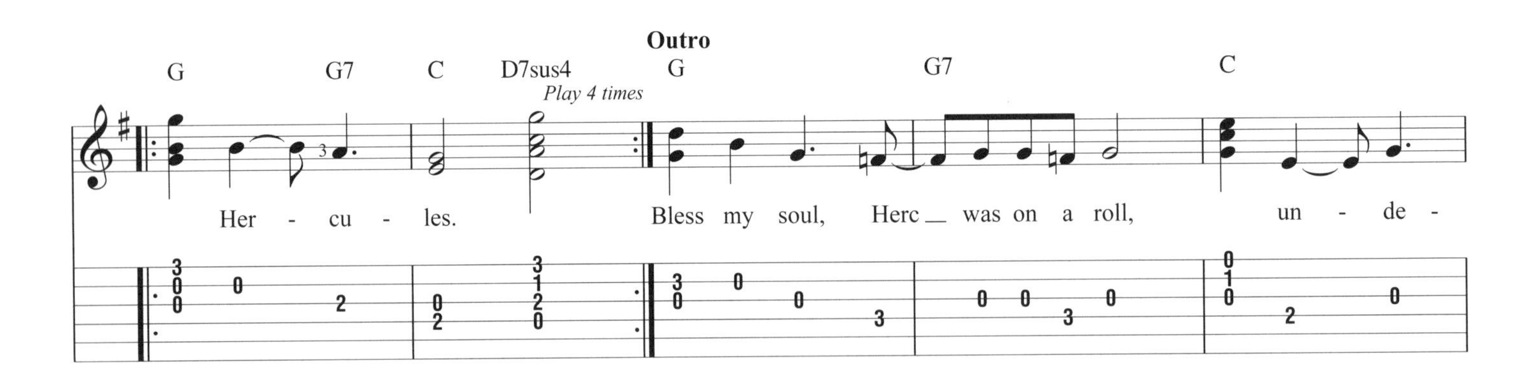
Outro
G G7 C D7sus4 G G7 C
Play 4 times
Her - cu - les. Bless my soul, Herc_ was on a roll, un - de -

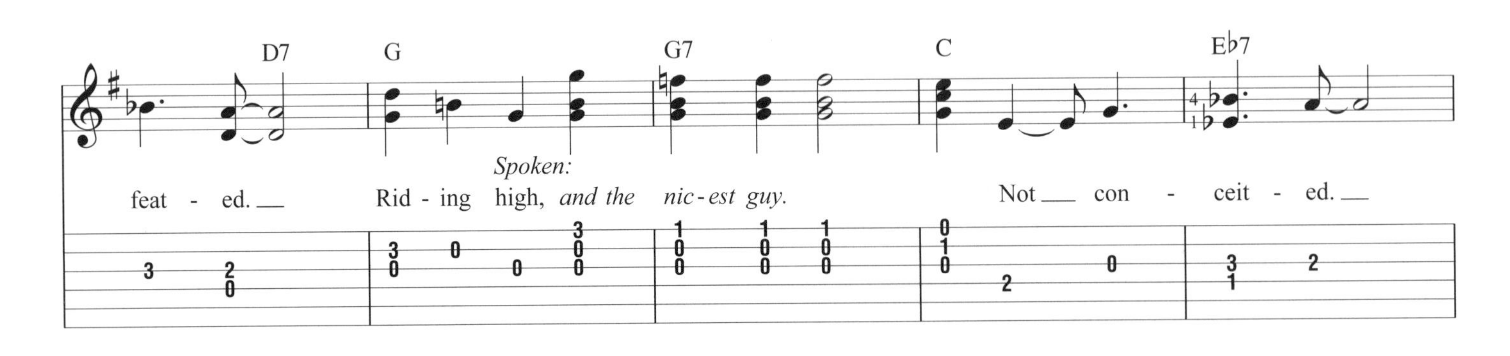
D7 G G7 C E♭7
Spoken:
feat - ed._ Rid - ing high, and the nic - est guy. Not_ con - ceit - ed._

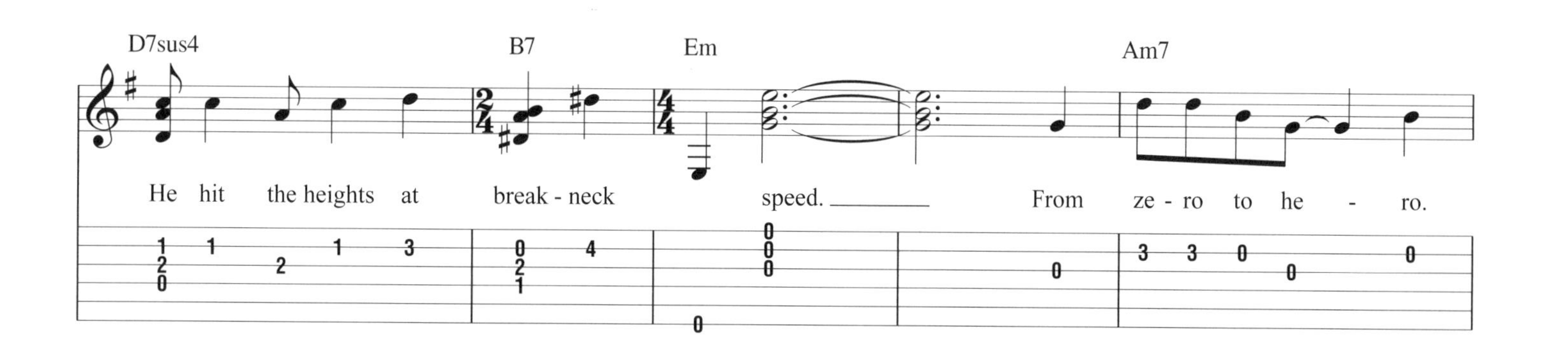

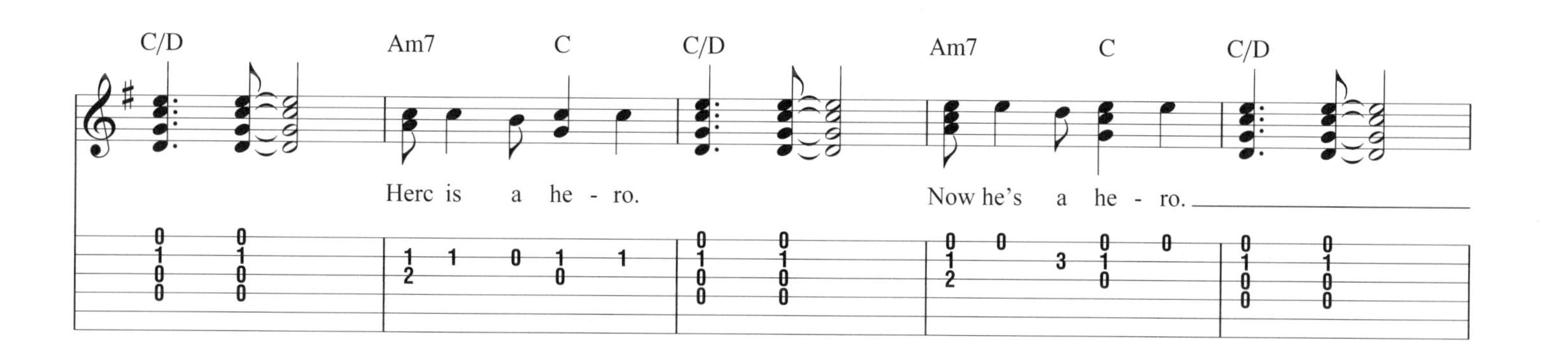

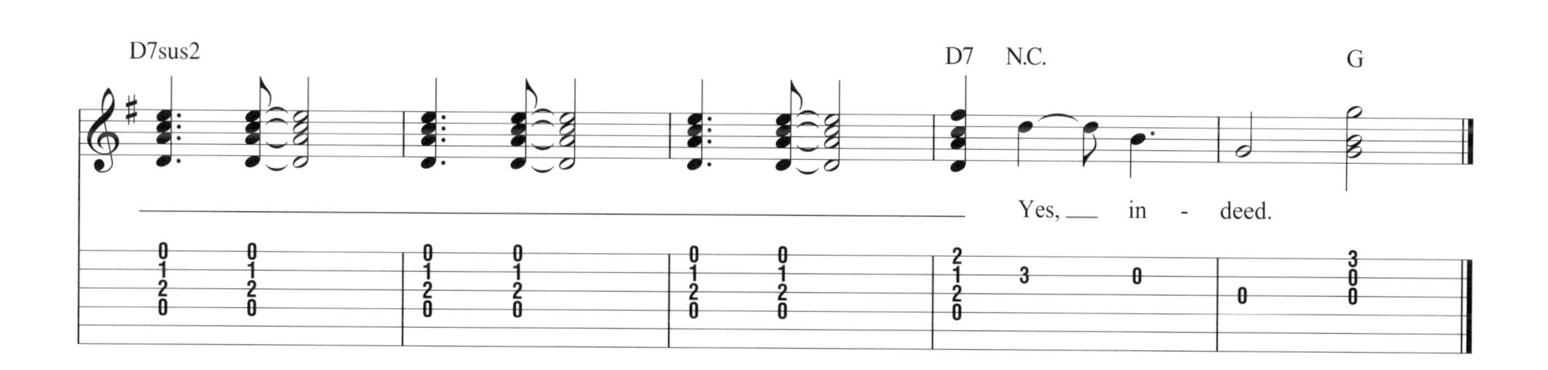

Additional Lyrics

3. Say amen there he goes again
   Sweet and undefeated and an awesome ten for ten
   Folks lined up just to watch him fles
   And this perfect package packed a pair of perfect pecs
   Hercie he comes he sees he conquers
   Honey the crowds were going bonkers